T0235751

Lecture Notes of the Institute for Computer Sciences, Social Informatics and Telecommunications Engineering 379

More information about this series at http://www.springer.com/series/8197

Nguyen-Son Vo · Van-Phuc Hoang ·
Quoc-Tuan Vien (Eds.)

Industrial Networks and Intelligent Systems

7th EAI International Conference, INISCOM 2021
Hanoi, Vietnam, April 22–23, 2021
Proceedings

Springer

Editors
Nguyen-Son Vo
Faculty of Electrical and
Electronics Engineering
Duy Tan University
Da Nang, Vietnam

Van-Phuc Hoang
Le Quy Don Technical University
Hanoi, Vietnam

Quoc-Tuan Vien
Middlesex University
London, UK

ISSN 1867-8211 ISSN 1867-822X (electronic)
Lecture Notes of the Institute for Computer Sciences, Social Informatics and
Telecommunications Engineering
ISBN 978-3-030-77423-3 ISBN 978-3-030-77424-0 (eBook)
https://doi.org/10.1007/978-3-030-77424-0

This Springer imprint is published by the registered company Springer Nature Switzerland AG
The registered company address is: Gewerbestrasse 11, 6330 Cham, Switzerland

Preface

We are delighted to introduce the proceedings of the 7th European Alliance for Innovation (EAI) International Conference on Industrial Networks and Intelligent Systems (INISCOM 2021). This conference brought together researchers, developers, and practitioners from around the world who are leveraging and developing industrial networks and intelligent systems. The focus of INISCOM 2021 was the state of the art in all areas of Big Data, 5G Networks and beyond, the Internet of Things (IoT), Artificial Intelligence (AI), and Cyber-Security towards risk reduction and resilience to natural disasters and extreme climate events globally.

The technical program of INISCOM 2021 consisted of 39 full papers in oral presentation sessions at the main conference tracks. There were five conference tracks: Track 1 – Telecommunications Systems and Networks; Track 2 – Hardware, Software, and Application Designs; Track 3 – Information Processing and Data Analysis; Track 4 – Industrial Networks and Intelligent Systems; and Track 5 – Security and Privacy. Aside from the high-quality technical paper presentations, the technical program also featured one keynote speech given by Dr. Harish Viswanathan, Head of the Radio Systems Research Group at Nokia Bell Labs, USA, and Prof. Trung Q. Duong, Chair of Telecommunications at Queen's University Belfast, UK, and Research Chair of the Royal Academy of Engineering, UK.

Coordination with the steering chairs, Prof. Imrich Chlamtac and Prof. Trung Q. Duong was essential for the success of the conference. We sincerely appreciate their constant support and guidance. It was also a great pleasure to work with such an excellent Organizing Committee team and we thank them for their hard work in organizing and supporting the conference. Particular thanks go to the Technical Program Committee (TPC), who completed the peer-review process for the technical papers and put together a high-quality technical program. We are also grateful to the conference manager, Natasha Onofrei, for the support and all the authors who submitted their papers to INISCOM 2021.

We strongly believe that INISCOM provides a good forum for all researchers, developers, and practitioners to discuss all science and technology aspects that are relevant to industrial networks and intelligent systems. We also expect that the future editions of INISCOM will be as successful and stimulating as this year's conference, as indicated by the contributions presented in this volume.

May 2021

Nguyen-Son Vo
Van-Phuc Hoang
Quoc-Tuan Vien

Organization

Steering Committee

Imrich Chlamtac	University of Trento, Italy
Trung Q. Duong	Queen's University Belfast, UK

Organizing Committee

General Chair

Van-Phuc Hoang	Le Quy Don Technical University, Vietnam

General Co-chairs

Cong-Kha Pham	University of Electro-Communications, Japan
Dinh Quoc Nguyen	Vietnam Institute of Geosciences and Mineral Resources, Vietnam

Technical Program Committee Chair and Co-chair

Nguyen-Son Vo	Duy Tan University, Vietnam
Quoc Tuan Vien	Middlesex University, UK
Trung Q. Duong	Queen's University Belfast, UK

Publicity and Social Media Chairs

Tomohiko Taniguchi	Fujitsu Laboratories, Japan
Dinh Quoc Nguyen	Vietnam Institute of Geosciences and Mineral Resources, Vietnam

Workshops Chairs

Koichiro Ishibashi	University of Electro-Communications, Japan
Sylvain Guilley	Telecom Paris, France
Quang Kien Trinh	Le Quy Don Technical University, Vietnam

Sponsorship and Exhibits Chairs

Hoa Le-Minh	Northumbria University, UK
Do Thanh Quan	Le Quy Don Technical University, Vietnam

Publications Chairs

Luong Duy Manh   Le Quy Don Technical University, Vietnam
Doan Van Sang   Naval Academy, Vietnam

Panels Chairs

Berk Canberk   Istanbul Technical University, Turkey
Tran Cong Manh   Le Quy Don Technical University, Vietnam

Tutorials Chairs

Tuan Le   Middlesex University, UK
Jean-Luc Danger   Telecom Paris, France

Demos Chairs

Zoran Hadzi-Velkov   Ss. Cyril and Methodius University, Macedonia
Le-Nam Tran   University College Dublin, Ireland
Truong Xuan Tung   Le Quy Don Technical University, Vietnam

Local Chair

Hoang Minh Thien   Le Quy Don Technical University, Vietnam

Technical Program Committee

Ali Shahrabi   Glasgow Caledonian University, UK
Cong Hoang Diem   Hanoi University of Mining and Geology, Vietnam
Dac-Binh Ha   Duy Tan University, Vietnam
Dao Thi-Nga   Le Quy Don Technical University, Vietnam
Huu Hung Nguyen   Le Quy Don Technical University, Vietnam
Huy T. Nguyen   Nanyang Technological University, Singapore
Kien Nguyen   Chiba University, Japan
Kien Dang   Ho Chi Minh City University of Transport, Vietnam
Leandros Maglaras   De Montfort University, UK
Pham Ngoc Son   Ho Chi Minh City University of Technology and Education,
                          Vietnam
Tuan Nguyen   University of Buckingham, UK
Ta Minh Thanh   Le Quy Don Technical University, Vietnam
The Nghiep Tran   Le Quy Don Technical University, Vietnam
Toan Doan   Thu Dau Mot University, Vietnam
Truong Khoa Phan   University College London, UK
Van-Ca Phan   Ho Chi Minh City University of Technology and Education,
                          Vietnam
Van-Phuc Hoang   Le Quy Don Technical University, Vietnam
Xuan Nam Tran   Le Quy Don Technical University, Vietnam
Xuan Tung Truong   Le Quy Don Technical University, Vietnam
Yuanfang Chen   Hangzhou Dianzi University, China

Contents

Hardware, Software, and Application Designs

Information Processing and Data Analysis

Industrial Networks and Intelligent Systems

Telecommunications Systems
and Networks

T4PW: TSCH in WBAN for Real-Time Monitoring of Pregnant Women

Amy Sene[1]([⊠]), Ibrahima Niang[1]([⊠]), Alassane Diop[2], and Assane Gueye[3]

[1] Cheikh Anta Diop University, Dakar, Senegal
amy.sene@uadb.edu.sn
[2] Alioune Diop University, Bambey, Senegal
[3] Carnegie Mellon University Africa, Kigali, Rwanda

Abstract. Most developing countries are face to a deficit of doctors and qualified medical staff. This situation poses a real problem for population, especially pregnant women who are at a much greater risk. The use of biosensors can be an alternative solution to overcome these deficiencies. This article presents a new protocol called T4PW (TSCH For Pregnant Woman). T4PW uses the Wireless Body Area Networks (WBANs) and is based on 802.15.4e TSCH standard. Our new protocol aims to provide a real-time remote monitoring to pregnant woman during the pregnancy period and at childbirth. The woman health state is determined from the values measured by the biosensors. Several slotframe templates are proposed according to the health status and the 802.15.4e default timeslot length is reduced.

Keywords: Network · Biosensors · Health · T4PW · 802.15.4e · TSCH · QoS · WBAN

1 Introduction

Most developing countries fall below the WHO (World Health Organization) standards for the minimal threshold of doctors, midwives and nurses per population. Countries below this threshold struggle to provide required healthcare to their population. In addition to that, the distribution of the health staff often reveals significant disparities between regions. Furthermore, most health structures do not have an adequate technical platform and often staff have limited expertise and skills to properly analyze and diagnose some medical conditions.

This deficit of health workers causes many problems to the population, especially pregnant women. Often, pregnant women residing in some areas must make displacement (sometimes long distances) to regions to receive healthcare services. WHO recommends [1] women to consult their health providers at least 8 times during pregnancy to identify potential problems, manage them and reduce the risk of death or neonatal death. Frequent and quality consultations for all women during pregnancy [2] will facilitate the application of preventive measures and the early detection of risks, avoid complications as much as possible, and help to overcome health inequalities. Unfortunately, most

© ICST Institute for Computer Sciences, Social Informatics and Telecommunications Engineering 2021
Published by Springer Nature Switzerland AG 2021. All Rights Reserved
N.-S. Vo et al. (Eds.): INISCOM 2021, LNICST 379, pp. 3–15, 2021.
https://doi.org/10.1007/978-3-030-77424-0_1

pregnant women are not able to comply with these recommendations due to the issues mentioned above.

Another problem arises during childbirth, where midwives do not always have all the physiological information about the woman. For example, childbirth often causes bleeding and unfortunately most women don't know their blood type. Unfortunately, the time required for a blood test and a laboratory analysis to determine the blood type is often quite long, which usually leads to loss of life.

To provide a solution to the problems mentioned above and ensure a continuous real-time monitoring of pregnant women (during pregnancy period and at childbirth), we propose a new protocol called T4PW (TSCH for Pregnant Woman). T4PW is based on the IEEE 802.15.4e TSCH (Time Slotted Channel Hopping) standard. TSCH is an amendment of IEEE 802.15.4e and uses a mechanism of channel hopping that permit access for multiple devices and avoid the cross-technology interference, which can decrease the network reliability. Our protocol T4PW uses a Wireless Body Area Network (WBAN) which [3] is a kind of wireless network composed of biosensors worn by the patient to collect his/her health information such as vital signs.

In IEEE 802.15.4e TSCH network [14], all nodes are synchronized. The time is subdivided into equal interval called timeslot and a succession of timeslot represents a slotframe.

The medical data transmission, required time constraints. The data must be transmitted with low latency times. Also, WBAN networks use a wireless link and can be subject to interference that can affect the performance.

Taking these constraints into consideration, T4PW inherits all the advantages of TSCH, while adding several improvements. To achieve this, several health states are defined for the measurements taken by the biosensors. Then, in order to provides the appropriate medical information, T4PW can dedicate a number of slotframes depending on the health status of the pregnant woman. To reduce the transmission latency, T4PW shortens the timeslot length of the IEEE 802.15.4e TSCH standard by eliminating individual acknowledgments which are to be replaced by cumulative acknowledgment.

The rest of the document structured as follows: Sect. 2 described in detail the IEEE 802.15.4e TSCH standard. Section 3 discusses some related works. Section 4 presents the detailed operation of T4PW. And, finally, the document ends with simulation results and a conclusion.

2   Overview of 802.15.4e TSCH

The IEEE 802.15.4e TSCH, published [4, 5] in 2012, was design to improve the IEEE 802.15.4 standard (2011) Medium Access Control (MAC) protocol. The main objective of the new design was to to improve the IEEE 802.15.4 standard performance in two main fronts: latency and reliability. It does this by operating multiple channels simultaneously. In the TSCH design, IEEE 802.15.4 nodes are allowed to support many applications including industrial ones. TSCH integrates a technique that uses time synchronization and channel hopping to ensure low-power operation, reliability robustness, reliability, availability and security. This integration of frequency hopping and the uses of Time Division Multiple Access (TDMA) [4, 6] makes the network robustness against effects such as noise, interference, and multipath fading.

2.1 TimeSlot

In TSCH, time is divided into [7] fixed periods that are called timeslots. The timeslot, [8, 12] typically 10 ms long, is a sufficient interval of time needs to ensure the following functionalities: the transmission of a data frame from the sender to the recipient, the reception of an acknowledgment to inform the sender that the frame has been successfully received, the operations required for security and the turning the radio to on or off. Each frame is [13] composed by application data (the payload) and information needed to identify it in the network. The maximum size is 127 bytes. TSCH network defines a default a Timeslot Template Structure that is illustrated in Fig. 1.

Transmitter

			wait (RX on) + RX Ack
macTsTxOffset	TX data	macTsRxAckDelay	macTsAckWait

Receiver

macTsRxOffset	macTsRxWait		macTsTxAckDelay	<macTsMaxAck
	wait (RX on) + RX of data			TX Ack

Fig. 1. Default timeslot template

By default, for all transmitted data, acknowledgment is expected. In a timeslot, data is transmitted by the transmitter after macTsTxOffset from the beginning of the timeslot. The receiver waits macTsRxOffset and then goes into receive mode, and starts listening for incoming data for macTsRxWait. If no data has not received from the transmitter after macTsRxWait, the receiver may turn off its radio. After transmitting the data, the transmitter waits macTsRxAckDelay and then enables the receiver mode to await the acknowledgment from the receiver. Once the data has been received, the receiver waits macTsTxAckDelay and then sends an acknowledgment to tell that the packet is successfully received.

2.2 SlotFrame

A slotframe [8] is a succession of timeslots that automatically and periodically repeats over the time. Each node knows the necessary information about the network by receiving the EB (Enhanced Beacon) message sent by the coordinator. The message contains all the required information for a device to be synchronize with the network. This information specially concerns the channel hopping and the timeslot structure. TSCH does not require [4] a fixed length for slotframe. This length must be adapted according to the needs of the application. The slotframe size [5, 8] depends on the application needs.

2.3 TSCH Node Scheduling

Communication between the nodes [8] is done according to a scheduling strategy that is composed by several cells in the form of a mathematical matrix. The number of timeslots represents the rows and the columns are determined by the number of the channelOffset. During a timeslot a node can transmit, receive, or sleep as details below:

- transmit: for this, the device checks on its buffer if a matching corresponding to the scheduling is found. If yes the device sends the data. Otherwise, the device turns off its radio (sleep) to save power.
- receive: the device puts itself into listening mode and waits for incoming data. If a packet is received, the device generates an ACK to confirm the success reception. Otherwise, it turns off his radio (sleep) as before.

We have different types of cell communication with TSCH [8, 9]:

- Dedicated: 2 nodes (transmitter/receiver) can exchange information without collisions. Nodes that are not affected may turn off they radio.
- Shared: the same timeslot can be used by one or several devices to send data. With this mode, collisions can occur.
- Free: any node is assigned to a free cell: it is an available resource for scheduling.
- Advertisement: cells are dedicated for sending synchronization frames or Enhanced Beacons. The broadcast Transmissions is use.

2.4 Channel Hoping

TSCH standard [8, 9] uses 16 channels for communication numbered from 0 to 15 that defines the channelOffset. A communicating between devices is represented by a combination of slotOffset and channelOffset. The frequency is determined as follow (1).

$$f = F[(ASN + channelOffset)\%Nchannels] \tag{1}$$

where, NChannels and ChannelOffset represent respectively the available channels and the channelOffset; ASN (Absolute Slot Number) defines the timeslot counter executed since the network is set up (when network is launched for the first time, the ASN is fixed to 0. After each timeslot, the value is incremented by 1. The de-vices obtain the current value through the EB message); and F defines the available channels that can be use.

Figure 2 descripts an example of SlotFrame with 28 timeslots length.

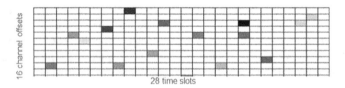

Fig. 2. Example of SlotFrame

3 Related Works

Despite its recent publication, IEEE 802.15.4e TSCH has been subject of many research studies recently.

Rasool Tavakoli et al. [7] presented a new template of timeslot named hybrid timeslot. With their solution, each timeslot is dedicated to one node and at the same time shared by other nodes. Before using the channel, the none-owner nodes must wait Δt to be sure that the dedicated node is not sending or receiving. If the dedicated node is active (sending or receiving), none-owners cancel their planned transmission. Otherwise, they can use the channel. As a consequence, the hybrid timeslot has a length greater than the default length of TSCH.

In Ref. [10] the authors worked on the use of a heart rate sensor for monitoring patients. They consider that the amount of generated data is determined by the health status of the patient to be monitored. The more the patient health status becomes critical, the more the quantity of generated data increases. To manage this variation of data, they improve the use of TSCH by proposing a dynamic allocution for timeslot. When data increase, they allocate additional timeslots to the concerned node. When the status returns to normal, the coordinator recovers the additional allocated timeslots.

After arguing that the existing planning approaches in IoT sensor systems fail to satisfied the different requirements, the authors of [10] propose an adaptive scheduling algorithm (PASA) for quality of service (QoS) of heterogeneous applications. The service cycle (ST) of each node is managed adaptively according to several criteria like priority traffic (RP) that is calculated based on data throughput and delay requirements. As the priority becomes high, so does the corresponding ST.

This article in [11] presents a slotframe partitioning-based cell scheduling (SPCS) planning procedure. SPCS is based on the IEEE 802.15.4 TSCH standard. It subdivides a slotframe into several subframes of different sizes and the allocation of these partitions is determined by the depth of a node and the number of slotOffsets required for each partition. SPCS uses a network information table (NIT) containing all the routing information for all sensor nodes allowing the root to have all the information concerning the network.

In Ref. [6] the authors made a detailed study of several communication protocols used in WBAN network. They also explain the importance of using the standard TSCH technology in WBANs due to its operation based on TDMA and channel hopping, in addition of inheriting of basic advantages offered by the 802.15.4 standard such as resilience low noise. WBANs uses wireless communication and operate on the same frequency band (2.4 GHz) as many other devices. With this constraint, working with a protocol using a single frequency channel can cause interference. This situation can lead to a loss of synchronization for biosensors and can impact on the performance of application and increase energy consumption and latency time with packet retransmissions. The use of several channels is a solution to avoid interference. The results of its simulations show good performance for TSCH in WBAN networks.

4   T4PW Operation

T4PW is based on the 802.15.4e TSCH standard. T4PW provides a regular monitoring to pregnant woman by providing a real-time communication between the biosensors and the coordinator. In T4PW, our Wireless Body Area Network (WBAN) uses 6 biosensors (blood pressure, blood glucose, blood type, oxygen saturation, temperature, pulse). The biosensor for blood group will not be permanently worn by the woman. Since it's a factor with a static value. Each biosensor measures a physiological parameter and processes the data for use by the medical staff. The data measured by the biosensors are transmitted to the coordinator. The coordinator collects all the data coming from the different biosensors and acts as a gateway for outside.

Figure 3 shows the woman with the biosensors and the coordinator.

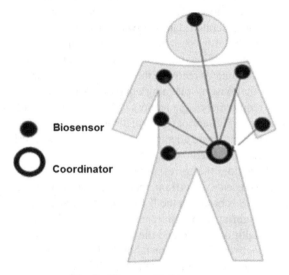

Fig. 3. Woman with biosensors

4.1   Data Classification

For each biosensor, in collaboration with a doctor, a range of values is defined to indicate the health status of the pregnant woman.

The following Table 1 shows the thresholds set for each class:

The class 1 corresponds to the normal thresholds. The class 2 refers to weakly critical data. The class 3 shows critical data. The class 4 corresponds to very critical data. This classification is used to determine the health status of the pregnant woman.

The normal status refers to the situation in which all values are in class 1. Therefore, the status health of the woman presents no abnormality.

The weakly critical status: at least one measured value belongs to class 2 and no value belongs to classes 3 and 4.

Table 1. Data classification

Type	Class 1	Class 2	Class 3	Class 4
Blood pressure	$7 \leq D \leq 8$ and $12 \leq S \leq 13$	$6 \leq D < 7$ or $13 < S \leq 14$	$5 \leq D < 6$ or $14 < S \leq 15$	$5 < D$ or $S > 15$
Blood glucose (G) g/l	$0,7 \leq G \leq 1$	$1 < G \leq 1,1$	$1 < G \leq 1,25$	$G > 1,25$ or $G < 0,7$
Pulse (P) beats/min	$80 \leq P \leq 120$	$120 < P \leq 140$	$140 < P \leq 160$	$P > 160$
Temperature	$37.6° \leq T \leq 38$	$38 < T \leq 39$	$39 < T \leq 40$	$T > 40$
Oxygen saturation (SO2)	$94 < SO2 \leq 99\%$	$94 < SO2 \leq 92$	$92 < SO2 \leq 90$	$SO2 < 90\%$

The critical status: at least one measured value belongs to class 3 and no value corresponds to class 4. This situation requires the intervention of the medical staff.

The very critical status: at least one measured value belongs to class 4. In such situation, an urgent intervention must be do.

4.2 Measuring Frequency

For each state, a measuring periodicity validated by a doctor is predefined. This periodicity indicates the interval time between 2 successive measuring for each biosensor. The following Table 2 shows the measuring frequency used for each state.

Table 2. Measuring frequency

Status	Interval between 2 measures
Normal status	F1 every 15 min
Weakly critical status	F2 every les 5 min
Critical status	F3 every minute
Very critical status	F4 every 30 s

We have a measuring sequence every 30 s when the woman's health status is very critical. At childbirth, the frequency F4 will be retained. The care during childbirth meets very precise monitoring criteria and requires careful monitoring of the woman.

4.3 T4PW Detail

Medical applications require real-time, availability and guarantees. A delay in intervention can lead to a loss of life. Medical staff must have all the required information, especially in urgent situations. Taking into account all these important factors, T4PW proposes to reduce the length of the timeslot which is by default equal to 10ms and SlotFrames with a duration of 15 min which corresponds to the maximum time interval between two consecutive measurements. The SlotFrame template is determined by the status health according to the measuring frequencies defined for each state. T4WP opted for dedicated timeslot to avoid collisions, so for a given timeslot only the dedicated biosensor can transmit.

T4PW TimeSlot Template
Since T4PW uses a network whose composition is determined beforehand, the number of nodes is known in advance, in other words for each measurement sequence, we know the number of packets that the coordinator must receive. So instead of sending an acknowledgment to each biosensor during its timeslot, the coordinator waits to receive all the data from the biosensors before responding to all of them with a broadcast message. Therefore, to reduce the transmission latency, T4PW eliminates the acknowledgment generation by the receiver. Consequently, the coordinator after receiving the data measured by a biosensor, will not send an acknowledgment and the transmitter which corresponds to the biosensor may idle the radio after sending its data, it does not wait for the reception of an acknowledgment. From the timeslot template, we can see that the time Δack required for the receiver to prepare and transmit an acknowledgment can be calculated as follows:

$$\Delta ack = macTsTxAckDelay + macTsMaxAck. \tag{2}$$

The corresponding values [15] are respectively 1 ms and 2,4 ms. Then we can deduce that

$$\Delta ack = 1\,ms + 2, 4\,ms = 3, 4\,ms. \tag{3}$$

Therefore, the T4PW timeslot length is obtained by:
IEEE 802.15.4e default length timeslot

$$\Delta ack = 10\,ms - 3, 4\,ms = 6, 6\,ms \tag{4}$$

T4PW SlotFrame Templates
After any measuring, the coordinator dedicates a timeslot TS with the length 6,6 ms to each biosensor for transmission of his data. In total 5 timeslot are granted. For a given timeslot, the biosensors that are not concerned turn off their radio to save energy. The first timeslot is reserved for sending the EB (Enable Beacon) by the coordinator to biosensors. After receiving the EB, each biosensor has information about when to transmit, receive or sleep.

After having received all the data from the biosensors, the coordinator generates and sends a broadcast message EB + to all the biosensors. The 7th timeslot will be used for sending this EB + broadcast message. So all the biosensors must wake up on the 7th timeslot to receive the EB + and check if their transmission during their dedicated timeslot was successful. Each biosensor that the coordinator has not received its package during its dedicated timeslot, will be allocated another TS + (timeslot +) for the retransmission of its package. A biosensor that has not benefited a TS + will know that its transmission was successful.

The retransmission is proved to improve the performance of T4PW by reducing packet error rates. This makes T4PW more stable.

The EB + is also used by the coordinator to inform the biosensors about the time of the next measuring. This can help to intervene more quickly in critical situation. For example, a very critical status can occur suddenly after a normal. With the sending of EB +, biosensors will be informed that the next measuring must be taken in 30 s. To ensure the permutation between the different SlotFrames templates, after each measuring sequence, the coordinator checks if the health status has changed. If yes, the template corresponding to the new state is loaded otherwise the coordinator continues with the template of the current SlotFrame.

To represent the different templates defined for SlotFrames, we consider the following parameters:

- Biosensors are numerated from S1 to S5.
- C defines the coordinator.
- T means that the biosensor is in transmission mode.
- R means that the biosensor is on receiving mode.
- Seq represents a measuring sequence.

Normal Status

In this status only one measuring is taken by the biosensors throughout the duration of the SlotFrame (Fig. 4).

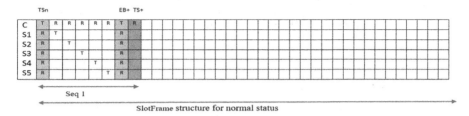

Fig. 4. SlotFrame template for normal status

Weakly Critical Status

In this state, the biosensors can take 3 successive measuring at regular intervals of 5 min during the SlotFrame (Fig. 5).

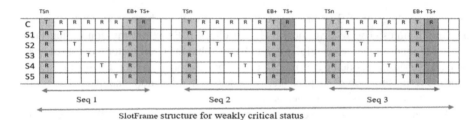

Fig. 5. SlotFrame template for weakly critical status

Critical Status

Measuring should be done every minute. SlotFrame can support 15 measuring sequences numbered from Seq1 to Seq15 (Fig. 6).

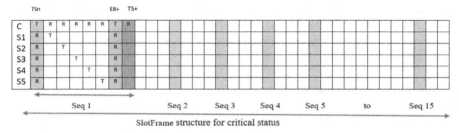

Fig. 6. SlotFrame template for critical status

Very Critical Status

Measuring become more frequent. The coordinator must allocate timeslots every 30 s. This allows to get 30 measuring sequences numbered from Seq1 to Seq30 (Fig. 7).

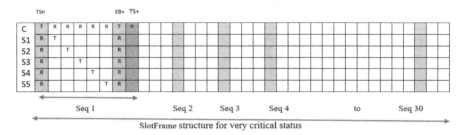

Fig. 7. SlotFrame template for very critical status

5   Performance Evaluation

This section presents the performance of the T4PW protocol in comparison with the traditional IEEE 802.15.4e TSCH.

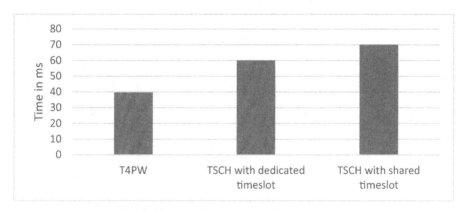

Fig. 8. Time use by each protocol for 1 sequence

This Fig. 8 compares the time used by each protocol for 1 sequence, to allow all biosensors to transmit their packet. We observe that the time uses by T4PW is less than the 802.15.4e TSCH time.

This Fig. 9 illustrates the average time required for retransmission in situation where packet loss has occurred. By default, in TSCH, for dedicated timeslot, retransmission of packet waits until the next assigned transmit timeslot occurs. For shared timeslot, a sender waits for the arrival of the first shared link to retransmit. For our case, we suppose that the dedicated TSCH timeslot uses an EB + which informs a biosensor when to retransmit.

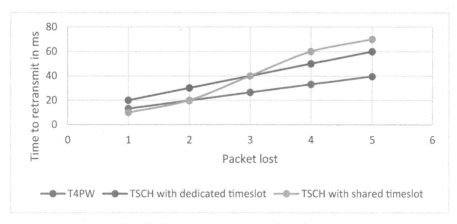

Fig. 9. Time average to retransmit packet loss

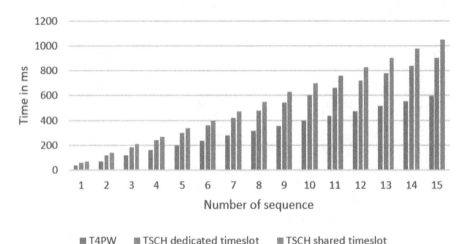

Fig. 10. Average time to send respectively 15 measurements sequences

In this Fig. 10, we have the evolution of the average time required to send respectively the 15 measurement sequences corresponding to the critical state. Through this figure, we can observe that the average delay for the proposed protocol T4PW is far less than that the 802.15.4e TSCH.

Technology grows so fast, T4PW takes account the scalability. Thus with T4PW, the coordinator can allocate additional timeslots in situation where other biosensors need to be integrated. This graph shows the evolution according to the number of deployed biosensors (Fig. 11).

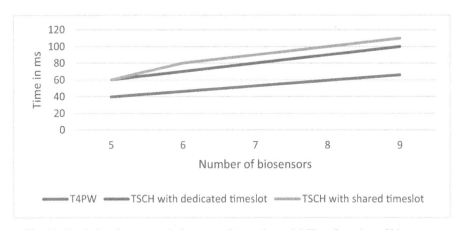

Fig. 11. Evolution time transmission according to the scalability of number of biosensors

6 Conclusion

The effective use of biosensors can participate to the development, by providing quality care to pregnant women. In this paper, we proposed a new protocol called T4PW. This protocol is based on the 802.15.4e TSCH standard and provides SlotFrames whose templates are determined by the health status of the pregnant woman to be monitored. To reduce the transmission delays, the default timeslot length proposed by the 802.15.4e TSCH standard has been reduced. Simulations results show that T4PW offers lower latency times than 802.15.4e TSCH.

References

1. OMS, Santé de la mère et des enfants: 10 moyens d'améliorer la qualité des soins. 17 février 2017
2. OMS, Les femmes enceintes doivent pouvoir bénéficier de soins adaptés au bon moment, 7 novembre 2016
3. Pushpan, S., Velusamy, B.: Fuzzy-Based Dynamic Time Slot Allocation for Wireless Body Area Networks, 7 May 2019
4. Hissein, M.H.S.: Etude et prototypage d'une nouvelle méthode d'accés aléatoire multi-canal multi-saut pour les réseaux locaux sans fil, 12 juillet 2017
5. Watteyne, T., Palattella, M., Grieco, L.: Using IEEE 802.15.4e Time-Slotted Channel Hopping (TSCH) in the Internet of Things (IoT): Problem Statement, Internet Engineering Task Force (IETF), May 2015
6. Veisi, F., Nabiy, M., Said, H.: An Empirical Study of the Performance of IEEE 802.15.4e TSCH for Wireless Body Area Networks
7. Tavakoli, R., Nabi, M., Basten, T., Goossens, K.: Hybrid Timeslot Design for IEEE 802.15.4 TSCH to Support Heterogeneous WSNs
8. Hammoudi, S., Aliouat, Z., Harous, S., Louail, L.: Time slotted channel hopping with collision avoidance. Int. J. Ad Hoc Ubiquitous Comput. (2018)
9. Morin, E.: Interopérabilité de protocole de communication adaptatifs basse-consommation pour des réseaux de capteurs, HAL Id: tel-01903194 (2018)
10. Ngo, M.V., La, Q.D., Leong, D., Quek, T.Q.S.: User Behavior Driven MAC Scheduling for Body Sensor Networks
11. Kwon, J.-H., Kim, E.-J., Kim, D.: Slotframe partitioning-based cell scheduling for IEEE 802.15.4 time slotted channel hopping. Sens. Mater. 31(5) (2019)
12. Duquennoy, S., Nahas, B.A., Elsts, A., GOikonomou, A.: TSCH and 6TiSCH for Contiki: Challenges, Design and Evaluation (2017)
13. Gaillard, G.: Opérer les réseaux de l'Internet des Objets à l'aide de contrats de qualité de service (Service Level Agreements) (2016)
14. Shi, K., Zhang, L., Qi, Z., Tong, K., Chen, H.: Transmission scheduling of periodic real-time traffic in IEEE 802.15.4e TSCH-Based Industrial Mesh Networks, September 2019
15. IEEE-SA Standards Board, IEEE Standard for Low-Rate Wireless Networks (2015)

Design of a Compact and High-Efficiency 5.8 GHz Microwave Power Amplifier for Wireless Communication Systems

Luong Duy Manh[1(✉)], Nguyen Thanh Hung[1], Nguyen Thi Anh[1], Dai Xuan Loi[2], and Nguyen Huy Hoang[1]

[1] Le Quy Don Technical University,
236 Hoang Quoc Viet, Co Nhue 1, Hanoi, Vietnam
duymanhcs2@mta.edu.vn
[2] Military Institute of Science and Technology,
17 Hoang Sam, Cau Giay, Hanoi, Vietnam

Abstract. In this paper, a compact and low-cost, high-efficiency microwave power amplifier is proposed and designed. The proposed amplifier operates at the 5.8 GHz band for wireless communications systems. The amplifier is designed on a low-cost 5 W GaN HEMT transistor from Qorvo and a RO4350B substrate from Rogers. The high-efficiency can be obtained by treating the second harmonic at the input side. The output side is treated up to the third harmonic. Both small-signal and large-signal performance of the proposed amplifier were evaluated by both simulation and experiment. The simulated and measured results validate that the designed power amplifier can be realized in a compact size and delivered 5 W power with a high-efficiency at 5.8 GHz band.

Keywords: Power amplifier · GaN · HEMT · High-efficiency

1 Introduction

Power amplifiers (PA) play an essential role in radio systems. It is the element which consumes the most energy in the transmitter to ensure the required output power level of the system. Therefore, the PA must have high efficiency in order to save power supply as well as reduce the heat loss, increase operating duration and improve the stability of the PA performance. Recently, along with the method of improving linearity, improving efficiency is one of the main methods in the design of the PA. The typical method used to improve the efficiency of the PA includes using the class-E, class-F [1–4]. These two methods utilize short and open-circuit transmission lines to minimize the power loss at harmonics. In addition, the voltage and current waveform at the transistor are engineered to ensure they have no intersections in the time-domain, resulting in reduction

This research is funded by Vietnam National Foundation for Science and Technology Development (NAFOSTED) under grant number 102.04-2018.14.

of the power loss at the transistor. The advantage of these two methods is that they ensure high efficiency because the power loss at the harmonics as well as the power loss at the transistor can be reduced simultaneously. However, these two methods have difficulties when PA works in the high-frequency range because the realization of the short- and open-circuited conditions at the high-frequency range is a challenging task.

Another typical efficiency improvement method is to make a phase adjustment between current and voltage at harmonics so that the phase difference between them is 90° [5–7], hence reducing the power consumption at the harmonics. The phase adjustment in the high-frequency range is easier to realize than creating short- and open-circuited condition. Therefore, this method is more suitable than using the class-E and class-F methods when designing PA operating in the high-frequency range.

Based on the above analysis, the research team has designed a high-efficiency PA operating at 5.8 GHz for use in the radio communication systems. Phase control method at the harmonics is used to improve the efficiency of the designed PA. The PA in this paper is designed using a low-cost GaN High-electron-mobility transistor (HEMT) device from Qorvo based on a microwave hybrid circuit technology.

The rest of the paper is structured as follows. In Sect. 2, the design procedure of the input and output matching networks of the PA is presented. In the Sect. 3, the simulated results will be experimentally verified at both small and large signal levels. Finally, Sect. 4 concludes the paper.

2   Impedance Matching Networks Design

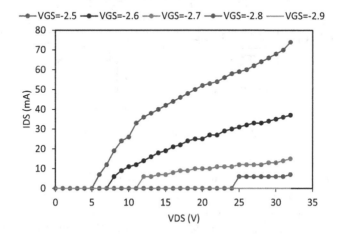

Fig. 1. Output characteristic of the real device.

In this paper, the simulation of the designed circuit is performed on Advanced Design System (ADS) [8] simulator from Keysight. The small-signal and large-signal models of the transistor are provided by Qorvo [9]. The transistor used a GaN HEMT device. This device is packaged in a quad-flat no-leads (QFN) with a size of 3.0 cm × 3.0 cm. This device is low-cost and it has a wide operating frequency range from DC to 12 GHz with 5 W output power at 1 dB compression point. For the design process, we first determine the quiescent point or operation condition based on the transistor's characteristics. The bias condition as recommended by the manufacturer is: drain voltage $\mathbf{V_{ds}}$ = 32 V and drain current $\mathbf{I_{ds}}$ = 25 mA. Since the static characteristic of the model provided by Qorvo may differ from the actual transistor, the actual static characteristic of the actual transistor has to be measured. Figure 1 depicts the static output characteristic through actual measurement of the real transistor. Based on this characteristic, to set a bias drain current to 25 mA as recommended by the manufacturer, the gate voltage is set to $\mathbf{V_{gs}}$ = −2.73 V. This is equivalent to the class-AB operation.

After setting up the operation condition, the impedance matching networks and bias circuit will be designed. These circuits are all made on the microstrip line technology using Rogers RO4350B material. The material parameters are as follows: dielectric constant: 3.66; dielectric loss: 0.0035; dielectric thickness: 30 mil; conductor thickness: 35 μm.

2.1 Input Matching Network

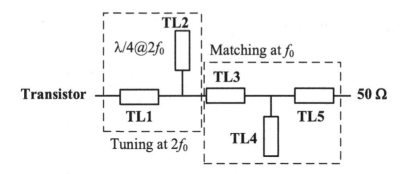

Fig. 2. Input matching network circuit.

The input circuit is responsible for transmitting the RF signal from the signal source to the input of the transistor so that the signal loss is minimal. This means that the input matching network (IMN) performs the impedance matching condition: $\mathbf{Z_S} = \mathbf{Z^*_{in}}$; where $\mathbf{Z_S}$ and $\mathbf{Z_{in}}$ are the source impedance and input impedance of the transistor, respectively. In this study, an additional stub to suppress quadratic harmonics at the input of the IMN is employed in order to further improve the efficiency of the designed PA. Circuit diagram of the IMN is shown in Fig. 2. Here, TL1, TL2 lines are used for the second harmonic

Fig. 3. Fabricated prototype of the IMN.

control while TL3, TL4 and TL5 lines are tuned to for impedance matching
at the fundamental frequency. The fabricated prototype of the IMN is given in
Fig. 3. The circuit shown in the figure includes the designed bias circuit. The
circuit size is quite compact 2.0 cm × 2.8 cm. The optimum input impedance
at the fundamental frequency and the second harmonic was determined using
a Source Pull technique based on the large-signal model of the TGF2977-SM
device provided by Qorvo. The results of the simulation of the electromagnetic
(EM) level and the measured impedance results of the IMN are shown in Fig. 4.
It can be seen the good agreement of the simulation results and the measurement
of the impedance of the IMN, the impedance difference at the second harmonic
is caused by the tolerance in the fabrication process of the microstrip lines. This
causes the phase deviation between simulated and measured impedances. It is
noted that the impedance at the second harmonic is located near the edge of the
Smith chart, indicating that the phase difference between voltage and current
at the second harmonic is approximately 90°, leading to a decrease in the power
loss at the harmonic.

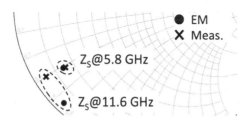

Fig. 4. Simulated and measured input impedances of the IMN.

In addition to the impedance, another important requirement of the matching
network is the insertion loss which needs to be checked. Simulated and measured
insertion losses of the IMN are shown in Fig. 5. It can be seen that the measurement of the insertion loss is greater than that of the simulation due to the loss

in the actual circuit taking into account the effect of the SMA connectors as well as the tolerance in the fabrication of microstrip lines. This difference will lead to a decrease in the output power as well as the power gain of the whole circuit.

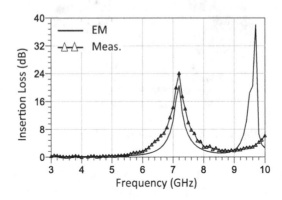

Fig. 5. Simulated and measured insertion loss of the IMN.

2.2   Output Matching Network

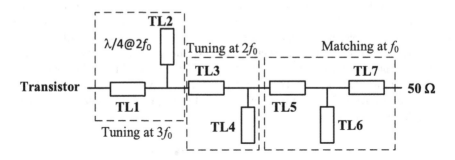

Fig. 6. OMN diagram.

The output matching network (OMN) plays a critical role in the design of the PA because it determines most of the important parameters of the PA such as output power, efficiency and power gain. Basically, the OMN is responsible for two main tasks: power matching to deliver the required output power to the load and compressing the high-order harmonics to improve the efficiency of the circuit. The OMN in this study, in addition to power matching task, will compress both the second and third harmonics. A Load Pull technique in ADS is used to determine the optimum impedances at the fundamental frequency and at the second harmonic and third harmonic. Schematic diagram of the OMN is shown in Fig. 6. Here, TL1, TL2 transmission lines adjust impedance for third harmonic

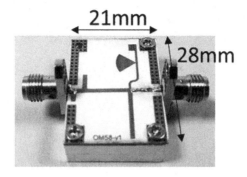

Fig. 7. Fabricated prototype of the OMN.

while TL3, TL4 adjust the second harmonic while TL5, TL6 and TL7 adjust the power matching at the fundamental frequency. The fabricated prototype of the OMN is shown in Fig. 7. It can be seen that the size of the OMN is also quite compact 2.1 cm × 2.8 cm. Simulated and measured impedances of the OMN are shown in Fig. 8. It is easy to see once again the good agreement between the simulation and measurement of the impedance of the OMN. This confirmed the accuracy of the design of the OMN. The impedances at the second and third harmonics of the OMN are also located near the edge of the Smith chart, implying that the power loss at these harmonics has been reduced, resulting in an enhanced efficiency. The losses in the OMN are shown in Fig. 9. The measurement results show that the insertion loss of the OMN is quite large compared to the simulation results, the same reason as with the IMN. This will lead to a decrease in the output power as well as the performance of the actual circuit compared to the simulation results.

3   Entire Circuit Evaluation

3.1   Small-Signal Evaluation

The results of simulation and measurement of the small signal parameters, or the scattering parameters, are shown in Fig. 10. It can be seen that the small signal measurement results is close to the simulation result at the electromagnetic field level. At the 5.8 GHz band, the input and output return losses are quite small, the small signal power gain is approximately 16 dB. Notably, the results of the small signal gain (S21) between the measurement and simulation are very close to each other. These results reflect the accuracy and suitability of designed circuits at the small signal level.

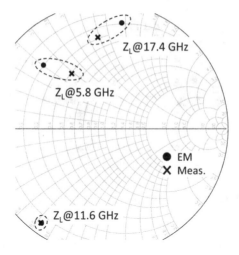

Fig. 8. Simulated and measured impedances of the OMN.

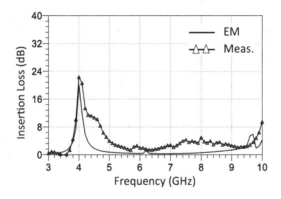

Fig. 9. Simulated and measured insertion loss of the OMN.

3.2   Large-Signal Evaluation

The results of the simulation and measurement of the large signal parameters are shown in Fig. 11. The evaluated criteria include: output power (Pout), efficiency (PAE) and power gain (Gain). It is noted that, the Qorvo's large signal model is used for the TGF2977-SM device, however the input/output matching networks use measured data as shown in the previous section. Another point is that the frequency used in the actual measurement is 5.72 GHz instead of 5.8 GHz as in the simulation. The frequency of 5.72 GHz is used because the actual measured insertion of the OMN is minimal. Observing the results in Fig. 11, it can be seen that, the output power and power gain between simulation and measurement have small differences. As indicated above, this difference is due to the difference in the insertion loss of the input and output matching circuits. However, the difference in PAE performance differs greatly in the large signal area. This

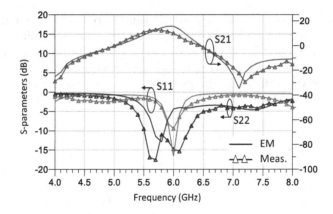

Fig. 10. Simulated and measured small-signal results.

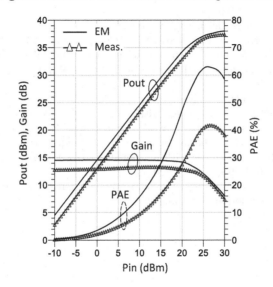

Fig. 11. Simulated and measured large-signal results.

difference is partly caused by the difference in output power. However, the bigger difference is due to the discrepancy between simulation and experiment in the drain current I_{ds}. This deviation comes from the difference in the static characteristic between the simulation model and the actual device.

4   Conclusion

In this paper, we have presented the design method of a 5.8 GHz high-efficiency, microwave power amplifier. To improve efficiency, open-circuited stub are used to adjust the phase difference between the voltage and current at the second harmonic at the input and the second and third harmonic at the output. The measurement results at the small signal level are close to the simulation results of the electromagnetic field level. Experimental results at the large signal level for the output power and power gain agree well with the simulation results. However, the PAE performance is quite different from the simulation because the DC model of the transistor is different from the actual model.

References

1. Sokal, N., et al.: Class EA new class of high-efficiency tuned single ended switching power amplifiers. IEEE J. Solid-State Circuits **SC-10**, 168–176 (1975)
2. Grebennikov, A.: High-efficiency class-e power amplifier with shunt capacitance and shunt filter. IEEE Trans. Circuits Syst. I Regul. Pap. **63**(1), 12–22 (2016)
3. Colantonio, P., et al.: On the class-F power amplifier design. Int. J. RF Microwave Comput.-Aided Eng. (1999)
4. Jin, X.X., et al.: High-efficiency filter-integrated class-F power amplifier based on dielectric resonator. IEEE Microwave Wirel. Compon. Lett. **27**(9), 827–829 (2017)
5. Kamiyama, M., et al.: 5.65 GHz high-efficiency GaN HEMT power amplifier with harmonics treatment up to fourth order. IEEE Microw. Wirel. Compon. Lett. **22**(6), 315–317 (2012)
6. Yao, T., et al.: Frequency characteristic of power efficiency for 10 W/30 W-class 2 GHz band GaN HEMT amplifiers with harmonic reactive terminations. In: Proceedings of the Asia-Pacific Microwave Conference, pp. 745–747 (2013)
7. Enomoto, J., et al.: Second harmonic treatment technique for bandwidth enhancement of GaN HEMT amplifier with harmonic reactive terminations. IEEE Trans. Microw. Theory Tech. **65**(12), 1–6 (2017)
8. https://www.keysight.com/zz/en/products/software/pathwave-design-software/pathwave-advanced-design-system.html
9. https://www.qorvo.com/

CLAN: A Robust Control Link for Aerial Mesh Networks in Contested Environments

Firat Rozkan Kilic[1,2(✉)], Mehmet Ozgen Ozdogan[1,2], Gokhan Secinti[1], and Berk Canberk[1]

[1] Department of Computer Engineering, Istanbul Technical University, Istanbul, Turkey
{kilicf18,ozdogan18,secinti,canberk}@itu.edu.tr
[2] Aselsan Inc., Ankara, Turkey

Abstract. Huge increase in the availability of commercial off-the-shelf unmanned aerial vehicles drastically shifts the way these devices operate and interact, enabling easy and affordable deployment of multiple drones to form a mesh network to perform aerial multi-robot missions such as 3D mapping, surveillance. This trend led to the development of unique applications and services relying on aerial mesh networks in contested environment, but also enables adversaries to improve their ability to counteract using simple techniques such as jamming. In this paper, we propose a robust Control Link for Aerial mesh Networks, namely CLAN, jointly disseminating mesh and UAV control traffic, to ensure reliable control communication for aerial mesh networks, via multi-path, multi-hop control links in contested environment. CLAN forms a dynamic tree topology, where control traffic is forwarded through multiple hops and utilizes multiple access technologies enabling multi-path end-to-end links in order to mitigate the effects of decreased signal power in longer ranges and the possibility of jamming attacks. Computer simulations of the contested environment show that the proposed CLAN algorithm that uses modified B.A.T.M.A.N. algorithm to selectively rebroadcast traffic control messages in order to significantly reduce the traffic control message number by 90% while improving the connectivity of the nodes compared to single hop MAVLink communication up to 72% in simulation results.

Keywords: Wireless mesh networks · B.A.T.M.A.N. · Proactive routing · Traffic control messages · Connectivity · Dynamic tree topology · Jamming · MAVLink

1 Introduction

Unmanned Air Vehicles (UAVs) are getting more affordable, smaller and more capable everyday, extending their domain from military to public and civil use with various new applications such as crowd monitoring, surveillance, traffic

© ICST Institute for Computer Sciences, Social Informatics and Telecommunications Engineering 2021
Published by Springer Nature Switzerland AG 2021. All Rights Reserved
N.-S. Vo et al. (Eds.): INISCOM 2021, LNICST 379, pp. 25–36, 2021.
https://doi.org/10.1007/978-3-030-77424-0_3

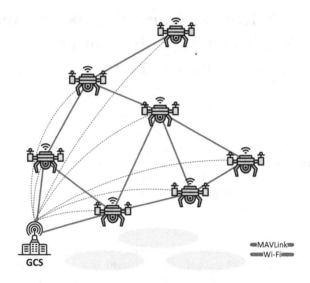

Fig. 1. Both MAVLink and UAV-to-UAV mesh links are up

control, cellular data offloading and logistics [1–4]. This trend also enables having multiple UAVs cooperating in order to perform shared tasks such as reconnaissance or monitoring hostile environments [5,6]. In most of these applications, UAVs require an active direct one-hop link with a Ground Control Station (GCS) for downstreaming sensor data to GCS and getting command and control parameters from GCS. Due to the nature of electromagnetic waves, the received power is inversely proportional to the square of the distance between the source and the destination, thus limiting the operation range of a UAV. This communication channel becomes susceptible for a jamming attack since the received power weakens as the UAV travels farther from the GCS. With above challenges in mind, we propose to use ad-hoc links between UAVs that are used to forward UAV-to-UAV messages in order to create and maintain logical e2e connections for the control messages between the GCS to UAV. However, any proactive mesh network protocol relies on its own control traffic to be generated and forwarded periodically in order to maintain an up-to-date topology. Considering this mesh control traffic is flooded through network, this traffic alone poses a risk to saturate ad-hoc links in larger networks. This, additional control traffic of UAVs burden de-facto protocol (shown in Sect. 3 and Sect. 4). Therefore, we develop a robust Control Link for Aerial mesh Networks, abbreviated as CLAN, that forms employing selective rebroadcast mechanisms in order to reduce the amount of traffic control messages. As our target scenario, we assume that the leaves in the formed tree structure are *mission nodes* that perform the main task of the multi-UAV system and the rest of the nodes, called *network nodes* act as a backbone to relay these messages to the GCS.

The CLAN framework that we propose uses the information from received traffic control (TC) packets at each drone and therefore operate using local information of that drone. Since the network is highly dynamic that has three degrees of freedom of movement, we think that the topology would change before having every information of the current state. Furthermore, CLAN framework designed to work in contested environments where jammers exist against drone surveillance missions. We propose a heuristic approach to move the network nodes in order to maintain connectivity of the mission nodes to the GCS while being able to sense and escape from jammers in such contested areas. The network nodes move autonomously with respect to the changing position of the other nodes or sensing a high received signal power that is interpreted as jamming attack with respect to proposed movement algorithms in order to increase connectivity and to form possible multiple paths from a node to the GCS to provide more resiliency.

We list the main contributions of the paper as follows:

– We conduct set of preliminary experiments, showcasing how existing mesh protocols suffers in maintaining e2e connection due to the large overhead of traffic control messages saturating the network containing multi-hop links and how long range links are vulnerable to jamming attacks.
– We design and implement CLAN framework, jointly optimizing the dissemination of both mesh and UAV control traffic, where MAVLink and B.A.T.M.A.N. protocols are used together as the baseline approach.
– We evaluate the performance of CLAN through extensive simulations, showing CLAN allows UAVs to operate in longer range, provide resilience against jammer attacks and improve connectivity.

The rest of the paper is structured as follows. Section 2 layouts the related works. The system overview and the details of CLAN are explained in Sect. 3. The evaluation results are presented in Sect. 4 and we conclude the paper with Sect. 5.

2   Related Work

In [7–9] researchers propose using the cellular network for both UAV-to-UAV (U2U) and UAV-to-GCS (U2G) communication for better performance. [10,11] study the network structure when there is no need for communicating with a central infrastructure node. Multicast trees in AODV [12] introduce packet delay, OLSR [17] makes the nodes learn the complete view of network and computationally more complex and active tree route finding mechanism in IEEE 802.11s [13] required three messages back and forth to complete tree finding. Instead of these protocols, we have changed the structure of OGM messages in B.A.T.M.A.N. and rebroadcasting of TC messages to form a node tree with low computational complexity.

In [14], OLSR (proactive) and DSR (reactive) protocols are compared in MANET with nodes having low mobility and it is shown that OLSR has outperformed DSR in terms of packet delays. The drawback of reactive protocols

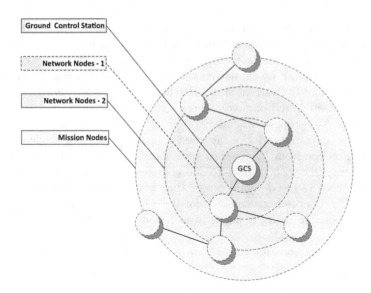

Fig. 2. Tree structure of nodes

is that there is a route finding delay before being able to send packets to their destination[14]. We have opted to use a proactive routing protocol because a) it ensures fresh and ready route tables and b) there is no route finding delay. However, the TC messages and the data traffic in the network can cause packet losses due to interference. In addition to this, Flying Ad-Hoc Networks (FANETs) have different challenges than MANETs and VANETs in terms of mobility and three degrees of freedom in the movement. To tackle with this situation [15,16] have proposed using directional antennas.

In [17] a wireless mesh network based on B.A.T.M.A.N. protocol with multiple ground potential receivers has been used to improve resiliency at the cost of compromising network throughput. These approaches are not suited for small rotary wing UAVs in a hostile environment. In this study, we propose a method to maintain UAV-GCS communication using the available wireless mesh network where the C2 Link fails. We achieve this by creating a tree structure of nodes with minimal Traffic Control messages by modifying the B.A.T.M.A.N. protocol [17] (Fig. 3).

3   System Model

In this paper, we approach the problem of UAV-GCS communication using wireless mesh network , where there are multiple drones in the system. We are mainly motivated by B.A.T.M.A.N. protocol [18] used for routing in multi-hop Mobile Ad-Hoc Networks (mhMANET). We modify this existing protocol to suit our needs. The system model that we study here is as follows: The drone network that performs the mission is initialized with at least one drone in each branch. The

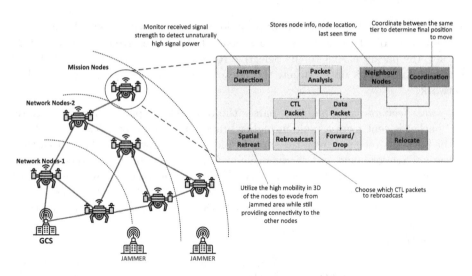

Fig. 3. CLAN concept

network drones are prohibited from their initial mission in order to ensure that there are drones closer to the Ground Control Station to relay the messages from further nodes. In the next section we will compare the original B.A.T.M.A.N. with our modified approach. The system model in normal situation is shown in Fig. 1. In the scenario of hardware fail on the GCS or an intentional disruption on the MAVLink is present, the communication can only be achieved by using the present wireless mesh network.

As mentioned above, in order to decrease the number of the traffic control messages and the data messages we form a tree of nodes. The OGMs, also called originator messages, in B.A.T.M.A.N. is only rebroadcasted if the received OGM has come from a node in the lower branches. Therefore, the source of this origi-nator node designates the node in the upper branches as the best next hope. In the Fig. 2 the tree formed in the example scenario is shown.

This selective rebroadcast of messages decrease the number of TC packets in the network. Downstream messages from the UAVs to the GCS is aggregated along the tree. This way, total number of data packets are reduced. Similarly, upstream messages from the GCS to the UAVs are sent as a one big packet and disaggregated along the way, also helping reducing the number of packets in the network. Since we decrease both the TC messages and command-and-control messages we decrease the packet loss rate.

Jammer Detection: Jammer detection block analyses the received signal levels and checks if a packet is received successfully. If the received signal power is high and the UAV doesn't receive a packet, it triggers spatial retreat.

Spatial Retreat: Randomly move to another position within the signal range of nodes in lower branch in order to evade the jammed area while maintaining connectivity of the nodes.

Packet Analysis: The packet analysis module checks if the received packet is a traffic control (TC) packet or a data packet. If the received packet is a TC packet, the packet is sent to the Selective Rebroadcast block as an input. If the received packet is a data packet, the packet is sent to the upper layers in the network.

Selective Rebroadcast: The block parses the received TC packet. If the received TC packet is sent from a node in higher branch, immediately drops the packet. If the packet is received from the same branch or from lower branches, check the "Original Sender" field and "Sequence Number" field in the TC message header to determine if the node has rebroadcasted this message recently by checking the circular buffer allocated for recently sent messages. If the buffer doesn't contain this message, i.e., the received message is fresh, then the node rebroadcasts this TC message to its neighbours. The selective rebroadcast algorithm is described in Algorithm 1.

Neighbour Nodes Table: Stores and updates the list of neighbour node information from the received TC packets. The information contains the location of the node, last time a message is received from the node and the branch of the node. If a connection is lost to a previously connected node, the information about the lost neighbour node is sent to the coordination block.

Coordination: When a previously existing connection fails between the neighbouring nodes, this block uses the information in the Neighbour Nodes Table block to determine a new position a node should be placed in order to restore the broken connection. The output of this block is the new position of the node in order to try to restore the recently broken connection.

Relocate: Gets the input from Neighbour Nodes and Coordination blocks to decide to stay or compute the next position to move.

Algorithm 1 Selective Rebroadcast Algorithm

1: $m_j \leftarrow received\ traffic\ control\ message\ from\ node_j$
2: **if** m *is not in the messages set* **then**
3:      $orgSender \leftarrow Originator\ Address\ field\ in\ the\ packet\ header$
4:      $seqNo \leftarrow Sequence\ Number\ field\ in\ the\ packet\ header$
5:      **if** $nodeTier_j > nodeTier_i\ or\ TTL == 0$ **then**
6:          drop m
7:      **else if** *didn't receive m before* **then**
8:          decrease TTL by one
9:          Rebroadcast m
10:         add (orgSender, seqNo) pair to sent messages set
11:     **else**
12:         drop m
13:     **end if**
14: **end if**

The selective rebroadcast algorithm significantly reduces the number of TC messages in the network especially where the operation area is smaller and the number of nodes is higher.

Algorithm 2 Movement Algorithm of the Network Nodes in CLAN

1: **for** time = 1 to SimulationTime **do**
2:   **for** each node i **do**
3:     **if** $(senseJammer(i))$ **then**
4:       Move(i)
5:     **end if**
6:     **if** $(nodetier_i < \text{MAX\_TIER\_NUMBER})$ **then**
7:       **for** each node j != i **do**
8:         **if** $(receive\ packet\ from\ node_j)$ **then**
9:           $Add\ node_i\ to\ recentlyCommunicatedList\ of\ node_j$
10:           lostTimer[i, j] = 0
11:         **else**
12:           increment lostTimer[i, j] by 1
13:         **end if**
14:         **if** $(lostTimer[i,j] == TIMEOUT\_THRESHOLD$ and $j\ is\ in\ list$ $recentlyCommunicatedList\ of\ node_i)$ **then**
15:           Move(i, j)
16:           giveUpCounter(j)++
17:           **if** $(giveUpCounter(j) == TIMEOUT\_THRESHOLD)$ **then**
18:             $Remove\ node_j\ from\ recentlyCommunicatedList\ of\ node_i$
19:           **end if**
20:         **end if**
21:       **end for**
22:     **end if**
23:     **if** $(recentlyCommunicatedList\ of\ node_i\ is\ empty)$ **then**
24:       MoveRandomlyInsideOperatingArea()
25:     **end if**
26:   **end for**
27: **end for**

---

4 Performance Evaluation

In this section, we compare the experimental results with the current approach in order to demonstrate the performance improvements. Mainly, CLAN provides two major improvements to the overall performance of UAV-GCS communication. The first improvement is the reduced number of the traffic control messages in the network using a proactive routing protocol. We validate this by comparing the number of the traffic control messages between the original B.A.T.M.A.N. algorithm and our proposed selective rebroadcast method. We generate the nodes randomly while guaranteeing that there is at least one node in each branch. Then, we record the initial position of the nodes in order to simulate the both B.A.T.M.A.N. and CLAN algorithm using the same initial parameters. The simulations are run with varying maximum area and the number of nodes. Each simulation is run for 100 seconds and the simulations are run 1000 times and the average number of generated traffic control messages are shown in Fig. 4.

We observe that as the area gets smaller and the number of nodes gets larger, the selective rebroadcast algorithm significantly reduces the number of

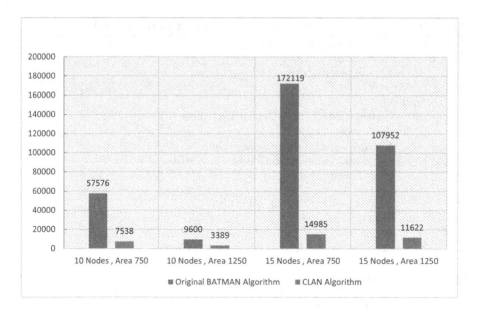

Fig. 4. Number of traffic control messages in proactive routing

traffic control messages. In larger areas with lower number of nodes, the nodes are sparse and there are less loops between the nodes, so the number of traffic control messages in B.A.T.M.A.N. is fewer.

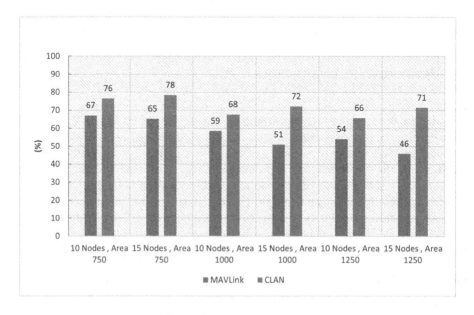

Fig. 5. Average connectivity

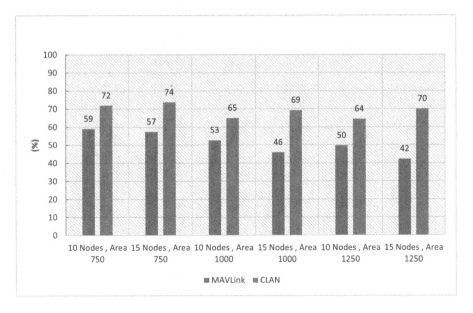

Fig. 6. Average connectivity (1 Jammer)

However, even in this situation CLAN algorithm reduced the number of the traffic control messages greatly. This improvement reduces the traffic control messaging overhead in the proactive routing in the mesh network between the nodes.

Secondly, we compare the connectivity of the system using CLAN algorithm that enables multi-hop transmission of the UAV messages and the system using individual MAVLink links to connect each node to the ground control station with a direct link. Connectivity of a node is "1" if a node can reach to the GCS and "0" if the node cannot. Total connectivity is the ratio of connected nodes over the total number of nodes, shown in Eq. 1 where N represents the number of total UAVs in the network. Both methods are simulated in order to get the average connectivity with the same initial node positions in each simulation run. Each simulation is run for 100 seconds and the simulation is run 1000 times to get the average results. The average percent of the connectivity is shown in varying area size, number of nodes and number of jammers are shown in Figs. 5–7 within the range of 95% confidence interval.

$$Connectivity = \frac{\sum_{i=1}^{N} c_i}{N} \qquad (1)$$

It can be seen that when the operation area of the group of drones is small, CLAN framework outperforms the single-hop communication by merely 10%. However, as the area increases, our proposed algorithm performs better by up to 50%. In the presence of standing jammers -that are randomly distributed in each simulation- the improvement is larger since the network nodes in CLAN relocate themselves in order to maintain connectivity while the communication in single-hop MAVLink is disrupted.

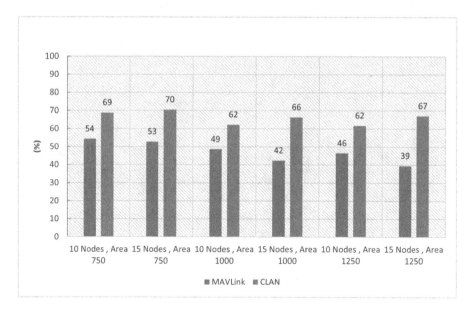

Fig. 7. Average connectivity (3 Jammers)

5   Conclusion

In this paper, we proposed an algorithm in order to increase the connectivity of multiple UAV systems by dividing the nodes into branches with respect to their distance to the ground control station and form a ad-hoc mesh network between the nodes. In our approach, we used an proactive ad-hoc routing in order to combat highly dynamic network topology due to the nature of UAV networks. We modified the B.A.T.M.A.N. algorithm to reduce the number of traffic control messages and according to our simulations we reduce these messages by up to 90%. With the reduced overhead of the traffic control messages, this ad-hoc mesh network is used to provide communication between the UAVs and the ground control station. The messages are sent over multiple hops and over possible multiple paths which increases the operation range and connectivity of multiple UAV systems. Our heuristic algorithm to relocate the node relies on local information and allows the node to act faster to broken links and possible jamming attacks. According to our results, CLAN algorithm does perform 10% better where the both the operation area and the number of nodes is smallest when no jammers are present and the improvements go up to 72% compared to single-hop communication using individual MAVLinks for each drone.

References

1. Bozkaya, E., Canberk, B.: BS-on-air: optimum UAV localization for resilient ultra dense networks. In: IEEE Conference on Computer Communications Workshops, INFOCOM 2018, pp. 877–881 (2018). https://doi.org/10.1109/INFOCOMW.2018. 8406903
2. Barrado, C., Meseguer, R., Lopez, J., Pastor, E., Santamaria, E., Royo, P.: Wildfire monitoring using a mixed air-ground mobile network. IEEE Pervasive Comput. 9(4), 24–32 (2010). ISSN 15361268. https://doi.org/10.1109/MPRV.2010.54
3. Sun, Z., Wang, P., Vuran, M.C., Al-Rodhaan, M.A., Al-Dhelaan, A.M., Akyildiz, I.F.: BorderSense: border patrol through advanced wireless sensor networks. Ad Hoc Netw. 9(3), 468–477 (2011). ISSN 15708705. https://doi.org/10.1016/j.adhoc. 2010.09.008
4. Hayat, S., Yanmaz, E., Muzaffar, R.: Survey on unmanned aerial vehicle networks for civil applications: a communications viewpoint. IEEE Commun. Surv. Tutor. 18(4), 2624–2661 (2016). ISSN 1553877X. https://doi.org/10.1109/COMST.2016. 2560343
5. Busnel, Y., Caillouet, C., Coudert, D.: Self-organized UAV-based supervision and connectivity: challenges and opportunities. In: 2019 IEEE 18th International Symposium on Network Computing and Applications, NCA 2019, pp. 1–5 (2019). https://doi.org/10.1109/NCA.2019.8935060
6. Menouar, H., Guvenc, I., Akkaya, K., Uluagac, A.S., Kadri, A., Tuncer, A.: UAV-enabled intelligent transportation systems for the smart city: applications and challenges. IEEE Commun. Mag. 55(3), 22–28 (2017). ISSN 01636804. https://doi.org/ 10.1109/MCOM.2017.1600238CM
7. Huang, Y., Mei, W., Xu, J., Qiu, L., Zhang, R.: Cognitive UAV communication via joint maneuver and power control. IEEE Trans. Commun. 67(11), 7872–7888 (2019). ISSN 15580857. https://doi.org/10.1109/TCOMM.2019.2931322. arXiv:1901.02804
8. Zhang, S., Zhang, H., Di, B., Song, L.: Cellular UAVTo-X communications: design and optimization for multi-UAV networks. IEEE Trans. Wirel. Commun. 18(2), 1346–1359 (2019). ISSN 15582248. https://doi.org/10.1109/TWC.2019.2892131. arXiv:1801.05000
9. Nguyen, H.C., Amorim, R., Wigard, J., Kovacs, I.Z., Mogensen, P.: Using LTE networks for UAV command and control link: a rural-area coverage analysis. In: IEEE Vehicular Technology Conference, vol. 2017-Septe, pp. 1–6 (2018). ISSN 15502252. https://doi.org/10.1109/VTCFall.2017.8287894
10. Dong, S.Y.: Optimization of OLSR routing protocol in UAV ad HOC network. In: 2016 13th International Computer Conference on Wavelet Active Media Technology and Information Processing, ICCWAMTIP 2017, pp. 90–94 (2017). https:// doi.org/10.1109/ICCWAMTIP.2016.8079811
11. Rosati, S., Kruzelecki, K., Heitz, G., Floreano, D., Rimoldi, B.: Dynamic routing for flying ad hoc networks. IEEE Trans. Veh. Technol. 65(3), 1690–1700 (2016). ISSN 00189545. https://doi.org/10.1109/TVT.2015.2414819. arXiv:1406.4399
12. Perkins, C.E., Park, M., Royer, E.M.: Adhoc on-demand distance vector routing. In: Mobile Computing Systems and Applications (WMCSA 1999), pp. 90–100 (1999)
13. Guesmia, M., Guezouri, M., Mbarek, N.: Performance evaluation of the HWMP proactive tree mode for IEEE 802.11s based wireless mesh networks. In: 3rd International Conference on Communications and Networking, ComNet 2012, vol. 2, no. 1 (2012). https://doi.org/10.1109/ComNet.2012.6217743

14. Appiah, M., Cudjoe, R.: A comparative study of reactive and proactive routing protocols on a mobility model in mobile ad hoc network (MANET). In: 2018 International Conference on Smart Computing and Electronic Enterprise, ICSCEE 2018, pp. 1–7 (2018). https://doi.org/10.1109/ICSCEE.2018.8538398
15. Britton, M., Coyle, A.: Performance analysis of the B.A.T.M.A.N wireless ad-hoc network routing protocol with mobility and directional antennas, pp. 1–6, November 2011. ISBN 978-1-4673-5727-2. https://doi.org/10.1109/MilCIS.2011.6470393
16. Alshbatat, A.I., Dong, L.: Adaptive MAC protocol for UAV communication networks using directional antennas. In: 2010 International Conference on Networking, Sensing and Control, ICNSC 2010, pp. 598–603 (2010). https://doi.org/10.1109/ICNSC.2010.5461589
17. Pandi, S., Gabriel, F., Zhdanenko, O., Wunderlich, S., Fitzek, F.H.: MESHMERIZE: an interactive demo of resilient mesh networks in drones. In: 2019 16th IEEE Annual Consumer Communications and Networking Conference, CCNC 2019, pp. 1–2 (2019). https://doi.org/10.1109/CCNC.2019.8651795
18. Neumann, A., Aichele, C., Lindner, M., Wunderlich, S.: Better approach to mobile ad-hoc networking (BATMAN). IETF Draft, pp. 1–24 (2008)

Energy-Efficient Mobility-Aware Clustering Protocol in WBASN for eHealth Applications

Thien T. T. Le[1]([⊠])[iD], Nguyen-Duy Lai[2], LeminhThien Huynh[1], and VanCuu Ho[1]

[1] Saigon University, Ho Chi Minh City, Vietnam
thien.lett@sgu.edu.vn
[2] Cao Thang Technical College, Ho Chi Minh City, Vietnam

Abstract. Wireless body area sensor networks (WBASN) becomes an emerge network which is now implemented for eHealth applications. The WBASN consists of multiple embedded biosensors and the coordinator. The biosensors collect vital data of human body, which will be transmitted to the coordinator; then, the coordinator forwards the vital data to doctor via the Internet. Because many sensors may select the same routing path to the coordinator, the collision of transmission may occur which leads to degrade network performance. In this paper, we proposed an energy-efficient mobility-aware clustering protocol (EMAC) which allows the sensors to form into clusters, then only cluster heads forward data to the coordinator. The results show that network performance has been improved in terms of high residual energy at the sensor nodes and high received packets at the coordinator.

Keywords: Wireless body area sensor network · Energy-efficient · Clustering · eHealth applications

1 Introduction

Wireless body area sensor networks (WBASN) are implemented for eHealth applications which will monitor the vital data of human for medical treatment at the hospital or at home [1–3]. The wireless biosensors can be attached or deployed on-in the human body to collect vital signals, such as heart rate, blood pressure, or temperature [3]. These biosensors can transmit data via the wireless link, the human can move freely at home or the hospital which is very convenient and helpful to the elderly. The typical network for eHealth applications can be described as in Fig. 1 [1,3]. In Fig. 1 the WBASN topology consists of one coordinator at the center of network, and many biosensors which can be deployed at the arm, leg, or shoulder of human body. The vital data from the human body can be transmitted to the gateway which forwards data to the medical

N.-S. Vo et al. (Eds.): INISCOM 2021, LNICST 379, pp. 37–47, 2021.
https://doi.org/10.1007/978-3-030-77424-0_4

server or the doctor through Internet for eHealth applications. In the situation where many biosensor nodes transmit data to the coordinator at the same time, many nodes may select the same routing path to transmit data to the coordination. Therefore, collision may occur which cause re-transmission packets. As a consequence, the energy consumption at node may increase while transmitting data [4].

Many routing protocols have been developed to reduce the energy consumption at node by selecting the forwarder or forming into a cluster [5]. In [6], the Mobility-supporting Adaptive Threshold-based Thermal-aware Energy-efficient Multi-hop ProTocol (M-ATTEMPT) has been investigated which results in low energy consumption at nodes while considering the mobility and the rise of temperature at node. The node will select the neighbors to forward data to the sink, the node may have more than one route to the sink. In M-ATTEMPT, node selects the routing path to the sink node according to the path with less hop-counts or less energy consumption. In [7], the author applie multi-hop routing protocol in WBASNs which called the Stable Increased-throughput Multi-hop Protocol for Link Efficiency (SIMPLE). The SIMPLE protocol ensures the network efficiency in terms of high throughput, reliable and power efficient protocol in which the node selects the forwarder according to a cost function of distance to the sink and the residual energy of node. The clustering protocol has shown the benefits of preserving the energy consumption and increasing the throughput of the network.

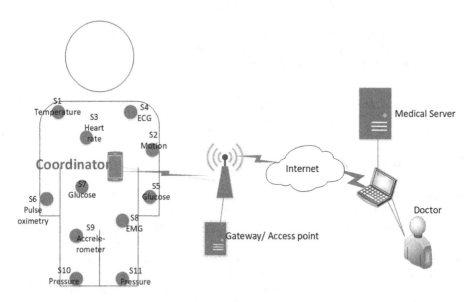

Fig. 1. WBASN topology for e-Health application.

In this paper, we proposed an Energy-efficient Mobility-Aware Clustering protocol (EMAC) protocol for WBASN. We assume that the topology of

WBASN is divided into multiple-hop communication. The algorithm aims to find the cluster in which the nodes can forward data to the coordinator with the lowest energy consumption. Our contribution can be explained as follows. Sensor nodes will form into the cluster by considering the residual energy and the network topology. The sensor node can elect to become the cluster head, then, the cluster head sends the HELLO message to its neighbors. The other nodes request to join the cluster by sending the REPLY messages. The cluster is updated after some rounds because the network topology changes according to the human mobility. We evaluate our proposed algorithm by comparing to other clustering protocols in terms of received packets at the coordinator, the number of dead nodes, and residual energy at node. The rest of paper is organized as follows. In Sect. 2, the energy-efficient mobility-aware clustering protocol (EMAC) protocol for WBASN is introduced. In the next section, the network performance is evaluated. Finally, the paper is concluded in Sect. 4.

2   Energy-Efficient Mobility-Aware Clustering Protocol in WBASN

2.1   Network Model

The network of WBASN is considered as in [6,7] in which a WBASN consists of a coordinator and M biosensor nodes in e-Health application. The network topology is shown as in Fig. 1. Biosensor node can transmit vital data to the coordinator via either one-hop communication or multi-hop communication. The sensor node is denoted as s_i. We assume that several sensor nodes can form a cluster in which the cluster head collects data packets of its cluster members then forwarding to the coordinator. The biosensor nodes can be categorized into cluster head (CH) or cluster members (CM). The network can be divided into C clusters in which each cluster has one CH and K CMs. The cluster head will be selected according to the residual energy and bandwidth of node. We define the bandwidth of cluster head as the total number of successfully received packets at the cluster head which cluster head will forward to the coordinator. Because of the limitation of the battery, the node will change the role of cluster head after some rounds.

In WBASN, each sensor node collects data according to the type of sensors such as heart rate, blood pressure. Data can be categorized into emergency data or periodic data which have different requirements of throughput, latency, and data rate. In our work, some reasonable assumptions can be adopted as follows:

- Nodes are dynamic with the same initial energy 0.5J and are deployed in or on the human body.
- The network consists of only one coordinator node and the location of coordinator node is known by all the sensor nodes. The distance between coordinator node to the sensor may change by time because of the movement of human body.

- The sensor nodes have a certain limitation as energy, storage, radio communication capabilities, and bandwidth.
- The depth of node is defined as the number of hops to reach to the sink node.
- After the cluster is formed, the sensor node will transmit data to the cluster head and, then, the cluster head forward aggregated data to the sink.

2.2 Energy Consumption Model

In WBASN, if nodes transmit data to the coordinator via one-hop transmission, the model of energy consumption for transmitting b-bits messages is calculated as in [6,7]. The energy expended to transmit the b-bits message (Etx) and to receive this message (Erx) are respectively given as follows:

$$E_{tx} = b * (E_{tx-elec} + E_{amp} * d^2) \tag{1}$$

where $E_{tx-elec}$ is the electronics energy dissipated per bit, d denotes the distance between transmitter and receiver, E_{amp} is the energy required for the amplified circuit.

$$E_{rx} = b * E_{rx-elec} \tag{2}$$

where $E_{rx-elec}$ is the electronics energy dissipated per bit.

In our algorithm, after sending data to the cluster head, the cluster member turn off the radio then enters the idle state in order to save energy. If the sensor node si transmits data to the coordinator; the energy consumption for one-hop transmission is calculated as follows

$$E_{tx}(i, S) = D_i * (E_{tx}) = D_i * b * (E_{tx-elec} + E_{amp} * d^2) \tag{3}$$

where D_i is the depth of node s_i, b is the total bits of data.

If node s_j is the cluster head; the depth of cluster j is denoted as D_j . The number of cluster member of cluster j is denoted as K; b denotes the total bits of data. The total energy consumption for receiving data from K cluster members is calculated as follows:

$$E_{rx}(CH_j) = D_j * K * E_{rx} = D_j * K * (b * E_{rx-elec}) \tag{4}$$

Energy consumption for transmitting b-bits data from cluster head to the sink is calculated as follows:

$$E_{tx}(CH_j, S) = D_j * K * E_{tx} = D_j * K * b * (E_{tx-elec} + E_{amp} * d^2) \tag{5}$$

The total energy consumption for transmitting and receiving at the cluster head is denoted as follows

$$E_{consump}(CH_j, S) = E_{tx}(CH_j, S) + E_{rx}(CH_j) \tag{6}$$

2.3   Energy-Efficient Mobility-Aware Clustering Protocol

In our proposed protocol, each node stores information of the sensor ID, distance to the coordinator, list of neighbors, residual energy, number of generated packets, and the current bandwidth. Let assume that bandwidth at node s_j is calculated as total of all packet data needed to send to the cluster head or the coordinator node. The maximum bandwidth in the network is defined as $BW_{threshold}$. If node s_j is the cluster head and the total number of cluster members is K; each member node s_j generates packet with length of b_{ij}. Total bandwidth at node s_j is calculated as follows:

$$BW_j = \sum_{i=1}^{K} b_{ij} \tag{7}$$

In order to balance the energy consumption at node and maximize the total bandwidth, the sensor nodes use the value of energy consumption and the total bandwidth in the history to calculate the probability to elect cluster head as follows

$$P(CH_i(t)) = \alpha \frac{E_{consump}(t-1)}{E_{res}} + \beta \frac{BW_i(t-1)}{BW_{threshold}} \tag{8}$$

where α and β are the coefficient in which $\alpha + \beta = 1$; $E_{consump}(t\text{-}1)$ is the energy consumption at round $(t\text{-}1)$ which is calculated as (9); $BW_i(t\text{-}1)$ is the bandwidth at round $(t\text{-}1)$.

Our main contribution aims to select the cluster head according to the energy consumption and the total received packet in the past. Assume that node si is currently a cluster head, then node may become cluster head or cluster member at the next round. If energy consumption of node $E_{consump}$ increases ΔE and $BW_i(t)$ increases ΔBW, then $P(CH_i)$ increases. In this case, due to the rise of energy consumption may lead to the short lifetime at node s_i, node s_i will become a cluster member in the next round.

The sensor nodes select the cluster head to join according to the distance to the cluster head. Each node creates the list of cluster head nearby as $N_{HELLO} = \{s_i \,|\, d(m,i) \le TRx, P(CH_i) \le P_{th}\}$, in which $d(m,i)$ is the distance between node s_m and cluster head s_i, TRx is the transmission range of node s_m, P_{th} is the threshold value to elect to cluster head. After receiving the HELLO messages of the neighbors, the sensor node select the cluster head with the shortest distance to join in order to reduce the energy consumption in trasmitting packets. The sensor s_m will select the cluster head amongst the list of N_{HELLO} as follows:

$$min_{dist-to-CH} = min\{d(m,i) \,|\, s_i \in N_{HELLO}\} \tag{9}$$

The cluster formation algorithm is shown in The Algorithm 1. Each sensor node calculates the probability to elect the cluster head, shown from line 1 to line 8. If the $P(CH_i)$ is smaller than the threshold value, node elects to become cluster head and broadcast the *HELLO* message. We assume that the number of cluster heads in the network can be selected as in [8]. For all nodes do not send

---
Algorithm 1. Energy-efficient mobility-aware clustering protocol

---
Input: Input: N nodes, node ID, neighbors of node
Output: Output: list of cluster head $LstCH$ and cluster members of each cluster head
 1: Assign $LstCH = \emptyset$; $LstCM = \emptyset$
 2: **for all** $s_i \in N$ **do**
 3:     Calculate the probability to elect cluster head $P(CH_i)$ as in (8)
 4:     **if** $P(CH_i) \leq P_{th}$ **then**
 5:         Node s_i broadcast HELLO message
 6:         Update $LstCH = LstCH \cup s_i$
 7:     **else**
 8:         Wait for HELLO message
 9:         Update $LstCM = LstCM \cup s_i$
10:     **end if**
11: **end for**
12: **for all** $s_m \in LstCM$ **do**
13:     **if** node s_m receives HELLO message **then**
14:         Node s_m waits for HELLO message from neighbors, create a list N_{HELLO}
15:         Node s_m finds the CH with $min_{dist-to-CH}$ as in (9)
16:         Node s_m sends REPLY message to node s_i
17:         Node s_i updates its cluster member $LstCM(s_i) = LstCM(s_i) \cup s_m$
18:     **else**
19:         Node s_m directly send data to the coordinator
20:     **end if**
21: **end for**

---

the *HELLO* message, nodes will wait for the *HELLO* message then select the cluster to join, shown from line 10 to line 17. The node may receive more than one *HELLO* messages from its neighbors as in line 11. Node selects the cluster head with the least distance comparing to others as in line 12. After selecting cluster head, node sends the REPLY message to the cluster head as in line 13. By receiving the *REPLY* from the other neighbors, the cluster head updates the cluster members as in line 14. Because of the mobility, some nodes may out of the transmission range of the cluster head; then they does not receive any *HELLO* message. These nodes will directly send data to the sink node.

3   Performance Evaluation

In this section, the energy-efficient mobility-aware clustering protocol (EMAC) protocol is evaluated and compared to the ATTEMP and SIMPLE algorithm [7] by using Matlab. The ATTEMP and SIMPLE also deploy the clustering protocols which select the cluster head based on the distance to the sink and the residual energy of node.

3.1   Simulation Environment

In our simulations, nodes are uniformly deployed at random body as in [7]. The sink node is fixed at the center of the network area. We also deploy the energy consumption model for transmitting and receiving data as in [7]. The detailed simulation parameters are listed in Table 1. We assume that the network deployment is changed after 1000 rounds in order to evaluate the network mobility. Each sensor node randomly generates packets to send to the coordinator.

Table 1. Simulation environment.

Parameter	Value
Network size	2 m * 2 m
Number of nodes	20
Data rate	250 kbps
Initial energy	0.5 J
$E_{tx-elec}$	16.7 nJ/b
$E_{rx-elec}$	36.1 nJ/b
E_{amp}	1.97e−9 nJ/b
α	0.5
β	0.5
Pth	0.2

3.2   Simulation Results and Discussion

The network performance is evaluated with respect to total received packets at the sink, number of dead nodes, and the residual energy of node [7]. In order to evaluate the stability of network performance in the dynamic environment, we evaluate the EMAC in three difference scenarios of mobility. The network deployment changes after 1000 rounds, the nodes mobility follows the Random waypoint mobility model with different velocity as in [5–7]. Three values of velocity are selected as 0.1 m/s, 0.2 m/s, and 0.3 m/s for low mobility, average mobility, and high mobility, respectively. The number of dead nodes is shown in Fig. 2. In the worst scenario, the nodes start to die at round 2500th, but half of the nodes die at round 8000th.

The average residual energy of each node is shown in Fig. 3. The residual energy declines quickly in case of high mobility. Despite that, the residual energy remains higher than 0.05 Joules at the round 8000th. As a consequence, the network lifetime of nodes remains longer. Because the high mobility scenario cause changes in the network topology, the nodes may out of transmission range of its cluster head then they require more energy consumption for data transmission. However, high mobility requires the cluster to re-establish which the sensors send more HELLO and REPLY messages.

The total received packets at the coordinator are calculated by total packets successfully receiving at the coordinator node. The simulation result in Fig. 4

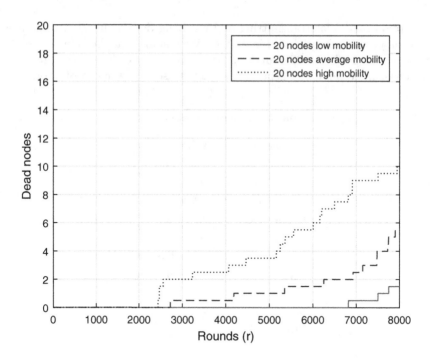

Fig. 2. Number of dead nodes in different network scenarios.

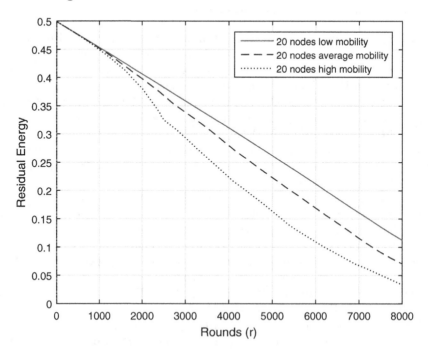

Fig. 3. Residual energy of nodes in different network senarios.

shows that our proposed EMAC performs better than SIMPLE and ATTEMP with respect to the higher number of received packets. In EMAC, nodes only transmit data to the cluster head which is already in the transmission range of node. Therefore, the probability of packet transmission is high. As a result, the total received packet at the coordinator is higher comparing to other protocols.

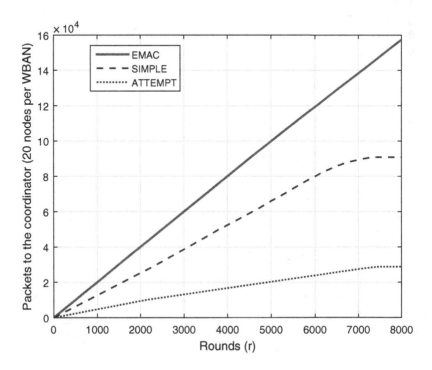

Fig. 4. Number of received packets at the coordinator node.

In Fig. 5, the number of dead nodes is used to evaluate the network lifetime. The dead node is calculated when nodes die due to energy depletion of battery. The simulation result in Fig. 3 shows the number of dead nodes along with the rounds. Our proposed EMAC performs better than ATTEMP and SIMPLE in which the nodes start to die in the 4500th round, while in the nodes dies in the 2000th and 3800th round as in the ATTEMPT and SIMPLE, respectively. In EMAC, the nodes change the role of cluster head after some time according to the history of bandwidth, which allows the nodes reduce the traffic. The non-cluster head will elect to be cluster head in the future, therefore, the traffic is kept balance in the network.

In the EMAC, the cluster head only communicates with only cluster members in each round, the number of overhead packets such as HELLO and REPLY messages are limited within K cluster members. The cluster member only transmits to the cluster head via the assigned time slot, the collision can be reduced.

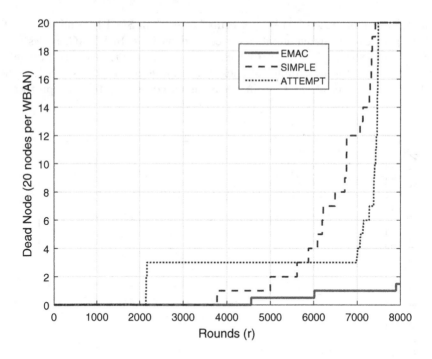

Fig. 5. Number of dead nodes.

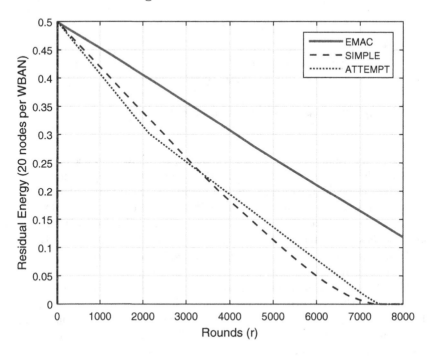

Fig. 6. Residual energy at one node.

Therefore, the consumption energy is reduced at cluster head per round. If the network topology change, the cluster will be re-selected with new cluster head and cluster members. In EMAC, the nodes select its cluster head according the least distance which results in low energy consumption in transmitting. Figure 6, shows that the average residual energy of EMAC is higher than ATTEMPT and SIMPLE.

4 Conclusion

In this paper, we have proposed the EMAC protocol to maintain the cluster with the change of network topology due to mobility. The biosensors nodes offer low dead nodes as well as high energy residual. However, the low dead nodes results in longer network lifetime which guarantees high packets received at the coordinator. The simulation evaluation shows that the EMAC outperforms other protocols in terms of higher residual energy and higher successful received packets at the coordinator node. In our future works, we will improve the cluster head selection based on the temperature rise at nodes in order to balance energy of nodes.

References

1. Vera, D., Costa, N., Roda-Sanchez, L., Olivares, T., Fernández-Caballero, A., Pereira, A.: Body area networks in healthcare: a brief state of the art. Appl. Sci. **9**(16), 3248 (2019)
2. Meharouech, A., Elias, J., Mehaoua, A.: Future body-to-body networks for ubiquitous healthcare: a survey, taxonomy and challenges. In: 2015 IEEE 2nd International Symposium on Future Information and Communication Technologies for Ubiquitous HealthCare (Ubi-HealthTech), pp. 1–6, May 2015
3. Meharouech, A., Elias, J., Mehaoua, A.: Moving towards body-to-body sensor networks for ubiquitous applications: a survey. J. Sens. Actuator Netw. **8**(2), 27 (2019)
4. Alkhayyat, A., Thabit, A.A., Al-Mayali, F.A., Abbasi, Q.H.: WBSN in IoT health-based application: toward delay and energy consumption minimization. J. Sens. (2019)
5. Qu, Y., Zheng, G., Ma, H., Wang, X., Ji, B., Wu, H.: A survey of routing protocols in WBAN for healthcare applications. Sensors **19**(7), 1638 (2019)
6. Javaid, N., Abbas, Z., Fareed, M.S., Khan, Z.A., Alrajeh, N.: M-ATTEMPT: a new energy-efficient routing protocol for wireless body area sensor networks. Procedia Comput. Sci. **19**, 224–231 (2013)
7. Nadeem, Q., Javaid, N., Mohammad, S.N., Khan, M.Y., Sarfraz, S., Gull, M.: Simple: stable increased-throughput multi-hop protocol for link efficiency in wireless body area networks. In: 2013 Eighth International Conference on Broadband and Wireless Computing, Communication and Applications, pp. 221–226. IEEE, October 2013
8. Heinzelman, W.R., Chandrakasan, A., Balakrishnan, H.: Energy-efficient communication protocol for wireless microsensor networks. In: Proceedings of the 33rd annual Hawaii IEEE International Conference on System Sciences, pp. 10-pp, January 2000

An Optimized Pilot-Assisted Channel Estimation Method for Low-Dispersive Channels

Quang-Kien Trinh[1]([⊠]), Thi-Hong-Tham Tran[1], Thi-Bac Dang[1], and Van-Thanh Nguyen[2]

[1] Le Quy Don Technical University, 236 Hoang Quoc Viet Street, Hanoi, Vietnam
kien.trinh@lqdtu.edu.vn
[2] Posts and Telecommunications Institute of Technology, Hanoi, Vietnam

Abstract. In this paper, we present a novel pilot-assisted channel estimation algorithm for orthogonal frequency-division multiplexing (OFDM) wireless communication systems. The proposed method uses fewer pilots, which helps to increase the bandwidth (BW) efficiency while maintaining the adequate bit-error-rate (BER). A systematical approach for optimization of the pilot pattern applied in the low-dispersive channels is proposed and the performances using both the proposed and conventional estimation methods are quantitatively compared the performance in terms of BER for a case study of DVB-T/T2 system in 2K mode. MATLAB simulations are performed to evaluate the methods in the cases of the specific channel models (urban and rural models). From the simulation results, the novel estimation method gives out mostly the same BER while requiring only about 25% pilot number per symbol, compared with the conventional methods.

Keywords: Channel estimation · OFDM · Comb-type · Pilot · DVB-T

1 Introduction

The multipath effect in wireless/over-the-air communication can lead to inter-symbol interference, attenuation in amplitude, and shift in phase of the signal at the receiver side. One of the main solutions to reduce the aforementioned effect and increase system efficiency is using the equalizer. In an OFDM system, the equalizer task requires preliminary information from the channel frequency response (CFR). The latter is often achieved by using pilot signal with two typical types of arrangements, block-type [1, 2] and comb-type [3–5]. With the block-type arrangement, the pilot signal is assigned to a particular OFDM block, which is sent periodically in the time-domain. The frequency-domain interpolation is used to estimate the channel response and this method typically is adopted for slowly fading channels [1, 2, 6]. In the fast-fading channels, comb-type pilot, where the pilot signals are uniformly distributed within each OFDM block, is adopted since and the channel information can be updated every OFDM symbol [3–5]. With the comb-type pilot arrangement, the channel response at data subcarriers can be interpolated from the CFR value at pilot subcarriers.

© ICST Institute for Computer Sciences, Social Informatics and Telecommunications Engineering 2021
Published by Springer Nature Switzerland AG 2021. All Rights Reserved
N.-S. Vo et al. (Eds.): INISCOM 2021, LNICST 379, pp. 48–56, 2021.
https://doi.org/10.1007/978-3-030-77424-0_5

To reconstruct CFR from the scattered pilot information, several interpolation techniques such as linear, spline, cubic interpolation, can be used. The higher and more complex methods usually offer better accuracy and efficiency [6]. Other than interpolation, in [7], the author presented a new approach for indirectly calculating CFR from the channel impulse response (CIR) estimation, which works well for the static channel. As a further extension from that approach, in [8], the authors proved that, with certain modifications, this method is promising for wide-band transmission in the low-dispersive channels. However, in [7, 8], the authors did not present the method for finding optimized pilot frequency spacing, and the evaluation was not quantitatively conducted for channel bit-error-rate (BER), especially with realistic channel models. In this paper, we proposed a systematical approach for optimization of the pilot pattern applied in the low-dispersive channel based on the original approach in [7, 8]. Also, we quantitatively compared the performance in terms of BER between the proposed method and the conventional interpolation ones for a case study of the DVB-T/T2 system in 2K mode. The result shows that the proposed pattern achieves similar accuracy while having much better spectral efficiency.

The remaining of the paper is organized as follows. Section 2 describes conventional channel estimation methods based on interpolation techniques. Section 3 proposes a novel pilot pattern. Section 4 presents bandwidth extension and simulation results and Sect. 5 concludes the paper.

2 Background of Conventional Estimation in the OFDM System

For comb-type pilot subcarrier arrangement, the N_p pilot signals $x_p(m)$, $m = 0 \div N_p - 1$ are uniformly inserted in $X(k)$ according to the following equation [6]:

$$X(k) = X(mL + l) = \begin{cases} x_p(m), & l = 0 \\ inf.data & l = 1, \ldots .L - 1 \end{cases} \tag{1}$$

where L = (number of carriers/N_p) and $x_p(m)$ is the mth pilot subcarrier value. Figure 1 illustrates the pilot arrangement in an OFDM system.

We define $\{H_p(k), k = 0, 1, \ldots .N_p\}$ as the CFR at pilot subcarriers. The estimate of the channel at pilot subcarriers based on LS estimation is given by:

$$H_e = \frac{Y_p}{X_p} k = 0, 1, \ldots .N_p - 1 \tag{2}$$

where $Y_p(k)$, $X_p(k)$ are output and input at the kth pilot subcarrier respectively.

A good example of the OFDM system that uses pilot-aided channel estimation is the DVB-T/T2 system, where the pilots will be used with interpolation techniques in the time domain and frequency domain. The channel estimation, which is performed independently at each symbol in the frequency domain, is called one-dimensional (1D) estimation, while the estimation in both time and frequency domain is two-dimensional (2D) estimation.

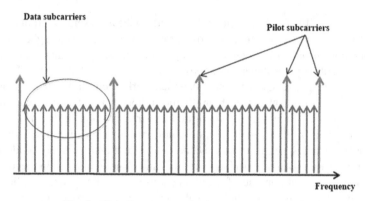

Fig. 1. The pilot arrangement in the OFDM system

In 1D channel estimation, the CFR will be estimated by using different interpolation methods such as: linear, cubic, spline interpolation… in the frequency domain. This method is easy to implement as it bases on the correlation function between the subcarriers in the frequency domain to estimate the CFR of the current symbol.

To increase the accuracy, the pilot information in both time and frequency domains will be used, which is called the 2D channel estimation. The 2D estimation method is illustrated in Fig. 2. The choice of 2D channel estimation gives a good tradeoff between performance and complexity [6]. First, the estimation is performed in the time domain using interpolation and pilot subcarriers of some OFDM symbols. The second step is to use these estimated values as pilots to estimate the channel response for all of the remaining subcarriers on each OFDM symbol.

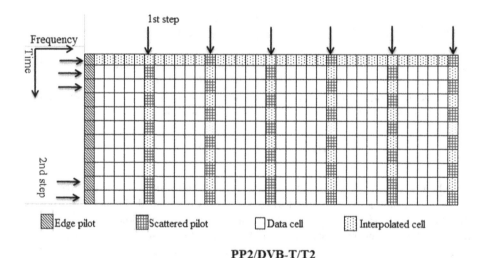

PP2/DVB-T/T2

Fig. 2. Two-dimensional channel estimation in the DVB-T system

3 Optimized Pilot Pattern for Low-Dispersive Channel

In [7] the multipath channel with N rays is considered, each of which has a delay of τ_n, phase - φ_n, and intensity - μ_n. In this case, the CFR of a multipath channel can be presented as:

$$H(\omega) = \sum_{n=1}^{N} \mu_n e^{-j(\varphi_n + \omega\tau_n)} \tag{3}$$

Transmitting K of pilot signals through this channel on the known frequencies on the receiving side it is possible to define V_k of the voltages generated by pilot signals.

$$V_k = \sqrt{\rho_s} H(\omega_k) + n_k \tag{4}$$

where ω_k is the frequency of the k pilot carrier, n_k is a component of Gaussian noise power, and ρ_s is the signal-to-noise ratio (SNR) for k^{th} component of the received pilot signal. Estimation of the CFR of a multipath channel (3) is described as a delay line with $K-1$ taps, with the same delay $\Delta\tau$ between them [7]

$$\hat{H}_k = \sum_{m=1}^{K} z_m e^{-j\omega_k(m-1)\Delta\tau}, \quad \Delta\tau = \frac{\tau_{max}}{K}, \tag{5}$$

where z_m - complex parameters defining amplitude and signal phase for tap m of a delay line, τ_{max} - possible maximum time delay in the channel. In the estimation process, this value (τ_{max}) will be substituted by T_{max} and the relation between these two values will be evaluated in Sect. 4.

Determination of the multipath channel characteristics is reduced to an estimate of z_m by the measured values of voltages V_k generated by pilot signals on the receiver. The approaches of the theory of potential noise immunity [9] are based on the methods of mathematical statistics, which allows us to evaluate the unknown parameters of the signal. Estimation of z_k the parameter is performed by the maximum likelihood method. In this case, the logarithm of the likelihood function (6) for the kth component of the signal is expressed as

$$L_k(z_1, z_2, \ldots, z_K) = \left| V_k - \sqrt{\rho_s} \left[\sum_{m=1}^{K} z_m e^{-j\omega_k(m-1)\Delta\tau} \right] \right|^2 \tag{6}$$

The Maximum likelihood estimates of parameters $z_1, z_2, \ldots z_K$, are determined from K equations as follows

$$\frac{\partial L_k(z_1, z_2, \ldots, z_K)}{\partial \overline{z}_k} = \sqrt{\rho_s} e^{-j\omega_k(m-1)\Delta\tau} \cdot \left(V_k - \sqrt{\rho_s} \left[\sum_{m=1}^{K} z_m e^{-j\omega_k(m-1)\Delta\tau} \right] \right) \tag{7}$$

Using the vector form, we have the main Eq. (8), connecting the columns of measured values $\overrightarrow{V}$ and estimated parameters $\overrightarrow{Z}$, $\overrightarrow{Z}$ is the estimate of CIR

$$\vec{Z} = \left(\frac{1}{\sqrt{\rho_s}} \right) \left[\overline{A^T}.A \right].\overline{A^T}.\vec{V} \tag{8}$$

where $\overrightarrow{V} = \|V_k\|$, $\overrightarrow{Z} = \|Z_k\|$, $A = \|a_{mk}\|$ - the phase shift matrix, with $a_{mk} = e^{-j\omega_k(m-1)\Delta\tau}$.

The main difference between interpolation methods and the proposed method is the calculating procedure. The accuracy of the interpolation essentially depended on the number of the interpolated points, in other words, the greater number of pilots, the better the estimation results. With the proposed method, CFR is reconstructing via CIR by mathematical transformation, it is crucial to determine the right pilot spacing for accurately estimating CIR, the latter depends on the maximum delay τ_{max} of the channel.

Figure 3 illustrates the result CIR and CFR using the proposed method with 24 pilot subcarriers.

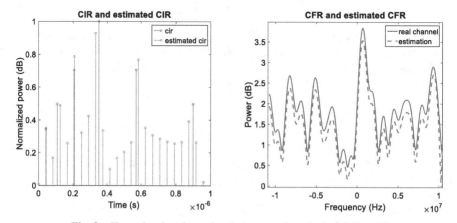

Fig. 3. Channel estimation using the proposed method with K = 24

4   A Case Study: Channel Estimation for DVB-T/T2 System

In the following, we present a case study for a practical commercial DVB-T/T2 system with major parameters listed in Table 1. We use MATLAB simulation with the Rayleigh

Table 1. Simulation setup using DVB-T system parameters.

Parameters	Specifications
Guard interval	1/8
The type of guard interval	Cyclic extension
Model of the channel	"Urban type channel", Rayleigh
Bandwidth	6 MHz
Speed of the transmitter	60 km/h
Type of modulation	QPSK

channel model, the detailed power spectrum density and path delays of the channel are from [10]. Other simulation parameters (modulation type, bandwidth, subcarrier spacing, the central carrier frequency) are from the system DVB-T in 2K mode. Our model simulates not only the CIR, CFR estimation but also evaluates the BER of the system, which is the major performance metric for the optimization process.

4.1 Optimizing the Pilot Spacing

In [7], the value τ_{max} in (5) was substituted by the estimated value T_{max}, in which the author proposed the ratio $\tau_{max}/T_{max} = (0.7 - 0.9)$. The work in [8] surveyed the method with the quasi-static channel [10], and this ratio was reduced to get better estimation results. As presented in [7, 8], when applied to a specific system, the ratio must be adjusted with the condition of the channel (maximum delay) and the system (bandwidth and subcarrier spacing).

In the following, we present an empirical approach to optimized pilot spacing in the case of the low-dispersive channel profile. A system model using the proposed method is simulated with the parameters taken from the DVB-T/T2 system, working in 2K mode, with QPSK modulation as presented in Table 1. These MATLAB simulations are performed with different values of the ratio τ_{max}/T_{max} using some channel models from [10] to find out the optimal τ_{max}/T_{max} range based on BER.

Figure 4 shows BER performance with the changes of the ratio τ_{max}/T_{max}. In the specific case of a low-dispersive channel, the ratio $\tau_{max}/T_{max} \leq 0.7$ give the best BER performance, compared to other ranges. It is important to keep the first and the last pilot signals at the edge frequencies of the band, otherwise the estimated CFR might be incorrect at these locations. The number of pilots in use K depends on the spacing of two adjacent pilots and the width of the frequency band.

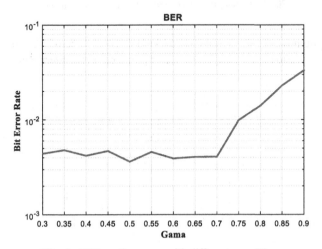

Fig. 4. BER performance with different τ_{max}/T_{max}

4.2 Performance Evaluations

This section presents the detailed simulation results and the comparison between the methods' efficiency using the BER parameter. With the analysis above, we simulate those estimation methods in MATLAB. The detailed parameters are presented in Table 1. Figure 5 shows the results using 1D and 2D channel estimation. The simulation result in Fig. 5 shows that 1D channel estimation and 2D channel estimation both give adequately accurate results, but the 2D curve fits the actual CFR more closely than 1D with the tradeoff is the higher implementation complexity.

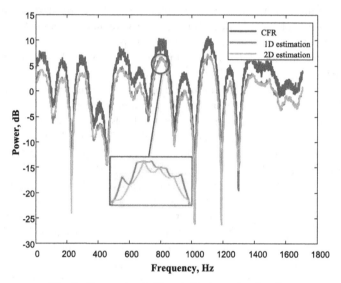

Fig. 5. Conventional 1D and 2D channel estimation

Applying the novel method in the case of the DVB-T system in 2K mode with the above-mentioned ratio of $\tau_{max}/T_{max} \leq 0.7$, an optimized pilot pattern can be achieved as

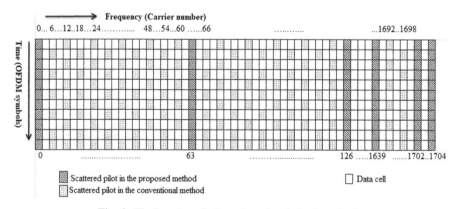

Fig. 6. The location of pilot subcarriers in both methods

presented in Fig. 6. As can be seen from the pilot location, the proposed pattern has only about one fourth of the conventional pattern pilot number. Besides, with these locations, the calculation procedure will be simpler, as the receiver does not need to recognize the order of the symbol for the pattern identification as in 1D and 2D methods.

To evaluate and compare the efficiency of the estimation methods, we simulated the conventional methods and the proposed method on the same system configuration. Figure 7 shows the BER performance in the cases of AWGN and the fading channel.

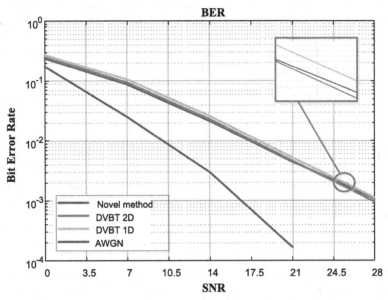

Fig. 7. BER performance of the channel with AWGN, 1D, 2D of the conventional estimation and the novel channel estimation.

In Fig. 7, the AWGN is the lowest line – as it is the ideal transmission condition. Other BER lines show that the performance of the novel pattern is better than 1D channel estimation but a little inferior to 2D channel estimation. When comparing the conventional method and the novel method, with the same SNR (at 28 dB), the BER performance of conventional 1D channel estimation is $1.146 * 10^{-3}$, while of novel method achieved $1.109 * 10^{-3}$ and BER of the 2D method is $9.9 * 10^{-4}$. From the results, it is clear that the proposed pattern gives similar accuracy while using a significantly less number of pilots (only one-fourth of the DVB-T/T2 pilot number – per symbol), which also means higher spectral efficiency. Besides, regarding the complexity of the estimation, with the constant location at every OFDM symbol, the proposed pattern using the novel method is less complex than those conventional ones as the symbol order identification is not required.

5 Conclusion

In this paper, we studied the channel estimation using the comb-type pilot arrangement and proposed an approach for optimization of the pilot pattern applied in the low-dispersive channel, where the CFR is indirectly calculated from the estimated CIR. The performance of the estimation method is quantitatively evaluated in terms of BER and compared with the conventional methods in DVB-T/T2 system in 2K mode. The simulation results show that the BER performances of the two methods are mostly equivalent while the proposed pilot pattern using significantly fewer pilots and a simpler calculation procedure, which essentially helps to save the system bandwidth and energy. With the inherent advantage in spectral efficiency, the proposed approach could be suited for other OFDM systems, especially for wide-band ones, though the broader study and analysis are still required for the solid validation.

Acknowledgement. The authors thank HTP HITECH CORP for sponsoring this research.

References

1. Yang, F., Wang, J., Wang, J., Song, J., Yang, Z.: Channel estimation for the Chinese DTTB system based on a novel iterative PN sequence reconstruction. In: IEEE International Conference on Communications, pp. 285–289 (2008)
2. Zaier, A., Bouallègue, R.: Channel estimation study for block- pilot insertion in OFFDM systems under slowly time-varying conditions. Int. J. Comput. Netw. Commun. (IJCNC), vol. 3, no. 6, November 2011
3. Mahmoud, H.M., Mousa, A.S., Saleem, R.: Channel estimation based in comb-type pilots arrangement for OFDM system over time varying channel. J. Netw. **5**(7) (2010)
4. Edris, F.A.F., Elsid, A.G., Nerma, M.H.M.: A study of channel estimation in fast fading environments. Int. J. Sci. Technol. Res. **4**(08) (2015)
5. Zettas, S., Lazaridis, P.I., Zaharis, Z.D., Kasampalis, S., Cosmas, J.: A Pilot Aided Averaging Channel Estimator for DVB-T2. IEEE (2013)
6. Bahai, A.R.S., Saltzberg, B.R., Ergen, M.: Multi-Carrier Digital Communications Theory and Application of OFDM, 2nd ed (2004)
7. Bykhovskiy, M.A.: Method opredeleniya parametrov mnogoluchevogo kanala svyazi [Method for determining the parameters of multipath communication channel]. Electrosvyaz [Telecommunication] **3**, 46–49 (2010). [In Russian]
8. Tran, T., Prokopchuk, M., Dvorkovich, A.: Study of channel response estimation method based on theory of optimum noise immunity, Engineering and Telecommunications - En&T-2019 (2019)
9. Kotelnikov, V.A.: The theory of optimum noise immunity. Mineola (1960)
10. Digital Radio Mondiale (DRM), ETSI System Specification ES 201 980 V4.1.2, April 2017

Performance Analysis of Mobile Edge Computing Network Applied Uplink NOMA with RF Energy Harvesting

Van-Truong Truong[1,2(✉)], Minh-Thong Vo[1,2], and Dac-Binh Ha[1,2]

[1] Faculty of Electrical-Electronic Engineering, School of Engineering and Technologies, Duy Tan University, Da Nang 550000, Vietnam
{truongvantruong,vominhthong}@dtu.edu.vn
[2] Institute of Research and Development, Duy Tan University, Da Nang 550000, Vietnam
hadacbinh@duytan.edu.vn

Abstract. In this paper, we study a mobile edge computing (MEC) network based on uplink non-orthogonal multiple access (NOMA) scheme with radio frequency energy harvesting (RF EH). Due to the energy and compute resources constraint, two users cannot complete their tasks by themselves within the maximum time delay. Therefore, they harvest the RF energy from a nearby access point (AP) and use all that energy to offload their tasks to the AP. We derive the closed-form expressions of the successful computation probability (SCP) of the users to evaluate system performance. We propose a algorithm based on genetic algorithm (GA) that determines the system's optimal time switching ratio to achieve the maximum SCP, namely MSCP-GA. Furthermore, we consider the numerical results to thoroughly understand the impact of parameters such as transmit power, time switching ratio on the system performance. Monte Carlo simulation is used to confirm the validity of our analysis.

Keywords: Mobile edge computing · Non-orthogonal multiple access · Uplink NOMA · Successful computation probability · MEC server · Genetic algorithm · Optimization

1 Introduction

In recent years, the next generation of wireless technology, i.e., 5G, has overgrown with outstanding supports of extreme speeds and capacity [1]. Technological breakthroughs in 5G have paved the way for developing many high-bandwidth applications such as virtual reality, augmented reality, autonomous cars, mobile online games, massive connected Internet of Things (IoT) [2]. However, mobile devices (MD) are currently not keeping up with the demand from these computation-intensive and latency-critical applications. It encouraged the

© ICST Institute for Computer Sciences, Social Informatics and Telecommunications Engineering 2021
Published by Springer Nature Switzerland AG 2021. All Rights Reserved
N.-S. Vo et al. (Eds.): INISCOM 2021, LNICST 379, pp. 57–72, 2021.
https://doi.org/10.1007/978-3-030-77424-0_6

development of Mobile Edge Computing (MEC), with the idea of shifting computation and data storage servers closer to MD [3].

Many technologies and scenarios in the 5G pattern integrated with MEC, in which NOMA and RF EH are two critical enabling technologies that researchers are very interested in. Applying NOMA in the MEC network has many benefits, including supporting many users, reducing latency and system energy consumption [4–7].

Ye *et al.* proposed NOMA MEC network in [4], in which two users offload their tasks to a MEC server located access point (AP) to ensure system delay constraint. Authors have used the derivative approach to maximize system performance in terms of successful computation probability (SCP) with three schemes: complete local computation, partial computation offloading, and complete offloading. In [5], Fang *et al.* proposed a multi-user NOMA MEC network, in which M users are randomly distributed in a single cell and computed by a MEC server located at BS center cell. The authors examined the system over Rayleigh fading and perfect channel state information (pCSI) conditions. A bisection searching algorithm is used to solve the problem of minimizing task computation time. Ha *et al.* in [6] proposed a downlink NOMA MEC network with two MEC APs to assist computation for a limited energy user. The authors proposed an APS algorithm based on channel gain to enhance the system's security performance. All of the above studies confirm the advantages of adopting NOMA over OMA when operating under the same schemes.

Besides, integrating RF EH techniques in MEC networks will solve limited battery lifetime, unstable grid power supply, and low computing capability [8–11]. Min *et al.* in [8] investigated the RF EH IoT healthcare monitoring system based on MEC. Multiple sensors use their battery and RF energy to gather parameters like blood pressure and electrocardiograms. They can operate their tasks by themselves or receive computational help from the MEC server to make urgent recommendations. The reinforcement learning algorithm is proposed to use CSI information, input tasks, and computational resources to optimize the sensors' offloading strategy. In [9], the authors proposed the RF EH NOMA MEC network operated with a two-phase protocol: wireless power transfer phase and computation phase. Algorithms based on the iterative algorithm and an alternative optimization algorithm are proposed to solve the problem of maximizing the system's computational performance. Garcia *et al.* in [11] wireless-powered multi-user NOMA MEC system assisted by a power beacon (PB) and AP in the presence of an eavesdropper. Specifically, AP and PB broadcast the RF energy to M users. Then, the users simultaneously offload the tasks to the MEC server located at the AP using NOMA. The authors assume the AP has considerable computational resources, so they ignore the computation time here. A solution based on particle swarm optimization (PSO) is proposed to maximize the system secrecy computation efficiency (SCE).

In this study, we consider the RF EH NOMA MEC system over Rayleigh fading channel. The main contributions of our paper are as follows.

- We investigated the RF EH NOMA MEC over Rayleigh fading.
- We derived the closed-form expression of successful computation probability for this system. Furthermore, we provided numerical results to investigate the impact of the network parameters, i.e., transmit power, time switching ratio, the task length, bandwidth, to verify RF EH NOMA deployment's effectiveness in the MEC network.
- We proposed an optimization algorithm based on a genetic algorithm to find the optimal time switching so that the SCP is maximized. Simulation results show that our proposed algorithm can improve the SCP.

The rest of this paper is organized as follows. Section 2 presents the system model. The performance of this considered system is analyzed in Sect. 3. We present the optimization problem in term of SCP in Sect. 4. The numerical results and discussion are shown in Sect. 5. Finally, we conclude our work in Sect. 6.

2   System Model

The system model for an uplink NOMA mobile edge computing network with energy harvesting is depicted as Fig. 1, in which two energy-constrained users (i.e., U_1 and U_2) offload their tasks to MEC access point (AP) through uplink NOMA by using the harvetsed energy from AP. All devices are assumed to have a single antenna and operate in the half-duplex mode. Assuming that U_1 and U_2 have L_1-bit and L_2-bit tasks, respectively, to be executed and they may not be able to execute their tasks locally within the latency budget due to the limited computational ability. Therefore, U_1 and U_2 offload their tasks to AP's server through wireless links subject to quasi-static Rayleigh fading. However, due to energy constraint, before transmission, U_1 and U_2 harvest the RF energy from AP and use this for offloading.

We propose a new protocol, called RF EH Uplink NOMA MEC scheme, for MEC network as follows.

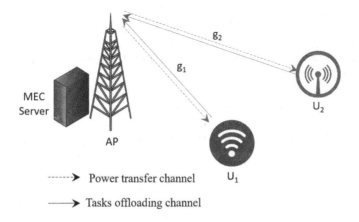

Fig. 1. System model for uplink NOMA MEC using RF EH network

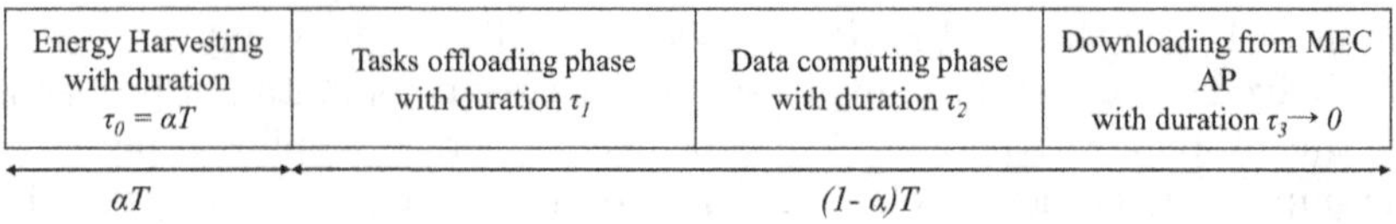

Energy Harvesting with duration $\tau_0 = \alpha T$	Tasks offloading phase with duration τ_1	Data computing phase with duration τ_2	Downloading from MEC AP with duration $\tau_3 \to 0$

αT $(1-\alpha)T$

Fig. 2. Time flow chart for proposed system

- In the first phase (energy harvesting phase), the users harvest energy from AP during the duration of $\tau_0 = \alpha T$, where α denotes the time switching ratio, i.e., $0 < \alpha < 1$, and T stands for transmission block time. During this energy harvesting phase, the harvested energy of U_i, ($i \in (1,2)$) is obtained by

$$E_i = \eta P_0 g_i \alpha T, \tag{1}$$

where $0 < \eta \leq 1$ stands for the energy conversion efficiency of the energy receiver [12], P_0 denotes the transmit power of AP, g_i denotes the channel power gain of link $U_i - AP$.

- In the second phase (offloading phase), U_i apply uplink NOMA scheme to offload their tasks to the AP's server during duration τ_1. On the basis of the principle of NOMA, the received signal of offloading tasks at MEC server is expressed as

$$y_{MEC} = h_1 \sqrt{P_1} x_1 + h_2 \sqrt{P_2} x_2 + n_{MEC}, \tag{2}$$

where h_i denotes the channel coefficient, x_i stands for the offloading task of the ith user, , $i \in \{1,2\}$. $n_{MEC} \sim \mathcal{CN}(0, \sigma^2)$ represents the AWGN at the MEC server. Note that $g_i = |h_i|^2$. The transmit power P_i calculated as follows

$$P_i = \frac{E_i}{(1-\alpha)T - \tau} = a P_0 g_i, \tag{3}$$

where $a \triangleq \frac{\eta \alpha T}{(1-\alpha)T - \tau}$. τ stands for the computing time at MEC server defined as follows:

$$\tau = \frac{\rho(L_1 + L_2)}{f}, \tag{4}$$

where ρ and f denote the number of required CPU cycles for each bit and the CPU-cycle frequency of MEC server, respectively.

- In the third phase (computing phase), according to the principle of uplink NOMA, AP first decodes the task x_i with larger power level by treating the remain with smaller power level as noise and then subtracts this component in duration τ_2. Hence, the signal-to-interference-plus-noise ratio (SINR) and the signal-to-noise ratio (SNR) for the MEC server to decode x_i are written as

if $g_1 > g_2$:

$$\gamma_{11} = \frac{a \gamma_0 g_1^2}{a \gamma_0 g_2^2 + 1}, \tag{5}$$

$$\gamma_{12} = a \gamma_0 g_2^2, \tag{6}$$

else

$$\gamma_{22} = \frac{a\gamma_0 g_2^2}{a\gamma_0 g_1^2 + 1}, \tag{7}$$

$$\gamma_{21} = a\gamma_0 g_1^2, \tag{8}$$

where $\gamma_0 = \frac{P_0}{\sigma^2}$. Then, these tasks are executed on the MEC server in duration τ_3.

- Finally, in the last phase (result returning phase), U_i downloads the results from AP during τ_3.

The time flow chart for EH Uplink-NOMA MEC protocol is as Fig. 2, in which τ_3 is assumed very small compared to transmission time and thus is neglected [4,7,13].

The i.i.d. quasi-static Rayleigh channel gains g_i, $i \in \{1,2\}$, follows exponential distributions with parameters λ_i. Therefore, the cummulative density function (CDF) and probability density function (PDF) of g_i are respectively given by

$$F_{g_i}(x) = 1 - e^{-\frac{x}{\lambda_i}}, \tag{9}$$

$$f_{g_i}(x) = \frac{1}{\lambda_i} e^{-\frac{x}{\lambda_i}}. \tag{10}$$

3   Performance Analysis

In order to characterize the performance of a NOMA-MEC system, the successful computation probability, namely $\boldsymbol{\Phi}_s$, is used as an important performance metric [4,6,7]. It is defined as the probability that all tasks are successfully executed within a given time $T > 0$, which is expressed as

$$\boldsymbol{\Phi}_s = \Pr\left(\max\{t_1, t_2\} + \tau \le (1 - \alpha)T\right), \tag{11}$$

where t_1 and t_2 are the transmission latency of U_1 and U_2, respectively and calculated as follows:

$$\begin{cases} t_1 = \frac{L_1}{(1-\alpha)B\log(1+\gamma_{11})}, t_2 = \frac{L_2}{(1-\alpha)B\log(1+\gamma_{12})}, & g_1 > g_2 \\ t_1 = \frac{L_1}{(1-\alpha)B\log(1+\gamma_{21})}, t_2 = \frac{L_2}{(1-\alpha)B\log(1+\gamma_{22})}, & g_1 < g_2 \end{cases} \tag{12}$$

where B denotes the channel bandwidth.

In order to evaluate the performance of this considered NOMA MEC system, we obtain the following lemmas.

Lemma 1

Under quasi-static Rayleigh fading, the closed-form expression of the SCP $\Phi_s^{U_1}$ for this considered uplink RF EH NOMA MEC system is given by

$$
\Phi_s^{U_1} =
\begin{cases}
\frac{\pi}{N\lambda_2} \sum_{j=1}^{N} \exp\left(-\frac{\sqrt{\gamma_{th1}\left(\theta_j^2 + \frac{1}{a\gamma_0}\right)}}{\lambda_1} - \frac{\theta_j}{\lambda_2} \right) \sqrt{\frac{1-\phi_j}{1+\phi_j}} \\
\quad + \frac{\lambda_2}{\lambda_1+\lambda_2} \exp\left[-\left(\frac{1}{\lambda_1} + \frac{1}{\lambda_2}\right)\sqrt{\frac{\gamma_{th1}}{a\gamma_0}} \right], & \gamma_{th1} > 1 \\[2ex]
\frac{\pi c}{2N\lambda_2} \sum_{j=1}^{N} \exp\left(-\frac{\sqrt{\gamma_{th1}\left(x_j^2 + \frac{1}{a\gamma_0}\right)}}{\lambda_1} - \frac{x_j}{\lambda_2} \right) \sqrt{1-\phi_j^2} \\
\quad + \frac{\lambda_1}{\lambda_1+\lambda_2} \exp\left[-\left(\frac{1}{\lambda_1} + \frac{1}{\lambda_2}\right)c \right] + \frac{\lambda_2}{\lambda_1+\lambda_2} \exp\left[-\left(\frac{1}{\lambda_1} + \frac{1}{\lambda_2}\right)\sqrt{\frac{\gamma_{th1}}{a\gamma_0}} \right], & \gamma_{th1} < 1
\end{cases}
\tag{13}
$$

where $\gamma_{th1} = 2^{\frac{L_1}{\Omega_1(1-\alpha)B}} - 1$, $\Omega_1 = (1-\alpha)T - \frac{\rho L_1}{f}$, $c = \sqrt{\frac{\gamma_{th1}}{a\gamma_0(1-\gamma_{th1})}}$, $\theta_j = -\ln\left(\frac{\phi_j+1}{2}\right)$, $x_j = \frac{(\phi_j+1)c}{2}$, $\phi_j = \cos\left(\frac{2j-1}{2N}\pi\right)$, and N is the complexity-vs-accuracy trade-off coefficient.

Proof. See Appendix A.

Lemma 2

Under quasi-static Rayleigh fading, the closed-form expression of the SCP $\Phi_s^{U_2}$ for this considered uplink RF EH NOMA MEC system is given by

$$
\Phi_s^{U_2} =
\begin{cases}
\frac{\pi}{N\lambda_1} \sum_{j=1}^{N} \exp\left(-\frac{\sqrt{\gamma_{th2}\left(\theta_j^2 + \frac{1}{a\gamma_0}\right)}}{\lambda_2} - \frac{\theta_j}{\lambda_1} \right) \sqrt{\frac{1-\phi_j}{1+\phi_j}} \\
\quad + \frac{\lambda_1}{\lambda_1+\lambda_2} \exp\left[-\left(\frac{1}{\lambda_1} + \frac{1}{\lambda_2}\right)\sqrt{\frac{\gamma_{th2}}{a\gamma_0}} \right], & \gamma_{th2} > 1 \\[2ex]
\frac{\pi c}{2N\lambda_1} \sum_{j=1}^{N} \exp\left(-\frac{\sqrt{\gamma_{th2}\left(x_j^2 + \frac{1}{a\gamma_0}\right)}}{\lambda_2} - \frac{x_j}{\lambda_1} \right) \sqrt{1-\phi_j^2} \\
\quad + \frac{\lambda_2}{\lambda_1+\lambda_2} \exp\left[-\left(\frac{1}{\lambda_1} + \frac{1}{\lambda_2}\right)c \right] + \frac{\lambda_1}{\lambda_1+\lambda_2} \exp\left[-\left(\frac{1}{\lambda_1} + \frac{1}{\lambda_2}\right)\sqrt{\frac{\gamma_{th2}}{a\gamma_0}} \right], & \gamma_{th2} < 1
\end{cases}
\tag{14}
$$

where $\gamma_{th2} = 2^{\frac{L_2}{\Omega_2(1-\alpha)B}} - 1$, $\Omega_2 = (1-\alpha)T - \frac{\rho L_2}{f}$, $c = \sqrt{\frac{\gamma_{th2}}{a\gamma_0(1-\gamma_{th2})}}$, $\theta_j = -\ln\left(\frac{\phi_j+1}{2}\right)$, $x_j = \frac{(\phi_j+1)c}{2}$, $\phi_j = \cos\left(\frac{2j-1}{2N}\pi\right)$, and N is the complexity-vs-accuracy trade-off coefficient.

Proof. The proof of Lemma 2 is similar to the proof of Lemma 1; see Appendix A.

Lemma 3

Under quasi-static Rayleigh fading, the closed-form expression of the SCP Φ_s for this considered uplink RF EH NOMA MEC system is given by

$$
\Phi_s = \begin{cases}
\frac{\pi}{N\lambda_2} \sum_{j=1}^{N} \exp\left(-\frac{\sqrt{\gamma_{th}\left(\theta_j^2 + \frac{1}{a\gamma_0}\right)}}{\lambda_1} - \frac{\theta_j}{\lambda_2}\right) \sqrt{\frac{1-\phi_j}{1+\phi_j}} \\
-\frac{\pi b}{2N\lambda_2} \sum_{j=1}^{N} \exp\left(-\frac{\sqrt{\gamma_{th}\left(x_j^2 + \frac{1}{a\gamma_0}\right)}}{\lambda_1} - \frac{x_j}{\lambda_2}\right) \sqrt{1-\phi_j^2}, \\
+\frac{\pi}{N\lambda_1} \sum_{j=1}^{N} \exp\left(-\frac{\sqrt{\gamma_{th}\left(\theta_j^2 + \frac{1}{a\gamma_0}\right)}}{\lambda_2} - \frac{\theta_j}{\lambda_1}\right) \sqrt{\frac{1-\phi_j}{1+\phi_j}} \\
-\frac{\pi b}{2N\lambda_1} \sum_{j=1}^{N} \exp\left(-\frac{\sqrt{\gamma_{th}\left(x_j^2 + \frac{1}{a\gamma_0}\right)}}{\lambda_2} - \frac{x_j}{\lambda_1}\right) \sqrt{1-\phi_j^2}, \quad \gamma_{th} > 1 \quad (15) \\
\frac{\pi(c-b)}{2N\lambda_2} \sum_{j=1}^{N} \exp\left(-\frac{\sqrt{\gamma_{th}\left(y_j^2 + \frac{1}{a\gamma_0}\right)}}{\lambda_1} - \frac{y_j}{\lambda_2}\right) \sqrt{1-\phi_j^2} \\
+\frac{\lambda_1}{\lambda_1+\lambda_2} \exp\left[-\left(\frac{1}{\lambda_1} + \frac{1}{\lambda_2}\right)c\right] \\
+\frac{\pi(c-b)}{2N\lambda_2} \sum_{j=1}^{N} \exp\left(-\frac{\sqrt{\gamma_{th}\left(y_j^2 + \frac{1}{a\gamma_0}\right)}}{\lambda_1} - \frac{y_j}{\lambda_2}\right) \sqrt{1-\phi_j^2} \\
+\frac{\lambda_1}{\lambda_1+\lambda_2} \exp\left[-\left(\frac{1}{\lambda_1} + \frac{1}{\lambda_2}\right)c\right], \quad \gamma_{th} < 1
\end{cases}
$$

where $\gamma_{th} = 2^{\frac{L}{\Omega(1-\alpha)B}} - 1$, $\Omega = (1-\alpha)T - \frac{\rho L}{f}$, $b = \sqrt{\frac{\gamma_{th}}{a\gamma_0}}$, $c = \sqrt{\frac{\gamma_{th}}{a\gamma_0(1-\gamma_{th})}}$, $\theta_j = -\ln\left(\frac{\phi_j+1}{2}\right)$, $x_j = \frac{(\phi_j+1)c}{2}$, $y_j = \frac{(\phi_j+1)(c-b)}{2} + b$, $\phi_j = \cos\left(\frac{2j-1}{2N}\pi\right)$, and N is the complexity-vs-accuracy trade-off coefficient.

Proof. See Appendix B.

4   SCP Optimization Problem and Solution

Based on the proposed system above, maximal the successful computation probability problem (MSCP) of users are declared the following:

$$(\text{MSCP}) : \max_{\alpha} \ (\Phi_s) \tag{16a}$$

$$\text{subject to} : \max\{t_1, t_2\} + \tau \le (1-\alpha)T \tag{16b}$$

$$0 < \alpha < 1 \tag{16c}$$

where constraints (16b) ensure that all tasks are processed within the maximum allowed delay. Constraints (16c) describe the time switching ratio.

To solve the MSCP, we propose to use the genetic algorithm (GA), namely MSCP-GA, described in Algorithm 1. GA is classified in evolutionary algorithms, simulating biological evolution in nature and following Darwin's theory of evolution, [14,15]. In GA, each chromosome in the population is the problem solution. We initialized a population with 50 random individuals. We deploy the uniform crossovers for the population as follow:

$$\alpha \leftarrow \epsilon \alpha_{p1} + (1 - \epsilon)\alpha_{p2} \tag{17}$$

where α is the offspring time switching ratio, α_{p1} and α_{p2} are parents, ϵ is the random number from 0 to 1 that determine how many of the genes needed from parents, $\epsilon \sim U(0, 1)$.

We use the roulette wheel selection technique [14] for selecting the individual parents. That means the better the fitness value will have more opportunities to be selected for the crossover process. Next, the random mutation was used on the population as follow:

$$\alpha \leftarrow \alpha \mu \beta \tag{18}$$

where μ is mutation rate, and β is the same length as the chromosome, and the elements in it are randomly selected 0 and 1.

Finally, the new population is formed based on the best fitness value. We get an optimal time switching ratio when the algorithm reaches the maximum number of iterations.

Algorithm 1. Maximal the successful computation probability based on Genetic Algorithm (MSCP-GA)

1: **procedure** MSCP-GA(Φ_s)
2:     **Input** $N, P_s, f, \rho, B, T, L_1, L_2$
3:     **Output** α^*
4:     Initialize population size $nPop$, crossover rate χ, mutation rate μ, the maximum evolutionary generation $MaxIt$.
5:     **while** $i < MaxIt$ **do**
6:         Use the fitness function (15) to evaluate the population.
7:         Crossover using (17) and Mutation using (18).
8:         Selection new populations.
9:         i = i + 1
10:    **end while**
11:    Return α^*

In the next section, we discuss the proposed algorithm complexity. The Heap Sorting algorithm is used to order the population and to get the best solutions. The number of operations required for the selection process is $nPop \log(nPop)$. The number of operations required for crossover process and mutation process is $\xi \frac{nPop}{2}$ and $\mu.nPop$. Thus, the algorithm complexity of MSCP-GA is given by:

$$TC = MaxIt.(nPop.\log(nPop) + \xi.\frac{nPop}{2} + \mu.nPop) \tag{19}$$

5 Numerical Results and Discussion

In this section, we provide the numerical results in terms of successful computation probability Φ_s to reveal the impact of key system parameters to the system performance. The simulation parameters used in this work are provided in Table 1 [6,16].

Table 1. Simulation parameters

Parameters	Notation	Typical Values
Number of antennas of each device	N	1
Transmit power	P_s	0–30dB
CPU-cycle frequency of MEC server	f	1 GHz
The number of CPU cycles for each bit	ρ	10
Channel bandwidth	B	1 GHz
The threshold of latency	T	10 ms
The number of data bits of U_1	L_1	60 Kbits
The number of data bits of U_2	L_2	20 Kbits
The population size	$nPop$	50
Crossover rate	χ	0.6
Mutation rate	μ	0.001
The maximum evolutionary generation	$MaxIt$	50

The impact of average transmit SNR (γ_0) and time switching ratio (α) on system performance in terms of successful computation probability Φ_s is shown in Fig. 3, 4 and 5. It is easy to observe that both user's SCP increases as γ_0 increases. It demonstrates that increasing the transmit power can improve the system performance. Next, the effect of α is also clearly shown in the two pictures above. When increasing α from 0 to 1, the SCP tends to increase gradually, achieving its maximum value and gradually decreasing. It can be explained that when α increases, the users will have more time to harvest RF energy and use that plentiful energy in offloading tasks. However, when α gets closer to 1, users do not have enough time to offload their tasks, resulting in an SCP decrease. It also proves the existence of α^* makes the SCP reach maximum value.

Figure 6 depicts the impact of the length of task of U_1 and bandwidth on system performance. In this experiment, we gradually increase the U_1 task length while keeping the task length of U_2. We observed that the increase in the length of the task of U_1 reduces its performance. However, it contributes to improving the probability of successful computation for U_2. Another observation is that increasing the bandwidth can improve system performance. In the case of very high bandwidth, the task's length does not affect system performance much.

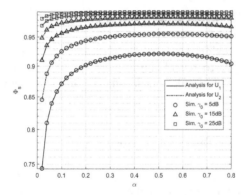

Fig. 3. $\Phi_s^{U_1}$ and $\Phi_s^{U_2}$ vs. time switching ratio α with different γ_0.

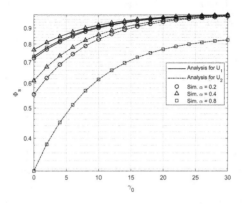

Fig. 4. $\Phi_s^{U_1}$ and $\Phi_s^{U_2}$ vs. average transmit SNR γ_0 with different α.

Figure 7 describes MSCP-GA rapidly converges with the setting parameters given in Table 1. Figure 8 describes comparison among the optimal algorithm and non-optimal approach in term of SCP. With the non-optimal approach, we use fixed time switching ratio, 0.1, 0.4 and 0.8, respectively, to evaluate system performance. The results show that the use of the MSCP-GA algorithm gives higher efficiency than not using the optimal algorithm. Furthermore, to highlight the advantages of MSCP-GA, we also compared it to the MSCP-based on brute force optimization (MSCP-BF) [17] case. The results show that two optimal algorithms give the same results. However, it should be noted that the algorithm complexity of MSCP-BF is higher than that of MSCP-GA. The results show that our proposed algorithm improves system performance.

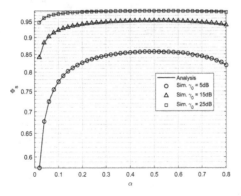

Fig. 5. Φ_s vs. time switching ratio α with different γ_0.

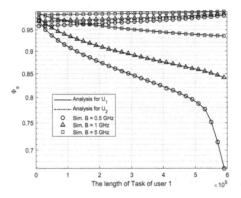

Fig. 6. Φ_s vs. the length of task of U_1 with different B.

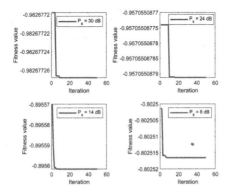

Fig. 7. Algorithm convergence when operating with different transmit power.

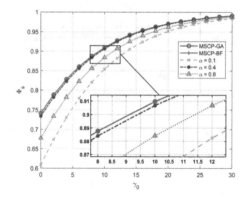

Fig. 8. System performance comparison among the optimal algorithm and non-optimal approach.

6   Conclusion

In this paper, we considered the uplink RF EH NOMA MEC network. Specifically, two energy-constraint users harvest RF energy from AP to offload their tasks. We derived the expression of the successful computation probability of two users and of system. We proposed a low-complexity approach based on the GA and achieved optimal system performance. Simulation results confirmed the superiority of the proposed algorithm in comparison with the traditional approach.

Appendix A: Proof of Lemma 1

Here, we derive the closed-form expression of $\Phi_s^{U_1}$ as follows.

$$
\begin{aligned}
\Phi_s^{U_1} &= \Pr\left(g_1 > g_2, \gamma_{11} > \gamma_{th1}\right) + \Pr\left(g_1 < g_2, \gamma_{21} > \gamma_{th1}\right) \\
&= \underbrace{\Pr\left(g_1 > g_2, \frac{a\gamma_0 g_1^2}{a\gamma_0 g_2^2 + 1} > \gamma_{th1}\right)}_{I_1} + \underbrace{\Pr\left(g_1 < g_2, a\gamma_0 g_1^2 > \gamma_{th1}\right)}_{I_2} \quad \text{(A-1)}
\end{aligned}
$$

$$I_1 = \Pr\left(g_1 > g_2, g_1 > \sqrt{\gamma_{th1}\left(g_2^2 + \frac{1}{a\gamma_0}\right)}\right)$$

$$= \begin{cases} \Pr\left(g_1 > \sqrt{\gamma_{th1}\left(g_2^2 + \frac{1}{a\gamma_0}\right)}\right), & \gamma_{th1} > 1 \\ \Pr\left(g_1 > \sqrt{\gamma_{th1}\left(g_2^2 + \frac{1}{a\gamma_0}\right)}, g_2 < \sqrt{\frac{\gamma_{th1}}{a\gamma_0(1-\gamma_{th1})}}\right) \\ \qquad + \Pr\left(g_1 > g_2, g_2 > \sqrt{\frac{\gamma_{th1}}{a\gamma_0(1-\gamma_{th})}}\right), & \gamma_{th1} < 1 \end{cases}$$

$$= \begin{cases} \int_0^\infty \left[1 - F_{g_1}\left(\sqrt{\gamma_{th}\left(x^2 + \frac{1}{a\gamma_0}\right)}\right)\right] f_{g_2}(x)dx, & \gamma_{th} > 1 \\ \int_0^c \left[1 - F_{g_1}\left(\sqrt{\gamma_{th}\left(x^2 + \frac{1}{a\gamma_0}\right)}\right)\right] f_{g_2}(x)dx \\ \qquad + \int_c^\infty \left[1 - F_{g_1}(x)\right] f_{g_2}(x)dx, & \gamma_{th} < 1 \end{cases}$$

$$\overset{(a)}{=} \begin{cases} \frac{\pi}{N\lambda_2} \sum_{j=1}^N \exp\left(-\frac{\sqrt{\gamma_{th}\left(\theta_j^2 + \frac{1}{a\gamma_0}\right)}}{\lambda_1} - \frac{\theta_j}{\lambda_2}\right)\sqrt{\frac{1-\phi_j}{1+\phi_j}}, & \gamma_{th} > 1 \\ \frac{\pi c}{2N\lambda_2} \sum_{j=1}^N \exp\left(-\frac{\sqrt{\gamma_{th}\left(x_j^2 + \frac{1}{a\gamma_0}\right)}}{\lambda_1} - \frac{x_j}{\lambda_2}\right)\sqrt{1 - \phi_j^2} \\ \qquad + \frac{\lambda_1}{\lambda_1+\lambda_2} \exp\left[-\left(\frac{1}{\lambda_1} + \frac{1}{\lambda_2}\right)c\right], & \gamma_{th} < 1 \end{cases} \qquad (A-2)$$

where $c = \sqrt{\frac{\gamma_{th}}{a\gamma_0(1-\gamma_{th})}}$, step (a) is obtained by applying the Gaussian-Chebyshev quadrature method [18] in which $\theta_j = -\ln\left(\frac{\phi_j+1}{2}\right)$, $x_j = \frac{(\phi_j+1)c}{2}$, $\phi_j = \cos\left(\frac{2j-1}{2N}\pi\right)$, and N is the complexity-vs-accuracy trade-off coefficient.

Next, we obtain the expression of integral I_2 as follows:

$$I_2 = \Pr\left(\sqrt{\frac{\gamma_{th1}}{a\gamma_0}} < g_1 < g_2\right) = \int_{\sqrt{\frac{\gamma_{th1}}{a\gamma_0}}}^\infty \left[F_{g_1}(x) - F_{g_1}\left(\sqrt{\frac{\gamma_{th1}}{a\gamma_0}}\right)\right] f_{g_2}(x)dx$$

$$= \frac{\lambda_2}{\lambda_1 + \lambda_2} \exp\left[-\left(\frac{1}{\lambda_1} + \frac{1}{\lambda_2}\right)\sqrt{\frac{\gamma_{th1}}{a\gamma_0}}\right].$$

$$(A-3)$$

From (A-1), (A-2), (A-3), we obtain the result as (13). This concludes our proof.

Appendix B: Proof of Lemma 3

Here, we derive the closed-form expression of Φ_s as follows.

$$\Phi_s = \Pr\left(g_1 > g_2, \gamma_{11} > \gamma_{th}, \gamma_{12} > \gamma_{th}\right) + \Pr\left(g_1 < g_2, \gamma_{21} > \gamma_{th}, \gamma_{22} > \gamma_{th}\right)$$

$$= \underbrace{\Pr\left(g_1 > g_2, \frac{a\gamma_0 g_1^2}{a\gamma_0 g_2^2 + 1} > \gamma_{th}, a\gamma_0 g_2^2 > \gamma_{th}\right)}_{I_3}$$

$$+ \underbrace{\Pr\left(g_1 < g_2, a\gamma_0 g_1^2 > \gamma_{th}, \frac{a\gamma_0 g_2^2}{a\gamma_0 g_1^2 + 1} > \gamma_{th}\right)}_{I_4}$$

$$\hspace{10cm} \text{(B-1)}$$

$$I_3 = \Pr\left(g_1 > g_2, g_1 > \sqrt{\gamma_{th}\left(g_2^2 + \frac{1}{a\gamma_0}\right)}, g_2 > \sqrt{\frac{\gamma_{th}}{a\gamma_0}}\right)$$

$$= \begin{cases} \Pr\left(g_1 > \sqrt{\gamma_{th}\left(g_2^2 + \frac{1}{a\gamma_0}\right)}, g_2 > \sqrt{\frac{\gamma_{th}}{a\gamma_0}}\right), & \gamma_{th} > 1 \\[2em] \Pr\left(g_1 > \sqrt{\gamma_{th}\left(g_2^2 + \frac{1}{a\gamma_0}\right)}, \sqrt{\frac{\gamma_{th}}{a\gamma_0(1-\gamma_{th})}} > g_2 > \sqrt{\frac{\gamma_{th}}{a\gamma_0}}\right) \\[1em] \quad + \Pr\left(g_1 > g_2, g_2 > \sqrt{\frac{\gamma_{th}}{a\gamma_0(1-\gamma_{th})}}\right), & \gamma_{th} < 1 \end{cases}$$

$$\overset{(c)}{=} \begin{cases} \frac{\pi}{N\lambda_2}\sum_{j=1}^{N}\exp\left(-\frac{\sqrt{\gamma_{th}\left(\theta_j^2 + \frac{1}{a\gamma_0}\right)}}{\lambda_1} - \frac{\theta_j}{\lambda_2}\right)\sqrt{\frac{1-\phi_j}{1+\phi_j}} \\[1em] \quad - \frac{\pi b}{2N\lambda_2}\sum_{j=1}^{N}\exp\left(-\frac{\sqrt{\gamma_{th}\left(x_j^2 + \frac{1}{a\gamma_0}\right)}}{\lambda_1} - \frac{x_j}{\lambda_2}\right)\sqrt{1-\phi_j^2}, & \gamma_{th} > 1 \\[2em] \frac{\pi(c-b)}{2N\lambda_2}\sum_{j=1}^{N}\exp\left(-\frac{\sqrt{\gamma_{th}\left(y_j^2 + \frac{1}{a\gamma_0}\right)}}{\lambda_1} - \frac{y_j}{\lambda_2}\right)\sqrt{1-\phi_j^2} \\[1em] \quad + \frac{\lambda_1}{\lambda_1+\lambda_2}\exp\left[-\left(\frac{1}{\lambda_1} + \frac{1}{\lambda_2}\right)c\right], & \gamma_{th} < 1 \end{cases}$$

$$\hspace{10cm} \text{(B-2)}$$

where $b = \sqrt{\frac{\gamma_{th}}{a\gamma_0}}$, $c = \sqrt{\frac{\gamma_{th}}{a\gamma_0(1-\gamma_{th})}}$, step (c) is obtained by applying the Gaussian-Chebyshev quadrature method in which $\theta_j = -\ln\left(\frac{\phi_j+1}{2}\right)$, $x_j = \frac{(\phi_j+1)c}{2}$, $y_j = \frac{(\phi_j+1)(c-b)}{2} + b$, $\phi_j = \cos\left(\frac{2j-1}{2N}\pi\right)$, and N is the complexity-vs-accuracy trade-off coefficient.

Similarly, we obtain the expression of integral I_4 as follows:

$$
I_4 = \begin{cases}
\frac{\pi}{N\lambda_1} \sum_{j=1}^{N} \exp\left(-\frac{\sqrt{\gamma_{th}\left(\theta_j^2 + \frac{1}{a\gamma_0}\right)}}{\lambda_2} - \frac{\theta_j}{\lambda_1} \right) \sqrt{\frac{1-\phi_j}{1+\phi_j}} \\
\quad - \frac{\pi b}{2N\lambda_1} \sum_{j=1}^{N} \exp\left(-\frac{\sqrt{\gamma_{th}\left(x_j^2 + \frac{1}{a\gamma_0}\right)}}{\lambda_2} - \frac{x_j}{\lambda_1} \right) \sqrt{1 - \phi_j^2}, \quad \gamma_{th} > 1 \\
\frac{\pi(c-b)}{2N\lambda_1} \sum_{j=1}^{N} \exp\left(-\frac{\sqrt{\gamma_{th}\left(y_j^2 + \frac{1}{a\gamma_0}\right)}}{\lambda_2} - \frac{y_j}{\lambda_1} \right) \sqrt{1 - \phi_j^2} \\
\quad + \frac{\lambda_2}{\lambda_1+\lambda_2} \exp\left[-\left(\frac{1}{\lambda_1} + \frac{1}{\lambda_2}\right) c \right], \quad \gamma_{th} < 1
\end{cases}
$$

$$(B\text{-}3)$$

From (B-1), (B-2), (B-3), we obtain the result as (15). This concludes our proof.

References

1. Chettri, L., Bera, R.: A comprehensive survey on internet of things (IoT) toward 5G wireless systems. IEEE Internet Things J. **7**(1), 16–32 (2019)
2. Mao, Y., You, C., Zhang, J., Huang, K., Letaief, K.B.: A survey on mobile edge computing: the communication perspective. IEEE Commun. Surv. Tutor. **19**(4), 2322–2358 (2017)
3. Pham, Q.V., et al.: A survey of multi-access edge computing in 5G and beyond: fundamentals, technology integration, and state-of-the-art. IEEE Access **8**, 116974–117017 (2020)
4. Ye, Y., Lu, G., Hu, R.Q., Shi, L.: On the performance and optimization for MEC networks using uplink NOMA. In: IEEE International Conference on Communications Workshops (ICC Workshops), Shanghai, China. IEEE (2019)
5. Fang, F., Xu, Y., Ding, Z., Shen, C., Peng, M., Karagiannidis, G.K.: Optimal resource allocation for delay minimization in NOMA-MEC networks. IEEE Trans. Commun. **68**, 7867–7881 (2020)
6. Ha, D.-B., Truong, V.-T., Ha, D.-H.: A novel secure protocol for mobile edge computing network applied downlink NOMA. In: Vo, N.-S., Hoang, V.-P. (eds.) INISCOM 2020. LNICST, vol. 334, pp. 324–336. Springer, Cham (2020). https://doi.org/10.1007/978-3-030-63083-6_25
7. Ye, Y., Hu, R.Q., Lu, G., Shi, L.: Enhance latency-constrained computation in MEC networks using uplink NOMA. IEEE Trans. Commun. **68**(4), 2409–2425 (2020)
8. Min, M., et al.: Learning-based privacy-aware offloading for healthcare IoT with energy harvesting. IEEE Internet Things J. **6**(3), 4307–4316 (2018)
9. Zhou, F., Wu, Y., Hu, R.Q., Qian, Y.: Computation efficiency in a wireless-powered mobile edge computing network with NOMA. In: ICC 2019–2019 IEEE International Conference on Communications (ICC), pp. 1–7. IEEE (2019)
10. Hoang, T.M., Van Son, V., Dinh, N.C., Hiep, P.T.: Optimizing duration of energy harvesting for downlink NOMA full-duplex over Nakagami-m fading channel. AEU-Int. J. Electron. Commun. **95**, 199–206 (2018)

11. Garcia, C.E., Camana, M.R., Koo, I.: Particle swarm optimization-based secure computation efficiency maximization in a power beacon-assisted wireless-powered mobile edge computing NOMA system. Energies **13**(21), 5540 (2020). ISSN: 1996-1073

12. Ha, D.B., Tran, D.D., Tran-Ha, V., Hong, E.K.: Performance of amplify-and-forward relaying with wireless power transfer over dissimilar channels. Elektron. ir Elektrotechnika J. **21**(5), 90–95 (2015)

13. Zhou, F., Wu, Y., Hu, R.Q., Qian, Y.: Computation efficiency in a wireless-powered mobile edge computing network with NOMA. In: IEEE International Conference on Communications (ICC), Shanghai, China, pp. 20–24, May 2019

14. Guo, X., Su, J., Zhou, H., Liu, C., Cao, J., Li, L.: Community detection based on genetic algorithm using local structural similarity. IEEE Access **7**, 134583–134600 (2019)

15. Fang, P., Zhao, Y., Liu, Z., Gao, J., Chen, Z.: Resource allocation strategy for MEC system based on VM migration and RF energy harvesting. In: 2020 IEEE 91st Vehicular Technology Conference (VTC2020-Spring), pp. 1–6. IEEE (2020)

16. Hassanat, A., Almohammadi, K., Alkafaween, E., Abunawas, E., Hammouri, A., Prasath, V.: Choosing mutation and crossover ratios for genetic algorithms a review with a new dynamic approach. Information **10**(12), 390 (2019)

17. Chen, L., Wu, J., Long, X., Zhang, Z.: Engine: cost effective offloading in mobile edge computing with fog-cloud cooperation. arXiv preprint arXiv:1711.01683 (2017)

18. Truong, V.T., Vo, M.T., Lee, Y., Ha, D.B.: Amplify-and-forward relay transmission in uplink non-orthogonal multiple access networks. In: 2019 6th NAFOSTED Conference on Information and Computer Science (NICS), pp. 1–6. IEEE (2019)

Popularity-Based Hierarchical Caching for Next Generation Content Delivery Networks

Nima Najaflou[1][✉], Selin Sezer[3], Zeynep Gürkaş Aydın[1], and Berk Canberk[2]

[1] Istanbul University - Cerrahpasa, Istanbul, Turkey
nima.najaflou@ogr.iu.edu.tr
[2] Istanbul Technical University, Istanbul, Turkey
[3] Medianova CDN, Istanbul, Turkey

Abstract. More than half of the content over the Internet is carried by content delivery networks (CDNs). CDNs cache popular and most requested contents on the edges of the network. Thus helping to increase Quality of Experience (QoE), e.g., by decreasing time to first byte (TTFB) for different contents. In the present paper, we focus on developing a hierarchical caching structure for CDNs to improve their QoE. We focus on unpopular content here, since it accounts for a big portion of content over the Internet. Our novel data-driven method forms caching clusters or hierarchies to deal with unpopular contents. In order to form our clusters and assign edge servers into these clusters, we consider the pattern in which contents have been requested including the total number of requests, similar objects between two edge servers, and requests for those objects. Using $tf - idf$ method, which is widely used in information retrieval, we find the similarities between requests landed on each of our edge servers and use these similarities to form clusters using the Markov Clustering algorithm. We evaluate our approach using different hierarchical models, and with real-world requests from a large-scale global CDN. We demonstrate that our hierarchical caching approach improves cache hit ratio by 9.05%. Additionally, a 7.39% decrease in TTFB is observed.

Keywords: Hierarchical caching · User generated content · Long tail · Content delivery network · Clustered caching

1 Introduction

With the increasing number of Internet users and devices connected to the Internet, network data consumption has seen a tremendous growth [10]. Content providers heavily rely on Content Delivery Networks (CDNs) to reduce the latency by placing the content at the network's edges, closer to the end-users, and benefit from in-network content caching. Thus content benefits from improved availability and boosted performance.

© ICST Institute for Computer Sciences, Social Informatics and Telecommunications Engineering 2021
Published by Springer Nature Switzerland AG 2021. All Rights Reserved
N.-S. Vo et al. (Eds.): INISCOM 2021, LNICST 379, pp. 73–87, 2021.
https://doi.org/10.1007/978-3-030-77424-0_7

Numerous studies have focused on content caching in the literature. Web caching has extensively been studied [25,32]. Some studies have focused on caching in the Base Stations(BSs) [3] as well as caching in Heterogeneous Networks (HeNets) [33]. To cope with some of the challenges in content caching, several studies have suggested a hierarchical caching architecture to improve the amount of content that can be served from the cache clusters. These hierarchical caching architectures also reduce latency and bandwidth consumption.

Though there have been many studies in various areas of content caching, most of which have focused on delivering popular content since it is economically more feasible for CDN companies to deal with popular content instead of dealing with unpopular contents which will be consumed by a small fraction of the users. But with the rise of Online Social Networks (OSNs) the amount of User-Generated Contents(UGCs) produced proliferated. A big portion of the content produced by OSNs is having the characteristics of unpopular content. Moreover, today we see a transformation from a limited number of content producers, to where everybody is a content producer and publisher. Consider for example e-commerce (online classified advertisement) platforms such as Facebook Marketplace, eBay, or Alibaba.com where users can publish their contents. Here again, the characteristic of the content and its' popularity is different from a news website such as The New York Times. The long tail of the content in OSNs or UGC providers such as classified advertisement platforms make it harder to keep these contents in the cache pool of a CDN without the content getting evicted by cache replacement algorithms. The result is a lower hit ratio for unpopular content, which in some cases may even add to overall Time to First Byte (TTFB) by adding another hop. This low cache hit ratio will consequently affect QoE and QoS provided by CDNs.

Despite the explosive growth of UGCs and OSNs and the importance caching these content play for CDNs and the challenges they may face, there have only been few works on caching unpopular long-tailed content such as the work in [1,7,28]. But most of these studies have focused on video and explicitly YouTube platform and less has been done for images or other formats of contents which are different in many aspects from the video. In this paper, we will focus on unpopular content and we will propose a new approach for efficiently caching this type of content. Our data-driven approach will provide this flexibility to react to the changes in content access patterns over time and adapt accordingly. Our proposed method is a dynamic hierarchical caching topology which may change over time if the content access pattern changes. Moreover, instead of defining a fixed topology for all content providers and serving all content using this structure, we try to group content providers with similar access patterns and construct unique topologies for each of the groups. We will enforce similar patterns into these groups and will increase the chance of a cache hit.

1.1 Our Contribution

Firstly we will introduce a new data-driven two-level hierarchical caching topology to deal with unpopular content. To form our clusters we use info about the characteristic of the requests landed on surrogate servers. This method in contrast to other arbitrary methods tries to cluster edges with similar behavior into the same cluster. Secondly, this design, in contrast to arbitrary two-level hierarchical caching topology suggested in previous works, and those used by major CDN companies are dynamic and adaptive and have the capability to change and reshape based on the changes in content access patterns. Thirdly we will use a novel low-complexity approach to model this access pattern and group similar patterns at the same clusters. The approach we use is a combination of the well-known tf-idf method used in natural language processing and the Markov clustering algorithm. Finally, We benchmark our proposed method against the static origin shield method used by many CDNs. To do so we use data from a large-scale global CDN which consists of more than a million requests for various contents.

2   Related Work

There have been several studies focusing on content caching in the literature. Web caching has extensively been studied, see for example [32] and [25] for background information about web caching and its application. Several studies have focused on caching at the base stations (BSs) in mobile networks and the so-called edge caching. Authors in [3,16,31] and [34] deal with the issue of caching contents, mostly popular contents, at the BSs, user devices or intermediate servers, routers or gateways to bring the content closer to the client. In addition to caching popular contents at BSs, the concept of the heterogeneous network (HeNets) and techniques to redirect the user into less busy networks with higher capacity have studied widely [13]. In [33] the authors suggest a scheme where popular contents are pushed and pre-cached into BSs during off-peak hours of the network to be ready.

Many of the challenges in content caching have been discussed in [12,17,22]. Between the challenges mentioned in those articles cache replacement strategies have gained lots of attention. Though several other variations of LRU such as LRFU [14], CFLRU [21], xLRU [19] and ARC [18] have been proposed, but LRU is still the cache replacement algorithm of choice in many systems due to its simplicity and effectiveness.

To tackle the problems with traditional architectures, a tree-like cooperative and uncooperative hierarchical caching was suggested in [8] and they demonstrated that cooperative hierarchical caching architecture outperforms the traditional uncooperative one. The work in [20] suggests a cooperative hierarchical caching scheme that considers link latency while fetching the contents from origin servers. Authors in [4] suggest a content replication method which aims at reducing the handover latency and packet loss. Authors in [5] formulate and design a cooperative cache management algorithm aiming at minimizing bandwidth cost and maximizing cache hit ratio in CDNs. [11] considers a joint cache content placement and request routing problem and seeks for an efficient approximate solution. A content placement algorithm based on the popularity is suggested in [9]. Their algorithm decides whether to cache or not to cache the content. It caches a number of chunks of the content determined in chunk marking window (CMW) and updates CMW based on the number of requests received for the file. [2] and [24] also deals with the problem of content placement across hierarchical caching networks. In [2] authors focus on content placement across heterogeneous distributed servers. They formulate disk space, bandwidth, and other constraints and their algorithm suggest a number of copies needed and the location they should be placed (Fig. 1).

Reference	Objective	Topology	Content Type	Technique	Solution	Content Type
[4]	Maximize traffic volume served from cache, Minimize Bandwidth cost	Hierarchical, with leaf and parent node	IPTV, VoD content	Linear Programming	Optimal	Popular
[10]	Maximize amount of supported traffic with respect to link utilization	Collaborative Hierarchical Caching	IPTV	Lagrangian Relaxation	Optimal	Popular
[8]	Minimizing Cache management overhead, Maximizing cache usage efficiency	Arbitrary	Chunk-based caching in Content Centric Networks	Greedy	Sub-Optimal	Popular
[2]	Minimize System resource usage (Disk, Bandwidth)	Arbitrary	IPTV, VoD content	Mixed Integer Programming combined with Lagrangian Relaxation	Near Optimal Solution	Popular
[22]	Minimize server load	m-level Hierarchy, m >2	IPTV, VoD content	Linear Programming, Submodular maximization	Optimal	Popular
This Paper	Maximize Long-tail content delivery from cache, Minimize System Load	2-level Dynamic Hierarchical	Object delivery over CDN	Unsupervised Clustering Algorithm	Optimal	Popular and Unpopular

Fig. 1. Comparison of different works done on hierarchical caching

3 Problem Description

Content Delivery Networks deploy several geographically distributed heterogeneous cache servers, namely *surrogate servers* or *edge servers*, to serve the contents to the clients from the nearest location. This architecture which only consists of surrogate servers and origin servers is shown in Fig. 2a. There are several drawbacks to this architecture such as limited capacity of surrogate servers, flow of numerous requests from surrogate servers to the origin server, and the spike of traffic and load these requests might cause in origin servers.

Some CDN companies such as Akamai and Fastly use a secondary layer of caching called *Origin Shields* to rule out the problems mentioned earlier. They assign a certain and perpetual number of surrogate servers to these origin shield servers. This architecture is also shown in Fig. 2b. Origin shields in this architecture have higher caching capacity (space) which provides redundancy and a bigger pool of cached contents. This will result in a higher HIT ratio for CDN companies because those contents which can't normally be cached on edges due to their unpopularity and lower frequency of use, now can be cached in this

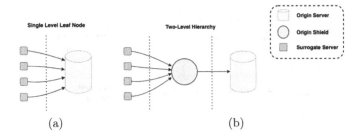

Fig. 2. Cache clusters for a network of edge servers (a) before forming a cluster each edge acts independently and in cache MISS situation they request content from origin server, while in (b) by forming clusters, in cache MISS situation they form a shield for origin server.

redundant area. But there are few problems with these architectures which CDNs have to deal with: Firstly these architectures assign a certain number of edge servers to an origin shield. The number is regardless of content providers' (CP) content types and behavior of their clients. While some CPs may have a limited number of contents with a high volume of requests for these contents, others may have numerous contents with few requests for each of these contents. This will lead to a problem which we call it *battle for survival*. Those contents with fewer requests will be in a battle for survival with more popular content. This situation is shown in Fig. 3. This figure shows the requests made for three different CPs' objects over a certain period of time. Objects belonging to content provider A have lower popularity (lower number of requests per object) compared to content provider B and C.Therefore if we serve all these contents from the same cache pool, cache replacement algorithms such as LRU or others [23] will evict contents with lower popularity (more likely contents belonging to content provider A.) to open up space for upcoming traffic. The behavior of content provider A is very similar to OSN, with a large number of contents and a few requests per content. Hereby the problem with caching UGCs arises. This is what we called earlier a battle for survival, and it makes it hard to cache these contents.

Second problem with this architecture is that when you assign an origin shield to a few edge servers perpetually, in fact, you restrain this capacity. Due to the static nature of these architectures, inefficiencies in handling requests and sub-optimal usage of capacity will be inevitable.

Thirdly, since they don't have a data-driven architecture, they can't react autonomously to any changes such as changes in the number of requests, edge servers load, content popularity, and other metrics, and adapt themselves accordingly.

To deal with long-tailed contents and use our distributed and heterogeneous infrastructure optimally and deliver UGCs efficiently, we propose to form cache clusters dynamically and assign shielding responsibility to one of the surrogate servers within the cluster.

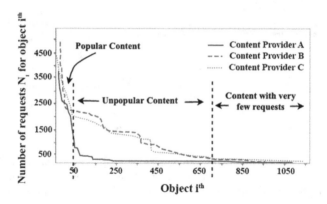

Fig. 3. Problem with the current architecture.

4   Proposed Architecture

As discussed earlier, instead of assigning a fixed number of surrogate servers to their corresponding origin shields which are typically used by many CDN companies, our architecture constructs these building blocks dynamically considering the volume of the requests and different parameters in the surrogate server and underlying network. Additionally, we calculate and form these clusters separately for each customer with unique behavior, so for example customer A's cluster is different from customer B's cluster. These calculations are done in certain time intervals. These clusters may vary from time i to time j $(i \neq j)$. Figure 4 depicts the overall system architecture and it gives a detailed representation of how our system works.

In each cluster C_i we have two types of nodes: A Selected Surrogate Server (SSS) and one or more Distribution Surrogate Servers (DSS). Requests from clients first land on DSS, in case of a cache MISS in DSS, the request will be handed to that cluster's SSS. If SSS has that content, it will pass it to DSS, otherwise, SSS will ask the origin server of the content provider for the content, gets it, and delivers it to DSS that had asked for it. A copy of the content will be cached on SSS. SSS here will also act as a shield for the origin server by reducing the number of requests for the same content from the same cluster to only one. These role assignments are done after doing the measurements and calculations depicted in Fig. 5. The final output of these two modules is the roles for edge servers which will consequently form clusters of edge servers with DSS and SSS. Figure 5 shows these two modules and their components. We will explain these modules after giving preliminary information about the graph we constructed for our network and related topics, then Edge Side and Calculation modules are explained.

We model our geo-distributed CDN as a set of heterogeneous nodes with different capacities and resources. These nodes are connected through heterogeneous network connections or links. Each of these links has different inbound

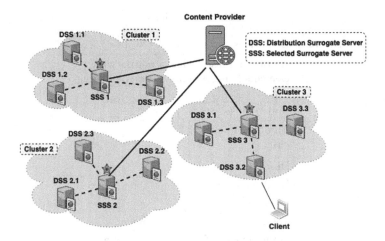

Fig. 4. Proposed Architecture and corresponding components

and outbound bandwidth and latency. We assume that all these nodes and the links between them have a similar reliability rate. Additionally, we assume that between each pair of nodes there is a routing path, which emphasizes that the graph forming our network is strongly connected. These links are weighted and undirected.

4.1 Edge Side Module

In order to collect data from our edge servers, we designed a module called the Edge Side module which is located on each edge server (Fig. 5). For all of our customers, the TailStat unit measures the number of requests received for each of the contents. It will give us the total number of received requests (TLR) and the total number of requested objects (TRO). This info can give us an insight into frequently requested content and less frequent ones. Edge Resources unit measures available resources of the edge server such as disk usage, bandwidth, and other load-related metrics of the server (D, B, LA, P). All these data are collected and sent to the Calculation module in some time intervals.

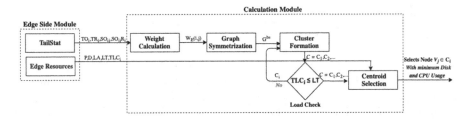

Fig. 5. A scheme showing our modules and their corresponding sub-modules.

Table 1. Notations

Symbols	Definitions
G	A graph represented as a matrix with elements being weights on corresponding edges
i, j	Node indices, $1 \leq i, j \leq n$
n	Number of nodes in G
P	CPU Usage
D	Disk I/O Usage
LA	Load Average
LT	Load Threshold
TO_i	Total number of objects at node i
TR_i	Total number of requests received at node i
SO_{ij}	Similar objects between node i and node j
$SO_{ij}R_i$	Number of requests at node i for Similar objects between node i and node j
TLC_i	Total load average of cluster C_i
NVC_i	Number of vertices in cluster C_i

4.2   Calculation Module

The calculation module is made of four units each of which does a certain job to finally obtain the clusters and their corresponding centroids. These units are shown in Fig. 5.

Initially, a directed weighted graph is created. Each of the nodes V of this graph are our surrogate servers and we have an edge between all the nodes of this graph, in another word it is a complete digraph. For each edge E_{ij} of the digraph $\mathcal{G}$ which is connecting vertices v_i to v_j a weight W_E is calculated using our weight formula.

We use the Weight Calculation unit (1) to calculate the weight $W_E(i, j)$ for each directional edge E_{ij} from node v_i to node v_j. For doing so we adapt *tf-idf* [26] which is mainly used as a weighting factor in information retrieval or text mining. In order to prevent confusion we simply call it $W_E(i, j)$ and it can be obtained by:

$$W_E(i, j) = \frac{SO_{ij}}{TO_i} \times \log(\frac{TR_i}{SO_{ij}R_i + 1})$$

In this phase of our research we will continue with limited attributes, but adding further attributes to our weighting factor would't change the main concept (Table 1).

The graph $\mathcal{G}$ which is obtained from the Weight Calculation unit is a directed graph. Since many of the works done in community detection or graph partitioning are applicable on an undirected graph and only a few of them are concerned with a directed graph, we would transform our directed graph into an undirected one in the Graph Symmetrization unit (2). The work done in [27] suggests two methods for graph symmetrization; namely *bibliometric symmetrization* and *degree-discounted symmetrization*. Since our graph is a complete digraph we are going to use bibliometric symmetrization. So for original directed graph $\mathcal{G}$ with associated adjacency matrix A, bibliometric symmetrized graph G^{bs} can be obtained as follow:

$$G^{bs} = AA^T + A^T A$$

All the steps and operations below are applied on Graph G^{bs}. We use Cluster Formation unit (3) to find clusters in our network. Inside this unit, we use the Markov Clustering algorithm (MCL) which was proposed by Stijn van Dongen [30] and is based on stochastic flow through a network. MCL computes stochastic flow through a network by iteratively applying two operators called *inflation* and *expansion* on the initial stochastic matrix till it reaches convergence. MCL has shown to be very effective in problems such as bacterial molecular network clustering [29] as well as biological networks [6,15]. Using MCL you can't define the number of clusters but you can control the reinforcement step by *inflation*. By playing with *inflation rate* you can obtain clusters with different levels of granularity.

Algorithm 1. ClusterFormation

Require: Graph $\mathcal{G}^{bs} = (\mathcal{V}, \mathcal{E})$, $Adjacency matrix A$
Ensure: Clusters $\mathcal{C} = C_1, C_2, ..., C_k$ such that $\bigcup C_i = \mathcal{V}$
1: $A := A + I$ #Adding Self-loops to the graph
2: $M := AD^{-1}$ #Calculate Initial Stochastic matrix M
3: **while** M hasn't converged **do**
4:     $M := M_{exp}$ #Expand M by taking power e of M
5:     $M := M_{inf}$ #Inflate M with parameter r
6:     $M := M_{Pru}$ #Prune M
7: **end while**
8: Interpret resulting Matrix M to detect Clusters
9: **return** $\mathcal{C}$

Though our first goal is to find communities inside our network of edge servers, we also would like each cluster to be capable of handling the load inside the cluster without getting overwhelmed. If any of our clusters get over-loaded it will result in it the requests being dropped which will affect that cluster's availability. Availability is an important factor for CDN companies since their customers highly rely on the availability provided by CDNs.

In this unit, we provide our bibliometric symmetrized graph G^{bs} with node set $\mathcal{V}$ and edge set $\mathcal{E}$ respectively as the input to our $Cluster Formation$ algorithm. A is adjacency matrix where $A(i, j)$ denotes the weight between node v_i and node v_j and M is the initial stochastic matrix and represents the transition probability

Algorithm 2. LoadCheck

Require: Clusters $\mathcal{C} = C_1, C_2, ..., C_k$ with their corresponding load data
Ensure: Load of each cluster C_i is below a threshold LT
1: **for all** Cluster $C_i \in \mathcal{C}$ **do**
2:    **if** $TLC_i \leq LT$ **then**
3:        $CentroidSelection(C_i)$
4:    **else**
5:        $LoadCheck(ClusterFormation(C_i))$
6:    **end if**
7: **end for**
8: **return** $\mathcal{C}$

---

of a random walk or in other words Markov chain on the graph. Additionally, we make sure that the load of each cluster is below a threshold through *LoadCheck* algorithm. If any of the clusters has load above the threshold LT we recalculate clusters for the nodes inside that cluster separately. We calculate the total load average for each cluster C_i denoted by TLC_i as follow:

$$TLC_i = \frac{\sum\limits_{v_j \in C_i} LA(v_j)}{NVC_i}$$

Algorithm 3. CentroidSelection

Require: Set v_j of vertices belonging to cluster C_i
Ensure: Load of each cluster C_i is below a threshold LT
1: **for all** Vertices $v_j \in C_i$ **do**
2:    **if** $LA(v_j) \leq TLC_i$ **then**
3:        Select Node with Min Disk I/O D and CPU P
4:    **end if**
5: **end for**
6: **return** Centorid CN_i for Cluster C_i

In order to create a hierarchical topology and reduce the number of requests flowing to the origin server, we need to select a centroid for each of our clusters. We do so using the Centroid Selection unit (4). The centroid of each cluster which we call the Selected Surrogate Server (SSS), depicted in Fig. 4, will act as an origin shield, providing a higher hit ratio and lower latency.

5   Numerical Evaluation

Here in this section, we will present the implementation results of our proposed architecture in a realistic testbed. Throughout the tests we assume, there are $NON = 7$ edge nodes each assigned a cache size CS which is less than what is needed to store all the objects in the cache. The reason for this decision is to create a cache competition situation explained earlier. All these seven nodes have similar hardware such as CPU, RAM, etc., and have the same caching configurations. These nodes are located at the same location, all in a data center in Germany which means the latency value from the origin server to these edges and vice versa are almost the same.

We use a collection of $N = 100$ objects with identical size of OS. For simplicity we assume all the objects belong to one origin server. Therefore the number of objects which can be stored on each edge node can be calculated as $NOO = CS/OS$. It's good to know that in real deployments there are more than one origin servers.

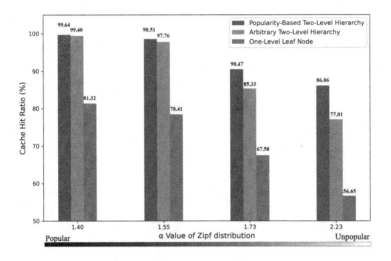

Fig. 6. Total Hit Ratio of all edge servers over different shape parameter α

We assume that the popularity of the contents follows Zipf Distribution with shape parameter α. We use five different values for parameter α as $\alpha = \{1.35, 1.45, 1.85, 2.00, 2.15\}$ and use $NumPy$ library to generate numbers with following Zipf distribution. In each test, we generate seven sets of numbers using a single α value. We repeat this for all the α values given above. In all of our edge servers, we run LRU for cache replacement. We set the load threshold TL needed for $LoadCheck$ algorithm to be 75%.

The main objectives of our tests are to observe the effect of our proposed architecture on Cache Hit ratio and Latency. We can describe Cache Hit ratio as the ratio between the number of requested contents served from the cache to the total number of contents requested. Similarly, we measure the latency here through a metric called Total download time. Since all the objects in the cache are similar and of the same size, this will give us the time in which the requested object has been retrieved.

We conducted three sets of experiments, one using one-level leaf node, another with arbitrary hierarchy structure and the third one was formed as the output of our *ClusterFormation* algorithm. Also in our second set of experiments we randomly chose a node as the origin shield, but in the third set we used *CentroidSelection* algorithm for this purpose. The number of requests and other data in the first set were given as input to form the clusters and choose centroids in the third set.

Finally We performed 10 tests and calculated the Cache Hit ratio and latency with 95% confidence interval.

5.1   Test Results

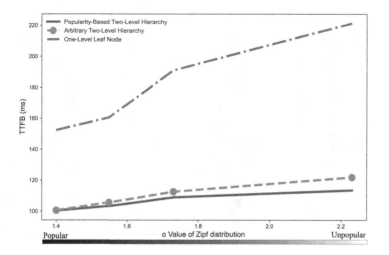

Fig. 7. Average content access time latency (ms) for different shape parameter α

The results of our tests are shown in Figs. 6 and 7. Figure 6 shows Hit ratio measurements of three different topologies used. As you can see here, though our proposed popularity-based two-level hierarchical topology outperforms other topologies in popular contents (contents with low α value) this difference gets more significant when the value of α grows and it deals with unpopular content. Our proposed method shows 9.05% improvement compared to the arbitrary two-level topology. We believe this is due to the pattern-sensitivity of our algorithm and the way it clusters edges into different groups.

Additionally, looking at Fig. 7 we can see similar effect. As you can see here, our proposed algorithm has lead to 7.39% improvement in TTFB. It's good to know that this result may vary in similar tests. Since TTFB value between Client-Edge, Edge-OriginShield and OriginShield-Origin may vary due to network situation and the distance of the servers to each other. Again what is obvious here is that our proposed method has taken away arbitrary two-level hierarchy in reducing TTFB for the contents.

6   Conclusion

In this paper, we have proposed a novel approach to form a hierarchical caching topology in content delivery networks. In particular, we focused on user-generated content which tends to have a long tail, and impose a challenge for CDNs. We have analyzed the performance of our approach with different Zipf distributions. We also found that our proposed scheme can significantly improve cache hit ratio for higher shape parameter α in Zipf distribution which is equivalent to long-tail contents. Numerical results showed this approach's performance benefits over other common cache hierarchies used by CDNs. To the best of our knowledge, this work is the first to address the problem of user-generated content caching. We hope this work will facilitate future research in this area.

References

1. Ager, B., Schneider, F., Kim, J., Feldmann, A.: Revisiting cacheability in times of user generated content. In: 2010 INFOCOM IEEE Conference on Computer Communications Workshops, pp. 1–6. IEEE (2010)
2. Applegate, D., Archer, A., Gopalakrishnan, V., Lee, S., Ramakrishnan, K.K.: Optimal content placement for a large-scale VoD system. IEEE/ACM Trans. Netw. **24**(4), 2114–2127 (2015)
3. Bastug, E., Bennis, M., Debbah, M.: Living on the edge: the role of proactive caching in 5G wireless networks. IEEE Commun. Mag. **52**(8), 82–89 (2014)
4. Bilen, T., Canberk, B.: Handover-aware content replication for mobile-CDN. IEEE Netw. Lett. **1**(1), 10–13 (2018)
5. Borst, S., Gupta, V., Walid, A.: Distributed caching algorithms for content distribution networks. In: 2010 Proceedings IEEE INFOCOM, pp. 1–9. IEEE (2010)
6. Brohee, S., Van Helden, J.: Evaluation of clustering algorithms for protein-protein interaction networks. BMC Bioinform. **7**(1), 488 (2006). https://doi.org/10.1186/1471-2105-7-488
7. Cha, M., Kwak, H., Rodriguez, P., Ahn, Y.Y., Moon, S.: I tube, you tube, everybody tubes: analyzing the world's largest user generated content video system. In: Proceedings of the 7th ACM SIGCOMM Conference on Internet Measurement, pp. 1–14 (2007)
8. Che, H., Tung, Y., Wang, Z.: Hierarchical web caching systems: modeling, design and experimental results. IEEE J. Sel. Areas Commun. **20**(7), 1305–1314 (2002)
9. Cho, K., Lee, M., Park, K., Kwon, T.T., Choi, Y., Pack, S.: Wave: popularity-based and collaborative in-network caching for content-oriented networks. In: 2012 Proceedings IEEE INFOCOM Workshops, pp. 316–321. IEEE (2012)
10. Cisco: Cisco annual internet report (2018–2023) white paper (2020). https://bit.ly/3e8MYuk
11. Dai, J., Hu, Z., Li, B., Liu, J., Li, B.: Collaborative hierarchical caching with dynamic request routing for massive content distribution. In: 2012 Proceedings IEEE INFOCOM, pp. 2444–2452. IEEE (2012)
12. Dehghan, M., et al.: On the complexity of optimal routing and content caching in heterogeneous networks. In: 2015 IEEE Conference on Computer Communications (INFOCOM), pp. 936–944. IEEE (2015)

13. ElSawy, H., Hossain, E., Haenggi, M.: Stochastic geometry for modeling, analysis, and design of multi-tier and cognitive cellular wireless networks: a survey. IEEE Commun. Surv. Tutor. **15**(3), 996–1019 (2013)
14. Lee, D., et al.: LRFU: a spectrum of policies that subsumes the least recently used and least frequently used policies. IEEE Trans. Comput. **12**, 1352–1361 (2001)
15. Li, L., Stoeckert, C.J., Roos, D.S.: OrthoMCL: identification of ortholog groups for eukaryotic genomes. Genome Res. **13**(9), 2178–2189 (2003)
16. Liu, D., Chen, B., Yang, C., Molisch, A.F.: Caching at the wireless edge: design aspects, challenges, and future directions. IEEE Commun. Mag. **54**(9), 22–28 (2016)
17. Maddah-Ali, M.A., Niesen, U.: Fundamental limits of caching. IEEE Trans. Inf. Theory **60**(5), 2856–2867 (2014)
18. Megiddo, N., Modha, D.S.: ARC: a self-tuning, low overhead replacement cache. Fast **3**, 115–130 (2003)
19. Mokhtarian, K., Jacobsen, H.A.: Caching in video CDNs: building strong lines of defense. In: Proceedings of the Ninth European Conference on Computer Systems, pp. 1–13 (2014)
20. Najaflou, N., Arış, A., Canberk, B., Aydın, Z.G.: The nearest origin-shield (NOS): a jitter-free overlay routing framework for content delivery networks. In: 2019 International Symposium on Networks, Computers and Communications (ISNCC), pp. 1–6. IEEE (2019)
21. Park, S.Y., Jung, D., Kang, J.U., Kim, J.S., Lee, J.: CFLRU: a replacement algorithm for flash memory. In: Proceedings of the 2006 International Conference on Compilers, Architecture and Synthesis for Embedded Systems, pp. 234–241 (2006)
22. Paschos, G.S., Iosifidis, G., Tao, M., Towsley, D., Caire, G.: The role of caching in future communication systems and networks. IEEE J. Sel. Areas Commun. **36**(6), 1111–1125 (2018)
23. Podlipnig, S., Böszörmenyi, L.: A survey of web cache replacement strategies. ACM Comput. Surv. (CSUR) **35**(4), 374–398 (2003)
24. Poularakis, K., Tassiulas, L.: On the complexity of optimal content placement in hierarchical caching networks. IEEE Trans. Commun. **64**(5), 2092–2103 (2016)
25. Rabinovich, M., Spatscheck, O.: Web Caching and Replication, vol. 67. Addison-Wesley, Boston (2002)
26. Ramos, J., et al.: Using TF-IDF to determine word relevance in document queries. In: Proceedings of the First Instructional Conference on Machine Learning, New Jersey, USA, vol. 242, pp. 133–142 (2003)
27. Satuluri, V., Parthasarathy, S.: Symmetrizations for clustering directed graphs. In: Proceedings of the 14th International Conference on Extending Database Technology, pp. 343–354 (2011)
28. Traverso, S., Huguenin, K., Trestian, I., Erramilli, V., Laoutaris, N., Papagiannaki, K.: Tailgate: handling long-tail content with a little help from friends. In: Proceedings of the 21st International Conference on World Wide Web, pp. 151–160 (2012)
29. Van Dongen, S., Abreu-Goodger, C.: Using mcl to extract clusters from networks. In: van Helden, J., Toussaint, A., Thieffry, D. (eds.) Bacterial Molecular Networks, vol. 804, pp. 281–295. Springer, Heidelberg (2012). https://doi.org/10.1007/978-1-61779-361-5_15
30. Van Dongen, S.M.: Graph clustering by flow simulation. Ph.D. thesis (2000)
31. Wang, X., Chen, M., Taleb, T., Ksentini, A., Leung, V.C.: Cache in the air: exploiting content caching and delivery techniques for 5G systems. IEEE Commun. Mag. **52**(2), 131–139 (2014)

32. Wessels, D.: Web Caching. O'Reilly Media, Inc., Sebastopol (2001)
33. Yang, C., Yao, Y., Chen, Z., Xia, B.: Analysis on cache-enabled wireless heterogeneous networks. IEEE Trans. Wirel. Commun. **15**(1), 131–145 (2015)
34. Zeydan, E., et al.: Big data caching for networking: moving from cloud to edge. IEEE Commun. Mag. **54**(9), 36–42 (2016)

A Real-Time Internal Calibration Method for Radar Systems Using Digital Phase Array Antennas

Hung Tran Viet and Thien Hoang Minh[(✉)]

Le Quy Don Technical University, 236 Hoang Quoc Viet, Hanoi, Vietnam
thienhm.isi@lqdtu.edu.vn

Abstract. This paper proposed a real-time internal calibration method for receiving channels of radar systems using phased array antennas with real-time digital beam-forming. In most calibration methods, the frequency of the calibration signal (CalSig) is different from that of the echo signal, leading to some disadvantages in the calibration procedure. This paper analyzed and proposed a novel solution to solve those disadvantages. In the solution, we use the CalSig with the same frequency as the echo signal. The CalSig is a binary phase-shift keying (BPSK) signal and amplitude-modulated by an on-off keying (OOK) code sequence. The proposed CalSig has peak power equivalent to noise power but its average power is much lower than noise power by using OOK modulation with a small duty cycle D such that it does not affect the echo signal significantly. Measurement of receiving parameters is based on correlation properties of the signal. The performance of the proposed method is analyzed using the statistical theory and verified by Matlab simulation. Results show the effectiveness of the method with high accuracy, satisfying the real-time requirement while affecting receiving quality insignificantly. Phase and amplitude errors can be achieved values below $0.5°$ and 0.2 dB, respectively.

Keywords: Phased array antenna · Real-time calibration · Radar system · Digital beam-forming

1 Introduction

Nowadays, phased array antennas are used widely in radar applications because they have many advantages over the previous systems such as highly spatial selection ability, good interference suppression, high-speed beam scanning, SNR improvement [1]. Systems using the phased array antennas also have more demands about the number of transceiver modules (TRM), directional error, real-time digital beam scanning, etc. Therefore, monitoring amplitude and phase differences between channels is required with higher accuracy. Because parameters of the channels vary continuously under the impacts of aging, temperature and many other factors, real-time monitoring of channel parameters is compulsory. Most of the conventional periodic calibration methods have

© ICST Institute for Computer Sciences, Social Informatics and Telecommunications Engineering 2021
Published by Springer Nature Switzerland AG 2021. All Rights Reserved
N.-S. Vo et al. (Eds.): INISCOM 2021, LNICST 379, pp. 88–103, 2021.
https://doi.org/10.1007/978-3-030-77424-0_8

become inappropriate as they do not meet the real-time specification [2–10]. Thus, a real-time approach of calibration is demanded. Real-time calibration is necessary especially for systems that require monitoring parameters with high accuracy during operation, the process of parameter calibration does not interrupt the operation of the systems. In [11–15], the structure and algorithm of the real-time internal calibration were described clearly for 5G communications or SweepSar radars. In general, calibration procedures presented in those papers are based on coupling to receiving channels a single-tone signal, its frequency is in-band of the receivers but different from echo signal frequency. The echo signal and the CalSig after digitizing will be separated by digital filters, parameters of receiving channels are determined by measuring parameters of the CalSig, the results will be used to complement phase and amplitude differences between channels.

Nevertheless, calibration frequency must be near and far enough from operation frequency. Being near enough to get the best results of calibration and far enough to avoid interference for the echo signal. How near and far the calibration frequency depends on the range of operational frequencies and bandwidth of the system. In [11], the calibration structure was proposed for 5G systems with the frequency range of 27–29 GHz, the difference between the calibration frequency and the operation frequency is 2 MHz. The experiment showed good results with 0.9° phase error and 0.5 dB amplitude error. However, for systems with the spectrum spread principle, signal bandwidth can be up to several tens MHz [16], the errors might be much higher. Obviously, the method in the paper provided experiment results with a simple structure of the signal, which is not appropriate for systems with large signal bandwidth.

In [12–15], real-time calibration was applied on the SweepSar radar with the operating frequency range of 1215 MHz–1300 MHz. The gain-frequency characteristic of its receiver module over temperature is shown in Fig. 1 [15].

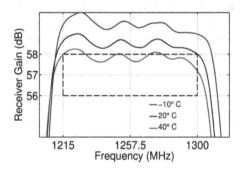

Fig. 1. Gain vs. frequency characteristic with different temperatures.

The above characteristic shows that the gain of the receiving channel is not flat over the range of operational frequencies, the ripple is larger than 0.5 dB and varies with different temperatures. This effect is typical because the specifications of electronic components change over frequency and temperature. Thus, when the calibration frequency is different from the operational frequency and the characteristics of receivers are unknown, determining receiving channel parameters by measuring parameters of the CalSig might lead to significant errors. Similarly, the phase-frequency characteristics are non-linear and also different from channel to channel, the phase differences can be up to several degrees. These differences are unavoidable, we cannot reduce these errors by measuring multiples times and averaging them. For systems with high accuracy requirements, these errors must be suppressed by characterizing all receiver modules in the whole frequency and temperature range, then set up lookup tables to compensate errors when calibrating in real-time. For systems with a large number of modules, this method is very difficult to realize. We need to arrange sensors to acquire exactly desired temperatures of the modules with the real-time requirement. These solutions demand expensive effort to implement and increase system complexity when the number of modules is large.

To cope with the disadvantages of internal calibration methods, in which frequencies of the CalSig and echo signal are different as mentioned above, we propose a novel calibration scheme with frequencies of the CalSig and echo signal are the same. In Sect. 2, the structure of the CalSig is proposed. Section 3 analyzes measurement errors and the impact of the CalSig on the quality of the system. Verification by Matlab simulation is presented in Sect. 4 and the last one is the conclusion.

2   Structure of the CalSig

In this paper, we select an internal calibration method as presented in [11–15] and focus on receiver calibration. The structure of a TRM according to this calibration method is shown in Fig. 2, including paths of the signals in the receive-and-calibration mode. In this mode, the signal generator will generate the CalSig (blue) to input the RF port of the TRM, the SW1 switch directs the CalSig to the RS and CR connectors. Then the CalSig will be fed to the input of a directional coupler. The CalSig will enter the entire receiving channel together with the echo signal (red) from the antenna. The pink line indicates the combined signal of the CalSig and the echo signal. The high-frequency signal in the receiving channel is down-converted to an intermediate frequency (IF), digitized by an analog-to-digital converter (ADC).

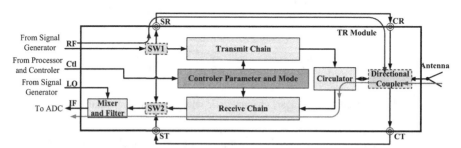

Fig. 2. Structure of a TRM with the signal paths in receiving-and-calibration mode. (Color figure online)

To overcome the disadvantages of the calibration method outlined in [11–15], we propose a solution that the CalSig frequency and the echo signal frequency are equal. The

CalSig is shifted by 180° in phase from pulse to pulse according to a random binary code sequence $C(n) = e^{\pm j\theta} = \pm 1$ ($\theta = 0°$ or 180°) such that the bandwidth of the CalSig and the echo signal is equivalent. It means that the CalSig and the echo signal exist simultaneously in the entire receiving channel including both analog and digital signal processing parts. The IF signal after the ADC does not need digital filters to separate the CalSig and echo signal as in [11–15], it is demodulated down to baseband (DDC) to produce a quadrature complex signal. This complex signal is a combination signal (ComSig) consisting of three components: the CalSig, the echo signal and the internal noise. In which the CalSig contains phase and amplitude information of the receiving channel. When performing calibration, the ComSig is sampled in the time the OOK modulation code equals "1" and stored in buffers along with the sequence $C(n)$. By correlating the ComSig sample sequence with the $C(n)$ phase code sequence, we obtain the amplitude and phase of the receiving channel. These parameters are used to compensate for phase and amplitude errors between the receiving channels.

When two signals have the same frequency and bandwidth, the determination of the channel parameters through measuring the CalSig will be more accurate. Nonetheless, it leads to interference between two signals, affecting calibration performance and quality of the echo signal processing. Following we will describe solutions to solve these two problems.

The first problem is to ensure the quality of echo signal processing, the CalSig must have a very low average power [17]. However, the ADCs have a limited number of bits and internal noise in radar receivers occupies only several LSB bits, the small echo signal even occupies only 1–2 LSB bits. If we reduce the peak power of the CalSig so that it is much smaller than the noise level, the CalSig may be less than the value of the LSB bit of ADC. Therefore, we choose the CalSig with the peak power equivalent to noise power and amplitude-modulated according to an OOK code with a small duty cycle D, in which the value "1" appears randomly. Then, the average power of the CalSig is much lower than the noise power. The selection of the value of D and the significance of CalSig generation will be analyzed in Sect. 3. The CalSig is illustrated in Fig. 3 with $D = 1/16$.

The second problem is to ensure calibration performance. We have known that the echo signal in the radar receiver appears randomly. When the echo signal is large, the calibration quality will be impacted. To solve this problem, we use a threshold detector for the ComSig in the receiver, when it exceeds an arbitrary threshold, the ComSig is not sampled (although the CalSig is still present in the receiving channel). Threshold selection will be analyzed in Sect. 3, it depends on the requirement of measurement errors. Figure 4 illustrates different situations of the echo signal, if the echo signal is much higher than the noise level, the CalSig is not sampled and stored.

From the above discussions, we can formulate the process of generating the CalSig, measuring parameters and calibrating the receiving channels as shown in Fig. 5.

In Fig. 5, the CalSig is applied to the receiving channel, combined with the echo signal, then passes to ADC and DDC. The ComSig is divided into 3 branches. The noise power measuring unit and the ComSig power measuring unit are used to filter and reject samples with large echo signals. Then, the ComSig is registered into buffers along with

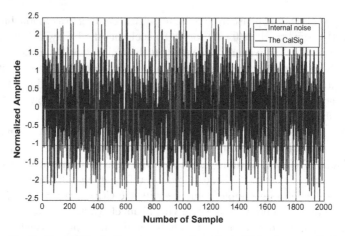

Fig. 3. The CalSig (red) and system noise (blue). (Color figure online)

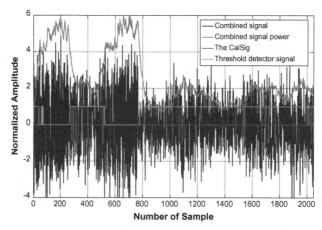

Fig. 4. The CalSig (red) is disable when the echo signal is larger than the threshold. (Color figure online)

the C(n) sequence. When the required set of N samples is sufficient, the correlation processing and receiving channel parameter estimation is performed. Phase and amplitude parameters of all receiving channels are sent to the calibration unit to compensate for channel errors. The theoretical basis for the selection of CalSig modulation parameters is analyzed in detail in Sect. 3.

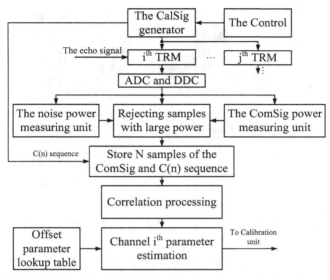

Fig. 5. Measurement and calibration procedure for the receiving channels.

3   Analyzing Measurement Errors and the Impact of the CalSig on the Quality of the System

3.1   Analyzing Measurement Errors

Three types of signals in the receiving channel are illustrated in Fig. 6. The nth sample of the ComSig is represented as follows:

$$S_{Comb}(n) = S_{Cal}(n) + S_{Echo}(n) + N(n) \tag{1}$$

where $S_{Cal}(n) = Ae^{j\varphi}C(n)$ is the CalSig, φ and A denote phase and amplitude of the receiving channel, $C(n) = \pm 1$ is the BPSK modulation code sequence. $N(n) = N_I(n) + jN_Q(n)$ is the internal noise and $S_{Echo}(n) = S_{IEcho}(n) + jS_{QEcho}(n)$ is the echo signal. Assume that $S_{NEcho}(n)$ is a combination of the echo signal and the internal noise:

$$S_{NEcho}(n) = S_{Echo}(n) + N(n) = S_{INEcho}(n) + jS_{QNEcho}(n)$$

$$S_{Comb}(n) = S_{Cal}(n) + S_{NEcho}(n) \tag{2}$$

The C(n) sequence is known, multiplying two sides of (2) by C(n), we obtain:

$$\begin{aligned}
S_{Comb}(n)C(n) = S'_{Comb}(n) &= S_{Cal}(n)C(n) + S_{NEcho}(n)C(n) \\
&= Ae^{j\varphi} + S_{INEcho}(n)C(n) + jS_{QNEcho}(n)C(n) \\
&= Ae^{j\varphi} + (S'_{INEcho}(n) + jS'_{QNEcho}(n))
\end{aligned} \tag{3}$$

where C(n) is a binary stochastic sequence with zero expectation, therefore the sequences $S'_{INEcho}(n) = S_{INEcho}(n)C(n)$ and $S'_{QNEcho}(n) = S_{QNEcho}(n)C(n)$ are also

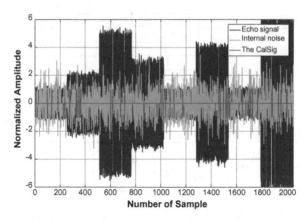

Fig. 6. Illustrate three types of signals in the receiving channel.

stochastic with zero expectation according to [18]. These two sequences have zero expectation for any echo signals $S_{Echo}(n)$. From (3), it can be realized that $S'_{Comb}(n)$ contains phase and amplitude information of the receiving channel in $Ae^{j\varphi}$ expression, while the complex component $S'_{INEcho}(n) + jS'_{QNEcho}(n)$ is the factor causing measurement errors. Define that σ^2_{INEcho} and σ^2_{QNEcho} are variances of the sample sequences $S'_{INEcho}(n)$ and $S'_{QNEcho}(n)$, respectively. In general, measurement error is determined by 3 times standard deviation, then $S'_{Comb}(n)$ is presented with measurement error as follows:

$$S'_{Comb}(n) = Ae^{j\varphi} \pm (3\sigma_{INEcho} + j3\sigma_{QNEcho}) \tag{4}$$

We have known that the random error decreases when averaging over many observations [18], averaging over N observations, the standard deviation decreases by $\sqrt{N}$. Considering the mean of N samples $S'_{Comb}(i), i = 1 \div N$, we obtain:

$$\overline{S'_{Comb}} = Ae^{j\varphi} \pm (3\sigma_{INEcho} + j3\sigma_{QNEcho})/\sqrt{N}$$
$$= (A\cos\varphi \pm 3\sigma_{INEcho}/\sqrt{N}) + j(A\sin\varphi \pm 3\sigma_{QNEcho}/\sqrt{N}) \tag{5}$$

According to (5), $3\sigma_{INEcho}/\sqrt{N}$ and $3\sigma_{QNEcho}/\sqrt{N}$ are two factors causing errors. The amplitude and phase errors depend on the relationship between φ and two above error components. In this work, without loss of generality, by supposing that $\sigma_{INEcho} = \sigma_{QNEcho} = \sigma_{NEcho}$, we have:

$$\overline{S'_{Comb}} = Ae^{j\varphi} \pm 3\sigma_{NEcho}(1+j)/\sqrt{N} \tag{6}$$

To facilitate transformation, we suppose that peak power of the CalSig (equivalent to noise power) equals 1 ($A^2 \approx 2\sigma^2_N = 1$), then $2\sigma^2_{NEcho}(2\sigma^2_{NEcho} \geq 1)$ indicates the ratio of the receiving channel power to the CalSig power, transform (6) we acquire:

$$\overline{S'_{Comb}} = e^{j\varphi} \pm 3\sigma_{NEcho}(1+j)/\sqrt{N} = e^{j\varphi} \pm (3\sqrt{2}\sigma_{NEcho}/\sqrt{N})e^{j\pi/4}$$

Considering the following expression:

$$BT = \overline{S'_{Comb}/e^{j\varphi}} = 1 \pm \frac{3\sqrt{2}\sigma_{NEcho}}{\sqrt{N}}cos(\frac{\pi}{4}-\varphi) \pm j\frac{3\sqrt{2}\sigma_{NEcho}}{\sqrt{N}}sin(\frac{\pi}{4}-\varphi) \quad (7)$$

Thus, BT is the basis for evaluating the measurement errors of the phase and amplitude of the receiving channel with two variables N and σ_{NEcho}. From (7), the amplitude error is given by:

$$amplitude\_error = |BT|^2 = (1 + 18\sigma_{NEcho}^2/N \pm 6\sqrt{2}\sigma_{NEcho}cos(\pi/4 - \varphi)/\sqrt{N})$$

We only consider the case of the largest error, i.e. $\pm cos(\pi/4 - \varphi) = 1$, then the amplitude error in dB is given by:

$$amplitude\_error\_dB = 10\lg(1 + 18\sigma_{NEcho}^2/N + 6\sqrt{2}\sigma_{NEcho}/\sqrt{N}) \quad (8)$$

Illustrating the Eq. (8) with the power levels of S_{NEcho}, $P(S_{NEcho}) = 2\sigma_{NEcho}^2 = 1, 2, 4, 8$, the number of samples $N = 5000 \div 100{,}000$ gives the results as shown in Fig. 7.

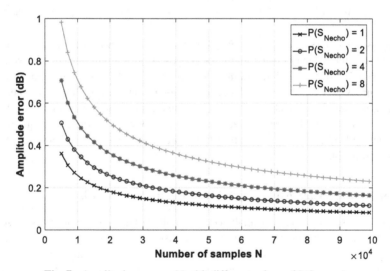

Fig. 7. Amplitude error vs. N with different values of $P(S_{NEcho})$.

Similarly, the phase error is:

$$phase\_error = \Delta\varphi = |Arg(BT)|$$

We only consider the case of the largest error, i.e. $\pm sin(\pi/4 - \varphi) = 1$, then:

$$phase\_error = \Delta\varphi = |Arg(1 + j\frac{3\sqrt{2}\sigma_{NEcho}}{\sqrt{N}})| \quad (9)$$

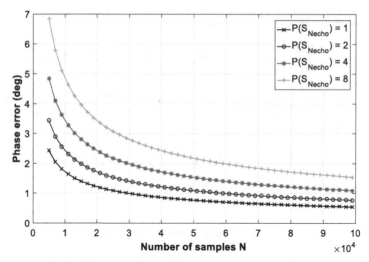

Fig. 8. Phase error vs. N with different values of P(S$_{NEcho}$).

Illustrating the Eq. (9) with the power levels of S_{NEcho}, $P(S_{NEcho}) = 2\sigma^2_{NEcho} =$ 1, 2, 4, 8, the number of samples N = 5000 ÷ 100,000 gives the results as shown in Fig. 7.

Expressions (8), (9), and Fig. 7, Fig. 8 provide evaluation results of amplitude and phase errors of the receiver channel with the proposed calibration method. It is clear that the larger number of accumulated samples (N) and the smaller echo signal power is, the higher accuracy is. Conversely, the larger echo signal power is, the larger the measurement error is, therefore detecting a large echo power and removing the CalSig as described in Sect. 2 will improve measurement accuracy. Depending on requirements of accuracy and calibration time, the threshold value and the number of samples (N) are selected appropriately.

3.2 Impact of the CalSig on the Quality of Receiving Channels

In two previous sections, we have analyzed the problem of measurement errors caused by noise and echo signals when calibrating. In contrast, the CalSig also interferes with the receiving channel, affecting the quality of the receiver. As described in Sect. 2, the CalSig is a BPSK modulated signal, combined with the OOK modulation (Fig. 9a). It has been known that in pulse radar engineering, the signal is typically processed averagely over cycles of repetition. Figure 9b illustrates that the signals are averaged over some cycles. Hence, putting the CalSig with the duty cycle D to the receiving channel is equivalent to applying a continuous CalSig with an average power reduced by M = 1/D. In this case, interference in the receiving channel includes the CalSig and internal noise. Calculation of probability distribution function of signals gives results as shown in Fig. 10.

As we can see, the probability density function of interference has a normal distribution with a standard deviation σ_N. σ_N decreases if M increases, when M = 4, 8, 16, 32, value of σ_N is 1,118, 1,061, 1,031, 1,016 and power of the interference increases by

0.97, 0.51, 0.26, 0.13 (dB), respectively. It is clear that when M = 32, the interference power increases negligibly (0.13 dB). To evaluate more comprehensively the impact of the CalSig on the quality of the receiver, we calculate for an active radar system. In a radar system, the most important parameter is the detection range. The relationship of the maximum detection range R_{max}, sensitivity P_{min} and noise power P_N of the receiver is described by the following expression:

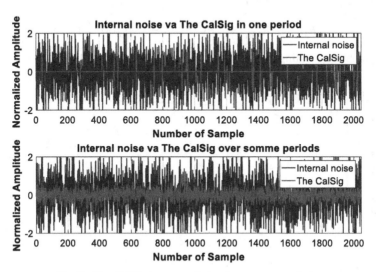

Fig. 9. The CalSig in one period and over some periods.

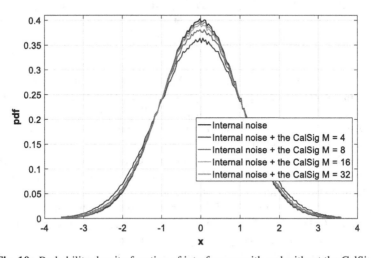

Fig. 10. Probability density function of interference with and without the CalSig.

$$P_{Rmin} = \frac{A}{R_{Max}^4} = P_N \cdot SNR_{Min} \qquad (10)$$

where SNR_{min} determines the value of true detection probability and false alarm probability. When the CalSig is applied to the receiving channel, expression (10) is rewritten as:

$$P_{RminCal} = \frac{A}{R^4_{MaxCal}} = P_{NCal} \cdot SNR_{Min} \tag{11}$$

From (10) and (11), we obtain:

$$R_{MaxCal}/R_{Max} = \sqrt[4]{P_N/P_{NCal}} = \sqrt[4]{M/(M+1)} \tag{12}$$

The graph representing the ratio R_{MaxCal}/R_{Max} (%) vs. M is shown in Fig. 11.

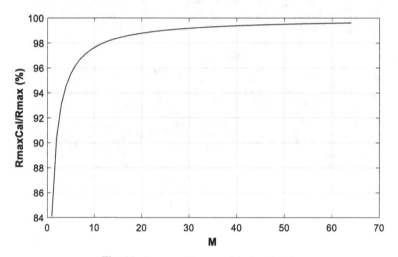

Fig. 11. R_{maxCal}/R_{max} vs. blank ratio M.

The result indicates that when $M > 24$ ($D < 4.2\%$) the ratio R_{maxHC}/R_{max} exceeds 99%. Thus, the proposed CalSig provides good calibration results and its impact on the detection range of the radar is negligible with a small value of D.

It is obvious that the proposed calibration method will take a long processing time because the required number of samples N is large. In addition, during the time that the echo signal exceeds the threshold, sampling the ComSig must be paused. The following example illustrates the time duration necessary to acquire a sufficient number of samples. With phase and amplitude errors are required below 1° and 0.2 dB, we need a number of samples: $N = 131{,}072$ (2^{18}) over some receiving/transmiting cycles, the blank ratio of the CalSig: $M = 32$, a cycle has 2048 range cells. Then through about 1600 cycles, we will have enough N samples. Suppose that in half of a cycle, the echo signal exceeds the threshold at which the ComSig is not sampled, therefore we need 3200 receiving/transmiting cycles. If each cycle is about 1 ms, then after 3.2 s, N samples will be acquired entirely. That time completely meets the real-time requirement of the calibration for radar systems. Parameters of electronic components in the operational process mainly vary due to temperature, this change is relatively slow, even performing calibration in a few tens of seconds still meets the real-time requirement. Hence, to improve the measurement accuracy, we can increase the number of samples (N), particularly if the phase and amplitude errors are required below 0.5° and 0.1 dB, we need to acquire $N = 2^{20}$ samples.

4 Evaluation of the Proposed Calibration Method by Simulation

In this section, we verify the proposed calibration method by Matlab simulation for independent receiving channels of a radar system using digital beamforming. Assume that the system has four receiving channels with different phase and amplitude (gain) parameters, the phase parameters are 0, 60, 120, 180 degrees and the amplitudes are 0, 1.58, 2.92, 4.08 dB, respectively. The echo signals on the receiving channels are segments of random signals in the time domain with a random level in the range of 0–5 in comparison to the noise level. The CalSig has $M = 32$, peak power equivalent to the noise level (Noise has the normal distribution). Since the CalSig average power is very low, the ComSig power is considered to be approximately equal to the S_{NEcho} signal power. The threshold level of the ComSig power to stop sampling is four times the noise power (6 dB), the required number of samples is $N = 100,000$. Each calibration process is started when we have enough N samples, calculating the phase and the amplitude errors of the channels, compensating for those errors, then continuing to acquire N samples for the next calibration. Results before and after calibration are shown in Figs. 12 and 13.

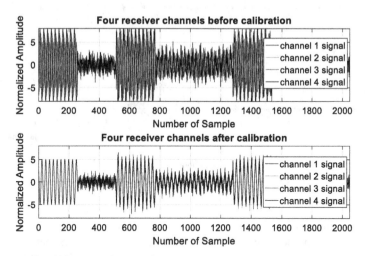

Fig. 12. Signals in receiving channels before and after calibration.

It is clear that after calibration, signals at the outputs of the receiving channels have the same phase and amplitude. The phase and amplitude errors of the channels in comparison with the first channel are shown in Figs. 14. The measurement results were recorded after each calibration. Figures 14 indicates errors of 100 calibrations. The results show that the amplitude and phase errors are smaller than 0.1 dB and 0.8°, respectively.

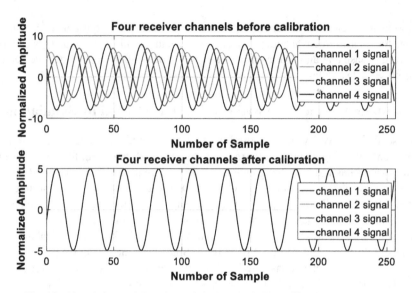

Fig. 13. Signals in receiving channels before and after calibration (Zoom out).

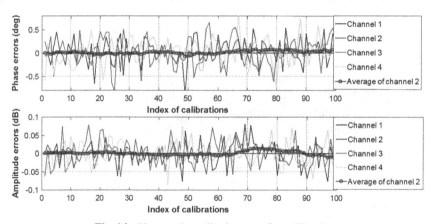

Fig. 14. Phase and amplitude error after calibration.

The calibration method presented in [11] achieves experimental results with a phase error of 0.9° and amplitude error of 0.5 dB. Result comparison shows that the proposed solution is feasible, achieving high accuracy in phase and amplitude adjustment.

To evaluate the impact of the CalSig on the detection ability of the radar system, we suppose that the radar uses signal coded by maximum length sequences with a pulse compression ratio of 256, the CalSig has a blank ratio M = 32. Figure 15 illustrates signals in a receiving channel.

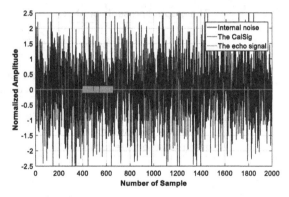

Fig. 15. Illustration of signals in the receiving channel.

The received signal is pulse-compressed in two situations with and without the CalSig, averaged over 32 receiving/transmiting cycles. SNR ratio is calculated in the two cases, giving the reduction of SNR in the case of the CalSig presence. Figure 17 shows the compressed signal. It can be seen that the noise background after the compression filter is higher when the CalSig is applied to the system. Figure 17 indicates the reduction of SNR due to the CalSig, it is approximately 0.13 dB, matching the calculation result. 0.13 dB reduction of SNR causes a decrease of the maximum detection range of the radar by below 1%. Thus, the impact can be neglected.

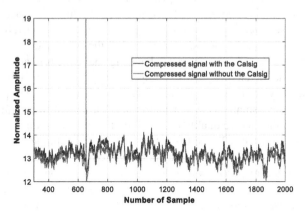

Fig. 16. Compressed signal with and without the CalSig.

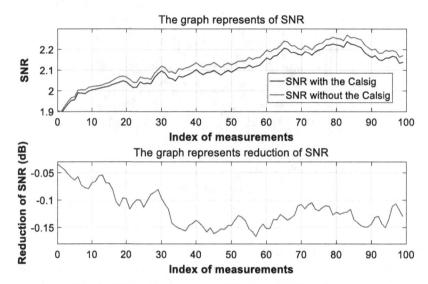

Fig. 17. SNR and reduction of SNR with the CalSig presence.

5 Conclusion

Real-time calibration in radar systems using digital phased array antennas is essential, especially for systems that require high precision in controlling the parameters of the TRMs while the system is in operation. There are various solutions to meet this require-ment. In the proposed method, the CalSig frequency is the same operating frequency of the system. The advantage of the method is that the measured parameters reflect more accurately the channel's characteristic, but a big challenge is interference between signals. To overcome the challenge, the CalSig is generated as a random phase-coded signal, simultaneously it is pulse-modulated with a large blank ratio. The proposed cali-bration method achieves small measurement errors, ensuring real-time requirements and negligible effect on the receive quality of the system. The simulation results show that calibration errors can reach 0.8° and 0.1 dB in phase and amplitude, respectively. The simulation results have demonstrated that calibration errors can reach 0.8° and 0.1 dB in phase and amplitude, respectively. However, as indicated in Figs. 14 and 15, it is easy to see that to reduce measurement errors, we can average through several calibrations (equivalent to increase the number of samples N). This should be done when the system operates stably, if averaging over 16 calibrations the phase and amplitude errors may be less than 0.2° and 0.02 dB.

References

1. Skolnik, M.I.: Radar Handbook, 3rd edn. The McGraw-Hill, New York (2008)
2. Pawlak, H., Charaspreedalarp, A., Jacob, A.F.: Experimental investigation of an external calibration scheme for 30 GHz circularly polarized DBF transmit antenna arrays. In: European Microwave Conference, pp. 764–767. Manchester (2006)

3. Takahashi, T., Konishi, Y., Makino, S., Ohmine, H., Nakaguro, H.: Fast measurement technique for phased array calibration. IEEE Trans. Antennas Propagation **56**(7), 1888–1899 (2008)
4. Pawlak, H., Jacob, A.F.: An external calibration scheme for DBF antenna arrays. IEEE Trans. Antennas Propagation **58**(1), 59–67 (2010)
5. Lee, K.-M., Chu, R.-S., Liu, S.-C.: A built-in Performance-Monitoring Fault Isolation and Correction (PM/FIC) system for active phased-array antennas. IEEE Trans. Antennas Propagation **41**(11), 1530–1540 (1993)
6. Van Werkhaven, G.H.C., Golshayan, A.K.: Calibration aspects of the APAR antenna unit. In: IEEE International Conference on Phased Array Systems and Technology, pp. 425–428. Dana Point, CA (2000)
7. Shipley, C., Woods, D.: Mutual coupling-based calibration of phased array antennas. In: IEEE International Symposium on Phased Array Systems and Technology, pp. 529–532. Dana Point, CA (2000)
8. Fulton, C., Chappell, W.: Calibration techniques for digital phased arrays. In: IEEE International Conference on Microwaves, Communications, Antennas and Electronics Systems, pp. 1–10. Tel Aviv (2009)
9. Aumann, H.M., Fenn, A.J., Willwerth, F.G.: Phased array antenna calibration and pattern prediction using mutual coupling measurements. IEEE Trans. Antennas Propagation **37**(7), 844–850 (1989)
10. Steyskal, H., Herd, J.S.: Mutual coupling compensation in small array antennas. IEEE Trans. Antennas Propagation **38**(12), 1971–1975 (1990)
11. Kim, D., Park, S., Kim, T., Minz, L., Park, S.: Fully digital beamforming receiver with a real-time calibration for 5G mobile communication. IEEE Trans. Antennas Propagation **67**(6), 3809–3819 (2019)
12. Hoffman, J.P., Veilleux, L., Perkovic, D., Peral, E., Shaffer, S.: Digital calibration of TR modules for real-time digital beamforming SweepSAR architectures. In: IEEE Aerospace Conference, pp. 1–8. Big Sky, MT (2012)
13. Horst, S.J., et al.: Implementation of RF circuitry for real-time digital beam-forming SAR calibration schemes. In: IET International Conference, pp. 1–6. Glasgow, UK (2013)
14. Hoffman, J.P., Horst, S., Veilleux, L., Ghaemi, H., Shaffer, S.: Digital calibration system enabling real-time on-orbit beamforming. In: IEEE Aerospace Conference, pp. 1–11. Big Sky, MT (2014)
15. Hoffman, J.P., Horst, S., Ghaemi, H.: Digital calibration system for the proposed NISAR (NASA/ISRO) mission. In: IEEE Aerospace Conference, pp. 1–7. Big Sky, MT (2015)
16. Hoffman, J.: Modular Ku/Ka-band actively calibrated antenna tile. In: IEEE Aerospace Conference, pp. 1–6. Big Sky, MT (2016)
17. Jens, R.: Technique for concurrent internal calibration during data acquisition for SAR systems. Remote Sens. **12**(11) (2020)
18. Standard_deviation Homepage. https://en.wikipedia.org/wiki/Standard_deviation. Accessed 17 Dec 2020

Micro-motion Target Classification Based on FMCW Radar Using Extended Residual Neural Network

Hai Le[1], Van-Sang Doan[2], Dai Phong Le[1], Thien Huynh-The[3], and Van-Phuc Hoang[1(✉)]

[1] Institute of System Integration, Le Quy Don Technical University, Hanoi, Vietnam
phuchv@lqdtu.edu.vn
[2] Faculty of Communication and Radar, Naval Academy, Nhatrang, Vietnam
[3] ICT-CRC, Kumoh National Institute of Technology, Gumi, Korea
thienht@kumoh.ac.kr

Abstract. Micro Doppler (m-D) effect is a phenomenon that provides signatures to discriminate different moving objects. Accordingly, this paper presents a novel residual convolutional neural network that can classify different moving targets based on m-D analysis of reflected frequency modulation continuous wave (FMCW) radar signals. The proposed network is optimized through the experiments of varying number of residual blocks. As a result, the proposed network yields the average classification accuracy of 93.48% with five residual blocks, 64 filters per convolution layer, and the filter size of 3 × 3. Moreover, thanks to the residual connection, our network remarkably outperforms two other existing networks in terms of accuracy.

Keywords: Convolution neural network · Micro Doppler · Moving target

1 Introduction

Autonomous vehicles have been yielding significant interest in the last decade, with considerable attention and investment from technology companies (such as Tesla, Waymo, and Baidu), governments, and academic research community [1]. To be able to complete driving autonomy on the road, the autonomous vehicles have to be equipped different types of sensors to provide the capability of sensing the surrounding environment and other moving objects, for example vehicles, humans, and animals. Indeed, various popular sensing technologies have been proposed, typically such as camera, LiDAR, or Radar [2]. The camera sensor [3] is used for objects classification based on color and texture signatures. They can be relatively cheap compared to the other types of sensors,

© ICST Institute for Computer Sciences, Social Informatics and Telecommunications Engineering 2021
Published by Springer Nature Switzerland AG 2021. All Rights Reserved
N.-S. Vo et al. (Eds.): INISCOM 2021, LNICST 379, pp. 104–115, 2021.
https://doi.org/10.1007/978-3-030-77424-0_9

however, camera devices suffer from limited depth of view, adverse weather, and light conditions. The second sensor is LiDAR (Light Detection and Ranging) [4], which uses steering laser arrays to produce an accurate 3-dimensional map of the surrounding environment around the autonomous vehicle. However, this sensor is still rather expensive and requires significant computational complexity to address the adverse effect of light and weather (for example, rainy, foggy, and snowy conditions). With above-mentioned disadvantages, cameras and LiDAR are not sufficient for a completely autonomous vehicle driving; therefore, radar sensor becomes a potential solution to overcome those disadvantage. Besides not being affected by light and weather conditions, the radar sensor can exploit the range-Doppler signature for entity classification processing [5].

Any movement of target poses a frequency shift in the radar return due to Doppler effect. Therefore, a moving target can be detected and recognized based on Doppler shift signatures. Since a target, for example, a helicopter flies, its blades rotate, or when a person walks, their arms swing naturally. These micro scale movements produce additional Doppler shifts, referred to as micro-Doppler (m-D) effects, which are useful to identify target features [6]. Furthermore, the m-D effects are modeled and simulated in some cases of micro-motion dynamics, such as vibration and rotation [7].

Recently, deep learning (DL) has been exploited to address many challenging detection and classification tasks in various applications, from computer vision [8–11] to medical informatics [12–14] and wireless communications [15–19]. For instance, Samaras et al. [20] have exploit DL for classifying different types of drone through a dataset handled from a surveillance radar. The classification method based on Deep Neural Network (DNN) was validated and reached the accuracy up to 95%. Not only drone, human motion also produces Doppler shift of reflected radar signal. Therefore, m-D radar is able to be applied to detect human motion, which is usually employed in automotive vehicle application [21]. In another scenario of parking monitoring application, Garcia et al. [22] have presented an effective convolutional neural network to classify radar images in order to detect vacant parking spaces with a 77-GHz imaging radar. Not only the convolutional neural network, the recurrent neural network is also considered for m-D target classification task, as presented in [23]. In addition, Angelov et al. [24] and Mento et al. [25] have demonstrated that the combination of convolution and LSTM (Long Short Term Memory) can facilitate the network model to be more stable.

Despite improving classification accuracy, the above-mentioned models reveal several weak points, including vanishing, over-fitting, and more computational complexity. Therefore, to effectively handle those limitations, a novel neural network for classifying m-D radar targets is proposed in this paper. Accordingly, the proposed network uses skip-connections to extract more strong features at many former layers, which can improve the classification accuracy. Additionally, the convolution layer is configured with grouped convolution operation that can noticeably reduce the number of network parameters. As a result, our network with five residual blocks attains high classification accuracy and remarkably outperforms two other existing models.

2 Doppler Effect and Time-Frequency Spectrogram

The Doppler effect occurs if a target has relative movement to the radar. In that case, the corresponding frequency shift is described as follows:

$$f_d = f_0 \cdot \frac{2 \cdot \boldsymbol{v} \cdot \boldsymbol{r}}{c}, \tag{1}$$

where f_d is the Doppler frequency shift, f_0 is the center carrier frequency of the radar signal, $\boldsymbol{v}$ is the target velocity, $\boldsymbol{r}$ is the radial range vector from the radar to the target, and c is the speed of electromagnetic wave. For a non-rigid target (for example human and bicycle), micro-motions have mechanical vibrations and rotations which usually exist along with bulk translation. As a result, the spectrogram transformed from a radar signal of a moving target will contain different Doppler signatures unexpectedly. Therefore, the Doppler signatures of radar signals reflected from walking pedestrian and running bicycle are important information for detection and classification.

The m-D signature can be visually plotted as a spectrogram using the short-time Fourier transform (STFT) that given as follows:

$$X(\tau, \omega) = \text{STFT}\{x(t)\} = \int_{-\infty}^{+\infty} x(t) \, w(t - \tau) e^{-j\omega t} dt \tag{2}$$

where $x(t)$ is the input signal of transformation and $w(t - \tau)$ is the kernel (so-called window) function. The resolution of STFT spectrogram is identified via the window function and the overlapping rate.

3 Proposed Neural Network

In this study, we propose a neural network for recognizing various types of FMCW radar target, including human, bicycle, and combination. The network model is designed with residual connection to reuse the former feature maps, which increase the classification accuracy via enhancing learning efficiency. As shown in Fig. 1a, the proposed network architecture consists of an input block, a series of residual blocks, and an output block. The blocks are built from several function layers which are connected to each other in certain flows. Generally, each layer can be formalized by a function as follows:

$$y^l = f\{x^l, w^l\} + b^l \tag{3}$$

where y^l is the output of l-th layer, $f\{\}$ denotes a layer function, x^l is the input of l-th layer, w^l is the set of weights of l-th layer, and b^l is the bias of l-th layer.

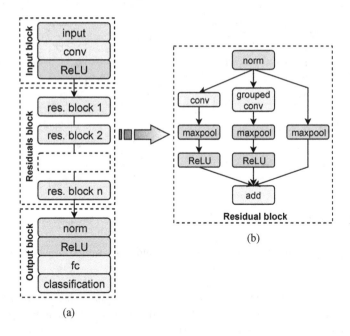

Fig. 1. Structure of the proposed network model: (a) Overall; (b) Residual block.

The input block is structured by an input layer, a convolution layer, and a ReLU (Rectified Linear Unit) activation layer. Specifically, the input layer is designated with the size of 400×144 to be appropriate to the size of spectrogram image. The input layer is followed by a convolution layer (conv) specified by 64 filters of size 1×1 to provide 64 channels at the output. Then, a ReLU activation layer is added to return the identical value with the positive input and the zero value with the negative input.

As the primary components to learn representational features at multi-scale resolutions, several residual blocks are organized in a cascade. Each residual block consists of three branches as shown in Fig. 1b. The first branch has three layers, including conv, max pooling (maxpool), and ReLU layers. The conv layer is designed by 64 filters of size 3×3. The maxpool layer follows the conv layer, which is configured by the pool size of 3×3 and the stride of (2,2). The spatial size of feature maps halves at the output of maxpool layer. The second branch also contains three layers with the same structure of the first one. However, the convolution layer of the second branch is a grouped type. The difference between the standard convolution and the grouped convolution is indicated in Fig. 2. Obviously, a grouped convolution with g groups uses g times fewer parameters and g times lower computational cost than a standard one. In particular, in this study we divide 64 filters into 8 groups with 8 filters of each. As a result, the number of learnable parameters in grouped conv layer reduces by 8 times if compared with a standard conv layer besides consuming a lower cost. The last branch is so-call a skip-connection from the output of normalization layer

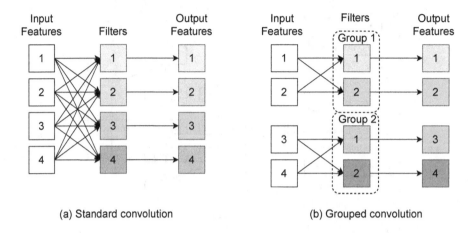

(a) Standard convolution   (b) Grouped convolution

Fig. 2. Difference between (a) standard and (b) grouped convolution.

to the input of addition layer. Because the feature map size at the output of the first and second branches equal to a half of their input, a maxpool layer should be inserted in the skip-connection that produces a feature map with the same spatial size of the two other branches. Notably, each residual block is started with a normalization layer (norm) and finalized with addition layer. The normalization layer is used to accelerate the neural network training progress with a more stable weight update scheme through normalization of the input features by re-centering and re-scaling. The addition layer performs an element-wise addition operation with three inputs resulted from three branches, wherein they have the same volume size. Accordingly, the useful features can be enhanced through each residual block.

The last block of our model is output block, which contains in turn norm, ReLU activation, fully connected (fc), softmax, and classification layers. The fc layer performs flattening its input feature maps into a vector. The output of fc layer is assigned 5 classes being identical to the number of targets in a given dataset (Ped, Bic, Ped + Ped, Bic + Pred, and Bic + Bic). The output values of fc layer is transferred to the softmax layer, where the probability (score) of each class is calculated by the following equation:

$$\rho_i(\mathbf{z}) = \frac{e^{z_i}}{\sum\limits_{j=1}^{C} e^{z_j}} \tag{4}$$

where $\mathbf{z}$ is the input vector, C is the number of classes, and i and j are the indices of a element in the vector $\mathbf{z}$. At the end, the Classification layer is the last one which executes the target judgement based on the highest score provided by the softmax layer. Accordingly, the predicted target is defined as follows:

$$Target_{predicted} = \arg\{\max\{\rho_i(\mathbf{z})\}\} \tag{5}$$

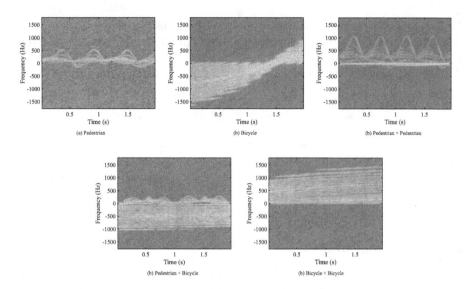

Fig. 3. m-D Spectrograms of several types of targets

4 Experiment Results and Discussion

4.1 Dataset Generation

In this study, we perform evaluation of the designed model based on the synthesized dataset, which is generated using the Matlab simulation program. Accordingly, we designed a radar simulation platform that transmits the FMCW signals to measure different types of target, including walking human (denoted Pedestrian - Ped) and cycling human (denoted Bicycle - Bic). Here, we assume that the swing movements of human hands and legs when walking produce the m-D effect in the spectrogram figure (Fig. 3a). Whereas, the cycle movement of bicycle wheels when running pose the m-D effect (Fig. 3b). The Doppler shift due to translation movements of pedestrian and bicyclist are also analyzed. In addition, several combination scenarios are taken into account to make more challenging to the network. In particular, the combinations of two walking people (denoted as Ped + Ped, Fig. 3c), walking people with running bicycle (denoted as Ped + Bic, Fig. 3d), and two running bicycles (Bic + Bic, Fig. 3e).

The radar used in the simulation platform transmits FMCW signal at 24 GHz band, the bandwidth of 250 MHz, and the waveform repetition time of 1 μs. The bicycle moves with speed less than 10 m/s. The simulation scenario is realized with varying properties, for example, bicyclists pedaling at different speeds and pedestrians with different heights walking at different speeds. As another assumption, the radar is fixed at the origin coordinate, meanwhile moving targets are uniformly distributed in a rectangular area of [5, 45] and [−10, 10] m from the origin location. Detailed other configurable parameters of dataset generation are listed in Table 1. It is noted that U{·} presents the uniformly contribution.

As a result, there are total 25,000 spectrogram images transformed from radar signals using STFT in the synthesized dataset, in which each target class has 5,000 images. We divide whole dataset into 20,000 images (80%) for training CNN model, and the remainder (20%) for testing the model performance.

Table 1. Crucial parameters of dataset generation.

Radar		Human		Bicycle	
Frequency	24 GHz	Height	U{1.5, 2} (m)	Gear rate	U{0.5, 6}
Bandwidth	250 MHz	Heading	U{−180, 180} (deg.)	Heading	U{−180, 180} (deg.)
Rep. frequency	2 μs	Speed	U{0.1, 2.8} (m/s)	Speed	U{1, 10} (m/s)

4.2   Experiment Results

The proposed model is trained in 20 epochs with the mini batch-size of 32, the initial learning rate of 0.01 with a drop factor of 0.1 after every 4 epochs. The stochastic gradient descent optimizer is applied in the training process with the computer hardware: CPU Core i5-9300H @2.4 GHz, RAM 8 GB Bus @2667 MHz, and GPU NVIDIA GeForce GTX 1660ti 6 GB.

In the first experiment, we train the network model with different residual blocks (from one to six blocks) on the training set without additive Gaussian noise. However, the trained network is then evaluated on the test set with adding the artificial Gaussian noise. The result of this experiment is shown in Fig. 4, where the classification accuracy of the network is improved along with the increment of the number of residual blocks (where the network goes deeper). Interestingly, the accuracy is significantly improved with smaller number of residual blocks (for example, two blocks is better than one block around 7.00%), while a tiny gap is deducted if increasing from five to six blocks). It is worth noting that the network complexity increases further as the number of blocks increases. Accordingly, the network with five residual blocks should be chosen for a good trade-off between the classification accuracy and the network complexity.

From the first experiment result, the network with five residual blocks is selected to classify the m-D radar targets of the test set when adding the Gaussian noise of different SNR (signal to noise ratio) levels. As a result, Fig. 5 shows the target classification accuracy of proposed network under SNRs ranging from −10 dB to 30 dB with step size of 5 dB. Obviously, the accuracy is improved with the increment of SNR, especially from 5 dB to 20 dB. The trained network yields the high accuracy for SNR $\geq$ 20 dB.

In the second experiment, we compare the performance of deep network trained on the training with and without additive noise. It should be noted that the accuracy is evaluated on the test set with noise. The comparison result is given in Fig. 6, where the network training with noise performs classification better than the network training without noise. Particularly, the network training with noise obtains the classification accuracy of $\geq$80% for SNR $\geq$ 0 dB and can

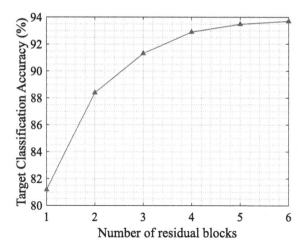

Fig. 4. The target classification accuracy of the proposed network with different number of residual blocks.

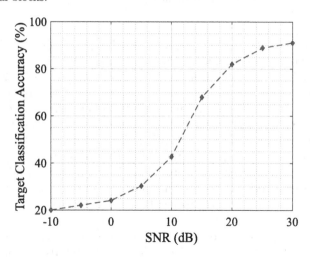

Fig. 5. The network performance in terms of classification accuracy when trained with dataset without noise.

achieve up to >90% for SNR ≥ 15 dB; whereas, the network training without noise yields accuracy of >80% for SNR ≥ 20 dB. It is observed that training with noise is significantly better than training without noise at SNR ≤ 20 dB. Therefore, it can be suggested that the network model should be trained with a diverse dataset to improve accuracy and prevent the over-fitting problem.

In the final experiment, we compare the proposed network of five residual blocks with two other existing models, including so-called Net01 in [26], and Net02 in [27].

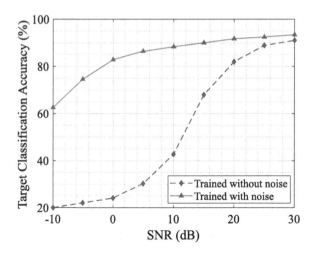

Fig. 6. Comparison of accuracy performance of proposed network when trained with different dataset options (with and without noise).

- Net01 is proposed for identifying indoor walking person using FMCW radar. The Net01 model consists of four conv layers with a filter size of 3×3 and number of filters in turn raising from 8 to 64. Each convolution layer is followed by 2 × 2 non-overlapping maxpool layer. Inserting to output of maxpool layer is an eLU (Exponential Linear Unit) activation layer that improves learning characteristics. Two fully connected layers are used as a classifier. The first fully connected layer is defined with output of 128, and second one is designed for five output classes. To prevent the over-fitting problem, the network is configured by a dropout layer with factor of 0.5 following the first fully connected layer. In this competition, the size of input layer of the Net01 model is modified from 256 × 45 to 400 × 144 to satisfy with the size of spectrogram images in our dataset.
- Net02 model is proposed for classifying different objects, including trolley, bike, cone, mannequin, sign and dog, based on 300 GHz radar data. The Net02 network is structured by three consecutive layer groups (where each group: conv + ReLU + maxpool). Three conv layers have the numbers of filters of 16, 32, and 64 with filter size of 5 × 5, 6 × 6, and 6 × 6, respectively. The maxpool layers has the pool size of 2 × 2. The third group is followed by a dropout layer with a factor of 0.5 that is employed to avoid the over-fitting problem in the training process. Following the dropout layer is conv and ReLU layers with 128 filters of size 3 × 3. The last convolution is designated by five filters of size 3 × 3 for being compatible with the number of classes in our dataset. In addition, the size of the input layer is modified to 400 × 144 for processing the spectrogram images.

Table 2. Performance comparison of the neural networks.

Networks	No. params	Accuracy (%)
Net01	418K	87.9
Net02	309K	88.2
Our model	230K	93.5

The above-mentioned networks are trained on the same dataset and the same configuration of the training process. The performance comparison of those networks is reported in Table 2, in which our proposed network remarkably outperforms two other ones. Specifically, Net01 is the largest network with the number of parameters of approximately 418K but obtains the lowest classification accuracy of 87.9%. Despite having the smallest number of learnable parameters of around 230K, our network achieves the highest accuracy due to leveraging residual connections to effectively re-usage highly meaningful features extracted from many former layers.

5 Conclusion

In this paper, we have proposed and designed a novel network architecture that is inspired by the residual convolutional neural network. The network is configured not only with skip-connection, but the grouped convolution is also employed to remarkably reduce the learnable parameters. Through experiments with different numbers of residual blocks, our network achieves the best trade-off performance with the 5-block configuration. In competition with other models, the proposed network of five residual blocks has significantly outperformed two other existing ones. For future works, we intend to design the model for more types of m-D radar targets and simultaneously improve the network performance in terms of classification accuracy and computational cost. Moreover, other signal pre-processing techniques will be taken into account to enhance the target classification accuracy.

References

1. Granath, E.: 5 Top Autonomous Vehicle Companies to Watch in 2020. Intelligent Mobility Xperience, 1 September 2020. www.intelligent-mobility-xperience.com/5-top-autonomous-vehicle-companies-to-watch-in-2020-a-958065/
2. RADAR, Camera, LiDAR and V2X for Autonomous Cars. NXP. www.nxp.com/company/blog/radar-camera-lidar-and-v2x-for-autonomous-cars:BL-RADAR-LIDAR-V2X-AUTONOMOUS-CARS
3. Rosique, F., Navarro, P.J., Fernández, C., Padilla, A.: A systematic review of perception system and simulators for autonomous vehicles research. Sensors **19**(3), 648 (2019)

4. Zhang, Y., Wang, J., Wang, X., Dolan, J.M.: Road-segmentation-based curb detection method for self-driving via a 3D-LiDAR sensor. IEEE Trans. Intell. Transp. Syst. **19**(12), 3981–3991 (2018)

5. Belgiovane, D., Chen, C.: Micro-Doppler characteristics of pedestrians and bicycles for automotive radar sensors at 77 GHz. In: 11th European Conference on Antennas and Propagation (EUCAP), Paris, pp. 2912–2916 (2017)

6. Chen, V.C.: The Micro-Doppler Effect in Radar. Artech House, Norwood (2011)

7. Chen, V.C., Li, F., Ho, S.-S., Wechsler, H.: Micro-Doppler effect in radar: phenomenon, model, and simulation study. IEEE Trans. Aerosp. Electron. Syst. **42**(1), 2–21 (2006)

8. Hua, C.-H., Huynh-The, T., Lee, S.: Convolutional networks with bracket-style decoder for semantic scene segmentation. In: Proceedings of IEEE International Conference on Systems, Man, and Cybernetics (SMC), Miyazaki, Japan, pp. 2980–2985 (2018)

9. Huynh-The, T., Hua, C.-H., Ngo, T.-T., Kim, D.-S.: Image representation of pose-transition feature for 3D skeleton-based action recognition. Inf. Sci. **512**, 112–126 (2020)

10. Huynh-The, T., Hua, C., Kim, D.: Encoding pose features to images with data augmentation for 3-D action recognition. IEEE Trans. Industr. Inf. **16**(5), 3100–3111 (2020)

11. Huynh-The, T., Hua, C.H., Tu, N.A., Kim, D.S.: Learning 3D spatiotemporal gait feature by convolutional network for person identification. Neurocomputing **397**, 192–202 (2020)

12. Huynh-The, T., Hua, C.H., Tu, N.A., Kim, D.S.: Physical activity recognition with statistical-deep fusion model using multiple sensory data for smart health. IEEE Internet Things J. (2020). https://doi.org/10.1109/JIOT.2020.3013272

13. Hua, C.-H., et al.: Bimodal learning via trilogy of skip-connection deep networks for diabetic retinopathy risk progression identification. Int. J. Med. Informatics **132**, 103926 (2019)

14. Hua, C.-H., Huynh-The, T., Lee, S.: DRAN: Densely reversed attention based convolutional network for diabetic retinopathy detection. In: Proceedings of the 42nd International Engineering in Medicine and Biology Conference (EMBC), Montréal, Québec, Canada, 20–24 July 2020 (2020)

15. Huynh-The, T., Hua, C., Kim, J., Kim, S., Kim, D.: Exploiting a low-cost CNN with skip connection for robust automatic modulation classification. In: Proceedings of 2020 IEEE Wireless Communications and Networking Conference (WCNC), Seoul, Korea (South), pp. 1-6 (2020)

16. Doan, V.-S., Huynh-The, T., Kim, D.-S.: Underwater acoustic target classification based on dense convolutional neural network. IEEE Geosci. Remote Sens. Lett. (2020). https://doi.org/10.1109/LGRS.2020.3029584

17. Huynh-The, T., Hua, C., Pham, Q., Kim, D.: MCNet: an efficient CNN architecture for robust automatic modulation classification. IEEE Commun. Lett. **24**(4), 811–815 (2020)

18. Doan, V.-S., Huynh-The, T., Hua, C.-H., Pham, Q.-V., Kim, D.-S.: Learning constellation map with deep CNN for accurate modulation recognition. arXiv preprint arXiv: 2009.02026 (2020)

19. Huynh-The, T., Doan, V.S., Hua, C.H., Pham, Q.V., Kim, D.S.: Chain-Net: learning deep model for modulation classification under synthetic channel impairment. arXiv preprint arXiv: 2009.02023 (2020)

20. Samaras, S., Magoulianitis, V., Dimou, A., Zarpalas, D., Daras, P.: UAV classification with deep learning using surveillance radar data. In: Tzovaras, D., Giakoumis, D., Vincze, M., Argyros, A. (eds.) ICVS 2019. LNCS, vol. 11754, pp. 744–753. Springer, Cham (2019). https://doi.org/10.1007/978-3-030-34995-0_68
21. Ma, X., Zhao, R., Liu, X., Kuang, H., Al-Qaness, M.A.A.: Classification of human motions using micro-doppler radar in the environments with micro-motion interference. Sensors (Basel) **19**(11), 2598 (2019)
22. García, J.M., Zoeke, D., Vossiek, M.: MIMO-FMCW radar-based parking monitoring application with a modified convolutional neural network with spatial priors. IEEE Access **6**, 41391–41398 (2018)
23. Han, L., Feng, C.: Micro-doppler-based space target recognition with a one-dimensional parallel network. Int. J. Antennas Propag. **2020**, 1–10 (2020)
24. Angelov, A., Robertson, A., Murray-Smith, R., Fioranelli, F.: Practical classification of different moving targets using automotive radar and deep neural networks. IET Radar Sonar Navig. **12**(10), 1082–1089 (2018)
25. Minto, M.R.I., Tan, B., Sharifzadeh, S., Riihonen, T., Valkama, M.: Shallow neural networks for mmWave radar based recognition of vulnerable road users. In: 12th International Symposium on Communication Systems, Networks and Digital Signal Processing (CSNDSP) (2020)
26. Vandersmissen, B., et al.: Indoor person identification using a low-power FMCW radar. IEEE Trans. Geosci. Remote Sens, **56**(7), 3941–3952 (2018)
27. Sheeny, M., Wallace, A., Wang, S.: RADIO: Parameterized generative radar data augmentation for small datasets. Appl. Sci. **10**(11), 3861–3873 (2020)

Hardware, Software, and Application Designs

Left Hand and Right Hand Circularly Polarized Antenna for 5G Devices

Tan Minh Cao[1], Hong Son Vu[1], Thi Duyen Bui[2], and Minh Thuy Le[1(✉)]

[1] School of Electrical Engineering (SEE), Hanoi University of Science and Technology (HUST), Hanoi, Vietnam
thuy.leminh@hust.edu.vn
[2] Faculty of Control and Automation, Electric Power University, Hanoi, Vietnam

Abstract. A novel wideband circularly polarized reconfigurable antenna for 5G devices is presented in this paper. Left hand and right-hand circular polarizations were achieved using the sequential phase rotation feeding network based on 90° hybrid coupler. The proposed antenna has a bandwidth (with AR $\leq$ 3 dB) of 24.8% and 4% for right hand circular polarization (RHCP) and left-hand circular polarization (LHCP) mode, respectively. At 3.75 GHz, the degree of circular polarization is 42° in LHCP mode and 51° in RHCP mode showing the potential of this proposed antenna for modern 5G terminal devices.

Keywords: 5G antenna · LHCP antenna · RHCP antenna · 90° hybrid · Circular polarization · Sequential phase rotation technique

1 Introduction

Nowadays, 5G is one key technology attracting many attentions of industrials and researchers over the world, especially after the finalization of the 3GPP release 15. However, when the 5G bandwidth is considering for commercial products, the wideband (3.3–4.2 GHz) antenna is required for 5G research and development phase in the laboratories. In telecommunication systems where the base station antenna requires the dual polarizations $\pm 45°$, from the terminated devices point of view, the circularly polarized (CP) antennas provide the low polarization loss factor over linearly polarized (LP) antennas. In recent years, CP antennas with the capability of switching polarization between RHCP and LHCPstates have increasingly been used in wireless communication systems [1–3] but these antennas have CP in a narrow band. In general, there are two reconfigurable polarization methods for CP antennas: reconfigurable radiating element and reconfigurable feeding network [3–7]. RF switches such as PIN diodes [4] and RF-MEMS [5], have been used to create an effective radiating structure for different polarization. The latter approach is the polarization reconfigurable antenna based on the switchable 90° phase shifter feeding into the radiation elements using RF switches shown in [6, 7] but the low efficiency of radiator element is a disadvantage of these works.

© ICST Institute for Computer Sciences, Social Informatics and Telecommunications Engineering 2021
Published by Springer Nature Switzerland AG 2021. All Rights Reserved
N.-S. Vo et al. (Eds.): INISCOM 2021, LNICST 379, pp. 119–127, 2021.
https://doi.org/10.1007/978-3-030-77424-0_10

This paper proposes a RHCP and LHCP antenna based on two 90° hybrid couplers and an array antenna at 5G band. Switching between RHCP and LHCP mode is conducted by adjusting the position of exciting port so PIN-diodes element is ignored to avoid the loss and non-linear effect. The proposed antenna has an outstanding bandwidth with 37% at both two modes with total dimensions of 85 × 85 × 40 mm^3. The 3dB AR bandwidths at RHCP and LHCP mode are 24.8% and 4%, respectively. A detailed antenna design is presented in Sect. 2. Section 3 is the conclusions.

2 5G LHCP and RHCP Antenna Design

2.1 Printed Dipole Antenna Element

The 5G ground-cut dipole element with "J"-balun is proposed in Fig. 1 but having wider bandwidth and higher gain than the dipole element in [8]. The high efficiency of the dipole antenna is the advantage so that this kind of element is chosen to design LHCP and RHCP antenna. "J"-balun consists of L_b and L_{ab} microstrip line, the perfect matching is achieved when $L_b = L_{ab} = \lambda/4$. The parameters of the proposed ground-cut printed dipole antenna element with "J"-balun are listed in Table 1:

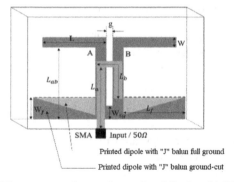

Fig. 1. The structure of ground-cut printed dipole with "J"-balun.

Table 1. Parameters of printed dipole with integrated "J" balun

Parameters	Values (mm)	Parameters	Values (mm)
L	15.5	W	2.5
L_S	14.5	W_g	8
L_g	20	g	0.9
L_a	12.92	W_{Sg}	2.5
L_b	12	W_a	1.85

The reflection coefficient of ground-cut and full ground dipole antennas is depicted in Fig. 2. The bandwidth (at $S11 \leq -10\,dB$) of full ground and ground-cut dipole antenna is from 3.6 GHz to 4 GHz and from 3.45 GHz to 4.14 GHz, respectively. The S11 of cutting ground dipole antenna is −39.5 dB at 3.75 GHz. The radiation pattern results are presented in Fig. 3 with the peak gain of 6.48 dBi and angular width (at −3dB) of 129.30° and the total radiation efficiency of 96.63% for full ground printed dipole antenna. The ground-cut dipole has the peak gain of 4.84 dBi, wider angular width (at −3dB) of 177.10° and the total radiation efficiency is 96.88%.

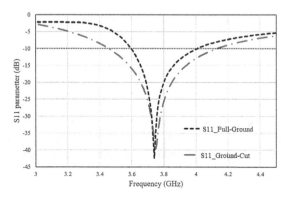

Fig. 2. Reflection coefficient of printed dipole with "J"-balun.

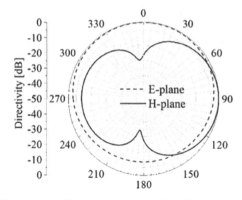

Fig. 3. Radiation pattern of the proposed ground-cut dipole element at 3.75 GHz

2.2 Proposed LHCP and RHCP Antenna

The sequential phase rotation feeding technique is used to obtain the wideband CP antenna. The difference of excitation phases at four antenna elements are arranged 0°, 90°, 180° and 270° at dipole 1, 2, 3 and 4, respectively as in Fig. 4. The RHCP or LHCP mode is chosen by selecting SMA_1 and SMA_2 through an RF switch circuit. In RHCP mode, SMA_1 is selected and SMA_2 is connected to a short circuit, that is the opposite of LHCP mode. The exciting phases of four dipoles elements at LHCP and RHCP modes are listed in Table 2. The parameters of a feeding network are listed in Table 3.

Table 2. Excited phases of antenna elements

	Dipole 1	Dipole 2	Dipole 3	Dipole 4
LHCP	0°	90°	180°	270°
RHCP	180°	90°	0°	270°

Table 3. Parameters of feeding network

Parameters	Values (mm)	Parameters	Values (mm)
W1	0.423	W2	0.95

The feeding network composes of two 90° hybrids to make the desired phase shift among dipoles as in Table 2, and the 70.7 Ω quarter-wavelength transmission lines are used to match impedance between element and feeding as in Fig. 4b.

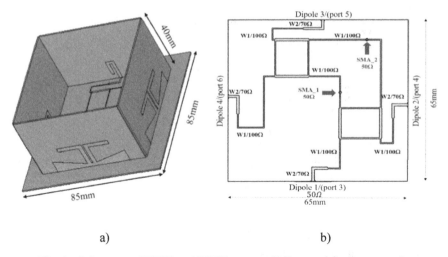

a)   b)

Fig. 4. a) Structure of LHCP and RHCP antenna. b) Proposed feeding network.

The simulated S-parameters of the feeding network corresponding with four exciting amplitudes and phases of four dipoles at RHCP mode are shown in Fig. 5a. The amplitude difference between the four ports is less than 1.6 dB and 1.8 dB at the center frequency for the RHCP and LHCP modes of operation, respectively. Meanwhile, the phases between the two adjacent elements are about 84° to 98° at RHCP mode and 80° to 100° at LHCP mode (Fig. 5b).

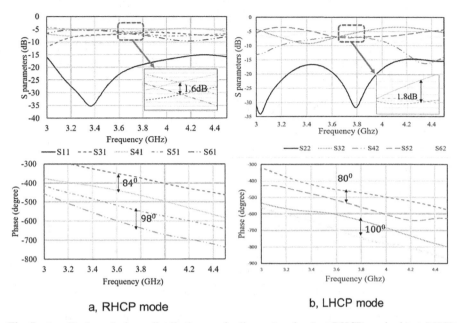

a, RHCP mode   b, LHCP mode

Fig. 5. Amplitude and phase distribution on feeding network. a) at RHCP mode; b) at LHCP mode

The RHCP and LHCP antenna is designed on the Rogers 4003C substrate with a dielectric constant of 3.55 and a height of 0.813 mm. The proposed 5G LHCP and RHCP antenna is shown in Fig. 6 with the dimension of $85 \times 85 \times 40$ mm^3. This configuration of LHCP and RHCP antenna has low mutual coupling between elements. To achieve RHCP or LHCP mode, the RF sources is selected to SMA_1 and SMA_2, respectively. The reflection coefficients of LHCP and RHCP antenna are shown in Fig. 7. It is seen that the operating band of the antenna at LHCP mode is slightly higher than the operating band of an antenna at RHCP mode. At LHCP mode, the simulated bandwidth is 1.38 GHz withS11 below −10 dB. Meanwhile, the simulated bandwidth of RHCP antenna is 1.24 GHz with S11 under −10 dB. The measured bandwidth (at S11 ≤ −

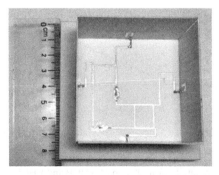

Fig. 6. RHCP and LHCP antenna prototype.

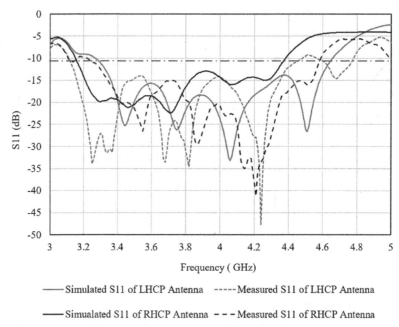

Fig. 7. Measured and simulated reflection coefficients for RHCP and LHCP modes.

10 dB) for the LHCP mode is 37.3% and the corresponding values of the RHCP mode is 37.3%. The overlapped bandwidth for both modes are 34.7% covering 3.3–4.2 GHz band for 5G technology according to 3GPP standard.

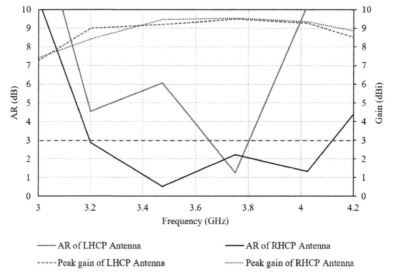

Fig. 8. Simulated AR and Gain of RHCP and LHCP antenna.

The AR and the realized peak gain of LHCP/RHCP is presented in Fig. 8. The AR of an antenna at RHCP mode is less than 3 dB from 3.2 GHz to 4.13 GHz (24.8%). Meanwhile, the AR of the antenna at LHCP mode is less than 3 dB from 3.65 to 3.81 GHz (4%).

The peak gain over the 3.2–4.2 GHz band is more than 8 dBi with a maximum value of 9.5 dBi at 3.7 GHz for both polarizations. The total radiation efficiency is up to 91.54% at LHCP mode and 91.66% at RHCP mode. At 3.7 GHz, the width of circular polarization is 42° in LHCP mode and 51° in RHCP mode as in Fig. 9.

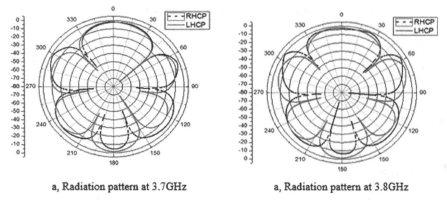

a, Radiation pattern at 3.7GHz   a, Radiation pattern at 3.8GHz

Fig. 9. Simulated AR in RHCP and LHCP mode of the proposed antenna at 3.7 GHz and 3.8 GHz.

Table 4 summarizes several proposed LHCP and RHCP antennas. In [9], the mmWave antenna is designed with a wideband and higher peak gain than the proposed RHCP/LHCP antenna, but the radiation efficiency and total efficiency is smaller than

Table 4. Comparison with related works

Ref.		Center Freq (GHz)	Bandwidth at		Gain (dBi)
			S11 ≤ −10 dB (%)	AR ≤ 3 dB (GHz)	
[9]	LHCP	28	2.85–10.17%	27.74–29.05	14.16
	RHCP		3.1–11.07%	27.76–28.95	13.52
[10]	LHCP	2.15	0.8–37.21%	2.05–2.27	8.01
	RHCP		0.8–37.21%	2.05–2.27	8.99
[2]	LHCP	2.45	0.11–4.5%	2.34–2.57	6.4
	RHCP		0.11–4.5%	2.35–2.61	6.5
[11]	LHCP	1.6	1.5–93.75%	1.5–2.2	4.8
	RHCP		1.5–93.75%	1.45–1.9	4.8
This work	**LHCP**	**3.75**	**1.4–37.3%**	**3.65–3.81**	**9.47**
	RHCP		**1.4–37.3%**	**3.2–4.13**	**9.52**

this work. In [2, 10, 11], the antennas are designed at sub 6 GHz frequencies. They are wideband but the peak gain is smaller than the proposed antenna.

3   Conclusions

A wideband RHCP and LHCP antenna using the printed dipole antenna elements and the sequential rotation feeding technique based on 90° hybrid coupler have been studied and presented in this paper. Based on 90° hybrid coupler feeding network, the proposed antenna has a wideband CP in both RHCP and LHCP modes. The bandwidth of the antenna is 37.3% (at −10 dB) for both RHCP and LHCP modes, respectively. The antenna has 42° of circular polarization in LHCP mode and 51° of CP in RHCP. The peak gain of antenna is up to 9.5 dBi over the operating frequencies. The simple antenna is easy to be applied for 5G devices which need high gain and wideband CP antenna characteristics.

Acknowledgment. This research is funded by the Ministry of Education and Training (MOET) under grant number B2020-BKA-11.

References

1. Le, T., Park, H.-Y., Yun, T.-Y.: Simple reconfigurable circularly polarized antenna at three bands. Sensors **19**(10), 2316 (2019). https://doi.org/10.3390/s19102316
2. Lu, Y., Wang, Y., Gao, S., Hua, C., Liu, T.: Circularly polarised integrated filtering antenna with polarisation reconfigurability. IET Microw. Antennas Propag. **11**(15), 2247–2252 (2017). https://doi.org/10.1049/iet-map.2017.0283
3. Le, M.T., Nguyen, Q.C., Vuong, T.P.: Design of a high gain antenna at 5.8 GHz using a new metamaterials structure. In: The Fourth IEEE International Conference on Communications and Electronics, pp. 411–416, August 2012. https://doi.org/10.1109/CCE.2012.6315940
4. Row, J.-S., Chan, M.-C.: Reconfigurable circularly-polarized patch antenna with conical beam. IEEE Trans. Antennas Propag. **58**(8), 2753–2757 (2010). https://doi.org/10.1109/TAP.2010.2050436
5. Kovitz, J.M., Rajagopalan, H., Rahmat-Samii, Y.: Design and implementation of broadband MEMS RHCP/LHCP reconfigurable arrays using rotated e-shaped patch elements. IEEE Trans. Antennas Propag. **63**(6), 2497–2507 (2015). https://doi.org/10.1109/TAP.2015.2417892
6. Chen, H., Yang, X., Yin, Y.Z., Fan, S.T., Wu, J.J.: Triband planar monopole antenna with compact radiator for WLAN/WiMAX applications. IEEE Antennas Wirel. Propag. Lett. **12**, 1440–1443 (2013). https://doi.org/10.1109/LAWP.2013.2287312
7. Cao, Y., Cheung, S.W., Yuk, T.I.: A simple planar polarization reconfigurable monopole antenna for GNSS/PCS. IEEE Trans. Antennas Propag. **63**(2), 500–507 (2015). https://doi.org/10.1109/TAP.2014.2382091
8. Duyen, B.T., Thuy, L.M., Cuong, N.Q.: Novel wideband circularly polarized antenna for wireless applications. In: The 2017 IEEE Asia Pacific Microwave Conference (APMC), pp. 430–433 (2017). https://doi.org/10.1109/APMC.2017.8251472
9. Park, S.-J., Park, S.-O.: LHCP and RHCP substrate integrated waveguide antenna arrays for millimeter-wave applications. IEEE Antennas Wirel. Propag. Lett. **16**, 601–604 (2017). https://doi.org/10.1109/LAWP.2016.2594081

10. Yoon, W.-S., Han, S.-M., Baik, J.-W., Pyo, S., Lee, J., Kim, Y.-S.: Crossed dipole antenna with switchable circular polarisation sense. Electron. Lett. **45**(14), 717 (2009). https://doi.org/10.1049/el.2009.0391

11. Lin, W., Wong, H.: Wideband circular polarization reconfigurable antenna. IEEE Trans. Antennas Propag. **63**(12), 5938–5944 (2015). https://doi.org/10.1109/TAP.2015.2489210

Examination of Investigation Method of Malware Spreading State

Anh Son Pham[(✉)] and Yasuhiro Nakamura

Cyber Security, Graduate School of Science and Engineering,
National Defense Academy, 1-10-20, Hashirimizu, Yokosuka, Japan
{em59043,yas}@nda.ac.jp
http://www.nda.ac.jp/cc/gsse, http://www.nda.ac.jp/~yas/

Abstract. In recent years, there have been many studies and reports on malware infection activities. These studies and reports focused on the number of source IP addresses with malware characteristics. By measuring the number of source IP addresses per day, we can determine the status of malware infection activity. The results were used to alert the public. However, such studies are unable to distinguish between source IP addresses that appear on multiple days and newly appearing source IP addresses, and the circumstances under which malware infections spread or shrink are unknown. Here, we measured the number of newly appearing source IP addresses over a long period of time to reveal the spread or shrinking of the malware.

Keywords: Malware spreading · Malware infection · Mirai · Hajime

1 Introduction

As of 2011, it was estimated that there would be about 50 billion IoT devices in 2020 [1]. On the other hand, it is known that embedded network devices such as IoT devices have many vulnerabilities [2–4]. In recent years, malware that uses these vulnerabilities to infect IoT devices, build overlay networks, and perform DoS attacks has become widespread. For example, in Sep. 2016, a large-scale and destructive DDoS attack was carried out by the malware Mirai. The appearance of botnets that enable large-scale attacks attracted attention. In the United States in 2019, many medical and educational institutions suffered about $7.5billion from the ransomware attack. Data from the 2020 Ransomware Resiliency Report also shows that 35% of organizations suffered between $1million and $5million [5].

In order to prevent such attacks, it is very important to analyze the behavior of malware and monitor the infection status. In particular, research on the infection activity of worm-type malware targeting IoT devices that spread destructively and actively, such as Mirai, is drawing attention. Darknet observation and honey port installation are effective methods for grasping the attack activity of

N.-S. Vo et al. (Eds.): INISCOM 2021, LNICST 379, pp. 128–141, 2021.
https://doi.org/10.1007/978-3-030-77424-0_11

these malwares. However, many general observation reports count the number of unique daily IP addresses that arrive at the sensor. The method can capture the activity of the worm that day, observing the source addresses for each day can be used to investigate the increase or decrease in infection activity, but it cannot distinguish between source addresses that appeared on multiple days and newly appearing source IP addresses, and the actual spread of infection is unknown. Therefore, this paper decided to investigate the infection status of worm-type malware. Using a specific day as the observation starting point, we measure the number of newly appearing source IP addresses for each day since that day. The number of newly appearing source IP addresses per day from that day is measured, and the increase or decrease in the number of infections can be determined by comparing it to the previous and following days. Furthermore, by measuring over a long period of time, it is possible to clarify the expansion and contraction of malware infections.

2   Related Works

2.1   Definitions

Each term is defined as follows.

(1) Darknet
    A darknet is an IPv4 address space advertised in BGP, and is a set of addresses to which devices are not connected.
(2) Darknet Observation
    Darknet observation refers to the acquisition and accumulation of packets that arrive at an address to which a device is not connected.
(3) The number of Sender Address
    The number of source addresses in total number of unique addresses obtained by extracting malware-characteristics from all packets observed during the day and excluding duplicate source addresses.
(4) The number of new source address
    The number of source addresses in total number of newly appearing source addresses in D days.

2.2   Related Works

The results of observing the activity of multiple malware that infects IoT devices have been reported in many reports. NICT reported the observation result of the number of packets that arrived on the darknet [6]. This report indicates the days when infectious activity was observed based on the communication characteristics of ransomware such as WannaCry, Petya [7] and BadRabbit [8]. In addition, the date and time when the infection activity of the IoT malware Mirai variant and Hajime was observed and the country statistics of the sender are reported. Also, NICT extracted observational data featuring the malware Mirai and Hajime and reported an increase or decrease in the number of source

IP addresses on a daily basis [9]. As a result, it was found that the number of Hajime infections was on the order of several times the number of Mirai infections. This report also clarified the scale of infection of Hajime and Mirai and the date when the infection activity was activated.

IIJ-SECT Security Report 2018 [10] investigated the infection activity of Mirai, qBot, and Hajime using packets that arrived at Honey Port, and measured changes in the number of IP addresses of these sources. The report clarified the tendency of malware infection activity and showed the number of source IP addresses for each port. In addition, in IIJ-SECT Security Report 2019 [11], it investigated the activity status of Mirai, Hajime, and qBot based on the packet data received at a honeypot. It measured the activity status and infection scale of Mirai variants, and indicated the relationship with the case where the DDoS attack using moobot in September 2019 caused damage to the services of Wikipedia, Twitch, and Blizzard.

These reports focus on the source IP addresses of packets that have the communication characteristics of malware, and grasp the activity of malware infection activity by finding the unique number of source IP addresses for each day. However, with this method, it is not possible to distinguish between a source address that appears on multiple days and a newly appearing source address, so it is not possible to determine the daily increase or decrease of infected addresses. Therefore, in this study, we propose a method to identify a newly infected source address and measure the increase or decrease of infection by finding a unique source address over the entire observation period.

2.3   Communication Features of Hajime and Mirai

Worm-type malware, such as Mirai and Hajime, may have unique characteristics in their scan packets. In this section, we determine that an incoming packet is a connection request from Mirai or Hajime based on the following already known features.

Features of Mirai
The destination port is 23 or 2323, the sequence number and destination address of the TCP packets are the same [9].

Features of Hajime
A lot of research has been done on Hajime, and the communication characteristics of Hajime have been divided into two main categories and studied. In this study, we take these two features and consider them as separate malware:

Hajime - Sequence Number: The upper or lower 16 nits of the sequence number of TCP packets will be zero [12].

Hajime - Window size: The window size of TCP packets is fixed at 14600 [9].

3   Proposal Method

This study analyzes the data that allowed us to observe unauthorized communication in the darknet. The analysis method is divided into five major steps, as shown in Fig. 1.

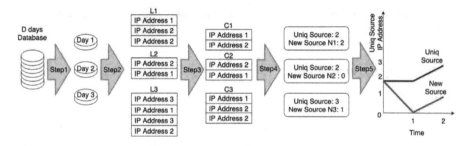

Fig. 1. Proposal method.

Step1: Divide the whole of the D-day's data observed from the darknet into one day's worth of data.

Step2: Extract the source IP addresses of the target packets with malware communication characteristics from the observed data for one day and create the source list Li for day i.

Step3: Use the source list Li created in step 2 to create a unique source list Ci for day i.

Step4: Find the number of new appearing senders Ni from the Ci list for day D.

Step5: Calculate the number of IP addresses in the Ci and Ni lists and draw a graph.

In the resulting graph, the blue line is the daily number of source addresses based on the existing method of NICT, and the red line is the number of newly appearing source addresses based on the proposed method of this study.

4   Experiment

4.1   Experiment Data

This study utilizes data from observations of unauthorized communication in the darknet. The dataset is a darknet observation dataset provided by NICT. The observation period is from 01/01/2016 to 12/31/2018. In addition, the target of this study is the IoT malware Mirai and Hajime, which have become active in recent years. We measure the number of daily source addresses of packets with Mirai and Hajime feature communications and the number of newly appearing source addresses. In this study, we use darknet observation data provided by NICT.

4.2   Experimental Results

Hajime
Results Based on the Characteristics of the Sequence Numbers
Figure 2 shows the infection activity from 01/01/2016 to 12/31/2018 and the measurement started on 01/01/2016. According to the results, it was confirmed that Hajime was presented even before 2016 and in Oct. 2016 the infection activity started to increase. At this time, the spread of Hajime infection increased along with the increase in infectious activity. The peak of spread of the infection was on 01/12/2017, when approximately 140,000 newly appearing source IP addresses of transmission were identified. It has gradually shrunk until August 2017 but infection activity began to spike in August 2017 and continued until April 2018. On the other hand, Fig. 3 shows that the number of newly appearing source IP addresses decreased and the infections began to shrink. After April 2018, the number of sender addresses became almost non-existent, and it could be confirmed that the number of source IP addresses did not increase again. Figure 3 also shows that the largest number of newly appearing source IP addresses per day in 2018 was about 170,000.

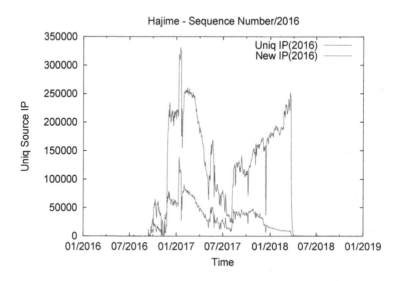

Fig. 2. Spreading of Hajime - Sequence Number from 01/01/2016 to 12/31/2018.

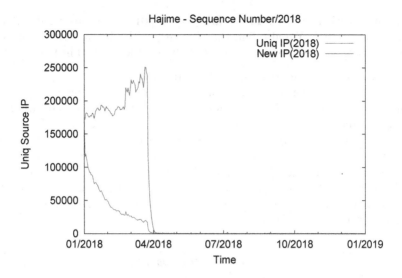

Fig. 3. Spreading of Hajime - Sequence Number in 2018.

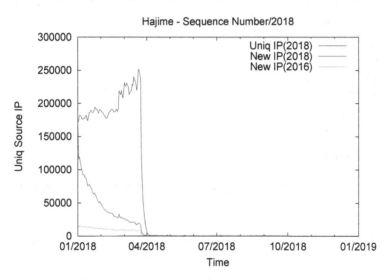

Fig. 4. Spreading of Hajime - Sequence Number in 2018 and newly source IP line 2016.

Figure 4 shows the trend of new source addresses of transmission, with 01/01/2016 as the measurement starting point, introduced into Fig. 3. New IP(2016) is a transition line for the number of newly appearing source addresses for 2018 with starting point on 01/01/2016. We can see that the actual number of new source IP addresses is a small fraction of the total number of source IP addresses that participated in the infection activity. Most of the senders that engaged in infectious activity in the first half of 2018 were those that had also appeared before 2018. We also find that the largest number of newly appearing source IP addresses per day was about 15,000, not the 170,000 in Fig. 3.

Results Based on the Characteristics of the Window Size
The trend in the number of source addresses of packets with the characteristics of window size is shown in Fig. 5 below. The observation period is 01/01/2016– 12/31/2018, and the observation start point is set to 01/01/2016. Hajime was confirmed to have been presented even before 2016, it was active in just a few host units until May 2016. From May 2016 onwards, Hajime's infection has been spreading along with a gradual increase in infection activity. The peak of the spread was on 1/12/2017. Approximately 140,000 hosts could be identified as newly appearing source addresses. Since then, the infections have been gradually decreasing until August 2017.

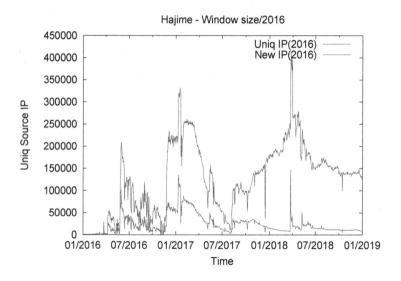

Fig. 5. Spreading of Hajime - Window size from 01/01/2016 to 12/31/2018.

From August 2017 to the end of March 2018, it appeared that the infection was active from August 2017 to the end of March 2018, and a large scale of infection activity took place in April. On the other hand, the number of new source addresses decreased during this period, and the scale of infection decreased. Figure 6 shows that Hajime's infection expanded rapidly on 3/25/2018. More than 148,000 newly appearing source IP addresses were identified, exceeding the peak of 1/12/2017. Since then, the infection has shrunk a bit, but the infection activity was still maintained.

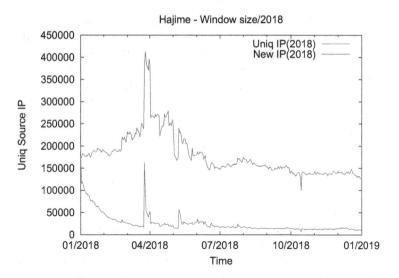

Fig. 6. Spreading of Hajime - Window size in 2018.

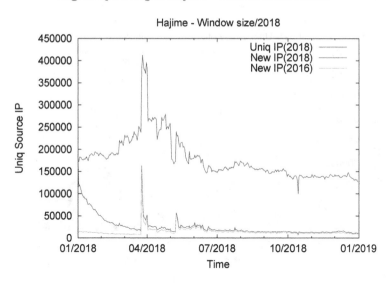

Fig. 7. Spreading of Hajime - Window size in 2018 and newly source IP line 2016.

To get a more accurate picture of the number of new source addresses, Fig. 6 inserts trend of newly appearing source IP addresses starting from 1/1/2016 and Fig. 7 shows that the error in the number of new source addresses up to April was very large. New IP(2016) is a transition line for the number of newly appearing source addresses for 2018 with starting point on 01/01/2016. We can also see that most of the source IP addresses of infection activity in 2018 also appeared before 2018.

Comparison of Results by Window Size and Sequence Number
While the number of source IP addresses having the feature of Window size began to increase from May of 2016, Fig. 8 showed that the number of source addresses with the TCP sequence number feature is from October 2016. The number of source addresses with the TCP sequence number feature from October was the same as the number of source addresses with the window size feature. The number of source addresses with the TCP sequence number feature decreased sharply from the end of March 2018, while the number of source addresses with the window size feature increased rapidly.

In addition, although newly appearing source addresses with characteristics of Window size from Fig. 9, Hajime infections began to spread from March 2016. The results of the study on the characteristics of TCP sequence numbers confirmed that it was from October 2016. From December 2016 to the end of March 2018, we confirmed that the results were the same as those studied in the Window size feature. In April 2018, fewer source addresses have the characteristics of the TCP sequence number, and the infection has shrunk, but a sharp increase in the number of source addresses that had the characteristics of Window size could confirm that the infection had spread rapidly.

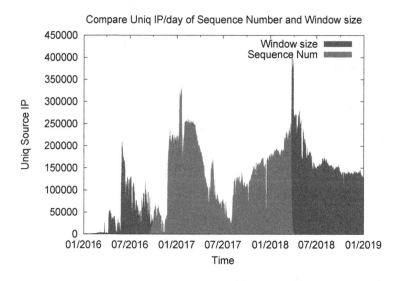

Fig. 8. Comparing of Uniq Source IP/day.

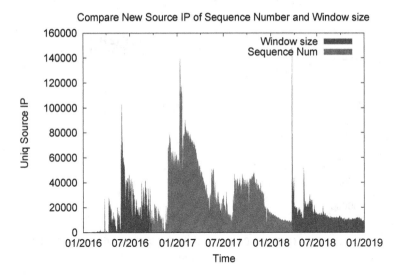

Fig. 9. Comparing of Newly Source IP.

Mirai

Results Based on the Characteristics of Mirai
Mirai was not presented at all until 08/01/2016. Figure 10 shows that it appeared from 08/01/2016 and the infection increased in activity and spread. The peak of the spread of the infection was on 09/21/2016. On that day, about 760,000 hosts participated in the infection activity, and about 380,000 were newly appearing source IP addresses. Since the peak, the infection situation has expanded and shrunk again.
In the second half of 2017 it had shrunk considerably, but on 11/30/2017, we can confirm that there was again a large scale infection activity. On that day, about 680,000 hosts participated in the infection activity, among which about 380,000 were new source IP addresses. The number of new source addresses was found to be almost equal to the number of new senders at the first peak. And after 11/30/2017, infection activity dropped sharply, and Mirai's infections also shrank.

Figure 11 shows that in 2018, tens thousands of new source addresses per day appeared without a sudden spread of infection. In 2018, the largest number of new source addresses per day was about 50,000 on the first day.

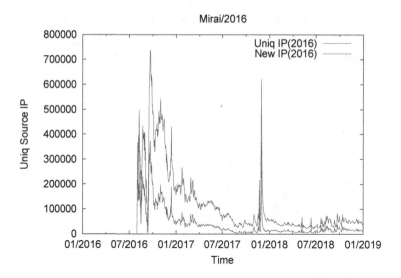

Fig. 10. Spreading of Mirai from 01/01/2016 to 12/31/2018.

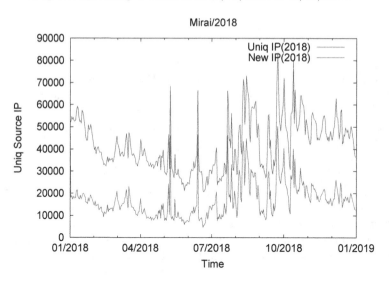

Fig. 11. Spreading of Mirai in 2018.

According to Fig. 12, the trend line for the number of newly appearing source addresses with 2016/01/01 as the observation starting point and the trend line for the number of new source address with 2018/01/01 as the observation starting point appear to almost overlap. New IP(2016) is a transition line for the number of newly appearing source addresses for 2018 with starting point on 01/01/2016. Most of the new source IP addresses in 2018 are real new source addresses and hosts that were infected before 2018 and are not believed to have participated

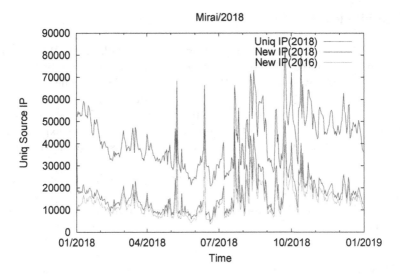

Fig. 12. Spreading of Mirai in 2018 and newly source IP line 2016.

in the infection activity again. Also, the largest number of new source addresses in one day was not 50,000 on the first day, but about 40,000 on May 9, 2018.

5   Discussion

The packets communicated by Hajime were characterized by a fixed window size over a long period of time. Hajime was reportedly infecting telnet with a method of repeated attempts using a prepared list of passwords. Around October 2016, a massive outbreak occurred soon after the appearance of the TCP sequence number feature. At this time, the addition of the TCP sequence number feature and the update of the password list suggested that Hajime had been improved.

As well as April, after the TCP sequence number features were removed and the password list was updated and improved for the second time, large scale infection activity occurred in early April 2018.

We tend to believe that the malware infections will spread along with the increased infection activity of Hajime and Mirai. Looking at the period from Oct. 2017 to April 2018, we can see that while Hajime's infection activity increased, the malware infection shrank. Therefore, an increase in infection activity does not imply an increase in malware infection, it is important to ensure that the number of newly appearing source addresses is investigated to determine the spread and shrinking of the malware.

The reason for Mirai's peak and then decline or increase again is likely due to the release of Mirai's source code, which led to a spike in infection activity each time a variant appeared.

6　Conclusion

This paper analyzes long-term observation data in the darknet. We were able to determine the source addresses of packets with characteristics of Mirai and Hajime, the IoT malware analyzed. We also confirmed that Hajime is a malware that existed long before Mirai, and showed the modified and improved period of the TCP sequence number feature of the packets communicated by Hajime. The results of this study provided a lot of information and clarified the expansion and contraction of malware with characteristic features, thus achieving the purpose of the study.

However, when the experiment was conducted, it was difficult and time consuming to compute due to the very large amount of observed data. Future problems should change the algorithm for this extraction and devise a way to process it efficiently.

References

1. Evans, D.: The Internet of Things - How the Next Evolution of the Internet Is Changing Everything. CISCO White Paper, April 2011. http://www.cisco.com/web/about/ac79/docs/innov/IoT_IBSG_0411FINAL.pdf
2. Cui, A., Stolfo, S.J.: A quantitative analysis of the insecurity of embedded network devices: results of a wide-area scan. In: ACSAC 2010, Austin, Texas, 6–10 December (2010). https://doi.org/10.1145/1920261.1920276
3. Costin, A., Zaddach, J., Francillon, A., Balzarotti, D.: A large-scale analysis of the security of embedded firmwares. In: Proceedings of the 23rd USENIX Security Symposium, pp. 95–110, August 2014. ISBN 978-1-931971-15-7
4. Costin, A., Zarras, A., Francillon, A.: Automated dynamic firmware analysis at scale: a case study on embedded web interfaces. In: ASIA CCS 2016, 30 May–03 June 2016. https://doi.org/10.1145/2897845.2897900
5. Crane, C.: Recent Ransomware Attacks: Latest Ransomware Attack News in 2020. https://securityboulevard.com/2020/08/recent-ransomware-attacks-latest-ransomware-attack-news-in-2020/
6. Cyber Security Labo: National Institute of Information and Communications Technology: NICTER Observation report (2017). https://www.nict.go.jp/cyber/report/NICTER_report_2017.pdf, (in Japanese)
7. Threat Hunter Team, Symantec: Petya ransomware outbreak: Here's what you need to know. BROADCOM Symantec Enterprise Blogs/Threat Intelligence. Accessed 24 October 2017. https://symantec-enterprise-blogs.security.com/blogs/threat-intelligence/petya-ransomware-wiper
8. Trend Micro: Bad Rabbit Ransomware Spreads via Network - A ransomware campaign hits Eastern European countries with what seems to be a variant of the Petya ransomware dubbed Bad Rabbit. Trend Micro Research. Accessed 24 October 2017. https://www.trendmicro.com/en_us/research/17/j/bad-rabbit-ransomware-spreads-via-network-hits-ukraine-russia.html
9. Cyber Security Labo, National Institute of Information and Communications Technology: NICTER Observation report 2018. https://www.nict.go.jp/cyber/report/NICTER_report_2018.pdf, (in Japanese)

10. IIJ Group Security Coordination Team: IIJ-SECT Security Report 2018, 28 January 2019. https://sect.iij.ad.jp/d/2019/01/288147.html, (in Japanese)
11. IIJ Group Security Coordination Team: IIJ-SECT Security Report 2019, 4 February 2020. https://sect.iij.ad.jp/d/2020/02/030029.html, (in Japanese)
12. IIJ Group Security Coordination Team: Hajime bot observation status, 1 September 2017. https://sect.iij.ad.jp/d/2017/09/293589.html, (in Japanese)

Improving Power Efficiency of AESA System with GaN Supply-Modulated Power Amplifier

Pham Cao Dai[✉], Le Dai Phong, Luu Van Tuan, and Nguyen Hoang Nguyen

Institute of System Integration, Le Quy Don Technical University, 236 Hoang Quoc Viet, Hanoi, Vietnam
daipc.isi@lqdtu.edu.vn

Abstract. This paper presents an analysis of using GaN supply-modulated (SM) power amplifier (PA) in an active electronically scanned array (AESA) system to improve system power efficiency. Specifically, the paper details a 4-W X-band GaN SM PA with power-added efficiency (PAE) of above 50% at 9.4 GHz frequency. The proposed PA achieves the PAE of above 35% over 800 MHz bandwidth and 40% in 10 dB output power back-off range. The simulation results show that the system PAE increases about 14–18% at the same condition of the array amplitude distribution and array scales by using GaN SM PA.

Keywords: Active electronically scanned array · GaN · Supply-modulated power amplifier · Power distribution · Operation range

1 Introduction

Recently, the active electronically scanned array (AESA) system [1–3] is widely researched, developed, and applied in radar and multi-function wireless systems. An AESA system uses solid-state devices and consists of an active phased array antenna where each of its elements is connected to a transceiver. This design can bring about high reliability, a wide dynamic range, high sensitivity, anti-electromagnetic interference, flexibility, and versatility, etc. [2, 4] whereas conventional models cannot because they utilize only one transceiver for all the antenna elements. For instance, the beamforming technique in an AESA system allows to synthesis transmitting/receiving pattern flexibly, scan the antenna spatially, and establish the multichannel for communication, detection, or tracking of different targets simultaneously.

However, there exist some disadvantages in an AESA system. The systematic design of AESA is incredibly complicated to achieve a wide scanning range, and avoid grating lobes, the distance between modules usually ranges from half-wavelength to wavelength [5]. It's only about 1.6 to 3.2 cm at 9.4 GHz. This makes the placement of the transceiver modules and system cooling more difficult.

Furthermore, the process of synthesizing the desired antenna pattern and reducing the side-lobe level usually leads to an unequal power distribution over the antenna aperture. This differs the output power of transmitter modules, which is the unwanted effect.

N.-S. Vo et al. (Eds.): INISCOM 2021, LNICST 379, pp. 142–155, 2021.
https://doi.org/10.1007/978-3-030-77424-0_12

Figure 1 illustrates a Taylor-$\bar{n}$ distribution [5] with $n = 3$ and a side-lobe level of -25 dB used in an AESA system with the 16×16-element array.

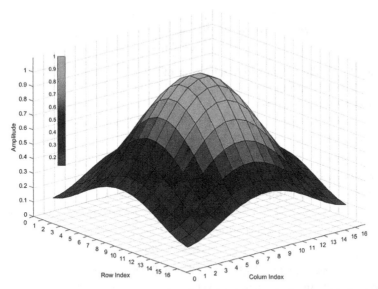

Fig. 1. Taylor $\bar{n}$ distribution with n = 3 and -25 dB side lobe level of a 16×16-elements Array

Due to the limited system space and the varied power distribution, it is necessary to improve the power efficiency and decrease the power consumption of the system, especially to enhance the quality of power amplifier (PA) because they are the largest power-consuming components in the system. In the AESA system, the PA is required to achieve high efficiency and this parameter must be maintained when the PA operates in the wide range of the output power.

The paper analyzes the power efficiency of an AESA system with beamforming, power distribution to result in a low side-lobe level, and changing of transmitting power according to its operating range. In addition, the paper introduces a design of an X-band GaN supply-modulated power amplifier (SM PA) [6, 7] used in an AESA system, which can improve the system power efficiency. The power efficiency of system is evaluated by simulating its operation in different power distributions and diverse array scales.

2 Power Efficiency of AESA System

2.1 Power-Added Efficiency of AESA System

The power efficiency of an AESA system depends on many units of system as PAs, Process unit, Power supply unit, etc. In this paper, we only consider the largest power-consuming components [8] in the AESA system, the PAs.

The power-added efficiency (PAE) of the PAs, given by:

$$PAE(\%) = \frac{P_o - P_i}{P_{DC}} \cdot 100(\%) \tag{1}$$

in which P_o is the output power; P_i is the input power; P_{DC} is the supplied DC power consumption.

Thus, the total PAE of an N-Transceiver AESA system PAE_{AESA} is as follows:

$$PAE_{AESA}(\%) = \frac{\sum_{k=1}^{N}(P_{ok} - P_{ik})}{\sum_{k=1}^{N} P_{DCk}} \cdot 100(\%) \tag{2}$$

where P_{ok}, P_{ik} are the output and input power of the kth PA, respectively, P_{DCk} is the supplied DC power consumption of the kth PA.

By applying Eq. (1), we have:

$$P_{DCk} = \frac{P_{ok} - P_{ik}}{PAE_k} \cdot 100 \tag{3}$$

where PAE_k is the PAE of the kth PA.

Substituting Eq. (3) in Eq. (2), we obtain:

$$PAE_{AESA}(\%) = \frac{\sum_{k=1}^{N}(P_{ok} - P_{ik})}{\sum_{k=1}^{N} \frac{P_{ok} - P_{ik}}{PAE_k}} (\%) \tag{4}$$

Equation (4) shows that the PAE of the system directly depends on the PAE of every PA in the array with the same output power.

2.2 Beamforming and Power Distribution

It is known that an AESA radar is able to gain the desired beam pattern of shape and direction with a reduced side-lobe ratio by controlling amplitude and phase of signals in receiver/transmitter modules using the appropriate coefficients. The formula synthesizing a beam pattern [5] for a linear antenna-element array is below:

$$F(u) = \sum_{n=1}^{N} A_n \cdot exp\left[j2\pi (n-1)u\right] \tag{5}$$

where $F(u)$ is a function of angle θ; A_n is the excitation coefficient of the nth element; N is the length of array; u is a variable given by:

$$u = \frac{d}{\lambda} \cdot (sin\theta - sin\theta_0) \tag{6}$$

in which θ_0 is the desired angle of the beam pattern.

In order to synthesize a specific beam pattern and reduce the side-lobe level, we exploit a certain distribution of excitation coefficients. A 16×16-element array using the Taylor $\bar{n}$ distribution with $n = 3$ and -25 dB side-lobe level (see Fig. 1) on both dimensions creates a beam pattern as illustrated in Fig. 2.

The Taylor $\bar{n}$ distribution shows that to achieve the -25 dB side-lobe level of beam pattern, the element of array edge is only 0.1314 in signal amplitude if normalizing signal amplitudes (the magnitude of the center element is 1.0). Thus, the signal power distribution over the array antenna aperture ranges in 17.63 dB.

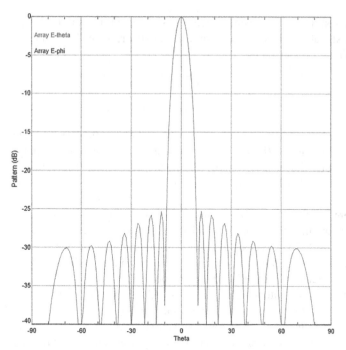

Fig. 2. The beam pattern of 16×16-element array antenna using 2D Taylor $\bar{n}$ distribution

In fact, the beamforming is implemented by using either the entire array or its sub-arrays depending pre-defined requirements. These beamforming methods are used in different functions and have different power distributions.

2.3 Operation Range and Transmitting Power

A wireless system does not always operate at its designed maximum distance in a real application to guarantee its functional stability. During operation, the operation range can be changed due to actual requirements. In addition, the changes in encoding, signal bandwidth, data rate etc. lead to change in receiver sensitivity, resulting in change in maximum operation range of system. According to the Friis transmission formula [9], the operation range formula of wireless system is given by:

$$R_{max} = \sqrt{\frac{P_t \cdot G_t \cdot G_r \cdot \lambda^2}{P_{sen} \cdot (4\pi)^2}} \tag{7}$$

where R_{max} is the operation range, P_t is the transmitter power, P_{sen} is the receiver sensitivity, G_t, G_r are the gain of the transmitting and receiving antennas, respectively, and λ is the wavelength.

In a radar system, the transmitter radiates signals out into space. When they meet a target, such signals are reflected and come back to the receiver. Therefore, the operating range formula [10] is given by:

$$R_{max} = \sqrt[4]{\frac{P_t \cdot G_t \cdot G_r \cdot \lambda^2 \cdot \sigma}{P_{sen} \cdot (4\pi)^2 \cdot L_{ges}}} \tag{8}$$

where σ is the target's effective reflection area, and L_{ges} is the loss coefficient.

From Eq. (7) and Eq. (8), the system's operating range is proportional to the square root (fourth root in the radar systems) of the transmitting power. Theoretically, if a system operates at a short distance, its transmitting power can be reduced corresponding to the square root (or fourth root) ratio while the system still works normally.

A current solution for radar systems whose operating ranges change is to properly modify their repetitive frequency, in which the duty of signal is varied but the output peak-power is remained. Thus, PAs always operate at their maximum power levels. However, this is not an optimum solution due to the restriction on controlling parameters of signal pulses and characteristics of the modulation code.

In short, the array antenna elements of an AESA system have inequivalent output power varied with time and position in a wide range during the process synthesizing a beam pattern and changing the operating function/range. Hence, PAs should have high PAEs and maintain them in a broad range of output power to improve the power efficiency for an AESA system. The PAE of a conventional PA achieves the highest value with the maximum output power and decreases rapidly with the decrease of the input power (output power, respectively). From Eq. (7), as a result, the AESA system will not achieve high performance with conventional amplifiers. By exploiting the advantages of GaN technology [11] with the controllable drain bias voltage corresponding to the required output power, the GaN SM PA could satisfy the above requirements. Therefore, it would be appropriate for the AESA system.

3   GaN Supply-Modulated Power Amplifier Design

We propose to use a GaN SM PA whose schematic is shown in Fig. 3.

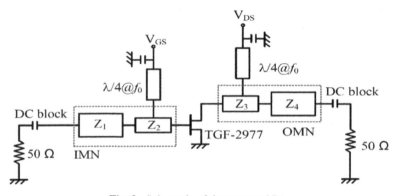

Fig. 3. Schematic of the proposed PA.

The input matching network (IMN) and output matching network (OMN) are implemented using two transmission lines with different characteristic impedances. These transmission lines function as low-pass filters [12]. It is noted that the IMN and OMN are designed at the fundamental frequency without using any harmonic termination elements. Here, $Z1 = Z4 = 20\ \Omega$; $Z2 = Z3 = 150\ \Omega$. The low pass filter technique [13] is employed to increase the PA bandwidth.

The optimum source and load impedance at the fundamental frequency (9.4 GHz) are: $25 - j92.8\ \Omega$ and $9.4 - j5$ Ohm, respectively. These values were returned by using the Load Pull simulation in ADS software in which a GaN HEMT TGF2977-SM small-signal and large-signal models are provided by Qorvo [14]. Besides, the large-signal model of the GaN HEMT is constructed relying on a non-linear Angelov model. Figure 4 exhibits the EM model of the proposed schematic (see Fig. 3). The IMN and OMN are realized as microstrip lines with a RO4350B substrate in this figure.

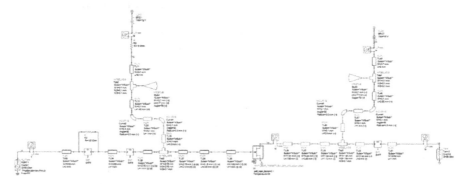

Fig. 4. Schematic of the proposed PA in ADS software.

The layout design of the proposed PA is shown in Fig. 5. The total PA dimension is $27.4 \times 11.4\ \mathrm{mm}^2$.

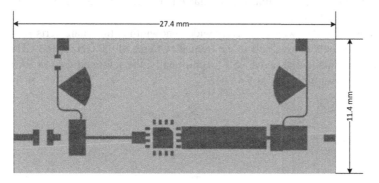

Fig. 5. The layout of the PA

Figure 6 indicates the simulated small-signal performance of the designed PA including input/output return losses, small-signal gain and stability. It can be seen that, both input and output return losses exhibit low from 9 GHz to 10 GHz. The PA is stable in the frequency range with relatively high power gain.

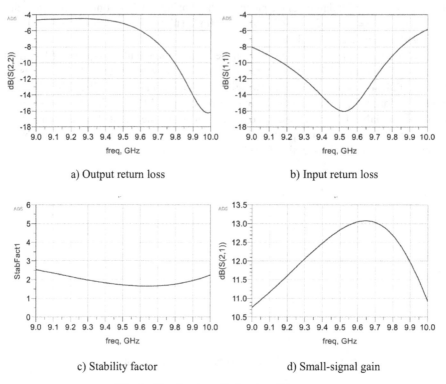

Fig. 6. Simulated small-signal performance.

The following Fig. 7 exhibits the simulated performance of the PA versus frequency for the large-signal model.

Obviously, the PA owns a relatively wide bandwidth in this characteristic. The variation of Pout is only below 2 dB in the frequency range of 9.0 GHz to 9.8 GHz and the PAE can be maintained at above 35%. Additionally, the saturated gain of PA is 12 dB with a 36-dBm output power at 9.4 GHz.

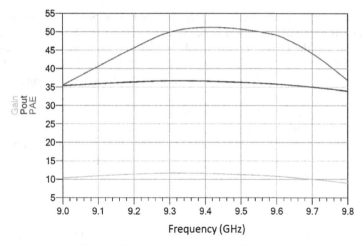

Fig. 7. Simulated large-signal performance

To maintain the high efficiency of PA for a wide range of output power, we utilize the supply modulation. The large-signal performance of the designed PA is evaluated and optimized by using a Harmonic Balance analysis in the ADS software. Figure 8 shows the large-signal performance of the designed PA for ten different fixed values of the drain bias voltage and modulated drain bias voltage at 9.4 GHz. When a drain bias voltage is properly controlled in range from 14 V to 32 V, the PA maintains a value of PAE higher than 40% in 10 dB of the output power back off.

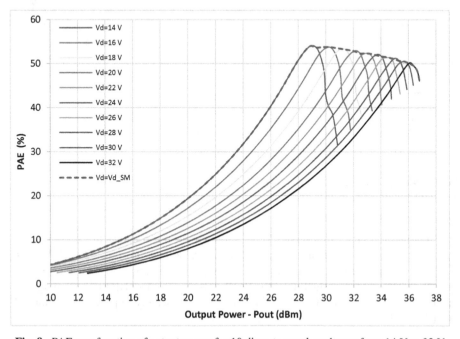

Fig. 8. PAE as a function of output power for 10 discrete supply voltages from 14 V to 32 V.

At the maximum output power trace, the PAE peak is about 50.1%, and it drops to 26.75% at 6 dB of the output power back off and 17.2% at 10 dB of the output power back off. However, the PAE of PA can reach 53.25% at 6 dB of the output power back off and 40.65% at 10 dB of the output power back off if using the supply modulation. This demonstrates that the PAE of PA is improved in a wide range of output power back off.

The PA is designed and optimized by using a priority criterion of high efficiency with low drain bias voltage and output power. This can improve the system performance even the AESA system works at its maximum distance because there are only a few of PAs (in the center of the array/sub-array) operates at the maximum output power and other PAs operates at the low output power.

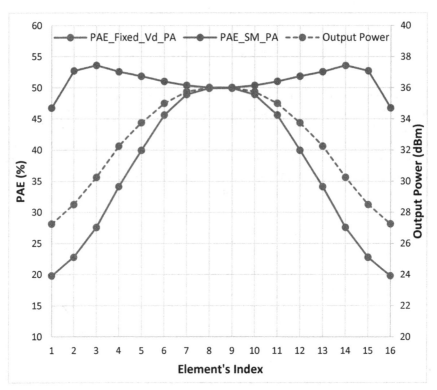

Fig. 9. PAE of a linear 16-element array using Taylor $\bar{n}$ distribution with n = 3 and −25 dB side lobe level (Color figure online)

Figure 9 shows the variation of PAE according to the position on a linear 16-element array using Taylor $\bar{n}$ distribution with $n = 3$ and a side-lobe level of −25 dB. We can see that the output power of array element declines from the center to edge of array (the dash line). This leads to reduction of the PAE of PAs using a fixed drain bias voltage Vd (the blue line). In contrast, the PAE of PAs can be significantly improved by using SM PAs (the red line).

4   Analysis Improvement Power Efficiency of AESA System with Designed GaN SM PA

In this section, we analyze the power efficiency of the AESA system using the proposed power amplifier (see Sect. 3) with various power distributions at different array scales and transmitting power levels. Here, we consider an AESA system working at the frequency of 9.4 GHz and using planar rectangular uniform arrays. The used power distributions for the side-lobe levels of -20, -25 and -30 dB are Chebyshev distributions denoted as Cheb_20, Cheb_25 and Cheb_30 respectively, and Taylor $\bar{n}$ distributions with $n = 2$, 3 and 4 abbreviated to TayN2_20, TayN3_25 and TayN4_30, respectively. Such power distributions are applied to both dimensions of the arrays.

Figure 10 shows the PAE variation of the AESA system with different array sizes: 4 × 16, 8 × 16 and 16 × 16 (rows x columns), where the dash lines indicate the systematic PAE when the PAs are supplied with fixed drain bias voltage for the maximum output power, the solid lines indicate the systematic PAE if using the SM PAs. Obviously, the solution using GaN SM PAs returns a significantly improved PAE (always higher than 48%) compared with the one using a fixed supply voltage (always lower than 37%).

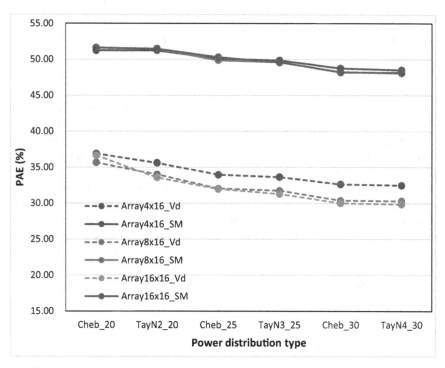

Fig. 10. PAE of AESA system with difference array scales and power distributions

Additionally, the lower side-lobe level, the lower PAE. The reason for that is that a lower side-lobe level needs a wider range of power distribution over the array aperture.

It means that there are many PAs working with the deeply low output power levels, corresponding to a low PAE.

The systematic PAE improvement is determined by the difference between the systematic PAEs using SM PA and using conventional PA, at the same other conditions (array size, output power etc.).

$$PAE_{Imp}(\%) = PAE_{SMPA}(\%) - PAE_{Conv}(\%) \tag{9}$$

where, PAE_{Imp} is the systematic PAE improvement, PAE_{SMPA} is the systematic PAE using the SM PA, and PAE_{Conv} is the systematic PAE using the conventional PA.

With the same output power condition, the systematic PAE improvement with the distribution types and array sizes is revealed in Table 1.

Table 1. The systematic PAE improvement (%) of AESA system by using GaN SM PAs.

Array size	Chebyshev distribution			Taylor $\bar{n}$ distribution		
	−20 dB	−25 dB	−30 dB	−20 dB (n = 2)	−25 dB (n = 3)	−30 dB (n = 4)
4 × 16 element	14.33	16.14	16.13	15.62	16.22	16.03
8 × 16 element	15.97	17.83	17.82	17.44	17.85	17.87
16 × 16 element	14.95	18.31	18.23	17.91	18.28	18.24

As shown in Table 1, the systematic PAE is improved from 14.33% to 18.28%. In most cases that systems with larger array (16 × 16 element) have efficiency better than others with smaller arrays (4 × 16 and 8 × 16 element) with the same power distribution.

In next step, we consider the systematic PAE improvement by using SM PA according to the variation of transmitting power.

Figure 11 shows the systematic PAE of an AESA system with 16 × 16-element array when the output power decreases 0 dB to 6 dB from maximum output power. It can be seen that its PAE also decreases when the output power decreases. However, the solution using GaN SM PAs outperforms the one using fixed drain bias voltage PAs because the power efficiency grows according to the reduced level of output power. This is shown in Fig. 12.

In short, the analysis results show that the use of GaN SM PAs significantly improves the power efficiency of an AESA system with using power distribution for synthesizing a beam pattern, reducing side-lobe level and transmitting power variation. The improved power efficiency is really meaningful for systems with a large number of elements and to reduce transmitting power.

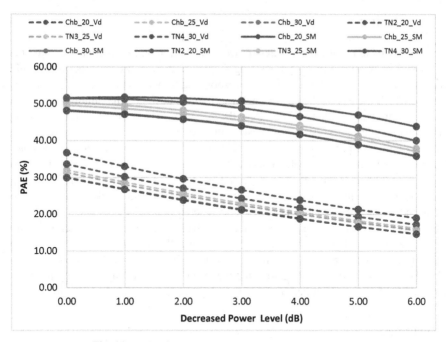

Fig. 11. PAE of AESA system vs decreased power level

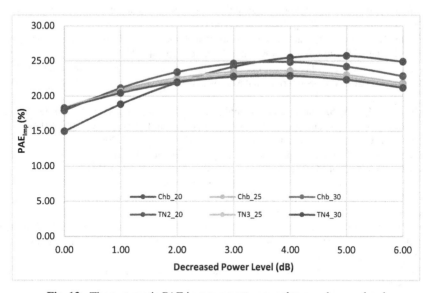

Fig. 12. The systematic PAE improvement versus decreased power level

5 Conclusion

The paper investigates the inequivalent power distribution on the antenna aperture of an AESA system resulting from synthesizing a beam pattern in order to reduce the side-lobe level and allow to alter its power corresponding to operating ranges. The working mode in which the established power is lower than its designed maximum level cannot achieve the highest efficiency. Therefore, the system can be heated up due to emitting useless energy during its operation. These challenges cooling the system, thus degrading it. Accordingly, the paper proposes using GaN SM PAs to improve the power efficiency. These PAs are high-efficiency elements and they can maintain a high efficiency in a wide range of output back off power. Moreover, a GaN PA needs a high drain bias voltage to function properly, thus allowing to control the PA conveniently in a wide range. The paper also introduces a 4-W X-band GaN SM PA designed for an AESA system. The low-pass filtering technique used in the proposed design provides the impedance-matching ability and expands the bandwidth. Thus, the PA can obtain a PEA of above 35% in a frequency range of 9.0 GHz to 9.8 GHz, and higher 40% in 10 dB of the output power back off at 9.4 GHz. The simulation results show that the proposed method significantly improves the power performance compared with current approaches using other amplifiers.

References

1. Hommel, H., Feldle, H.-P.: Current status of airborne active phased array (AESA) radar systems and future trends. In: Proceedings of IEEE MTT-S International Microwave Symposium Digest, Long Beach, CA, pp. 1449–1452 (2005)
2. Feldle, H.: State of the active phased array technology. In: Proceedings of 2007 2nd International ITG Conference on Antennas, Munich, pp. 241–245 (2007)
3. van Bezouwen, H., Feldle, H., Holpp, W.: Status and trends in AESA-based radar. In: Proceedings of IEEE MTT-S International Microwave Symposium, Anaheim, CA, pp. 526–529 (2010)
4. Mishra, A.K.: AESA radar and its application. In: Proceedings of 2018 International Conference on Communication, and Computing, Chennai, India, pp. 205–209 (2018)
5. Hansen, R.C.: Phased Array Antennas, 2nd edn. Wiley, Hoboken (2009)
6. Popovic, Z.: GaN power amplifiers with supply modulation. In: Proceedings of 2015 IEEE MTT-S International Microwave Symposium, Phoenix, AZ, pp. 1–4 (2015)
7. Cappello, T., Florian, C., Niessen, D., Paganelli, R.P., Schafer, S., Popovic, Z.: Efficient X-band transmitter with integrated GaN power amplifier and supply modulator. IEEE Trans. Microw. Theory Tech. 67(4), 1601–1614 (2019)
8. Yan, H., Ramesh, S., Gallagher, T., Ling, C., Cabric, D.: Performance, power, and area design trade-offs in millimeter-wave transmitter beamforming architectures. IEEE Circuits Syst. Mag. 19, 33–58 (2019)
9. Mailloux, R.J.: Phased Array Antenna Handbook, 2nd edn. Artech House Inc., Norwood (2005)
10. Skolnik, M.I.: Radar Handbook, 3rd edn. McGraw-Hill, New York (2008)
11. Winslow, T., et al.: Advances in GaN technology and design for active arrays. In: Proceedings of 2013 IEEE International Symposium on Phased Array Systems and Technology, Waltham, MA, pp. 1–19 (2013)
12. Hong, J.-S.: Microstrip Filters for RF/Microwave Applications, 2nd edn. Wiley, Hoboken (2011)

13. Rabbi, K., et al.: Highly efficient wideband harmonic-tuned power amplifier using low-pass matching network. In: Proceedings of 2017 47th European Microwave Conference (EuMC), Nuremberg, pp. 292–295 (2017)
14. https://www.qorvo.com/

Smart Shoe Based on Battery-Free Bluetooth Low Energy Sensor

Thanh Hung Nguyen, Minh Ngoc Tran, Quang Huy Le, Thi Anh Vu,
Quoc Cuong Nguyen, Dai Duong Nguyen$^{(\boxtimes)}$, and Minh Thuy Le$^{(\boxtimes)}$

Department of Instrument and Industrial Informatics (3I), School of Electrical Engineering,
Hanoi University of Science and Technology, Hanoi 100000, Vietnam
{duong.nguyendai,thuy.leminh}@hust.edu.vn

Abstract. In this work, we propose a smart shoe integrated with a very-low power wireless sensor node operating in Bluetooth Low Energy (BLE) 5.0 standard. The sensor node consists of a miniaturized printed inverted-F antenna, an accelerometer and a gyroscope being placed at the bottom of the shoe to measure footstep-length, running speed and foot landing angle. The maximum power consumption of the sensor is 11 mW and it is sustained by a triboeletric nanogenerator (TENG) which generates power from the friction causing by user's motion itself and an energy storage circuit. The triboelectric energy harvester, having the size of 6 cm × 6 cm, is made of multiple pairs of triboelectric materials can harvest up to 32 mW/m^2, enough to supply the sensor node.

Keywords: Smart shoe · Battery-less wireless sensor · BLE sensor · Triboelectric · Energy harvesting · Printed inverted-F antenna

1 Introduction

With the rapid development of big data, wireless sensors are becoming more and more important in data collecting. Wireless sensor nodes are useful thank to their mobility, independent operation, compactness, and interconnection, suitable to various measuring objects. Recently, many applications are being developed based on wireless sensors such as health monitoring, security or smart home. Currently, the majority of wireless sensors are being supplied by battery. However, due to the limited lifespan, they are not sustainable. Instead, other solutions must be made to increase the using time while reducing the number of batteries needed. Harvesting energy from the environment is a potential candidate to replace, or at least support, the batteries as primary power source for low power wireless sensor nodes. Among various power sources available in the ambience, triboelectricity-the phenomenon in which electricity is generated from mechanical friction, proves to be a suitable option for wearable sensors. Earlier works have succeeded in collecting from 3.2 mW/m^2 up to 313 mW/m^2 [1], showing vast potential of this energy source. In this paper, we propose the design of a smart shoe integrated with a wireless sensor node, which in turn being powered in part by triboelectricity. The sensor node,

N.-S. Vo et al. (Eds.): INISCOM 2021, LNICST 379, pp. 156–166, 2021.
https://doi.org/10.1007/978-3-030-77424-0_13

with the size of 4.5 cm × 3 cm, consumes 11 mW at maximum, measures the running speed, step, landing angle, then transmits the information using BLE technology. The triboelectric generator, with the size of 5 cm × 5 cm is able to harvest up to 32 mW/m², correspond with 12 μJ for each footstep.

2 System Design

2.1 The Proposed Smart Shoe

The block function of the entire system integrated on the shoe is shown in Fig. 1. Three main functional blocks are: the triboelectric based energy harvesting and storafe, the sensors, and the BLE transceiver, in which the sensors and transceiver consume 11 mW in their normal operating mode.

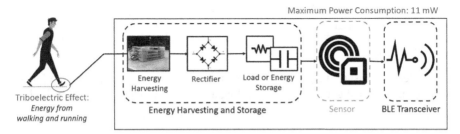

Fig. 1. Block diagram of the smart shoe.

The position of three main functional blocks on the shoe is depicted in Fig. 2, including the triboelectric nanogenerator, the energy harvesting and storage, and the BLE wireless sensor. These positions must be anaylsed to achieve maximum performance in term of the harvested power and power supply, the BLE antenna efficiency and the distance of communication of the BLE sensor.

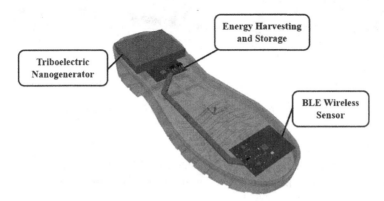

Fig. 2. The position of three functional blocks on the shoe.

2.2 Proposed Self-powered BLE Sensor

From the need of of runners, the parameters to be measured include running speed, the number of steps over time, the step length. The main criterion set for the smart shoe are shown in Table 1:

Table 1. The measured parameters, their ranges and the desired error.

Parameters	Range	Unit	Error (%)
Speed	0 ÷ 12.5	m/s	5 ÷ 10
Stepping rate	0 ÷ 300	Step/minute	5 ÷ 10
Step length	0 ÷ 2.7	M	5 ÷ 10
Landing angle	0 ÷ 90	Degrees	5 ÷ 10

In order to measure the above parameters, accelerometers (for speed, step length and stepping rate) and gyroscopes (for landing angle) are selected and listed in Table 2 (Fig. 3).

$$s = \sum \frac{1}{2} a_i t^2$$

(a)　　　　　　　　　　　　　　　　(b)

Fig. 3. The measured parameters of the BLE sensor node (a) foot landing angle and (b) speed, length and stepping rate.

The DA14585 wireless transceiver operates with BLE standard and has its power consumption provided in [2]. The power consumption in various operatin modes of the BLE transceiver is listed in Table 3:

Table 2. List of the selected devices.

Device	Selected model	Power consumption
Wireless transceiver	DA14585	11 mW
Accelerometer	MMA8451Q	10.8 uW
Gyroscope	BMG250	1.53 mW

Table 3. Power consumption in various operating modes of the BLE transceiver.

Device	Power consumption
Power-down Mode	1.56 uW
Sleep-mode (@retain 16 kB RAM)	3.6 uW
TX mode (@ 0dBm)	10.2 mW
RX mode (@ 1Mbps)	11 mW

When design the sensor node, the integration of antenna is a crucial step that determines the quality of BLE communication between the node and other BLE devices. We evaluate the printed inverted-F antenna via two main criterias: radiation pattern and reflection coefficient S_{11}. Here the miniaturized IFA antenna is designed, with the dimensions shown in Table 4 (Fig. 4).

Table 4. Dimensions of the IFA antenna (unit: mm)

Parameters	Value
w_s	2
w	0.8
L_f	5
L_1	2.8
L_2	2.2
L_3	1.7
L_4	2
L_5	3.7

When the antenna is integrated on-board, the impact of the wires and lumped elements within the circuit, and the fact that the ground is heavily mutilated due to the introduction of the lumped components make the antenna's impedance deviates and thus shift the resonant frequency significantly. The parameter L_5 of 3.3 mm is reoptimized to change the frequency back to the desired value between 2.4 GHz and 2.5 GHz

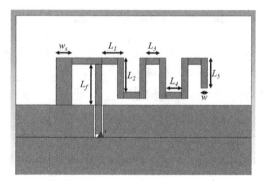

Fig. 4. The proposed miniaturized IFA antenna.

for BLE communication. As seen from Fig. 5, the antenna bandwidth and radiation pattern is still maintained after being placed inside the circuit. The antenna gain remains stable around 1.6 dBi.

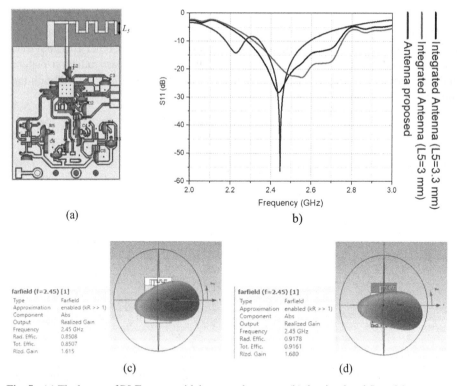

Fig. 5. (a) The layout of BLE sensor with integrated antenna, (b) the simulated S_{11} of the antenna standing alone and integrated in the BLE circuit, (c) the simulated radiation pattern of the standing alone antenna, and (d) the simulated radiation pattern of the antenna on-board.

The BLE sensor node is placed inside the shoes as we mentioned above, the influence of the shoes to antenna performance is considered, which is unveiled in Fig. 6a. The BLE sensor with integrated antenna is placed at three position: a) near the sole, b) near the arch and c) near the heel, corresponding with Fig. 6 a, b and c. If the antenna is close to the sole, the S_{11} of the antenna is slightly under -10 dB while reflection coefficients in two others positions are only under -7 dB in desired frequency.

When the heterogeneous environments are taken into account, the simulation of radiation pattern of the antenna on the BLE sensor placed near the sole is similar to the radiation pattern as in Fig. 5d but the peak gain is decreased from 1.6 dBi to 0.9 dBi. However, at two positions near the arch and near the heel the radiation pattern of the integrated antenna are not similar to the radiation pattern as in Fig. 5d as illustrated in Fig. 7. Therefore, the position near the sole is choosen to place BLE sensor node on the smart shoe.·

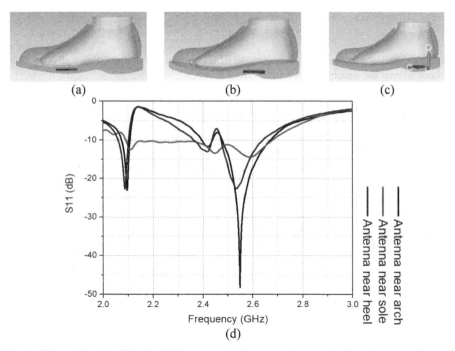

Fig. 6. The position in which the BLE sensor with integrated antenna is placed, a) near the sole, b) near the arch, c) near the heel, d) the simulated S_{11} of the antenna in 3 positions: the green line for near the sole, the blue line for near the arch, the red line for near the heel. (Color figure online)

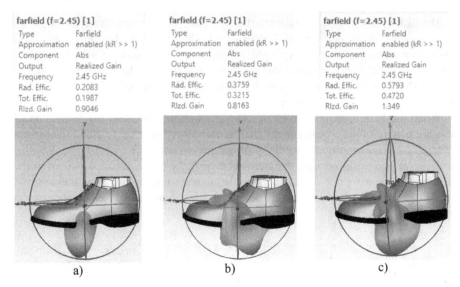

Fig. 7. The radiation patterns of the antenna on BLE sensor node corresponding with 3 position in shoes: a) near the sole, b) near the arch, c) near the heel

2.3 The Proposed Triboelectric Energy Harvester

The mechanical to electrical efficiency must be optimized to harvest energy from the runner footsteps. Due to the up-and-down motion of the foot, the harvester must consist of electrodes which contact to each other vertically. The structure is depicted in Fig. 8:

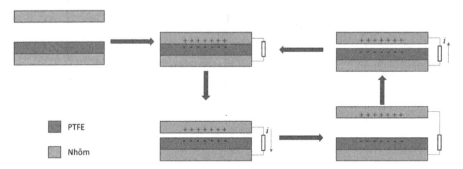

Fig. 8. Structure and operating principle of the triboelectric harvester.

To determine the energy generated by triboelectricity, the charge induced each time the pair of materials get into contact. The area of contact between the layers of PTFE and aluminum play a crucial role, determining how much charge are generated. This area A_r can be calculated from the applied force F, relative coefficient of friction between the two surfaces m_2, and elasticity coefficient E as follow [3]:

$$A_r = \frac{F}{E}\sqrt{\frac{\pi}{m_2}} \tag{1}$$

The relation between A_r and the amount of charge q generated is deduced from [3] as:

$$q = \frac{(\Phi_2 - \Phi_1)\varepsilon_0}{3ex_0}A_r \qquad (2)$$

where x_0 is the distance between two surfaces, e is the charge of an electron, Φ_i is the operating state of the two materials, and ε_0 is the permittivity of free space.

After the two surfaces collide, a voltage V_{OC} appears. The PTFE and aluminum layers form a capacitor, with the dielectric insulator consists the air gap of thickness $x(t)$ and the PTFE gap of thickness d_2 and permittivity ε_{r2}. V_{OC} is determined as follow:

$$V_{oc} = -\frac{Q}{S\varepsilon_0}\left(\frac{d_2}{\varepsilon_{r2}} + x(t)\right) + \frac{\sigma x(t)}{\varepsilon_0} \qquad (3)$$

where Q is the charge already station in the two metallic electrodes, and σ is the charge density induced by triboelectricity.

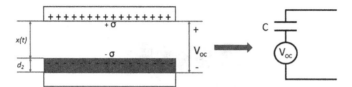

Fig. 9. Equivalent circuit of the TENG.

From the working principle explained above, a multilayer TENG, made of four stacked PTFE and aluminum layers is designed and the equivalent circuit of the TENG is presented in Fig. 9. The IC LTC3331 is employed for power management. Furthermore, the LTC3331 can switch between the TENG and battery, helps both sustain the sensor node, lengthen the using time before having to replace the battery and maintain a stable operation.

3 Device Testing

As seen in Fig. 10, the single layer TENG can harvests 11.26 µW and generates up to 30 V. Meanwhile, for the four layers TENG, these values are respectively 80 V and 80 µW, correspond with 12 µJ per footstep. The output voltage with 10 MΩ load of the single layer and four layers TENG are presented in Fig. 10 b and Fig. 11 b, the period of output voltage for the single layer and four layers TENG are shown in Fig. 10 c and Fig. 11 c. The four layers TENG is employed for the smart shoe as the output voltage is stable and potential to supply for BLE sensor node. The proposed energy harvester is compared to related works in Table 5.

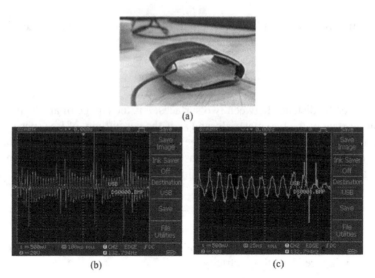

Fig. 10. (a) The single layer TENG, (b) the output voltage with 10 MΩ load, (c) a period of output voltage.

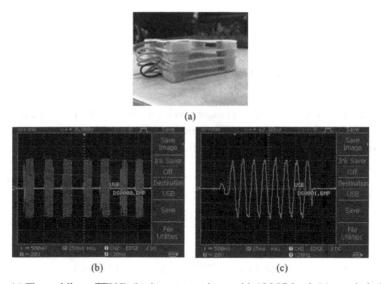

Fig. 11. (a) The multilayer TENG, (b) the output voltage with 10 MΩ load, (c) a period of output voltage.

The triboelectric nanogenerator is connected to the energy storage to power BLE sensor node as in Fig. 12. A comparison between the proposed BLE sensor node and earlier works is listed in Table 6. This work have lower power consumption than the works in [7–9]. At the distance of 10 m between the shoe and the smart phone, 100% measured data is transmited with 0 error showing the potential of the smart shoe.

Table 5. A comparison between the TENG of this work and earlier works.

	[4]	[5]	[6]	This work
Harvested power	19 uW	2294.17 uW	307.88 uW	80 uW
Size	13.1 cm × 9 cm	>5 cm × 5 cm	8 cm × 8 cm	6 cm × 6 cm

a)   b)

Fig. 12. (a) The low-powered sensor node, (b) the application to check the sensor broadcasting package.

Table 6. A comparison between the wireless sensor node of this work and earlier works.

	[7]	[8]	[9]	[10]	This work
Maximum power consumption	33.9 mW	57.09 mW	80 mW	25.37 mW	11.1 mW

4 Conclusion

In this work, idea of a smart shoe based on a wireless sensor node that operates in Bluetooth Low Energy standard, supplied by a triboelectric nanogenerator is investigated and validated. The sensor node consists of an accelerometer and a gyroscope, and consume 11 mW at maximum. The triboelectric nanogenerator harvest up to 32 mW/m^2 with 10 MΩ load, correspond with 12 μJ per footstep. The placed position in the shoe of BLE sensor node is proposed with 10 m of distance of communication withough error.

Acknowledgment. This research is funded by Hanoi University of Science and Technology under grant number T2020-SAHEP-003.

References

1. Wang, Z.L.: Triboelectric nanogenerators as new energy technology for self-powered systems and as active mechanical and chemical sensors. ACS Nano **7**(11), 9533–9557 (2013). https://doi.org/10.1021/nn404614z

2. Datasheet of DA14585, Dialog Semiconductor. https://www.dialog-semiconductor.com
3. Vasandani, P., Mao, Z.-H., Jia, W., Sun, M.: Relationship between triboelectric charge and contact force for two triboelectric layers. J. Electrost. **90**, 147–152 (2017). https://doi.org/10.1016/j.elstat.2017.11.001
4. Shamsuddin, et al.: Biomechanical energy harvesting by single electrode-based triboelectric nanogenerator. In: 2019 2nd International Conference on Computing, Mathematics and Engineering Technologies (iCoMET), Sukkur, Pakistan, pp. 1–5, January 2019. https://doi.org/10.1109/ICOMET.2019.8673493
5. Yingyong, P., Thainiramit, P., Vittayakorn, N., Isarakorn, D.: Performance and behavior analysis of single-electrode triboelectric nanogenerator for energy harvesting floor tiles. In: 2020 17th International Conference on Electrical Engineering/Electronics, Computer, Telecommunications and Information Technology (ECTI-CON), Phuket, Thailand, pp. 514–517, June 2020. https://doi.org/10.1109/ECTI-CON49241.2020.9157902
6. Jurado, U.T., Pu, S.H., White, N.M.: A contact-separation mode triboelectric nanogenerator for ocean wave impact energy harvesting. In: 2017 IEEE SENSORS, Glasgow, pp. 1–3, October 2017. https://doi.org/10.1109/ICSENS.2017.8234198
7. Nair, K., et al.: Optimizing power consumption in iot based wireless sensor networks using Bluetooth Low Energy. In: 2015 International Conference on Green Computing and Internet of Things (ICGCIoT), Greater Noida, Delhi, India, pp. 589–593, October 2015. https://doi.org/10.1109/ICGCIoT.2015.7380533
8. Zagan, I., Găitan, V.G., Petrariu, A.-I., Iuga, N., Brezulianu, A.: Design, fabrication, and testing of an IoT healthcare cardiac monitoring device. Computers **9**(1), 15 (2020). https://doi.org/10.3390/computers9010015
9. Sabatini, A., et al.: Design and development of an innovative sensor system for non-invasive monitoring of athletic performances. In: 2019 II Workshop on Metrology for Industry 4.0 and IoT (MetroInd4.0&IoT), Naples, Italy, pp. 162–166, June 2019. https://doi.org/10.1109/METROI4.2019.8792863
10. Nguyen, N., Nguyen, Q.C., Le, M.T.: A novel autonomous wireless sensor node for IoT applications. TELKOMNIKA (Telecommun. Comput. Electron. Control) **17**(5), 2276–2286 (2019). https://doi.org/10.12928/telkomnika.v17i5.12811

Highly Reliable PUFs for Embedded Systems, Protected Against Tampering

Jean-Luc Danger[1,2]([✉]), Sylvain Guilley[1,2][ID], Michael Pehl[3], Sophiane Senni[2], and Youssef Souissi[2]

[1] LTCI, Télécom Paris, Institut Polytechnique de Paris, Palaiseau, France
{jean-luc.danger,sylvain.guilley}@telecom-paris.fr
[2] Secure-IC S.A.S., Tour Montparnasse, 33 avenue du Maine, 75015 Paris, France
{sophiane.senni,youssef.souissi}@secure-ic.com
[3] Department of Electrical and Computer Engineering, Chair of Security in Information Technology, Technical University of Munich (TUM), Munich, Germany
m.pehl@tum.de

Abstract. Physically Unclonable Functions (PUFs) are well-known to be solutions for silicon-level anti-copy applications. However, as they are sensitive components, they are the obvious target of physical attacks. Thus, they shall be well protected. In this work we discuss the use case of key generation with a Loop PUF. We discuss the Loop PUF's efficiency and efficacy. We analyze it with respect to several known attacks like side-channel and machine learning attacks, and show that in all considered cases it either natively resists or can be protected. We also show that perturbation attempts should be within the scope of likely attacks, hence the PUF shall be protected against tampering attacks as well. Also for this attack scenario we highlight the salient features of the Loop PUF and explain how its mode of operation natively empowers it to resist such attacks.

Keywords: Physically Unclonable Function (PUF) · Loop PUF · Internet-of-Things (IoT) · Dependability · Anti-copy · Root-of-Trust · Tamper-Proof

1 Introduction

Physically Unclonable Functions (PUFs) are hardware structures that allow generating unique per chip values. This property arises from the amplification of tiny manufacturing variations, which become unambiguously quantifiable this way. The unique values derived by a PUF can be seen as "non-stored critical security parameters" and are used in different security applications detailed below.

The PUF's correct operation requires some pre-silicon dimensioning and even some post-silicon configuration (e.g., helper data generation and storage). The former prevents systematic bias and correlations predominantly through careful

N.-S. Vo et al. (Eds.): INISCOM 2021, LNICST 379, pp. 167–184, 2021.
https://doi.org/10.1007/978-3-030-77424-0_14

place and route, the latter helps to eliminate, e.g., remaining bias [17] and to guarantee high reliability. Although this life cycle management seems complex at a first glance, it fits nicely into that of today's system-on-chip (SoC) deployment model. Therefore, inclusion of PUFs into a SoC is not adding extra steps compared to those already in place in the industry.

PUFs are experiencing many commercial successes as intellectual property (IP) blocks. Large deployment is motivated by the need for defense in depth, but also because the PUFs allows for new use-cases: The key derived from a PUF, e.g., is not *injected*, it is rather *extracted* from silicon, which eases its management.

Owing to this successful dissemination, the standardization of PUFs has been following suit. In particular, at international standards organization (ISO), the project ISO/IEC 20897 is targeting to setting the ground for fair security evaluation of PUFs. Part 1 introduces the security problems and defines the goals. Part 2 tackles test and evaluation methodologies, in particular through quantitative metrics. The achievable security level of a PUF self-evidently depends on the PUF design itself as well as on possibly required processing of the PUF output, the PUF response. But also the use case plays an important role in the security considerations of the PUF based system. In this paper, we focus on the use case of deriving a device unique secret key from a PUF and discuss different aspects of this scenario given a specific PUF primitive, the *Loop PUF*.

Outline. The rest of the work is structured as follows: First, the motivation for using a PUF is provided in Sect. 2 together with an exemplar use case where the PUF is a cornerstone of the security. The model given for this use case simplifies the risk management in that only the PUF security shall be ensured, against all attacks across the board. Section 3 introduces the Loop PUF, the PUF used through this work as an architecture which complies to this requirement. The analysis of the reliability and the security of the Loop PUF is carried out afterwards. In Sect. 4 and Sect. 5 the Loop PUF's resistance against side-channel attacks and, respectively, machine learning attacks is discussed. Section 6 shows the innate advantage of the Loop PUF even if put at risk by tampering attempts. Eventually, Sect. 7 draws the conclusions of this paper.

2 Use Case

2.1 PUF Use Cases

Over the last years, many different applications have been suggested for PUFs. The most prominent of them are the use of PUFs in challenge-response protocols [26,33] and as Physically Obfuscated Key (POK) [9,13,18], i.e., to generate and to store keys. Further applications include key-based protocols [1,8] and key-exchange [24]. A generalization of theses and further use cases is provided in [3]. The generalization specifies in particular four PUF applications, which use the PUF

- To generate critical security parameters. This is the scenario, where the PUF is used to store or to derive a secret key.
- As device unfalsified identifier.
- For device authentication through a challenge-response protocol.
- For random source seeding.

2.2   PUF as a Master Key

We focus in the sequel on the first use-case. More precisely, we will investigate an innovative configuration for the case that an Internet of Things (IoT) device and its managing party shall be enabled to share a secret key. The PUF is used in the scenario to store a private key with the goal to reduce the attack surface.

Device Authentication Without PUF. In order to show the benefit of the PUF, consider the situation **without a PUF** first. This scenario is described in Fig. 1(a): A security owner generates a *secret key*, which is *provisioned* both to the chip and to the chip managing party. Therefore, an untrusted party can compromise the security model. For instance, since the security owner is not authenticated, a corrupted manager can provision several chips with the same key. Therefore, the dishonest manager in this "overbuilding" scenario can build indistinguishable clones of the IoT device when colluding with the foundry.

The regular process, however, consists in injecting a secret key both in the chip and in the manager. After this initial stage, the security owner, i.e., the trusted third party, is no longer needed. Rather, the provisioned chip can directly engage a communication based on a symmetric authentication protocol using the pre-shared key. The symmetric authentication protocol in this scenario is a strict requirement to ensure security both at end-point and at security manager side. One example for a (purely cryptographical) symmetric mutual authentication scheme is that the chip sends a random number[1] to the manager to check whether he is able to encrypt it correctly with the pre-shared secret key (remote authentication in Fig. 1). Vice versa, the manager sends a random number to the chip, to check that the chip encrypts it with the correct secret key (chip/IoT device authentication in Fig. 1).

Beyond the already discussed "overbuilding" risk, the described setup implies that both the end-point and the management company are properly protected against any attacker trying to come into the possession of the shared secret. This means, in particular: Also the keys managing company shall be protected, which happens to be not so obvious as the hack of Gemalto [19] shows, for example.

---

[1] The random number is usually termed a "challenge", and the encrypted response using the share secret key is customarily referred to as the "response". Please be aware that those shall not be confused with PUF challenge and responses. Indeed, there is no PUF in Fig. 1(a).

Device Authentication with PUF: Our Use Case. For this reason, there is a trend to transition from symmetric to asymmetric solutions. In the asymmetric case, each party has its own key pair (public and private key). The role of the third party is to endorse the chip, by signing its public key, which yields a certificate (in the sense of ITU-T X.509). Similarly, in the situation where the chip is expected to authenticate its manager, the third-party security owner shall also generate a certificate for the manager key pair. Therefore, later on, the third-party is no longer needed, and the chip and the manager can establish a secure channel using the respective key pairs, and can validate the other parties public key thanks to the certificate. For the sake of completeness, let us mention that in asymmetric authentication schemes each party has to prove it knows the private key associated with its public key. Again, and like for the symmetric case, each unilateral authentication is based on a challenge-response protocol (See footnote 1).

Please note that the asymmetric scenario implies that the chip is able to generate its own key pair. This is not taken for granted. Indeed, in the silicon manufacturing industry, chips are produced to be exact "functional" clones one of each other. Nevertheless, all chips differ from each other in practice due to minuscule manufacturing variations, which are the base to implement a PUF. The role of the PUF in the scenario **with a PUF** is to generate the chip unique private key. As a consequence, the end-point (IoT) device is the sole responsible for managing its root-of-trust key in this asymmetric case and the private key never leaves the device. This is illustrated in Fig. 1(b).

Obviously, in the novel use-case of Fig. 1(b), all the security of the IoT device is concentrated into the PUF itself. I.e., the PUF is the sole IP responsible for its security when in the field. Therefore, the PUF is a potential target of attacks. Notably, the PUF is also prone to physical attacks, since its application in the field allows the device to be tampered with from an attacker's perspective.

2.3 Motivation for This Work

The described scenario provides the motivation for this work: First, the PUF in this setting has to provide an unpredictable private key, which remains constant over time. I.e., the PUF shall be unique and reliable and shall not expose any information that helps an attacker to guess the PUF. Second, an attacker should not be able to extract the secret from the device. I.e., the PUF has to resist any form of tampering attempts, in particular it has to resist attacks observing side-channel leakage as well as perturbation attacks.

3 One Solution Based on the Loop PUF

The following shows that the requirements provided for the use case in Sect. 2 can be fulfilled with a real PUF. For this purpose, we consider the case of Loop PUF as one PUF primitive.

(a) Traditional use case (no PUF), with symmetric authentication.

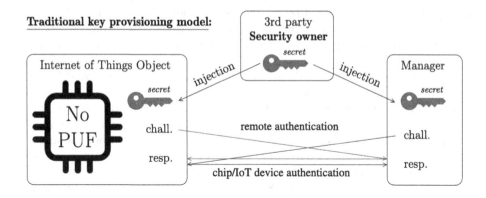

(b) Novel use case implemented by Secure-IC (leveraging a PUF), with asymmetric authentication.

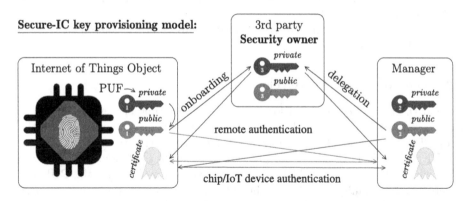

Fig. 1. Provisioning schemes, (a) traditional = symmetrical, (b) promoted by Secure-IC = asymmetrical. The third party is involved only at the key injection/extraction phases; afterwards, the manager is able to uniquely access its IoT object through a challenge/response protocol.

3.1 The Loop PUF Rationale

The Loop PUF [4] relies on a single loop structure. This loop is composed of n switch elements, which each allow to select a path (direct or crossed). Thus, the Loop PUF is strongly related to the Arbiter PUF [23]. However, while the signal traverses the path from the input to the output only once in the Arbiter PUF, it is inverted and feed back for the Loop PUF so that it repeatedly passes through the same structure. This way an oscillator is formed and the delay of a specific configuration is measured multiple times, accumulating process specific variations and decreasing the influence of noise. At the output the number of oscillations in a fixed period of time – the measurement time – is counted, which can be translated into a delay of the structure. The described process allows for the structure to improve the SNR for delay differences by increasing the measurement time.

To derive a secret bit from the Loop PUF, it is measured under two different challenges, i.e., two different configurations of the delay path. A bit is derived by comparing the difference of the delays, or equivalently the difference of the counter values, under the two challenges. The suggested method to select challenges for a Loop PUF is to derive the first challenge c_i based on Hadamard codes [27]; The second challenge $\neg c_i$ to compare with is the bitwise inverse of c. This way, as many challenge pairs $(c_i, \neg c_i)$ as stages are derived. Furthermore, the configurations of the Loop PUF between measurements differ as much as possible since all challenges c_i have Hamming distance $\frac{n}{2}$.

The Loop PUF has been well studied and, in particular, comes with a *stochastic model*. This formal model describes its expected properties. The Loop PUF shall be *dependable* [29], in particular:

- Its *entropy* shall be known[2]. An accurate analysis of the entropy of Loop PUFs is provided in [30];
- Its *reliability* shall be known. An accurate analysis of the reliability of Loop PUFs is provided in [28].

3.2   The Loop PUF Life-Cycle

Beyond the reliability achieved for a specific, design-time chosen measurement time, a self-assessment post-silicon test can further reduce the error rate in the Loop PUF's response. This test stage is customarily referred to as the *enrollment* in PUF parlance. This *enrollment* phase is to generate a reference key from the PUF and a "helper data" which is a public word to reconstruct the PUF key which may have faulty bits due to the extraction noise. This enrollment phase happens once just after the fabrication of the device. Figure 2 illustrates the two phases of enrollment and inference during which the PUF key is reconstructed by means of the helper data.

A simple helper data is to point out the most unreliable PUF bits in order to discard them during the inference phase. As the Loop PUF generates not only bit values but also their associated reliability level, this helper data is easy to obtain. The assessment of reliability by using the helper data to filter out unreliable elements is formalized in [30]. More details regarding the enrollment phases can be found in [25]. An attack on the helper data is possible if the attacker can read

---

[2] Notice that the entropy of the Loop PUF as well as of all strong PUF can be modelled reliably. Indeed, the number of challenge-response pairs is exponential in the number of delay elements. Thus Loop PUFs can be tested in principal using methods such as NIST SP 800-22 if a sufficient amount of carefully selected challenges is used to generate responses.

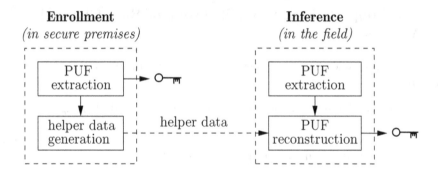

Fig. 2. The two phases of the Loop PUF life cycle to generate a private key.

and modify it, as explained in [7]. The same paper also shows that the attack is mitigated by using a double metric to extract the PUF response.

An efficient alternative to improve the reliability of the secret derived from the PUF is to generate an helper data by taking advantage of error correcting codes like in [10]. Section 4.3 discusses an attack using these helper data.

3.3 Test of Loop PUFs

Obviously, the PUF has become an industrial technology, meaning that it shall be tested. The tests shall consider the following two cases:

1. **Structural integrity test**, based on JTAG, can be implemented on the Loop PUF. This requires a simple mechanism to open the combinational loop. Such test allows to cover:
   - manufacturing issues, and
   - post deployment silicon manipulation detection.
2. **Behavioral test** to check *in situ* for security properties:
   - Health tests, and
   - Entropy test [6], using a partitioning of challenges between *application* and *service* challenges.

Effectively, only with these tests, not only the functional issues, but also security critical deviations in the PUF quality are detected.

3.4 Resistance to Attacks

From the sections above, we conclude, that the Loop PUF as a solution has all the requirements from the functional side and documentation side (for compliance to standards). It also comes with an accurate calibration procedure and testing capabilities. In the next section we discuss its robustness against attacks. In particular we detail in the next Sect. 4 the resistance to side-channel attack. Since the Loop PUF falls into the category of strong PUFs by nature, we also discuss its robustness to machine learning attacks in Sect. 5. Finally, we provide in Sect. 6 the explanation for the resistance against perturbation attacks.

4   The Loop PUF Security in Front of Side-Channel Attacks

Two scenarios of side-channel attacks are usually envisioned in the PUF context: The prediction of responses

- from unseen challenges based on the previously learned challenge-response pairs (see Sect. 4.1).
- from the power traces of PUF after having learned the relationship between some power traces and some responses (see Sect. 4.2).

The second scenario can be extended from attacks on the PUF itself to attacks on the processing of the PUF response (see Sect. 4.3).

4.1   Side-Channel Attacks on the Challenge-Response Pairs

This scenario assumes that an attacker can predict the PUF response for new challenge response pairs by observing – in this case via a side-channel – responses of previous challenges. Given these challenge-response pairs, e.g., machine learning can be applied to model the PUF and to eventually predict the responses also for unseen challenges. The attack scenario implies, that an attacker is able to configure the PUF with an unlimited amount of challenges since she is able to first train a model and has challenges left for which the response must be predicted. However, in the use-case of master key generation, this is not the case. In particular, the challenges shall be selected according to the Hadamard code as detailed above. I.e., the key bits are generated from the Loop PUF given a small set of fixed challenges. As a consequence, we do not consider this attack applicable.

4.2   Power Side-Channel Attacks Without Knowing Responses

The Loop PUF is designed with a single loop: having two loops would be prone to coupling between them, hence a decrease in reliability (if not a complete undermining of its rationale). However, from the side-channel perspective, measuring fewer oscillators at a time increases the signal-to-noise ratio (SNR) exploitable by an attacker. As a consequence, without surprise, some attacks manage to guess the PUF's frequency [34]. Those attacks on the primitive are getting more and more difficult with age mismatch [16], but remain likely [28]. Though, the direct readout can be easy countered, by exploiting the PUF's small variations [34] and implementing a temporal masking scheme. Recently demonstrated cross-PUF attacks [15] can be mitigated by this temporal masking scheme, either.

Compared to the Loop PUF, approaches like the parallel PUF [20], the ring oscillators PUF [33, §3], or the TERO PUF [2] have lower SNR for the attacker owing to the parallel processing of such PUFs. Parallelism here means, for example, that for ring oscillator and TERO PUFs, multiple instances are measured in parallel by different counters; Afterwards these counters are compared for bit derivation. Although the SNR for such PUFs is indeed lower, side-channel attacks were also presented for these structures. Effectively, shown attacks identify the counters and attack the PUF primitives by observing its oscillation frequency and oscillation duration [21, 35]. While the smaller SNR can make the attack harder in those cases, countermeasures suggested for those PUF types are normally more complex compared to the simple protection mechanism available for the Loop PUF: The suggested method for such PUFs is to interleave counters or to randomly permute the counter usage [21]. Of course, also the simple temporal masking scheme from the Loop PUF can be applied to such PUFs but if an attacker is able to resolve the individual PUF primitives, only the Loop PUF with temporal masking can resist such a side-channel attack.

4.3 Side-Channel Attacks on Error Correction

The key derived from a PUF must be reliable not only under nominal but also under different environmental conditions. Different temperatures, variations of the supply voltages, and aging of the circuit can cause a drift in the PUF response. Thus, although the Loop PUF allows for an enrollment procedure improving its reliability, the secret derived from the PUF might be still subject to post-processing. In particular, error correction is frequently required to derive a sufficiently stable key. This, however, adds another attack vector to the system: Similar to attacks on cryptographical ciphers, where the key-dependent processing is attackable by side-channel attacks, the processing of the secret PUF response can also be attacked. The efficiency of this attack introduced in [22] was demonstrated in [36]. The attack assumes that so called helper data, which is data used to map a random PUF response to the codeword of an error correcting code, are unprotected. I.e., read-out and manipulation of helper data is feasible in this setting. Consequently, from a side-channel perspective the helper data are equivalent to the data input of an algorithm processing a secret. Manipulation of the helper data allows for the derivation of secret dependent hypothesis. As a consequence, correlation power analyses of the error correcting code allows for extracting the secret key.

There are basically two countermeasures against this particular attack: First, write protection of helper data makes this attack impossible, since it hinders an attacker from observing the device under different inputs. Such a write protection might be achieved, e.g., by a locking bit implemented through a fuse blown after the enrollment phase. Second, the codeword masking strategy suggested in [22] hinders the attack. In particular, first order correlation power analysis is prevented through masking the secret while it is processed by the error correction code.

5   The Loop PUF Security in Front of Machine Learning Attacks

The Loop PUF in this work is used to store a secret key. For this use case, no challenge-response pairs are available to an attacker. Therefore, machine learning attacks were for a long time out of scope in this setting. However, [32] revealed that even in such scenarios machine learning attacks on PUFs with challenge-response behavior are possible. For this purpose, the existence of helper data in the key-storage scenario, which is explained in Sect. 4.3, is used:

Error correcting codes need redundancy. Consequently, the bits in a codeword have a known, well defined dependency on each other. The redundancy is ensured for PUFs by a helper data defined mapping from PUF response to codeword for which, most frequently, Fuzzy Commitment and Fuzzy Extractor schemes are used. For those schemes, the publicly known helper data reveal if a PUF bit is flipped or not in order to map the PUF response to a codeword. An attacker can now bring this information together: Through her knowledge about the used code, she can combine (XOR) helper data bits in a way so that the result only depends on specific PUF bits. This relation of different PUF bits are labels for a machine learning algorithm, which takes the corresponding publicly known challenges as features. As a consequence, an attacker is able to learn the relation of the bits of a PUF with challenge-response behavior. This way she can ultimately guess the key stored by the PUF or at least reduce the key entropy.

To hinder the attack, [32] suggest, besides others, two methods: (i) A limitation of the amount of challenge-response pairs can hinder the attack. (ii) High rate codes can make the attack more difficult. Countermeasure (i) is of particular interest for the Loop PUF construction. While other PUFs with challenge-response behavior use up to 2^n challenge-response pairs, where n is the number of stages, the Loop PUF uses only a very limited number of challenges. In particular, for the example in Sect. 6.2, up to $n = 64$ challenges can be used which are selected under consideration of optimal entropy exploitation. This, however, prevents machine learning attack on this PUF type completely. Furthermore, the high reliability achievable by a Loop PUF might allow for preventing the need of a concatenated code, which is capable to correct high errors down to an acceptable key error rate. This contributes to the resistance of the Loop PUF against such machine learning attack even if the number of challenge-response pairs would not be limited. The reason is, that concatenated codes typically comprise a low rate code which frequently contradicts (ii). As a consequence of the discussion we conclude, that the machine learning attack in [32] is not applicable to the Loop PUF construction analyzed in this work.

6   The Loop PUF Security in Front of Perturbations Attacks

Until now, the attacker in the previous sections was a passive one. She observed helper data or side-channel leakage in order to learn about the secret key. However, obviously the attacker can also get active. An active attacker can tamper with the device in order to enforce faulty behavior. While other means might be possible, the easiest way to tamper with the device is to intentionally manipulate operational parameters like the ambient temperature or the supply voltage of the device. These attacks we subsume under the term *perturbation attacks* and discuss their impact on the Loop PUF in the following. Please note, that further research is needed to analyze fault injection attacks on the PUF beyond this.

6.1   Criticality of Perturbation Attacks

The criticality of perturbation attacks is best explained with a concrete application scenario in mind. Let the PUF be used as a master key in a device. In this situation, the first operation at boot time is the derivation of this master key. Application code cannot start unless the key has been extracted. But for reliability reasons, most countermeasures are not on by default; They are activated by the application code. Through corrupting the master key, the start of application code is hindered and the countermeasures are not activated at boot. An example for how such a perturbation attack might practically work can be given, e.g., for SRAM PUFs: In this particular case, e.g., irradiating the charge pump can force the SRAM to zero. Clearly, if the SRAM is used as a PUF to store the master key but is forced to zero, the key cannot be derived correctly and the perturbation attack succeeds.

Due to the described process, an attacker disturbing the key derivation process can effectively hinder the activation of countermeasure, thus, enabling further attack. As a consequence perturbation attacks are an enabler for further attack vectors, which allow the attacker for more advanced tampering with the device that would be hindered as soon as countermeasures are active. The resulting criticality of perturbation attacks is qualitatively visualized in Fig. 3. The stages are security sub-system (denoted as "sec. sub-sys.") boot, followed by host system boot. Paradoxically enough, when the host has booted, it has all countermeasures activated (hence is very aware of the threats), and operates under secondary secrets (e.g., obtained thanks to key derivation functions). Therefore, the sweet spot for attacker is when the system starts, because at the same time the master key is handled and no (or few) countermeasures are active yet.

On top of the described scenario, an attacker can also try to gain information and to reduce entropy of the derived key from observing the system with a fault in the PUF response. The example shows, that stressing the PUF in particular at boot is a promising attack strategy for PUFs, which are not carefully protected.

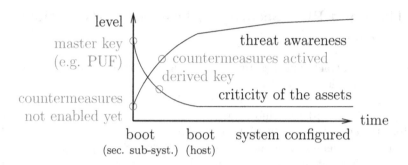

Fig. 3. Qualitative visualization of sensitivity level of keys (decreasing curve) and of the platform sensing capability (increasing curve) as a function of the boot process

6.2 The Loop PUF's Perturbation Resistance

This section shows experimental results to substantiate that the Loop PUF can be implemented so that it is resistant against perturbation attacks. The targeted PUF is an ASIC, implemented in 65 nm CMOS technology from STMicroelectronics [5]. For this purpose, the PUF is placed in a climate chamber (see Fig. 4(a)). The voltage and the temperature within the climate chamber are controlled (see Fig. 4(b)). Secure-IC Analyzr tool [31] is used to setup the experimental conditions and to query the PUF. A temperature range from $-10°$C to $+80°$C is considered. The Loop PUF under consideration is a Loop PUF with $n = 64$ stages, which is at the same time the challenge length. This PUF is configured to oscillate during $2^{18} = 262,144$ clock cycles.

We exemplify the robustness of the Loop PUF against perturbation attacks through manipulation of the ambient temperature for one particular challenge pair $(c, \neg c)$ in accordance to Sect. 3.1. The selected challenge pair in the experiment is $c = $ 0x6996966996696996, $\neg c = $ 0x9669699669969669. Please note, that an appropriate challenge selection strategy causes that showing the expected behavior for on particular challenge pair suffices. The enrollment strategy allows than for selecting challenges which behave similarly. The question, which percentage of challenges shows the expected behavior is another research question that is subject to future work.

Figure 5 shows the result of the experiment. The number of cycles, i.e., the counter values, after applying c and $\neg c$ is shown over the complete temperature range. Obviously the values are drastically affected by the temperature; They significantly decrease with increasing temperature. However, the values for c and $\neg c$ change similarly. In particular, for all temperatures the values for c are significantly larger than that for $\neg c$. As a consequence, the Loop PUF's response, which is defined through this difference, is constant over all temperatures.

To further improve the analysis with respect to noise, another data was collected for $+100°$C, a temperature for which a high noise level can be expected. The results of this experiment are give in Fig. 6. The Fig. 6(a) gives actually two insights: The two measurement results for c and $\neg c$ follow a global shape.

(a) PUF evaluation board inside of the climate chamber

(b) Control of the power supply and the climate chamber

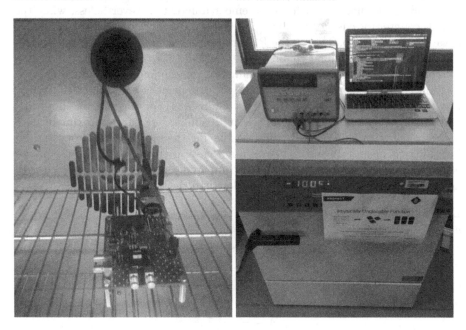

Fig. 4. Experimental setup in the PUF characterization laboratory

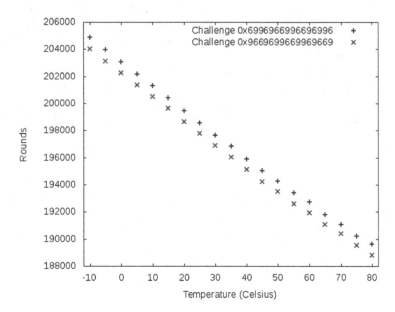

Fig. 5. Number of oscillation cycles (also denoted "rounds") of the PUF for two complementary challenges c and $\neg c$, over temperature

Since c and $\neg c$ are alternately measured, this indicates that the oscillations are affected by the same low frequency noise. The effect is overlaid with higher frequency noise affecting each measurement differently. Nevertheless, while the rounds counter for c is always above 138,000 the corresponding values for $\neg c$ are always below 126,000. This is, the PUF response would be for all measurements the same as under nominal conditions.

For a more quantitative understanding of this finding, a statistical approximation is provided. A histogram of the measurements for c and $\neg c$ is given in Fig. 6(b). The histograms can be fit by Gaussians. For the sake of simplicity, and since the standard deviations are quite similar, we can approximate both distributions with Gaussian distributions having the same standard deviation σ but different means μ_0 and μ_1. An error occurs, if the difference of the values observed for c and $\neg c$ flips its sign when compared to the nominal reference case, i.e., in our case if the value for c is smaller than the value of $\neg c$.

Lemma 1 ([28, Lemma 1, page 554]). *Under these considerations, the probability for this event, i.e., the error probability, is estimated to be*

$$P_e = \frac{1}{2} - \frac{1}{\sqrt{\pi}} \int_0^\delta e^{-t^2}\, dt$$

wherein

$$\delta = \frac{\mu_1 - \mu_2}{\sigma\sqrt{2}}.$$

Notice that P_e is also equal to $\frac{1}{2}(1 - \mathrm{erf}(\delta)) = \frac{1}{2}\mathrm{erfc}(\delta)$, where erf (resp. erfc) is the error function (resp. the complemented error function). For the distributions displayed in Fig. 6, the error probability, estimated with the formula of Lemma 1, is $P_e = 1.37 \times 10^{-264}$.

Please note that the model assumes that the two results of measuring c and $\neg c$ are independent. However, Fig. 6(a) already revealed that the noise of two subsequent measurements of the Loop PUF under c and $\neg c$ can be correlated (depending on the experimental protocol for the measurements). Therefore, the assumption of independence results likely in a worst case error estimate. A more accurate estimate considering the differences in the standard deviation and the correlation of the noise can be given using [12].

Summarizing, the result shows that the PUF response remains unaltered even if an attacker changes the temperature. The same conclusion can be drawn when the attacker instead manipulated the voltage. The cost for making the Loop PUF so reliable is a relatively long measurement time and possibly a preselection of stable challenges. Nevertheless, we can conclude that the Loop PUF indeed can be build so that it is insensitive to perturbation attacks, even if no additional processing step like error correction is used.

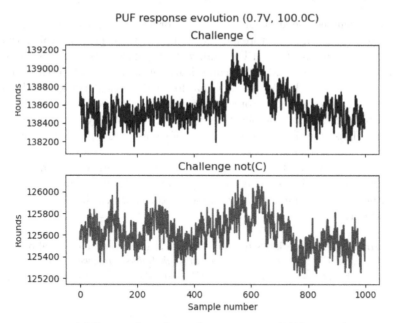

(a) Repeated numbers of measurements (1000 queries)

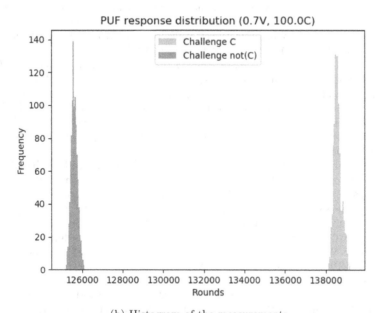

(b) Histogram of the measurements

Fig. 6. Number of rounds for two complementary 64-bit challenges

7   Conclusions and Perspectives

This work has discussed the application of PUFs for a specific use case: The Loop PUF is used to generate and to store a device unique key. Besides an explanation of the use case and of the Loop PUF, different attack vectors were discussed. In particular side-channel attacks, machine learning attacks, and perturbation attacks were considered. The results show that for all discussed attacks, the Loop PUF is able to resist or can be protected against. As a consequence, the Loop PUF is suitable for anti-copy application, while being natively anti-tamper at the same time. This is a highly desired feature for master key generation, when no system-level countermeasure is enabled yet.

As a perspective, we underline that in the current paper, we assumed only *global* perturbation, which they affect the full chip [11]. However, attacker with advanced or bespoke equipment can try for *local* attacks, which should be subject to future research.

Acknowledgments. This work has benefited from a funding via the bilateral project APRIORI (*Advanced PRivacy of IOT Devices through Robust Hardware Implementations*), from FR-DE cybersecurity 2020 call (MESRI-BMBF), managed by ANR from the French side.

References

1. Aysu, A., Gulcan, E., Moriyama, D., Schaumont, P., Yung, M.: End-to-end design of a PUF-based privacy preserving authentication protocol. In: Güneysu, T., Handschuh, H. (eds.) CHES 2015. LNCS, vol. 9293, pp. 556–576. Springer, Heidelberg (2015). https://doi.org/10.1007/978-3-662-48324-4_28
2. Bossuet, L., Ngo, X.T., Cherif, Z., Fischer, V.: A PUF based on a transient effect ring oscillator and insensitive to locking phenomenon. IEEE Trans. Emerg. Top. Comput. **2**(1), 30–36 (2014). https://doi.org/10.1109/TETC.2013.2287182
3. Bruneau, N., et al.: Development of the unified security requirements of PUFs during the standardization process. In: Lanet, J.-L., Toma, C. (eds.) SECITC 2018. LNCS, vol. 11359, pp. 314–330. Springer, Cham (2019). https://doi.org/10.1007/978-3-030-12942-2_24
4. Cherif, Z., Danger, J., Guilley, S., Bossuet, L.: An easy-to-design PUF based on a single oscillator: the loop PUF. In: 15th Euromicro Conference on Digital System Design, DSD 2012, Çeşme, Izmir, Turkey, 5–8 September 2012, pp. 156–162. IEEE Computer Society (2012). https://doi.org/10.1109/DSD.2012.22
5. Cherif, Z., Danger, J.L., Lozac'h, F., Mathieu, Y., Bossuet, L.: Evaluation of delay PUFs on CMOS 65 nm technology: ASIC vs FPGA. In: Proceedings of the 2nd International Workshop on Hardware and Architectural Support for Security and Privacy, HASP 2013, pp. 4:1–4:8. ACM, New York (2013). https://doi.org/10.1145/2487726.2487730
6. Dafali, R., Danger, J.L., Guilley, S., Lozac'h, F.: Embedded test circuit for physically unclonable function (December 1st 2020), USA patent US10855476B2
7. Danger, J., Guilley, S., Schaub, A.: Two-Metric helper data for highly robust and secure delay PUFs. In: IEEE 8th International Workshop on Advances in Sensors and Interfaces, IWASI 2019, Otranto, Italy, 13–14 June 2019, pp. 184–188. IEEE (2019). https://doi.org/10.1109/IWASI.2019.8791249

8. Frisch, C., Tempelmeier, M., Pehl, M.: PAG-IoT: a PUF and AEAD enabled trusted hardware gateway for IoT devices. In: 2020 IEEE Computer Society Annual Symposium on VLSI (ISVLSI), pp. 500–505. IEEE (2020)

9. Gassend, B.: Physical Random Functions (2003), msc thesis, MIT

10. Guajardo, J., Kumar, S.S., Schrijen, G.-J., Tuyls, P.: FPGA intrinsic PUFs and their use for IP protection. In: Paillier, P., Verbauwhede, I. (eds.) CHES 2007. LNCS, vol. 4727, pp. 63–80. Springer, Heidelberg (2007). https://doi.org/10.1007/978-3-540-74735-2_5

11. Guilley, S., Danger, J.L.: Global Faults on Cryptographic Circuits, Chapter 17 of [14]. https://doi.org/10.1007/978-3-642-29656-7_17

12. Hiller, M., Sigl, G., Pehl, M.: A new model for estimating bit error probabilities of ring-oscillator PUFs. In: International Workshop on Reconfigurable Communication-centric Systems-on-Chip (ReCoSoC). IEEE (2013)

13. Jacob, N., et al.: Securing FPGA SoC configurations independent of their manufacturers. In: Alioto, M., Li, H.H., Becker, J., Schlichtmann, U., Sridhar, R. (eds.) 30th IEEE International System-on-Chip Conference, SOCC 2017, Munich, Germany, 5–8 September 2017, pp. 114–119. IEEE (2017). https://doi.org/10.1109/SOCC.2017.8226019

14. Joye, M., Tunstall, M. (eds.): Fault Analysis in Cryptography. Information Security and Cryptography, Springer (2012). https://doi.org/10.1007/978-3-642-29656-7, ISBN 978-3-642-29655-0

15. Kroeger, T., Cheng, W., Guilley, S., Danger, J.L., Karimi, N.: Cross-PUF attacks on arbiter-PUFs through their power side-channel. In: 51st International Test Conference (ITC) sponsored by IEEE (November 3–5 2020)

16. Kroeger, T., Cheng, W., Guilley, S., Danger, J., Karimi, N.: Effect of aging on PUF modeling attacks based on power side-channel observations. In: 2020 Design, Automation & Test in Europe Conference & Exhibition, DATE 2020, Grenoble, France, 9–13 March 2020 pp. 454–459. IEEE (2020). https://doi.org/10.23919/DATE48585.2020.9116428

17. Maes, R., van der Leest, V., van der Sluis, E., Willems, F.: Secure key generation from biased PUFs. In: Güneysu, T., Handschuh, H. (eds.) CHES 2015. LNCS, vol. 9293, pp. 517–534. Springer, Heidelberg (2015). https://doi.org/10.1007/978-3-662-48324-4_26

18. Maes, R., Van Herrewege, A., Verbauwhede, I.: PUFKY: a fully functional PUF-based cryptographic key generator. In: Prouff, E., Schaumont, P. (eds.) CHES 2012. LNCS, vol. 7428, pp. 302–319. Springer, Heidelberg (2012). https://doi.org/10.1007/978-3-642-33027-8_18

19. Magazine, W.: Gemalto Confirms It Was Hacked But Insists the NSA Didn't Get Its Crypto Keys, 25 February 2015. https://www.wired.com/2015/02/gemalto-confirms-hacked-insists-nsa-didnt-get-crypto-keys/

20. Majzoobi, M., Koushanfar, F., Potkonjak, M.: Lightweight secure PUFs. In: Proceedings of the 2008 IEEE/ACM International Conference on Computer-Aided Desig, ICCAD 2008, pp. 670–673. IEEE Press, Piscataway (2008). http://portal.acm.org/citation.cfm?id=1509456.1509603

21. Merli, D., Heyszl, J., Heinz, B., Schuster, D., Stumpf, F., Sigl, G.: Localized electromagnetic analysis of RO PUFs. In: Proceedings of the IEEE International Symposium of Hardware-Oriented Security and Trust. IEEE, June 2013

22. Merli, D., Stumpf, F., Sigl, G.: Protecting PUF error correction by codeword masking. Cryptology ePrint Archive, Report 2013/334 (2013). http://eprint.iacr.org/2013/334

23. Pappu, R., Recht, B., Taylor, J., Gershenfeld, N.: Physical one-way functions. Science 297(5589), 2026–2030 (2002), https://doi.org/10.1126/science.1074376
24. Pehl, M., Frisch, C., Feist, P.C., Sigl, G.: KeLiPUF: a key-distribution protocol for lightweight devices using physical unclonable functions. In: 17th ESCAR Europe: Embedded Security in Cars (Konferenzveröffentlichung) (2019). https://doi.org/10.13154/294-6676
25. Pour, A.A., et al.: PUF enrollment and life cycle management: solutions and perspectives for the test community. In: 25th IEEE European Test Symposium, Tallinn, Estonia, 25–29 May 2020
26. Ranasinghe, D., Engels, D., Cole, P., et al.: Security and privacy: modest proposals for low-cost RFID systems. In: Auto-ID Labs Research Workshop, Zurich, Switzerland. Citeseer (2004)
27. Rioul, O., Solé, P., Guilley, S., Danger, J.: On the entropy of physically unclonable functions. In: IEEE International Symposium on Information Theory, ISIT 2016, Barcelona, Spain, 10–15 July 2016, pp. 2928–2932. IEEE (2016). https://doi.org/10.1109/ISIT.2016.7541835
28. Schaub, A., Danger, J., Guilley, S., Rioul, O.: An improved analysis of reliability and entropy for delay PUFs. In: Novotný, M., Konofaos, N., Skavhaug, A. (eds.) 21st Euromicro Conference on Digital System Design, DSD 2018, Prague, Czech Republic, 29–31 August 2018, pp. 553–560. IEEE Computer Society (2018). https://doi.org/10.1109/DSD.2018.00096
29. Schaub, A., Danger, J.L., Rioul, O., Guilley, S.: The big picture of delay-PUF dependability. In: 24th European Conference on Circuit Theory and Design, Sofia, Bulgaria, 7–10 September 2020
30. Schaub, A., Rioul, O., Danger, J., Guilley, S., Boutros, J.: Challenge codes for physically unclonable functions with Gaussian delays: a maximum entropy problem. Adv. Math. Commun. 14(3), 491–505 (2020). https://doi.org/10.3934/amc.2020060
31. Secure-IC S.A.S.: Analyzr® post-silicon security evaluation platform (2021). https://www.secure-ic.com/solutions/analyzr/
32. Strieder, E., Frisch, C., Pehl, M.: Machine learning of physical unclonable functions using helper data - revealing a pitfall in the fuzzy commitment scheme. IACR Trans. Cryptographic Hardw. Embedded Syst. 2021(2), 1–36 (2021)
33. Suh, G.E., Devadas, S.: Physical unclonable functions for device authentication and secret key generation. In: Proceedings of the 44th Design Automation Conference, DAC 2007, San Diego, CA, USA, 4–8 June 2007, pp. 9–14. IEEE (2007). https://doi.org/10.1145/1278480.1278484
34. Tebelmann, L., Danger, J.-L., Pehl, M.: Self-secured PUF: protecting the loop PUF by masking. In: Bertoni, G.M., Regazzoni, F. (eds.) COSADE 2020. LNCS, vol. 12244, pp. 293–314. Springer, Cham (2021). https://doi.org/10.1007/978-3-030-68773-1_14
35. Tebelmann, L., Pehl, M., Immler, V.: Side-channel analysis of the TERO PUF. In: Polian, I., Stöttinger, M. (eds.) COSADE 2019. LNCS, vol. 11421, pp. 43–60. Springer, Cham (2019). https://doi.org/10.1007/978-3-030-16350-1_4
36. Tebelmann, L., Pehl, M., Sigl, G.: EM side-channel analysis of BCH-based error correction for PUF-based key generation. In: Proceedings of the 2017 Workshop on Attacks and Solutions in Hardware Security, ASHES 2017, pp. 43–52. ACM, New York (2017). https://doi.org/10.1145/3139324.3139328

On Use of Deep Learning for Side Channel Evaluation of Black Box Hardware AES Engine

Yoo-Seung Won[(✉)] and Shivam Bhasin

Temasek Laboratories, Nanyang Technological University, Singapore, Singapore
{yooseung.won,sbhasin}@ntu.edu.sg

Abstract. With the increasing demand for security and privacy, there has been an increasing availability of cryptographic acclerators out of the box in modern microcontrollers, These accelerators are optimised and often black box. Thus, proper evaluation against vulnerabilities like side-channel attacks is a challenge in absence of architecture information and thus leakage model. In this paper, we show the use of deep learning based side-channel attack can overcome this challenge, allowing evaluation of black box AES hardware engine on a secure microcontroller, without the knowledge of precise leakage model information. Our results report full key recovery with only 3,000 traces under a profiling setting.

Keywords: Hardware AES engine · Side-channel analysis · Deep learning

1 Introduction

With the rise in need for security and privacy across applications, reliance on cryptography is ever growing. As a result, manufacturers integrate more and more cryptographic functions in modern microcontrollers to facilitate design of secure applications. For high performance applications, cryptographic functions are often available as in-built accelerators, accessible through an API. While these accelerators are secure in a classical setting, implementation security remains a concern. These accelerators may be used in sensitive applications requiring protection against attacks like side-channel attacks (SCA [8]) or faults attacks [13]. Thus, it must be carefully evaluated against such attacks when necessary. However, most if not all, accelerators are proprietary in nature and their architecture and related details are not available in public domain, making evaluation difficult. For instance, popular SCA like correlation power analysis is performed with a leakage model assumption [4]. If the leakage model is not precise, CPA is sub-optimal and may misguide security evaluation. The leakage model is better understood with knowledge of the architecture, which are not available in this setting.

© ICST Institute for Computer Sciences, Social Informatics and Telecommunications Engineering 2021
Published by Springer Nature Switzerland AG 2021. All Rights Reserved
N.-S. Vo et al. (Eds.): INISCOM 2021, LNICST 379, pp. 185–194, 2021.
https://doi.org/10.1007/978-3-030-77424-0_15

In this paper, we investigate the side-channel security of a black-box hardware AES engine on a commercial off the shelf microcontroller. The target microcontroller is recommenced for security critical applications like point of sale transactions. We demonstrate that using a deep learning based side-channel attack can allow better evaluation in the black box setting as compared to attacks like CPA where a precise leakage model is required.

The rest of the paper is organised as follows. Section 2 provides general background on SCA and deep learning for SCA. Section 3 describes the target device and evaluation platform. Section 4 reports experimental results and conclusions are drawn in Sect. 5.

2   Preliminaries

In this section, we provide background information on side-channel attacks (SCA) and use of deep learning for SCA.

2.1   Side-Channel Attacks

Side-Channel Analysis or Attacks (SCA) are a class of implementation level attacks which observe and exploit unintended physical leakages from target devices to gain information on underlying sensitive data. In context of cryptography, SCA aim at recovering the underlying secret key. The information can be observed by different channels including power consumption, electromagnetic emanation, timing, *etc.*

SCA can be widely classified as profiled and non-profiled. A profiled attack assumes a strong attacker with access to a clone device. By measuring traces corresponding to known plaintext and key, the adversary characterizes a model of the target device. On the victim device, the adversary captures only a few traces (ideally 1) with known plaintext but the key is unknown. These traces are then compared to the characterized model obtained from clone device to learn information on the secret key used by victim device. Initially, Gaussian templates [6] were used for model characterization but later machine learning and deep learning [1,11,12] were also shown to advantageous for profiled SCA.

Non-profiled attack on the contrary are directly applied on victim device, where adversary has access to plaintext or ciphertext but key is secret. Based on a leakage model like Hamming distance or Hamming weight, the adversary predicts a sensitive intermediate leakage value which depends on a part of secret kay (8-bits for AES) and known plaintext/ciphertext. The adversary test dependency of actual measurement with predicted leakage based on leakage model and all key hypothesis, using statistical tools. The correct key hypothesis is expected to show maximum dependency. In this work, we use Pearson correlation ρ as a statistical tool [4] to perform a correlation power analysis (CPA).

2.2 Deep Learning Based SCA

Recent profiled SCA have seen the application of deep neural networks [5,9]. Especially, convolution neural network (CNN) architectures are shown to be powerful for breaking countermeasures such as hardware jitter [5], shuffling [14], and masking [15]. Recent finding report CNN structures on various SCA open datasets [15] outperform the classical profiled SCA such as template attack [6].

3 Target Board and Setup

In this section, we report the target board and experimental setup. We target the Okdo E1 development board which is based on ARM Cortex-M33 chip.

The OKdo E1 development board which is an ultra-low-cost Development Board based on the NXP LPC55S69JBD100[1] dual-core Arm Cortex® M33 MCU. The intented application for this board are security sensitive like point-of-sale terminal. The security features of LPC55S69JBD100 are explained in the user manual [10]. It contains several hardware IPs such as an AES engine, a SHA engine, a random number generator, a PRINCE engine, and a key storage block that derive keys from an SRAM based Physically Unclonable Function (PUF). These IPs are accessible from the main processor as well as from a DMA engine for supporting functions like encryption and hashing. The hardware AES can be configured to operate with user defined or device specific key which is derived from the PUF. There are no security claims of the AES engine against physical attacks. The public information on specification of hardware AES engine is as follows.

- It supports key size: 128-bit, 192-bit or 256-bit key
- It supports following mode of operation: ECB, CBC, CTR, and ICB modes (ICB mode only supports to 128-bit key)
- AES functionality is combined with SHA block, referred to as SHA-AES
- When using 128-bit keys, the AES block takes 35 cycles for each block to encrypt, and additional 6 cycles for 192-bit key, and additional 12 cycles for 256-bit key.

We configure the main ARM Cortex® M33 MCU to run at the default frequency of 96 Mhz. The timing for AES-128 is determined by calling the encryption function between a LED toggle. The LED toggle then also serves as a trigger for the oscilloscope to synchronise the measurements. The side channel traces are measured on an oscilloscope via electromagnetic probe. We used a high-sensitivity low noise EM probe from Riscure [7] which has sufficient bandwidth to capture the activity at main clock frequency and clock frequency of hardware AES IP engine, since the probe is connected to a DC-powered Riscure amplifier with a frequency range of 100 kHz–2.5 GHz (Fig. 1).

---

[1] The chip manufacturers do not claim side-channel security for embedded AES engine. We have notified our findings to NXP PSIRT team and the details are under responsible disclosure.

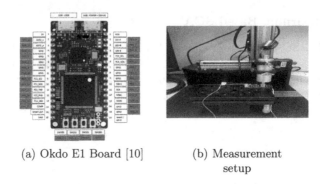

(a) Okdo E1 Board [10]   (b) Measurement
                                      setup

Fig. 1. Measurement setup for Okdo E1 development board.

While the trigger based on LED synchronises the traces, the trigger in itself is
$18.68\,\mu s$ but AES operation only takes 35 clock cycles which is about $0.35\,\mu s$.
On further analysis, we found that apart from I/O manipulation, the processor
also performs some key management task before the actual AES operation, causing a total execution time of $18.68\,\mu s$. The points corresponding to AES-128
operation only are thus determined by performing correlation power analysis on
side-channel traces with public information like plaintext and ciphertext. The
correlation peak corresponding to plaintext and ciphertext gives approximate
bounds on the AES operation, allows to significantly reduce the number of samples per trace by approximately $9\times$. Note that, the internal architecture of the
AES is not known and considered black box. Other techniques like normalised
inter-class variance (NICV [2]) can also be used.

3.1 Leakage Model

Since, the AES architecture is not known, it is hard to hypothesize the leakage
model. Based on available information, we know that its a hardware architecture
with 35 clock cyles. This means it is a parallel architecture which processes several bytes of the block per clock cycle. Previous works on hardware architecture
target the last round with Hamming distance model *i.e.* leakage corresponding
to state register being updated from last round input to output ciphertext [3].
However, given that 35 clock cycles also indicate that a complete round is not
processed in every clock cycle. Thus, we assume a weak leakage corresponding
to computation of last round Sbox. This is not optimal in hardware but still
requires less assumption on the underlying architecture which is always computed. The model can be written as Model 1: S-box$^{-1}[ct_i \oplus k^*]$, $i = 1, ..., 16$,
where S-box^{-1} indicate the inverse of AES S-box, ct_i, k^* mean the i-th byte of
ciphertext and the correct key respectively.

4   Experimental Results

In this section, we report the results of deep learning based side channel analysis for the OKdo E1 board. We measured 500, 000 traces corresponding to fixed key and random plaintext. All the analysis in this section are based on these traces.

4.1   Locating AES Activity

Since AES forms a small part of the triggered activity observed with toggling of the LED. We determine boundaries of the AES operation by computing correlation between traces and plaintext and ciphertext. As plaintext and ciphertext are first and last part of the computation respectively, activity corresponding to them will gives us bounds on AES activity in the trace. The result is shown in Fig. 2. The leakage of the plaintext and ciphertext is likely due to their transfer between main processor and hardware AES engine. For ciphertext, we observe leakage at 4 different instances, each time leaking 4 bytes. This indicate a 32-bit bus for data transfer between main processor and AES. The leakage of first, second, third, and fourth 32-bit words of ciphertexts was found between 12,000 and 14,000 points. The leakage of 16 plaintexts occurs at two instances respectively for first and last 8 bytes in Fig. 2b. This could be due to the loading of plaintext into hardware engine. The separate leakage of first 8 and last 8 bytes of the plaintext indicate a 64-bit architecture.

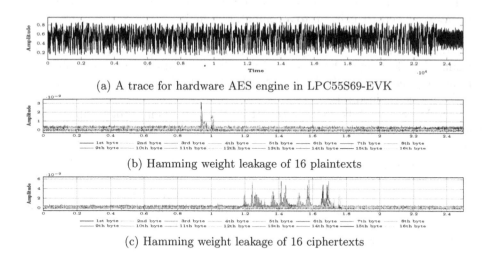

(a) A trace for hardware AES engine in LPC55S69-EVK

(b) Hamming weight leakage of 16 plaintexts

(c) Hamming weight leakage of 16 ciphertexts

Fig. 2. A trace of hardware AES engine and results for Hamming weight of plaintext and ciphertext.

4.2 Experimental Result for Deep Learning Based SCA

To perform a side-channel analysis based on deep learning, we use the state-of-the-art neural network structure of CHES 2020 [15]. More precisely, we consider the neural network structure as AES_HD structure since our main target is also hardware AES engine. As shown in Table 1, the CNN structure is quite simple.

Table 1. AES_HD architecture

Arch.	Convolution stage			MLP
	Filters	Kernel size	Pool size	
AES_HD	2	1	2	2

The attack is performed under a profiling setting. This means the adversary has access to a profiling or training dataset where the key and plaintext are known. The adversary then labels the dataset with the knowledge of key and plaintext and trains the deep learning architecture. Next, on the attack traces, where key is unknown, the unlabeled traces are queried against the trained model to predict the label. The predicted label for several traces are collected to determine the value of the secret key. The adversary then confirms the key with a known plaintext-ciphertext pair. In case, the attack is unable to find few key bytes, the attacker is able to brute force the remaining bytes using the known plaintext-ciphertext pair, up to a computation limit.

As stated earlier, the likely target leakage without much information on the hardware architecture can be tested with Model 1. We use Model 1 to label our training set, leading to 256 classes. Using 256 classes instead of commonly used Hamming weight of Model 1 (HW(Model 1)) will lead to an imbalanced dataset and must be avoided [11].

For Model 1, we take 45,000 traces (like [15]) as the number of profiling traces and 5,000 for the testing set. The testing set is unlabeled and queried against the trained model to predict labels which is then used for key recovery. The results are shown in Fig. 3a. It plots the guessing entropy of all the key bytes. A key byte is considered to be recovered, when the guessing entropy reaches minimum. In the current experiment, we can only recover 13 bytes of the 16 byte secret using all the 5,000 traces. As stated before, the remaining 3 bytes can be brute-forced using a known plaintext-ciphertext pair with a complexity of 2^{24}, which is easy to perform on a standard computer.

4.3 On the Power of Detailed Profiling

Now we consider a stronger attacker who has access to a bigger training dataset. For this, we used 200,000 traces for profiling. The rest of the experiments remain the same *i.e.* the unlabeled testing dataset is 5,000 traces and the labels are computed using Model 1. The results are shown in Fig. 4. As the deep learning

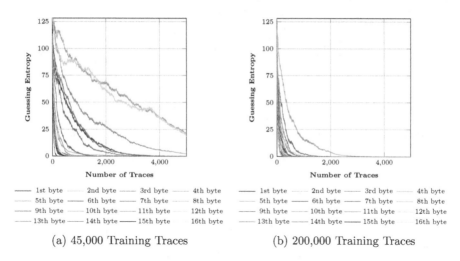

(a) 45,000 Training Traces   (b) 200,000 Training Traces

Fig. 3. Results of deep-learning based profiled SCA for 45,000 and 200,000 training dataset sizes.

model is now trained with a bigger training set, the attack in this case needs about 3,000 traces to recover the key. In fact, with less than 2,000 traces, 15 out of 16 bytes can be successfully recovered, leaving only one byte to guess. Care must be taken in choosing the training dataset size so as to not overfit the deep learning model.

4.4 Is Model 1 an Optimal Leakage Model

Finally, we verify if Model 1 actually fits well as the leakage model for the target black-box hardware engine. We performed correlation power analysis (CPA) in a known plaintext setting using all the 500,000 traces, with Model 1 as our leakage model. The results are shown in Fig. 4. The red line indicates the absolute correlation coefficient for correct key and the gray lines means the key candidates except for correct key. An attack is successful if red line stands out from all the grey lines. It can be observed that the attack is successful for only one byte (15th byte) and model Model 1 is not optimal for the given device. The brute force attack has to recover 15 bytes of the key which is beyond limit on standard computer, concluding the CPA to be unsuccessful.

Nevertheless, this highlights the power of deep learning based SCA. As shown previously, even without knowledge of the perfect model but only general information of the underlying architecture, deep learning based SCA could recover the key successfully.

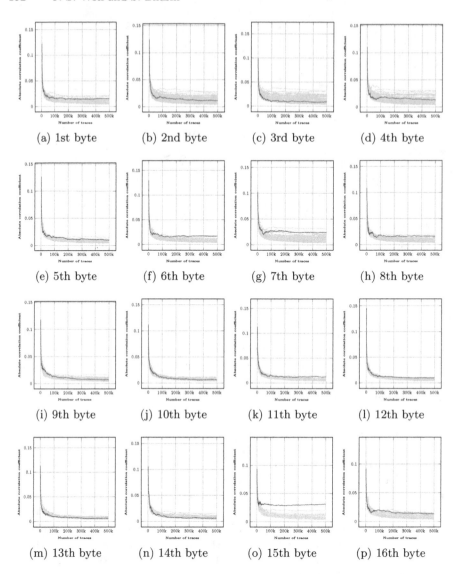

Fig. 4. CPA trend for 16 bytes. (Color figure online)

5   Conclusion

In this paper, we analyze the side-channel security of black box hardware AES engine integrated in NXP LPC55S69JBD100 microcontroller. The microcontroller is developed for security applications like point of sale. By minimum assumption on the AES architecture and considering a commonly manipulated sensitive value as leakage, we demonstrate successful attack using deep learning based SCA. The attack requires only 3,000 traces from the victim device when performed with a commonly known CNN architecture. We also confirmed that the leakage considered is not optimal for the architecture and could not recover the complete key using CPA. This demonstrates the advantages of using deep learning based SCA for targeting black box architecture. Further work can investigate precise leakage model and optimised CNN architecture for a worst case analysis on the underlying hardware AES.

Acknowledgement. We gratefully acknowledge the support of NVIDIA Corporation with the donation of the Titan XP GPU used for this research.

References

1. Benadjila, R., Prouff, E., Strullu, R., Cagli, E., Dumas, C.: Deep learning for side-channel analysis and introduction to ASCAD database. J. Cryptographic Eng. **10**(2), 163–188 (2019). https://doi.org/10.1007/s13389-019-00220-8
2. Bhasin, S., Danger, J.L., Guilley, S., Najm, Z.: NICV: normalized inter-class variance for detection of side-channel leakage. In: 2014 International Symposium on Electromagnetic Compatibility, Tokyo, pp. 310–313. IEEE (2014)
3. Bhasin, S., Guilley, S., Heuser, A., Danger, J.-L.: From cryptography to hardware: analyzing and protecting embedded Xilinx BRAM for cryptographic applications. J. Cryptographic Eng. **3**(4), 213–225 (2013). https://doi.org/10.1007/s13389-013-0048-4
4. Brier, E., Clavier, C., Olivier, F.: Correlation power analysis with a leakage model. In: Joye, M., Quisquater, J.-J. (eds.) CHES 2004. LNCS, vol. 3156, pp. 16–29. Springer, Heidelberg (2004). https://doi.org/10.1007/978-3-540-28632-5_2
5. Cagli, E., Dumas, C., Prouff, E.: Convolutional neural networks with data augmentation against jitter-based countermeasures. In: Fischer, W., Homma, N. (eds.) CHES 2017. LNCS, vol. 10529, pp. 45–68. Springer, Cham (2017). https://doi.org/10.1007/978-3-319-66787-4_3
6. Chari, S., Rao, J.R., Rohatgi, P.: Template attacks. In: Kaliski, B.S., Koç, K., Paar, C. (eds.) CHES 2002. LNCS, vol. 2523, pp. 13–28. Springer, Heidelberg (2003). https://doi.org/10.1007/3-540-36400-5_3
7. Doerr, C.: Side-channel based intrusion detection for industrial control systems. In: Critical Information Infrastructures Security: 12th International Conference, CRITIS 2017, Lucca, Italy, Revised Selected Papers, 8–13 October 2017, vol. 10707, p. 207. Springer (2018). https://doi.org/10.1007/978-3-319-99843-5_19
8. Kocher, P., Jaffe, J., Jun, B.: Differential power analysis. In: Wiener, M. (ed.) CRYPTO 1999. LNCS, vol. 1666, pp. 388–397. Springer, Heidelberg (1999). https://doi.org/10.1007/3-540-48405-1_25
9. Maghrebi, H., Portigliatti, T., Prouff, E.: Breaking cryptographic implementations using deep learning techniques. In: Carlet, C., Hasan, M.A., Saraswat, V. (eds.) SPACE 2016. LNCS, vol. 10076, pp. 3–26. Springer, Cham (2016). https://doi.org/10.1007/978-3-319-49445-6_1
10. NXP Semiconductors: UM11126 LPC55S6x/LPC55S2x/LPC552x User manual Rev. 1.8 - 24 October 2019. https://www.mouser.com/pdfDocs/NXP_LPC55S6x_UM.pdf
11. Picek, S., Heuser, A., Jovic, A., Bhasin, S., Regazzoni, F.: The curse of class imbalance and conflicting metrics with machine learning for side-channel evaluations. IACR Trans. Cryptographic Hardw. Embedded Syst. **2019**(1), 1–29 (2019)

12. Picek, S., Samiotis, I.P., Kim, J., Heuser, A., Bhasin, S., Legay, A.: On the perfor-
    mance of convolutional neural networks for side-channel analysis. In: Chattopad-
    hyay, A., Rebeiro, C., Yarom, Y. (eds.) SPACE 2018. LNCS, vol. 11348, pp. 157–
    176. Springer, Cham (2018). https://doi.org/10.1007/978-3-030-05072-6_10
13. Piret, G., Quisquater, J.-J.: A differential fault attack technique against SPN struc-
    tures, with application to the AES and KHAZAD. In: Walter, C.D., Koç, Ç.K., Paar,
    C. (eds.) CHES 2003. LNCS, vol. 2779, pp. 77–88. Springer, Heidelberg (2003).
    https://doi.org/10.1007/978-3-540-45238-6_7
14. Wu, L., Picek, S.: Remove some noise: on pre-processing of side-channel measure-
    ments with autoencoders. IACR Trans. Cryptographic Hardw. Embedded Syst.
    2020(4), 389–415 (2020)
15. Zaid, G., Bossuet, L., Habrard, A., Venelli, A.: Methodology for efficient CNN
    architectures in profiling attacks. IACR Trans. Cryptographic Hardw. Embedded
    Syst. **2020**(1), 1–36 (2020)

A New Method for Enhancing Software Effort Estimation by Using ANFIS-Based Approach

The-Anh Le[1,2], Quyet-Thang Huynh[1(✉)], Tran-Tuan-Nam Nguyen[1], and Minh-Hoa Tran Thi[3]

[1] School of Information and Communication Technology, Hanoi University of Science and Technology, Hanoi, Vietnam
thanghq@soict.hust.edu.vn
[2] Faculty of Information Technology, People's Police University, Bacninh, Vietnam
[3] University of Social Sciences and Humanities, VNU Hanoi, Hanoi, Vietnam

Abstract. The accurate estimation of the effort and cost becomes one of the important issues of project management. There are some algorithmic and non-algorithmic techniques are already developed to tackle the challenges of estimation tools in software project management such as Bayes probability-based approach, classification and regression, semantic analysis of software requirements, artificial neural networks, fuzzy logic, and hybrid methods. These techniques are unable to satisfy the management of modern and dynamic software development process. The aim of this paper is to propose a method of estimation by using the fuzzy logic's related functions and the fuzzy algorithm of the Adaptive Neuro-Fuzzy Inference System (ANFIS) model to improve the accuracy of Functional Point Analysis (FPA) to estimate the cost and effort of software development. A tool called ALBRE is also developed to support the calculation of the proposed method. Experimental results show that the proposed method based on the ANFIS model produces positive results, with less errors. The accuracy of VAF increases by up to 80% compared to the method proposed by Albrecht in Function Point Counting Practices Manual 4.2.1 by considering the Mean Magnitude of Relative Error (MMRE).

Keywords: ALBRE · Effort estimation · ANFIS · Function point · FPA · Software estimation · Neural-fuzzy

1 Introduction

The software industry has been developing rapidly in recent times, as a result, minimizing the development cost becomes a subject of interest [1]. Software development effort estimation is the process of evaluating the cost required to develop software in its early stages of development. It goes without saying that the more accurate estimation is, the more likely the project will succeed. Nevertheless, calculating accurate estimations is a difficult task [2]. Therefore, many software cost estimation models have been researched

© ICST Institute for Computer Sciences, Social Informatics and Telecommunications Engineering 2021
Published by Springer Nature Switzerland AG 2021. All Rights Reserved
N.-S. Vo et al. (Eds.): INISCOM 2021, LNICST 379, pp. 195–210, 2021.
https://doi.org/10.1007/978-3-030-77424-0_16

and developed for decades such as COCOMO, COCOMO II, UCP, SLIM, and FPA [2–4]. The methods provide an algorithmic model in the form of steps and calculation formulas drawn from the study of historical data of projects.

In recent years, the application of FPA has also been strongly researched and developed in many companies, organizations, and software enterprises. In 2009, NESMA published a document that applied FPA to the later phase of the project at maintenance and improvement phases with many positive results [22]. David W. Russel et al. [20] designed a variant of FPA to estimate software costs. The value of 14 GSC is adjusted to suit the specific settings. Archana Srivastava [21] changed the way to calculate VAF by adding the end-user programming with the same calculation as the VAF but with 16 GSC elements and new weighting with 0–5 weighting range. This has enabled freelance programmers or those who want to develop their own applications to estimate the exact cost of the application without having to know the entire system [21]. E. Praynlin and P. Latha [25] applied ANFIS to COCOMO estimation method of effort multiplier, the goal is to select the appropriate membership function through price MMRE treatment. The comparative results concluded that the paper selected the trapezoid function to give the lowest MMRE [25]. Shivakumar [23] proposed to apply ANFIS to the Class Point method to estimate software costs. The authors in [27] proposed the method that applied the modified ANFIS to improve effort estimation results and achieve accuracy up to 96% with training data and 89% with test data. Al-Hajri et al. [24] set up a new system of FP parameters using neural networks. The results were quite accurate although the correlation was still unsatisfactory with MMRE above 100%, derived from the wide variety of data points with much noise. Empirical studies by Abran and Robillard [26] show each relationship between the main part of FPA and effort. They proposed a model to use FPA in combination with ANFIS to make each relationship with effort. Therefore, effort estimation is supposed to be fateful because it is an infrequent, unique task with underestimation bias and different goals [3]. There are some factors that may impact the efficiency of software engineering such as product complexity, quality requirements, time pressure, process capability, team distribution, interrupts, feature churn, tools, and programming language [4]. The main purpose of this paper is to design an early effort estimating method based on FPA using ANFIS with customized Albrecht dataset to improve Function Point Counting Practices Manual 4.3.1 equation [6], compare between ANFIS model 6 membership functions to choose the best one and calculate the Value Adjustment Factor (VAF) of a specific software project with FPA by using results of the research.

The rest of this paper is organized as follows: In Sect. 2, the literature review will be presented. The proposed model and dataset description will be discussed in Sect. 3. In Sect. 4 and 5, the results and discussion of the proposed model will be presented.

2 Literature Review

2.1 Function Points Analysis (FPA)

Function points are proposed by a team under Allan Albrecht at IBM which is published in a book in 1979 [5, 10]. Albrecht states that function points are "an effective relative measure of function value delivered to our customer" [5]. Researchers have also found a strong relationship between the amount of function points and work effort. Function Points Analysis (FPA) is a common method for effort estimation [17]. It has many objectives and benefits that can be used as a vehicle to estimate the cost and resources during the phases of software development and maintenance.

Step 1. Determining the Unadjusted Function Point (UFP).

The UFP is a term used to describe the information of the specific countable functionality of the project or application to the user. The specific user functionality is evaluated what is delivered by the application, not how it is delivered. Only user-requested and defined components are counted with two types of functions: data types (Data Functions) and transactional types (Transactional Functions). Each of them is evaluated by assigning one of these three functional complexities: Low, Average and High. This calculation also depends on the quantity of each types-data and they will be translated to UFP. Table 1 will interpret this transformation. The total of these five UFPs will determine the overall UFP of this step.

Table 1. Transformation of functions to UFP

No	Type of functions		Functional complexity		
			Low	Average	High
1	*Transactional Functions*	External Input	3	4	6
2		External Output	4	5	7
3		External Inquiry	3	4	6
4	*Data Functions*	Internal Logical File	7	10	13
5		External Interface File	5	7	10

Step 2. Determining the Value Adjustment Factor (VAF).

The UFP will be adjusted by 14 technical factors or 14 General System Characteristics (GSC). These GSC will be interpreted in the Table 2 below with their brief description [5, 10].

$$VAF = (TDI \times 0,01) + 0,65 \tag{1}$$

There are 6 system influences, rated from to 5 to evaluate the weight of each GSC. These weights will be described in Table 3. In this research, we believe our VAF calculation will be at higher accuracy than the Eq. (2). The method will be demonstrated in later sections.

Table 2. General system characteristics

	General system characteristics	Brief description
1	Data communications	How many communication facilities are there to aid in the transfer or exchange of information with the application or system?
2	Distributed data processing	How are distributed data and processing functions handled?
3	Performance	Did the user require response time or throughput?
4	Heavily used configuration	How heavily used is the current hardware platform where the application will be executed?
5	Transaction rate	How frequently are transactions executed daily, weekly, monthly, etc.?
6	On-Line data entry	What percentage of the information is entered On-Line?
7	End-user efficiency	Was the application designed for end-user efficiency?
8	On-Line update	How many ILF's are updated by On-Line transactions?
9	Complex processing	Does the application have extensive logical or mathematical processing?
10	Reusability	Was the application developed to meet one or many user's needs?
11	Installation ease	How difficult are conversion and installation?
12	Operational ease	How effective and/or automated are start-up, backup, and recovery procedures?
13	Multiple sites	Was the application specifically designed, developed and supported to be installed and multiple sites for multiple organizations?
14	Facilitate change	Was the application specifically designed, developed and supported to facilitate change?

Step 3. Overall calculation – determining the Development project Function Point count (DFP).

The final calculation of the FPA process can be calculated by the following equation:

$$DFP = UFP \times VAF \tag{2}$$

Where DFP is the Development project Function Point count, UFP is Unadjusted Function Point and VAF is Value Adjustment Factor.

The FPA evaluation method is based on the opinion of the end-user, outside domain of the considering system, hence, the FPA is not depended on the technology used in the

Table 3. Degree of influence

Score as	System influence
0	Not present or no influence
1	Incidental influence
2	Moderate influence
3	Average influence
4	Significant influence
5	Strong influence throughout

system and not required the detail description of the system. It can be applied in the early stage of system development which based only on the system specification from the user so the project can be estimated and planned correctly. This will help the project manager in terms of cost management and control [8]. However, the FPA cannot be calculated automatically because of the end-user opinion-based method. Every input of the process is depended on the sense of the user and sometimes it is vague and imprecise. This can be adjusted by the user as an expert or a specialist. Thus, the FPA is a strong method for the design of the function-oriented system but it is not recommended for object-oriented systems design or scientific system with complicated algorithms and calculations [8].

2.2 Fuzzy Logic Membership Function

2.2.1 Classical Logic, Classical Set and Its Problems

Classical logic is used in the daily life of a human with only 2 values in opposition such as "no" – "yes", "0" – "1", "true" – "false", etc. In mathematics, the classical logic comes with the classical set. There are only 2 states of an element, "belong" or "not belong" to a specific set which is presented by the symbol $\in$ and $\notin$. By considering a membership function with an element x and a set A, the relationship of this logic will be interpreted by the following equation.

$$\mu A(x) = \begin{cases} 1 \ if \ x \in A \\ 0 \ if \ x \notin A \end{cases} 0 \le \mu A(x) \le 1 \qquad (3)$$

Hence, classical logic is absolute. However, if the other number sets, for instance, a set B is a set that contains rational numbers which are less than 9 and a set B' is a set that contain also rational numbers but much less than 9 or if the set of tall, average and short people are considered, there will be a problem. Is 1.51 m average enough, is 1.72 m tall enough. At this time, the classical logic is useless due to its limitation can never be cover all of the life situations of human. Human technology such as self-drive technology, artificial intelligence or human creative activities, the classical logic cannot support them to operate. Especially the machine learning technology, the knowledge is plenty of vague, uncertain situations with fuzziness in semantics and the machine needs an absoluteness. Thus, they cannot understand. That is the reason why fuzzy logic is needed to confront fuzzy problems. With fuzzy logic, the problem of the air-conditional, self-drive car and machine learning is resolved.

2.2.2 Fuzzy Logic, Fuzzy Set

Fuzzy logic is used to adjust the absoluteness of classical logic. If the classical logic states the certain theses as 100% or 0%, the fuzzy logic states the uncertain. Fuzzy logic is used to solve difficult problems that cannot be handled by a mathematical model due to its complex or unfeasible to construct. It is also applied to reduce the complexity of existing solutions and increase the accessibility of direct hypothesis [16]. The development of software has been measured by parameters that possess a certain level of fuzziness [18]. The fuzzy logic is applied to solve the problems that are inherent in existing effort estimation techniques [19].

In general, we can only give probabilistic rules for certain cases that are relatively perfect and cannot give only one rule to just one case. Now the rules are used together for continuous overlapping cases and what people do is perfect, round or approximate them. Combining rules can be typical when cases are repeated with the same or approximate state. People can do that through the flexibility of the language used to create rules as well as abstract thinking, logic coming from the human brain. However, that does not mean that we cannot use mathematics to model fuzzy logic theory. As shown in Sect. 2.2.1 on classical logic, we can use the membership functions to represent fuzzy logic theory. Membership function associates each point in the fuzzy set a real number in the interval [0,1] is called degree or grade of membership. Several types of fuzzy membership functions including Triangular, Gaussian bell, Trapezoidal, Sigma, S function and the function of Z. Among them, Triangular, Gaussian, and Trapezoidal are commonly used in software estimation models. These equations below will interpret the general type of membership function [11, 14].

$$\mu(x) = \begin{cases} \frac{x-l_1}{m-l_1}, & x \in [l_1, m] \\ \frac{l_2-x}{l_2-m}, & x \in [m, l_2] \\ 0, & x \notin [l_1, l_2] \end{cases} \qquad (4)$$

Where l_1 is the left boundary value of membership, m is the value of capital and l_2 is the right limit membership value ($l_1 < m < l_2$). Since all information contained in a fuzzy set is described by its membership function, it is useful to develop a lexicon of terms to describe various special features of this function [9]. This is a firm base for ANFIS training and represents the sense of "fuzzy", modeling from reality to logic model.

2.3 Anfis

ANFIS is an integrated model of Fuzzy Inference System (FIS) with Neural networks [12]. A generic rule in a Sugeno fuzzy pattern has the form: If Input1 $=$ x and Input 2 $=$ y, then output is z $=$ ax $+$ by $+$ c [12].

It needs 7 constrains:

Single output, defuzzied by the average center of weight method.

Membership functions of output must be the same type, linear or constant.

The number of output membership function and the number of the rule must be equal.

Each rule has its particular weight.

FIS structure will have an error if these constraints above are not satisfied.

Fuzzy membership functions and defuzzied method cannot be created by the user.

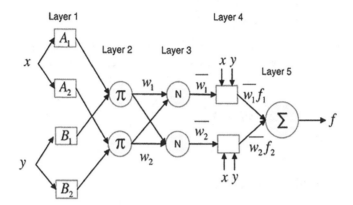

Fig. 1. ANFIS structure

ANFIS is a hybrid supervised method that leverages a hybrid learning algorithm to determine the parameters for fuzzy inference systems. It utilizes the least-squares method and propagation gradient descent method which is used for training FIS membership function parameters to investigate the given training data set. ANFIS can be executed by using an optional argument for model validation. This is called checking the model for overfitting. The argument used for this is called checking data set. The key is finding the FIS rule base. FIS converts human knowledge into a rule base in order to maximize performance and minimize the model error output [13]. ANFIS structure is described in Fig. 1.

The function of each node is described as follows:

Layer 1 Each node k in a square layer node with the function:

$$O_k^1 = \mu_{A_k}(x) \quad k = 1, 2 \tag{5}$$

$$O_k^1 = \mu_{B_{k-2}}(y) \quad k = 3, 4 \tag{6}$$

Where x, y is the input of node k, and A_k, B_k is a fuzzy set of rating the node function. O_k^1 is a membership function that determines the degree of membership B_{k-2} and A_k.

Layer 2 Each node labeled Π is a multiplier value, used AND operator to fuzzily inputs.

$$O_k^2 = w_k = \mu_{A_k}(x) \times \mu_{B_{k-2}}(y) \tag{7}$$

Layer 3 Normalized firing strength. Each node labeled N is calculated by taking the ratio of the k-th rule firing strength of the overall total of all rules firing strength.

$$O_k^4 = \overline{w}_k f_k = \overline{w}_k CD_{ik} \tag{8}$$

Layer 4 Setting the consequent parameters. Each node k in a square layer node with function:

$$O_k^4 = \overline{w}_k f_k = \overline{w}_k (p_k x + q_k y + r_k) \quad k = 1, 2 \tag{9}$$

where $\overline{w}_k$ is the output of Layer 3 and $p_k x + q_k y + r_k$ is the consequent parameters.

Layer 5 There is a single node with symbol Σ which calculates the overall output of the incoming signal. This stage is also called defuzzification.

$$O_k^5 = \sum_k \overline{w}_k f_k = \frac{\sum_k w_k f_k}{\sum_k w_k} \tag{10}$$

3 The Proposed Approach

3.1 Approach Description

According to Eq. (1), the calculation and estimation of the project cost based on FPA estimation depend on the two parameters UFP and VAF. These are the two factors that can cause relatively high errors in the cost and effort estimation. In this study, the VAF parameter will be fine-tuned to minimize errors through ANFIS in order to reduce the cost bias. The VAF value is calculated based on 14 GSC factors with the weights of DI influence (0–5). These DIs will also be tuned for accuracy in this study. To fine-tune the deviation of VAF, we use the adaptive neural-fuzzy network ANFIS to blur the VAF value calculated by Eq. (1). At the same time, the values of DI will also be improved through the introduction of a set of questions that are more semantically clear than the given CPM documents and Albrecht's research results.

The approaching model is illustrated in Fig. 2 below.

ANFIS is suitable for use in the proposal of this study. ANFIS learns from historical data sets and adjusts to minimize the factors that cause errors between the training model and real data of organizations. Users can provide the parameters of previous projects as input to ANFIS and from the training results, they can consider and select the most suitable results. The strength of ANFIS over conventional neural networks is its adaptability. ANFIS does not have a fixed model structure as a basis for the attributes of the variables in the system so users no need to know about the core technical issues nor waste time and effort to monitor the training process. However, ANFIS, like other neural networks, requires data from the past that is large enough to underpin an effective learning process. The greater the amount of data to learn, the more ANFIS will have accurate and closest calculations to reality.

The objective of the MMRE value achieved is minimum. For MMRE, it is calculated through MRE according to the following two-equation [7]. The relative error compared

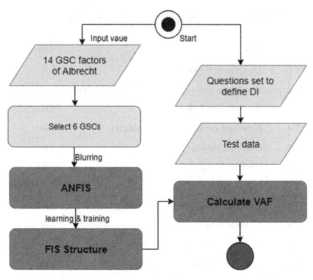

Fig. 2. Workflow of Software Effort Estimation by using ANFIS-based Approach

to the actual (5) and (6) average relative error. The algorithm for this method consists of 4 steps.

$$MRE_i = \frac{|Actual\ Effort_i - Estimated\ Effort_i|}{Actual\ Effort_i} \tag{11}$$

$$MMRE = \frac{1}{n} \sum_i^n MRE_i \tag{12}$$

Step 1. Reduce the Number of Input Values from 14 to 6 GSC

The reduction in numbers helps reduce ANFIS execution time as well as reduce resource utilization and exceed the computational power of the system. However, the VAF results remain the same to ensure that the inference from Eq. (1) does not change when ANFIS is trained. In fact, training with a data set of 5 GSCs takes only 15 min but when increasing to 6, the training time is 12 times. Based on recent research results, UCP estimation when comparing each GSC and based on practical experience, we choose 6 GSCs: 2, 3, 7, 9, 10 and 13. They are Distributed Data Processing (GSC2), Performance (GSC3), End-User Performance (GSC7), Complex Processing (GSC9), Reusability (GSC10), and Multi-Platform (GSC13). In the UCP estimation, the 13 factors and their weights, outlined in Table 4 below, affect the TCF value of a project under UCP. The 6 factors that are relevant and compared with the 6 GSCs are in bold.

Table 4. Technical Complexity Factor (TCF)

Factor	Description	Weight
T1	**Distributed system**	**2.0**
T2	**Response time/performance objectives**	**1.0**
T3	**End-user efficiency**	**1.0**
T4	**Internal processing complexity**	**1.0**
T5	**Code reusability**	**1.0**
T6	Easy to install	0.5
T7	Easy to use	0.5
T8	**Portability to other platforms**	**2.0**
T9	System maintenance	1.0
T10	Concurrent/parallel processing	1.0
T11	Includes special security objectives	1.0
T12	Provides direct access for third parties	1.0
T13	Special user training facilities are required	1.0

Step 2. Fuzzy 6 DI Values of 6 GSCs

6 DI values and VAF results calculated according to Eq. (1) will be put into ANFIS to implement fuzzy and training with different related functions according to 3 fuzzy language variables "small", "medium" and "large". From the recommendations and scoring criteria of CPM, this study will provide a more explicit set of questions and answers to assist the estimator. At the same time, the responses are weighted according to the CPM but will be relatively blurred through the statistical method of Albrecht's project data sets. The blurring is done by statistics across 240 projects, considering the percentage of occurrences of influences from 0 to 5. The calculation is rounded to 2 decimal places and the compensation is selected (Table 5).

Table 5. Statistics of the frequency offset ratio of DI of 6 GSCs

DI/GSC	2	3	7	9	10	13
0	0,98	0,97	0,92	0,83	0,83	0,83
1	0,82	0,94	0,88	0,87	0,78	0,63
2	0,7	0,76	0,69	0,78	0,76	0,75
3	0,69	0,74	0,62	0,72	0,8	0,88
4	0,85	0,79	0,88	0,86	0,88	0,93
5	0,97	0,8	0,99	0,93	0,94	0,98

$$DI = \text{Point } i \text{ is given by } CPM \times d \tag{13}$$

Where d is % of the compensation of the occurrence of point I.

Step 3. Estimate VAF Values

From the FIS data of ANFIS training in step 2 and the values in the data set, VAF values will be estimated using a new method. The ANFIS input values are 18 fuzzy sets of 6 GSCs and 3 linguistic variables. The output is the VAF value required. Thus, ANFIS will develop a total of 36 or 729 rules according to the "if-then" format as shown in the Table 6 below.

Table 6. The truth table of the ruleset

Input 1	Input 2	Input 3	Input 4	Input 5	Input 6	Output
Small	Small	Small	Small	Small	Small	Small
...	...	...	...	...	...	...
Small	Small	Large	Large	Small	Small	Medium
...	...	...	...	...	...	...
Large	Large	Large	Large	Large	Large	Large

Step 4. Use the VAF to Calculate Effort

After the VAF value has been calculated and with the UFP value available, we proceed to calculate the DPF value according to Eq. (2).

$$Effort = -13, 39 + 0, 0545 \times DFP \tag{14}$$

3.2 Dataset Description

Albrecht dataset is a famous and reliable dataset. It is an excel file sized 15×250 contained 240 actual software projects, estimated follow FPA method. Thus, it is included 14 columns of 14 GSCs and 1 column of VAF-calculated by Eq. (1). ANFIS requires a dataset for training as input and export the result to a test dataset as an output. The input is created by separating the original dataset–Albrecht dataset sized 15×240 into 3 types of a smaller train-test dataset, named A, B, and C, which will be interpreted as in Table 7.

Each dataset is considered as a metric of m x n. The training dataset will take more than the test dataset 1 column of VAF. The purpose of the train datasets is to 'teach' ANFIS with their input (GSCs) and output (VAF) then apply the knowledge (FIS) to calculate the output VAF with given GSCs in the test dataset. Reminded that the test and FIS metric columns must be exactly the same and the FIS will calculate only 1 project as its size of the row. These VAFs are the final results of this study that we are expected. Grouping the original 14 GSCs into smaller groups is considered because of the problem's complexity and computer capability issues. During the experiment,

Table 7. Dataset separation

#	Dataset	Size	Type	GSCs
1	A	6×70	Train	1–5
2		5×40	Test	
3		6×70	Train	6–10
4		5×40	Test	
5		6×70	Train	11–14
6		5×40	Test	
7	B	7×70	Train	2, 3, 7, 9, 10, 13
8		6×50	Test	
9	C	7×120	Train	
10		6×120	Test	

ANFIS cannot generate rules or 'learn' if the number of columns is greater than 8 or 9 due to the fact that a more powerful computer is required and the training time will also significantly increase, for example: training a dataset with 5 columns took 15 min, whereas training a dataset with 6 columns took 3 h, which means it possibly took up to 4 h to train with 7 columns. On the other hand, 2–4 grouping-columns are considered too few inputs for the result to be accurate. Therefore, 5 and 6 grouping-column has been chosen for this study (see step 2 in Sect. 3.1, Table 4).

In Table 7, the TCF and FPA have correlative factors with GSC2-T1, GSC3-T2, GSC7-T3, GSC9-T4, GSC10-T5, GSC13-T8, and factor T1 and T8 have the highest weight of 2 and the other weight of 1. It is believed that grouping 6 above GSCs can give out highly accurate results. As the pairing correlative factors above, there would be a considered pair: GSC11-T6, GSC12-T7 each has a weight of 0,5. Therefore, GSC11 and GSC12 have been eliminated from the grouping. It is reasonable to eliminate the remaining 6 GSCs, by studying the Albrecht dataset 150/240, it means that 62,5% projects are rated 0 or 1 with GSC14. So, GSC14 has also been eliminated. GSC6 and GSC8 are mostly applicable to online applications, which do not seem to be significant to every application, so we also eliminated these 2 GSCs. Besides, GSC1, GSC4, GSC5 can be chosen to replace any GSC from 6 chosen GSCs above (except GSC2 and GSC13). Therefore 6 GSCs that have been mentioned will be chosen as the basis of the dataset for this study (Fig. 3).

3.3 ANFIS Training

Firstly, in this study, every 10 datasets would be the input of ANFIS for training and testing with 6 different types of membership function, with 40, 60, 80, 90 and 100 epochs. Secondly, ANFIS will 'learn' through these training datasets then will generate rules and membership function parameters. Finally, ANFIS finishes training and generates the FIS file by grid partitioning method. The file was used for estimating the projects, which are numbers of the row in the test dataset and give the result as VAF value. It takes 3 h to obtain the expectation in the training. In the first stage, we conducted ANFIS training by using data from the previous stage. The training process allows the system to adjust the parameters as input/output. This process stops when the number of epochs is reached, or the number of error-rates achieved. In the second stage, a vector is created with the number of dimensions N where N is the number of membership functions that contains the parameters of membership functions. In each iteration, one of the parameters of the membership function will be updated [15]. Based on what ANFIS has studied, it will generate the VAF result with each project (row) in the test dataset. The FIS structure will show the result of the ANFIS training process, including the model of 36 fuzzy rules and a model of input and output of the structure. The simulation is conducted in MATLAB R2016a, Windows 10, 4 GB of RAM and INTEL Pentium G4400 3.3 GHz CPU. These following figures and tables will interpret the FIS structure (Table 8).

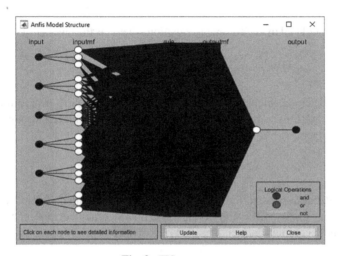

Fig. 3. FIS structure

3.4   ALBRE- Tool for Effort Estimation

ALBRE application is developed on MATLAB R2016a IDE. It is easy to deploy in an enterprise environment, company, small and medium organization. Individuals can also use the application to self-estimate the cost but requires a certain knowledge of software engineering. The main functions will be presented in this section: VAF Calculation, UFP Calculation, DI Calculation, Question set. Users can enter data into numeric fields in a variety of ways and perform calculations. In particular, entering data through the question set will have its own interface.

4   Results and Discussion

Evaluating the accuracy of estimation can be done by comparing the results of the production effort and the actual effort to calculate MRE (Magnitude of Relative Error) [7].

Table 8. The overall data of the training process with Gauss membership function

FIS structure	Number of inputs	6
	Number of outputs	1
	Type of membership function input	Gauss
	Type of membership function output	Linear
	Total fuzzy rule	729
Training structure	Number of epochs	80
	Error tolerance	0
Learning method		Hybrid
Training time		3 h

MRE can be calculated by the following equation where i is the number of observations:

$$MRE_i = \frac{|Actual\ Effort_i - Estimated\ Effort_i|}{Actual\ Effort_i} \tag{15}$$

The MRE value is calculated for each observation whose effort is estimated. The aggregation of MRE over multiple observations (N) can be achieved through the mean MMRE as follows:

$$MMRE = \frac{1}{n}\sum_i^n MRE_i \tag{16}$$

The Table 9 below presents the MMRE values for the set of inputs Tripmf and Gbellmf which has a very low MMRE value compared to all other membership functions with a group of 5 and 6 columns dataset.

Table 9. MMRE for various membership function with a group of 5 and 6 columns dataset

Membership function	MMRE (group 5)	Epochs	MMRE (group 6)	Epochs
trimf	0.1203	40	0.2309	40
trapmf	0.2965	60	0.2862	60
gbellmf	0.1259	80	0.4594	100
gaussmf	0.1183	100	0.2183	80
gauss2mf	0.2767	90	0.3690	90
pimf	–	–	0.3735	100

MMRE value of 0.1183 and 0.2183 for the Gaussian curve membership function is the lowest among all the membership functions of 2 groups prediction is based on available data. If there are errors in the actual data, then the result's accuracy will be affected. The fuzzification is based on certain membership functions. The selection of a particular membership function depends on the nature of data value to be used. If the selected membership function is incorrect, the input fuzzy data will be wrong and as a result, the output fuzzy data will also be wrong and the defuzzied output data will be imprecise and the error rate will be very high. Hence the selection of membership functions plays a very important role in the Estimation model.

5 Conclusion and Future Work

Software effort estimation involves dealing with the uncertainty of inputs. ANFIS is able to handle this uncertainty, and selecting correct membership functions plays a crucial role in effort estimation. Comparison between membership functions such as the Gaussian curve, Gaussian combination membership, and generalized bell-shaped membership, Trapezoidal membership and Triangular membership was done. The results show the Gaussian curve membership function has produced the smallest MMRE value compared to the other member function. The purpose of this study is to identify the membership function is to be used in ANFIS and give the most accurate effort estimation and claim the improvement of the Function Point Counting Practices Manual 4.2.1 equation (Eq. (2)). The proposed method is effective in estimating the cost development of new software. However, the current study was limited by computer capability issues and still has much remained to be improved. The study can point out the representation of this 6 selected GCSs but still cannot be 100% precise about the limitation of the random columns above. MATLAB is not a good platform for developing interfaces and applications, so it is very limited in targeting users, although it is heavily used in science or in a fuzzy neural network. by the simulation capabilities.

For future works, similar studies can be done to estimate software cost based on fuzzy logic and neural network by using ANFIS such as:

1) Analyzing the performance of the model by varying the number of epochs, the number of membership functions.
2) Analysis can also be done using an artificially generated dataset.
3) Another improvement for training by ANFIS to gain a higher VAF accuracy.

Acknowledgments. This research is funded by Hanoi University of Science and Technology under Grant number T2018-TĐ-009.

References

1. Grimstad, S., Jorgensen, M.: The impact of irrelevant information on estimates of software development effort. In: Proceedings of the 2007 Australian Software Engineering Conference, ASWEC 2007, pp. 359–368. IEEE Computer Society (2007)
2. Chulani, S.: Bayesian analysis of software cost and quality models. Ph.D. Dissertation, University of Southern California, Los Angeles (1999)

3. Sinhal, A., Verma, B.: Software development effort estimation: a review. Int. J. Adv. Res. Comput. Sci. Softw. Eng. **III**(6), 1120–1135 (2013)
4. Bourque, P., Fairley, R., (eds.): SWEBOK 3.0: Guide to the Software Engineering Body of Knowledge. IEEE Computer Society Press (2014)
5. Albrecht, A.J.: Measuring application development productivity. In: Proceedings of the Joint SHARE, GUIDE, and IBM Application Development Symposium, Monterey, California, 14–17 October, pp. 83–92. IBM Corporation (1979)
6. Timp, A.: Function point counting practices manual. International Function Point Users Group (2010). Release 4.3.1. ISBN 978-0-9753783-4-2
7. Foss, T., Stensrud, E., Kitchenham, B., Myrtveit, L.: A simulation study of the model evaluation criterion MMRE. IEEE Trans. Softw. Eng. **29**, 985–995 (2003)
8. Thang, H.Q.: Software Engineering Economics. Hanoi University of Science and Technology Publishing House (2016). (in Vietnamese)
9. Ross, T.J.: Fuzzy Logic with Engineering Applications, 3 ed, 606 p. Wiley (2010)
10. Jones, C.: Software economics and function point metrics. In: Thirty years of IFPUG Progress. http://www.ifpug.org/wp-content/uploads/2017
11. Kaur, M.: A fuzzy logic approach to software development effort estimation. Int. J. Adv. Res. Dev. **3**(1), 125–127 (2018). ISSN 2455-4030
12. Iraji, M.S.: Hypermedia web software effort estimate with adaptive neuro fuzzy inference system. J. Theoret. Appl. Inf. Technol. **93**(1), 133–142 (2016). ISSN 1992-8645
13. Bedi, R.P.S., Singh, A.: Software cost estimation using fuzzy logic technique. Indian J. Sci. Technol. **10**(3), 1–5 (2017)
14. Batra, G., Trivedi, M.: A fuzzy approach for software effort estimation. Int. J. Cybern. Inform. (IJCI) **2**(1), 9–15 (2013)
15. Sweta, K., Shashankar, P.: Comparison and analysis of different software cost estimation methods. Int. J. Adv. Comput. Sci. Appl. (IJACSA) **4**(1), 153–157 (2013)
16. Razaz, M., King, J.: Introduction to Fuzzy Logic - Information Systems - Signal and Image Processing Group (2004). http://www.sys.uea.ac.uk/king/restricted/boads/
17. Symons, C.R.: Function point analysis: difficulties and improvements. IEEE Trans. Softw. Eng. **14**(1), 2–11 (1988)
18. Moon Ting, S., Ling, T., Phang, K., Liew, C., Man, P.: Enhanced software development effort and cost estimation using fuzzy logic model. Malaysian J. Comput. Sci. **20**(2), 199–207 (2007)
19. Agustin Gutierrez, T., Cornelio Yanez, M., Pasquier, J.L.: Software development effort estimation using fuzzy logic: a case study. In: Proceedings of the Sixth Mexican International Conference on Computer Science (ENC 2005) (2005)
20. Russell, D.: A metric for rating the effectiveness of industrial automation systems using a derivative of function point analysis. Robot. Comput.-Integr. Manuf. **26**(6), 551–557 (2010)
21. Srivastava, A., Qamar Abbas, S., Singh, S.K.: Enhancement in function point analysis. Int. J. Softw. Eng. Appl. (IJSEA) **3**(6), 129–136 (2012)
22. NESMA: Function point analysis for software enhancement guidelines version 2.2.1 (2009)
23. Shivakumar, N., Balaji, N., Ananthakumar, K.: A neuro fuzzy algorithm to compute software effort estimation. Glob. J. Comput. Sci. Technol.: C, **16**(1) (2016). Version 1.0
24. Mokri, F.D., Molani, M.: Software cost estimation using adaptive neuro fuzzy inference system. Int. J. Acad. Res. Comput. Eng. **1**(1), 34–39 (2016)
25. Praynlin, E., Latha, P.: Estimating development effort of software projects using ANFIS. In: International Conference on Recent Trends in Computational Methods. Communication and Controls, Ongole, Andhra Pradash, India, pp. 15–20 (2012)
26. Abran, A., Robillard, P.N.: Function points analysis: an empirical study of its measurement processes. IEEE Trans. Softw. Eng. **22**(12), 895–910 (1996). https://doi.org/10.1109/32.553638
27. Mokri, F.D., Molani, M.: Software cost estimation using adaptive neuro fuzzy inference system. Inter. J. Acad. Res. Comp. Eng. **1**(1), 34–39 (2016)

A New Method to Improve Quality Predicting of Software Project Completion Level

The-Anh Le[1,2], Quyet-Thang Huynh[1(✉)], and Thanh-Hung Nguyen[1]

[1] School of Information and Communication Technology, Hanoi University of Science and Technology, Hanoi, Vietnam
{thanghq,hungnt}@soict.hust.edu.vn
[2] Faculty of Information Technology, People's Police University, Bacninh, Vietnam

Abstract. Earned Value Management (EVM) is a powerful tool for estimating costs and evaluating a software project. Many methods have been used to improve the effectiveness of EVM in evaluating a software project, in which the method of applying the Gompertz growth model (GGM) is one of the effective directions. The paper studies the method of combining the Gompertz growth model and the earned value management method (GGM-EVM) to predict the cost to complete the software project. The team experimented with modeling a number of software project data sets in practice, running and testing and analyzing the results. Several improvements have been proposed to increase the effectiveness of the GGM-EVM method, resulting in relatively positive research results.

Keywords: Project management · EVM · Growth models · Gompertz

1 Introduction

Earned value management (EVM) is one of the well-known techniques for controlling the time and cost of a project [1, 6]. This method is based on a set of metrics to measure and evaluate the overall health of a project in order to provide an early warning to the project administrator of project problems. However, this method has some limitations such as: based only on past costs, the prediction lacks reliability in the early stage of the project and does not take into account forecasting statistics [6]. These three limitations are the main reason for the development of new methods [1, 6]. One of the methods is the use of linear or nonlinear regression analyzes to develop regression models, also known as GM-Growth Models [2].

Currently, there are many models that predict the cost of completion of a project, as well as models that predict the end of a project. Different models have been adequately studied and compared with Batselier, J et al. In [4]. Some related studies using EVM method can be mentioned as: Khamooshi and Golafshani (2014) in [5] proposed new method EDM improved than most ESM methods, while Lipke and Watt (2011) in [6] and Elshaer (2013) in [7] extended the old ESM method which was very effective in the early phase of the project, but less effective in the later stages of the project. The authors

N.-S. Vo et al. (Eds.): INISCOM 2021, LNICST 379, pp. 211–219, 2021.
https://doi.org/10.1007/978-3-030-77424-0_17

Narbaev T.; De Marco A. (2014) [3] proposed a method that combines growth models and EVM methods for some positive results.

There are a number of studies related to project completion time forecasting and project completion cost prediction by applying different performance factors in the combined growth model and EVM approach to improve forecast quality [4, 6, 8]. Each of the models above has its own advantages and disadvantages and is applicable to specific datasets. In the framework of this paper, we focus on research on growth model Gompertz and apply on the data of real projects in [9]. We inherit the results of the methods that have been studied in the article [2, 4, 8] by testing and evaluating the experimental results, then propose to improve the value management technique to obtain the results with Gompertz growth model to improve the quality of project completion prediction. [10] proposed a method for improvement the parameter estimation of non-linear regression in growth model to predict project cost at completion.

The next content in the paper is presented as follows: Sect. 2 presents the value management method and growth model Gompertz; Sect. 3 presents project completion cost estimation and proposes I-GGM methodology to improve predictive quality; Sect. 4 presents project completion time prediction and suggested improved I-Regression method; Finally, in Sect. 5 presents conclusions, scientific contributions and development directions of the next research.

2 Background

2.1 The Earned Value Management Method

UML is most generally used to provide a standard way to visualize a system's design and is also widely used for test case generations. There are many types of research in recent years about various techniques for generating test cases from UML diagrams.

Earned Value Management is an efficient tool used to predict project completion time and cost based on current project status. EVM has 06 main parameters as follows [6]:

- PV (Planned Value): Value as planned, PV = BAC *% of expected work.
- AC (Actual Cost): Actual cost, which is the actual cost spent at the time of monitoring the project.
- EV (Earned Value): The earned value, EV = BAC *% of the actual work, is the sum of the PV values that have been completed, from the start of the project to the time of project monitoring.
- ES (Earned Schedule): Time as planned, is the time spent by AC according to PV plan.
- BAC (Budget at Completion): Funding to complete the project.
- PD (Plan Duration): Project duration.

Project performance in terms of time and cost, determined by comparing the key parameters PV, AC, EV, and ES provides the following performance measurement results:

- CPI (Cost Performance Index): Cost performance index. Formula for calculating CPI = EV / AC;
- SPI (Schedule Performance Index): Index of planned performance. The formula for calculating SPI = EV / PV;
- SPI (t): Adjustment plan performance index (symbol (t) to specify that this formula relates to time). Formula to calculate SPI (t) = ES / AT;

Cost Estimate at Completion (CEAC) is calculated by the following formula:

$$CEAC = AC + PCWR = AC + \frac{(BAC - EV)}{PF} \tag{1}$$

Where:

AC: Actual cost at the present moment (i.e. actual time AT).

PCWR: Estimated costs for the remaining works (estimates for the future).

PF (Performance Factor): Performance factor.

The CEAC estimation methods based on the different efficiency coefficients of the EVM model are shown in Table 1.

Table 1. Overview of EVM-based project completion cost prediction methods

	CEAC1	CEAC2	CEAC3	CEAC4	CEAC5
SPI	PF = 1	PF = CPI	PF = SPI	PF = SCI	PF = 0.8 * CPI + 0.2 * SPI
SPI(t)			PF = SPI(t)	PF = SCI(t)	PF = 0.8 * CPI + 0.2 * SPI(t)

Estimated time to complete the project (TEAC - Time Estimate at Completion) is calculated [4.6]:

$$TEAC = AT + PDWR \tag{2}$$

Where:

AT: Current time;

PDWR: Estimated time of remaining jobs, calculation is also based on PE coefficient.

To predict the time to complete the project, one of three methods based on PV, ED and ES [4] can be used.

2.2 Gompertz Growth Model (GGM)

Gompertz function is used in combination with EVM to increase efficiency estimates TEAC and CEAC, this function is often used to describe the phenomenon with model S-shaped growth [2, 4]:

$$G(t) = \alpha \exp[-e^{\beta - \gamma t}] \tag{3}$$

where α, which represents the asymptotic value ($t \to \infty$) of the Gompertz function and is therefore related to the final budget of the project. The parameter γ, which characterizes the growth rate of the cumulative curve, allows the study of a variety of different project cost profiles

For $\beta = \gamma T$, where T is the vertex of the distribution function, we have the Gompertz function and the distribution function:

$$G(t) = \alpha \exp[-e^{-\gamma(t-T)}] \tag{4}$$

$$g(t) = \frac{dG(t)}{dt} \alpha \gamma G(t) e^{-\gamma(t-T)} \tag{5}$$

We can define the end of the project as a specific part of the asymptotic value, such as 95% or 99%, in that case, at the intended end of the project.

$$G(T_1) = (1 - \varepsilon)G(t \to \infty) = (1 - \varepsilon)\alpha = \alpha exp[-e^{\beta - \gamma t}] \tag{6}$$

where ε is a constant. We define k satisfying:

$$1 - \varepsilon = exp[-e^{-k}] \tag{7}$$

deduce:

$$k = \lambda(T_1 - T) \tag{8}$$

Therefore, k is determined when we choose a specific endpoint of the project, eg, 99% of the asymptotic, α.

3   Research Methodology

3.1   Original Method

The authors in [3] have proposed the ES-GGM method to predict the cost of completing the project, including 3 steps as follows:

Step 1: Construct an S-curve of the growth model
The first step is to build an S-curve that combines actual cost (AC) and expected value (PV).

With the curve function GGM as follows:

$$G(t) = \alpha \exp[-e^{\beta\gamma - T}] \tag{9}$$

Use the least square regression algorithm to find three parameters of the GGM model: (α, β, γ) such that the smallest deviation from the reference data. With CEAC prediction, we need to construct a GGM curve regression for the value AC - the actual cost to predict AC at the end. Input data because if only taking AC until the time of making prediction, it will be too little and easily cause error in prediction. Therefore, in [1, 2], the authors take the PV data portion of the remaining time to compensate for the missing data. Specifically, the reference data as input to the regression are as follows:

AC data until the time of making prediction t.

PV data from the time of the prediction to the end of the project.

This data set is inserted as input to the least square regression algorithm and the output is a trio of parameters of the GGM model: (α, β, γ).

Step 2: Calculate project completion cost based on Gompertz growth model (GGM)

Performing CEAC calculation according to GGM:

$$CEAC(x) = AC(x) + [GGM(1.0) - GGM(x)] * BAC \tag{10}$$

Step 3: Calculate the cost of completing the project based on GGM plus ES:

According to ES-GGM:

$$CEAC(x) = AC(x) + [GGM(1/SPI(t)) - GGM(x)] * BAC \tag{11}$$

3.2 Proposed Method I-GGM

Because the calculation process of the regression model uses many PV values, the generated curve is very close to these values. This leads to when predicting according to GGM, the results are usually quite close to PV, which is mostly inaccurate.

We propose a method to improve the I-GGM. In which, instead of regression according to AC + PV, we will regress according to AC and the rest is the AC value predicted using EVM-CPI. Thus, GGM will calculate the trend of data via CPI and help improve the accuracy of the solution.

The improvement method I-GGM proposed by us will include the following steps:

Step 1: Construct an S curve of the growth model

The first step is to construct an S-curve that combines the actual cost (AC) and the AC value predicted through the CPI.

The S curve is constructed as a combination of the actual cost curve (AC) and the remainder the estimated AC values based on the CPI. This curve will reflect the past and future of the project.

In order to construct an S-curve and apply a growth model, it is necessary first to standardize project data as follows:

- Standardize all project time point values in terms of units (ie PD will be normalized to 1.00). Each successive timeline will be the cumulative part of this unit. These normalized values will be the predictor (x) variable of a GGM growth model.
- Standardize the actual cost values AC (from the beginning of the project to the present time AT) in terms of units (ie BAC = 1.00).
- Standardize the expected values of AC according to the CPI (from the time of AT to the PD of the project) in terms of units (BAC = 1.00).

After normalization, we proceed to combine the normalized values of actual AC and expected value AC above. Then we get a time-axis S curve from the inception to the

PD of a project, which is a combination of AC (historical data) and expected value AC according to CPI (future data) of project data.

Step 2: Calculate the growth model parameters Gompertz: (α, β, γ).

Step 3: Calculate the cost of completing the project: Calculate the CEAC according to the formula (12)

$$CEAC(x) = AC(x) + [GGM (1/SPI(t)) - GGM (x)] * BAC \qquad (12)$$

4   Experiment and Evaluation

4.1   Experimental Data

The actual project datasets are listed from the website: https://www.projectmanagement. ugent.be/research/data/realdata. In which, we have performed data filtering statistics to select 20 projects in the field of software engineering. The experimental data are shown in Table 2.

Table 2. Data on 20 projects in the field of software engineering

ID	Project name	BAC (€)	Duration (month)	tracking
1	C2011-07 Patient Transport System.xlsx	180759.44	12.9666	23
2	C15-10 Tax Return System (1).xlsx	18990	2.8333	3
3	C2015-11 Staff Authorization System.xlsx	14400	1.8333	3
4	C2015-12 Premium Payment System.xlsx	132570	6.1333	3
5	C2015-13 Broker Account Conversion System.xlsx	12735	3.9	4
6	C2015-14 Supplementary Pensions Database.xlsx	34260	4.1347	4
7	C2015-15 FACTA System.xlsx	11700	1.9	3
8	C2015-16 Generic Document Output System.xlsx	64620	9	6
9	C2015-17 Insurance Bundling System.xlsx	281430	6.9388	5
10	C2015-18 Tax Number system (2).xlsx	39450	4.2666	3
11	C2015-20 Policy Numbering System.xlsx	12645	5.7	4
12	C2015-21 Investment Product (1).xlsx	4020	1.2333	2
13	C2015-22 Risk Profile Questionnaire.xlsx	29880	5.0361	4
14	C2015-23 Investment Product (2).xlsx	46920	4.0388	4
15	C2015-24 CRM System.xlsx	44130	7.7666	6

(continued)

Table 2. (*continued*)

ID	Project name	BAC (€)	Duration (month)	tracking
16	C2015-25 Beer Tasting.xlsx	1210	0.4402	3
17	C2015-26 Debt Collection System.xlsx	458112.3683	4.9388	5
18	C2015-28 Website Tennis Vlaanderen.xlsx	219275	6.7	4
19	C2016-08 SCM System.xlsx	375253.343	24.1666	34
20	C2016-09 Data Loss Prevention System.xlsx	584951.7688	6.5	9

4.2 Evaluation Criteria

a) **Percentage error measure (PE)**

The PE reflects the efficiency of each method in predicting the cost of completing the project. The PE is the difference between the actual cost and the estimated cost as a percentage:

$$PE\% = \frac{(CEAC - AC)}{AC} 100\% \tag{13}$$

where:

CEAC: estimated cost at the time of project completion.
AC: the actual cost of completing the project.

b) **Mean Absolute Percentage Error measure (MAPE)**

The Mean Absolute Percentage Error (MAPE): corresponding to the average value of PE on different projects is calculated by the formula:

$$MAPE\% = \frac{100\%}{n} \sum_{i=1}^{n} \frac{|CEAC_i - AC_i|}{AC_i} = \frac{1}{n} \sum_{i=1}^{n} |PE_i|\% \tag{14}$$

4.3 Result of Assessment According to MAPE

The calculated MAPE value is evaluated through 5 main phases:

- The beginning of project, Tracking 0;
- The first half of project, Tracking ¼;
- Between Project Tracking ½;
- The second half of project, Tracking ¾;
- At the end of project, the Tracking last.

At each phase, average the PE value across all 20 projects with each algorithm.

The MAPE results when predicting the CEAC of the 5-phase methods from 0 to 4 are shown in Fig. 1. The horizontal axis represents the project phases and the vertical axis shows the value of MAPE (%).

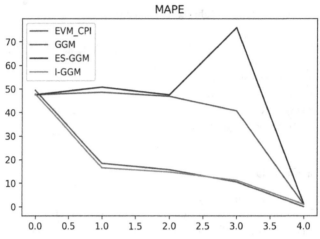

Fig. 1. MAPE results when predicting CEAC

In which, EVM-CPI predicts EVM-CPI, GGM and ES-GGM are predicted by GGM regression using the method in [1, 2], and I-GGM is the proposed improved regression model. Realizing that, GGM and ES-GGM showed ineffective results compared to EVM, while the improved I-GGM model was effective compared to EVM. The explanation given is similar to the above, partly because the CPI volatility of software engineering projects is too high, making it harder to predict GGM meth-od. Besides, the fact that projects have a relatively low tracking number also significantly affects the regression quality. After applying the innovation, I-GGM better captured the uptrend by CPI to give more stable results than using pure GGM and ES-GGM. Considering the average MAPE results obtained in the above figure, I-GGM can be rated slightly better than EVM-CPI (due to the higher and more significant predictive importance at the beginning of the project. than predicted at the end of the project).

5   Conclusions

In this paper, a methodology was proposed that combines Gompertz growth model and EVM techniques to improve the quality of predicting software project completion. The improvement method I-GGM uses a cost-performance index (CPI) that predicts future costs instead of the PV value that builds the S curve closest to reality to predict the cost of completion most accurate project. Conducted experiments on 20 data sets of actual software projects published on the website [9]. The test results show significant and relatively good improvements of the I-GGM improvement methods compared to the previous models such as GMM, ES-GGM, EVM. Overall, the results obtained confirm that the proposed improvement has theoretical basis and is justified by experiment with actual data sets.

Development direction: In the future, we will continue to improve the algorithm and collect more real data for more accurate testing.

Acknowledgments. This research is funded by Hanoi University of Science and Technology under Grant number T2018-TĐ-009.

References

1. Simion, C.P., Marin, I.: Project cost estimate at completion: earmed value management versus earned schedule-based regression models. A comparative analysis of the models application in the construction projects in Romania. Econ. Comput. Econ. Cybern. Stud. Res. **52**(3) (2018)
2. Nannini, G., Warburton, R.D.H., De Marco, A.: Improving the accuracy of project estimates at completion using the Gompertz function. In: International Research Network on Organizing by Projects (IRNOP) 2017, UTS ePRESS, Sydney: NSW, pp. 1–15 (2017)
3. Narbaev, T., De Marco A.: Combination of growth model and earned schedule to forecast project cost at completion. J. Constr. Eng. Manag. **140**(1), Article number 04013038 (2014). ISSN 0733–9364.
4. Batselier, J., Vanhoucke, M.: Evaluation of deterministic state-of-the-art forecasting approaches for project duration based on earning value management. Int. J. Proj. Manag. **33**(7), 1588–1596 (2015)
5. Khamooshi, H., Golafshani, H.: EDM: earned duration management, a new approach to schedule performance management and measurement. Int. J. Proj. Manag. **32**, 1019–1041 (2014)
6. Fleming, Q.W., MeKoppelman, J.: Earned value project management. Project Management Institute Newtown Square, Pennsylvania, USA (2015)
7. Elshaer, R.: Impact of sensitivity information on the prediction of project's duration using earning schedule method. Int. J. Proj. Manag. **31**(4), 579–588 (2013)
8. Le, T.A., Huynh, Q.T., Nguyen, T.H., Nguyen, N.H., Cao, P.N.: Correction for future performance factor PF in EVM-GM method evaluating the completion of software projects: testing and evaluation. In: Proceedings of the Association National Workshop XXI: Selected issues of Information and Communication Technology, pp. 137–143. Scientific and Technical Publishing House, Hanoi (2018)
9. Batselier, J., Vanhoucke, M.: https://www.projectmanagement.ugent.be/research/data/realdata
10. Huynh, Q.T., Le, T.A., Nguyen, T.H., Nguyen, N.H., Nguyen, D.H.: A method for improvement the parameter estimation of non-linear regression in growth model to predict project cost at completion. In: 2020 RIVF International Conference on Computing and Communication Technologies. IEEE (2020)

An Embedded Digital Multi-channel Analyzer for Radiation Detection Based on FPGA

Quang-Kien Trinh[1(✉)] ⓘ, Van-Ninh Trinh[1], Thanh-Bang Le[1], Tien-Hung Dinh[2], and Van-Hiep Cao[2]

[1] Le Quy Don Technical University, Hanoi, Vietnam
{kien.trinh,banglt}@lqdtu.edu.vn, phongvan.tomsk@gmail.com
[2] Military Institute of Chemistry and Environment/High Command of Chemical, Hanoi, Vietnam
dinhtienhungnbc@gmail.com, caovanhiep123@gmail.com

Abstract. In recent years, digital processing algorithms have been widely applied in spectrum processing applications. Besides, FPGA technology, thanks to its undeniable advantages in flexibility, high integration, and cost-effectiveness, is seriously considered as a practical platform for the realization of embedded digital signal processing (DSP) systems.

This work conducts a study on the practical implementation of Digital Multi-channel Analyzer (DMCA) based on reconfigurable hardware (FPGA). We proposed a modular reconfigurable DMCA design that is ready to be integrated into portable radiation detecting equipment and is still capable to handle high-speed signal sampling as well as could be extended to further functions such as remote sensing and classifying. This module could be integrated into the real-time radiation monitoring system. The algorithms of pulse shaping filter, detecting peaks and spectrum histogram processing are optimized and implemented entirely using available FPGA logic resources.

The design is experimentally verified in a system using Lanthanum Bromide Scintillation Radiation LaBr3(Ce) detector. The results are compared with commercial products (DSPEC of ORTEC), where isotopes ^{137}Cs and ^{60}Co gamma-ray spectra show that its performance partially is superior to the DSPEC in terms of full width at half maximum (FWHM), received and lost count rate, integral non-linearity. This prototype system is highly promising for the multi-DMCA system in considering performance, cost, and form factors. Regarding resource utilization and performance, the whole design utilizes only 5% LEs, 24% memory resources of 10M50SAE144I7G FPGA from Intel and the DMCA core is capable to handle up to 97 MSPS sampling rates.

Keywords: Digital multi-channel analyzer (DMCA) · DPP · FPGA

1 Introduction

1.1 The Development of Digital Pulse Processing

In recent years, studies of digital pulse processing (DPP) algorithms have shown a valuable benefit over analog signal processing systems. Indeed, the digital approach

N.-S. Vo et al. (Eds.): INISCOM 2021, LNICST 379, pp. 220–232, 2021.
https://doi.org/10.1007/978-3-030-77424-0_18

offers designs with high accuracy and good performance, hence, DPP has been widely applied in many applications such as recording, radiation spectrum analysis [1], isotope identification [2], dose rate measurement [3], and so on. Particularly, the DPP approach is well suited for radiation detection algorithms, and it currently is primarily adopted in the nuclear electronics study.

Recent applications of DPP are showing significant improvements over traditional models, various DPP algorithms, such as pulse-shaping filters, peak detector, or amplitude spectral analysis, have been recommended [3–6]. The incorporation of DPP techniques into Digital Multichannel Analyzer (DMCA) allows transforming 512 to 8192 the number of channels [4, 5]. Besides, the adoption of digital improves the system's anti-interference capabilities and increases the sampling rate for real-time processing [5].

The enhanced capability of DPP algorithms essentially comes with an increase in computationally complexity and diversity, thus a high-performance hardware platform is required. In this context, there is a timely need to promptly reform DPP's mapping strategy into the hardware platform and support scalable and modular hardware customization for specific applications without sacrificing design functionality and performance. Among the available platforms, FPGA is the widely applied selection in addition to using the traditional off-the-shelf DPPs implementations.

1.2 Reconfigurable Hardware-Based Approaches for DMCA Accelerators

Technology vendors and researchers constantly put enormous efforts to improve FPGA integration, functionality, and performance. State-of-the-art FPGA undoubtedly is an ideal platform for embedding multi-task, heavy-computing, and customized algorithms on the same single chip. FPGA-based multichannel analyzers, in particular, have become increasingly popular thanks to their high reconfigurability, fast response time, and very high energy efficiency [6]. ZENG Weihua et al. in work [6] implemented a 1024-channel DMCA system on EP3C40Q240 FPGA from Intel, which occupies only 30% of the total logic resources. They experimentally showed that ^{137}Cs nuclear signals detected by NaI(Tl) detector have a resolution of ~ 8% and 0,8% integral nonlinearity. Research by Dang et al. [5] successfully implemented 8192-channel DMCA, with 0,23% integral nonlinearity, on EPM7160E FPGA from Intel (32-bit value resolution) for HPGe Detector using 14-bit 62.5 MSPS ADC.

This work presents a design and implementation of the real-time and high-resolution DMCA, specialized for scintillation detectors, based on moderate off-the-shelf FPGA. The combination of the finite impulse response (FIR) for shaping filter, detecting peaks, and spectral histogram processing is optimized to increase throughput, energy resolution, and minimize logic resources of FPGA.

The main contributions of this work are summarized as follows.

- A very resource-efficient and high-performance FPGA-based embedded DCMA design. (combining software for rendering gamma spectra). Our DCMA core could run signal processing and filtering algorithm with the sampling rate up to 97 MSPS and deliver relatively good peak detection efficiency using only 5% logic elements,

24% memory resources on Intel 10M50SAE144I7G FPGA, i.e., significantly better than implementation on [5] and [6].

- This design experimentally tested with a LaBr3(Ce) detector using ^{137}Cs and ^{60}Co radiation sources and has been compared to the results from a commercial detector from DSPEC. The initial results show that obtained results from our low-cost FPGA-based DMCA exhibit almost the same accuracy as DSPEC and is partially superior in terms of full width at half maximum (FWHM), received and lost count rate, integral nonlinearity.
- The proposed DMCA is highly scalable and reconfigure (i.e., using FPGA) and is ready for deploying a full multi-DMCA system-on-chip and/or further extending to complex features such as classification and recognition.

The remainder of this paper is organized as follows: Section 2 introduces the basic background of DMCA. Section 3 presents the results of the simulation system performed on the software. Section 4 proposes a generic design for the digital pulse processing problem on the hardware and describes our FPGA-based implementation details upon this proposed design. Section 5 concludes the paper.

2 Background

Digital Multi-Channel Analyzer (DMCA) includes two parts, the first one is ADC, the main component of radiation measurements and the second is nuclear analysis instruments. The main function of the DMCA consists of three parts [7]: (1) Data acquisition and (2) Data processing, which are performed by hardware, (3) Control and indicator, which are usually performed by software running on computer communicated via standard interfaces such as USB, Ethernet or Serial port.

Signals from the detector in analog spectroscopy systems are being shaped, filtered, and amplified by pulse amplifier module and digitized by the ADC at the end of the processing sequence. Some basic limitations on these systems are the correction and expansion of filter functions, the impact of interference on analog electronic components such as resistors, capacitors, inductors, analog connectors, and high energy consumption.

The digital signal processing system (DSP) is an effective solution to overcome these limitations. In these systems, the signal from the detector is pre-amplified and filtered before being digitalized and subsequent processing are done in the digital domain. Digital processing algorithms are used to filter and optimize the digitized and sampled data. Data are processed by numerical methods to find the peak value and transfer it to the MCA memory for analysis and indication. The functional block diagram of a DMCA is shown in Fig. 1.   •

Some of the DMCA's outstanding advantages are high processing speed, high throughput, improving resolution and temperature stability, along with its highly configurable capacity, FPGA provides the ability to build and expand filtering functions without changing hardware. Comparable resolution features coupled with significantly smaller overall processing times can be provided by efficient filtering and processing algorithms. This result improves the ability to process high throughput without reducing resolution as in analog spectroscopy systems.

Besides, in DSP-based systems, processing in the digital domain minimizes the uncertainty of shifting and instability normally associated with analog processing. Spectrometers developed based on DSP can provide the ability to load frequencies exceeding 100000 pulses per second with sufficient resolution to obtain a good gamma spectrum [17].

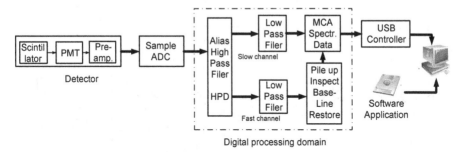

Digital processing domain

Fig. 1. The functional block diagram of a DMCA

3 DMCA Function Design and Verification

This section describes in detail our DMCA design, which starts with the mathematical model that is rigorously verified by MATLAB-Simulink before actually implemented on hardware (i.e. FPGA).

3.1 The Analytical Model of DMCA

One of the most important factors affecting the quality of the DMCA and a digital gamma spectrometer is the algorithm that shapes (filters) the digitized pre-amplification input signal into a suitable signal form for precisely determines the input signal amplitude. There are three most widely employed algorithms: Gaussian deformation algorithm [9], bipolar pulse deformation algorithm "cups" [10], and the isosceles trapezoidal pulse deformation algorithm, isosceles triangle [10–12]. Each algorithm has certain advantages and disadvantages, in which the optimal and most practically applied algorithm is the trapezoidal pulse transformation algorithm due to the advantages on the signal-to-noise ratio (peak resolution), which is close to optimal for many practical digital spectroscopy systems [8].

In this work, we also applied an isosceles trapezoidal filter, considering that it is well-suited for processing radiation signals and the feasibility for embedded hardware implementation. The filter transfer function can be factorized as follows:

$$F_{TPZ} = \left(1 - \beta z^{-1}\right) * \left(\frac{1 - z^{-R}}{1 - z^{-1}}\right) * \left(\frac{1 - z^{-(R+M)}}{1 - z^{-1}}\right) * \left(\frac{z^{-1}}{R}\right) \qquad (1)$$

where constants R specify the rise time duration of trapezoidal pulse and M specify the flat-top duration of the trapezoidal pulse. β is the time constant depending on the input signal and clock period. After the input samples are filtered and delivered in the form of trapezoidal-shaped signal, its peak amplitude is detected and statistically accumulated for constructing the final histogram. Correspondingly, the DMCA functional diagram is depicted in Fig. 2. In which, the three key components in the digital domain are the Energy filter, the Peak detector, and the Histogram builder. Detailed functional implementations of those components will be described in the following Subsection.

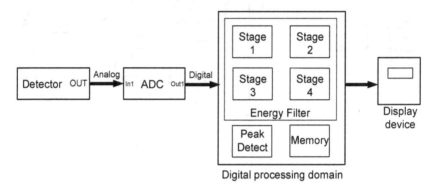

Fig. 2. The structural diagram of a DMCA system

3.2 Design the DMCA Model on MATLAB-Simulink

We further implemented the whole processing DMCA algorithm on MATLAB-Simulink (R2019a version used in this work) for evaluating DMCA-based models and that is being used as the reference design for the subsequent hardware implementation phase.

Based on the model of the digital pulse signal processing system, we proceed to build the DMCA model with three functional blocks, Energy filter, which is used to increase the signal to noise ratio (SNR), minimize the baseline drifts and reduce pileup [14]. The peak detector for measuring the signal amplitude and the Histogram builder for constructing the final amplitude spectrum. The trapezoidal pulse shaping block with the transfer function in the complex frequency domain z is represented by formula (1). We divide the Energy filter into 4 sub-filters with the corresponding transfer function. An example of 4-stage filter outputs is illustrated in Fig. 3. The results show that input the signal from the pulse generator on a relatively large noise background, after going through the filter the noise is effectively phased out and the final signal is shaped into an isosceles trapezoidal. The final signal shape greatly reduces the complexity as well as increases the accuracy of the subsequent block.

Peak detector: As from the name, this block uses a threshold discriminator to treat the trapezoidal signal after the filter. Once the peak level is detected, this block creates a logic pulse for measuring the amplitude and sends this value to the histogram builder.

Histogram builder: In the histogram builder the detected peak value is accumulated and stored into a histogram memory. Specifically, when there is an event that needs to be stored, the pulse amplitude is used as the address for access and increases the current value in the memory cell by one. i.e., the contents of the cell are retrieved, added by one, and saved back to the same address. This process is performed for sufficient time (in this case, ~ 1 ms) the histogram will be constructed and stable. Figure 4 shows an example of the final histogram using a DMCA model on MATLAB-Simulink.

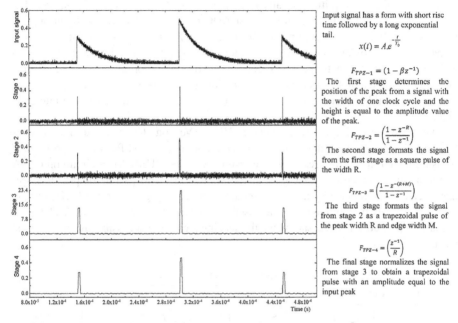

Input signal has a form with short rise time followed by a long exponential tail.

$$x(t) = A.e^{-\frac{t}{T_0}}$$

$$F_{TPZ-1} = (1 - \beta z^{-1})$$

The first stage determines the position of the peak from a signal with the width of one clock cycle and the height is equal to the amplitude value of the peak.

$$F_{TPZ-2} = \left(\frac{1 - z^{-R}}{1 - z^{-1}}\right)$$

The second stage formats the signal from the first stage as a square pulse of the width R.

$$F_{TPZ-3} = \left(\frac{1 - z^{-(R+M)}}{1 - z^{-1}}\right)$$

The third stage formats the signal from stage 2 as a trapezoidal pulse of the peak width R and edge width M.

$$F_{TPZ-4} = \left(\frac{z^{-1}}{R}\right)$$

The final stage normalizes the signal from stage 3 to obtain a trapezoidal pulse with an amplitude equal to the input peak

Fig. 3. Simulated signal transformation corresponding to four filter stages.

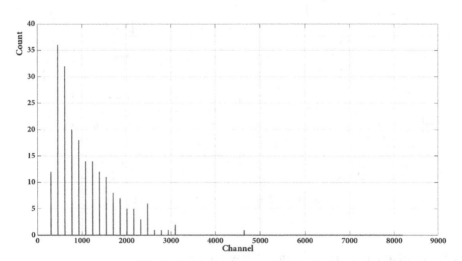

Fig. 4. Histogram of simulation signals.

4   Design of DMCA System

4.1   The Structural Design of the DMCA System

Based on the functional block in the previous section, the hardware implementation block diagram is constructed in detail (see Fig. 5). As can be seen from the figure, signals from the preamplifier (usually integrated inside the detector) are transferred to the sampling circuit and digitized by a fast ADC [13]. The ADC output signal will be processed by digital circuits entirely embedded in FPGA. This circuit consists of Energy Filter, Peak detector, and the Histogram builder. The output signal of the Energy Filter is transferred to peak-detection circuits, consist of a differentiator, a level discriminator, a peak counter, and a pile-up detector block and finally used to create the energy spectrum in Histogram builder. The latter consists of pulse height analyzer, controlling interface, and memory.

All those processing is encapsulated in VHDL/Verilog. The whole design is simulated by (Altera Quartus) functionally verified before porting to FPGA for experimental measurement. Finally, for presenting the result, we added a USB driver circuit on FPGA to communicate and transfer the final histogram to a PC. This part in the practical scenarios can easily replace by a more compact alternative (e.g. integrated LCD) or data can be wirelessly transferred to the end-user components or even to the cloud. The latter scenario is particularly necessary when the sensing area is not accessible due to radiation hazards.

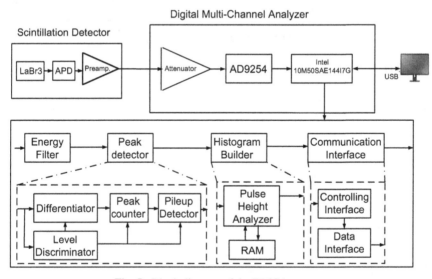

Fig. 5. Block diagram of the DMCA system.

4.2   Scintillation Detector and the Analog Frontend

The scintillation detector [15] consists of a scintillation crystal, an avalanche photodiode (APD) to convert the light from the scintillation crystal into electrical pulses, which is amplified by an integrated pre-amplifier circuit. In this work, we employed a detector with LaBr3(Ce) crystal with a size of $10 \times 10 \times 30$ mm, APD type S8664–1010, charge-sensitive pre-amplifier type eV5093. For the analog frontend, we adopted commercial 14-bit AD9254 ADC from Analog Device [16], which has a maximum sampling rate of 150 MSPS. The ADC converts analog signal amplitude from $-1 \div +1$V, the 14-bit parallel output which is directly fed to FPGA inputs.

4.3 Pulse Processing System Design

The incoming signal from the detector is digitized by ADC and the digital samples are passed directly to the digital pulse processing circuit inside FPGA. Especially to the input of the pulse-shaping filter of the Energy filter. After the energy filter, the signal is shaped into a series of trapezoidal and passed through the threshold discriminator to create a logic pulse for controlling subsequent functional blocks, including differentiator, peak counter, pileup detector, and pulse height analyzer. The differentiator is used to reveal peaks and detect pileup. While the signal larger than a given threshold, the peak counter counts the number peak in one pulse cycle by using a logic pulse from a differentiator. Spectral storage memory is configured from Dual Port Random Access Memory-DPRAM, which is built into the FPGA. The memory is organized with 13 bits address bus, capacity 8192 locations; 32 bits data bus, recording range $0 \div 2^{32}-1$ count; and includes memory select signals, read/write data control bus.

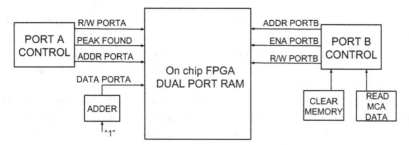

Fig. 6. Block diagram of memory and interface.

Block diagram of memory and interface is shown in Fig. 6. When there is an event that needs to be stored, the pulse amplitude is used to generate the memory address, the contents of the cell are retrieved to add a count before updating to the same location. The above operations are performed with port A. The memory clear operations, reading spectrum analysis results are performed independently via port B through the interface between this port and the computer.

4.4 FPGA Implementation and Experimental Results

The design in previous Sections after functional evaluation by logic simulation has been fully ported into a commercial FPGA board using Intel Max 10 FPGA. We also developed an in-house software program on PC to communicate with the board for reading the final histogram and plot it on the computer. The hardware implementation on FPGA is summarized in Table 1.

Table. 1. Analysis and synthesis summary.

	This work	[5]	[6]
Chip Family	Intel MAX 10	Intel MAX 7000	Intel Cyclone III
Device	10M50SAE144I7G	EPM7160E	EP3C40Q240
Logic resources	2,380/49,760 (5%)	1,050/3,200 usable gates	11,880/39,600 (30%)
Total pins	24/101 (24%)	–	–
Total memory bits	423,936/1,677,312 (25%)	–	–
Multiplier	3 / 288 (1%)	–	–
Max frequency	97 MHz	62.5 MHz	65 MHz

The results obtained found that the hardware resources used by the logic elements, memory elements, RAM, and DSP are reasonably small, i.e., occupies only 5% (2,380 LEs on 10M50SAE144I7G), which is much smaller than the DMCA design in [6][1]. The result indicates that our design is capable to extend to multiple channels (i.e., multiple ADCs and detectors). The maximum frequency of this design can up to 97 MHz, which allows to speed up the algorithm with real-time tasks.

Furthermore, we conducted the experimental tests on the implemented DMCA. In this test, we use the available LaBr3(Ce) detector in our Institute of Chemistry and Environment. The detected signal is passed through the AD9254 daughter board before processing in FPGA. The final recorded spectra are sent to the computer via a USB interface. We use isotopes ^{137}Cs and ^{60}Co as the calibration sources for experimenting. Figure 7 (a) shows the histogram of the natural background (no active radiation), (19, 20) shows the recorded gamma spectra of ^{137}Cs and ^{60}Co, respectively. The graph shows that the spectrum obtained is consistent with the radioisotopes reference sample results (Fig. 8).

Finally, the functionalities of the DMCA were compared to an ORTEC commercial digital system (DSPEC). The output of the detector has simultaneously connected to DMCA and DSPEC. The interaction rate in the detector was adjusted by using ^{137}Cs and ^{60}Co sources in a different activity and also by adjusting the distance between the source and the detector to achieve the desirable count rates.

An important characteristic of a multi-channel analyzer is the width of the total energy peak. It is usually measured on the full width half maximum (FWHM) [18]. In an ideal case, pulses caused by monoenergetic radiation would all be the same height, and the multichannel analyzer would display a single line that would represent the radiation

---

[1] We did not compare resource utilization of our work with [5] since that work used CPLD device that is not based on Logic Element primitives.

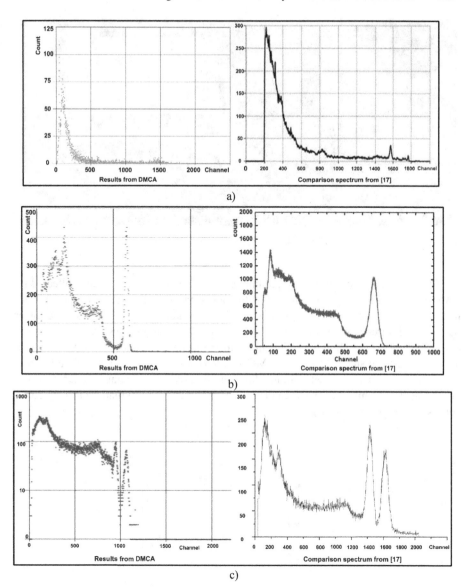

Fig. 7. The display of the spectrum on the computer (left) and comparison spectrum (right) [17], a) Naturally occurring background radiation, b) Gamma spectrum of ^{137}Cs source; c) Gamma spectrum of ^{60}Co source.

energy. In practice, a peak with a measurable width is observed. To evaluate the quality of the DMCA, the FWHM must be as small as possible.

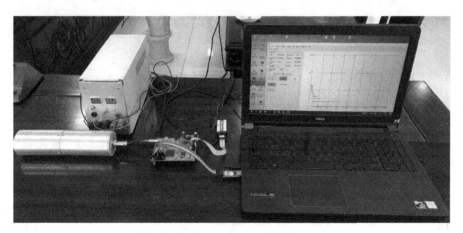

Fig. 8. Design testing on FPGA board

The spectra and spectroscopic parameters of ^{137}Cs and ^{60}Co sources collected by DMCA and DSPEC are shown in Fig. 9, the upper part is different spectra which were measured simultaneously at count rates of 25kcps, 30kcps, and 35kcps; and the lower part is the difference of spectroscopic parameters. The graph shows that the spectrum obtained between two digital multichannel amplitude analyzers does not differ much in terms of spectrum shape. However, DMCA's FWHM is about 10% better than DSPEC jr. 2.0, 15% better at peak elevation. The peak area of ^{60}Co obtained by DMCA was about 5% more, while the peak area of ^{137}Cs was about 7% more than DSPEC jr. 2.0 at counts of 25kcps and 30kcps.

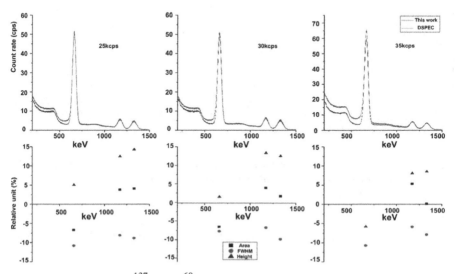

Fig. 9. The spectra of ^{137}Cs and ^{60}Co sources were collected by DMCA and DSPEC.

Another important DMCA parameter examined is integral nonlinearity ($INL = CH_{max}/CH_{total}$) [5], where CH_{max} is the maximum difference (channel unit) of the spectral peak position relative to the theoretical linear line over the entire measuring range; CH_{total} is the number of channels of the DMCA. Using Gwintek standard pulse generator GDS 303587, the survey results of the spectral peak position dependence when changing input signal amplitude are shown in Fig. 10. According to the experimental data, the integral nonlinearity of DMCA is 0.1367%.

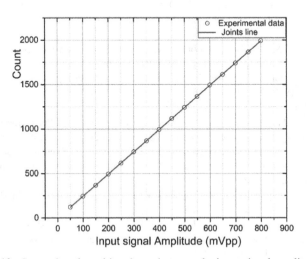

Fig. 10. Spectral peak position dependence on the input signal amplitude.

5 Conclusion

This study presents an embedded reconfigurable DMCA that has been systematically designed and experimentally verified in conjunction with the LaBr3(Ce) scintillation detector. The major results indicate that our design exhibits the almost equivalent performance of the commercial off-the-shelf DSPEC jr. 2.0 DMCA while experimenting on standard isotopes of ^{137}Cs and ^{60}Co.

Our working prototype has been fully developed on FPGA that offers a small form factor, low-cost, and low-energy DCMA, thus, being ready embedded in practical systems. Also, regarding resource utilization, our design not only superior some prior arts in the area-efficiency but the reconfigurable platform (FPGA) allows further deploying more features using complex data processing algorithms such as on-device classification and recognition. The latter paved the way for design a new class of smart DCMA where intelligent computing tasks can be performed right at the analyzer. It is also feasible to adopt this design for different application scenarios, e.g., by integrated wireless module, this device can interact in the radiation-/bio- hazard environments or the devices can push the detected data directly to the cloud as an IoT device for storing and further analyzing and processing at a larger scale.

References

1. Ma, Y., Fischer, W.-J., Henniger, J., Weinberger, D., Kormoll, T.: System noise of a digital pulse processing module for nuclear instrumentation. In: EPJ Web of Conferences, vol. 225, p. 01012 (2020). ANIMMA, Inc. 2019

2. Warburton, W.K., Momayezi, M., Hubbard-Nelson, B., Skulski, W.: Digital pulse processing: new possibilities in nuclear spectroscopy. Appl. Radiat. Isot. **53**, 916–920 (2000)

3. Moline, Y., Thevenin, M., Corre, G., Paindavoine, M.: A novel digital pulse processing architecture for nuclear instrumentation. In: 2015 4th International Conference on Advancements in Nuclear Instrumentation Measurement Methods and their Applications (ANIMMA), Lisbon, pp. 1–4 (2015)

4. Lanh, D., Son, P.N., Son, N.A.: In-house development of an FPGA-based MCA8K for gamma-ray spectrometer. Springerplus **3**(1), 1–12 (2014). https://doi.org/10.1186/2193-1801-3-665

5. Quy, D.H.N., Tuan, P.N., Dien, N.N.: Design and construction of a digital multichannel analyzer for HPGe detector using digital signal processing technique. J. Anal. Sci. Methods Instrum. **09**(02), 22–29 (2019)

6. Zeng, W.: The design of digital multi-channel analyzer based on FPGA. Energy Procedia **39**, 428–433 (2013). Asian Nuclear Prospects 2012 (ANUP2012). ScienceDirect

7. Qin, Z.J., Chen, C., Luo, J.S., Xie, X.H., Ge, L.Q., Wu, Q.F.: A pulse shape discrimination method for improving Gamma-ray spectrometry based on a new digital shaping filter. Radiat. Phys. Chem. **145**, 193–201 (2018)

8. Bogovac, M.: Implementation of a Trapezoidal filter in an FPGA by using MATLAB & Xilinx design tools. IAEA, Vienna, Austria (2013)

9. Ge, Q., Ge, L.-Q., Wu, J.-P., Li, X.-L.: Research on digital Gaussian shaping filter for nuclear signals based on sampling theorem. Hedianxue Yu Tance Jishu/Nucl. Electron. Detect. Technol. **34**, 1201–1203, 1212 (2014)

10. Jordanov, V.T., Knoll, G.F., Huber, A.C., Pantazis, J.A.: Digital techniques for real-time pulse shaping in radiation measurements. Nucl. Instrum. Methods Phys. Res. Sect. A: Accelerators, Spectrometers, Detect. Assoc. Equip. **353**(1–3), 261–264 (1994)

11. Jordanov, V.T., Knoll, G.F.: Digital synthesis of pulse shapes in real-time for high-resolution radiation spectroscopy. Nucl. Instrum. Methods Phys. Res. Sect. A **345**(2), 337–345 (1994)

12. Georgiev, A., Gast, W.: Digital pulse processing in high resolution, high throughput, gamma-ray spectroscopy. IEEE Trans. Nucl. Sci. **40**(4), 770–779 (1993). https://doi.org/10.1109/23.256659

13. Lee, P.S., Lee, C.S., Lee, J.H.: Development of FPGA-based digital signal processing system for radiation spectroscopy. Radiat. Meas. **48**, 12–17 (2013)

14. Knoll, G.F.: Radiation Detection and Measurement, 4th edn. Wiley, Hoboken (2010)

15. Knoll, G.F.: Radiation Detection and Measurement. 3rd ed. Chapters 16 to 18. Wiley (1999)

16. Analog Devices: 14-Bit, 150 MSPS, 1.8 V. Analog-to-Digital Converter. AD9254 Datasheet

17. Hung, D.T., Hiep, C.V., Khang, P.D., et al.: Gamma spectrum tabilization for environmental radiation monitoring stations using NaI(Tl) detector. Radiat. Protect. Dosimetry, 1–8 (2020)

18. Rozsa, C.M.: Measuring Radiation: An Introductory Discussion. Saint-Gobain Ceramics & Plastics, Inc. (2014)

19. L. Swiderski, R. Chandra, A. Curioni et al.: Scintillation response of Xe gas studied by gamma-ray absorption and Compton electrons. J. Instrum. (2015)

20. CASSY Lab 2: User manual. Appendix, Cobalt60

A Design of CMOS PUF Based on Ring Oscillator and Time-to-Digital Converter

Van-Phuc Hoang[✉], Quang Phuong Nguyen, Van Trung Nguyen,
Thanh Trung Nguyen, and Xuan Nam Tran

Le Quy Don Technical University, 236 Hoang Quoc Viet, Hanoi, Vietnam
phuchv@lqdtu.edu.vn

Abstract. Physical unclonable functions (PUF) is a promising technique in the field of hardware security with the main principle based on the random variations of inherent semiconductor devices during the fabrication process to provide the secret keys for cryptography or IC identification/authentication. In this paper, we present a new, efficient design of CMOS PUF based on ring oscillators and a time-to-digital converter (TDC). The proposed PUF design provides higher number of respond bits for each challenge, better reliability and uniqueness compared with conventional RO PUF designs. The proposed PUF design is implemented with TSMC 180 nm CMOS process using Cadence Virtuoso tool. The detailed design, simulation and evaluation results are also presented and discussed. The experimental results have clarified the efficiency of the proposed PUF design.

Keywords: PUF · Ring oscillator · TDC

1 Introduction

The issue of information system security is becoming emerging, especially in the context toward the smart cities based on Internet of Things (IoT). Especially, in IoT systems, with huge number of resource constrained nodes, the security threat (in both hardware and software aspects) becomes critical. There have been many studies reporting the possibility to use hardware circuits and tools to collect the information illegally and attack the information systems. Moreover, integrated circuit (IC) fabrication technologies have developed quickly so that it could implement complicated algorithms and intelligent processing techniques, but also leads to the hardware security threats at any step of the IC design and fabrication flow. Besides, the issue of IC counterfeit is becoming emerging when the outsourcing is more and more popular in semiconductor industry today. Hence, the research topics on hardware security assurance for IoT systems are becoming emerging.

Physical unclonable functions (PUF) is a new technique in hardware security with the main principle based on the random variations of the inherent semiconductor devices during the IC fabrication process. A PUF is considered as the hardware implementation of a mathematical one-way function with the basic operating principle based on the

© ICST Institute for Computer Sciences, Social Informatics and Telecommunications Engineering 2021
Published by Springer Nature Switzerland AG 2021. All Rights Reserved
N.-S. Vo et al. (Eds.): INISCOM 2021, LNICST 379, pp. 233–242, 2021.
https://doi.org/10.1007/978-3-030-77424-0_19

relationship of challenge-respond pairs (CRPs) as shown in Fig. 1. PUFs can be used to provide the hardware based secret keys for cryptography applications by exploiting the random characteristics of PUFs. Moreover, a PUF provide an efficient means for IC identification/authentication since it can be considered as the fingerprint of the IC chip [1–4]. PUF is also a promising solutions for device authentication in IoT systems with resource constrained nodes.

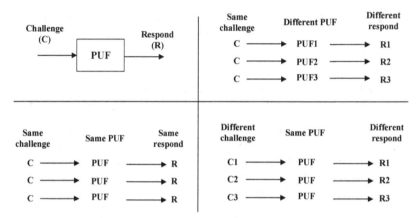

Fig. 1. Basic operating principle of PUFs based on CRPs.

Among number of PUF design structures, Ring Oscillator (RO) based PUFs provide an efficient tool for the issue of IC counterfeit in semiconductor industry [5]. RO PUF utilizes the difference in the frequencies of two identical ROs. One of the disadvantages of RO PUF is that it requires very larger hardware resources to provide enough CRPs for key extraction applications. Hence, there have been many papers presenting RO based PUF designs with the solutions to maximize the number of challenge-respond pairs (CRPs) which can be extracted. However, there are very few papers aiming to provide minimal number of extracted bits per challenge while remaining the PUF performance [5]. Moreover, there is not any paper mentioning the use of TDCs for RO based PUFs.

Therefore, in this paper, we aim to propose a new RO PUF design using a time-to-digital converter (TDC) to improve the CRPs and number of bits for each challenge. With n ROs used, the maximum number of CPRs is 2 C_2^n and the respond bit number depends on the frequency or the number of RO stages used. The proposed PUF design is implemented with TSMC 180 nm CMOS process using Cadence Virtuoso tool.

The rest of this paper is organized as follows. The conventional RO based PUF designs and related works are described in Sect. 2. In Sect. 3, we will introduce the proposed TDC based RO PUF and its operation principle. Then, in Sect. 4, we present the implementation results of the proposed PUF design and compare with previous ones. Finally, the paper is concluded in Sect. 5.

2   Conventional RO Based PUF Designs and Related Works

Firstly, we consider the operating principle of the ROs. When an even number of inverters are connected in series with suitable initial condition (such as active enable signal), the output of the RO will provide one signal with a specific frequency. The RO PUF utilizes the special characteristics that the frequencies of the ROs with identical layout are random but with static differences which are caused by the variations in the semiconductor fabrication process. The output of RO PUF is created by comparing the frequencies of the RO pair [5]. A conventional RO Based PUF structure is presented in Fig. 2 in which the frequencies of a random pair of oscillators are selected by the challenge input (*C*). Due to the random variations in the IC fabrication process, the frequencies of this pair are different and they are compared so that one output bit is generated (as the respond, or *R*) to show their relationship (smaller or greater) [4]. The signed function style of this method causes the information lost and requires a large number of ROs to extract the reliable and unique chip identification information. In addition, the fluctuation in absolute RO frequencies caused by operating conditions and other sources make this conventional scheme not practical.

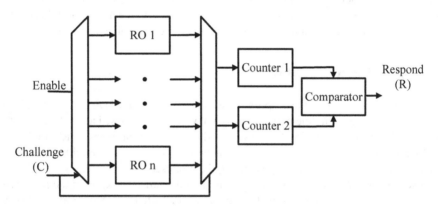

Fig. 2.   Traditional RO PUF architecture.

Many works have been carried out to improve the conventional RO PUF by two main directions. The first direction is to increase the flexibility in RO PUF hardware configurations, so equivalent to retrieve more RO pairs (ROp), and the second direction is to improve data processing technique to enhance the efficiency of RO PUF data extraction. Authors in [5] proposed the configurable FPGA-based RO PUFs that allow the inverters to be flexibly selected by a multiplexer (Fig. 2). Accordingly, a N stage ROs could be configured to generate 2^N different frequencies. Gao *et al.* in [6] proposed a similar structure, where the number of stage inverters can be adjusted by multiplexer. Therefore, metastable outputs can be avoided. Moreover, C. Gu et al. from Queen's University Belfast proposed and evaluated the efficiency of two PUF design types based on ring oscillator (RO) and PicoPUF including 127 Xilinx Artix-7 28 nm FPGA boards [7]. Moreover, our research team has successfully developed an FPGA based PUF design using ring oscillator and proposed a new ID extraction scheme for IC with the proposed

RO PUF. The proposed ID extraction scheme in FPGA has fully employed the local variations independent with the fabrication technology [8].

Authors in [9] produced longer PUF output using less ROs by latching the counter value in Gray code of slower RO (Fig. 2) of each pair. The disadvantage of this method locates in the complexity of data processing caused by choosing the significant bit string locations. In general, these designs lead to the high complexity in the circuit layout caused by the integration of many multiplexers so maintaining the layout symmetry and regularity is especially challenging. In addition, the evaluation methods in those works follow the conventional way as described in [6]. On the other hand, J. Agustin et al. [10] proposed a RO PUF exploiting the variability of the duty cycle instead of measuring deviations of the output frequency so that the number of ROs needed to implement a robust PUF is decreased.

It can be seen that one disadvantage of the conventional RO PUF designs is the small number of respond bits. Hence, it needs to be replicated to provide high key length in modern cryptographic applications, such as AES, so that the circuit complexity becomes very high. Besides, the number of independent CRPs is very low. As mentioned above, the previous papers focus on improving the maximum number of independent CRPs which can be extracted from one challenge. There are very few papers concerning the issue of respond bit number for each challenge [5]. Hence, in the next part of this paper, we will introduce a new technique of TDC based RO PUF to solve this issue.

3 Proposed TDC Based RO PUF

In this section, we describe the proposed PUF based on ROs and TDC. It is well known that a TDC converts each time period to a digital word. Our proposed idea of using TDC for RO PUF, as shown in Fig. 2, is based on the time characteristics of RO PUFs. In this PUF design, the MUXs are used separately and ROs are configured by K scaling method [7]. Instead of using an edge counter, the proposed structure employs the TDCs to convert the delay time of two oscillators to digital words. The CRP in the proposed TDC based RO PUF is composed by the pair $(C_1, C_2/R)$ where C_1 and C_2 are the MUX selecting signals enabling two stages to work among n oscillator stages. The use of the synchronous DEMUX and MUX signals in this RO PUF approach helps to reduce the power consumption since only two ROs work among n oscillator stages. The first stage with the minimal duty cycle is used as the comparator.

Due to the random variations in the IC fabrication process, the frequency and duty cycles of two outputs o_1 and o_2 (at two MUXs) are not the same. Basically, a TDC works properly if the Start signal arrives before the Stop signal [11]. Hence, two TDCs are required with the crossed connection as shown in Fig. 3. These TDCs work sequentially to measure the delay time values of o_1 and o_2 signals controlled by RESET signal (at '0' value). The bit sequence at the TDC output is encoded into the binary format by a tree encoder [12], then passed through the binary subtractor to provide the respond sequence R. In this proposed RO PUF, the TDC with Vernier delay line structure is used as shown in Fig. 4 [11]. This structure includes N stages in which each stage comprises of two delay units (τ_1, τ_2) and one D-FF. With this operation principle, the resolution of the TDC is LSB $= \tau_1 - \tau_2$.

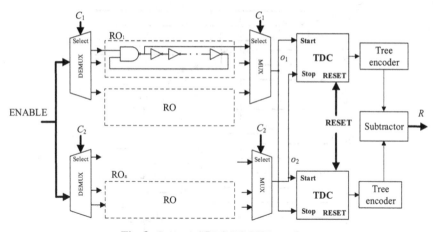

Fig. 3. Proposed TDC RO PUF structure.

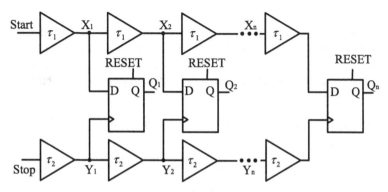

Fig. 4. TDC with Vernier delay line structure.

Figure 5 illustrates the operation principle of the TDC with Vernier delay line structure. The Start and Stop signals are fed to the D and Clock inputs of the D-FF element. Both signals are then propagated through each stage of this TDC provided that the condition of ($\tau_1 > \tau_2$) is satisfied. Hence, after each stage, the Start signal tends to be in-phase with the Stop signal. If its phase is lower, the value of the output D is '1'. Otherwise, the output value becomes '0'.

In this design, the Vernier TDC output is in the form of the thermometer code. It can be converted into the binary format (such as in Gray or ordinary binary form) by the tree encoder [9]. This tree encoder converts from the 2^k bit thermometer code to the k-bit binary format.

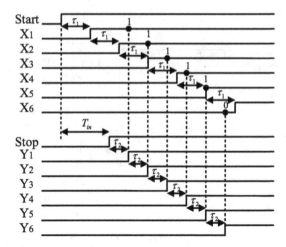

Fig. 5. Operation of the TDC with Vernier delay line structure.

Figure 6 presents the RESET signal generation circuit in which the truth table of the logic function block is presented in Table 1. Figure 7 depicts the simulated waveform of RESET signal generated by the circuit in Fig. 6. By employing the adaptive RESET signal generator, the PUF outputs are extracted with high level of the stability.

Table 1. Truth table of the logic function block used in the adaptive RESET signal generation circuit.

Input	Output
0..000	0
0..001	1
...	...
1..110	1
1..111	0

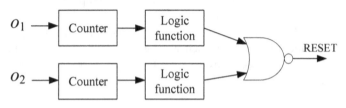

Fig. 6. Adaptive RESET signal generation circuit.

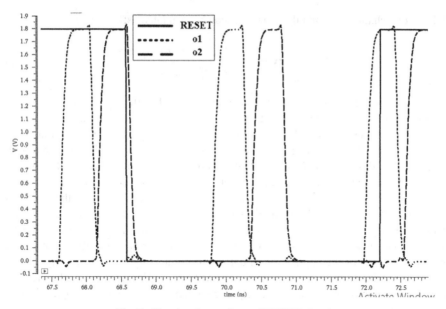

Fig. 7. Simulated waveform of RESET signal.

4 Implementation Results

In this section, we evaluate the performance of the proposed TDC based RO PUF with K = 5 and implemented with TSMC 180 nm CMOS process. The PUF output is extracted by Cadence Virtuoso tool, then processed by Matlab software to provide the performance evaluation metrics. In this work, we use two performance metrics including uniqueness and reliability for the proposed and previous PUF designs.

For the uniqueness, when the same challenge sets are given to different PUFs, the PUF outputs should be different. In other words, the uniqueness indicates how different the generated IDs are among the devices with PUF designs. Specifically, the uniqueness is calculated by the different bits in the respond (R) generated by different PUFs with the same C input and evaluated by the mean Hamming distance (HD) of R values. With k different PUFs having the n-bit respond, the uniqueness is expressed as:

$$\textbf{Uniqueness} = \frac{2}{k(k-1)} \sum_{i=1}^{k-1} \sum_{j=i+1}^{k} \frac{HD(R_i, R_j)}{n} \tag{1}$$

Monte Carlo simulation is used with device mismatch models based on (1) at typical temperature condition (25 °C). As a results, the uniqueness of the proposed PUF design is 48.56%. Moreover, the reliability evaluates the stability of the PUF respond under variations of different parameters including temperature, supply voltage and device aging. If the PUF$_i$ generates an n-bit respond (R_i) at the normal condition, it also generates the respond R_i' at different conditions. We perform this measurement m times with one

PUF for one challenge C and the reliability can be evaluated as:

$$\text{Reliability} = 1 - \frac{1}{m} \sum_{t=1}^{m} \frac{HD(R_i, R'_{i,t})}{n} \qquad (2)$$

We have performed the Monte Carlo simulation with different design corners and temperature in the range of $(25, 35, 45, 55, 65)$ °C. Figure 8 shows the output waveform of the proposed TDC based PUF with the 4-bit respond by Monte Carlo simulation. Moreover, Table 2 shows the experiment results of the proposed PUF compared with other RO PUF designs. It can be seen that the proposed TDC based RO PUF achieves higher value of the uniqueness with an acceptable value of the reliability. The challenge bit C selects 2 among n RO stages randomly, hence the number of CRPs in the proposed TDC based RO PUF is C_2^n. By using C_1 independent with C_2 for selecting the first and second RO stages, combined with a full binary subtractor, the higher number of CRPs can be provided as above. With the achieved results, the proposed PUF design shows its high potential for the application in data encryption using symmetrical algorithms such as the Advanced Encryption Standard (AES) [13]. However, for authentication applications, more improvements are required so that they becomes the topics for our future works.

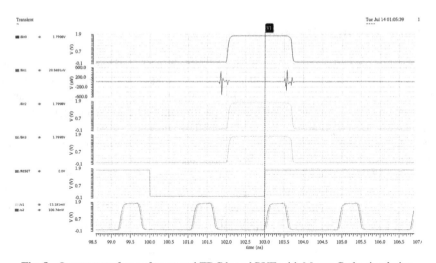

Fig. 8. Output waveform of proposed TDC based PUF with Monte Carlo simulation.

Table 2. Comparison with other RO PUF designs.

Parameter	Number of CRPs	Number of generated bits per challenge	Uniqueness (%)	Reliability (%)
Idea value	2^n	n	50	100
[4]	$\frac{n}{8}$	1	46.15	99.52
[9]	$n-1$	1	47.31	99.14
Proposed PUF	$2 \times C_2^n$	4	48.56	96.56

5   Conclusion

In this paper, we have presented a new, efficient design of CMOS PUF based on the ring oscillators and a time-to-digital converter. The proposed PUF design provides more respond bits for each challenge, higher reliability and uniqueness compared with other works. The proposed PUF design is implemented with TSMC 180 nm CMOS process using Cadence Virtuoso tool. The detail design, simulation and evaluation results are also presented and discussed. The implementation results have clarified the efficiency of the proposed PUF design. In the future work, we will propose other methods to increase the respond bit-width, complete the layout design for the proposed PUF and perform the comprehensive PUF evaluation analysis. Moreover, the applications of the proposed PUF design in the authentication and data encryption will be considered in our future work.

Acknowledgment. This research is funded by Vietnam National Foundation for Science and Technology Development (NAFOSTED) under grant number 102.02–2020.14.

References

1. Halak, B.: Physically Unclonable Functions: From Basic Design Principles to Advanced Hardware Security Applications, 1st edn. Springer (2018). https://doi.org/10.1007/978-3-319-76804-5
2. Herder, C., et al.: Physical unclonable functions and applications: a tutorial. Proc. IEEE **102**(8), 1126–1141 (2014)
3. Rührmair, U., Holcomb, D.E.: PUFs at a glance. In: 2014 Design, Automation & Test in Europe Conference & Exhibition (DATE), Dresden, pp. 1–6 (2014)
4. Suh, G.E., Devadas, S.: Physical unclonable functions for device authentication and secret key generation. In: Proceedings of 44th ACM/IEEE Design Automation Conference (DAC), pp. 9–14, June 2007
5. Delavar, M., et al.: A ring oscillator-based PUF with enhanced challenge-response Pairs. Can. J. Electr. Comput. Eng **39**(2), 174–180 (2016)
6. Gao, M., Lai, K., Qu, G.: A highly flexible ring oscillator PUF. In: Proceedings of the 51st Annual Design Automation Conference. ACM (2014)
7. Gu, C., Chang, C.H., Liu, W., Hanley, N., Miskelly, J., O'Neill, M.: A large scale comprehensive evaluation of single-slice ring oscillator and PicoPUF Bit cells on 28 nm Xilinx FPGAs. In: IEEE Workshop on Attacks and Solutions in Hardware Security (ASHES), pp.1–6 (2019)

8. Tran, V.-T., Trinh, Q.-K., Hoang, V.-P.: Enhanced ID authentication scheme using FPGA-based ring oscillator PUF. In: 2019 IEEE 13th International Symposium on Embedded Multicore/Many-core Systems-on-Chip (MCSoC), Singapore, pp. 320–327 (2019)
9. Kodýtek, F., Lórencz, R., Buček, J.: Improved ring oscillator PUF on FPGA and its properties. Microprocess. Microsyst. **47**, 55–63 (2016)
10. Agustin, J., Lopez-Vallejo, M.L.: A temperature-independent PUF with a configurable duty cycle of CMOS ring oscillators. In: 2016 IEEE International Symposium on Circuits and Systems (ISCAS), Montreal, QC, pp. 2471–2474 (2016)
11. Henzler, S.: Time-to-Digital Converters, Springer (2010). https://doi.org/10.1007/978-90-481-8628-0_2
12. Madhumati, G.L., Rao, K.R., Madhavilatha, M.: Comparison of 5-bit thermometer-to-binary decoders in 1.8 V, 0.18 μm CMOS technology for flash ADCs. In: 2009 International Conference on Signal Processing Systems, Singapore, pp. 516–520 (2009)
13. Phan, T., Hoang, V., Dao, V.: An efficient FPGA implementation of AES-CCM authenticated encryption IP core. In: 2016 3rd National Foundation for Science and Technology Development Conference on Information and Computer Science (NICS), pp. 202–205 (2016)

Information Processing and Data Analysis

A Bufferless Non-exact Matching Hardware Accelerator for Processing Large Non-uniform Stream Data

Quang-Manh Duong$^{(\boxtimes)}$, Quang-Kien Trinh, Dinh-Ha Dao, and Trung-Nguyen

Le Quy Don Technical University, Hanoi, Vietnam
manhdq@lqdtu.edu.vn

Abstract. Recently, problems related to big data processing are becoming more and more popular and place great demands on the processing ability of the systems. The common feature of these problems is the need to find and compare data patterns in a large input data stream in real-time. Algorithms for data processing and pattern matching have been studied for a long time, including both exact and inaccurate (non-exact) solutions, at the same time, the searching data type can be uniform or heterogeneous (non-uniform). Among the proposed data processing platforms, the solution using specialized hardware accelerators proved to be superior in performance and power consumption compared to traditional solutions that combining software and the computing power of the conventional CPUs. In this study, we proposed a bufferless non-exact matching hardware accelerator for processing large non-uniform stream data on reconfigurable hardware (FPGA) combining pipeline architecture and a parallel processing approach. We analyzed the evaluation of hardware resource utilization and the data searching speed on different hardware chips, thereby giving the optimal solution for the hardware design. Finally, we practically demonstrated a design on the Kintex 7-XC7K325T FPGA device that performs pattern matching for shaping large raw input stream data. The hardware implementation from hundreds to thousands of times faster than that on software show the high applicability of the accelerator in practice.

Keywords: FPGA accelerator · Pattern matching · Parallel processing · Pipelined architecture

1 Introduction

In recent times, the problem of dealing with big data, which is prominent among these is the pattern matching problem, has become increasingly popular and has great practical value. This problem has existed for a long time, starting from the classical problems related to communication in computer networks, in which deciding the packet next hop requires reliable and timely matching (of IP/MAC and other components) algorithms. The next problems are safety and security in computer networks, requiring the system to be able to detect malicious packets, computer viruses, etc., these are the premises for

© ICST Institute for Computer Sciences, Social Informatics and Telecommunications Engineering 2021
Published by Springer Nature Switzerland AG 2021. All Rights Reserved
N.-S. Vo et al. (Eds.): INISCOM 2021, LNICST 379, pp. 245–258, 2021.
https://doi.org/10.1007/978-3-030-77424-0_20

the development of Network intrusion detection systems (NIDS) [1], is an important research direction in the scope of Deep Packet Investigation (DPI) [2].

Many solutions have been introduced to solve such problems. In the early stage, when there are not many options available, software solutions combined with the computing power of a shared processor (CPU) are often applied. However, the number of matching patterns was becoming larger and larger, accompanied by complex processing algorithms, making the solution using the software to face many limitations: firstly, the parallel computation on software is not effective; secondly, the bus size when using the software is fixed and small, leading to time-consuming for matching; thirdly, memory access speed on software is not high due to cumbersome architecture. Regarding the last problem, the matching process itself does not take much time, but other backend work is expensive, for example, retrieving a pattern requires a lot of memory-read operations and sometimes has to go to level catches to get data. From the aforementioned analysis, the solution using the software in combination with a conventional CPU may not be suitable for problems that require intensive or real-time computing, thus dedicated hardware solutions are a good alternative. However, hardware accelerators as well can assist but not be a substitute for the whole system, and a combination of specialized hardware and software solutions [3, 4] will be the complete approach to solve the DPI problems.

Let's take a look at a few recent case studies on pattern matching used in DPI on recently advanced hardware platforms. Wang et al. [5] proposed a pattern matching algorithm based on a skip counting automata, implemented through a three-state CAM (TCAM), which helps increasing effectiveness when the TCAM is used for regular expression-based pattern matching; Hung et al. [6] presents an efficient GPU-based multiple pattern matching algorithm for packet filtering, whereas Lin et al. [7] describe an architecture utilizing CPUs and GPUs, implementing a Length-bounded Hybrid Pattern-Matching Algorithm (LHPMA) for DPI. However, these approaches do not consider the approximate matching (they allow false positive but not the random bit error rate), while we are targeting the problem of big data where the preprocessing or data mining allows.

In the scope of this study, we primarily focus on the solution using reconfigurable hardware (FPGA) [8–12], considering their powerful computation capability and flexible customization capability, which are suitable for problems that have strict requirements in latency and bandwidth. Although the computation speed is not compared with ASIC [13], current FPGA devices are adequately powerful enough to solve problems with large bandwidth and their logical resources are sufficient for implementing massive parallel processing. The outstanding feature of FPGA compared to ASIC is that it allows for rapid development, can be easily reconfigured, and is much more cost-effective. Recent reports [14–17] show that the FPGA-based accelerators are capable to handle not only high bandwidth (i.e., up to 400 Gbps [18, 19]) for network packet parser and classification but can easily adapt to rapidly changing and development of the network protocols. The majority of prior arts are consistent in the view that classical signature-based approaches, e.g., Aho-Coasick DFA [20] in conjunction with additional techniques such as the Bloom filter (BF) [21] and Locality Hashing (LSH) [22] are extensively and practically applied [23]. Nonetheless, applying inference-based (Machine Learning) and Neural Network [24, 25] also are merely proposed, which may pave the way for revolutionalized approaches for solving modern big data problems.

In this work, we also focus on the matching problems applied for non-deterministic input stream patterns (i.e., raw binary stream) as opposed to network traffic where the flow of data is segmented/formatted into packets/frames. Besides we also consider a very practical application scenario that has not been covered in most of the previous work. First, the matching is done in a non-exact manner, i.e., the matched is considered with a certain variable permitted error threshold. Second, the design is targeted for memory-constrained devices, i.e., there is no buffering for a gigabit-level stream bandwidth but only a small on-chip cache (a few tens of Kb) serving as the interface elastic buffers[1].

The main contributions of this work are summarized as follows:

- A parallel pipelined architecture of a bufferless non-exact matching hardware accelerator for processing large non-uniform stream data on reconfigurable hardware (FPGA).
- An in-depth analysis based on implementation results on parallelism strategy and technological feasibility and limitation for applying the FPGA-based pattern matching accelerators.
- On-board demonstration of the proposed FPGA implementation using the proposed design that achieves processing speed hundreds of times higher (approximately can up to 945 times faster) on our available Digilent NETFPGA CML board (Kintex 7-XC7K325T) than on the equivalent software implementation.

The rest of this paper is organized as follows. Section 2 introduces the hardware design of the data searching accelerator. Section 3 proposes a design evaluation on dedicated reconfigurable hardware (FPGA) and gives discussions on further improvements. Section 4 presents the practical verification of the proposed design on the Kintex 7-XC7K325T FPGA device. Section 5 concludes the paper.

2 Hardware Design of Data Searching Accelerator

2.1 The Data Matching Problem

In recent years, with the development of transmission technologies, the transmission speed, as well as the data flow, have increased dramatically, so the problem of searching data in a large input data stream becomes more and more urgent. There are two main solutions in big data processing architecture: batch processing and stream-based processing, and stream-based processing is normally chosen when it is necessary to have an immediate response to the event in which data is just generated.

The requirement for big data processing problems in general, as well as the streaming processing problem is that the time of processing must be very short. The amount of data to be processed increases rapidly while the processing ability of the software is limited by the performance of the processors. The viable solution to this problem is to transfer high-speed and real-time responses to specialized hardware. Processed data will be stored for data visualization, data reporting, or data analysis later. In this work, we

---

[1] Due to confidential agreement, we could not go into detail or name of the specific application, but the common technical aspects are described.

designed an FPGA-based accelerator that processes and search for data from large input streaming data using pipelined architecture and parallel data processing. The problems of data searching can be solved thanks to the mentioned advantages of FPGA technology, including the working frequency is large enough to processing high-speed data flows with small latency; hardware-based parallel computing capability is the basis for data processing acceleration; flexible reconfiguration ability ensure to adapt to changes in the data flow structure.

2.2   The Architecture of the Design

In this paper, we propose a hardware design then evaluate parameters to optimize the data searching speed and resource utilization. The main part of the design is a parallel searching block called Matching Engine (ME) as shown in Fig. 1.

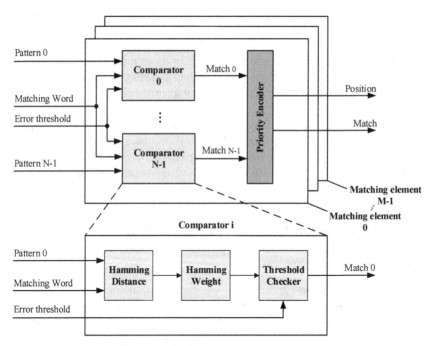

Fig. 1. Block diagram of matching engines

Input streaming data to ME is compared with pre-configured data patterns with comparators, each ME contains N such blocks. The comparator computes the required parameters such as Hamming distance, Hamming weight and compares the last parameter with the permitted deviation threshold. Finally, the Priority Encoder will decide whether to select the current data or not (by the Match signal at the output of the ME), in case the data is selected, its position in the streaming data (Position signal) will be stored. To accelerate the searching process, we arranged an array of MEs with the described working principle, i.e. having (NxM) comparators working simultaneously (in parallel).

Design of the Non-exact Comparator

For the reason that the error threshold is permitted, the comparator in this architecture is designed for signature-based matching and in the scope of circuit design. Other algorithmic enhancements are considered at other design layers. Each comparator works with two vectors of the same size x and y as shown in Fig. 2, where y is the sample binary bit string and x is the binary bit string to be compared. First, the Hamming Distance (HD) block calculates the distance between the two vectors x and the vector y, the output of this block is a binary vector, and also the input of the Hamming Weight (HW) block, which has the function of counting the number of bit 1 and the output represents the number of different positions between the original two input vectors. The comparator sets an initial fixed threshold value E (Error threshold), depending on which the comparison is classified as either an exact comparison ($E = 0$) or non-exact (inaccurate) comparison ($E \neq 0$).

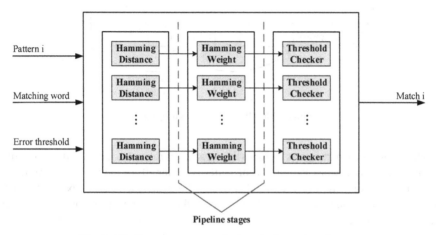

Fig. 2. Pipeline structure to calculate the hamming distance

We focused on the architectural optimizing for comparators to accelerate the computation speed for the overall ME block. In the case of exact matching, the comparator will perform a direct comparison of two input vectors, if they matched, then conclude the correct search result and vice versa, hence there is no need to use HW blocks, which greatly reduces resources and speeds up the computation. However, since the matching problem allows for a certain error threshold, in the case of non-exact matching, it is necessary to optimize the design for the bit error computation block.

Based on the above analysis, a tree adder structure capable of automatically adjusting the input data size is selected for the bit error computation. The first stage of the tree adder is optimized using the 6-input LUT of the FPGA Series 7, at the second stage, the two results are added together and moved to the following stage. This process is repeated until the final result is computed, using the inter-stage pipeline technique to ensure timing optimization with the number of the used adder stage is [log2([L/6])] in total.

The threshold checker is used to filter the input data by comparing them to a threshold value which can be set at run time. In practice, small Hamming distance values are of interest (since the input data is quite close together), large values are not considered to save processing time as well as memory during filtering the results. To ensure the best possible performance, ME and all design elements are described and optimized by the hardware description language (HDL) with the primary task of creating a customizable (extensible) design to apply for different problems. Accordingly, the parameters of the design can be generically configured. The model of the structure of comparison data and related parameters is described in Fig. 3.

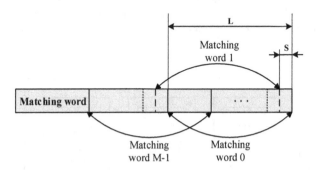

Fig. 3. Structure of the matching data

The set of design parameters includes the parameters related to the input data structure (length of matching word L, number of patterns N, length of symbol S); parameters related to the design architecture (number of matching elements M, number of pipeline stages C, system frequency F); parameter related to the searching type (exact or non-exact searching - error threshold E).

3   Design Evaluation on FPGA

We conduct the design evaluations of computation speed and resource utilization according to the parameter groups presented in Sect. 2.2, including the group of parameters involving the input data structure (L, N, S); the group of parameters related to the design architecture (M, C, F) and the parameter involving the searching method (E). These evaluations were made on the 2016.4 Xilinx Vivado software version.

3.1   Evaluation on the Impact of Parameters Related to the Input Data Structure

In this sub-section, we have chosen some representative and active FPGA families from Xilinx, including the low-cost (Artix-7), the best price/performance (Kintex-7), the performance-optimized (Virtex-7) solutions to evaluate the resource utilization when changing the length of matching word L. The graph represents the resource utilization is shown in Fig. 4 with fixed parameter set (M = 8, C = 2, F = 100 MHz).

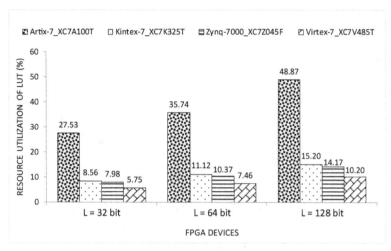

Fig. 4. Number of LUTs utilized on different FPGA devices and lengths of matching word with fixed parameter set (M = 8, C = 2, F = 100 MHz, E ≠ 0)

The evaluation results obtained show that with the same length of the matching word LUT resource utilized on different FPGA series decreases from Artix-7 to Virtex-7, which can predict through the hardware resources available on these chips announced by the manufacturer. However, the most expected result is the effect of the matching word length on resource consumption, which makes a significant difference in considered cases. For example, when the length value increased from 32 bits to 128 bits, the number of LUTs utilized in the Kintex-7 XC7K325T FPGA device almost doubled (8.56% vs 15.2%), thus reducing the length of matching word is an aspect that needs more attention.

3.2 Evaluation on the Impact of Parameters Related to the Design Architecture

Furthermore, we evaluated resource utilization on the same Kintex-7 device (XC7K325T) with different values of the number of matching elements M ranging from 2 to 32. Evaluations are conducted in both exact searching (E = 0) as well as non-exact searching (E > 0), the corresponding results of different utilized resources are shown in Fig. 5.

Theoretically, as the M value increases, the number of concurrent operations, as well as the number of logical resources utilized increases accordingly, the number of LUT utilized reaches the maximum value when the number of matching elements M = 32 (correspondingly 256 simultaneous comparisons), which accounts for less than 50%, an indication that the design is completely feasible on this FPGA platform. The analysis is evaluated in both cases of exact matching and non-exact matching.

In the case of the exact matching, there is no need to compare the results against a given error threshold, the Hamming weight block is omitted, resulting in a consequential decrease in the number of utilized logic resources. The graph showing the correlation between the percentages of utilized LUT in both cases is shown in Fig. 5. The difference in logic resource consumption is insignificant when the number of matching elements

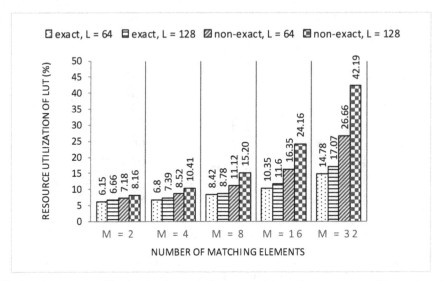

Fig. 5. The resource utilization for the cases of exact matching and non-exact matching evaluated on Kintex-7 XC7K325T with a fixed parameter set (C = 2, F = 100 MHz)

is small (M = 2; 4) and becomes quite large (about 25%) when M increases to the maximum value (M = 32). Based on the shape of the charts it is possible to comment that the LUT count grows in qua quasi-exponential manner and the parameter M has a significant influence on resource utilization.

Predictably, the resource utilized in non-exact searching is greater than in exact searching since the last one does not require the bit error counter. For example, with the same number of matching elements M = 32, non-exact searching requires 2.5 times more logical resources than an exact searching, which poses the need for optimization of the bit error calculator (HW block) to reduce the utilized hardware resources. In this study, we propose an HW block designed for the matching word of length L = 128 bits, so four design schemes for Hamming weight counter have length 128 × 1; 64 × 2; 32 × 4, and 16 × 8 respectively (see Fig. 6).

Among the designs mentioned, the one that uses four blocks with a 32-bit computational string length gives the best results, which can be explained based on the characteristics of the 7 series FPGA chips that are optimal for 6-input LUT.

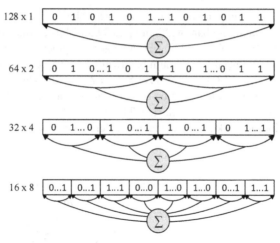

Fig. 6. Design diagram of the hamming weight counter

3.3 Performance Evaluation

The Actual Time of the Pattern Matching Process
In this section we calculate and examine the change of actual time spent on the non-exact pattern matching process, T_{actual}, calculated by the difference of theoretical time $T_{desired}$ and setup time T_{setup} (slack) on FPGA chip series. On each FPGA chip series at this time, we choose a typical device, all the time-related figures are given in Table 1.

Table 1. Actual time spent on the non-exact pattern matching process

M = 8	Artix-7	Kintex-7	Zynq-7000	Virtex-7	Kintex ultrascale
Device	XC7A100T	XC7K325T	XC7Z045F	XC7V485T	XCKU095
Actual time (ns)	13.16	9.12	8.93	9.00	6.91
Desired time (ns)	20	20	20	20	20
Slack time (ns)	6.84	10.88	11.07	11.01	13.09

Maximum Bandwidth and Comparison with Software Implementation
The data processing speed of the design (bandwidth - BW) depends on parameters including the length of symbol S, the number of matching elements M, and the system frequency F according to the formula $BW = S \times M \times F$. The maximum bandwidth of the board circuit is estimated based on the maximum value of the mentioned above parameters and depends greatly on the type of FPGA chip.

Here, we calculated the bandwidth based on the core of the design, therefore the actual value of the BW which can be achieved depends on the type of communication between the FPGA board and the computer and this is merely a technical issue. Theoretically, the design can achieve a maximum bandwidth of up to 39.36 Gbps on the Kintex Ultrascale FPGA series (XCKU095). XC7K325T FPGA board for practical verification of the proposed design can achieve the maximum bandwidth of 10.53 Gbps corresponding to the set of parameters (M = 48, L = 128, N = 8, S = 2, E $\neq$ 0), which about 945 times higher than the equivalent implementation on software, the actual bandwidth can reach a higher value by employing a larger device. The graphs of the maximum bandwidth, as well as the maximum clock frequency on the different series of FPGA, are shown in Fig. 7.

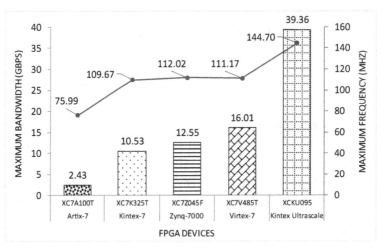

Fig. 7. The maximum bandwidth and the maximum frequency of the design on the different FPGA devices with a fixed set of parameters (M = 48, L = 128, N = 8, S = 2, E $\neq$ 0)

3.4 The Multilayer Optimizing Solutions to Improve the Overall Performance of the Searching System

In this study, our solutions related to the matching core design and optimizing them for data searching belong to the under solution layer. In this solution layer, we have proposed a parallel pipelined architecture of a bufferless non-exact matching hardware accelerator, and evaluations of the impact of the various parameters on searching performance have been fully conducted in Subsects. 3.1, 3.2, and 3.3. For a general data searching problem, design proposals often target such matching cores.

However, a data searching system generally has different multiple design layers, to get the best performance, all of the design layers must be improved and optimized. Although located at different layers, the general purpose of the solutions is saving resource utilization and accelerating the data processing and in practice, these two criteria are often achieved simultaneously. Sometimes, a good solution at the upper layer, i.e. the system design level, can solve a lot of problems, including problems related to the matching core. Therefore, optimal solutions at the system design level should be fully considered, which is also the future development direction of the research besides matching core improvement solutions.

Based on the analysis and preliminary survey of recent studies on similar problems shown in Sect. 1 of this paper, two groups of solutions are viable for the system design level, the first is the applying of classical algorithms in conjunction with additional techniques such as Bloom Filter and Locality-Sensitive Hashing to reduce the size of the data in comparison and matching processes. Some typical studies can be outlined for instance: Prya et al. [21] present a combined hierarchical approach based on an all-length Bloom filter for the source prefix field and an H-trie data structure for the destination prefix field; Lim et al. [22] extend the tuple pruning algorithm for traffic filtering; Ahmandi et al. [23] introduced a k-stage pipelined Bloom filter to improve power efficiency.

The second group of solutions deals with an area of interest recently, using Artificial Intelligence combined with Machine Learning techniques to create Neural Networks that help classify the raw (non-uniform) data from the input, which can significantly reduce the amount of data to be processed on the hardware. Neural Networks can be completely constructed on software platforms while some stages in the network requiring intensive-computation can be transferred to hardware for acceleration. Zhou et al. [24] proposed a network based on 10–30 neurons for the traffic classification task in which the difference in accuracy when using neurons 30 and 10 is negligible, compared the Naive Bayesian method with the Feed-Forward Neural Network model and found that the latter method proved more effective. Zelina et al. [25] proposed a packet-size-based classification model using early detection which classifies the flow based on the first few packets, in which the first 6 packets of the flow were used to train the NN model and classify 5 applications (SSH, Skype, HTTP, POP3, Bittorrent) with an average of 60–70% accuracy.

The solution groups related to the system design level presented above are potential options for us in improving the overall searching system, for example, hashing data before comparing, using Bloom Filters or Neural Networks to classify and reduce the size of raw data at the input of the searching system. These solutions will be considered and applied in upcoming studies.

4 The Practical Verification of the Matching Core

We finally evaluated the effectiveness of the accelerator core via a real-world application. Specifically, the core has to perform in-exact matching with a variable threshold and has matched for different types of data with a total of 512 patterns. During the practical experiment on the Kintex-7 XC7K355T FPGA device, the input of the non-uniform data flow is pushed down to the FPGA board via AXI protocol to perform the searching. The design will adjust accordingly according to the values of the general parameters outlined as mentioned above in Subsect. 2.2.

With specific design parameters, the test results show the number of utilized resources including 54% of LUT, 1% of memory elements, and 33% of RAM (Fig. 8).

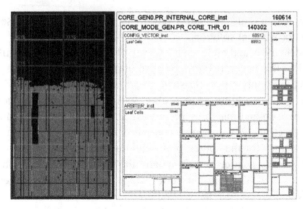

Fig. 8. Resource utilization on Kintex7-XC7K355T FPGA device for a matching core including peripherals with a fixed set of parameters (F = 100 MHz, L = 128, M = 8, N = 512, E ≠ 0)

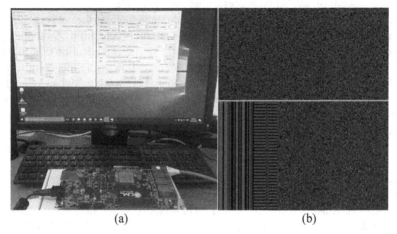

(a)   (b)

Fig. 9. Design verification on digilent NETFPGA CML board (Kintex7-XC7K355T FPGA) (a) and the bit view of the data before and after processing (b)

The process of searching the data transmitted from the computer to the FPGA board (Fig. 9a) gave accurate results, confirming the correctness of the design, but the bandwidth was limited to about 800 Mbps. This can be partly explained by the non-uniform data type at the input leading to bit-by-bit processing, and the rest due to the bandwidth limitation of the Ethernet 1 Gbps port. Figure 9b shows a bit-view image of the data before processing (top image) with a chaotic arrangement and after processing (bottom image), which has been arranged in order and formatted.

5   Conclusion

In this paper, we have proposed a design for the data matching accelerator implemented on reconfigurable hardware (FPGA) due to its outstanding technological advantages.

Design parameters were considered to evaluate the resource utilization and the data searching speed. As a case study, an implementation on the Kintex 7-XC7K325T FPGA device has been conducted, using the exact and non-exact searching method.

The solutions to improve the search speed can be using multiple parallel comparators or reducing the size of the input data, the last one is the premise for applying data hashing algorithms to reduce the size of the matching patterns, thereby speeding up the data searching on the hardware. In addition to such improvements of the hardware design, other promising solutions are the applications of classical data searching algorithms in conjunction with Bloom filter, Locality-Sensitive Hashing, or Neural Networks to reduce the size of the input data stream and we will consider their adoption for improvement of the design in the future work.

Acknowledgment. This research is funded by the Vietnam National Foundation for Science and Technology Development (NAFOSTED) under grant number 102.01–2018.310.

References

1. Huang, N.F., Hung, H.W., Lai, S.H., Chu, Y.M., Tsai, W.Y.: A GPU-based multiple-pattern matching algorithm for network intrusion detection systems. In: Proceedings of the 22nd International Conference on Advanced Information Networking and Applications (AINA), pp. 62–67 (2008)
2. Thinh, T.T., Hieu, T.N., Van Quoc, D., Kittitornkun, S.: A FPGA-based deep packet inspection engine for network intrusion detection system. In: 9th International Conference on Electrical Engineering/Electronics, Computer, Telecommunications and Information Technology, Phetchaburi, pp. 1–4 (2012). https://doi.org/10.1109/ECTICon.2012.6254301.
3. Fiessler, A., Hager, S., Scheuermann, B., Moore, A.W.: HyPaFilter – a versatile hybrid FPGA packet filter. In: Proceedings of the ACM/IEEE Symposium on Architectures for Networking and Communications Systems (2016)
4. Fiessler, A., Lorenz, C., Hager, S., Scheuermann, B., Moore, A.W.: HyPaFilter+: enhanced hybrid packet filtering using hardware assisted classification and header space analysis. IEEE/ACM Trans. Netw. **25**, 3655–3669 (2017)
5. Wang, F., Hong, Y., Jin, J.: Research on regular expression data packet matching algorithm based on three state content addressable memory. Int. J. Simul. – Syst. Sci. Technol. vol. **16**(5A) p. 8.1–8.5 (2015)
6. Hung, C.-L., Lin, C.-Y., Wu, P.-C.: An Efficient GPU-based multiple pattern matching algorithm for packet filtering. J. Sig. Proc. Syst. **86**(2–3), 347–358 (2016). https://doi.org/10.1007/s11265-016-1139-0
7. Lin, Y.S., Lee, C.L., Chen, Y.C.: Length-Bounded hybrid CPU/GPU pattern matching algorithm for deep packet inspection. Algorithms **10**(16), 1–13 (2017)
8. Baker, Z.K., Prasanna, V.K.: Time and area efficient pattern matching on FPGAs. In: FPGA, pp. 223–232 (2004)
9. Clark, C.R., Lee, W., Schimmel, D.E., Contis, D., Kone, M., Thomas, A.: A hardware platform for network intrusion detection and prevention. In: Proceedings of Workshop on Network Processors and Applications, pp. 136–145 (2005)
10. Clark, C.R., Schimmel, D.E.: Efficient reconfigurable logic circuits for matching complex network intrusion detection patterns. Proceedings of International Conference on Field Programmable Logic and Applications, pp. 956–959 (2003)

11. Sourdis, I., Pnevmatikatos, D.: Pre-decoded CAMs for efficient and high-speed NIDS pattern matching. In: 12th Annual IEEE FCCM, April 2004
12. Clark, C.R., Schimmel, D.E.: Scalable pattern matching for high speed networks. In: 12th Annual IEEE FCCM, April 2004
13. Liu, R.T., Huang, N.F., Chen, C.H., Kao, C.N.: A fast string-matching algorithm for network processor based intrusion detection system. ACM Trans. Embed. Comput. Syst. 3(3), 614–633 (2004)
14. Pus, V., Kekely, L., Korenek, J.: Low-Latency modular packet header parser for FPGA. In: Proceedings of the 9th ACM/IEEE Symposium on Architecture for Networking and Communications Systems. Austin, Texas, pp. 77–78 (2012)
15. Benácek, P., Pus, V., Kubátová, H.: P4-to-VHDL: automatic generation of 100 Gbps packet parsers. In: Proceedings of the IEEE 24th Annual International Symposium on Field-Programmable Custom Computing Machines (2016)
16. Benácek, P., Pus, V., Korenak, J., Kekely, M.: Line rate programmable packet processing in 100Gb networks. In: Proceedings of tthe 27th International Conference on Field Programmable Logic and Applications, Ghent, Belgium (2017)
17. da Silva, J.S., Boyer, F.-R., Langlois, J.M.P.: P4-compatible high-level synthesis of low latency 100 Gb/s streaming packet parsers in FPGAs. In: Proceedings of the 26th ACM/SIGDA International Symposium on Field-Programmable Gate Arrays (FPGA 2018), February 2018. Monterey, California
18. Attig, M., Brebner, G.: 400 Gb/s programmable packet parsing on a single FPGA. In: Proceedings of the ACM/IEEE Seventh Symposium on Architectures for Networking and Communications Systems. pp. 12–23 (2011)
19. Pus, V., Kekely, L., Korenek, J.: Design methodology of configurable high performance packet parser for FPGA. In: Proceedings of the 17 International Symposium on Design and Diagnostics of Electronic Circuits and Systems. Warsaw, Poland (2014)
20. Kumar, S., Turner, J., Williams, J.: Advanced algorithm for fast and scalable deep packet inspection. In: Proceedings of the ACM/IEEE Symposium on Architecture for Networking and Communications systems. San Jose, CA (2006)
21. Priya, A.G.A., Lim, H.: Hierarchical packet classification using a bloom filter and rule-priority tries. Comput. Commun. 33(10), 1215–1225 (2010)
22. Lim, H., Kim, S.Y.: Tuple Pruning Using Bloom Filter for Packet Classification, pp. 48–58. IEEE, Micro (2010)
23. Ahmadi, M., Wong, S.: K-Stage Pipelined bloom filter for packet classification. In: Proc. International Conference on Computational Science and Engineering. Vancouver, Canada, pp. 64–70 (2009)
24. Zhou, W., Dong, L., Bic, L., Zhou, M., Chen, L.: Internet traffic classification using feed-forward neural network. In: Proceedings of the International Conference on Computational Problem-Solving (2011)
25. Zelina, M., Oravec, M.: Early Detection of Network Applications using Neural Networks. IEEE, Elmar (2011)

A New User Recommendation Model Within the Context of the Covid-19 Pandemic

Thanh Trinh[✉]

Center for Remote Sensing and Geohazards, Vietnam Institute of Geosciences and Mineral Resources, Hanoi, Vietnam

Abstract. Event-based social networks provide people with fantastic platforms to improve their relationships and make friends through offline and online activities. Predicting the event attendance of users is a challenging problem and solved by many techniques. Recently, the outbreak of Covid-19 changes the ways that users participate in events, from offline to online. In this paper, we study the problem of user recommendation within the context of the Covid-19 pandemic. To address this problem, we first analyze the information of events to obtain three factors, i.e., content, time, and location. Then, we propose a new recommendation model to compute scores of new events with respect to participated events of each user. Finally, the top N events with the highest scores are recommended to the user. Extensive experiments were conducted on a real Meetup event dataset, and the results have shown that our model outperforms comparison methods.

Keywords: Recommendation · Covid-19 · EBSNs

1 Introduction

Event-based social networks (EBSNs) [7,11] enhance the interactions and relationships among people by providing flexible platforms for them. People use these platforms to make offline activities and invite others to attend with them. Meetup[1] is considered as a famous example of EBSNs. Figure 1 demonstrates an example of EBSNs and descriptions of events in EBSNs. We can observe that the information of events includes content, time, location, as well as a list of attendees. When an event appears in Meetup, the event will be recommended to a user if it is relevant to the user's participated events. Users can attend several events with different contents, and events can be hosted in different places. Several research problems are listed in EBSNs, such as event recommendation and user recommendation. Many works [4,8,9,11,13,16] have been proposed to address these problems. The Covid-19 pandemic recently appears and affects

---

[1] meetup.com.

© ICST Institute for Computer Sciences, Social Informatics and Telecommunications Engineering 2021
Published by Springer Nature Switzerland AG 2021. All Rights Reserved
N.-S. Vo et al. (Eds.): INISCOM 2021, LNICST 379, pp. 259–267, 2021.
https://doi.org/10.1007/978-3-030-77424-0_21

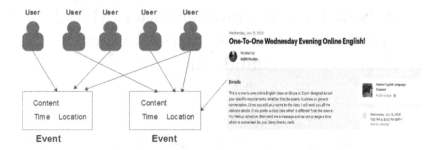

Fig. 1. Example of event-based social networks.

almost all outdoor activities across the world in the year 2020. For example, many football matches are delayed or even canceled. By investigating a crowded city, London, UK, we find that the topics and the types of events are significantly changed. Particularly, outdoor activities change from offline to online, or even they are canceled. And, the numbers of participants are fluctuated due to the Covid-19 crisis. These facts also make users change the way to take part in events.

Therefore, in this paper, we study the user recommendation problem within the context of the Covid-19 through an investigation of EBSNs. We formulate this problem as follows: *Given a user u with a list of participated events, the goal is to recommend the top N upcoming suitable events to user u.*

We study this problem in the context of the Covid-19 pandemic, which happens in London in the first nine months of 2020, from January to September. The information of events is extracted into content, location, and time factors. We first convert contents into vectors of terms in order to measure the similarity between events contents. Cosine similarity is adopted to measure the relevance between events' contents. Then, similarities between events based on time and location factors are measured. Finally, we propose a new recommendation to compute the relevance score of a new event with respect to a list of participated events of a user u. Events with higher scores will be recommended to user u.

An empirical study was conducted on the real world dataset. The experimental results have shown that the improvement of our proposed model over three baseline methods. We also find that the content factor is the most critical one that affects the decisions of users.

The remainder of this paper is organized as follows. Section 2 analyzes Meetup event characteristics. The proposed model is presented in Sect. 3. Section 4 presents the empirical study. Related work is included in Sect. 5. Section 6 gives conclusions and new research directions of this work.

2   Meetup Event Analysis

In this section, we discuss three essential factors, i.e., text (or content), time, and location, that influence users to join events. The relevance score between two events, e^i and e^j, can be represented by the three factors.

2.1   Text Factor

Since an event's text can be represented as a vector of terms, we compute the similarity between events' contents. Given two events e^i and e^j with two vectors of terms T^i and T^j, the similarity between them is defined as the following Eq. 1:

$$t(e^i, e^j) = \frac{T^i \cdot T^j}{\|T^i\|\|T^j\|} \tag{1}$$

where $t(.,.)$ is the cosine similarity score between two events, the value of t is from $[0, 1]$. The higher value of t indicates that two events are much relevant.

2.2   Time Factor

We divide the time factor of events into two factors: the day of week factor and the time of day factor. The temporal similarity score between events can be defined as the following equations:

$$w(e^i, e^j) = \begin{cases} 1 & \text{if day}(e^i) = \text{day}(e^i) \\ 0 & \text{otherwise} \end{cases} \tag{2}$$

where $w(.,.)$ is the similarity score between two events based on the day of week factor, and $day(.)$ presents weekly days (for instance Sunday). The similarity based on the time of day factor between two events is computed as Eq. 3.

$$h(e^i, e^j) = e^{-\frac{(e^i(t) - e^j(t))^2}{2}} \tag{3}$$

where $e^i(t)$ is the time of day of event e^i, for instance, $7pm$.

2.3   Location Factor

We calculate the location similarity between events as Eq. 4:

$$d(e^i, e^j) = e^{\frac{-l(e^i, e^j)^2}{2}} \tag{4}$$

where $l(e^i, e^j)$ is the distance in miles between the two locations of two events.

3   Recommendation Model

We propose a new recommendation model to provide a user with a list of N new events. Given a list of new events E^n and a user u with a list of participated events E^p, the goal is to offer user u the top N new events relevant to E^p.

Each event e^j in E^n, Algorithm 1 is first used to calculate relevance score s_j of e^j w.r.t. E^p. Then, all events in E^n are sorted by the relevance score s in descending order. Finally, the proposed model will recommend the top N new events with the highest scores s to user u. If two events have the same score s, one event with a higher score d will be selected. Score d is computed by Eq. 8.

Algorithm 1. Relevance score (e^j, E^p)

Initial: Given a set of participated events E^p, a new event e^j.
Given a threshold α, the value of α is from 0 to 1.
for *each event e^i in E^p* **do**
  | $t_j^i(e^i, e^j)$ is computed by Eq. 1; $w_j^i(e^i, e^j)$ is computed by Eq. 2;
  | $h_j^i(e^i, e^j)$ is computed by Eq. 3; $d_j^i(e^i, e^j)$ is computed by Eq. 4
end

$$w_j = \frac{\Sigma^{|E^p|} w_j^i}{|E^p|}; \tag{5}$$

$$h_j = \frac{\Sigma^{|E^p|} h_j^i}{|E^p|}; \tag{6}$$

$$t_j = \frac{\Sigma^{|E^p|} t_j^i}{|E^p|}; \tag{7}$$

$$d_j = \frac{\Sigma^{|E^p|} d_j^i}{|E^p|}; \tag{8}$$

$$s_j = \alpha \times t_j + (1 - \alpha) \times (w_j \times h_j) \tag{9}$$

---

4   Empirical Study

We have collected a real Meetup event dataset of London city from Meetup, from January to September 2020. That contained 19761 events and 18237 users, in which each event had at least five attendees, and each user engaged in at least five events in the time period. We used Lucence[2] to generate terms for events contents. Figure 2 describes the total number of events (19761) and only the number of online events (8580) in the first nine months of 2020. Figure 3 illustrates the distribution of users and events in the dataset. We can observe that the majority of users attend less than 15 events and the majority of events have less than 20 attendees. For more details, the average number of attendees per event is 19, and the average number of participated events per user is 12.

4.1   Setup

We split the collected dataset into three datasets and used them in experiments as follows:

- **Dataset 1.** Events that were collected from January to March were considered as the participated events. All events were obtained from April to June as the new events.

---

[2] https://lucene.apache.org/.

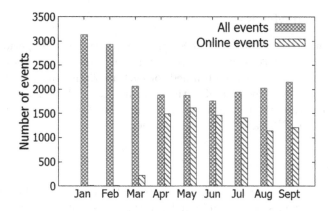

Fig. 2. Number of events in the first nine months of 2020.

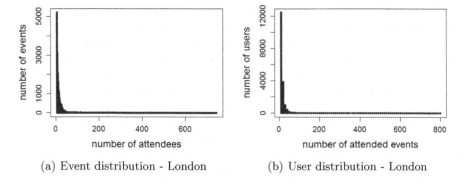

(a) Event distribution - London   (b) User distribution - London

Fig. 3. Distribution of events and users in the first nine months of 2020.

- **Dataset 2.** Events from April and June were taken as the participated ones, and events from July to September were treated as the new ones.
- **Dataset 3.** Events from January to June were used as attended ones, and events from July to September were considered as the new ones.

4.2   Baseline Methods

We compare the proposed model with three baseline methods; they are listed as follows:

- Location-based model (**LM**). The relevance score of each new event e^j is computed by Eq. 8.
- Text-based and location-based model (**TLM**). The score of event e^j is calculated as $t_j \times d_j$; t_j is defined by Eq. 7, and d_j is expressed by Eq. 8.
- Text-based model (**TM**). The score of event e^j is calculated by Eq. 7.
- The proposed model(**PM**). The score is computed in Algorithm 1 and described in Eq. 9.

4.3   Evaluation Metrics

We use precision $P@N$ and recall $R@N$ metrics to evaluate the performance of recommendation models, where N is the number of top events recommended to each user. The two metrics are obtained for each user, and the overall precision and recall are achieved by averaging these accuracies of all users.

Algorithms were implemented in Java and executed on a machine with 2.6 GHz dual-core CPU and 8 GB main memory.

4.4   Experimental Results

We compare the performance of the proposed method with three baseline methods. The experiments were conducted on the three different split datasets. Figure 4 shows the recall and the precision metrics of the four comparison methods, and the number of events is set to 5, 10, and 15.

We can observe that the proposed model outperforms the other methods in the three datasets. **LM** is the worst method because **LM** gives a list of events without considering contents to users. Moreover, these events are created in the same places or can be held online; hence, LM produces the worst results. In event-based social networks, users often engage in events on similar topics; therefore, **TM** produces accuracies of recall and precision much higher than **LM** and **TLM**. However, one factor is not enough to predict the event attendance of users because their decisions also depend on location and time factors.

The proposed model **PM** is formed by the combination of terms, time, and location. In other words, the location, time, and text scores are taken into account for computing the relevance score of each new event with respect to a set of participated events. Therefore, **PM** can select relevant events in terms of contents, time, and location. Moreover, we evaluate different values of parameter α to achieve the best performance; the value of $\alpha = 0.95$ is an optimal value in our proposed model for three datasets. That is why **PM** yields the best results in the two metrics.

Dataset 2 and Dataset 3 have the same list of new events that are extracted from July to September; hence, the results from these two datasets are not much different. Moreover, the results of these two datasets are much higher than those of Datasets 1. We explain that as follows: 1) Dataset 1 contains a part of the number of online events while the other datasets contain all online events (seen in Fig. 2). 2) At the end of March, London was lockdown; so, people could not join some common outdoor activities. These facts reduce the performance of all methods in Dataset 1.

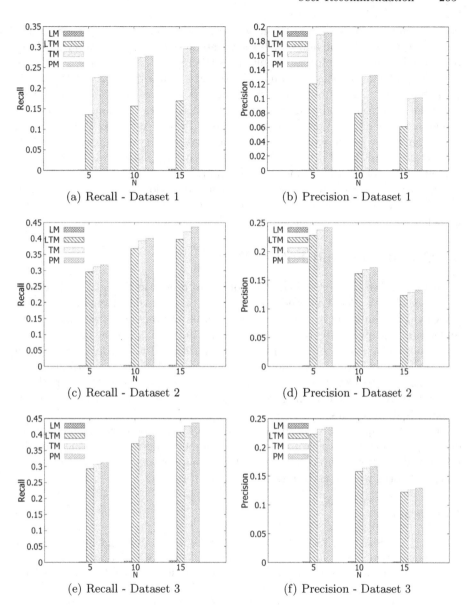

Fig. 4. Performance of the four methods.

5   Related Work

Several research problems were defined in event-based social networks [5], such as recommendation and group activeness [12]. The problems of event recommendation and user recommendation have attracted a lot of interest from researchers [8,17,19]. Event recommendation provides an event with a list of users by investigating the behaviors of users and influences on them [8,11,13], and analyzing the online and offline social interactions with geographical places to be used in matrix factorization methods [10,18].

The problem of user recommendation was studied in [2,7,9,18]. They exploited the social contexts and the behaviors of users in event-based social networks to recommend suitable events to each user. Hannon [3] defined a friend recommendation problem by studying Twitter network. This problem was extended by some works [6,13–15], such as activity recommendation [14] and active friend [13]. The problem of friend recommendation was addressed by exploiting the relationships among users, and the interactions between users and events contexts in those works. Multiple recommendation problems were studied and solved in one framework, such as a graph-based model [9] and a probabilistic model [1].

6   Conclusions and Future Work

In this paper, we have presented the problem of user recommendation in event-based social networks. This study is conducted on the real collected data within the Covid-19 pandemic in London. Three factors of events are first analyzed to understand the event attendances, i.e., content, location, and time factors. Then, we propose a new model to provide each user with a list of proper events. The empirical results have shown that the proposed model outperforms the baseline methods. Due to Covid-19, many events are held online via Zoom or Skype services; therefore, the content factor is the key feature in the decisions of users to participate in events.

This work opens two promising directions for future work: 1) recommendation problems within this pandemic in different countries; 2) changes of the relationships between users and the interactions between users and events in social networks when a certain crisis happens in real life.

References

1. Dong, C., Shen, Y., Zhou, B., Jin, H.: I2Rec: an iterative and interactive recommendation system for event-based social networks. SBP-BRiMS 2016. Lecture Notes in Computer Science, pp. 250–261. Springer International Publishing, Cham (2016). https://doi.org/10.1007/978-3-319-39931-7_24
2. Du, R., Yu, Z., Mei, T., Wang, Z., Wang, Z., Guo, B.: Predicting activity attendance in event-based social networks. In: Proceedings of the 2014 ACM International Joint Conference on Pervasive and Ubiquitous Computing - UbiComp 2014 Adjunct. pp. 425–434. ACM Press, New York (2014). https://doi.org/10.1145/2632048.2632063
3. Hannon, J., Bennett, M., Smyth, B.: Recommending twitter users to follow using content and collaborative filtering approaches, pp. 199–206 (2010)
4. Jhamb, Y., Fang, Y.: A dual-perspective latent factor model for group-aware social event recommendation. Inf. Process. Manage. 53(3), 559–576 (2017). https://doi.org/10.1016/j.ipm.2017.01.001,https://linkinghub.elsevier.com/retrieve/pii/S0306457316302357

5. Li, R., Lei, K.H., Khadiwala, R., Chang, K.C.C.: TEDAS: A twitter-based event detection and analysis system. Proceedings - International Conference on Data Engineering, pp. 1273–1276 (2012). https://doi.org/10.1109/ICDE.2012.125

6. Li, S., Cheng, X., Su, S., Jiang, L.: Followee recommendation in event-based social networks. In: Gao, H., Kim, J., Sakurai, Y. (eds.) DASFAA 2016. LNCS, vol. 9645, pp. 27–42. Springer, Cham (2016). https://doi.org/10.1007/978-3-319-32055-7_3

7. Liu, X., He, Q., Tian, Y., Lee, W.C., McPherson, J., Han, J.: Event-based social networks. In: Proceedings of the 18th ACM SIGKDD International Conference on Knowledge Discovery and Data Mining - KDD 2012, p. 1032. ACM Press, New York (2012). https://doi.org/10.1145/2339530.2339693

8. Ogundele, T.J., Member, S.: SoCaST *: personalized event recommendations for event-based social networks : a multi-criteria decision making approach. IEEE Access 6(1), 27579–27592 (2018). https://doi.org/10.1109/ACCESS.2018.2832543

9. Pham, T.A.N., Li, X., Cong, G., Zhang, Z.: A general graph-based model for recommendation in event-based social networks. In: 2015 IEEE 31st International Conference on Data Engineering, pp. 567–578 (2015). https://doi.org/10.1109/ICDE.2015.7113315

10. Qiao, Z., Zhang, P., Cao, Y., Zhou, C.: Combining heterogenous social and geographical information for event recommendation. In: Twenty-Eighth AAAI Conference on Artificial Intelligence, pp. 145–151 (2014). http://www.aaai.org/ocs/index.php/AAAI/AAAI14/paper/view/8451

11. Trinh, T., Nguyen, N.T., Wu, D., Huang, J.Z., Emara, T.Z.: A new location-based topic model for event attendees recommendation. 2019 IEEE-RIVF International Conference on Computing and Communication Technologies (RIVF), pp. 1–6 (2019). https://doi.org/10.1109/rivf.2019.8713716

12. Trinh, T., Wu, D., Huang, J.Z., Azhar, M.: Activeness and loyalty analysis in event-based social networks. Entropy 22(1), 119 (2020). https://doi.org/10.3390/e22010119,https://www.mdpi.com/1099-4300/22/1/119

13. Trinh, T., Wu, D., Wang, R., Huang, J.Z.: An effective content-based event recommendation model. Multimedia Tools Appl. 1–20 (2020). https://doi.org/10.1007/s11042-020-08884-9

14. Tu, W., Cheung, D.W., Mamoulis, N., Yang, M., Lu, Z.: Activity-partner recommendation. In: Cao, T., Lim, E.-P., Zhou, Z.-H., Ho, T.-B., Cheung, D., Motoda, H. (eds.) PAKDD 2015. LNCS (LNAI), vol. 9077, pp. 591–604. Springer, Cham (2015). https://doi.org/10.1007/978-3-319-18038-0_46

15. Yin, H., Zou, L., Nguyen, Q.V.H., Huang, Z., Zhou, X.: Joint event-partner recommendation in event-based social networks. In: 2018 IEEE 34th International Conference on Data Engineering (ICDE), pp. 929–940. IEEE, April 2018. https://doi.org/10.1109/ICDE.2018.00088, https://ieeexplore.ieee.org/document/8509309/

16. Yin, Z., Xu, T., Zhu, H., Zhu, C., Chen, E., Xiong, H.: Matching of social events and users: a two-way selection perspective. World Wide Web 23(2), 853–871 (2020). https://doi.org/10.1007/s11280-019-00724-7

17. Zhang, S., Lv, Q.: Hybrid EGU-based group event participation prediction in event-based social networks. Knowl.-Based Syst. 143, 19–29 (2018). https://doi.org/10.1016/j.knosys.2017.12.002

18. Zhang, W., Wang, J.: A collective bayesian poisson factorization model for cold-start local event recommendation categories and subject descriptors, pp. 1455–1464 (2015)

19. Zhu, Z., Shi, L., Liu, B., Ma, Z.: Multi-feature based event recommendation, 11, 618–633 (2018)

Enhancing the Capacity of Detecting and Classifying Cavitation Noise Generated from Propeller Using the Convolution Neural Network

Hoang Nhat Bach[1(✉)], Duc Van Nguyen[2], and Ha Le Vu[1]

[1] Institute of Electronics, Military Institute of Science and Technology, Hanoi, Vietnam
[2] Communication Engineering Departments, School of Electronics and Telecommunications, Hanoi University of Science and Technology, Hanoi, Vietnam

Abstract. One of the biggest concerns of underwater research is improving the ability to detect and classify sound sources. The Machine Learning and Deep Learning models often require a very large amount of data, while the data sources of the passive sonar system are limited; therefore, it is very important to pre-process data to improve data quality. This paper proposes a solution to improve the detection and classification of cavitation noise generated from propeller by improving the Detection of Envelope Modulation on Noise (DEMON) algorithm before using a modified Convolution Neural Network. The testing result shows that the accuracy of the modified model reaches around 90%, which is better than the results of existing methods, and it is prospectively developed and applied in practicalities.

Keywords: Passive sonar · DEMON · Convolution neuron network

1 Introduction

The role of marine control and defense for Vietnam, a country with 3,200-km coastline, is significantly important. The classification of underwater signals obtained from passive sonar systems is one of the challenges, due to the complex changes in time and spectral features in signals even from the same source. According to Nielsen [1] the typical noise sources for a ship include: noise from engines, machines and equipment on the ship while in motion (distant shipping), noise of hydrodynamic flows on the ship hull, propeller noise. Each type of signals has its own characteristics and can be detected by experienced surveyors by hearing or seeing the signal spectrum. During the movement, the main noise source of each ship is the cavitation of the propeller blades. The characteristics of this noise depend on the rotation frequency of the propeller blades, i.e. depend on frequency components that are varied by the speed of the blades. The cavitation noise increases proportionately with the speed of the blades and decreases as the depth increases. The repetition of such process produces vessel-specific features. Based on that

N.-S. Vo et al. (Eds.): INISCOM 2021, LNICST 379, pp. 268–275, 2021.
https://doi.org/10.1007/978-3-030-77424-0_22

linear relationship, the analysis of main frequency components will allow the calculation of the remaining parameters. The most popular and useful detection method is to use DEMON algorithm. DEMON algorithm was first proposed by Nielsen in 1991; since then, there have been many variations proposed to solve different specific problems, for example, tracking of multiple sources in a decoupled way [2], or 3/2D spectral analysis to extract propeller features from acoustic vector sensor data [3]. The basic DEMON algorithm has been tested in practice [4] and has also been used to detect the breathing pattern of divers from recorded data [5], etc. Based on the aforementioned research, we use a modified DEMON to analyse the propeller characteristic frequency components, and demonstrate the result under spectrogram (also called DEMONgram), which is a graphical representation of frequency in terms of time and magnitude. Spectrograms that possess characteristics of each object are fed into Convolution Neural Network (CNN) for analysis and processing.In recent years, Deep Learning (DL) has formed new break-throughs; the DL model has the ability to process hidden features of the target signals through a multi-layer network. From the proposals of Fukushima (1980) [6] and LeCun (1989), the CNN completed in 2012 [7] was the first multi-layer structure using relative relationships in space to reduce the dimensions of parameters and improve training per-formance. LeNet [8] (1998) was the first network to apply 2-dimensional convolution. AlexNet [9] (2012) has broken the previous stereotype that learned features will not be as effecient as manually created features (through the SUFT, HOG, SHIFT algorithms). VGG-16 [10] (2014) formed a trend to improve the accuracy of DL networks by increas-ing the depth of the model. Variations of GoogleNet [11] (2014), by combining multiple filters of different sizes into the same block, produced the block architecture for the later CNN. ResNet-50 [12] (2015) used identified "short-cut" connection to map inputs from the previous layers to the following layers. It is a very deep network architecture, but has a smaller number of parameters, based on techniques from GoogleNet. DenseNet [13] (2016) is the next generation of ResNet which inherits the block architecture and develops the "short-cut" connection for a dense network.

The next parts of the paper will be organized as follows: part 2 will introduce the DEMON pre-processing method and its improvements, part 3 will analyze the CNN structure and the improved network model, and part 4 will be the conclusion.

2   Pre-processing by Modified DEMON

In the basic DEMON algorithm as defined by Nielsen, $x(t)$ is the acoustic signal that contains noise of the propeller and the environment, presented by:

$$x(t) = s(t) + n(t) \tag{1}$$

$$s(t) = m(f, t) w(t) \tag{2}$$

In which, $s(t)$ is a broadband signal formed by the modulation of a carrier wave-form $w(t)$ by a modulating waveform $m(f, t)$, while $n(t)$ is environmental noise. The modulating waveform $m(f, t)$ is periodic with frequency f, thus $m^2(f, t)$ is also periodic which can be expressed under a cosine formula as follows:

$$m^2(f, t) = \sum_{l=0}^{L} A_l \cos(lcft + l\theta) \tag{3}$$

Where $c = 2\pi/f_s$, f_s is the sampling frequency, A_l is the expansion coefficient of $m^2(t)$, θ is phase, and L is the number of coefficients. Because the square makes the left side of Eq. (3) always positive, the coefficient A_l must be selected to make the right side also positive (Fig. 1).

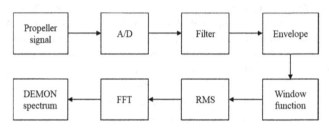

Fig. 1. DEMON algorithm

We propose the following solution: the signal spectrum is calculated by Short Time Fourier Transform (STFT). From that, we calculate a 2-dimensional spectral matrix, among which, one dimension is frequency, the other is the number of samples. The frequency amplitude of each segment is averaged to obtain a unique representative value. This technique divides the acoustic signal into consecutive overlapping segments. The result of this process is a set of filtered spectrogram images, which will be put into DL network for training. When the signal is unstable, the detection and classification accuracy will be reduced significantly. DL models can solve this problem more easily, because they extract hidden features using layers. On the other hand, as there are various types of noise, suitable selection of features plays an important role in guaranteeing the performance of the model. Thus, the result of modified DEMON reduces noise while retains sufficient features to increase detection accuracy. Our proposal can clearly separate characteristic frequencies and harmonics, as well as can decrease false alarm. Figure 3a, b are corresponding spectrograms of Fig. 2a, 2b.

In both methods, computation requires the definition of a target frequency window; unsuitable selection of input parameters can make the detection task unfeasible. Each sample is smoothed by window fuction, and the corresponding standard deviations are calculated. Signal is detected whenever the corresponding signal exceeds the corresponding detection threshold. Our simulation uses the dataset from the project: "An underwater vessel noise database" by Research center for Telecommunication Technologies – Universida de Vigo [14], as well as the dataset recorded by ourselves – Institute of Electronics, Military Institute of Science and Technology – in Lan Ha Bay, Hai Phong, Vietnam. Datasets include various types of underwater ship sounds. The sounds are recorded in shallow waters and in real conditions, which contain both natural and anthropogenic environment noise (Fig. 4).

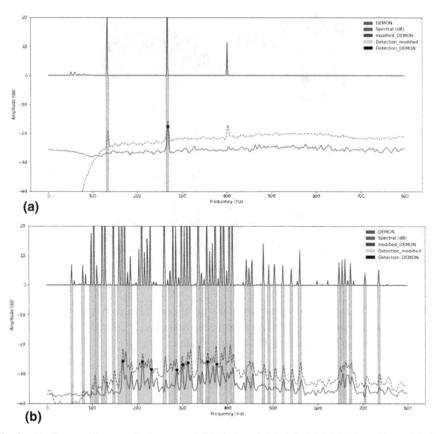

(a)

(b)

Fig. 2. (a) Comparision result between DEMON and Modified DEMON at Record-1 (b) Comparision result between DEMON and Modified DEMON at Record-2

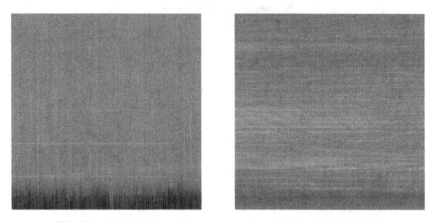

Fig. 3. a, b Spectogram after pre-processing with Modified DEMON

Fig. 4. Data recorded in Lan Ha Bay

Detection accuracy is calculated from the numbers and percentages of correct and incorrect ship detections. Table 1 shows two confusion matrices displaying the detection accuracy, and Table 2 summarizes the accuracy rates.

Table 1. Detection accuracy on a database of 3300 1-min audio samples

DEMON	Reality	No ship
	Ship	
Ship	1463	198
No ship	337	1302
Total samples	1800	1500
Modified DEMON	Reality	
	Ship	No ship
Ship	1768	45
No ship	32	1455
Total samples	1800	1500

Table 2. Accuracy rates and also the false-alarm rates

	DEMON (%)	Modified DEMON(%)
Detection accuracy	81.28%	98.22%
False alarm	13.2%	3%

3 CNN Comparision

We separate the samples into 70% for training set, 20% for validation set, and 10% for test set. We also use the spectrograms size of $3 \times 224 \times 224$ to include in the CNN model for training. From analyzing results between the models, the accuracy of LeNet, AlexNet, VGG is only around 65–75% (Fig. 5).

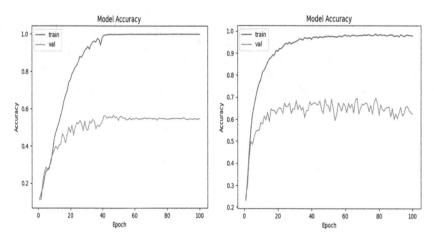

Fig. 5. a, b Training result our dataset with LeNet and VGG model

Proposed network model structure diagram (Fig. 6):

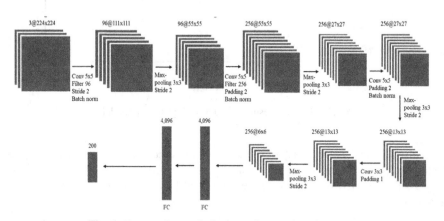

Fig. 6. Proposed convolution neural network architecture

The tuning is a challenge with a deep learning complicated structure. Because underwater datasets are insufficient, the deep model network is hard to be trained. Therefore, we propose a neural network using batch normalization with 1 input layer, 4 convolution layers, 4 maxpooling layers, and 2 fully connected layers. The batch normalization layers which are placed just after defining the sequential model and after the convolution layer will reduces the internal covariate shift of the model. The internal covariate shift is a change in the input distribution of an internal. The inputs received from the previous layer are always changed. Adding batch normalization layers ensure that the mean and standard deviation of the inputs will always remain the same, and minimize the fluctuation of the distribution. Batch norms don't compute the entire data, and the model's data distribution will make some noise. This can help overcome overfitting and help learn better. The first convolution layer has 1 convolution [5 × 5], the stride is 2, and 96 kernels. Using a smaller size of convolution matrix [5 × 5] will retain more information on the spectrogram. Filter size of the pooling layers is [3 × 3]; stride is 2. Extending the size of the convolution layers, reducing the dimensions of the feature map and making the filter size and stride smaller increase the accuracy of our model (Fig. 7).

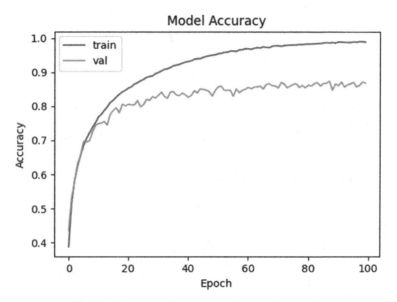

Fig. 7. Training result accuracy with proposed model

With our model, the accuracy of validation increases around 90%. After testing with the test set, the result shows that the accuracy has been greatly improved. It proves that the classification network can be further improved by the modification of the neural networks.

4 Conclusion

This paper describes a method for acoustic recognition of ships. It is a spectrogram domain analysis for passive sonar based on DEMON with a modified Convolution Neural Network which attains an accuracy percentage of 94.25%. The proposed model which is provided for cavitation noise from propeller, has a better performance in recognizing and preventing false detection. Based on the classification results, we conclude that: (1) deep learning models provide good results for detecting and classifying underwater and surface targets, and these models still process well in low SNR environments; (2) while DEMON algorithm focuses on fundamental frequency, our modified model additionally recognizes variations in the amplitude of fundamental frequencies; (3) the transformation of data from signal sequence to spectrogram enables the system to process a large amount of complicated data on a real-time basis; (4) datasets are still limited due to some security reasons. Therefore, preprocessing datasets and finding ways to increase the number of samples are the two main problems that shall be improved in the future.

Acknowledgment. This study was funded by the Vietnam National Foundation for Science and Technology Development (NAFOSTED) under the project number 102.04–2018.12.

References

1. Nielsen, R.O.: Sonar signal processing. Artech House Inc. (1991)
2. Fillinger, L., Sutin, A., Sedunov, A.: Acoustic ship signature measurements by cross-correlation method. J. Acoustical Soc. Am. **129**(2), 774–778 (2011)
3. Li, S.: DEMON feature extraction of acoustic vector signal based on 3/2-D spectrum. In: IEEE Conference on Industrial Electronics and Applications, pp. 2239–2243 (2007)
4. Tao, R., Feng, Y., Wang, Y.: Theoretical and experimental study of a signal feature extraction algorithm for measuring propeller acceleration in a port surveillance system. IET Radar Sonar Navig **5**(2), 172–181 (2011)
5. Lennartsson, R., Dalberg, E., Persson, L., Petrovic, S.: Passive acoustic detection and classification of divers in harbor environments. In: OCEANS 2009, Biloxi, pp. 1–7 (2009)
6. Fukushima, K.: Neocognitron: a hierarchical neural network capable of visual pattern recognition. Neural Netw. **1**, 119–130 (1988)
7. Alom, M.Z., et al.: A state-of-the-art survey on deep learning theory and architectures. Electronics **8**(3), 292 (2019)
8. LeCun, Y., Bottou, L., Bengio, Y., Haffner, P.: Gradient-based learning applied to document recognition. Proc. IEEE **86**, 2278–2324 (1998)
9. Krizhevsky, A., Sutskever, I., Hinton, G.E.: Imagenet classification with deep convolutional neural networks. In: Advances in Neural Information Processing Systems NIPS, vol. 25 (2012)
10. Simonyan, K., Zisserman, A.: Very deep convolutional networks for large-scale image recognition. In: arXiv:1409.1556 (2014)
11. Szegedy, C., et al.: Going deeper with convolutions. In: Proceedings of the IEEE Conference on Computer Vision and Pattern Recognition, Boston, MA, USA, 7–12, pp. 1–9 (2015)
12. He, K., Zhang, X., Ren, S., Sun, J.: Deep residual learning for image recognition. In: Proceedings of the IEEE Conference on Computer Vision and Pattern Recognition, Las Vegas, NV, USA, 27–30, pp. 770–778 (2016)
13. Huang, G., Liu, Z., van der Maaten, L., Weinberger, K.Q.: Densely connected convolutional networks. In: Proceedings of the IEEE Conference on Computer Vision and Pattern Recognition, Honolulu, HI, USA, pp. 4700–4708 (2017)
14. Research center for Telecommunication Technologies - Universida de Vigo homepage. http://atlanttic.uvigo.es/underwaternoise/

A Feature-Augmented Deep Learning Model for Extractive Summarization

Bui Thi Mai Anh and Nguyen Thi Thu Trang[(⊠)]

Software Engineering Department, School of Information and Communication
Technology, Hanoi University of Science and Technology, Hanoi, Vietnam
{anhbtm,trangntt}@soict.hust.edu.vn

Abstract. Extractive text summarization can be seen as a classification
task in which sentences from the document are labelled with either *in-summary* or *not-in-summary*. The most salient sentences (i.e., with highest ranking score) from the original document will be selected to generate
the summary. Recent success of deep learning in the field of Natural Language Processing (NLP) has raised a trending research direction for text
summarization task. Many neural models have been proposed in which
applying recurrent neural network (rNN) for extractive summarization
is also becoming increasingly popular. In this paper, we aim to improve
the baseline sequence to sequence model proposed by Nallapati et al. by
augmenting more sentence features so that the generated summary can
benefit from potential features of the whole document. On one hand,
the additional sentence-based features enrich the representation vector
resulting from the sentence-level RNN of the baseline model. On the
other hand, the relevant information from word-level will also be added
to the final vector to increase the accuracy of the classification task. The
experiment has been conducted for the DailyMail/CNN dataset to evaluate our proposed method and the state of the art works. The empirical
results show that the proposed model with augmented features increases
about 0.3-0.4 points of ROUGE-1 and ROUGE-2 in comparison with
related works.

Keywords: Extractive summarization · Sequence to sequence model ·
Recurrent neural networks

1 Introduction

Text summarization is a process of automatically generating summaries from
an input document while preserving the overall meaning as well as the coherence of the original. Automatic text summarization can be categorized into
two main approaches: (i) *extractive* and (ii) *abstractive* [10]. The extractive-based approaches form summaries by selecting the most salient sentences from
the input document and assembling them in a coherent way. In contrast, the
abstractive-based approaches aim to generate *human-written* summaries by

© ICST Institute for Computer Sciences, Social Informatics and Telecommunications Engineering 2021
Published by Springer Nature Switzerland AG 2021. All Rights Reserved
N.-S. Vo et al. (Eds.): INISCOM 2021, LNICST 379, pp. 276–286, 2021.
https://doi.org/10.1007/978-3-030-77424-0_23

applying linguistic methods to rephrase sentences which convey the most important information of the original document. Although the abstractive summarization is better than the extractive one, it requires to understand the semantic as well as the structure of the input document, which in turn results into a difficult task for a computer. The extractive summarization, therefore, has attracted much more attention of researchers. An extractive method can be considered as a classification task, which decides whether or not each sentence of the input document belongs to the summary. Traditional methods mainly focus on scoring sentences using graph-based models [7,15], rule-based methods [3,22] to explore the relation between text components (i.e., words or sentences). Some approaches apply evolutionary algorithms to calculate sentence scores on the basis of relevant sentence features such as relation to title document, sentence position, proper noun etc. [1,13,14]. The ranking model is defined as a linear combination of features whose weights are typically determined through experiments.

With the recent emergence of deep neural models, many studies have adopted neural networks for extractive summarization task. Yin and Pei proposed to use *Convolutional Neural Network* (CNN) to learn sentence representation and process the classification of sentences as an optimization problem (in which sentences with high prestige and diverseness would be selected) [24]. This work was however devoted to multi-document summarization. In another work of Cheng et al., a CNN was also applied to encode sentences together with a *Recurrent Neural Network* (RNN) to represent the input document as a sequential of encoded sentences [6]. The classification task was performed by another RNN to take into account previously labeled sentences. Nallapati et al. proposed a similar architecture to encode documents at both word- and sentence-levels [16]. The labelling task is then explicitly enhanced with document features including sentence content, salience, novelty and position.

It is observable that the RNN architecture matched and outperformed the state of the art studies for extractive summarization [6,16,24]. We however argued that the ability of RNNs to take into account previous information of only last few steps to describe the present state might affect the quality of generated summaries. Indeed, it is likely that the relevant information which might be stored at some first words of the underlying sentence cannot be taken into account to represent the state of this sentence. In this case, the probability to be chosen for the summary of the sentence might be reduced. Moreover, the ability to capture the whole context of the document, which could be regarded as a shortcoming of the sequence to sequence architecture, is also required to improve the saliency of the generated summary. In order to address this problem, we propose to integrate several context features so that the summary representation can be augmented with the whole sentence features. More concisely, we adopt two bi-directional RNN models to describe the input document at both word and sentence levels, inspiring from the work of Nallapati et al. [16]. The probability of being selected for the summary of each sentence is then augmented with six proposed word/sentence-based features (see details in Sect. 3). With these features, the meaning of the whole input sentences would contribute to the output result of the RNN, increasing the accuracy of generated summaries.

The rest of this paper is organized as follows. We first introduce closely related works on the topic of analyzing sentences features for improving summarization techniques in Sect. 2. Section 3 describes our proposed approach with some improvements based on six word/sentence features. We finally present the empirical results in Sect. 4 and conclude the paper with remarks on our future direction in Sect. 5.

2   Related Work

This section gives a short overview of related works under the context of applying deep learning in automatic text summarization.

Rush et al. [20] were the first to successfully apply deep learning to text summarization task. They proposed an attentional-based sequence to sequence model to generate abstractive summaries. Inspired by the neural machine translation model [2], novel words of the summary are generated on the basis of a conditional probability on encoded input sentences. Some following works on neural abstractive models of Nallapati et al. [17], See et al. [21], Paulus et al. [19] focused particularly on addressing the out-of-vocabulary problem and on improving the degree of freedom when generating novel words for summaries.

Recent studies have considered also neural networks for the extractive summarization task yielding promising results [4,6,12,16,18,23,24]. Most extractive summarization models are typically processed as a binary-classification in which each sentence of the original document is labeled either *in-summary* or *not-in-summary*. In the same fashion, neural extractive summarization models assign to each sentence a probability of being selected to the output summary. CNNs were first proposed for encoding input sentences with the aim of extracting the most relevant information from the document [24]. RNN models were then adopted for the classification task to take into account previously labeled sentences which are also importance for deciding whether or not the current sentence should be selected for the summary [6]. Wu et al. [23], Narayan et al. [18] then proposed to improve the RNN extractive model with reinforcement learning for the better discrimination among sentences when building summaries. Nallapati et al. have replaced the CNN architecture by two bi-directional RNN models (i.e., backward and forward RNNs) to capture the document at word-level as well as at sentence-level [16]. The chance of being included in the summary of each sentence is calculated based on the hidden state of such models. The obtained result out-performed or was comparable to the state-of-the-art deep learning models.

In this paper, we consider the similar architecture of RNNs integrating with some word and sentence features to give an extra reward to each sentence. Sentences with high rewards are more likely to be selected for the generated summary. Our proposed model will be detailed in the next section.

3   Proposed Approach

3.1   Baseline Model

The baseline model of our work is the SummaRuNNer model proposed by Nallapati et al., the state-of-the-art one for neural extractive summarization [16]. In this model, extractive summaries are generated through a two-layer bi-directional GRU-RNN. The input sentences from the original document are sequentially passed into the model. The first layer, working at the word-level, aims to extract the relationship between words of each input sentence. The second layer, which takes the hidden states of the first layer as inputs, focused on encoding the representation of the whole sentences of the document. The hidden states of the second layer rNN are then used to represent the entire document through a non-linear transformation (i.e., a `tank` function). The classification layer decides whether or not a sentence belongs to the summary through a probability as shown in Eq. 1.

$$
\begin{aligned}
P(y_j = 1 | h_j, s_j, d) = \sigma(&W_c h_j \ \#(\texttt{content}) \\
&+ h_j^T W_s d \ \#(\texttt{salient}) \\
&- h_j^T W_r tanh(s_j) \ \#(\texttt{novelty}) \\
&+ W_{ap} p_j^a \ \#(\texttt{abs. pos. imp.}) \\
&+ W_{rp} p_j^r \ \#(\texttt{rel. pos. imp.}) \\
&+ b), \ \#(\texttt{bias term})
\end{aligned}
\tag{1}
$$

where the binary variable y_j indicates whether or not the j-th sentence belongs to the summary. h_j denotes the encoding representation of the j-th sentence and s_j dynamically represents the current summary at the j-th sentence position, given by:

$$
s_j = \sum_{i=1}^{j-1} h_i P(y_i = 1 | h_i, s_j, d)
\tag{2}
$$

3.2   Proposed Model

The problem of the RNNs is that they practically can only look back a last few steps. In other words, they cannot store a large number of hidden states of previous steps. Hence, the presentation of the j-th sentence at the j-th hidden state (h_j) cannot represent all necessary information of that sentence.

In this paper, we propose to augment more sentence features so that the summary presentation can be augmented with the whole sentence features, illustrated in Fig. 1. After doing some empirical experiment, we propose to augment six features which can be computed at the word and sentence level. The word-level feature score WF_j is computed from the word sequences of input sentences. The sentence-level features are explored after the second layer of the model, i.e. Sentence-level GRU. These two types features are then combined with SummaRuNNer ones to build up a complex feature layer. The sentence distribution

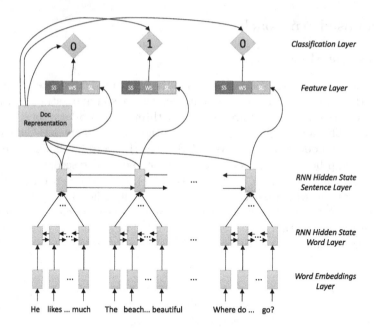

Fig. 1. Proposed extractive summarization model with augmented sentence and word-level features

is modeled and computed based on these features with their weights. This can be viewed as a probability distribution over the input sentences, which represents the output summary.

The logistic layer to determine whether a sentence belongs to the summary (see Eq. 1) now becomes:

$$
\begin{aligned}
P(y_j = 1 | h_j, s_j, d) = \sigma(W_c h_j & \ \#(\texttt{content}) \\
+ h_j^T W_s d & \ \#(\texttt{salient}) \\
- h_j^T W_r tanh(s_j) & \ \#(\texttt{novelty}) \\
+ W_{ap} p_j^a & \ \#(\texttt{abs. pos. imp.}) \\
+ W_{rp} p_j^r & \ \#(\texttt{rel. pos. imp.}) \\
+ W F_j & \ \#\texttt{score of word-} \\
& \ \ \ \texttt{based features} \\
+ S F_j & \ \#\texttt{score of sentences-} \\
& \ \ \ \texttt{based features} \\
+ b), & \ \#(\texttt{bias term})
\end{aligned}
\tag{3}
$$

where SF_j is the augmented feature score at the sentence-level and WF_j is the one at the word-level for the j-th sentence.

The sentence features which can be computed at word-level WF_j is given by individual feature scores and their corresponding weights:

$$
WF_j = W_{tfisf} TFISF_j + W_{sl} SL_j + W_{sr} SR_j
\tag{4}
$$

where $TFISF_j$ is Term Frequency-Inverse Sentence Frequency (TF-ISF) of the sentence, SL_j is the sentence length feature, and SR_j is the stop word ratio of the j-th sentence.

In the same manner, the sentence features which can be computed at word-level SF_j is given by:

$$SF_j = W_{fd}FD_j + W_{pr}PR_j + W_{sf}ST_j \tag{5}$$

where whether FD_j the sentence is the first in the document, FR_j is the sentence score using PageRank algorithm [9], and ST_j is the similarity of the sentence to the topic sentence. These sentence features will be explained in detail in the next sub-sections.

3.3   Word-Based Features

Term Frequency - Inverse Sentence Frequency. When investigating each sentence in a single document, a variant of TF-IDF (Term Frequency – Inverse Document Frequency) is typically proposed, TF-ISF (Inverse Sentence Frequency) [5], in which the word frequencies are investigated at the sentence level. A sentence with higher TF-ISF might contain more meaningful information, therefore could be a good candidate in summary. Given a document D, the TF-ISF score of the j-th sentence can be calculated by summing TF-ISF of all words as indicated in Eq. 6.

$$TFISF_j = \sum_{i=1}^{N}(TF_{ij} * log(\frac{M}{sf_j})) \tag{6}$$

where TF_{ij} is the number of occurrences of the i-th word in the j-th sentence, sf_i (sentence frequency) is the number of sentences in the document D contains the i-th word, M is the number of sentences in document D and N is the number of words in the jth sentence.

Sentence Length. The length of a sentence can be considered as an useful feature. Indeed, recent studies have indicated that short sentences are less likely to appear in the summary [13]. In order to qualify this characteristic, we calculate the length (measured by words) of the j-th sentence in the document D as in Eq. 7.

$$SL_j = \frac{L_j - \mu}{\sigma} \tag{7}$$

where L_j is the number of words of the j-th sentence, μ and σ are the average length and standard deviation of all the sentences in the document respectively.

Stopword Ratio. Stop words are generally the most common words in a natural language. They are typically used to express grammatical relationships among words of a sentence [8], therefore, have little lexical meaning. A sentence with a high rate of stop words should not be chosen as part of summary. We therefore take into account the stop word ratio of a sentence as a feature. It is computed as the number of stop words in the sentence compared to the total number of stop words in the whole document.

$$SR_j = \frac{SW_j}{SW_D} \tag{8}$$

where SW_j is the number of stop words of the sentence j-th, SW_D is the total number of stop words in the document D.

3.4   Sentence-Based Features

First in Document. As indicated in some recent studies, the most relevant information of the document tends to appear at the beginning part of the document [8]. The lead-3 summarization (which extracts the first 3 sentences of the document) even gave good results. Therefore, we propose to use this feature to emphasize the role of the first sentence in the document.

$$FD_j = \begin{cases} 1 \text{ if } h_j \text{ is the first sentence} \\ 0 \text{ otherwise} \end{cases} \tag{9}$$

where h_j is hidden state of the j-th sentence, h_0 is hidden state of the first sentence.

Sentence Score with PageRank. PageRank is an algorithm to rank the importance of website pages in Google search engine results [9]. Therefore, in this paper, we propose to use PageRank algorithm to measure the importance of sentences in the document, given by:

$$PR_j = \frac{1-d}{N} + d * \sum h_i \in C(h_j) \frac{PR_i}{L(h_j)} \tag{10}$$

where:

- $h_1, h_2. \ldots h_j. \ldots h_N$ are hidden states of the first, second,..., j-th,..., N sentences in the document D
- $C(h_j)$ is the collection of the hidden states linking to the hidden state h_j, corresponding to the j-th sentence
- $L(h_j)$ is the number of outbound links on the hidden state h_j
- d is the coefficient, which is empirical found as 0.85
- N is the number of sentences of the document D

Similarity to the Topic Sentence. The topic sentence plays an important role in the document as it summaries the main idea of the document. All the sentences belonging to the summary should be semantically related to the topic sentence. In this paper, we consider the similarity score between a sentence in the document and the topic as a sentence-based feature. The similarity of two sentences, S_i and S_j, is calculated using Cosine as following:

$$similarity_{cos}(S_i, S_j) = \frac{\sum_{k=1}^{M}(w_{ik} \times w_{jk})}{\sqrt{\sum_{k=1}^{M}(w_{ik}^2) \times \sum_{k=1}^{M}(w_{jk}^2)}} \qquad (11)$$

where M refers to the total number of terms in the document, w_{ik} denotes the weight of the term k in the sentence S_i and w_{jk} denotes the weight of the term k in the sentence S_j. In almost English articles, the topic sentence is usually appeared as the first sentence of the document. We therefore calculate the similarity to the topic sentence of the j-th sentence as $ST_j = similarity_{cos}(S_j, S_0)$.

4 Experimentation

4.1 Dataset

In this work, we employ the widely used corpus, Daily Mail/CNN dataset [11], which contains online news articles (27.2 sentences or 680.0 tokens on average) paired with gold summaries (human-written with 3.8 sentences or 52.3 tokens on average). The corpus has 277,554 training pairs of origin document and gold summary; 13,367 validation pairs and 11,443 test pairs. Besides, in the corpus, each sentence has a label: either "0" indicating not in summary, either "1" indicating in summary, or "2" indicating either in or not in summary. In this work, we consider the sentence with the label "2" is the sentence not in summary.

4.2 Empirical Settings

In order to train our proposed model, we used a single GTX-1080Ti GPU and fixed the batch size as 32. In the prediction phase, the summaries are generated using a probability threshold of 0.5 (i.e., $P(s_j) > 0.5$ meaning that the sentence s_j is chosen for the summary). We trained both the baseline model and our proposal model with 150k vocabulary for about 9,000 iterations (5 epochs), similar to the 5 epochs required by the baseline model [16]. For all experiments, our model has 200-dimensional hidden states and 100-dimensional word embeddings.

4.3 Experimental Results

Our experiments are performed on two measurement metrics: (i) the standard ROUGE metric on the gold summaries and the generated summary, reporting the F1 scores for ROUGE-1, ROUGE-2 and ROUGE-L (which respectively measure the word-overlap, bigram-overlap, and longest common sequence between the reference summary and the summary to be evaluated), and (ii) the absolute metric using sentence labels. We obtain our ROUGE scores using the pyrouge[1].

---

[1] https://pypi.org/project/pyrouge/.

Table 1. Result on DailyMail/CNN corpus using full-length F1 variants of absolute metrics

Models	Dailymail/CNN (11443 documents)		
	F1(%)	Recall (%)	Precision (%)
SummaRuNNer (re-run)	73.1	69.0	77.6
SummaRuNNer + 3 word-level features	73.1	69.0	77.8
SummaRuNNer + 3 sen.-level features	73.1	69.0	77.8
SummaRuNNer 6 features+	**75.2**	**72.4**	**78.3**

Table 2. Result on DailyMail/CNN corpus using full-length F1 variants of Rouge

Models	Dailymail/CNN (11443 documents)		
	R-1(%)	R-2 (%)	R-L (%)
Cheng et al. 2016 [6]	35.4	13.3	**32.6**
SummaRuNNer + (re-run)	39.7	16.6	30.5
SummaRuNNer + 3 word-level features	40.0	16.8	30.0
SummaRuNNer + 3 sen.-based features	40.0	16.8	30.0
SummaRuNNer + 6 features	**40.1**	**16.9**	30.1

Table 3. Result on Daily Mail corpus use limited length (75 bytes and 275 bytes)

Models	Recall at 75 bytes (%)			Recall at 275 bytes (%)		
	R-1	R-2	R-L	R-1	R-2	R-L
Cheng et al. 2016 [6]	22.7	8.5	12.5	**42.2**	17.3	**38.4**
SummaRuNNer + (re-run)	25.3	10.8	13.5	41.7	17.4	33.9
SummaRuNNer + 3 word-level features	25.2	10.8	13.3	41.8	17.5	34.0
SummaRuNNer + 3 sen.-based features	25.2	10.8	13.3	41.8	17.5	34.0
SummaRuNNer + 6 features	**25.5**	10.9	13.5	42.0	17.6	34.2

We re-run the baseline model, and then compare with the results obtained from our proposal models with augmented sentence features.

Table 1 shows the absolute performance based on labels with Precision, Recall and F1 scores of the proposed model comparing with the baseline model SummaRunNer and some other previous models. The sentence was chosen as in summary if the $P > 0.5$ (after some empirical experiments). The experimental results show that the proposed model with augmented features outperformed about 2–3% to the previous ones in all three metrics of Precision, Recall and F1.

Table 2 shows the ROUGE Scores of the proposed models comparing with the baseline model SummaRunNer and some other models. The evaluation was performed by comparing the generated summaries with the associated gold references, in terms of ROUGE. A sentence was chosen in summary is it is in the top-four sentences and $P > 0.6$ (after some empirical experiments). The experimental results show that the proposed model with augmented features increases about 0.3-0.4 points of ROUGE-1 and ROUGE-2 (F1 score).

Table 3 shows the performance of various models on the DailyMail corpus using the limited length recall variants of Rouge with respect to the abstractive ground truth at 75 bytes and 275 bytes.

5 Conclusion

In this paper, we investigate some words- and sentences-based features to improve the quality of an extractive text summarization model. Our work is based on the baseline model SummaRUNNer, proposed by Nallapati et al. [16]. With these features, the meaning of the whole input sentences has been better captured, rather than relying on only the RNNs. The experimental results on Daily Mail/CNN dataset shows that our proposed model, the performance of the summarization in absolute metric as well as the ROUGE one increases about 2–3% or 0.3–0.4 point compared to the baseline one. In the future, we plan to study more on the DNN network to have a better representation of the whole document. Furthermore, we have argued that the Rouge measures are typically built based on the character matching, thus cannot reveal the semantical similarity (i.e., two sentences with similar meaning may be considered as different according to some lexical differences). Improving the Rouge measures is therefore a promising research direction in the future.

Acknowledgement. This research is supported by Hanoi University of Science and Technology under the project entitled *"Intent Classification and Slot Tagging Dataset Construction and Conversational Model Development"*.

References

1. Anh, B.T.M., My, N.T., Trang, N.T.T.: Enhanced genetic algorithm for single document extractive summarization. In: Proceedings of the Tenth International Symposium on Information and Communication Technology, pp. 370–376 (2019)
2. Bahdanau, D., Cho, K., Bengio, Y.: Neural machine translation by jointly learning to align and translate. arXiv preprint arXiv:1409.0473 (2014)
3. Carbonell, J., Goldstein, J.: The use of mmr, diversity-based reranking for reordering documents and producing summaries. In: Proceedings of the 21st annual international ACM SIGIR conference on Research and development in information retrieval, pp. 335–336 (1998)
4. Chatterjee, N., Jain, G., Bajwa, G.S.: Single document extractive text summarization using neural networks and genetic algorithm. In: Arai, K., Kapoor, S., Bhatia, R. (eds.) SAI 2018. AISC, vol. 858, pp. 338–358. Springer, Cham (2019). https://doi.org/10.1007/978-3-030-01174-1_26
5. Chatterjee, N., Mittal, A., Goyal, S.: Single document extractive text summarization using genetic algorithms. In: 2012 Third International Conference on Emerging Applications of Information Technology, pp. 19–23. IEEE (2012)

6. Cheng, J., Lapata, M.: Neural summarization by extracting sentences and words. In: Proceedings of the 54th Annual Meeting of the Association for Computational Linguistics (vol.1: Long Papers). pp. 484–494 (2016)
7. Erkan, G., Radev, D.R.: Lexrank: graph-based lexical centrality as salience in text summarization. J. Artif. Intell. Res. **22**, 457–479 (2004)
8. Ferreira, R., et al.: Assessing sentence scoring techniques for extractive text summarization. Expert Syst. Appl. **40**(14), 5755–5764 (2013)
9. Gustavsson, P., Jönsson, A.: Text summarization using random indexing and pagerank. In: Proceedings of the third Swedish Language Technology Conference (SLTC-2010), Linköping, Sweden (2010)
10. Hahn, U., Mani, I.: The challenges of automatic summarization. Computer **33**(11), 29–36 (2000)
11. Hermann, K.M., et al.: Teaching machines to read and comprehend. In: Advances in neural information processing systems, pp. 1693–1701 (2015)
12. Liu, Y.: Fine-tune bert for extractive summarization. arXiv preprint arXiv:1903.10318 (2019)
13. Meena, Y.K., Gopalani, D.: Evolutionary algorithms for extractive automatic text summarization. Procedia Comput. Sci. **48**, 244–249 (2015)
14. Mendoza, M., Bonilla, S., Noguera, C., Cobos, C., León, E.: Extractive single-document summarization based on genetic operators and guided local search. Expert Syst. Appl. **41**(9), 4158–4169 (2014)
15. Mihalcea, R.: Graph-based ranking algorithms for sentence extraction, applied to text summarization. In: Proceedings of the ACL Interactive Poster and Demonstration Sessions, pp. 170–173 (2004)
16. Nallapati, R., Zhai, F., Zhou, B.: Summarunner: A recurrent neural network based sequence model for extractive summarization of documents. In: AAAI, pp. 3075–3081 (2017)
17. Nallapati, R., et al.: Abstractive text summarization using sequence-to-sequence rnns and beyond. arXiv preprint arXiv:1602.06023 (2016)
18. Narayan, S., Cohen, S.B., Lapata, M.: Ranking sentences for extractive summarization with reinforcement learning. arXiv preprint arXiv:1802.08636 (2018)
19. Paulus, R., Xiong, C., Socher, R.: A deep reinforced model for abstractive summarization. In: International Conference on Learning Representations (2018)
20. Rush, A.M., Chopra, S., Weston, J.: A neural attention model for abstractive sentence summarization. arXiv preprint arXiv:1509.00685 (2015)
21. See, A., Liu, P.J., Manning, C.D.: Get to the point: Summarization with pointer-generator networks. arXiv preprint arXiv:1704.04368 (2017)
22. Suanmali, L., Salim, N., Binwahlan, M.S.: Fuzzy logic based method for improving text summarization. arXiv preprint arXiv:0906.4690 (2009)
23. Wu, Y., Hu, B.: Learning to extract coherent summary via deep reinforcement learning. arXiv preprint arXiv:1804.07036 (2018)
24. Yin, W., Pei, Y.: Optimizing sentence modeling and selection for document summarization. In: Twenty-Fourth International Joint Conference on Artificial Intelligence (2015)

Proposing Chatbot Model for Managing Comments in Vietnam

Phat Nguyen Huu[1](✉) (iD), Cam Do Manh[1], and Hieu Nguyen Trong[2]

[1] School of Electronics and Telecommunications, Hanoi University of Science
and Technology (HUST), Hanoi, Vietnam
phat.nguyenhuu@hust.edu.vn, cam.dm165801@sis.hust.edu.vn
[2] National Institute of Patent and Technology Exploitation (NIPTECH),
Vietnamese Ministry of Science and Technology, Hanoi, Vietnam
nthieu@most.gov.vn

Abstract. Today, the behavioral culture on social networks is a painful
issue. State agencies have been trying to clean up the network environment of country. Many policies are proposed to process videos and clips
with offensive content. However, it is a small part of cleaning up the network environment. We often see hateful comments on social media sites.
It exists anywhere from social media to online games that are difficult
to control and punish because of their big data. There are not too many
social networking sites and online games until now. Therefore, it is not
too difficult for communities to limit inappropriate words. Therefore, we
offer a chatbot model to manage the comments that helps to clean the
network environment in the paper. The results show that the proposal
model achieves up to 75% accuracy with 100,000 comments.

Keywords: Chatbot · Impolite comment · Natural language
processing · AI · Machine learning

1 Introduction

With the explosion of internet, the number of users is increasing. There are about
2.6 billion Facebook users and 1.7 billion people use daily [15,18]. In Vietnam,
there are 64 million Facebook accounts per 90 million people. However, there is
no shortage of ingredients that always leave offensive comments and go against
public opinion that makes readers uncomfortably. In order to avoid harmful
effects on society, we need to remove it. Therefore, we propose a chatbot model
to help solve this problem.

ChatBot is a computer program that conducts a conversation through instant
messaging [12]. It can automatically answer questions or handle situations. Scope
and complexity of chatbot are determined by the algorithm of their creators. It is
used for many areas such as e-commerce, customer service, healthcare, banking
and finance, and entertainment services.

© ICST Institute for Computer Sciences, Social Informatics and Telecommunications Engineering 2021
Published by Springer Nature Switzerland AG 2021. All Rights Reserved
N.-S. Vo et al. (Eds.): INISCOM 2021, LNICST 379, pp. 287–297, 2021.
https://doi.org/10.1007/978-3-030-77424-0_24

Chatbot is divided into two categories:

1. The system targeting on an application domain (Task-Oriented) is called open domain (OP).
   Auto-responder model on OP allows users to participate any topic. Social media networks (Facebook or Twitter) are usually OP and they have many topics. Consequently, the requiring knowledge is created to answer OP dialogues that becomes more difficult. However, the collection and extraction of data from this domain is quite large and simple.
2. The system without a target orientation is called close domain (CD).
   Auto-responder model often focuses on answering questions relating to a specific domain such as health, education, travel, and shopping. In the model, the space for input and output patterns is limited since these systems try to achieve a very specific goal. Technical customer support or shopping assistants are closed to domain applications. These systems are unable to communicate and they only perform specific tasks in the most efficient way. Users are able to ask and answer anything. However, the system is not required to handle them.

Each approach to the problem has a different solution. Inappropriate sentences appear more and more with the growing popularity of social media and comments. However, the difficult problem is that Vietnamese have the ability to magically combine together to create extremely diverse sentences. Depending on the context, it can be understood as an offensive sentence if listing all those words into forbidden and controlling words is completely possible. However, it requires a very large database. Besides, people often try to circumvent the law. They can explain other ways such as antonyms, synonyms, spelling, abbreviations, adding or subtracting words, etc. with the same idea.

In the paper, we propose a method to solve the diversity of objectionable online based on chatbot model that can identify and classify inappropriate statements on the Internet. The rest of the paper includes ve parts and is organized as follows. Section 2 presents the proposal algorithm. Section 3 will evaluate the proposal model and analyze the results. In final section, we give conclusions and future research directions.

2 Proposal Algorithm

2.1 Theoretical Basis

Firstly, we need to set out the requirements for our algorithm. In the paper, our request will be:

1. Automatically detecting sentences that do not match with high accuracy.
2. The program can be integrated into many different languages that is able to be used widely.
3. The maximum amount of time to process per comment is less than 30 s.

Fig. 1. System structure diagram.

From the above requirements, we propose the structure diagram of system as shown in Fig. 1.

In Fig. 1, we have:

Pre-processing Block: Converting the input sentence into an array containing meaningful words. It includes the steps, namely separating Vietnamese words, data cleaning, handling nonsense words, and defining the meaning of each word.

Determining Block: Based on a defining array and a set standard, the system determines the level of whole sentence.

Responding Block: From the level of sentence and components, chatbot will proceed to give the most appropriate answer.

In the scope of study, we have not found any documents for processing sensitive words in Vietnamese. More detail of system structure will be presented below.

Data Collection

The difficulty for testing effectiveness of chatbot is the dataset of comments on social networking sites. We do not have the comments data since we create them from Facebook. Our self-built dataset has 100,000 comments.

Pre-processing Data

Separating Vietnamese Words

Natural language processing includes a lot of problems such as machine translation, text summarization, information retrieval, information extraction, etc. To solve the problems, the word segmentation is very important. It will determine the success of system.

To solve the problem, we need to analyze properties of words of Vietnamese as follows:

- Infinitive word: form and meaning of words are syntactically independent.
- Words include single words, complex words, and compound words.
- Words are structured from language. The recognition of words of Vietnamese is called clustering as shown in Fig. 2.

In Fig. 2, there is more than one way to understand this sentence where the second way has no meaning.

As we all know, Vietnamese text often puts spaces between syllables. A word has more syllables since there are many ways to divide it. This causes ambiguity. This ambiguous resolution is called the word separation problem.

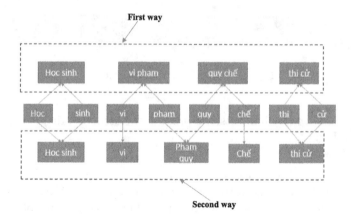

Fig. 2. The problem of clustering in Vietnamese [16].

The most important criterion in word separation is accuracy. We have achieved 97% accuracy on words. However, if calculating according to the sentence, the accuracy is only about 50%. The difference is caused by the complexity of Vietnamese.

Currently, there are several approaches to word separation problem as follows [13]:

- *Maximum match* [11,17]: We put words to cover all the sentences and satisfy certain heuristic. The advantage of method is very fast. However, there are many limitations such as low accuracy or inability to handle words that are not in the dictionary.
- *Rules* develops a manual or automatic rule set to distinguish allowing and authorizing combinations.
- *Graphization* builds a graph to represent the sentence and solve the problem of finding the shortest path on the graph.
- *Machine learning* considers the problem of string labeling. The way is used in JVNSegmenter [14].
- *Language model* gives several ways for separating whole sentences. This is the approach of vnTokenizer [2,3].

In this article, we use the *Maximum matching* method based on [14].

Data Cleaning
After separating words, text appears many special characters and punctuation. These ingredients reduce the efficiency of treatment process. In this section, we convert all capital words to low case and remove punctuation marks.

Solving Meaningless Words
This is the key point of the paper. In online comments, acronyms are often used.

If we only split and categorize words, we will miss many offensive sentences that still exist on social networks. There are several avoiding ways to use as:

- Using alternative words to describe the sentence.
- Using marks to center sentences.

These writing styles can fully express the meaning of offensive word. It will not create an offensive word when separating them. The common point of two ways is that the separating words are nonsensical or single words. Therefore, we need to process the separating words.

As shown in Fig. 2, we will have two steps to handle the problem.

- *Matching words:* Applying to words with one to two letters. We put them together into a new word. If that word makes sense, we will re-assemble it. Otherwise, we perform step 2.
- *Swap:* Vietnamese letters are divided into vowels and consonants. There are many Vietnamese words that have no meaning. However, their vowels and consonants are similar to the offensive sounds. Therefore, it will be used as a substitute for offensive words and the reader can still understand their meaning. Based on this point, we separate the vowels and consonants. If the system can match words with offensive meanings, we will update them into dictionary.

As a result, we improve the accuracy of separating from daily comments.

Classify Meaning of Words

As mentioned above, one of the most common ways to be offensive is to use synonyms and antonyms. To solve the problem, we propose to group commonly using synonyms and antonyms. We are dividing them into the following groups: offensive words, bad words, proverbial pronouns, animals, names of vocation, general, body, sensitive words, comparison words, negative words, activity, other words.

Determining Level of Word

Based on the division of antonyms, there are many groups of words that are not offensive. We can see that a few words is able to create offensive statements. There are offensive statements to this person that are extremely vulgar. However, it feels normal. To solve this problem, we proceed to create a norm to determine the level of objectionable sentences. Regulations are shown in Table 1.

The offensive score will be the sum of all vulgarities. Based on that result, we propose to divide it into six levels as follows:

- Level 0 (0–3 points): The sentence is not offensive.
- Level 1 (4–7 points): The sentences do not use disparaging words. A lot of repetition can go up to level 2.
- Level 2 (8–11 points): The sentences are intended to offend others and need to conduct warnings and sanctions.
- Level 3 (12–15 points): The sentences contain vulgar words and need punishment.
- Level 4 (16–19 points): The sentences contain highly offensive words and need a strong punishment

Table 1. The normative table determines the inappropriate sentence.

Word meaning	Example	Lowest mark	Highest mark	Condition
Offensive word	***	14		
Cursing and criticizing words	Stupid	7	14	
Pronouns	Father, mother	2	2	
Animal	Dog, cat	2	2	
Scold	Shut up, go away	3	9	
Body word	Eyes, nose, mouth	1	2	Cursing word or animal
Comparing word	Like, as	2	2	Mark of words is more than 3
Negative	Having negative meaning	2	2	When going with meaningful compliments
Canoe words are not suitable	Damn, fuck	4	8	
Curse	Die, go away	7	7	Going with the pronouns

- Level 5 (≥20 points): The sentence is full of unacceptable offensive words and need deterrent to be an example.

Through the step, we have identified the objectionable as well as the objectionable level of the separate comments. We then can give appropriate handling measures as well as warnings.

2.2 Database Design

Social networks are written by many languages. Therefore, it needs to be able to use for all languages and libraries. Besides, people are intelligent and know how to circumvent the law by different ways of speaking to express objection without violating. Therefore, it is necessary to constantly update and expand in order to ensure the effectiveness of chatbot.

There will be two factors required to ensure:

- The amount of Vietnamese words must be large in order not to lead to confusion,

– The program is able to facilitate frequent updates without cumbersome manipulations.

The first element is a very difficult task. With twelve vowels and seventeen consonants, the number of words is an extremely large number that is hard to enumerate. We can only constantly update and improve over time with the increasing number of comments. Therefore, we focus on the second one. It is be updated regularly without maintaining each time.

We perform the step based on the existing database as shown in Fig. 3 where:

– *Diem_minanddiem_max* are minimum and maximum points for each group,
– *Diem_hien_tai* is score of each meaningful group,
– *Dieu_kien* is condition of meaning group,
– *Tu_chui_tuc* is the word that reacts to group.

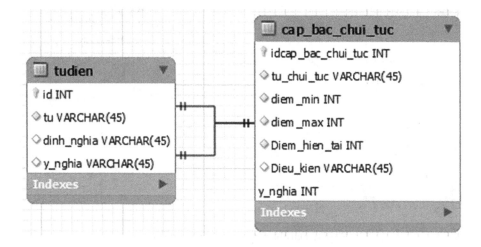

Fig. 3. Database for determining comment level.

Based on the dictionary table, sentences can be divided into meaningful words and phrases. As a result, we update the current score into table corresponding to meaning groups. Therefore, we are able to determine the offensive level of sentence. Answer and level can be used for different penalties. Therefore, the database presenting for penalty function will consist of three tables with two $1 - n$ relations as shown in Fig. 4 where:

– *thoi_gian_phat* is time to punish each punishment level per minute,
– *bot_dap* is answer of bot,
– *isbot, istuc, ischui, iscoquan* etc. are existence of factors to check whether the sentence is offensive.

As such, we have dataized the ranking and how the chatbot responds. Depending on user, it is possible to adjust according to them.

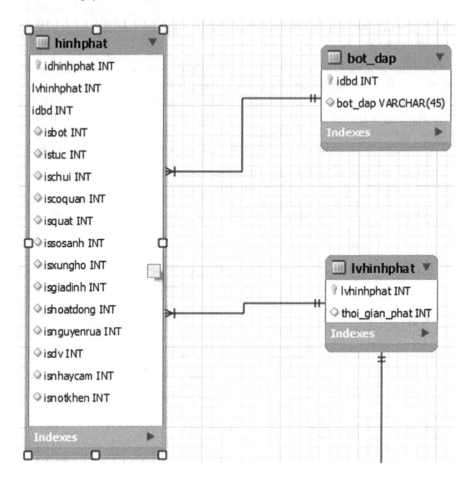

Fig. 4. Database for penalty function.

3   Simulation and Results

We perform for 100,000 comments based on [5]. The training process is as follows:

- Data input includes 100,000 comments taking from articles on Facebook and stored as .xlsx files. We divide into five types (4254 comments are level 1; 2627 comments are level 2; 1574 comments are level 3; 1021 comments are level 4; and 735 comments are level 5).
- Programming language uses php.
- Database system uses my Sql.
- Training tool uses php programming language that will read comments from input data. It then runs through the chatbot program to proceed to get the output data and save it.
- We use Intel Core i7 with 8192 Ram, Inspiron 3543.

– Data output is 5 files corresponding to offensive ranks. The program will divide the comments into offensive ranks and save them to each respective file.

Since we are not able to screen all 100,000 questions, we will conduct an assessment based on the results that are obtained for each level. The results are shown in Table 2.

Table 2. Training statistics and evaluation results.

Number of comments	Expecting processing time (Max)	Number of offensive comments	Exact number of ranks among offensive comments	Correct detection rate	Actual processing time
100,000	80 h	10,211	7696	75.36%	115 h

Detailed results with each level of comments are shown in Table 3. The correct detection rate is estimated by

$$correct\ detection\ rate = \frac{the\ correct\ number\ of\ comments}{total\ number\ of\ comments}. \tag{1}$$

Table 3. Statistics of the results obtained for each level.

Level	Number of comments	Correct detection rate (%)
1	4254	63.3
2	2627	77.54
3	1574	80.74
4	1021	94
5	735	100

In Table 3, we can see that the results are not high with 75% accuracy. The reasons are as follows:

– There are many sentences that do not have offensive meanings but still have offensive words.
– Many words in abbreviations are ignored and cannot be detected.
– The processing speed is still low. The maximum processing time is about 83 h (about 3.5 days) with 100,000 comments.

To solve the problems, it is necessary to improve as follows:

- Reseting comment level splits to be even stricter that helps to cover bad cases.
- Optimizing code, reduced processing time to an appropriate level. Maximum processing for comment is 30 s.
- Keeping to update dictionary in order to get the best accuracy from non-meaning words.
- Applying machine learning and AI to chatbot based on [6,7,10].

Therefore, we can develop the program that can be applied for practice.

4   Conclusion

Today, popular games have several ways to mask inappropriate comments. However, they have not put any effort into the issue. Most of those programs are based on specific words to identify and their effect is not great. Therefore, we propose the chatbot program to manage this comment based on:

- using antonyms.
- separating words with spaces or punctuation marks.
- using alternative words.

Besides, we set a standard to be able to determine the level of comment since optimal treatment can be taken. In the future, we will integrate new algorithms to improve the accuracy based on artificial intelligence (AI) [1,4,8,9].

References

1. Albayrak, N., Özdemir, A., Zeydan, E.: An overview of artificial intelligence based chatbots and an example chatbot application. In: 2018 26th Signal Processing and Communications Applications Conference (SIU), pp. 1–4 (2018)
2. Bakar, J.A., Omar, K., Nasrudin, M.F., Murah, M.Z.: Tokenizer for the Malay language using pattern matching. In: 2014 14th International Conference on Intelligent Systems Design and Applications, pp. 140–144 (2014)
3. Barcala, F.M., Vilares, J., Alonso, M.A., Grana, J., Vilares, M.: Tokenization and proper noun recognition for information retrieval. In: Proceedings. 13th International Workshop on Database and Expert Systems Applications, pp. 246–250 (2002)
4. Bozic, J., Tazl, O.A., Wotawa, F.: Chatbot testing using AI planning. In: 2019 IEEE International Conference On Artificial Intelligence Testing (AITest), pp. 37–44 (2019)
5. Burtsev, M., et al.: DeepPavlov: Open-source library for dialogue systems, July 2018
6. Chen, Y.N., Asli, C., Hakkani-Tur, D.: Deep learning for dialogue systems, pp. 8–14, January 2017
7. van Deemter, K., Krahmer, E., Theune, M.: Plan-based vs. template-based NLG: a false opposition?, August 1999
8. du Preez, S.J., Lall, M., Sinha, S.: An intelligent web-based voice chat bot. In: IEEE EUROCON 2009, pp. 386–391 (2009)

9. Khin, N.N., Soe, K.M.: University chatbot using artificial intelligence markup language. In: 2020 IEEE Conference on Computer Applications (ICCA), pp. 1–5 (2020)
10. Klüwer, T.: From Chatbots to Dialogue Systems, pp. 1–22, July 2011
11. Liu, B., Zhang, T., Han, F.X., Niu, D., Lai, K., Xu, Y.: Matching natural language sentences with hierarchical sentence factorization. In: Proceedings of the 2018 World Wide Web Conference, pp. 1237–1246, WWW 2018, International World Wide Web Conferences Steering Committee, Republic and Canton of Geneva, CHE (2018)
12. Mauldin, M.: Chatbot (2020). https://en.wikipedia.org/wiki/Chatbot. Accessed 11 Dec 2020
13. Nguyen, C.T., Nguyen, T.K., Phan, X.H., Nguyen, L.M., Ha, Q.T.: Vietnamese word segmentation with CRFs and SVMs: an investigation. In: Proceedings of the 20th Pacific Asia Conference on Language, Information and Computation, pp. 215–222. Tsinghua University Press, Huazhong Normal University, Wuhan, November 2006
14. Nguyen, T., Le, A.: A hybrid approach to Vietnamese word segmentation. In: 2016 IEEE RIVF International Conference on Computing Communication Technologies, Research, Innovation, and Vision for the Future (RIVF), pp. 114–119 (2016)
15. Phillips, S.: A brief history of Facebook. The Guardian, January 2007
16. Hông Phuong, L., Thi Minh Huyên, N., Roussanaly, A., Vinh, H.T.: A hybrid approach to word segmentation of Vietnamese texts. In: Martín-Vide, C., Otto, F., Fernau, H. (eds.) LATA 2008. LNCS, vol. 5196, pp. 240–249. Springer, Heidelberg (2008). https://doi.org/10.1007/978-3-540-88282-4_23
17. Zhong, M., Liu, L., Lu, R.: Shallow parsing based on maximum matching method and scoring model. In: 2008 3rd International Conference on Innovative Computing Information and Control, pp. 408–408 (2008)
18. Zuckerberg, M.: Facebook (2020). https://www.facebook.com/. Accessed 11 Dec 2020

Industrial Networks and Intelligent Systems

Social Hybrid Reciprocal Velocity Obstacle-Based Socially Aware Mobile Robot Navigation Framework

Duy Thao Nguyen, Van Bay Hoang, Trong Nghia Le, Tran Hiep Nguyen, and Xuan Tung Truong[(⊠)]

Le Quy Don Technical University, Hanoi 6000000, Vietnam

Abstract. In this paper, we propose a social hybrid reciprocal velocity obstacle (SHRVO)-based navigation framework which allows a mobile robot to avoid safely and socially humans or groups of humans in dynamic social environments. The integration of social behaviors, including passing to the right of humans or human groups and selecting the left to overtake, into the original hybrid reciprocal velocity obstacle algorithm is the key idea of our proposed framework. The developed frame work is evaluated by conducting a sequence of experiments in simulation environment. The experimental results have demonstrated the success of the proposed framework in safely navigating a mobile robot in dynamic social environment while still adhering to the social manners.

Keywords: Socially aware robot navigation · Cooperative navigation · Motion planning · Collision avoidance

1 Introduction

Recently, many socially aware navigation frameworks [7,13] and [1] have been presented to address the problem of navigating mobile robots autonomously in public environments such as museums, airports, commercial centers and urban areas. Depending on how to integrate the human information and social restraints into the navigation systems, these current humanly aware systems can be relatively separated into: (i) social costmap-based approaches and (ii) motion planning system-based approaches. While the methods in the first category incorporate the human data and social behaviors to build the costmap function, the techniques in the second category directly integrate the social restriction into the motion planning systems.

Several navigation systems for mobile robots [6,9,10] and [18] have been introduced based on the social costmap techniques in recent times. In these systems, the 2-D Gaussian and linear techniques are applied to combine the human information and social constraints with the aim of building the social costmap. After that, the path planning algorithms [4,16] and dynamic window

© ICST Institute for Computer Sciences, Social Informatics and Telecommunications Engineering 2021
Published by Springer Nature Switzerland AG 2021. All Rights Reserved
N.-S. Vo et al. (Eds.): INISCOM 2021, LNICST 379, pp. 301–314, 2021.
https://doi.org/10.1007/978-3-030-77424-0_25

approach [3] are utilized to generate a feasible trajectory and a motion command to drive the robots to their targets. When these techniques are installed, the robots not only can avoid safely the surrounding humans, but also behave socially such as ensuring no violation of private space and social interaction area and selecting a appreciate side to overtake a person. However, when operating in crowded and dynamic environments [9] and [8], the computation process of these methods to determine a feasible path for mobile robots is very complicated and takes a lot of time.

In term of approaches based on motion planning system, the recent proposed navigation frameworks [2,14,17] and [12] have been developed by incorporating the information of human into the conventional motion planning algorithms, for instance social force model [5] and velocity obstacles [15]. The computation time to generate the optimal path for mobile robots has been significantly improved and these techniques also have been verified in real-world environments. However, the social constraints such as taking the right side to pass and selecting the left to overtake are not considered in these systems.

In this paper, a human-like navigation system for mobile robots is proposed by incorporating the social rules into the original hybrid reciprocal velocity obstacle (HRVO) approach [15], which is a real-time algorithm considering the cooperation between robots operating in the shared environments. Particularly, we incorporate the social behaviors including selecting the right side to pass a human or a human group and taking the left side when overtaking, into the HRVO model, and propose a social hybrid reciprocal velocity obstacle (SHRVO) model. When equipped the proposed SHRVO model, the mobile robots are capable of behaving humanly when avoiding humans and human groups, and navigating safely towards their targets.

The remainder of the paper is arranged as follows. Section 2 introduces the proposed social hybrid reciprocal velocity obstacle model. The simulation experiments are presented in Sect. 3. The conclusion of the paper is provided in Sect. 4.

2   Proposed Framework

2.1   Problem Description

Considering a socially dynamic environment which consists of a mobile robot and N surrounding humans. The mobile robot has a fixed radius r_A, a current position p_A, an actual velocity $\mathbf{v}_A$, a goal situated at p_A^{goal} and a preferred speed p_A^{pref}. The goal can be directly selected as a fixed position in the plane or be the consequence of some algorithms, for instance global planning or scheduling algorithms. The preferred speed is identified as the speed taken by the robot when there are no humans or obstacles in its path. Similar to choosing the goal of the mobile robot, this speed can be pre-selected or be the output of some external methods. In addition, humans presenting around the robot can be denoted as $\mathbf{P} = \{\mathbf{p}_1, \mathbf{p}_2, ..., \mathbf{p}_N\}$, where $\mathbf{p}_i$ is the ith person. Each human also has a constant radius r_i, a current position p_i, an actual velocity $\mathbf{v}_i$, a goal situated at p_i^{goal} and a preferred speed p_i^{pref}.

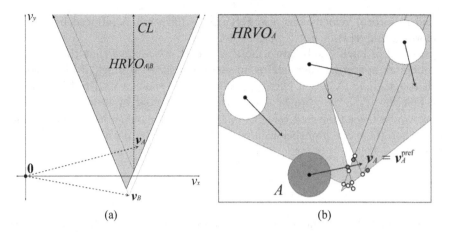

Fig. 1. (a) The configuration of HRVO. (b) The construction of the combined hybrid reciprocal velocity obstacle for the dark robot.

The objective of the mobile robot is to independently and concurrently compute a new velocity at each time step to generate an optimal trajectory towards its desired destination while not only ensuring the collision-free and oscillation-free with any human or obstacle in the environment but also following the social rules such as overtaking to the left of a human or a human group and passing them on the right side.

2.2 Hybrid Reciprocal Velocity Obstacle Model

The hybrid reciprocal velocity obstacle concept [15] is a real-time navigation algorithm for multiple mobile robots or virtual agents in which the reciprocity between robots is specially considered. The hybrid reciprocal velocity obstacle was developed to resolve one of the particular limitations of the reciprocal velocity obstacle formulation which is known as "reciprocal dance", and this algorithm has been successfully applied to mobile robots in an real-world environment. A brief review of the concept of the hybrid reciprocal velocity obstacle will be described in this section.

To counter the situation of "reciprocal dances", the hybrid reciprocal velocity obstacle combines the velocity obstacle and the reciprocal velocity obstacle to discourage robots from passing each other on different sides. For two robots A and B, if $\mathbf{v}_A$ is to the right of the centerline of the reciprocal velocity obstacle for robot A induced by robot B ($\mathbf{RVO}_{A|B}$), with the aim of encouraging robot A to pass on the right side of robot B, the reciprocal velocity obstacle will be expanded to the left side by replacing the left edge of $\mathbf{RVO}_{A|B}$ with the left edge of the velocity obstacle $\mathbf{VO}_{A|B}$. The intersection point between the right side of $\mathbf{RVO}_{A|B}$ and the left side of $\mathbf{VO}_{A|B}$ will be the apex of the hybrid reciprocal velocity obstacle. We exchange right and left and mirror the procedure if $\mathbf{v}_A$ is to the left of the centerline. The geometric interpretation of constructing a hybrid reciprocal velocity obstacle $\mathbf{HRVO}_{A|B}$ for robot A induced by robot B is shown in Fig. 1(a).

In stead of having only two robots A and B, we assume that there is a set of robots $\mathbf{A}$ operating together in an environment with a set of obstacles $\mathbf{O}$. Each robot A_i in $\mathbf{A}$ has a current position p_{Ai}, velocity $\mathbf{v}_{Ai}$, radius r_{Ai} and goal position p_{Ai}^{goal} that can be recognized or measured by other robots. Each robot A_i also has a preferred velocity $\mathbf{v}_{Ai}^{pref}$ toward its goal (velocity that a robot takes when there are no other robots or obstacles in its path) which is defined as follow:

$$\mathbf{v}_{Ai}^{pref} = v_{Ai}^{pref} \frac{\mathbf{p}_{Ai} - \mathbf{p}_{Ai}^{goal}}{\|\mathbf{p}_{Ai} - \mathbf{p}_{Ai}^{goal}\|2} \tag{1}$$

Each robot A_i will independently execute a continuous cycle including: (i) Sense positions and velocities of nearby robots; (ii) Select optimal new velocity outside union of HRVO's; (iii) Compute control input from new velocity; (iv) and Apply control input to robot's actuators until reaching its goal position.

Based on information from the sensing phase, the hybrid reciprocal velocity obstacles $\mathbf{HRVO}$ induced by each neighboring robot in $\mathbf{A}$ and the velocity obstacles $\mathbf{VO}$ generated by each obstacle in $\mathbf{O}$ for robot A_i will be constructed and then unified to form the combined hybrid reciprocal velocity obstacle.

$$\mathbf{HRVO}_{Ai} = \bigcup_{Aj \in \mathbf{A}} HRVO_{Ai|Aj} \cup \bigcup_{Oj \in \mathbf{O}} VO_{Ai|Oj} \tag{2}$$

Because the data that are obtained from sensors and used for calculating the hybrid reciprocal velocity obstacle contain uncertainty, the combined uncertainty-adjusted hybrid reciprocal velocity obstacle will be constructed to ensure the correct functioning of HRVO approach by applying a Kalman filter.

For collision avoidance, the robot A_i should select a new velocity $\mathbf{v}_{Ai}^{new}$ that is closest to its preferred velocity $\mathbf{v}_{Ai}^{pref}$ and outside the combined uncertainty-adjusted hybrid reciprocal velocity obstacle:

$$\mathbf{v}_{Ai}^{new} = arg \min_{v \notin \mathbf{HRVO}_{Ai}} \|\mathbf{v} - \mathbf{v}_{Ai}^{pref}\|2 \tag{3}$$

The ClearPath efficient geometric algorithm is used to compute this velocity. Due to the kinematic restrictions of the robot, the velocity $\mathbf{v}_{Ai}^{new}$ will be transformed into a control input (wheel speeds v_l and v_r) to allow the robot quickly reach the $\mathbf{v}_{Ai}^{new}$. This cycle will be continued until the robot reaches its goal position. This is illustrated in Fig. 1(b).

Algorithm 1 describes overall approach for navigating multiple mobile robots by applying the concept of HRVO, which is divided into three primary steps: (i) *perception* (Lines 3–4 of the Algorithm 1), *construction* (Lines 5–11 of the Algorithm 1), and (iii) *selection* (Lines 12–13 of the Algorithm 1). The input of the Algorithm 1 is the set of robots $\mathbf{A}$ and set of obstacles $\mathbf{O}$, and the output is the control input wheel speeds $\mathbf{v}_r, \mathbf{v}_l$ of the mobile robot. *The first step is perception and in which each robot in $\mathbf{A}$ acquires its own position and velocity, and those of*

Algorithm 1: Hybrid reciprocal velocity obstacle algorithm

---

    input : Set of robots **A**, set of obstacles **O**
    output: Motion control command $\mathbf{v}_r, \mathbf{v}_l$
1 **begin**
2   for all $\mathbf{A}_i \in \mathbf{A}$ **do**
3         $\mathbf{S} \leftarrow$ Sensing(**S**);
4         $\mathbf{G} \leftarrow$ Gaussiandistribution(**S**);
5         $\mathbf{VO} \leftarrow$ ContructVO(**A, O, S**);
6         $\mathbf{RVO} \leftarrow$ ConstructRVO(**VO, S**);
7         $\mathbf{LC} \leftarrow$ LocateCenterline(**RVO**);
8         $\mathbf{CH} \leftarrow$ ConstructHRVO(**VO, RVO**);
9         $\mathbf{AH} \leftarrow$ AdjustHRVO(**G, CH**);
10       $\mathbf{AVO} \leftarrow$ AdjustVO(**G, VO**);
11       $\mathbf{CAH} \leftarrow$ CombineAdjustHRVO(**AH, AVO**);
12       $\mathbf{PV} \leftarrow$ PrefVelocity(**A, S**);
13       $\mathbf{NV} \leftarrow$ NewVelocity(**CAH, PV**);
14   **end for**
15   Return $\mathbf{v}_r, \mathbf{v}_l$;

---

the surrounding robots and obstacles in **O**. Because sensors contain uncertainty, a Kalman filter is used to obtain the accurate estimation of the positions and velocities of the robots and obstacles by providing a Gaussian distribution of these information. *In the second step*, the velocity obstacles **VO** and reciprocal velocity obstacles **RVO** for each robot in **A** induced by other surrounding robots in **A** and velocity obstacles in **O** are constructed. Next, depending on the relative position between the centerline of **RVO** and the velocity of the robot, one of two edges of **RVO** will be replaced with a corresponding edge of **VO** to construct the hybrid reciprocal velocity obstacle **HRVO**. After that, the **HRVO** will be expanded to the uncertainty-adjusted hybrid reciprocal velocity obstacle **HRVO*** by using the Gaussian distribution to reduce the uncertainty in the perception step. The velocity obstacle $\mathbf{VO}_{A|O}$ for each obstacle in **O** in the environment are also transferred to uncertainty-adjusted velocity obstacle **VO***. The last part of this step will be the construction of the combined uncertainty-adjusted hybrid reciprocal velocity obstacle for each robot in **A**. *In the final selection step*, a new velocity for each robot will be computed by using the Clearpath algorithm before converting to the speeds of the wheels which are the control input of each robot.

2.3 Proposed Social Hybrid Reciprocal Velocity Obstacle Algorithm

In HRVO concept, for two robots A and B, whether robot A will choose a new velocity to the right or left of $\mathbf{RVO}_{A|B}$ depending on the relative position between $\mathbf{v}_A$ and the centerline of $\mathbf{RVO}_{A|B}$. In our social HRVO concept, in addition to relative position, we also consider the distance between the current velocity of robot A and the centerline of $\mathbf{RVO}_{A|B}$ when choosing the new

---

Algorithm 2: Social hybrid reciprocal velocity obstacle algorithm

---

    input : Set of robots **A**, set of obstacles **O**

    output: Motion control command $\mathbf{v}_r$,$\mathbf{v}_l$

1 **begin**

2   **for all** $\mathbf{A}_i \in \mathbf{A}$ **do** ;

3   **S** ← Sensing(**S**);

4   **G** ← Gaussiandistribution(**S**);

5   **T** ← setupThreshold();

6   **VO** ← ContructVO(**A, O, S**);

7   **AVO** ← AdjustVO(**G, VO**);

8   **RVO** ← ConstructRVO(**VO, S**);

9   **LC** ← LocateCenterline(**RVO**);

10   **if** distance ($\mathbf{v}_{Ai}$,centerline) < threshold;

11   **CHS** ← ConstructSHRVO(**VO, RVO, LC, T**);

12   **AHS** ← AdjustSHRVO(**G, CHS**);

13   **CASH** ← CombineAdjustSHRVO(**AHS, AVO**);

14   **else**

15   **CH** ← ConstructHRVO(**VO, RVO**);

16   **AH** ← AdjustHRVO(**G, CH**);

17   **CAH** ← CombineAdjustHRVO(**AH, AVO**);

18   **PV** ← PrefVelocity(**A, S**);

19   **NV** ← NewVelocity(**CAH, PV**);

20   **end for**

21   Return $\mathbf{v}_r, \mathbf{v}_l$;

---

velocity for robot A. We install a number that plays a role as a threshold for this selection. If the distance between the velocity and centerline of $\mathbf{RVO}_{A|B}$ is larger than the threshold, robot will follow the HRVO concept for choosing new velocity (Lines 14–17 of the Algorithm 2). If the distance is smaller than the threshold and the velocity is not to the side as we wish, the centerline of $\mathbf{RVO}_{A|B}$ will be moved an equal distance to the threshold and to the side that we do not wish the robot A to pass (Lines 10–13 of the Algorithm 2). This transfer ensures that $\mathbf{v}_A$ is to the desired side of the centerline of $\mathbf{RVO}_{A|B}$. By the symmetry, this is totally similar to robot B. Consequently, robots can pass others on the side that is in accordance with social rules. Because of adding the social rules to the HRVO concept, we call the result a social hybrid reciprocal velocity obstacle, and denote it $\mathbf{SHRVO}_{A|B}$. The method to construct the social hybrid reciprocal velocity obstacle is described specifically in Algorithm 3. The input of Algorithm 3 includes the radius, position, current velocity and preferred velocity of all robots in the environment, while the output will be the construction of social hybrid reciprocal velocity obstacle consisting of apex, left side and right side. The Algorithm 3 first calculates the parameters that will be used to create the **VO**, **RVO** and declares a threshold as a condition for constructing the **SHRVO** (Lines 4–9 of the Algorithm 3). If the velocity of robot is to the right (or left) of the centerline of the **RVO** but the distance between them is less

---

Algorithm 3: Construct SHRVO

---

input : Set of robots $\mathbf{A}$ with: robot position $\mathbf{p}_{Ai}$, robot velocity $\mathbf{v}_{Ai}$, robot preferred velocity $\mathbf{p}_{A_i}^{pre}$, robot radius $\mathbf{r}_{Ai}$

output: SHRVO (apex, side1, side2)

1 **begin**

2   **for all** $\mathbf{A}_i \in \mathbf{A}$ **do**

3   **for all** $\mathbf{A}_j \in \mathbf{A}(j \neq i)$ **do**

4   constant bias: **threshold**;

5   **Angle** $= atan(p_{Aj} - p_{Ai})$;

6   **openingAngle** $= \dfrac{asin(r_{Aj} - r_{Ai})}{abs(p_{Aj} - p_{Ai})}$;

7           $\mathbf{d} = 2^* sin(openingAngle)^* cos(openingAngle)$;

8   **VOSide1** $= (cos(Angle - openingAngle), sin(Angle - openingAngle))$;

9   **VOSide2** $= (cos(Angle + openingAngle), sin(Angle + openingAngle))$;

10   **if** $det(p_{Aj} - p_{Ai}, p_{A_i}^{pre} - p_{A_j}^{pre}) > 0$;

11   **if** $DispPointToSegment(p_{Aj} - p_{Ai}, p_{A_i}^{pre} - p_{A_j}^{pre}) < bias$;

12   **VBnew** $= ClosePointOnSegment(v_{Aj}, (v_{Aj} - bias))$;

13   **interPoint** $=$

$InterVectors(VBnew, VOSide2, 0.5^*(v_{Ai} + v_{Aj}), VOSide1)$;

14   **HRVOApex** $=$

$interPoint - norm(p_{Aj} - p_{Ai})^* \dfrac{unOffset^* abs(p_{Aj} - p_{Ai})}{r_{Aj} + r_{Ai}}$;

15   **else**

16                 $\mathbf{s} = 0.5^* det(v_{Aj} - v_{Ai}, VOSide2)$;

17   **HRVOApex** $=$

$v_{Aj} + s^* VOSide1 - norm(p_{Aj} - p_{Ai})^* \dfrac{unOffset^* abs(p_{Aj} - p_{Ai})}{r_{Aj} + r_{Ai}}$;

18   **else**

19              $\mathbf{s} = 0.5^* det(v_{Aj} - v_{Ai}, VOSide1)$;

20   **HRVOApex** $=$

$v_{Aj} + s^* VOSide2 - norm(p_{Aj} - p_{Ai})^* \dfrac{unOffset^* abs(p_{Aj} - p_{Ai})}{r_{Aj} + r_{Ai}}$;

21   **end for**;

22   **end for**;

23   Return SHRVO(**apex, side1, side2**);

---

than the threshold, the **SHRVO** will be generated to make the robot act like human in society (Lines 10–14 of the Algorithm 3). If this distance is larger than the threshold, the robot will follow the concept of **HRVO** (Lines 16–20 of the Algorithm 3).

The geometric interpretation of **R-SHRVO** for the right rule is illustrated in Fig. 2(a). Because the distance between $\mathbf{v}_A$ and CL is smaller than the threshold b, robot A will choose a new velocity to the right of $\mathbf{RVO}_{A|B}$ even though $\mathbf{v}_A$ is to the left of the centerline of $\mathbf{RVO}_{A|B}$. To encourage this, a right social HRVO

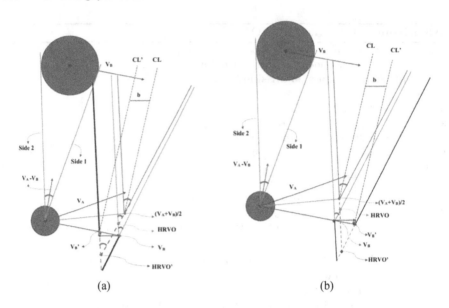

(a)   (b)

Fig. 2. The first figure is the geometric interpretation of R-SHRVO for the right rule and the second is the geometric interpretation of R-SHRVO for the left rule

is created by enlarging the reciprocal velocity obstacle to the left side. The steps are as follows:

Step 1 - Create a new velocity obstacle (VO'): From the apex of **VO** ($\mathbf{v}_B$), draw a vector $\mathbf{v}_b$ that is parallel to the Ox axis (origin of the coordinated axis is at the center of robot A), toward the left and has a length of threshold b.

$$\mathbf{v}_b = \mathbf{v}_B - (b, 0) \tag{4}$$

Project $\mathbf{v}_b$ onto velocity $\mathbf{v}_B$, we get point B'. This is the new apex of $\mathbf{VO}'_{A|B}$. And from this apex, draw two edges that are parallel to the edges of $\mathbf{VO}_{A|B}$ to form a new velocity obstacle $\mathbf{VO}'_{A|B}$.

*Step 2 - Create a **SHRVO** for right rule (R-SHRVO):* The apex of **R-SHRVO** is the intersection between the right side of $\mathbf{RVO}_{A|B}$ and the left side of $\mathbf{VO}'_{A|B}$.

$$\mathbf{apex} = \text{right } \mathbf{RVO}_{A|B} \cap \text{left } \mathbf{VO}'_{A|B} \tag{5}$$

As a result, the left boundary of **SHRVO** for right rule will be the left side of $\mathbf{VO}'_{A|B}$, and the right boundary will be the right side of $\mathbf{RVO}_{A|B}$.

For the left rule, the procedure is nearly the same as described above, just exchanging right and left. The $\mathbf{RVO}_{A|B}$ at that time will be expanded to the right to encourage robot A to take the left side of robot B to pass. Figure 2(b) will illustrate the steps to construct the **SHRVO** for left rule.

The apex of **L-SHRVO** is the intersection between the left side of $\mathbf{RVO}_{A|B}$ and the right side of $\mathbf{VO}'_{A|B}$. Two boundaries of **SHRVO** for left rule will be the right side of $\mathbf{VO}'_{A|B}$, and the left side of $\mathbf{RVO}_{A|B}$.

$$\mathbf{apex} = \text{left } \mathbf{RVO}_{A|B} \cap \text{right } \mathbf{VO}'_{A|B} \qquad (6)$$

3 Experiments

The effectiveness of the proposed social HRVO model is verified by implementing and testing in a simulation environment. The C/C++ programming language is applied to implement the proposed system, while the Robot Operating System (ROS) [11] is utilized to develop the entire navigation framework. The original HRVO package[1] was inherited and adjusted to develop the proposed social HRVO model.

3.1 Simulation Setup

We create scenarios, as shown in Figs. 3, 4, 5 and 6, in which the mobile robot need to cooperate with the behaviors of other humans in the environments to reach its goal. In addition to guarantee the collision-free, the robot is required to follow the social rules such as passing on the right side or left side of other humans. With the aim of demonstrating the performance of the proposed social HRVO model, we compare it with the original hybrid reciprocal velocity obstacle model HRVO [15]. Furthermore, the proposed socially aware navigation framework is validated by adopting the human comfortable safety indices (HCSI) introduced by Truong et al. [19], including *social individual index (SII)*, *social group index (SGI)*. The HCSI indices are used to estimate the human safety and comfort and socially acceptable behaviors of the mobile robot. Specifically, the SII value is applied to measure the physical safety and psychological safety of each individual, while the SGI is used to measure the comfortable safety of the human group.

3.2 Simulation Results

Videos with our simulation results can be found at the links[2,3,4] and[5].

Experiment 1 – Avoiding a Person: We first examine the proposed SHRVO model in a simulation environment with a person. The mobile robot is expected to move from left to right without any collision with a moving person. The simulation results are shown in Fig. 3. The first and third rows show the trajectory

---

[1] https://gamma.cs.unc.edu/HRVO/.
[2] https://youtu.be/wTTiu03l5Mw.
[3] https://youtu.be/6gm5oFtz0uo.
[4] https://youtu.be/GL03vP92J1Y.
[5] https://youtu.be/nPKkuFw4z0Y.

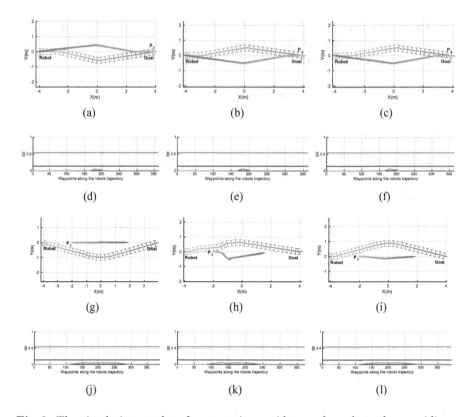

Fig. 3. The simulation results of cooperative avoidance of a robot when avoiding a person. The first and third rows, from left to right, show the trajectory of the robot and the human equipped with the R-SHRVO model, L-SHRVO model and the conventional HRVO model, respectively. The second and fourth rows illustrate the corresponding social individual index (SII).

of the robot and the person, and the second and fourth rows illustrate the SII value along the robot's trajectory.

In Figs. 3(a) and 3(b), the mobile robot equipped with the proposed SHRVO technique successfully cooperates with the moving person to avoid each other on the side that we preconfigure in the algorithm. In contrast, the robot and the person select the left side to avoid if it is installed the conventional HRVO model in Fig. 3(c). Similarly, in Figs. 3(g) and 3(h), the robot successfully overtakes on the side following the rule which is installed in the SHRVO model, whereas left side is the selection of the robot and the person with the HRVO model as shown in Fig. 3(i).

Figures 3(d), 3(e), 3(f), 3(j), 3(k) and 3(l) show that, when equipped with the SHRVO model, the mobile robot not only successfully cooperates with the moving person to overtake or avoid but also still maintains a safety distance with the person.

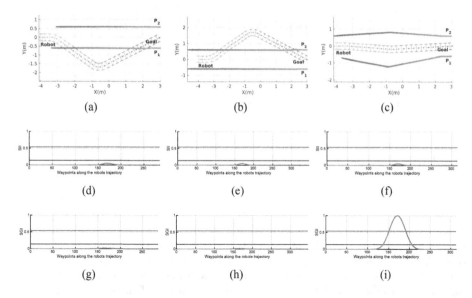

Fig. 4. The simulation results of cooperative avoidance of the robot and a group of two people in opposite directions. The first row, from left to right, shows the trajectory of the robot and the humans equipped with the R-HRVO model, L-HRVO model and the conventional HRVO model, respectively. The second and third rows illustrate the corresponding social individual index and social group index (SGI).

Experiment 2 – Avoiding a Group of Two People: In this experiment, we want to verify the avoiding behavior of the mobile robot when avoiding a group of two people moving towards the robot. The simulation results are shown in Fig. 4, in which the first row shows the trajectory of the robot when passing two people, while the second and last rows illustrate the SII and SGI values along the robot's trajectory, respectively. In the first row of Fig. 4, by cooperating with the behaviors of two people, the mobile robot equipped with the proposed SHRVO algorithm, as presented in Figs. 4(a) and 4(b), or the HRVO algorithm, as presented in Fig. 4(c), is able to safely navigate to its goal.

Although the SII values in Fig. 4(d), Fig. 4(e) and Fig. 4(f) are similarly low indicating that the robot equipped with both SHRVO and HRVO models often maintains a safety distance with each person, the trajectory of HRVO model goes through the interaction space between two people. This is the reason for the much higher SGI value of HRVO model in Fig. 4(i) in comparison with the SGI values in Fig. 4(g) and Fig. 4(h) of SHRVO model. Therefore, in this experiment, the robot installed the SHRVO model offers a higher safety distance with the group of two people than the HRVO model.

Experiment 3 – Avoiding Dynamic People: The successful performance of the proposed SHRVO model is further clarified in several crowded environment

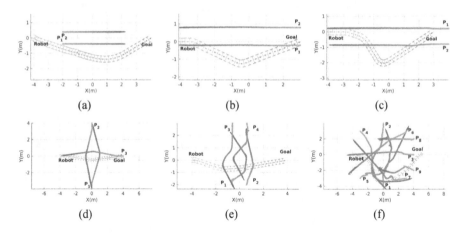

Fig. 5. The simulation results of cooperative avoidance of the robot equipped with R-SHRVO model when avoiding dynamic people. The first row shows the trajectory of the robot and two humans in different situations, while the second row, from left to right, illustrates the trajectory of the robot and three people, four people and a crowd of people, respectively.

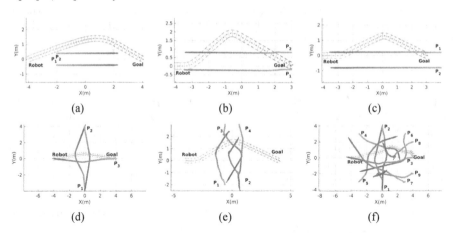

Fig. 6. The simulation results of cooperative avoidance of the robot equipped with L-SHRVO model when avoiding dynamic people. The first row shows the trajectory of the robot and two humans in different situations. Whereas, the second row, from left to right, illustrates the trajectory of the robot and three people, four people and a crowd of people, respectively.

scenarios, in which many people are moving toward the robot or in the same direction. The simulation results are shown in Fig. 5 and Fig. 6.

In Fig. 5, the simulation results show that the mobile robot equipped with the R-SHRVO algorithm successfully cooperates with the humans to guarantee the collision-free by selecting the right side to avoid each other. Especially, when one of two people is to the right of the robot as shown in Fig. 5(c) or there are a crowd of people in the environment as shown in Fig. 5(f), the robot still chooses the right side to avoid the humans if it is installed the R-SHRVO model.

Similarly, Fig. 6 illustrates that the robot equipped with the L-SHRVO model also succeeds in navigating to its goal without any collision by selecting the left side to avoid the humans. The successful performance of the L-SHRVO model is demonstrated even if one of two people is to the left of the robot as shown in Fig. 6(b) or there are a crowd of people as shown Fig. 6(f).

In summary, the simulation results illustrate that, the robot equipped with the proposed SHRVO model is capable of cooperating with the humans in the crowded environment, and safely and socially navigating to the given target.

4   Conclusion

We have presented a social hybrid reciprocal velocity obstacle (SHRVO)-based navigation framework which ensures the free collision and social behavior for a mobile robot while navigating in dynamic social environments. In our proposed system, the social rules are integrated into the conventional HRVO algorithm to construct the SHRVO model. We have executed many simulation experiments to verify the proposed framework and the results demonstrate that our developed system can be able to navigate the mobile robot safely and humanly in dynamic social environments.

In the future, we will install the proposed SHRVO model on our mobile robot platform, and conduct experiments in real-world environments.

Acknowledgment. This research is funded by Vietnam National Foundation for Science and Technology Development (NAFOSTED) under grant number 102.01-2018.10.

References

1. Cheng, J., Cheng, H., Meng, M.Q., Zhang, H.: Autonomous navigation by mobile robots in human environments: a survey. In: 2018 IEEE International Conference on Robotics and Biomimetics, pp. 1981–1986, December 2018
2. Ferrer, G., Sanfeliu, A.: Proactive kinodynamic planning using the extended social force model and human motion prediction in urban environments. In: IEEE/RSJ International Conference on Intelligent Robots and Systems, pp. 1730–1735, September 2014
3. Fox, D., Burgard, W., Thrun, S.: The dynamic window approach to collision avoidance. IEEE Trans. Robot. Autom. **4**(1), 23–33 (1997)
4. Hart, P.E., Nilsson, N.J., Raphael, B.: A formal basis for the heuristic determination of minimum cost paths. IEEE Trans. Syst. Sci. Cybern. **4**(2), 100–107 (1968)
5. Helbing, D., Molnár, P.: Social force model for pedestrian dynamics. Phys. Rev. E **51**, 4282–4286 (1995)
6. Kirby, R., Simmons, R., Forlizzi, J.: COMPANION: a constraint-optimizing method for person-acceptable navigation. In: Proceedings of the IEEE International Symposium on Robot and Human Interactive Communication, pp. 607–612, September 2009

7. Kruse, T., Pandey, A.K., Alami, R., Kirsch, A.: Human-aware robot navigation: a survey. Robot. Auton. Syst. **61**, 1726–1743 (2013)
8. Kruse, T., Kirsch, A., Khambhaita, H., Alami, R.: Evaluating directional cost models in navigation. In: Proceedings of the ACM/IEEE International Conference on Human-robot Interaction, pp. 350–357 (2014)
9. Lu, D.V., Smart, W.D.: Towards more efficient navigation for robots and humans. In: IEEE/RSJ International Conference on Intelligent Robots and Systems, pp. 1707–1713. IEEE (2013)
10. Pandey, A.K., Alami, R.: A framework towards a socially aware mobile robot motion in human-centered dynamic environment. In: IEEE/RSJ International Conference on Intelligent Robots and Systems, pp. 5855–5860, October 2010
11. Quigley, M., et al.: ROS: an open-source robot operating system. In: ICRA Workshop on Open Source Software, vol. 32, pp. 151–170 (2009)
12. Repiso, E., Garrell, A., Sanfeliu, A.: Adaptive side-by-side social robot navigation to approach and interact with people. Int. J. Soc. Robot. **12**, 909–930 (2020). https://doi.org/10.1007/s12369-019-00559-2
13. Rios-Martinez, J., Spalanzani, A., Laugier, C.: From proxemics theory to socially-aware navigation: a survey. Int. J. Soc. Robot. **7**, 137–153 (2015). https://doi.org/10.1007/s12369-014-0251-1
14. Shiomi, M., Zanlungo, F., Hayashi, K., Kanda, T.: Towards a socially acceptable collision avoidance for a mobile robot navigating among pedestrians using a pedestrian model. Int. J. Soc. Robot. **6**(3), 443–455 (2014). https://doi.org/10.1007/s12369-014-0238-y
15. Snape, J., Van den Berg, J., Guy, S., Manocha, D.: The hybrid reciprocal velocity obstacle. IEEE Trans. Robot. **27**(4), 696–706 (2011)
16. Stentz, A.: The D* algorithm for real-time planning of optimal traverses. Technical report, CMU-RI-TR-94-37. The Robotics Institute, Carnegie-Mellon University (1994)
17. Truong, X.T., Ngo, T.D.: Toward socially aware robot navigation in dynamic and crowded environments: a proactive social motion model. IEEE Trans. Autom. Sci. Eng. **14**(4), 1743–1760 (2017)
18. Truong, X.T., Ngo, T.D.: Dynamic social zone based mobile robot navigation for human comfortable safety in social environments. Int. J. Soc. Robot. **8**(5), 663–684 (2016). https://doi.org/10.1007/s12369-016-0352-0
19. Truong, X.T., Ngo, T.D.: "To Approach Humans?": a unified framework for approaching pose prediction and socially aware robot navigation. IEEE Trans. Cogn. Dev. Syst. **10**(3), 557–572 (2017)

Proposing Gesture Recognition Algorithm Using HOG and SVM for Smart-Home Applications

Phat Nguyen Huu$^{(\boxtimes)}$(iD), Tan Phung Ngoc, and Hoang Tran Manh

School of Electronics and Telecommunications, Hanoi University of Science and Technology (HUST), Hanoi, Vietnam
{phat.nguyenhuu,hoang.tranmanh}@hust.edu.vn,
Tan.PNCA190157@sis.hust.edu.vn

Abstract. Gesture recognition is one of the key aspects of robot communication systems. There are many image recognition techniques that are being developed to use in many different intelligent systems. In the paper, we perform the image processing techniques that include artificial intelligence technologies and deep learning in gesture recognition to apply for smart-home systems. We propose the gesture recognition model including the histogram of oriented gradient (HOG) and support vector machine (SVM) detection algorithms combining the kernel correlation filter (KCF) algorithm for tracking objects and a multi-layer convolution neural network (CNN) for classifications. The results show that the proposal algorithm is applicable for real environments with accuracy up to 99% per 6 seconds.

Keywords: Gesture recognition · Histogram of oriented gradient · Support vector machine · Kernel correlation filter · Convolution neural network

1 Introduction

With the development of automation applications, human-computer interaction (HMI) systems gradually become important and significant. HMI with smart-home control system is one of the core issues to create accuracy that is convenience and friendliness with civilian applications in the direction of getting closer to communication nature. Instead of living control, using voice controls or via gestures is developing.

Using gestures in HCI systems is an effective idea that helps people communicate in the real world. Gesture is the act of one or more combinations of different body parts that imply information. Hand gestures are commonly used body language comparing to other parts because of their flexibility. The various shapes and postures of hand bring a large amount of information to communicate in real environments.

© ICST Institute for Computer Sciences, Social Informatics and Telecommunications Engineering 2021
Published by Springer Nature Switzerland AG 2021. All Rights Reserved
N.-S. Vo et al. (Eds.): INISCOM 2021, LNICST 379, pp. 315–323, 2021.
https://doi.org/10.1007/978-3-030-77424-0_26

Therefore, we focus on new technologies in smart-home control using gesture language with limited hardware cost and quality in the paper. The goal of paper is to propose a gesture recognition algorithm using histogram of oriented gradient (HOG) and support vector machine (SVM) that is able to detect while minimizing noise and processing speed and reducing errors. Our static gestures are selected as on, off, up, and down. The dynamic gestures are as follows:

- Toggle state switching is hand from spread state upwards to re-grip state,
- Up order is hand from outstretched state up to left,
- Down order is hand from outstretched state up to right.

The rest of the paper includes five parts and is organized as follows. Section 2 presents several related works. Section 3 presents the proposal algorithm. Section 4 will evaluate the proposal model and analyze the results. In final section, we give conclusions and future research directions.

2   Related Work

The motion recognition problem can be solved by combining basic image processing, namely object detection, recognition, and tracking. There are many image processing algorithms that have been developed for detection and recognition. We divide into main groups, namely advanced machine learning and deep learning techniques.

Machine learning (ML) techniques are general terms commonly using with basic feature extraction methods from original data and then combining such as SVM, decision tree, nearest-neighbor to train identity models. There are several extraction techniques as follows

1. Viola – Jones's target detection technique [13] is the technique in real-time target detection based on Haar feature extraction. The technique is used in face detection.
2. Scale-invariant feature transform (SIFT) [10]: The special feature of SIFT is scale-invariant that will give stable results with different aspect ratios of image. Besides, it can be said that this algorithm is rotation-invariant to ensure the result with different rotation of object.
3. HOG [9] is calculated on a dense grid of cells and normalized the contrast among blocks to improve accuracy. It is used to describe the shape and appearance of objects.

Advanced deep learning techniques use multi-layered convolutional neural networks (CNNs) for training on labeled datasets. Several deep learning techniques are applied for object detection and recognition as follows:

1. Region proposals (R-CNN, Fast R-CNN, Faster R-CNN, cascade R-CNN) [8]: The method proposes areas capable of containing the object and performs identification to save computational capacity.

2. Single shot multibox detector (SSD) [3] such as YOLO, Refinedet: The main idea of SSD comes from using bounding boxes by pre-initializing boxes at each location on image. The SSD will compute and evaluate information at each location to see if there are any objects. If there are any objects, it will determine which one it is. Based on the results, SSD will compute an amalgamation box covering the object.

Since the detection and recognition algorithms require a large amount of computation and the accuracy is not able to reach 100%, the object tracking techniques for gesture recognition are also widely applied to ensure the continuous real-time recording of location and to avoid interference in multi-subject environments. There are many tracking algorithms for image processing such as BOOSTING [2], MIL, KCF [5], TLD, MEDIANFLOW [6], GOTURN [14], MOSSE [1], CSRT [7,12]. Therefore, we are able to select the suitable algorithm.

3   Proposal Algorithm

The proposal solution for motion detection is developed and performed based on three main problems, namely hand detection, grip, and position. In the paper, we propose the gesture recognition algorithm using HOG and SVM based on our previous results [11] as shown in Fig. 1.

Details of the steps are as follows:

1. **Pre-processing** is an essential step in reducing noise and increasing reliability for computation. In the paper, processing steps include in resizing and synchronizing images, balancing histogram to reduce the light effect, eliminating noise by median filter.
2. **Hand region detection** is performed based on the HOG characteristic extraction [4] combining with SVM classifier. The HOG characteristics are the shape of object characterizing by the distribution of intensity and direction of pixel value (a gradient vector). The gradient vector represents the change of luminance pixel when it is in the corner and edge areas of object. Therefore, the HOG feature is an effective choice for hand posture.

    The HOG method is to use information about the distribution of intensity gradients or edge directions to describe local objects of image. Its operators are implemented by dividing an image into sub regions calling cells. We compute histograms for points within cell. Combining them together, we get a representation of original image. To enhance recognition performance, local histograms is able to be normalized by calculating an intensity threshold in area larger than the cell (blocks) and using them to normalize. The result is a feature vector that is more invariant to changes in lighting conditions. Details of the steps for extracting the HOG features are as shown in Fig. 2.

    To detect hands, the next step is to use SVM algorithm for classification or regression problems. We use the pyramid method and sliding window to address the areas of image obtaining at different scales. Finally, the results are processed by the non-maximum suppression (NMS) algorithm to eliminate unreliable or overlapping area.

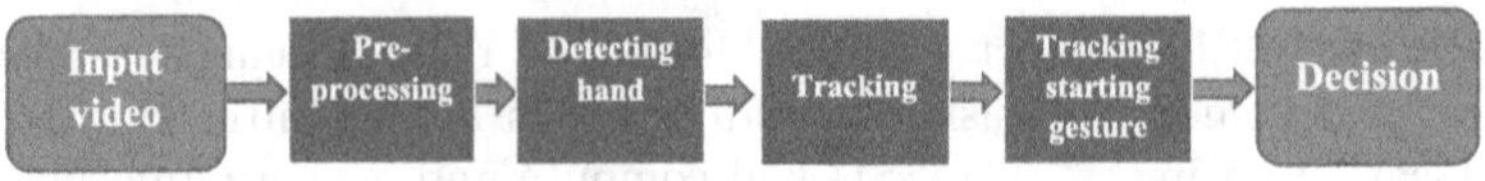

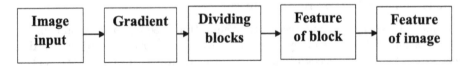

Fig. 1. Diagram of the proposal system.

| Image input | Gradient | Dividing blocks | Feature of block | Feature of image |

Fig. 2. Details of steps of HOG.

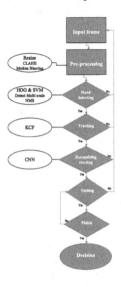

Fig. 3. Details of proposal algorithm.

3. **Tracking object** uses KCF technique. KCF method includes the following steps:
   - Determination of grip area: can be the initial user-defined area or an area detecting by the previous frame,
   - Description of features: defines the characteristics of image area,
   - Regression training: The detecting ROI features will be added to form a dataset including past and present features for training model,
   - The results after regression training is a new model. The model is the basis for the next step.
4. **Object classification** is one of the typical problems of image processing that has achieved many achievements by applying deep learning techniques to multi-layered CNN. We select a CNN model including 2-dimensional convolution layers (Conv2D) with sizes 32, 64, 128 (pyramid structure), Relu activation function, and 3 layers of MaxPooling2D, respectively. With a flatten layer, the output is a dense layer of size 128 and 4. The model output is

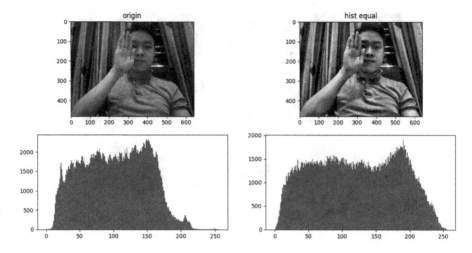

Fig. 4. Image results of adaptive histogram balancing process.

a list of expectations where each of them represents a classification. In the paper, we classify four postures for the four classifier outputs. Subject is classified based on ROI of image.

After detecting and recognizing the starting of gesture, subsequent frames will be continuously updated. The human hand will be categorized to find out what kind of ending or exiting gesture when the grip is lost.

As a result, we are able to implement each part of algorithm. The final step is to incorporate the algorithms into real-time frames from computer camera. Combining the algorithms increases the processing time since the program will not perform continuous object detection. We only perform at three frames to detect for one times. Details of the proposed algorithm are shown in Fig. 3.

4 Simulation and Results

4.1 Setup

Our program is built by Python on Jupyter Notebook platform. We use the OpenCV and Dlib libraries. The simulation is performed on a personal computer with a Core i5 4310 CPU configuration at 2 GHz without using GPU.

4.2 Training Result

Firstly, the images are pre-processed to increase reliability and accuracy as shown in Fig. 4.

The training samples will be performed on real time for smart indoor application. In the paper, the training sample is captured from the user of actual image.

Fig. 5. Results of samples using target detection.

The dataset with hand position is selected for training. Results are shown in Fig. 5.

For categorization of training dataset, we use 1000 images for one time. These images are only ROI regions containing the target without other details. Results are shown in Fig. 6.

Fig. 6. Results of images for the training dataset.

4.3   Detection Results

Besides, we perform to evaluate for detection results by HOG and SVM using images with many different backgrounds. The results are shown in Tables 1, 2,

Fig. 7. Result of detecting hand error.

Table 1. Result of training model.

Posture	Number of samples	Number of incorrect identification	Number of unrecognized samples	Identification time (Seconds/images)	Accuracy
Posture spread your arms up	1000	5	85	0.063471447	91.00%

Table 2. Result of detection model for **static gesture**.

Posture	Number of samples	Number of incorrect identification	Number of unrecognized samples	Identification time (Seconds/images)	Accuracy
Holding hands	1000	2	2	0.069411886	99.60%
Posture spread your arms up	1000	0	5	0.072152341	99.50%
Posture spread your arms left	1000	8	3	0.066520801	98.90%
Posture spread your arms right	1000	7	0	0.067326031	99.30%

and 3. When the background is constantly changing, the algorithm will fail. Results shown in Fig. 7.

According to CNN model above, the classifier output will be a 4-element sequence where each element represents a label. The elements have a value from 0 to 1. When the representative value of label is close to 1, the result of classifier will be more likely to be that label. We choose a limit of 0.85 that means the

Table 3. Result of detection model for **dynamic gesture**.

Posture	Number of test	Number of incorrect identification	Number of unrecognized samples	Accuracy
Switch state (on/off)	30	0	2	93.33%
Increasing	30	1	3	86.67%
Reducing	30	2	1	90%

label will be selected when the corresponding value is the largest and greater than 0.85. If there is no label with a corresponding value greater than 0.85, the result is counted as unrecognizable. In case, the result is counted as false identification.

We found that due to the limitations of experimental gesture samples, the effective proposal has not been completely evaluated. However, it is possible to evaluate through the accuracy of hand position detection steps and recognition of their starting and ending posture. The problems will be solved in the future.

5   Conclusion

In the paper, we have explored image processing and machine learning techniques to evaluate applicability in gesture recognition systems. Based on the techniques, we have synthesized and performed the gesture recognition model including detection algorithm using HOG and SVM, clinging algorithm by correlation filter with KCF, and the algorithm to classify the hand using CNN. The algorithm has been trained on datasets including labels with 1000 images. As a result, the algorithm ensures real-time processing speed at an acceptable level and high accuracy. Based on the obtaining results, we will develop and apply the method for smart-home applications.

Acknowledgement. This research is carried out in the framework of the project funded by the Ministry of Education and Training (MOET), Vietnam under the grant B2020-BKA-06. The authors would like to thank the MOET for their financial support.

References

1. Bolme, D.S., Beveridge, J.R., Draper, B.A., Lui, Y.M.: Visual object tracking using adaptive correlation filters. In: 2010 IEEE Computer Society Conference on Computer Vision and Pattern Recognition, pp. 2544–2550 (2010)
2. Breiman, L.: Bias, variance, and arcing classifiers. Technical Report 460, Statistics Department, University of California, November 2000
3. Ning, C., Zhou, H., Song, Y., Tang, J.: Inception single shot multibox detector for object detection. In: 2017 IEEE International Conference on Multimedia Expo Workshops (ICMEW), pp. 549–554 (2017)

4. Dalal, N., Triggs, B.: Histograms of oriented gradients for human detection. In: 2005 IEEE Computer Society Conference on Computer Vision and Pattern Recognition (CVPR 2005), vol. 1, pp. 886–893 (2005)
5. Dalei, L., Ruitao, L., Xiaogang, Y.: Object tracking based on kernel correlation filter and multi-feature fusion. In: 2019 Chinese Automation Congress (CAC), pp. 4192–4196 (2019)
6. Dattathreya, Han, S., Kim, M., Maik, V., Paik, J.: Keypoint-based object tracking using modified median flow. In: 2016 IEEE International Conference on Consumer Electronics-Asia (ICCE-Asia), pp. 1–2 (2016)
7. Feng, F., Wu, X., Xu, T.: Object tracking with kernel correlation filters based on mean shift. In: 2017 International Smart Cities Conference (ISC2), pp. 1–7 (2017)
8. Girshick, R.B.: Fast R-CNN. CoRR abs/1504.08083 (2015)
9. Lee, H.-J., Chung, J.-H.: Hand gesture recognition using orientation histogram. In: Proceedings of IEEE. IEEE Region 10 Conference, 'Multimedia Technology for Asia-Pacific Information Infrastructure' (Cat. No.99CH37030), TENCON 1999, vol. 2, pp. 1355–1358 (1999)
10. Lowe, D.G.: Object recognition from local scale-invariant features. In: Proceedings of the Seventh IEEE International Conference on Computer Vision, vol. 2, pp. 1150–1157 (1999)
11. Nguyen Huu, P., Quang, T.M., Hoang Lai, T.: An ANN-based gesture recognition algorithm for smart-home applications. KSII Trans. Internet Inf. Syst. **14**(5), 1967–1983 (2020)
12. Torregrosa Olivero, J.A., María Burgos Anillo, C., Guerrero Barrios, J.P., Montoya Morales, E., Gachancipá, E.J., Andrés Zamora de la Torre, C.: Comparing state-of-the-art methods of detection and tracking people on security cameras video. In: 2019 XXII Symposium on Image, Signal Processing and Artificial Vision (STSIVA), pp. 1–5 (2019)
13. Viola, P., Jones, M.: Robust real-time object detection. Int. J. Comput. Vis. - IJCV **57**, 137–154 (2001)
14. Wang, C., Galoogahi, H.K., Lin, C., Lucey, S.: Deep-LK for efficient adaptive object tracking. In: 2018 IEEE International Conference on Robotics and Automation (ICRA), pp. 627–634 (2018)

A Container-Based Edge Computing System for Smart Healthcare Applications

Tuan Le-Anh[(✉)], Quan Ngo-Van, Phuong Vo-Huy, Dang Huynh-Van,
and Quan Le-Trung

UiTiOt Research Group, Department of Computer Networks, University of Information
Technology, Vietnam National University – Ho Chi Minh City, Ho Chi Minh City, Vietnam
tuanla.14@grad.uit.edu.vn, {16520981,16520975}@gm.uit.edu.vn,
{danghv,quanlt}@uit.edu.vn

Abstract. Edge computing is evolving how data are processed and analyzed from
a large figure of various Internet of Things (IoT) devices globally. The rapid development of IoT, 5G, artificial intelligence (AI), and applications that require real-
time computing capability steadily propel edge computing systems. In this paper,
we propose a container-based edge computing system for smart healthcare applications. The smart care mobile and web-based applications aim to assist doctors
or nurses with intelligent monitoring and caring for patients in the recovery phase
in real-time. The proposed system's design takes advantage of edge computing's
capabilities to timely deal with the patient's facial emotion detection and heart
disease diagnosis AI applications and a robust cloud computing infrastructure to
centralize the patient's data in the secure, scalable, and fault-tolerance database.
Moving these AI applications to the edge outperforms cloud computing in processing time, energy efficiency, and bandwidth saving. Finally, implementing the
AI applications on a lightweight container orchestration platform for management
efficiency with high availability, scalability, and deployment automation.

Keywords: Edge computing · Cloud computing · IoT · Artificial intelligence ·
Container-based virtualization · Container orchestration platform

1 Introduction

In contemporary and prospective trends, IoT equipment has produced enormous data in
our daily lives over a large-scale range of sectors, such as agriculture, transportation,
energy, industrial, smart cities, and manufacturing. In 2016, the generated data was
about 220 zettabytes and an estimate to strike over 250 zettabytes by 2021 [1]. The
figures for appliances connected to the IoT application network can reach 34.2 billion
devices worldwide by 2025 [2]. In hindsight, cloud computing has been a widespread
technology trend and an indispensable component in the era of IoT with data analytics,
AI, and big data [3]. Despite its overall prosperity, cloud computing is not a good fit for
smart applications that require real-time data and low latency [4]. The advent of edge

© ICST Institute for Computer Sciences, Social Informatics and Telecommunications Engineering 2021
Published by Springer Nature Switzerland AG 2021. All Rights Reserved
N.-S. Vo et al. (Eds.): INISCOM 2021, LNICST 379, pp. 324–336, 2021.
https://doi.org/10.1007/978-3-030-77424-0_27

computing aims to overcome these challenges. It does not intend to replace, however, cloud computing rather than its complementation. Edge computing expects to place computing close to where the data originates and the fact that it yields some benefits of energy efficiency, latency, and bandwidth reduction. The advent of edge computing aims to overcome these challenges [25]

According to the IEEE Computer Society [5], AI at the edge is one of the leading study tendencies in 2020. With the innovation of smart IoT hardware, modern AI algorithms, and the proliferation of 5G, machine learning (ML) applications have significantly transformed to the edge for more efficiency at a more economical cost. In current years, the confluence of edge computing and AI [6] continually drive smart IoT applications to adapt our modern life with a broad range of use cases, such as landslides monitoring [7], poultry real-time monitoring [8], patients and elderly tracking [9], cattle behavior analysis [10], climatic enclosure [11] and pivot irrigation [12]. Concerning the edge virtualization trends [13, 14], they have innovated applications at the edge with flexibility and efficiency in provisioning services. Compared to hypervisors, the advent of containerization reduces a significant overhead by implementing process isolation at the operating system level.

This research proposes a container-based edge computing system for smart healthcare applications with cloud-edge-based computing solutions, modern deep learning algorithms, docker-based, and lightweight cluster technologies.

This paper is structured as follows. Section 1 presents an overview of IoT data trends and the edge computing's benefits, the AI deployment at the edge for smart IoT applications, and virtualization for the edge. Afterward, Sect. 2 describes related works on IoTs smart healthcare applications, AI deployment at the edge, and the container-based virtualization. Next, Sect. 3 provides insights into the design and implementation of the proposed system. Then, Sect. 4 demonstrates the experimental results to evaluate the system performance, the hardware usage, and the accuracy of the AI applications. Finally, Sect. 5 ends this paper with conclusions and future work.

2   Related Work

This section presents a literature review of smart healthcare, the AI deployment at the edge, and the virtualization for edge computing.

2.1   Smart Healthcare

These days, patients suffering from chronic diseases [15] continue to grow, while nurses and doctors are limited. Therefore, the efficient use of these resources is a step towards smart healthcare systems. The rapid growth of next-generation technologies, including cloud computing, edge computing, artificial intelligence, and the proliferation of 5G technologies, have transformed smart healthcare platforms. In some recent research, notably [16], the authors introduced an edge computing-based smart healthcare framework for resource management. Besides, [27] proposed a Cloud of Things (CoT) for smart healthcare, and [17] presented an effective training scheme for the deep neural network in edge computing that enabled the Internet of Medical Things (IoMT) systems. Finally, [26] introduced next-generation technologies: challenges, vision, model, and future directions for smart healthcare applications.

2.2 Artificial Intelligence at Edge Computing

Nowadays, developing AI applications at the edge has been significantly growing around the world. The AI on edge contributes to shining intelligent applications with low latency, bandwidth saving, and low energy usage. However, this approach faces a variety of challenges, especially handling and power consumption. In the cloud, energy-intensive training occurs, and then deploy trained applications at the edge for prediction tasks. In edge computing, training takes place at the edge, leads to a higher demand for edge hardware computing capabilities. Besides, data storage and security pose a challenge as edge devices will hold most of the data and transfer only a small portion to the cloud, and security standard for IoT devices. As a result, leading technology companies have continually researched and developed to create more powerful computing hardware with lower energy consumption, also focus on optimizing AI algorithms. Besides, organizations concentrate on smart IoT hardware consist of BrainChip (Akida Neuromorphic System-on-Chip), CEVA (NeuPro series), Google (Edge TPU), GreenWave (AI GAP8 Processor), Huawei (Ascend Chips), Intel (Xeon), Nvidia (Jetson TX2), Qualcomm (Vision Intelligence Platforms) and STMicroelectronics (STM32 microcontrollers). Besides, leading technology corporations building ecosystems create solutions for each industry and each specific scenario. These companies include Google (AI platform), Huawei (MindSpore), IBM (Watson), Intel (AI Developer Program), Microsoft (Azure), and enterprise IoT building blocks such as IoT Hub, Azure Databricks, ML Studio, and Power BI [18].

Some significant studies following this approach: Landslides monitoring [7], the author introduced AI with edge computing architecture on Kubernetes and Docker Platform, and others, which are monitoring poultry in real-time [8], cattle behavior analysis [10], and pivot irrigation, plant diseases, and pests identification [12]. Interestingly, the patients and elderly tracking [9], the authors presented a cloud-fog-IoT-based system that observes the health of the elderly and patients during the recovery phase that belongs to the healthcare sector that our research will introduce in this paper.

2.3 Edge Computing Virtualization

In recent years, applying virtualization technologies for applications at the edge has significantly increased [13, 14]. These virtualization technologies provide a platform for running various physical machine services, using either hypervisor or container techniques. However, container-based solutions and other emerging ones are challenging traditional hypervisor-based virtual machines. New technology trends are lightweight, more flexible, efficient, and efficient in the deployment of services. Recent studies focus on optimizing virtualization to increase its performance, like a bare-metal environment, also a comparison between virtualization technologies. According to [28], the authors found increasing container solutions on Platform as a Service (PaaS). In [19–23], the authors measured and compared the performance of KVM, Xen, and Linux Container (LXC), Docker, OSv, and compared the runtime of each environment with the bare metal server. In the article [24], the authors also explained comparing the performance of container-based technologies for the cloud with a diverse set of parameters. The results clearly showed that the performance of hypervisors had improved significantly over the past few years. Container solutions outperformed, however, and their overhead was almost negligible. Despite the container solution's flexibility and manageability, we may consider trading-off them with security matters.

3   Proposed System

This part will introduce the proposed system's design and implementation. The paragraph structure is as follows: Sect. 3.1 presents the system architecture and design, and Sect. 3.2 describes performing the proposed paradigm.

3.1   System Architecture and Design

The proposed system bases on the cloud-edge-based computing paradigm. Figure 1 illustrates the high-level architecture of the proposed system model. The design incorporates three components: cloud data center, edge, and end-device.

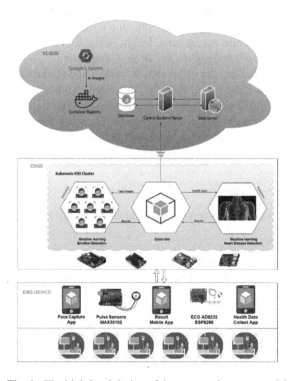

Fig. 1. The high-level design of the proposed system model.

- **Cloud data center:** The design embraces a private container registry to retain facial emotion detection and cardiovascular disease diagnosis AI images, databases, backend, and web servers for the patient's information and health data supervision. The cloud backend server processes data and stores the results in the database. Then, it refreshes data from the database to the webserver. Concerning the database, it is a NoSQL, reserves the patient's information and health data, including name, gender, age, heart rate, electrocardiogram (ECG), facial emotion, heart disease diagnosis, and other reports. Besides, the web application assists doctors in observing the patient's health statistics.

- *Edge:* The edge structure incorporates modern edge devices such as Raspberry PI's or other vendor hardware to form a lightweight container orchestration platform to coordinate the edge backend server, facial emotion detection, and cardiovascular disease diagnosis AI applications. Depending on hardware constraints and requirements, the cluster could involve more masters and multiple worker nodes for scalability, fault-tolerant, and high availability. The backend server listens and deals with data from end devices or dispatch them to the corresponding AI applications regarding the workflow. It then returns the results to the mobile application and the cloud backend server that updates the database and refreshes the web application. The patient's facial emotion detection AI application interprets the base64-encoded images to predict the current patient's mood (e.g., happy, sad, neutral, fearful, disgusted, angry, or surprised). Likewise, the heart disease diagnosis AI function analyzes and predicts the patient's percentage at risk based on age, gender, height, weight, systolic and diastolic blood pressure, cholesterol, smoking, glucose, alcohol, and activity.
- *End-device:* IoT appliances and smart sensors collect and send data to the edge backend server for data processing and analysis. The mobile application reflects the results in real-time. Next, Fig. 2 exhibits the context design of observing the patient's health data in hospitals. In this context, doctors or nurses can track the patient's information and data health status via mobile and web applications.

3.2 System Implementation

This paragraph summarizes implementing state-of-art technologies for the proposed system:

- *Cloud data center:* We deployed a private Docker registry to hold the AI application's images based on Google's AutoML with deep learning algorithms for training datasets and creating AI models. When it comes to the web application, it consists of a Node.js framework-based backend server, a NoSQL database using Google Firebase, and Flutter framework-based web server written in Dart language.
- *Edge:* We performed a lightweight Kubernetes cluster (K3S) rather than Kubernetes (K8S) to coordinate Docker-based containers for the backend server and AI applications.
- *End-device:* We implemented IoT functions written in C/C++ language with Arduino ESP8266 hardware, MAX30102 pulse, and ECG AD8232 ECG sensors to collect and send the patient's health data to the edge backend server. Figure 3 shows the mobile and web user interface. These applications help doctors and nurses to observe the patient's health status in real-time.

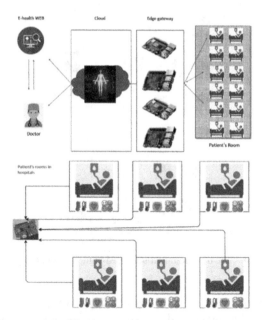

Fig. 2. The context design.

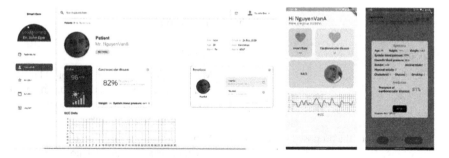

Fig. 3. The mobile and web application user interface.

4 Experimental Results

In this section, we demonstrate the experimental results. Section 4.1 measures and evaluates the proposed system's performance compared to the traditional cloud-based computing paradigm. Next, Sect. 4.2 assesses the AI training model's accuracy. Finally, Sect. 4.3 analyzes the hardware resource usage of the proposed system during the experiment.

4.1 Performance Comparison

This part compares the proposed system's processing time (see Fig. 1) with the traditional cloud-based computing paradigm (see Fig. 4).

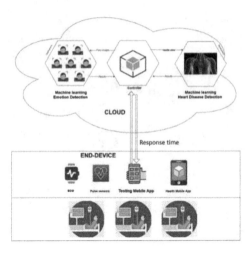

Fig. 4. The traditional cloud-based computing paradigm.

In the traditional cloud-based model, we deployed AI applications in the cloud. On the contrary, these AI functions we deployed at the edge of the proposed system. The specifications for the experiment were as follows (Table 1).

Table 1. Technical specifications

No.	Component	Specification
1	End devices	Mobile application (Dart, Android 11); Request: Facial emotion detection and heart disease diagnosis; Function: Send requests and measure response times
2	Edge server of the proposed system model (see Fig. 1)	Container-based nodes: Facial emotion detection, heart disease diagnosis, and backend server; Edge device: Raspberry Pi; Operating system: Raspbian; CPU: ARMv8 64-bit SoC @ 1.4 GHz; RAM: 1 GB; SD card: 32 GB
3	Cloud server of the cloud-based computing model (see Fig. 4)	Container-based nodes: Facial emotion detection, heart disease diagnosis, and backend server; Cloud provider: Google Cloud Platform; Operating system: Debian Buster; CPU: Intel Xeon; RAM: 2GB; Hard drive: 60 GB

This test was conducted on a network bandwidth of 96.64 Mbps download, and 92.98 Mbps upload speed. As a result, Fig. 5 illustrates the processing time of the AI applications of the proposed system was remarkably better.

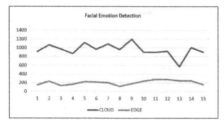
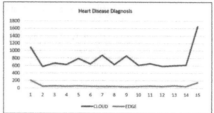

Fig. 5. Performance comparison: the proposed system vs. the traditional cloud-based paradigm

Table 2. Facial emotion detection's response time

No	Cloud-based paradigm	Proposed system model	Relative difference
1	913 ms	153 ms	760 ms
2	1062 ms	235 ms	827 ms
3	971 ms	134 ms	837 ms
4	869 ms	169 ms	700 ms
5	1118 ms	226 ms	892 ms
6	968 ms	218 ms	750 ms
7	1090 ms	206 ms	884 ms
8	960 ms	123 ms	837 ms
9	1197 ms	178 ms	1019 ms
10	898 ms	245 ms	653 ms
11	896 ms	283 ms	613 ms
12	921 ms	278 ms	643 ms
13	567 ms	251 ms	316 ms
14	1002 ms	248 ms	754 ms
15	900 ms	155 ms	745 ms

Table 2 shows the results of the facial emotion detection AI application over 15 runs. We can find a noticeable difference in terms of processing time between the two models. The proposed system is typically 4–5 times faster on average than the traditional cloud-based paradigm.

Table 3. Heart disease diagnosis's response time

No	Cloud-based paradigm	Proposed system model	Relative difference
1	1088 ms	205 ms	883 ms
2	577 ms	43 ms	534 ms
3	661 ms	51 ms	610 ms
4	625 ms	43 ms	582 ms
5	792 ms	53 ms	739 ms
6	647 ms	45 ms	602 ms
7	885 ms	47 ms	838 ms
8	629 ms	44 ms	585 ms
9	867 ms	33 ms	834 ms
10	614 ms	45 ms	569 ms
11	652 ms	51 ms	601 ms
12	586 ms	46 ms	540 ms
13	603 ms	63 ms	540 ms
14	624 ms	43 ms	581 ms
15	1648 ms	153 ms	1495 ms

Same as above, Table 3 displays the outcomes of the heart disease diagnosis AI application. As a result, the proposed system model performed ten times faster on average than the cloud-based computing model.

4.2 Accuracy Evaluation of Artificial Intelligence Applications

This section evaluates the AI model's accuracy for the facial emotion detection and cardiovascular disease diagnosis applications we deployed at the edge. We conducted the experiment with the datasets "fer2013.csv", "cardio_train.csv" provided by Kaggle with 80% of the datasets for training, 10% for PublicTest, and 10% for other purposes of AutoML. As a result, it shows in Fig. 6 below.

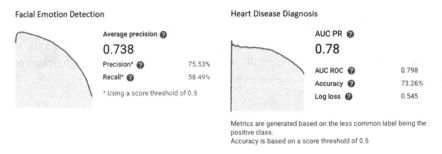

Fig. 6. The AI model's evaluation

About the facial emotion detection, the AI model's precision was about 0.738 on average. More details, precision, and recall were approximately 75.53 and 58.49%. Regarding the cardiovascular disease diagnosis, the area under the precision-recall (PR) curve and receiver operating characteristic (ROC) curve were around 0.78 and 0.798. More, its accuracy was proximately 73.26%.

4.3   Hardware Resource Usage and Evaluation

This paragraph analyzes and evaluates the hardware resource consumption corresponding to the proposed system model during the experimental test, with the number of connections increased from 1 to 200. The requests included the patient's facial emotion detection and health data diagnosis. Concerning the testing methodology, we employed Postman to create a series of HTTP POST requests with base64-encoded images and the mobile application to simulate patients' figures corresponding to data from IoT sensors. Table 4 manifests the hardware specification for the test.

Table 4. Hardware specifications

No.	Role	Description
1	Master	Debian Buster, Core i5-8250U 1.80 GHz, Memory 2 GB, Hard drive 15 GB
2	Worker 1	Debian Buster, Core i5-8250U 1.80 GHz, Memory 2 GB, Hard drive 15 GB
3	Worker 2	Raspbian, ARM Cortex-A53 1.4 GHz, Memory 2 GB, SD card 32 GB

The following outcomes (see Fig. 7) indicate that increasing the number of requests demands more CPU resources, and memory gains correspond to the number of connections. For every 40 connections, memory usage requires about 200 MB. Besides, the bandwidth significantly increased, corresponding to the number of sockets or requests.

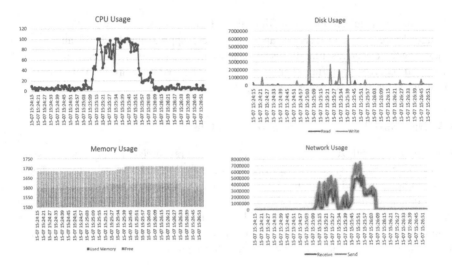

Fig. 7. Hardware resource statistics

5 Conclusion and Future Work

In this paper, we proposed the container-based edge computing system for smart health-care applications. In short, we introduced related works in terms of this research and exhibited insights into system design and architecture. Next, we demonstrated the implementation of the proposed system. Finally, we analyzed the experimental results to evaluate the proposed model. Forthcoming work is open to researching new smart healthcare services to enhance the design and innovative technologies to secure data compression in transit.

References

1. Cisco Global Cloud Index: Forecast and Methodology 2016–2021 (white paper) Cisco, pp. 2016–2021 (2016)
2. State of the IoT 2018: Number of IoT devices now at 7B – Market accelerating. https://iot-ana lytics.com/state-of-the-iot-update-q1-q2-2018-number-of-iot-devices-now-7b/. Accessed 09 Nov 2020
3. Verma, A.: The Relationship between IoT, Big Data, and Cloud Computing. Whizlabs Blog, 28 Nov 2018. https://www.whizlabs.com/blog/relationship-between-iot-big-data-cloud-com puting/. Accessed 09 Nov 2020
4. Caprolu, M., Pietro, R.D., Lombardi, F., Raponi, S.: Edge computing perspectives: architec-tures, technologies, and open security issues. In: 2019 IEEE International Conference on Edge Computing (EDGE), pp. 116–123, July 2019. https://doi.org/10.1109/EDGE.2019.00035
5. Exclusive Content – IEEE Computer Society's Tech Trends for 2020—IEEE Computer Society. https://www.computer.org/publications/tech-news/trends/exclusive-content-ieee-cs-tech-trends-for-2020/. Accessed 10 Nov 2020
6. Deng, S., Zhao, H., Fang, W., Yin, J., Dustdar, S., Zomaya, A.Y.: Edge intelligence: the confluence of edge computing and artificial intelligence. IEEE Internet Things J. **7**(8), 7457–7469 (2020). https://doi.org/10.1109/JIOT.2020.2984887

7. Elmoulat, M., Debauche, O., Saïd, M., Mahmoudi, S., Manneback, P., Lebeau, F.: Edge computing and artificial intelligence for landslides monitoring. Proc. Comput. Sci. **177**, 480–487 (2020). https://doi.org/10.1016/j.procs.2020.10.066
8. Debauche, O., Saïd, M., Mahmoudi, S., Manneback, P., Bindelle, J., Lebeau, F.: Edge computing and artificial intelligence for real-time poultry monitoring. Proc. Comput. Sci. **175**, 534–541 (2020). https://doi.org/10.1016/j.procs.2020.07.076
9. Debauche, O., Saïd, M., Manneback, P., Assila, A.: Fog IoT for health: a new architecture for patients and elderly monitoring. Proc. Comput. Sci. **160**, 289–297 (2019). https://doi.org/10.1016/j.procs.2019.11.087
10. Debauche, O., Saïd, M., Mahmoudi, S., Manneback, P., Bindelle, J., Lebeau, F.: Edge Computing for Cattle Behavior Analysis, April 2020
11. Debauche, O., Mahmoudi, S., Mahmoudi, S.A., Manneback, P., Lebeau, F.: Edge computing and artificial intelligence semantically driven. Application to a climatic enclosure. Proc. Comput. Sci. **175**, 542–547 (2020). https://doi.org/10.1016/j.procs.2020.07.077
12. Debauche, O., Saïd, M., Elmoulat, M., Mahmoudi, S., Manneback, P., Lebeau, F.: Edge AI-IoT pivot irrigation, plant diseases, and pests identification. Proc. Comput. Sci. **177**, 40–48 (2020). https://doi.org/10.1016/j.procs.2020.10.009
13. Morabito, R.: Virtualization on internet of things edge devices with container technologies: a performance evaluation. IEEE Access **5**, 8835–8850 (2017). https://doi.org/10.1109/ACCESS.2017.2704444
14. Jaiswal, K., Sobhanayak, S., Turuk, A.K., Bibhudatta, S.L., Mohanta, B.K., Jena, D.: An IoT-cloud based smart healthcare monitoring system using container-based virtual environment in edge device. In: 2018 International Conference on Emerging Trends and Innovations in Engineering and Technological Research (ICETIETR), pp. 1–7, July 2018. https://doi.org/10.1109/ICETIETR.2018.8529141
15. Kim, J.: The effect of patient participation through physician's resources on experience and wellbeing. Sustainability **10**, 2102 (2018). https://doi.org/10.3390/su10062102
16. Oueida, S., Kotb, Y., Aloqaily, M., Jararweh, Y., Baker, T.: An edge computing based smart healthcare framework for resource management. Sensors **18**, 4307 (2018). https://doi.org/10.3390/s18124307
17. Pustokhina, I.V., Pustokhin, D.A., Gupta, D., Khanna, A., Shankar, K., Nguyen, G.N.: An effective training scheme for deep neural network in edge computing enabled Internet of Medical Things (IoMT) systems. IEEE Access **8**, 107112–107123 (2020). https://doi.org/10.1109/ACCESS.2020.3000322
18. Koon, J.: How AI Changes the Future of Edge Computing. EE Times Europe, 24 June 2019. https://www.eetimes.eu/how-ai-changes-the-future-of-edge-computing/. Accessed 14 Nov 2020
19. Morabito, R., Kjällman, J., Komu, M.: Hypervisors vs. lightweight virtualization: a performance comparison. In: 2015 IEEE International Conference on Cloud Engineering, pp. 386–393, March 2015. https://doi.org/10.1109/IC2E.2015.74
20. Estrada, Z., Stephens, Z., Pham, C., Iyer, R.: A Performance Evaluation of Sequence Alignment Software in Virtualized Environments, pp. 730–737, May 2014. https://doi.org/10.1109/CCGrid.2014.125
21. Felter, W., Ferreira, A., Rajamony, R., Rubio, J.: An updated performance comparison of virtual machines and Linux containers, pp. 171–172, March 2015. https://doi.org/10.1109/ISPASS.2015.7095802
22. Kominos, C., Seyvet, N., Vandikas, K.: Bare-metal, virtual machines and containers in OpenStack, pp. 36–43, March 2017. https://doi.org/10.1109/ICIN.2017.7899247
23. Potdar, A.M., Dg, N., Kengond, S., Mulla, M.M.: Performance evaluation of Docker container and virtual machine. Proc. Comput. Sci. **171**, 1419–1428 (2020). https://doi.org/10.1016/j.procs.2020.04.152

24. Kozhirbayev, Z., Sinnott, R.O.: A performance comparison of container-based technologies for the cloud. Future Gener. Comput. Syst. **68**, 175–182 (2017). https://doi.org/10.1016/j.future.2016.08.025
25. Shi, W., Cao, J., Zhang, Q., Li, Y., Xu, L.: Edge computing: vision and challenges. IEEE Internet Things J. **3**(5), 637–646 (2016). https://doi.org/10.1109/JIOT.2016.2579198
26. Tuli, S., et al.: Next-generation technologies for smart healthcare: challenges, vision, model, trends and future directions. Internet Technol. Lett. **3**(2), e145 (2020). https://doi.org/10.1002/itl2.145
27. Mahmoud, M.M.E., et al.: Enabling technologies on cloud of things for smart healthcare. IEEE Access **6**, 31950–31967 (2018). https://doi.org/10.1109/ACCESS.2018.2845399
28. Pahl, C.: Containerisation and the PaaS cloud. IEEE Cloud Comput. **2**, 24–31 (2015). https://doi.org/10.1109/MCC.2015.51

Multi-object Detection by Using CNN for Power Transmission Line Inspection

Dinh Cong Nguyen[1,2]([✉]), The Cuong Nguyen[1,2], Dinh Hung Phan[2],
Nhan Tam Le[3], and Van Vien Tran[2]

[1] Hong Duc University, Thanh Hoa, Vietnam
{nguyendinhcong,nguyenthecuong}@hdu.edu.vn
[2] ThinkLABs JSC, Thanh Hoa, Vietnam
{hung,vientv}@thinklabs.com.vn
[3] IBM Vietnam, Hanoi, Vietnam
letam@vn.ibm.com

Abstract. Multi-object detection for power transmission line is one of the key tasks to control and monitor quality of the system. In the past, defective objects were found out by naked-eye inspection through aerial images and relied on the experienced workers. Due to harsh environmental conditions, manual observation might be a time-consuming and dangerous task. Recently, this task has been supported by machine learning where deep-learning algorithms are applied to increase the efficiency of detection/recognition phases. This paper discusses different approaches for multi-object detection based on Convolutional Neural Network (CNN) model to investigate the quality and condition of power lines in Vietnam. Our proposed system outperforms the state-of-the-art methods on our dataset.

Keywords: Power transmission inspection · Multi-object detection · Aerial image

1 Introduction

Power transmission system is composed of different types of components such as tower, insulator, conductor, so on. These components play a critical role in the safe transmission of the electric power system. Because these components endure extreme weather conditions (raining, storm, etc.), they have sometime suffered several damages such as: insulator faults, connectors corroded, conductor damaged Fig. 1. Moreover, material aging, overloading are also main factors to influence on them. The quality of the system is whereby decreased.

Therefore, to make the power supply system sustainable, reliable and available, these components need to periodic inspection throughout the year. This process helps to detect defective devices. Then, the experts will decide which parts should be repaired or replaced by the new ones. Previously, the conventional inspection was mostly based on a manual inspection. However, this task

N.-S. Vo et al. (Eds.): INISCOM 2021, LNICST 379, pp. 337–347, 2021.
https://doi.org/10.1007/978-3-030-77424-0_28

Fig. 1. Due to outdoor environment in complicate land forms and unpredictable weather, the power transmission system could be damaged frequently.

remains a challenge because of time-consuming, costly and life-threatening processes. Due to these reasons, it needs to find out an efficient method to cope with this problem. An automatic observation is an alternative solution [1], known as multi-object detection and recognition in the literature.

Recently, the development of Unmanned Aerial Vehicle (UAV) and new digital image processing technologies could support to capture images or videos with very high resolutions at different angles and distances. A new platform for power transmission inspection has been supported [2]. This process could be divided into two phases as data collection and data analysis. Although UAV inspection greatly decreases in works of inspectors, low cost, high security, efficiency, but it also creates enormous data. Moreover, a large number of transmission towers are built in the forests or mountains. Therefore, the collected aerial images are suffered from complex backgrounds, illumination changes, rotations, distances that directly impact on the quality of detection and recognition.

For our context, we collected images and videos from the power transmission line at The National Power Transmission Corporation (EVN NPT PTC2)[1] with different scenarios in order to detect those objects in this system. Therefore, we need to study several approaches to find out the best model to fit well with our own dataset. Recently, Convolutional Neural Network (CNN)-based detection approach has gained big achievements in terms of a very high detection accuracy and a strong robustness with gigantic datasets [3]. This highly motivates us to apply CNN model for multi-object detection of our problem.

In this paper, a new approach to automatically recognize different elements of power transmission devices is given. The main contributions are follows.

- A new standard dataset is produced by collected and manually labeled images from EVN NPT in Vietnam.
- A new system to automatically detect five types of components in the aerial images is proposed by adopting a deep convolutional neural network.

The remainder of this paper is given as follows. Section 2 revises several works related to this topic. Then, Sect. 3 describes our dataset. Next, Sect. 4 details multi-object detection tasks while Sect. 5 will present our system. Section 6 shows

---

[1] https://www.npt.com.vn.

and discusses the results. At last, Sect. 7 will conclude and discuss some perspectives.

2   Related Works

The existing solutions to deal with this task could be divided into two categories: hand-crafted feature-based approaches and deep learning-based approaches. In hand-crafted feature-based approaches, a variety of low-level features are applied such as color [4,5], shape [7], edge [8], texture [9] and so on. However, as summary from [10], the methods are less accurate in average. Basically, they are quite sensitive with noises, complex backgrounds. In addition, their performances have degraded in case of which electric devices are overlapped or by filming distances.

Over past few years, along with the development of hardware devices and deep neural network models, object detection and recognition have obtained a great achievement. Many of works were adopted convolutional neural network (CNN) model into the inspection of power lines. It could be listed in [3]. As [11] applied CNN into their work for detection process and the color/edge-based models for segmentation process. Although this contribution is robust to object detection, its effectiveness limits with a small number of scenarios due to the sensitiveness of low-level features. For insulator detection, [12,13] are applied either R-CNN or Faster R-CNN model. These works divided detection process into two steps in which the first step localized insulators and then the second step classified defective insulators. The main drawback is that two steps are strongly dependent. It results in poor classification if the first step does not perform well. Moreover, it could be hard to train an end-to-end system with a reasonable performance for the insulator fault detection due to complex backgrounds and various angles of shooting. To address this problem, [10,14] employed a CNN architecture and used either the segmentation of the insulator fault or the adaptive morphology method. However, these approaches are quite sensitive with the complex and uncontrollable scenarios, because they applied low-level feature-based model after the detection for classification.

It can be seen that most of the recent works on this topic employed two-stage strategy where CNN was applied in the first stage to detect objected, followed by segmentation with low-level features to classify whether faulty devices or not. As known that low-level features are quite sensitive, they therefore cannot be robust against the occlusion, various orientations, illumination changes, viewpoint changes, and complex background. Our approach differs from those, we consider faulty devices as individual objects, and hence, we just employ one-stage model.

3   Data Collection

At the best of our knowledge, there is no publicly available dataset that identifies the devices on the high-voltage transmission lines in Viet Nam. To make it, we have created a dataset called "ThinkLabs-data". ThinkLabs-data contains 1235 images taken from flying-cam devices (Phantom 4 Pro, Airiestronic XT8) with very high resolutions in range of 12–20 Mpx. The captured areas include of mountains, forests and flats. For the safety, the images were captured with at least 5 m from the devices with many different shooting angles. Then, they were uploaded automatically into our server in which images was labeled by used LabelIMG[2]. The dataset is composed of five components as described in the Table 1 and visualized in Fig. 2.

Table 1. Dataset description with training and testing sets.

Datasets	Numbers				
	Single insulators	Double insulators	Corona rings	Discharge guns	Insulator fault
Training set	904	868	2153	1212	213
Testing set	226	217	539	304	54

(a)   (b)   (c)   (d)   (e)

Fig. 2. Visualization of the dataset composing of: (a) Single insulator string, (b) Double insulator string, (c) Corona ring, (d) Discharge gun, (e) Insulator fault.

In our dataset, we considered the faulty parts as separate objects from original images. For example, we carefully annotated broken insulators from single/double insulator strings to create an insulator fault set with 213 and 54 images in training and testing sets, respectively. Followed this step, it is common in literature to use argumentation techniques to enrich the data.

4   Multi-object Detection

As reminder with the advent of the CNN network, object detection and recognition have been obtained a new breakthrough Fig. 3. Currently, there are many

---

[2] https://github.com/tzutalin/labelImg.

models using CNN to detect objects: R-CNN, Fast R-CNN, Faster R-CNN [15], YOLO [16].

We present here two different approaches to deal with our specific dataset. These approaches are well-known methods in multi-object detection in general and power transmission component inspection in detail as based on Faster R-CNN in Sect. 1, YOLOv4 in Sect. 4.2.

method	# box	data	mAP	aero	bike	bird	boat	bottle	bus	car	cat	chair	cow	table	dog	horse	mbike	person	plant	sheep	sofa	train	tv
SS	2000	07	66.9	74.5	78.3	69.2	53.2	36.6	77.3	78.2	82.0	40.7	72.7	67.9	79.6	79.2	73.0	69.0	30.1	65.4	70.2	75.8	65.8
SS	2000	07+12	70.0	77.0	78.1	69.3	59.4	38.3	81.6	78.6	86.7	42.8	78.8	68.9	84.7	82.0	76.6	69.9	31.8	70.1	74.8	80.4	70.4
RPN*	300	07	68.5	74.1	77.2	67.7	53.9	51.0	75.1	79.2	78.9	50.7	78.0	61.1	79.1	81.9	72.2	75.9	37.2	71.4	62.5	77.4	66.4
RPN	300	07	69.9	70.0	80.6	70.1	57.3	49.9	78.2	80.4	82.0	52.2	75.3	67.2	80.3	79.8	75.0	76.3	39.1	68.3	67.3	81.1	67.6
RPN	300	07+12	73.2	76.5	79.0	70.9	65.5	52.1	83.1	84.7	86.4	52.0	81.9	65.7	84.8	84.6	77.5	76.7	38.8	73.6	73.9	83.0	72.6
RPN	300	COCO+07+12	**78.8**	**84.3**	**82.0**	**77.7**	**68.9**	**65.7**	**88.1**	**88.4**	**88.9**	**63.6**	**86.3**	**70.8**	**85.9**	**87.6**	**80.1**	**82.3**	**53.6**	**80.4**	**75.8**	**86.6**	**78.9**

Fig. 3. Results on PASCAL VOC 2007 test set with Fast R-CNN and VGG-16.

4.1 Faster R-CNN-based System

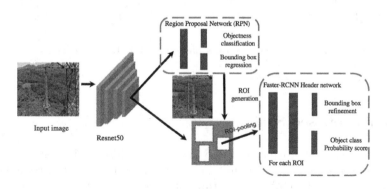

Fig. 4. The detection process bases on Faster R-CNN model.

With the advantage of the Faster R-CNN model [15], we have adopted it here of detection and recognition process with power transmission system devices (insulators, corona rings, discharge guns) Fig. 4. There are several works on this model [3,10,13]. We employ the Resnet50 network to extract image features. We use this network based on advantages of being not too large in size and providing high accuracy Table 2.

4.2 YOLO-based System

Recently, YOLOv4 [17] has appeared as the state-of-the-art object detector. For this reason, we employ the pre-trained weights of YOLOv4 model for our dataset.

Table 2. Pre-trained model (available online https://keras.io/api/applications/).

Model	Size	Top-1 accuracy	Top-1 accuracy	Parameters	Depth
Xception	88 MB	0.79 %	0.945%	22,910,480	126
VGG16	528 MB	0.713 %	0.901%	138,357,544	23
ResNet50	98 MB	0.74 %	0.92%	25,636,712	26
ResNet101	171 MB	0.764 %	0.928%	44,707,176	26
InceptionV3	92 MB	0.779%	0.937 %	23,851,784	159

For convenience, we remind here the main points of this model. YOLOv4 includes of three key parts as: backbone - CSPDarnet53, neck - SPP (Spatial pyramid pooling), and head - YOLOv3. YOLOv4 uses BoF (Bag of Freebies), BoS (Bag of Specials) for backbone and detector. This approach is shown in Fig. 5.

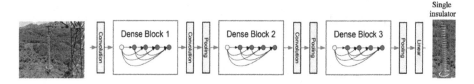

Fig. 5. The detection process based on YOLOv4 model [17].

5   Our Proposed System

Our overall system is provided in Fig. 6. Image acquisition is the first step of the inspection process in which captured images of power transmission components using a camera on the UAV. All captured images used in the paper were taken

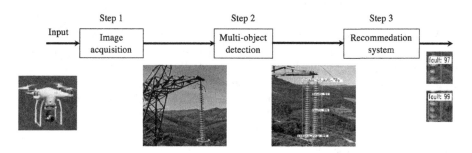

Fig. 6. Our proposed system for power transmission inspection based on CNN with three main steps.

on the Vietnam Electricity of The National Power Transmission Corporation (EVNNPT). The captured areas include of mountains, forests, making it difficult to traditional approaches. The collected images are then sent to our sever to trigger the second step.

In the second step, we propose to apply YOLOv4-based system. Compare to the Faster R-CNN-based system, YOLOv4-based system is faster and more accurate in average [17]. It therefore can perform this system in a near real-time processing. The acquired images are passed through this system to detect five given objects as listed in Table 1. In the third step, the situation of each component is observed by cropped it from detection regions. In the scope of this paper, we only used a case study for informing the broken insulators.

It is worth noting here that most of the state-of-the-art works on detecting faulty devices processed with segmentation problems [5,6,10]. However, the approaches are quite sensitive with complex backgrounds having a large similarity to the neighboring pixels. Therefore, we take into account the broken parts as particular objects (see Sect. 1). When the broken part is detected, this region will be located and informed. A report will guide for power companies to find exactly locations of the insulator faults.

6   Experiments

In this section, we present the performance evaluation of our system on the proposed dataset. For the multi-object detection task, we only concentrate on the step 2 of our system Fig. 6. Sections 6.1 and 6.2 detail the experimental setups and metrics. At last, Sect. 6.3 presents the results.

6.1   Experimental Setups

At the training step, the pre-trained weights of YOLOv4 was cloned from Darknet. By experimental loops and recommendation for customizing parameters from original paper with YOLOv4 [17], we modified the config file as follows: batch = 64, subdivisions = 32, max-batches = 10000, step = 8000,9000, classes = 5, filters = 30. In order to improve the robustness of the training model, image augmentation was deployed as hue variation (in range 0.9 to 1.1), exposure variation (in range 1 to 1.5), and rotation (in range $-60°$ to $60°$). In addition, we developed in dilation and erosion of training samples to enrich the dataset. The model was obviously trained by an open-source python environment using Darknet library.

6.2   Metrics

Object detection systems predict the outcome as bounding boxes and labels. For each bounding box we measure the overlap between the predicted box with the ground truth bounding box called the Intersection over Union (IoU) [18]. For each class we calculate precision and recall based on the IoU threshold (0.5). We define a prediction to be a True Positive (TP) if the IoU > 0.5, False Positives (TP) if the IoU > 0.5 and False Negative (FN) if a ground truth not detected. Average precision (AP) is the measurement calculated based on the Precision (P) - Recall (R) curves for all data points (M).

$$P = \frac{TP}{TP + FP} \qquad R = \frac{TP}{TP + FN} \qquad AP = \sum_{m=1}^{M}(R_m - R_{m-1})P_m$$

Table 3. Results on three approaches on the detection task (shown in the step 2 of Fig. 6), the proposed system using YOLOv4 outperforms other approaches on our dataset with big gaps.

Data	Objects				
	Fault insulator	Single insulator	Double insulator	Corona ring	Discharge gun
VGG16-based system- Average precision (AP %)					
Training set	71.8 %	53.5%	64.6%	79.3%	84/37%
Testing set	53%	61.2%	70.5%	61.65%	50.7%
Faster R-CNN-based system - Average precision (AP %)					
Training set	82.8%	80.8%	89.9%	68.6%	57.6%
Testing set	71%	64.3%	71.4%	50.5%	49.1%
Proposed system - Average precision (AP %)					
Training set	99.95%	99.54%	99.8%	99.66%	99.42%
Testing set	88.54%	93.25%	93.32%	81.06%	88.51%

6.3   Results

Our implementations were test on ThinkLabs-data with Tesla K80 GPU, 12 GB RAM architecture. The results are given in Table 3. It can see that our approach outperforms others on all objects. The results on single/double insulators are performed in best about 93.3%. It is true that the object detection system could fail to detect single insulator, double insulator, fault insulator in different scenarios. It could result from the different shooting angles from the flying-cam device. Next, the complexity of the background image also causes incorrect prediction results. Compare to the performance on single/double insulators, result on fault insulator is a bit smaller with 4% of gap. It could be explained that the faulty parts in the insulator strings are quite smaller, they could disappear in some angles of the flying-cam devices. Corona rings and discharge gun also occur several errors. This could result from the same reasons as the faulty parts of the insulators. The successful detection is visualized in Fig. 7.

In addition, Faster RCNN-based approach provides regions of interest for doing convolution, it is strongly dependent on the sizes of anchor points. Meanwhile, YOLO-based approach does detection and classification in one shot, it could affect the final results on our dataset.

For clarity, we measure the processing time in the testing phase. The results are shown in Table 4. It can be seen that our approach is almost ten times as fast as the VGG16-based system and five times as fast as the Faster R-CNN system. It could perform as a near real-time processing.

Table 4. Results on the processing time of three different approaches for the detection tasks (in second).

Methods	VGG16-based system	Faster R-CNN-based system	Our system
Processing time	1.12 (s)	0.68 (s)	0.158 (s)

Fig. 7. Visualization of our detection results.

7   Conclusions and Perspectives

In this paper we proposed a new standard dataset of electric power equipment for high-voltage transmission line inspection. Then, different approaches are re-implemented to automatically detect and recognize objects with a special focus on the insulator fault detection. Our proposed system performed as the best candidate for this task.

The proposed system performs in a near real-time processing. It could be embedded directly into UAV for detection and recognition tasks. Then, a new method for scheduling the flying direction could be embedded into the UAV to improve the quality of detection and recognition tasks.

Acknowledgments. This research was funded by ThinkLABs R&D[3] and the sample data was supported by EVN NPT2[4] in Da Nang.

References

1. Pagnano, A., Höpf, M., Teti, R.: A roadmap for automated power line inspection. Maintenance and repair. Proc. Cirp **12**, 234–239 (2013)
2. Shakhatreh, H., Sawalmeh, A.H., Al-Fuqaha, A., Dou, Z.: Unmanned aerial vehicles (UAVs): a survey on civil applications and key research challenges. IEEE Access **7**, 48572–48634 (2019)
3. Liu, X., Miao, X., Jiang, H., Chen, J.: Review of data analysis in vision inspection of power lines with an in-depth discussion of deep learning technology. Preprint arXiv:2003.09802 (2020)
4. Zhai, Y., Chen, R., Yang, Q., Li, X., Zhao, Z.: Insulator fault detection based on spatial morphological features of aerial images. IEEE Access **6**, 35316–35326 (2018)
5. Wang, Y.L., Yan, B.: Vision based detection and location for cracked insulator. Comput. Eng. Design **35**(2), 583–587 (2014)
6. Oberweger, M., Wendel, A., Bischof, H.: Visual recognition and fault detection for power line insulators. In: Computer Vision Winter Workshop (2014)
7. Hao-ran, J., Lin-jun, J.I.N.: Recognition and fault diagnosis of insulator string in aerial images. J. Mech. Electr. Eng. **32**(2) (2015)
8. Yin, J., Lu, Y., Gong, Z., Jiang, Y., Yao, J.: Edge detection of high-voltage porcelain insulators in infrared image using dual parity morphological gradients. IEEE Access **7**, 32728–32734 (2019)
9. Wang, M., Du, Y., Zhang, Z.R.: Study on power transmission lines inspection using unmanned aerial vehicle and image recognition of insulator defect. J. Electron. Meas. Instr. **26**, 1862–1869 (2015)
10. Han, J., et al.: A method of insulator faults detection in aerial images for high-voltage transmission lines inspection. Appl. Sci. **9**(10), 2009 (2019)
11. Siddiqui, Z.A., Park, U.: A drone based transmission line components inspection system with deep learning technique. Energies **13**(13), 3348 (2020)
12. Kang, G., Gao, S., Yu, L., Zhang, D.: Deep architecture for high-speed railway insulator surface defect detection: denoising autoencoder with multitask learning. IEEE Trans. Instr. Meas **68**(8), 2679–2690 (2018)
13. Ma, L., Xu, C., Zuo, G., Bo, B., Tao, F.: Detection method of insulator based on faster R-CNN. In: Annual International Conference on CYBER Technology in Automation, Control, and Intelligent Systems (CYBER), pp. 1410–1414 (2017)

---

[3] https://thinklabs.vn/vn/.
[4] https://www.npt.com.vn.

14. Tao, X., Zhang, D., Wang, Z., Liu, X.: Detection of power line insulator defects using aerial images analyzed with convolutional neural networks. IEEE Trans. Syst. Man Cybern. Syst. 1–13 (2018)
15. Ren, S., He, K., Girshick, R., Sun, J.: Faster R-CNN: towards real-time object detection with region proposal networks. In: Advances in Neural Information Processing Systems, pp. 91–99 (2015)
16. J., Redmon, S., Divvala, R., Girshick: You only look once: unified, real-time object detection. In: CVPR, pp. 779–788 (2016)
17. Bochkovskiy, A., Wang, C.Y., Liao, H.Y.M.: YOLOv4: optimal speed and accuracy of object detection. Preprint arXiv:2004.10934 (2020)
18. Nguyen Dinh, C., Delalandre, M., Conte, D., Pham, T.A.: Fast RT-LoG operator for scene text detection. J. Real-Time Image Process. **18**(1), 19–36 (2020). https://doi.org/10.1007/s11554-020-00942-7

Active Power Filter Under Imbalance and Distortion of Grid Connected Solution

Leminh Thien Huynh[1]([✉]), Thanh Vu Tran[2], Viet-Dung Do[2], and Van Cuu Ho[1]

[1] SaiGon University, Ho Chi Minh City, Vietnam
[2] University of Transport, Ho Chi Minh City, Vietnam

Abstract. This study proposes an APF grid-connecting solution to reduce harmonic at the moment of connecting transfer status. The work includes analyzing the system structure, the parameters of the passive LCL-filter system, the active power filter (APF) grid-connecting transfer status, the phase lock loop (PLL) for phase-matching connecting algorithms, and the Fuzzy-PI grid connection control based on *d-q* theory. To validate the accuracy of the proposed solution, simulation and experimental results shows that the power system is more stable by applying the transfer of the APF-connecting procedure. The proposed APF grid-connecting also reduces grid current's THD, and matches phase between grid voltage and grid current.

Keywords: Active Power Filter · APF grid connecting · LCL-filter · *d-q* control theory · PI controller · Fuzzy-PI controller · Power quality · PLL · Total Harmonic Distortion

1 Introduction

The electric welding facilities, the increasing of non-linear loads in both consumer electronics in household appliances and semiconductor devices in the factories are the facts that cause the negative effects on power systems, such as high order harmonics, the mismatching phase between grid current and grid voltage, leading low power electric quality and low power factor (PF). In particular, phase imbalance and waveform distortion cause significant total harmonic distortion (THD) [1] and generate high reactive power. Therefore, the power supply system is not fresh anymore, which is the cause of reducing the device's lifespan, increasing the energy consumption of the electronic devices, and lost in energy transmission. To deal with this challenge, the use of Active Power Filter (APF) has been one of the most effective and certified solutions since 1976 in Akagi's research works. Since then, the APF's control technique continuously improved. The p-q theory has been applied for modeling the APF's mathematical architectures of the APF's controller in [3]. In [4–6], the adaptive technique control has been presented to contribute the APF's control methodologies. In [6–8], the grid connecting of the active power filter is obviously required in filtering electrical source, that is also one of the effective solutions for handing out the suitable APF-grid-connecting. Besides, many studies have

N.-S. Vo et al. (Eds.): INISCOM 2021, LNICST 379, pp. 348–366, 2021.
https://doi.org/10.1007/978-3-030-77424-0_29

been promoting to develop the grid-connecting for distributed power systems together [7–13]. However, none of them shows a perfect APF grid-tie-connecting in details, it is needed to develop not only the APF grid-tie-connecting but also the associating of the renewable energy sources to the grid.

In order to improve the efficiency of electrical systems according to IEEE standard STD 519 [14], it is necessary to develop an effective method of APF grid connecting for both source harmonic filters and improving power factor, specially in the period of APF grid-tie-connecting transfering. The grid connecting can inject the APF for the grid-filtering out of high order harmonics from non-linear loads and makes in phase between grid voltage and grid current, but the procedure hardly requires the stability state. So in this study, we first mention about the negative effect of non-linear load on the three-phase grid system. Then, we propose a new solution to match phase for grid voltage called the APF grid-connecting transfering. This connecting transfering procedure aims to improve the stability state of the system as well as reducing the harmonic at the moment of connecting transfer status. The simulation and experiments show that the results of the APF grid-tie-connecting matches the requirements of the IEEE standard STD 519 in terms of the high quality of power, the low delay response and low overshot in the period of connecting transferring. According to IEEE standard STD 519, the total harmonic distortion (THD) is given by:

$$THD = \frac{\sqrt{\sum_{h=2}^{\infty} I_{hRMS}^2}}{I_{RMS}} \tag{1}$$

The rest of this paper is organized as follows. In Sect. 2, the topology of the proposed three-phase APF system working the three-phase grid is presented. In Sect. 3, the control policy in the duty of three-phase grid-tie-connecting is described in details. The simulation and experimental results are shown in Sect. 3.2. Finally, the conclusion is presented in Sect. 4.

2 Three-Phase-APF Grid-Tied-Connecting Control Policy

2.1 Topology of Proposed Three-Phase Grid-Connected APF

Figure 1 shows the configuration of three-phase grid-connected active filter system which consists of an Active Power Filter based on voltage source inverter (VSI-APF), a three-phase LCL-filter, and a three-phase grid with non-linear load. The Active Power Filter consists of the VSI-APF is connected to the three-phase grid system through the LCL-passive filter and the static-transfer-switch (STS).

In order to provide higher frequency harmonic extenuation with the same values of the inductor, we replace a filter made from inductance by a three-phase passive filter. The three-phase passive filter is constructed from an inductance-capacitor-inductance (LCL-filter) as shown in Fig. 1. Because the third-order is caused by the LCL-filter type, an easing of a resistor called R_d is used to eliminate this stability problem. A resistor R_d is defined as a passive damping method. As a result, by using an LCL-filter with APF, the DC link will be working with the reference voltage of 750 VDC with the parameters

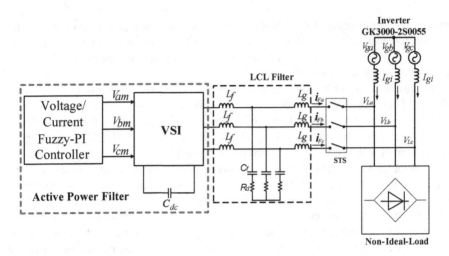

Fig. 1. Configuration of the three-phase grid-connected active filter system.

as follows: the nominal voltage (line-line RMS, $V_{g(ab,bc,ca)} = 220V = \sqrt{3}\, V_{g(a,b,c)}$) is 220 V generated by 5.5 kW single phase (220 V, 50–60 Hz) to the three-phase frequency inverter; model GK3000-2S0055; the output frequency range is 0–400 Hz; L_{gi} is the grid inductance before connecting with Non-Ideal-Load; after creating $V_{(a,b,c)m}$ of the controller, the VSI combines with the LCL-filter to generates i_{Fa}, i_{Fb}, i_{Fc} with 8 kHz of the switching frequency; V_{La}, V_{Lb}, V_{Lc}, are marked at the grid connecting points for three-phase a, b, and c respectively. STS is the controlled switch or so-called the static-transfer-switch.

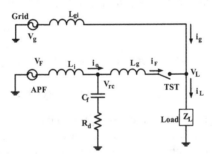

Fig. 2. Equivalent one-phase model.

With a three-phase symmetric system considering in the research, an equivalent one-phase modal can be employed for analysis as shown in Fig. 2. In which the circuit conditions, the base parameters of the system are determined in Table 1.

The LCL-filter is combined with the three-phase grid-connected APF to attenuate the ripples in the APF grid-connecting process. The parameters of the three-phase LCL-filter used in this study are summarized in Table 2.

Table 1. The per-unit system for the circuit condition

Parameters	Calculating	Value
Z_{base}	$V^2/P = 220^2 / 5000$	9.68[Ω]
C_{base}	$1/(2\pi f * Z_{base}) = 1/2\pi * 50 * 9.68$	328.83[uF]
L_{base}	$Z_{base}/2\pi f = 9.68/2\pi * 50$	30.816[mH]

Table 2. Summarized list of parameters of the three-phase LCL-filter

Parameters	Value
L_i	1.083[mH]
C_f	12[uF]
L_g	0.2[mH]
R_d	1.5[Ω]

Figure 2 shows the equivalent one-phase model which is the one-phase model of the three-phase grid-connected active filter system in Fig. 1. In Fig. 2, V_F is the output voltage of VSI, i_o is output current of VSI, V_{rc} is the voltage of filter capacitor C_f and small damp resistor R_d in series connection, i_F and V_L are output current and output voltage of stage power conversion, i_L is load current, i_g is the current of the grid, and V_g is the voltage of the grid. The APF inductance L_i and the grid inductance L_g are used as a function of the LCL-filter of the proposed power system. Z_{base} was defined as total equivalent impedance; C_{base} and L_{base} were total equivalent capacitor and total equivalent inductor of the system, respectively.

2.2 The Identification of Scheme

The instability problem of the third order harmonic is caused by an LCL-filter and higher-order harmonics are caused by non-linear loads, the Fuzzy-PI controller was designed to overcome this issue. Some existing works have applied LCL-filters as in [14–18]. In [15, 16], the authors used one extra response or by regulating the ratio of control frequency and the resonance frequency of the LCL-filter. Another work applies the active damping policies for LCL-filters in [17]. The passive damping procedure with a resistor is deployed to overcome the instability problem in [10, 18, 19].

Since the grid form signals and the VSI output form signals are in AC status, they need to be in-phase to make the APF harmonic eliminate function come true. The system negative effects occur suddenly which are the sag-voltage, the current distortion and the delay of calculating in the main controller. Those negative effects may seriously affect the d-q calculating result signals from rotation reference. The distortion and imbalance issue can be caused by the transferring from voltage control for the sag-voltage problem to the current control. In [20, 21], the authors associates the controller output current and voltage with the single-phase DGs (Distributed Generations – DGs), however, the

APF output signals with transferring situations need to have an algorithm to adapt with the changing in phase and amplitude of the grid signals.

Figure 3 shows the control loop's scheme of the gird current which consists of the Voltage Fuzzy-PI Controller and Current Fuzzy-PI Controller of the APF. In Fig. 3, the V_{dmc} and V_{qmc} will be the compensate components to reduce THD in the APF-grid-connecting procedure. These signals will be combined with the fixed grid voltage in d-q frame, V_{dmv}, and V_{qmv}, to generate V_{dm} and V_{qm} [22].

$$V_{dm} = V_{dmv} + V_{dmc} \tag{2}$$

$$V_{qm} = V_{qmv} + V_{qmc} \tag{3}$$

$$V_{dmc} = \zeta * \Delta V_{gd} + (1 - \zeta)\Delta I_{gd} \tag{4}$$

$$V_{qmc} = \zeta * \Delta V_{gq} + (1 - \zeta)\Delta I_{gq} \tag{5}$$

$$\text{When} \begin{cases} \zeta = 0, V_{g(k)}^{rms} \geq 0.7 * V_g^{rms} \\ \zeta = 1, V_{g(k)}^{rms} < 0.7 * V_g^{rms} \end{cases}$$

The control loop's scheme normally works with the current controller for eliminating high order harmonic, so that $V_{dmc} = \Delta I_{gd}$ and $V_{qmc} = \Delta I_{gq}$. In case of leaking grid voltage; if the magnitude of leaking grid voltage is less than 70% which is defined by the collecting of the *RMS* grid voltage amplitude $k^{th}(V_{g(k)}{}^{(rms)})$, the control loop's scheme will be controlled by the voltage controller denoted as $V_{dmc} = \Delta V_{gd}$ and $V_{qmc} = \Delta V_{gq}$.

In Fig. 2, while getting V_{am}, V_{bm}, and V_{cm} throughout the d-q to abc converter frame, the VSI plays the role of creating the filter current, $i_F(t)$, to do the active filter function given by:

$$i_F(t) = i_L(t) - i_g(t) \tag{6}$$

By using four Fuzzy-PI controllers instead of the conventional PI controller to get compensated signals, such as $\Delta Vg(d,q) = f_{Fuzzy\text{-}PI}(E_{v(d,q)})$ and $\Delta I_{g(d,q)} = f_{Fuzzy\text{-}PI}(E_{i(d,q)})$ [23], the positive sequence signals in $\alpha\beta$ frame is given by:

$$V_{g\alpha}^+ = (2/3)^{1/2}\left[V_{ga} - (1/2).V_{gb} - (1/2).V_{gc}\right] \tag{7}$$

$$V_{g\beta}^+ = (1/2)^{1/2}\left[0 + V_{gb} - V_{gc}\right] \tag{8}$$

The phase angle of the grid θ will be calculated by the PLL as in Fig. 4. At first, the $V_{g\alpha}{}^+$ and $V_{g\beta}{}^+$ are calculated as in (7) and (8), respectively. Then, the PLL use the positive sequence signals of $V_{g\alpha}{}^+$ and $V_{g\beta}{}^+$ to calculate the exact angle-grid phase.

The phase angle of the grid θ will be calculated by the PLL as in Fig. 4. At first, the $V_{g\alpha}{}^+$ and $V_{g\beta}{}^+$ are calculated as in (7) and (8), respectively. Then, the PLL use the positive sequence signals of $V_{g\alpha}{}^+$ and $V_{g\beta}{}^+$ to calculate the exact angle-grid phase. This step aims to synchronize the phase of grid voltage and grid current [24]. The PLL's

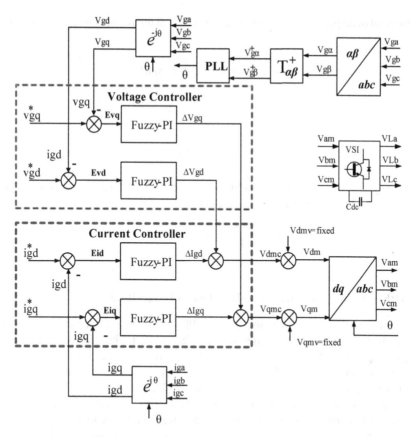

Fig. 3. Control loop's scheme of the grid current.

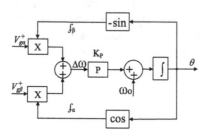

Fig. 4. The block-diagram of PLL controller.

operation applied the d-q theory to generate the θ angle with an unchanging of ωo, shown in Fig. 4. As a result of generating $V_{g\alpha}^{+}$ and $V_{g\beta}^{+}$, the value of θ is pure which is not affected by high order harmonics.

An angle frequency variation to a phase detector (PD), called Δω, is defined by Eq. (9). Grid voltages' components on a static reference frame in Fig. 3, which consist of $V_{g\alpha}^{+}$ and $V_{g\beta}^{+}$; the ∫αand ∫βare the sine-feedback and the cosine-feedback of the

PLL's output θ, respectively; V_P and θ_P are the original input respectively of voltage and phase.

$$\Delta\omega = V_{g\alpha}^{+}.f_\alpha + V_{g\beta}^{+}.f_\beta = V_P \sin(\theta_P - \theta) \tag{9}$$

$$V_{g\alpha}^{+} = \frac{2}{3}V_{gab} - \frac{1}{3}V_{gca} \tag{10}$$

$$V_{g\beta}^{+} = \frac{1}{\sqrt{3}}V_{gbc} \tag{11}$$

By integral calculation of the P-controller output and the feed-forward base angular frequency ω_o, the angle θ is the result from (12), where $\omega_o = 2\pi f_o$.

$$\theta = \int (K_P \Delta\omega + \omega_o)dt \tag{12}$$

2.3 APF in Grid-Tied Operation Mode Control Algorithm

In Fig. 3, the STS connects the three-phase-APF with the LCL-filter to the main grid, the main grid is in normal condition when the STS is closed. The grid current references in d-q form can be determined from the expected active and reactive powers as in the conventional PI controller in [25, 26]. The improvement works have applied the Fuzzy-PI controller to adjust the d-q APF reference currents [23, 27].

Figure 5 is the structural schematic diagram of the Fuzzy-PI controller in Fig. 3. The conventional PI controller with unchanged K_I and K_P parameters are not convenient for the fast complex instability systems. In [28], a fast adaptive Fuzzy-PI has been applied as in Fig. 5. The parameters in the Fuzzy-PI controller can be listed as follows: the E_μ is the input error; $dE_\mu/d\tau$ is the rate of input deviation; α_μ and α_d are the quantization factor of E_μ and $dE_\mu/d\tau$, respectively; the initialize values for K_I and K_P are K_I^* and K_p^*. The relationship between the two couple parameters (K_I and K_P) and ($dE_\mu/d\tau$ and ΔE_μ) will be estimated by the fuzzy control principle.

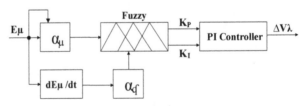

Fig. 5. Fuzzy-PI controller.

In Fig. 5, the Fuzzy-PI controller consists of a Fuzzy controller and a traditional PI controller. The combining of Fig. 3 and Fig. 5 indicates E_μ stands for E_{vq}, E_{vd}, E_{id} and E_{iq}, these signals are the inputs of the Fuzzy-PI; $\Re^*$ and $\Re$ are reference signals and natural signals in d-q frame consisting of (v_{gd}^*, v_{gq}^*), (i_{gd}^*, i_{gq}^*) and (v_{gd}, v_{gq}), (i_{gq}, i_{gd}) respectively. And certainly ΔV_λ represents $\Delta V_{g(d,q)}$ and $\Delta I_{g(d,q)}$.

$$\begin{cases} E_\mu = \Re^* - \Re \\ dE_\mu(\ell)/d\tau = E_\mu(\ell) - E_\mu(\ell - 1) = \vartheta_\mu \\ E_\mu(\ell) = E_\mu(\ell - 1) \end{cases} \qquad (13)$$

After Eqs. (13), furring of E_μ and $dE_\mu/d\tau$ are done, Mamdani fuzzy rule-based is used to regulate ηK_P and ηK_I.

$$\begin{cases} \eta K_P = \psi_1(E_\mu, \vartheta_\mu) \\ \eta K_I = \psi_2(E_\mu, \vartheta_\mu) \end{cases} \qquad (14)$$

The results of Eqs. (14) then can be used to determine the proportional K_P and integral coefficients K_I. By that way, the parameters for the PI controller are modified.

$$\begin{cases} K_P = K_P^* + \eta K_P \\ K_I = K_I^* + \eta K_I \end{cases} \qquad (15)$$

Finally, the adjustment signal ΔV_λ is calculated through PI controller.

$$\Delta V_\lambda = k_p E_\mu + k_i \int_0^t E_\mu dt \qquad (16)$$

In Fig. 5, the d-q Fuzzy-PI controllers' outputs is denoted as ΔV_λ which consists of ΔI_{gd}, ΔI_{gq}, ΔV_{gd} and ΔV_{gq}. The ΔV_λ indicates the grid variation which are supplemented to the fixed d-q grid voltages V_{dmv} and V_{qmv} to achieve good dynamic feedback with the grid voltage in feed-forward signals [29].

The phasor diagram in current control mode is shown in Fig. 6. At first, the V_{dmc} and V_{qmc} is calculated by using V_{mc}; then V_m is the addition of V_{dmc} and V_{qmc} which shows the changing of unexpected effecting from the non-linear load. At the transfer's instant from voltage control to current control mode, the outputs signals controller V_{dmc} and V_{qmc} are maintained during the on-grid-connecting operation. The APF output signals in d-q format can be controlled by the d-q current outputs of controller V_{dmc}, V_{qmc} around the fixed V_{dmv}, V_{qmv} (Fig. 3).

In the current control mode, the synchronization of the output-PLL's angle θ, the angle of grid voltage θ_g, and the α-β voltages' grid can be computed from the sized three-phase-line voltages' grid V_{gab}, V_{gbc}, V_{gca} through Eq. (10) and Eq. (11). In Fig. 7, V_{mc} is the compensating signal, V_{mv} is based on the grid and fixed, and V_m is a sensitive signal caused by an unexpected change of the system. The closed-loop scheme will control the phasor in the voltage control mode while the detecting range of the V_g^{rms} is in the range of (0[V], 154[V]). The Fuzzy-PI controller creates V_{dmv} and V_{qmv} by comparing them with the fixed V_{dmc} and V_{qmc} as in Fig. 7. At that time, the same d-q reference voltages will be fed to the input voltages of the PLL. The output $\Delta\omega$ will be determined by

$$\Delta\omega = 154 * \cos\theta \cdot (-\sin\theta) + 154 * \sin\theta \cdot \cos\theta = 0 \qquad (17)$$

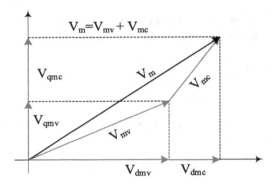

Fig. 6. Phasor diagram in current control mode.

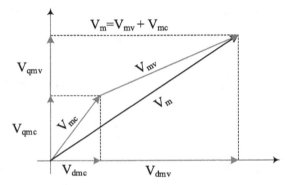

Fig. 7. Phasor diagram in voltage control mode.

Through the Fuzzy-PI control and PLL operation, the VSI can compensate an adding voltage to make getting high quality grid under the sensitive load and imbalance source condition.

3 Simulation and Experience Results

3.1 Simulation Results

In this section, a simulation is conducted using the PSIM program to demonstrate the system with and without the proposed algorithm, also the results of APF grid-connecting algorithm. Non-linear load's effects in a three-phase grid with and without the proposed APF connecting algorithm are shown in Fig. 8.

Figure 9 shows the details of APF-grid-connecting procedure, in which the three-phase load currents have a THD_i of about 30.75% on average with off grid-connecting and the off grid-connecting $THD_{ig(a,b,c)}$ is 30%. In grid-connected time, the grid currents become sine because of reducing high order harmonics, which makes grid currents' $THD_{ig(a,b,c)}$ cutoff to 3.5% in equilibrium. This simulation result indicates the effective working of the APF and the validity of the suggested seamless transfer algorithm.

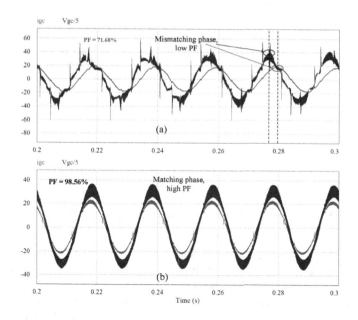

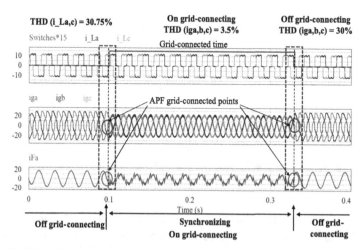

Fig. 8. Simulation results for Non-linear load's effects in three-phase grid: (a) without propose algorithm, mismatch phase between grid current i_{gc} and grid voltage v_{gc}; (b) with propose algorithm, match phase with high PF = 98.56%.

With the proposed algorithm, the synchronization of grid current signal and grid voltage signal is successful matched. Furthermore, when transferring from off grid-connecting to on grid-connecting operation, the in phased of the APF's signals and grid's signals are shown in Fig. 10.

Fig. 9. Simulation results for the proposed algorithm: grid-tie operating procedure.

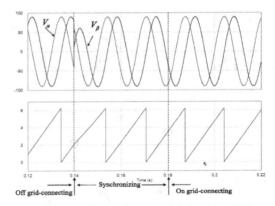

Fig. 10. Simulation results for the proposed algorithm: PLL operation.

Figure 11 shows the results of the transition from on grid-connecting to off grid-connecting operation when there are voltage sag situations in voltage on the main grid. If the $V_g^{(rms)}$ value drops below 70%, the APF recognizes the voltage sags. After regulating the d-q grid currents to zero, the STS turns to trip status. Because the compensating voltage mode operation is control by the APF controller, the load voltage is instantly gotten back to the expected voltage.

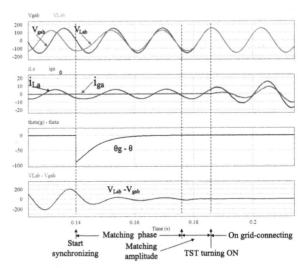

Fig. 11. The results in simulation for the transfer from Off grid-connecting to On grid-connecting with dedicated algorithm: transferring operation mode.

Figure 12 shows the PLL operation at the transition mode. The unbalanced node occurred due to the two-phase voltage sags in α-β grid voltages, the balanced α-β positive sequence voltages are deployed at the input of the PLL controller's voltages. Even though the grid voltage sags exist and in transfer-mode, the PLL controller's angle

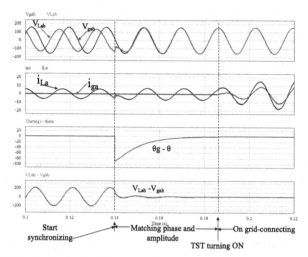

Fig. 12. The results in simulation for the transfer from Off grid-connecting to On grid-connecting operation without dedicated algorithm.

raises without any unexpected jump which is due to the balance of the PLL controller voltage inputs in the α-β reference system.

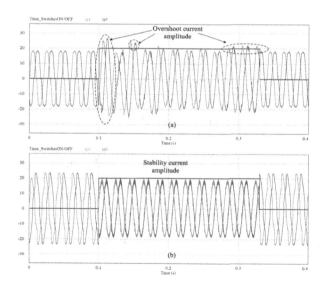

Fig. 13. The results in simulation for the transfer from Off grid-connecting to on grid-connecting operation without dedicated algorithm.

In spite of the little distortion of the load voltage during the short period of time between the sag-voltage occurrence point and the beginning point of the off grid-connecting operation, the APF can transfer evenly to the off-grid mode without the spike-voltages and rush-currents as shown in Fig. 13.

3.2 Experimentation Results

Figure 1 in the Sect. 2 declares the scheme for hardware design with a 5kW three-phase-APF grid-tie-connecting system. The system's controller is conducted by 32-bit STM32H743iiT6. Then, the three-phase-load voltages and grid-side's inductor currents, and three-phase-grid currents and voltages are determined by measurement.

The three-phase switch and the two IGBTs per phase are in anti-serial are considered as the STS, and an on-grid/off-grid signal for STS is created by the controller. A programmable three-phase source is applied to imitate the main grid such as sag-voltage existing. Figure 14 shows the in phase of the output VSI voltage and the grid voltage.

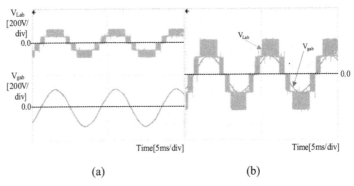

(a)   (b)

Fig. 14. Grid-tied operation experimental results with proposed algorithm: (a) grid voltage V_{gab} and VSI voltage V_{Lab}. (b) In phase of the two signals.

Figure 15 and Fig. 16 show the experimental signals when the system working in changing from on grid-connecting to off grid-connecting operation (Fig. 15) and the working's result of the PLL (Fig. 16) with the suggested algorithm.

Figure 17 and Fig. 18 show the results of experimentation for the transferring from on grid-connecting to off grid-connecting operation under a sag-voltage of 70% in the main grid during the on grid-connecting operation. In Fig. 17, after tripping STS, the load voltage immediately obtains its expected voltage at the off grid-connecting operation

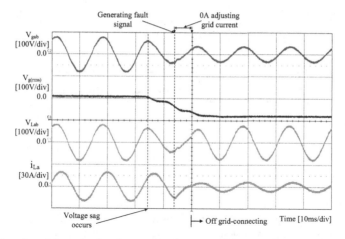

Fig. 15. Experimental results for the transfer from on-grid-connecting to off-grid-connecting operation with proposed algorithm: grid voltage and output voltage and current.

mode, the currents in *d-q* reference and also the current of a-phase-grid are regulated to zero before the STS turns to trip status. Figure 18 shows the input voltages' balanced in the α-β reference system and the synchronization of PLL's angle, which raises evenly during the sag-voltage and the transferring-mode.

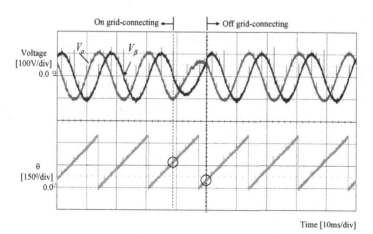

Fig. 16. Experimental results for the transfer from On-grid-mode to Off-grid-mode with proposed algorithm: PLL operation.

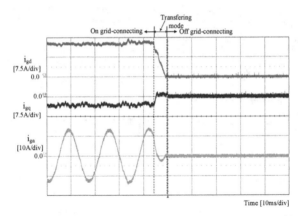

Fig. 17. The results of experimentation for the transferring status from on grid-connecting to off grid-connecting operation with suggested algorithm: d-q grid currents.

Figure 19 shows the results of experimentation for the transfer from off grid-connecting to on grid-connecting operation with the proposed algorithm: grid and load voltages. Figure 20 points out the results of experimentation for the transfer from off grid-connecting to on grid-connecting operation with the suggested algorithm with the signs of grid current and load currents. It is obvious that the result has low quality when the system works without the proposed algorithm (Fig. 21).

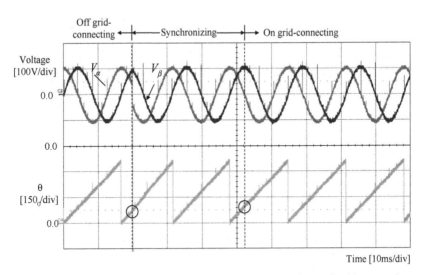

Fig. 18. The results of experimentation for the transferring status from off grid-connecting to on grid-connecting operation with suggested algorithm: the operation of PLL.

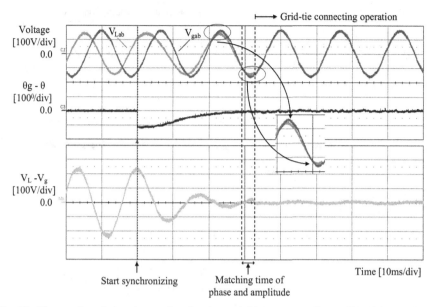

Fig. 19. The results of experimentation for the transferring status from off-grid-connecting to on-grid-connecting operation using proposed algorithm: grid-voltages and load-voltages.

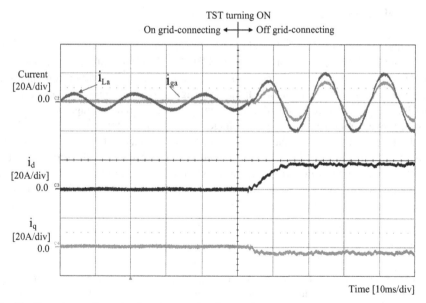

Fig. 20. Experimental results for the transfer from off-grid-connecting to on-grid-connecting operation with proposed algorithm: grid and load currents.

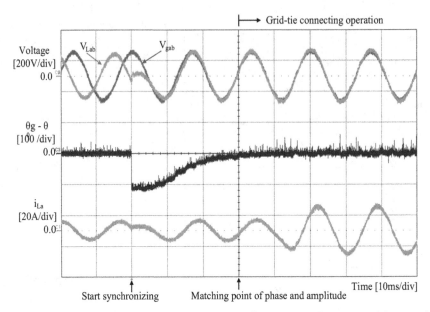

Fig. 21. Experimental results for the transfer from off-grid-connecting to on-grid-connecting operation without proposed algorithm.

4 Conclusion

After simulating the proposed algorithm in Psim software, the experiment in the active power filter hardware system using the STM32H743iiT6 microcontroller chip has been completed. With the results obtained, besides matching phase for grid current and grid voltage to increase power factor and eliminating high order harmonics to decrease THDi from 30.07% to 3.5%, it is seen that the magnitude of the load voltage and its phase are successively matched to the grid-voltage without any distortion and spike. Also, with the proposed algorithm, the active power filter's signals and the grid's ones have in-phase and equivalent values in amplitude, reducing the instantaneous overshot current amplitude at the time of the APF on grid transferring. In the future, this model can be improved to work with serious sag-voltage in the time of over tens fundamental cycle by using ultra-capacitor instead of C_{dc}-link.

References

1. Suhendar, Firmansyah, T., Maulana, A., Zuldiag, Dewanto, V.: Shunt active power filter based on P-Q theory with multilevel inverters for harmonic current compensation. Telkomnika (Telecommun. Comput. Electron. Control) **15**(4), 1632–1640 (2017)
2. Ucar, M., Ozdemir, E.: Control of a 3-phase 4-leg active power filter under non-ideal mains voltage condition. Electr. Power Syst. Res. **78**(1), 58–73 (2008)
3. Dang, X.K., Do, V.D., Nguyen, X.P.: Robust adaptive fuzzy control using genetic algorithm for dynamic positioning system. IEEE Access **8**(December), 222077–222092 (2020)

4. Do, V.-D., Dang, X.-K., Huynh, L.-T., Ho, V.-C.: Optimized multi-cascade fuzzy model for ship dynamic positioning system based on genetic algorithm. In: Duong, T.Q., Vo, N.-S., Nguyen, L.K., Vien, Q.-T., Nguyen, V.-D. (eds.) INISCOM 2019. LNICSSITE, vol. 293, pp. 165–180. Springer, Cham (2019). https://doi.org/10.1007/978-3-030-30149-1_14

5. Do, V., Dang, X.: Fuzzy adaptive interactive algorithm design for marine dynamic positioning system under unexpected impacts of Vietnam Sea. Indian J. Geo Mar. Sci. **49**(November), 1764–1771 (2020)

6. Zeng, Z., Yang, H., Zhao, R., Cheng, C.: Topologies and control strategies of multi-functional grid-connected inverters for power quality enhancement: a comprehensive review. Renew. Sustain. Energy Rev. **24**, 223–270 (2013)

7. Kamel, R.M.: New inverter control for balancing standalone micro-grid phase voltages: a review on MG power quality improvement. Renew. Sustain. Energy Rev. **63**, 520–532 (2016)

8. Mahmud, N., Zahedi, A.: Review of control strategies for voltage regulation of the smart distribution network with high penetration of renewable distributed generation. Renew. Sustain. Energy Rev. **64**, 582–595 (2016)

9. Santoso, H., Budiyanto, B.: Microgrid development using a grid tie inverter. MAKARA J. Technol. Ser. **17**(3), 121–127 (2014)

10. Eren, S.: Composite nonlinear feedback control and stability analysis of a grid-connected voltage source inverter with LCL filter. IEEE Trans. Ind. Electron. **60**(11), 5059–5074 (2013)

11. Zhang, X., Wang, Y., Yu, C., Guo, L., Cao, R.: Hysteresis model predictive control for high-power grid-connected inverters with output LCL filter. IEEE Trans. Ind. Electron. **63**(1), 246–256 (2016)

12. Singh, M., Chandra, A.: Real-time implementation of ANFIS control for renewable interfacing inverter in 3P4W distribution network. IEEE Trans. Ind. Electron. **60**(1), 121–128 (2013)

13. Hoevenaars, T., LeDoux, K., Colosino, M.: Interpreting IEEE STD 519 and meeting its harmonic limits in VFD applications. In: Record of Conference Papers - Annual Petroleum and Chemical Industry Conference, pp. 145–150 (2003)

14. Guzman, R., De Vicuna, L.G., Morales, J., Castilla, M., Miret, J.: Model-based control for a three-phase shunt active power filter. IEEE Trans. Ind. Electron. **63**(7), 3998–4007 (2016)

15. Vodyakho, O., Mi, C.C.: Three-level inverter-based shunt active power filter in three-phase three-wire and four-wire systems. IEEE Trans. Power Electron. **24**(5), 1350–1363 (2009)

16. Hogan, D.J., Gonzalez-Espin, F., Hayes, J.G., Lightbody, G., Egan, M.G.: Adaptive resonant current-control for active power filtering within a microgrid. In: 2014 IEEE Energy Conversion Congress and Exposition, ECCE 2014 (2014)

17. Zammit, D., Spiteri Staines, C., Apap, M., Licari, J.: Design of PR current control with selective harmonic compensators using Matlab. J. Electr. Syst. Inf. Technol. **4**, 347–358 (2017)

18. Srinath, S., Poongothai, M.S., Aruna, T.: PV integrated shunt active filter for harmonic compensation. Energy Proc. **117**, 1134–1144 (2017)

19. He, J., Li, Y.W., Blaabjerg, F., Wang, X.: Active harmonic filtering using current-controlled, grid-connected DG units with closed-loop power control. IEEE Trans. Power Electron. **29**(2), 642–653 (2014)

20. Tran, T.V., Chun, T.W., Lee, H.H., Kim, H.G., Nho, E.C.: PLL-based seamless transfer control between grid-connected and islanding modes in grid-connected inverters. IEEE Trans. Power Electron. **29**, 5218–5228 (2014)

21. Leminhthien, H., Thanhvu, T., Vancuu, H.: The effecting of non-ideal-load on three-phase-power systems using fuzzy control active power filter. J. Transp. Sci. Technol. **27+28**, (05/2018), 119–121 (2018)

22. Thien, H.L.M., van Huong, D., Tien, N.X., van Cuu, H., Vu, T.T.: Improving the electric quality of the back-to-back system on modern electric railways using active power filter algorithm. J. Mech. Eng. Res. Dev. **44**(1), 83–98 (2020)

23. Karuppanan, P., Mahapatra, K.K.: PLL with fuzzy logic controller based shunt active power filter for harmonic and reactive power compensation. In: India International Conference on Power Electronics, IICPE 2010 (2011)

24. Van, T.L., Huynh, L., Tran, T.T., Nguyen, D.C.: Improved control strategy of three-phase four-wire inverters using sliding mode input-output feedback linearization under unbalanced and nonlinear load conditions (2015)

25. Trinh, Q.-N., Lee, H.-H.: An advanced current control strategy for three-phase shunt active power filters. IEEE Trans. Ind. Electron. 60(12), 5400–5410 (2013)

26. Dehini, R., Benachaiba, C.: Improving the active power filter performance by robust self-tuning face to sudden change of load. J. Electr. Eng. 1–9 (2020)

27. Pitalúa-Díaz, N., Herrera-López, E.J., Valencia-Palomo, G., González-Angeles, A., Rodríguez-Carvajal, R.A., Cazarez-Castro, N.R.: Comparative analysis between conventional PI and fuzzy logic PI controllers for indoor Benzene concentrations. Sustainability 7(5), 5398–5412 (2015)

28. Bouzelata, Y., Kurt, E., Altin, N., Chenni, R.: Design and simulation of a solar supplied multifunctional active power filter and a comparative study on the current-detection algorithms. Renew. Sustain. Energy Rev. 43, 1114–1126 (2015)

Intelligent IoT Monitoring System Using Rule-Based for Decision Supports in Fired Forest Images

Hai Van Pham[1(✉)] and Quoc Hung Nguyen[2]

[1] Hanoi University of Science and Technology (HUST), Hanoi, Vietnam
haipv@soict.hust.edu.vn
[2] University of Economics Ho Chi Minh City (UEH), Ho Chi Minh City, Vietnam

Abstract. Recently, many investigations focus on studying to detect of forest fires using IoT devices such as remote sensors or conventional fire detector sensors. However, supports in fire forest in real-time are hard for current studies in large forests. This paper has presented a novel approach to forest fire detection implemented using an improved rule-based integrated with k-means algorithm to improve the detection of forest fires. The rules in knowledge based can be considered in a camera as forest fires in real-time detection. The research explores the construction of Time-Lapse Videos from cluttered consecutive image. Mechanisms have been developed to automatically render the images with these elements from the scenes to produce more 'truthful' videos which more accurately describe of forest fires. The experimental results show that our proposed IoT monitoring system achieves significant improvements in 'real-time' fire detection.

Keywords: Video time lapse · Rule-based · Clustering · K-means · IoT fire forest system · Intelligent forest monitoring

1 Introduction

Recently, remote sensing and image processing of IoT devices, including image segmentation [2] and machine learning [1], have been a feature of research over an extended period and there exists a large body of published research on these topics. Clustering is the process of classifying a group of abstract objects into classes of similar objects, the task of image segmentation function is to process the original image into many different clusters [3,4]. The processing of satellite images enables the segmentation [of satellite images] and the classification of entities into specific types such as trees, soil, and water.

In the K-means clustering algorithm [4,5], the simplest idea about a cluster is to gather points which close to each other in a defined space that can be applied to image processing in a domain of monitoring forest under uncertainty.

N.-S. Vo et al. (Eds.): INISCOM 2021, LNICST 379, pp. 367–378, 2021.
https://doi.org/10.1007/978-3-030-77424-0_30

Research has identified a number of proposals to improve the performance of the K-means algorithm [5]. The proposed methods have significantly enabled enhancement of the traditional K-means method. For example, Linde et al. [7] have proposed a method for vector quantizer design and C. Huang et al. have introduced an approach to enable direct search using a binary division method based on the principle of structural analysis [8,9].

Muhammad et al. considers the early detection of fires and introduced an approach based on Convolutional Neural Networks (CNN) to enable surveillance for effective disaster management. The proposed method uses fine-tuned CNN for tracking surveillance cameras with an adaptive prioritisation mechanism is used in surveillance systems to ensure the autonomous response [6,19]. Zhang et al. has introduced an approach to address 'wildland' forest fires and smoke detection based on faster R-CNN using Synthetic Smoke Images and video sequences [18]. In [19] the use of an approach based on unsupervised training is applied to the quantification of large historical data sets for use in decision-support for disasters and securities. The limitations of these approaches are high computational cost combined with large image and video large data sets for the monitoring of forests [11–13,15].

Santiago et al. [16] in a paper entitled "A Forest Fire Detection algorithm using a fuzzy system approach based on overlap indices to effectively control the fire detection" presents a study which employs the convex combination of several overlap functions and overlap indices to realise improved results based on the use of fuzzy Logic Systems. Haifeng Lin et al. [17] have introduced a fuzzy inference system combined with a big-data analysis algorithm to enable the prediction of forest fires based on rechargeable wireless sensor networks. The proposed approach applies an advanced quantitative technique to estimate the potential fire risk predicated on the conversion of the data into triangulated numbers. All wireless sensor derived weather data [captured over continuous 24 h periods] is used to illustrate prevailing status of forest environments [20–22].

In this paper has presented a novel approach to enable the effective detection of forest fires based on our proposed method called the BK-fired forest (BKFF) algorithm. It is based on a development of the K-means clustering algorithm using a rule-based approach. Our contribution lies in the development of an approach to the classification of satellite imaging based on a development of the K-means clustering algorithm using a rule-based approach. Rules in the knowledge based can be considered in a camera as forest fires extracted by video time lapse in real-time detection. When applied to the detection of forest fires through a camera.

This paper is organized as follows: Several related works are shown in Sect. 1. In Sect. 1, the theory of the K-means clustering algorithm and several evaluation methods are briefly reviewed. The details of the new method are discussed in Sect. 2. Experiment results which show the advantages of the algorithm are proposed in Sect. 3, as well. Finally, conclusions are drawn in Sect. 4.

2   The Proposed Model

In this section, Figure 1 shows an overview of the proposed model with the image segmentation method.

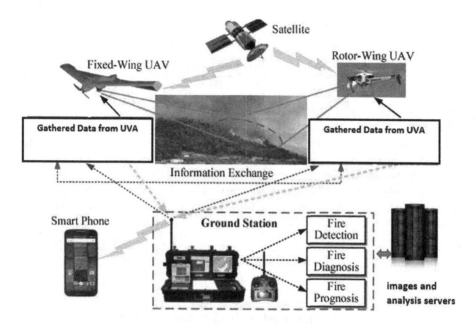

Fig. 1. The proposed model of image segmentation method using IoT devices

All data sets are collected from UAVs, including fired images of forests. All of image files are stored in image and analysis servers. The proposed model has presented fire detection and diagnosis. End users using smart phone can be given in decision making in real time under an uncertain environment.

2.1   The Proposed Algorithm to Color Image Segmentation Problem

In this paper, we have proposed a novel model called BK-means algorithm for color image segmentation problem based on the development of basic K-means clustering algorithm as follows:

Input Picture $\mathbf{X}$ and the number of clusters $\mathbf{K}$.

Output the center $\mathbf{M}$ and the label vector for each data point $\mathbf{Y}$.

Step 1: Read color image $\mathbf{X}$

Step 2: Pre-process image $\mathbf{X}$ is as follows: The processing photo step is to apply techniques for improvement of the image quality. This method uses Successive

Mean Quantization Transform (SMQT). The basic unit of SMQT is Mean Quantization Unit (MQU) that includes the average value of all pixels in the image, then the average value is used to quantify the value of the data either 0 or 1, depending on the value of the pixel [3], depending on the value of the pixel as shown in Eq. 1 and 2:

$$Pixel\,(D) \rightarrow Mean \rightarrow M\,\{0,1\} \tag{1}$$

$$M\,(x) = \begin{cases} 1, \, if D\,(x) > Mean \\ 0, \qquad esle \end{cases} \tag{2}$$

Step 3: Convert image **X** from RGB color space into $L*a*b*$ in the details as follows: The basic of segmenting images with the K-means clustering algorithm is to create clusters based on the color value of each pixel. It is possible to consider the color components of pixels see [4,10]. In this section we apply K-means clustering for identified images on color space $L*a*b*$. In the color space $L*a*b*$, it is possible to reduce features of brightness L and keep 2 color components of channels $a*$ and $b*$ [4,10]. Note that the method converts images from the color standard RGB to the color standard $L*a*b*$:

Step 4: Reduce data dimensions including image format and convert **X** from 3D space into 2D space [4,10] and then obtain the pixel matrix $\hat{\mathbf{X}}$ as shown in Eq. 3:

$$I\,(h,w,c) \rightarrow A\,(h \times w, c) \tag{3}$$

where h, w is size and c is the number of color channel of image I

Step 5: Select a parameter K from the matrix $\hat{\mathbf{X}}$: using Elbow and Silhouette methods. This is described as shown in Eq. 4:

$$wcss\,(C) = \sum_{i=1}^{K} \sum_{o \in c_i} d\,(o, cen_i)^2 \tag{4}$$

where o_i is the object and cen_i is the center of the ith cluster, d is the Euclidean distance, K is the number of clusters.

Step 6: Create an original **K** cluster centers: Arrange the matrix $\hat{\mathbf{X}}$ in non-decreasing order, divide the entire of sorted image data into **K** equal parts (**K** clusters are predicted in step 4). We calculate the average of each part in step 5 and the average value is assigned to the center for the corresponding cluster and is saved as the original cluster center.

Step 7: Apply K-means clustering algorithm to the image matrix with the number of clusters **K** and original cluster centers optimized in steps 5 and 6.

2.2 Applied Rule-Based to the Proposed Model by Detecting Fires in Photos and Videos

Vision-based fire detection has many advantages as follows: a large area can be monitored, determined the exact location of fire and be warned along with surveillance cameras. The image data is extracted from video by surveillance cameras. The video is continuously cut into frames, these frames continuously put into the image processing system in order to detect the fire area. When it recognizes the fire area in the image at any time, the video would immediately be alerted to the fire at the place where the surveillance camera is located. Rule-based methods minimize false alarm rate in comparison with fires/smoke sensors. These rules are described significantly as integrated with the camera, shown in Fig. 2.

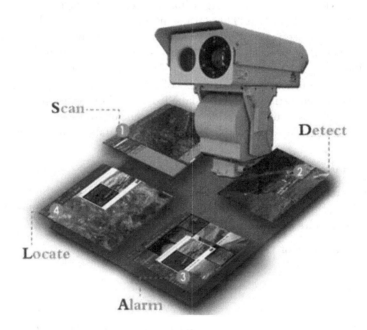

Fig. 2. Fire detection model using a camera.

Rule 1: For pixels at coordinates $e(x, y)$, if pixels are fire, the following rule must be satisfied [18] as shown in Eq. 5:

$$R_1(x, y) = \begin{cases} 1, & if\ R(x, y) > G(x, y) > B(x, y) \\ 0 & otherwise \end{cases} \tag{5}$$

Rule 2: Determination of threshold values for fire pixels [19] as shown in Eq. 6:

$$R_2(x, y) = \begin{cases} 1, & if\ (R(x, y) > 190) \cap (G(x, y) > 100) \cap (B(x, y) < 140) \\ 0, & otherwise \end{cases} \tag{6}$$

Rules 3 and 4: These rules are described as shown in Eq. 7 and Eq. 8 [19]. Additionally, these rules embedded in the demonstration with AI camera are shown in Fig. 2:

$$R_3\left(x,y\right) = \begin{cases} 1, & if\ Y\left(x,y\right) > Cb\left(x,y\right) \\ 0, & otherwise \end{cases} \tag{7}$$

$$R_4\left(x,y\right) = \begin{cases} 1, & if\ Cr\left(x,y\right) > Cb\left(x,y\right) \\ 0, & otherwise \end{cases} \tag{8}$$

3 Experiments

3.1 Data Sets in Experiments

The proposed model have been tested with datasets containing 600 Natural Images and 1000 Ground Truth images (manual segment image). All the images are (481 × 321) pixels in size. The data source is available from Berkeley University[1] [23,24]; the test dataset consists of 5331 images, including 2400 images with fire (labelled as *fire*) and 2931 images without fire [(labelled as *notfire*). The satellite image data sets are available from earthengine[2]. The dataset for satellite image segmentation problems is collected from Google Image; the outputs (for the segmentation steps) are labelled in areas of the forest images. In the detection of fires in pictures and videos, the outputs of images have been cut from the video time lapse in real-time detection then labeled as *fire* or *notfire*.

3.2 Evaluation Methods

Appropriate methods such as Mean Squared Error (MSE), Peak Signal-to-Noise Ratio (PSNR), Structural Similarity Index Metric (SSIM), and Evaluation based on clustering results are used to evaluate the proposed model.

– Mean Squared Error (MSE) as shown in Eq. 9 [6]

$$MSE = \frac{1}{M \times N} \sum_{i=1}^{M} \sum_{j=1}^{N} \left(I_{ij} - \hat{I}_{ij}\right)^2 \tag{9}$$

where $\hat{I}$ - the original image, I - the segmented image, M, N are the size of the image I. The smaller the $RMSE = \sqrt{MSE}$ value is, the better the output image will be.
– Signal-to-noise ratio calculation is shown in Eq. 10 (SNR) [6]:

$$SNR = \frac{\sum_{i=1}^{M} \sum_{j=1}^{N} I_{ij}^2}{\sum_{i=1}^{M} \sum_{j=1}^{N} \left(I_{ij} - \hat{I}_{ij}\right)^2} \tag{10}$$

where $\hat{I}$ - the original image, I - the segmented image, M, N are the size of the image I.

---

[1] https://people.eecs.berkeley.edu/.
[2] Earthengine: https://earthengine.google.com/timelapse/.

- Peak Signal-to-Noise Ratio (PSNR) calculation is shown in Eq. 11 [6]:

$$PSNR = 10 \times \log_{10} \left(\frac{MAX_j^2}{MSE} \right) \tag{11}$$

Note: the higher value of PSNR corresponds to a better quality image.
- Structural Similarity Index Metric (SSIM) calculation is shown in Eq. 12 [6]:

$$SSIM(x, y) = \frac{(2\mu_x + \mu_y)(2\sigma_{xy})}{(\mu_x^2 + \mu_y^2)(\sigma_x^2 + \sigma_y^2)} \tag{12}$$

in which : $\mu_x = \frac{1}{N} \sum_{i=1}^{N} x_i, \mu_y = \frac{1}{N} \sum_{i=1}^{N} y_i$

and $\sigma_x = \sqrt{\frac{1}{N-1} \sum_{i=1}^{N} (x_i - \mu_x)^2}, \sigma_y = \sqrt{\frac{1}{N-1} \sum_{i=1}^{N} (y_i - \mu_y)^2}, \sigma_{xy} = \frac{1}{N-1} \sum_{i=1}^{N} (x_i - \mu_x)(y_i - \mu_y)$

(N) is the total number of pixels, (x) is the segmented image, and (y) is the original image.

- Mean Absolute Error (MAE) [6]: this method is used to detect the 'blue effect' in any 'real-time' image, the most common is a satellite image. Normally, satellite images are blurred due to atmospheric disturbance. The computation of the MAE for an image is shown in Eq. 13:

$$MSE = \frac{1}{M \times N} \sum_{i=1}^{M} \sum_{j=1}^{N} \left| I_{ij} - \hat{I}_{ij} \right| \tag{13}$$

where $\hat{I}$ - the original image, I - the segmented image, M, N are the size of the image I.
- Structural Content (SC) [6]: the structure contents provides the similarity between two images. As the similarity between two images increases, the (SC) approaches (1) as shown in Eq. 14:

$$SC = \frac{\sum_{i=1}^{M} \sum_{j=1}^{N} I_{ij}^2}{\sum_{i=1}^{M} \sum_{j=1}^{M} \hat{I}_{ij}^2} \tag{14}$$

where $\hat{I}$ - the original image, I - the segmented image, M, N are the size of the image I.
- Evaluation based on clustering results: each $\frac{N(N-1)}{2}$ pair of pixels in the data layer is assigned to the same cluster IFF they are similar. A True Positive (TP) decision is to assign two similar pixels to the same cluster, a True Negative $(()TN)$ decision is to assign two different pixels to different clusters. There are two types of potential errors: (a) one is where a (FP) assigns two different pixels to the same cluster, and (b) the second is where

a (FN) decides to assign two similar pixels for different clusters. The index (RI) indicates the percentage of correct decisions as shown in Eq. 15:

$$RI = \frac{TP + TN}{TP + FP + TN + FN} \tag{15}$$

The method to determine a *positive* class, *Precision* [1] is defined as the rate at which (TP) points are correctly classified as *positive* $(TP + FP)$ as shown in Eq. 16:

$$Precision = \frac{TP}{TP + FP} \tag{16}$$

Recall [1] is defined as the rate at which (TP) points among those points that are actually *positive* $(TP + FN)$ as shown in Eq. 17:

$$Recall = \frac{TP}{TP + FN} \tag{17}$$

The value F_1 [6]: lies in the [0, 1] range where a higher value of (F_1) represents a better classification. When both *Recall* and *Precision* are equal to 1, $F_1 = 1$. Figure 3 models this evaluation based on clustering results is from as shown in Eq. 18:

$$F_1 = 2 \times \frac{Precision \times Recall}{Precision + Recall} \tag{18}$$

3.3   Experimental Result and Evaluation

The proposed BK-means and the basic K-means methods have been tested with the same data sets under the same conditions for image detection as shown in Fig. 3. The proposed method and K-means algorithm are used to automatically identify the lake area, forest area and vegetation area, land area, sandy area along the lake. We can also visually predict a forest image, categorized in five main colors: blue is the lake area, green is the forest and vegetation area, brown is the land area, white is the sand area, and gray is the swamp area.

The experimental results are shown in Fig. 4. The proposed model performance is better than traditional K-means's method according to Table 1. For further tests in the experiments, the proposed model has been performed with data sets consisting of 2 subsets, dealing with fire data sets contains 2400 images with fire labelled 1 and the not-fire test set contains 2931 images without fire labelled 0. The results of fire detection in photos are illustrated in Fig. 5

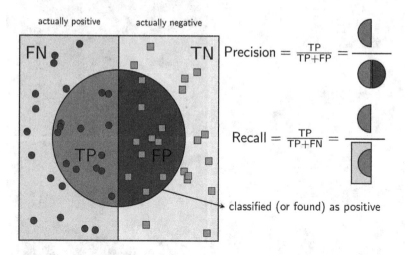

Fig. 3. Recall and precision calculation method for binary classification problem [1]

Fig. 4. Satellite image of Lake Chiquita Mar area

Table 1. Comparisons of the proposed BK-means and the K-means algorithm performance

	Time (s)	Iterations	RMSE	MAE	SNR	PSNR	SC	SSIM
K-means	30.8658	28	0.0486	0.0362	18.5860	26.2638	0.9863	0.8550
BK-means	29.2071	26	0.0944	0.0735	15.8679	20.5045	0.9768	0.8369

Fig. 5. Results of fire detection in photos

4 Conclusion

A novel approach has proposed to make real-time decisions caused by forest fire. K-means method does not work well for noisy or low qualitative images. While implementing image clustering with K-means, we have investigated in the quality of the input image, enhancing the features of pixels [14]. In order to distinguish smoke and images like fog, cloudy sky, and color-like images of such as image features and large intensity light, etc. the proposed model detects the movement of smoke in video explores the construction of Time-Lapse Videos from cluttered consecutive image. The novel approach enhance the performance of K-mean algorithm for forest detection problem. It is indicated that the proposed model achieves significant improvements in real-time detection.

Acknowledgment. This work was supported by the University of Economics Ho Chi Minh City under project CS-2020-15.

References

1. Tiep, V.H.: The base of machine learning (2018)
2. Wang, Z., Jensen, J.R., Im, J.: An automatic region-based image segmentation algorithm for remote sensing applications. Environ. Modell. Softw. **25**(10), 1149–1165 (2010)

3. González, J.C., Salazar, Ò.D.C.: Image enhancement with Matlab algorithms. Blekinge Institute of Technology Department of Applied Signal Processing SE-371 79, Karlskrona Sweden (2016)
4. Kajla, S., Bansal, R.: Efficient improved K means clustering for image segmentation. Int. J. Innov. Res. Comput. Commun. Eng. **4**(6) (2016)
5. Bisla, A., Yadav, P.: Image segmentation using K-means clustering algorithm. Machine Learning Project (2019)
6. Rajkumar, S., Malathi, G.: A comparative analysis on image quality assessment for real time satellite images. Indian J. Sci. Technol. **9**(34) (2016). School of Computing Science and Engineering, VIT University, Chennai, 600127, Tamil Nadu, India
7. Linde, Y., Buzo, A., Gray, R.M.: An algorithm for vector quantizer design. IEEE Trans. Commun. **COM–28**, 84–95 (1980)
8. Huang, C., Harris, R.: A comparison of several vector quantization codebook generation approaches. IEEE Trans. Image Process. **2**(1), 108–112 (1993)
9. John, N., Viswanath, A., Sowmya, V., Soman, K.P.: Analysis of various color space models on effective single image super resolution, August 2016
10. Mathur, G., Purohit, H.: Performance analysis of color image segmentation using K- means clustering algorithm in different color spaces. IOSR J. VLSI Signal Process. (IOSR-JVSP) **4**(6), 1–4 (2014). Ver. III
11. Aqil Burney, S.M., Tariq, H.: K-means cluster analysis for image segmentation. Int. J. Comput. Appl. (0975–8887) **96**(4) (2014)
12. Vipin, V.: Image processing based forest fire detection. Int. J. Emerg. Technol. Adv. Eng. **2**(2), 87–95 (2012)
13. Tuba, V., Capor-Hrosik, R., Tuba, E.: Forest fires detection in digital images based on color features. Int. J. Environ. Sci. **2** (2017)
14. Mehaboobsab, S.N., Alamgeer, A.K., Ahmed, M.M.N., Badruddin, A.M.S.: Fire detection system using image processing. Department of Electronics and Telecommunication Engineering Anjuman-I-Islam's Kalsekar Technical Campus, 2015–2016
15. Binti Zaidi, N.I., binti Lokman, N.A.A., bin Daud, M.R., Achmad, H., Chia, K.A.: Fire recognition using RGB and YCbCr color space. ARPN J. Eng. Appl. Sci. **10**(21), 9786–9790 (2015)
16. Garcia-Jimenez, S., Jurio, A., Pagola, M., De Miguel, L., Barrenechea, E., Bustince, H.: Forest fire detection: a fuzzy system approach based on overlap indices. Appl. Soft Comput. **52**, 834–842 (2017)
17. Lin, H., Liu, X., Wang, X., Liu, Y.: A fuzzy inference and big data analysis algorithm for the prediction of forest fire based on rechargeable wireless sensor networks. Sustain. Comput.: Inf. Syst. **18**, 101–111 (2018)
18. Zhang, Q., Lin, G., Zhang, Y., Gao, X., Wang, J.: Wildland forest fire smoke detection based on faster R-CNN using synthetic smoke images. Proc. Eng. **211**, 441–446 (2018)
19. Muhammad, K., Ahmad, J., Baik, S.W.: Early fire detection using convolutional neural networks during surveillance for effective disaster management. Neurocomputing **288**(2), 30–42 (2018)
20. Pham, H.V., Moore, P., Tran, K.D.: Context matching with reasoning and decision support using hedge algebra with Kansei evaluation. In: Proceedings of the fifth symposium on Information and Communication Technology (SoICT 2014), Hanoi, Vietnam, 4–5 December 2014, pp. 202–210 (2014)
21. Moore, P., Pham, H.V.: Intelligent context with decision support under uncertainty. In: Second International Workshop on Intelligent Context-Aware Systems (ICAS 2012), pp. 977–982 (2012)

22. Van Pham, H., Moore, P.: Emergency service provision using a novel hybrid SOM-spiral STC model for group decision support under dynamic uncertainty. Appl. Sci. **9**, 3910 (2019)
23. Image data sets in Berkely Univ. Libaray. https://people.eecs.berkeley.edu/yang/software/lossy_segmentation
24. Image forest data sets. https://earthengine.google.com/timelapse

Enhancing the Control Performance of Automatic Voltage Regulator for Marine Synchronous Generator by Using Interactive Adaptive Fuzzy Algorithm

Xuan-Kien Dang[1]([⊠]), Viet-Dung Do[1,2], Van-Tinh Do[1], and Le Anh-Hoang Ho[3]

[1] Ho Chi Minh City University of Transport, Ho Chi Minh City, Vietnam
dangxuankien@hcmutrans.edu.vn
[2] Dong An Polytechnic, Dĩ An, Vietnam
[3] Van Hien University, Ho Chi Minh City, Vietnam

Abstract. Currently, Adaptive Fuzzy Control is considered the most effective tool in the nonlinear control system. In this paper, we studied an automatic voltage regulator (AVR) system based on the Interactive Adaptive Fuzzy Algorithm (IAFA) to change the field excitation of the synchronous generator maintaining constant terminal voltage under the effect of unknown disturbances. The Fuzzy function calibrates the AVR controller to adapt to the varying output voltage of the generator, and its performance was compared with that of the recently used tuning methods for the same system configuration and operating conditions to validate the effectiveness of the proposed method. The results show that the proposed AVR-based IAFA method outperformed its conventional counterparts in terms of stability voltage response brings us high performance in simulation and experiment.

Keywords: Adaptive fuzzy control · Automatic voltage regulator · Interactive adaptive · Synchronous generator · Varying output voltage

1 Introduction

The certainty that electricity is now crucial to the work of all marine equipment. The Ship Power System (SPS) is a kind of 'nervous system' because it is covering not only energy but also the automation of modes that allow it to control systems composed of numerous elements that exceed the perceptual abilities of the sailor [1]. Moreover, the technical requirements currently being deployed for the management system, energy, water, or economic operation of the ship have significantly increased requirements for class and dependability of power source. The Automatic Voltage Regulator (AVR) is a key component of the power system owing to the purpose of improving power system stability, power quality, and power system economics [2].

© ICST Institute for Computer Sciences, Social Informatics and Telecommunications Engineering 2021
Published by Springer Nature Switzerland AG 2021. All Rights Reserved
N.-S. Vo et al. (Eds.): INISCOM 2021, LNICST 379, pp. 379–392, 2021.
https://doi.org/10.1007/978-3-030-77424-0_31

In general, there are two important control systems on board that are steering system and electric power system. Many researchers are devoted to developing enhanced technology and artificial intelligence in the autopilot on the steering system for its outstanding advantages [3–8]. Numerous proposed advanced control solutions, including Fuzzy [3], Hybrid Fuzzy [4] and Fuzzy Adaptive [5, 6], Neural Network [7], and Recurrent Cerebellar Model Articulation [8], have demonstrated the effectiveness and stability of these algorithms. Meanwhile, many classic controllers such as PID and LQR are applied for the electric power system yet. Moreover, there are not too many studies on modern control theory applied to increase the quality of the electrical system on board, especially voltage stabilizers for generators.

Related to Synchronous Generator to ensure the quality of the electrical system, the adaptive control strategy is proposed in [9] for Virtual Synchronous Generator, and the optimal damping ratio of the controller is maintained to suppress the oscillation of power and frequency of the generator. The authors clarified the performance of the system enhanced since the response time and overshoots are optimized. In order to enhance the adaptability and robustness of induction generator, the adaptive nonlinear controller built by adding the estimated uncertainty value is designed [10] to improve the regulation performance of the system in case of grid faults and parameter uncertainty.

In recent years, Adaptive Fuzzy Control (AFC) has got a great extension and lots of novel results to deal with problems of uncertainty and disturbance of nonlinear system in works of literature [5, 6], and [11–15]. The research results all have the same conclusion that is AFC strategy can guarantee that all the signals in the closed-loop system which are bounded under a class of switching signals with average dead-time. Moreover, adaptive reliability guaranteed the control performance of uncertain nonlinear systems. This is the reason that motivates us to use the novel AFC strategy for Marine Synchronous Generator because it always has to work in the harsh conditions of the environment and working mode.

In this paper, we aimed to enhance the control performance of AVR for Marine Synchronous Generator by using Interactive Adaptive Fuzzy Algorithm (IAFA). We carefully designed the IAFA controller for reducing the effect of uncertain parameters and disturbances. The main contributions of this paper are given as follow:

(i)   We first built the Automatic Voltage Regulator Model and then given some Remark and Assumption.
(ii)   By simulation, we determined that the Fuzzy PID controller design for AVR is not highly feasible under impacts of the drop voltage or time-delay caused by the nonlinear characteristics. However, our suggested solution, one kind of Hybrid Fuzzy Interactive algorithm, is Interactive Adaptive Fuzzy Algorithm.
(iii) Interactive Adaptive Fuzzy Algorithm is designed. By using the error between the output signal of the AVR ideal model and the AVR actual model, the compensation controller is added to the model.
(iv)   Finally, the hardware is designed for the experiments.

The rest of the paper is organized as follows. Section 2 shows the design of automatic voltage regulator model and Sect. 3 describes the structure of the proposed IAFA.

Section 4 presents the simulation, experimental results, and discussions. Finally, the concluding remarks are given in Sect. 5.

2 Automatic Voltage Regulator Model

An automatic voltage regulator (AVR) maintains a constant voltage across the synchronous generator output at different load levels. This scheme is solved by adjusting the output voltage of the synchronous generator based on regulating the excitation voltage [16]. The AVR model consists of four main components: the amplifier, the exciter, the generator, and the sensor. A schematic diagram of the AVR total principle [17] is illustrated in Fig. 1.

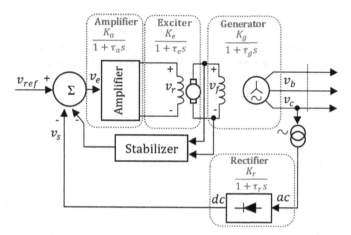

Fig. 1. The schematic diagram of the AVR total principle.

The Amplifier Model. v_e is the error voltage between the output voltage of the generator and the setpoint. Then the error $v_e = v_{ref} - v_s$ is amplified. The transfer function of the amplifier model is given by

$$G_a(s) = \frac{v_{ref}(s)}{v_e(s)} = \frac{K_a}{1 + \tau_a s} \tag{1}$$

Since the time constant τ_a of the stationary exciter is small, then the equivalent transfer function becomes the gain connected between the synchronous generator and the AVR controller [18]. Besides, K_a is the gain of the stationary exciter, used to adjust control signal.

The Exciter Model. The exciter model supplies the DC voltage to the excitation coil, which has a time constant τ_e and amplification coefficient K_e [19]. The excitation voltage v_r is performed to the excitation coil independent of the generator voltage. The v_f voltage is proportional to the output voltage of the synchronous generator. The transfer function of the exciter model is described below:

$$G_e(s) = \frac{v_f(s)}{v_r(s)} = \frac{K_e}{1 + \tau_e s} \tag{2}$$

The Generator Model. The output voltage of the synchronous generator depends on the excitation voltage v_f, the rotation speed of the traction motor, the load level, and the load characteristics [20]. The generator model consists of the time constants and gain constants of τ_g and K_g, respectively. The transfer function of the generator model is expressed as follows:

$$G_g(s) = \frac{v_t(s)}{v_f(s)} = \frac{K_g}{1 + \tau_g s} \tag{3}$$

The Rectifier Model. In the rectifier model, the transformer converts the AC voltage of the generator to a suitable AC voltage. Then, the rectifier transforms this voltage to DC voltage as the feedback signal (v_s) for the AVR system [21]. The transfer function of the rectifier model is described as

$$G_r(s) = \frac{v_s(s)}{v_t(s)} = \frac{K_r}{1 + \tau_r s} \tag{4}$$

Therefore, the transfer function of the AVR system is related to the generator output voltage $v_t(s)$ to the reference voltage $v_{ref}(s)$ defined as follows:

$$G(s) = \frac{v_t(s)}{v_{ref}(s)} = \frac{K_a K_e K_g K_r(1 + \tau_r s)}{(1 + \tau_a s)(1 + \tau_e s)(1 + \tau_g s)(1 + \tau_r s) + K_a K_e K_g K_r} \tag{5}$$

The open-loop transfer function of the AVR system can be rewritten as

$$K_g(s)H(s) = \frac{K_a K_e K_g K_r}{(1 + \tau_a s)(1 + \tau_e s)(1 + \tau_g s)(1 + \tau_r s)} \tag{6}$$

Remark: If the generator operates in the actual conditions under the characteristics of load-varying, the generator parameters will exhibit high nonlinearity.

Assumption: The excitation voltage usually remains in the fixed status. If the voltage drop occurs due to the load-varying characteristics, the output voltage is not stable. As such, the assumptions are more reasonable.

In this paper, the authors aim to suggest an Interactive Adaptive Fuzzy Algorithm for the AVR system under the condition of Assumptions. The goal is to keep the output voltage of the generator at precision level and stability, while the fuzzy function calibrates the AVR controller to adapt to the varying output voltage of the generator.

3   Interactive Adaptive Fuzzy Algorithm

3.1   Fuzzy PID Controller

Proportional-Integral-Derivative (PID) controllers are widely used in industrial applications, especially the AVR control systems [22–24]. This solution had the advantage of simple structural and stable output. However, these cover bounded activities without considering the voltage drop in the generator output. In this study, the authors propose a PID controller as the main controller whose transfer function is described as [23]

$$u_{PID}(s) = K_p + \frac{K_i}{s} + K_d s \tag{7}$$

To enhance the control quality of the AVR system, we propose the Fuzzy controller has a double-input $e(t)$, $de/d(t)$, and a triple-output, K_p, K_i and K_d [25]. The outputs of the fuzzy controller calibrate the coefficient K_p, K_i and K_d suitably, respectively. In this paper, the symbols {*NB, NBB, NS, NSS, ZE, PSS, PS, PBB, PB*} are the MFs notations, whose values correspond to big negative, near big negative, small negative, near small negative, zero, near small positive, small positive, near big positive and big positive. Thence, these fuzzy sets of the fuzzy controller are established as follows:

$$e = \{NB\ NBB\ NS\ NSS\ ZE\ PSS\ PS\ PBB\ PB\}$$
$$de/dt = \{NB\ NS\ ZE\ PS\ PB\}$$
$$K_p = \{ZE\ PSS\ PS\ PBB\ PB\}$$
$$K_i = \{ZE\ PSS\ PS\ PBB\ PB\}$$
$$K_d = \{ZE\ PSS\ PS\ PBB\ PB\}$$

The rule designation form B^i is a binary variable which makes out the rule consequence and B^i is expressed as

$$R_i : \text{If } \hat{e}_1 \text{ is } A_1^i \ \ldots \text{ and } \hat{e}_n \text{ is } A_n^i \text{ then } u \text{ is } B^i \tag{8}$$

where $A_1^i, A_2^i, \ldots A_n^i$ and B^i express the fuzzy sets. By applying the center average defuzzifier, the fuzzy response can be computed as

$$u_f = \frac{\sum_{i=1}^h B^i [\prod_{j=1}^n \mu_{A_j^i}(\hat{e}_j)]}{\sum_{i=1}^h [\prod_{j=1}^n \mu_{A_j^i}(\hat{e}_j)]} \tag{9}$$

for $\mu_{A_{kj}^i}(\hat{e}_j)$ is the membership functions, h is the number of If-Then rules [26, 27]. The fuzzy output can calibrate the K_p, K_i and K_d coefficients according to the error $e(t)$. The PID coefficients are calibrated by

$$\begin{cases} K_p(s) = K_p(s-1) + u_f(kp)\Delta K_p \\ K_i(s) = K_i(s-1) + u_f(ki)\Delta K_i \\ K_d(s) = K_d(s-1) + u_f(kd)\Delta K_d \end{cases} \tag{10}$$

Substituting Eq. 10 into Eq. 7, the Fuzzy PID (F-PID) controller [28] can be written as

$$u_{fPID}(s) = K_p(s)e(s) + K_i(s)\int_0^s e(s)ds + K_d(s)\frac{de(k)}{dk} \tag{11}$$

However, in case of the system is controlled by the F-PID controller under the impacts of the voltage drop out or time-delay, the system is obtained result is not highly feasible. Thus, we propose the Interactive Adaptive Fuzzy Algorithm to calibrate the AVRs response to adapt to the ideal model. Then, the operation mechanism of the IAFA solution begins in the continuation section and the adaptive fuzzy controller for the AVR model will be introduced in Fig. 2.

3.2 Interactive Adaptive Fuzzy Algorithm Solution

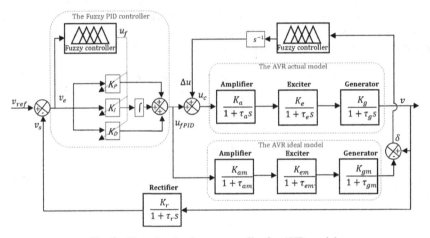

Fig. 2. The adaptive fuzzy controller for AVR model.

The weakness of the F-PID solution is only to carry out on the small range of input error. The control signal of the actual AVR model is adjusted by the adaptive coefficient Δu which is established by the fuzzy function [25]. The ideal model is given by

$$G_m(s) = \frac{K_{am}K_{em}K_{gm}}{(1+\tau_{am}s)(1+\tau_{em}s)(1+\tau_{gm}s)} \tag{12}$$

The adjustment performs corresponding to the error δ, i.e., the error between the output signal of the AVR ideal model and the AVR actual model. The error δ is computed as follows:

$$\delta = \left(\frac{K_aK_eK_g}{(1+\tau_a s)(1+\tau_e s)(1+\tau_g s)}\right)u_c - \left(\frac{K_{am}K_{em}K_{gm}}{(1+\tau_{am}s)(1+\tau_{em}s)(1+\tau_{gm}s)}\right)u_{fPID} \tag{13}$$

Table 1. The rules for Δu adaptive adjustment

Δu		$d\delta/d(t)$		
		Ns	Ze	Ps
$\delta(t)$	Ne	$Ne_{\Delta u}$	$Nss_{\Delta u}$	$Ns_{\Delta u}$
	Ns	$Nss_{\Delta u}$	$Ns_{\Delta u}$	$Ze_{\Delta u}$
	Ze	$Ns_{\Delta u}$	$Ze_{\Delta u}$	$Ps_{\Delta u}$
	Ps	$Ze_{\Delta u}$	$Ps_{\Delta u}$	$Pss_{\Delta u}$
	Po	$Ps_{\Delta u}$	$Pss_{\Delta u}$	$Po_{\Delta u}$

The control signal of the actual model is defined as

$$u_c = u_{fPID} + \Delta u \tag{14}$$

Coefficient Δu defines the adaptive adjustment force. It is well calibrated to remove the error of the actual model. In this paper, we apply the fuzzy control consisting of double-input: the error $\delta(s)$, and the velocity error $d\delta/ds$ for defining the Δu adaptive force. The fuzzy rules with 15 rules for Δu adaptive adjustment is given in Table 1.

The IAFA proposed aims to remove the error value δ. The control signal of the AVR actual model corrects Δu to adapt to the AVR ideal model. That is, $\delta \to 0$ when $t \to \infty$, respectively.

$$\left(\frac{K_a K_e K_g}{(1 + \tau_a s)(1 + \tau_e s)\left(1 + \tau_g s\right)}\right) u_c = \left(\frac{K_{am} K_{em} K_{gm}}{(1 + \tau_{am} s)(1 + \tau_{em} s)\left(1 + \tau_{gm} s\right)}\right) u_{fPID} \tag{15}$$

4 Simulations and Experiments

4.1 Configuration Parameter

In this paper, we accomplish the simulation of the designed model in the same parameters and conditions of AVRs in two cases, employed by using Matlab 2019a software. The simulation result shows the comparisons between the IAFA and the others strengthening

Table 2. The structure parameters for AVR model

Components	Range of coefficient	Selection value
Amplifier	$10 < K_a < 400; 0.02 < \tau_a < 0.1s$	$K_a = 10; \tau_a = 0.1$
Exciter	$1 < K_e < 400; 0.4 < \tau_e < 1s$	$K_e = 1; \tau_e = 0.4$
Generator	$0.7 < K_g < 1; 1 < \tau_g < 2s$	$K_g = 1; \tau_g = 0.4$
Rectifier	$0.001 < \tau_r < 0.06s$	$K_r = 1; \tau_r = 0.01$

the performance of the novel method. The IAFA solution (express in Sect. 3) with the adaptive goal (define at Eq. 15) performs on the AVR model, whose operation parameters are supplied by Table 2 [22] as

In case 1, the IAFA and others control, both methods are achieved the output voltage of the ship generator to the expected value (380 voltage) in around 100 s. This case performs the simulations under both non-disturbance and disturbance conditions. In case 2, we apply these solutions to adjust the output voltage down to 350 voltage from the current level is 380 voltage in the time range of the 50s to 100s. The simulation results are outlined in Figs. 3, 4, and Fig. 5 show that the IAFA (red line), F-PID (blue line), and PID (black line) can maintain the stability of the output voltage of the ship generator to the desired voltage. The disturbance vectors [29] take into account as $d(t) = J^T(\psi)b$ with the first-order Markov process that expresses the disturbances. In which, b shows the disturbance impacts with $b(0) = [0KN.m]^T$, and $T \epsilon R^{3 \times 3}$ expresses the diagonal matrix of time constant, $\omega \epsilon R^3$ is a zero-mean Gaussian white noise vector, and $\psi = 3 \times 10^2$ is the diagonal magnitude matrix of ω.

$$\dot{b} = -T^{-1}b + \psi\omega \qquad (16)$$

4.2   Simulation Results

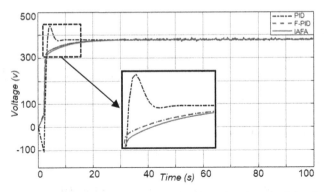

Fig. 3. The AVR response of simulation cases 1 without disturbance. (Color figure online)

The results comparisons of the AVR controllers demonstrate that the IAFA solution guarantees a stable response in every simulation case under disturbance impacts. After doing so, the proposed IAFA meets the questions according to Assumption and Remark. In the case of using a PID controller, the overshoot value is larger than the others. The classical solution cannot see the engineering requirements under disturbances operations. Besides this, the F-PID solution supplies a good performance within the limited range of disturbance. However, the F-PID results are not satisfactory in the case of the drop voltage impact. By using the IAFA solution, the output voltage does not fluctuate according to the disturbance impact. The erroneous is inside of the limited range. In the drop voltage, the response fluctuates in lower case and follow-up the desired value. The proposed

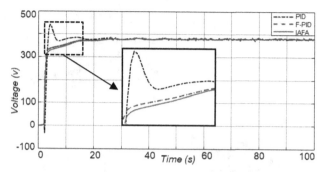

Fig. 4. The AVR response of simulation cases 1 with disturbance. (Color figure online)

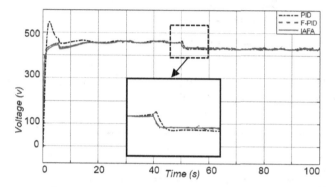

Fig. 5. The AVR responses of simulation cases 2.

IAFA has significantly enhanced the performance quality deal with the fluctuation level and erroneous.

4.3 AVR Experimental Model

We build the embedding IAFA controller on the AVR experimental model [30], which's structure and specification present in Fig. 6. The control program has been applied in full by Matlab software. This real-time controller realizes the control program directly into the STM32F4 Kit by the C+ software compiled. The STM32F4 Kit receives the setpoint value from the computer. Then the center processing compares it with the actual value to find the established error. Based on the established error, the IAFA real-time controller computes the control command for the AVR operation to keep the output voltage stable. The control signal converts into a corresponding voltage that acts as an IGBT firing angle. The amplitude of the IGBT firing angle will change the excitation voltage (0–72 VDC).

We experiment with the proposed solution in two cases. In case 1, the IAFA and F-PID solutions control the output voltage to reach a 180 VAC level around 100s. These experimental results are given the expression in detail by Figs. 7 and 8. Also, we apply these controllers to regulate the AC voltage of the ship generator down to the 150 VAC

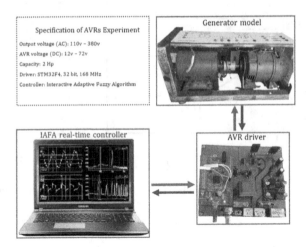

Fig. 6. The AVR experimental model

level at the 50th second. Figure 9 and 10 reveal that the proposed IAFA can correct the output voltage to achieve the desired level.

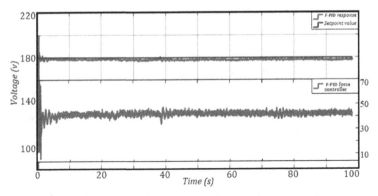

Fig. 7. The F-PID responses for the experiment cases 1

The output voltage is not feasible if the AVR applies the F-PID solution (described in Fig. 7). However, the proposed IAFA (expressed in Fig. 8) showing the result is less overshoot and more stable. In case 2, it is worth noting that the fluctuation of the IAFA is less than the F-PID at the switching time. The satisfactory results confirm that the IAFA can adapt to the disturbance impacts in the actual condition.

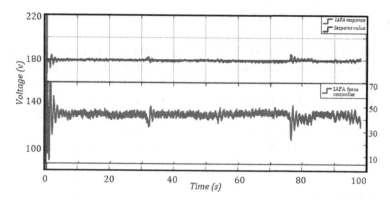

Fig. 8. The IAFA responses for the experiment cases 1

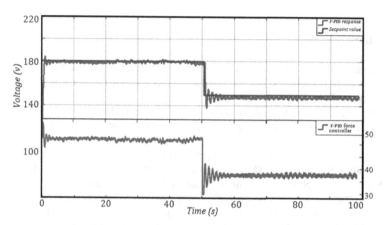

Fig. 9. The F-PID responses for the experiment cases 2

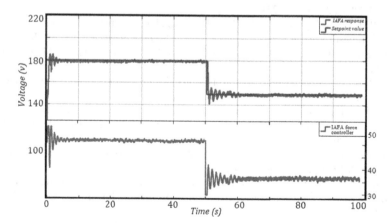

Fig. 10. The IAFA responses for the experiment cases 2

5 Conclusions

In this paper, we proposed the novel automatic voltage regulator model by combining the F-PID controller and Fuzzy controller to create the interactive adapt to adjust the field excitation of the ship's generator maintained the stable of voltage under the effect of disturbances. In case the amount of load-varying or voltage drops occur in the running process, the simulation and experiment demonstrated that the system attained the lowest fluctuation, and the IAFA can keep the voltage stable for a long time. The satisfactory results indicate that the IAFA is a promising study direction for maritime generator control in the actual operation.

Acknowledgements. This study was supported by the Applied Basic Research Program of Ministry of Transport of Vietnam DT203039 (2020).

References

1. Grzeczka, G., Piłat, T., Polak, A.: The parameters of excitation current of ship synchronous generator as the diagnostic symptoms of the propelling IC engine. J. Mar. Eng. Technol. **16**(4), 344–348 (2017)
2. Saravanan, G., Ibrahim, M.: Enhanced chaotic grasshopper optimization algorithm based PID controller for automatic voltage regulator system. Int. J. Recent Technol. Eng. **8**(4), 348–354 (2019)
3. Dang, X.K., Ho, L.A.H., Do, V.D.: Analyzing the sea weather effects to the ship maneuvering in Vietnam's Sea from BinhThuan province to Ca Mau province based on fuzzy control method. TELKOMNIKA (Telecommun. Comput. Electron. Control) **16**(2), 533–543 (2018)
4. Do, V.D., Dang, X.K.: The fuzzy particle swarm optimization algorithm design for dynamic positioning system under unexpected impacts. J. Mech. Eng. Sci. **13**(3), 5407–5423 (2019)
5. Dang, X.K., Truong, H.N., Nguyen, V.C., Pham, T.D.A.: Applying convolutional neural networks for limited-memory application. TELKOMNIKA (Telecommun. Comput. Electron. Control) **19**(1), 244–251 (2021)
6. Ta, V.P., Dang, X.K., Dong, V.H., Do, V.D.: Designing dynamic positioning system based on H∞ robust recurrent cerebellar model articulation controller. In: The 4th International Conference on Green Technology and Sustainable Development, Ho Chi Minh, Vietnam, pp. 652–658 (2018)
7. Dang, X.K., Do, V.D., Nguyen, X.P.: Robust adaptive fuzzy control using genetic algorithm for dynamic positioning system. IEEE Access **8**, 222077–222092 (2020)
8. Do, V.D., Dang, X.K.: Fuzzy adaptive interactive algorithm design for marine dynamic positioning system under unexpected impacts of Vietnam Sea. Indian J. Geo-Mar. Sci. **49**(11), 1764–1771 (2020)
9. Wang, F., Zhang, L., Feng, X.Y., Guo, H.: An adaptive control strategy for virtual synchronous generator. IEEE Trans. Ind. Appl. **54**(5), 5124–5133 (2020)
10. Mauricio, J.M., León, A.E., Antonio, G.E., Solsona, J.A.: An adaptive nonlinear controller for DFIM-based wind energy conversion systems. IEEE Trans. Energy Convers. **23**(4), 1025–1035 (2008)
11. Nguyen, S.D., Vo, H.D., Seo, T.T.: Nonlinear adaptive control based on fuzzy sliding mode technique and fuzzy-based compensator. ISA Trans. **70**, 309–321 (2017)
12. Wang, W., Tong, S.: Adaptive fuzzy bounded control for consensus of multiple strict-feedback nonlinear systems. IEEE Trans. Cyber. **48**(2), 522–531 (2017)

13. Tran, H.K., Chiou, J.S., Nguyen, T.N., Vo, T.: Adaptive fuzzy control method for a single tilt tricopter. IEEE Access **7**, 161741–161747 (2019)
14. Huo, X., Ma, L., Zhao, X.D., Zong, G.D.: Event-triggered adaptive fuzzy output feedback control of MIMO switched nonlinear systems with average dwell time. Appl. Math. Comput. **365**, 1–16 (2020)
15. Ma, L., Huo, X., Zhao, X.D., Zong, G.D.: Adaptive fuzzy tracking control for a class of uncertain switched nonlinear systems with multiple constraints: a small gain approach. Int. J. Fuzzy Syst. **21**, 2609–2624 (2019)
16. Zhang, Z., Liu, Y.H.: Stochastic small signal stability analysis of power system with automatic voltage regulator. In: Proceedings of the 36th Chinese Control Conference, Dalian, China, pp. 1907–1912 (2017)
17. Ayasun, S., UlaG, E.L., Sönmez, F.: Computation of stability delay margin of time-delayed generator excitation control system with a stabilizing transformer. Math. Probl. Eng. **2014**, 1–10 (2014)
18. Sonawane, P.R., Karvekar, S.S.: Optimization of PID controller for automatic voltage regulator system. In: Proceedings of the IEEE 2017 International Conference on Computing Methodologies and Communication, Erode, India, pp. 318–323 (2017)
19. Gozde, H., Taplamacioğlu, M.C., Ari, M.: Automatic Voltage Regulator (AVR) design with chaotic particle swarm optimization. In: Proceedings of ECAI 2014 - International Conference – 6th Edition, Bucharest, România, pp. 23–26 (2014)
20. Satpathi, K., Ukil, A., Pou, J., Zagrodnik, M.D.: Design, analysis and comparison of automatic flux regulator with automatic voltage regulator based generation system for DC marine vessels. IEEE Trans. Transp. Electrif. **4**(3), 694–706 (2018)
21. Sahu, J., Satapathy, P., Debnath, M.K., Mohanty, P.K., Sahu, B.K., Padhi, J.R.: Automatic voltage regulator design based on fractional calculus plus PID controller. In: Proceedings of 2020 International Conference on Computational Intelligence for Smart Power System and Sustainable Energy, Odisha, India (2020)
22. Puralachetty, M.M., Pamula, V.K., Akula, V.N.B.: Comparison of different optimization algorithms with two stage initialization for PID controller tuning in automatic voltage regulator system. In: Proceedings of the 2016 IEEE Students' Technology Symposium, Kharagpur, India, pp. 152–156 (2016)
23. Salih, A.M., Humod, A.Th., Hasan, F.A.: Optimum design for PID-ANN controller for automatic voltage regulator of synchronous generator. In: Proceedings of 4th Scientific International Conference Najaf (SICN), Al-Najef, Iraq, pp. 74–79 (2016)
24. Priyambada, S., Mohanty, P.K.: Performance evaluation of DEPSO algorithm on automatic voltage regulator using conventional PID & Fuzzy-PID controller. In: Proceedings of 2015 International Conference on Energy, Power and Environment: Towards Sustainable Growth (ICEPE), Shillong, India (2015)
25. Do, V.D., Dang, X.K., Le, A.T.: Fuzzy adaptive interactive algorithm for rig balancing optimization. In: International Conference on Recent Advances in Signal Processing, Telecommunication and Computing, Danang, Vietnam, pp. 143–148 (2017)
26. Sharma, R., Gopal, M.: A Markov game-adaptive fuzzy controller for robot manipulators. IEEE Trans. Fuzzy Syst. **16**(1), 171–186 (2008)
27. Do, V.-D., Dang, X.-K., Huynh, L.-T., Ho, V.-C.: Optimized multi-cascade fuzzy model for ship dynamic positioning system based on genetic algorithm. In: Duong, T.Q., Vo, N.-S., Nguyen, L.K., Vien, Q.-T., Nguyen, V.-D. (eds.) INISCOM 2019. LNICSSITE, vol. 293, pp. 165–180. Springer, Cham (2019). https://doi.org/10.1007/978-3-030-30149-1_14
28. Dang, X.K., Guan, Z.H., Li, T., Zhang, D.X.: Joint smith predictor and neural network estimation scheme for compensating randomly varying time-delay in networked control system. In: Proceedings of the 24th Chinese Control and Decision Conference, Tai Yuan, China, pp. 512–517 (2012)

29. Hu, X., Du, J., Shi, J.: Adaptive fuzzy controller design for dynamic positioning system of vessels. Appl. Ocean Res. **53**, 46–53 (2015)
30. Bal, G., Kaplan, O., Yalcin, S.S.: Artificial neural network based automatic voltage regulator for a stand-alone synchronous generator. In: Proceedings of 8th International Conference on Renewable Energy Research and Applications, Brasov, Romania, pp. 1032–1037 (2019)

Flood Prediction Using Multilayer Perceptron Networks and Long Short-Term Memory Networks at Thu Bon-Vu Gia Catchment, Vietnam

Duy Vu Luu[1], Thi Ngoc Canh Doan[2], Khanh Le Nguyen[2], and Ngoc Duong Vo[3(✉)]

[1] The University of Danang – University of Technology and Education,
48 Cao Thang, Danang, Vietnam
ldvu@ute.udn.vn

[2] The University of Danang – University of Economics, Danang, Vietnam
{canhdtn,khanh.le}@due.edu.vn

[3] The University of Danang – University of Science and Technology, Danang, Vietnam
vnduong@dut.udn.vn

Abstract. There is a significant change in the amplitude of rainfall between the rainy season and the dry season at Thu Bon-Vu Gia catchment in Vietnam. 65% to 80% of the annual rainfall is in the rainy season. Therefore, Thu Bon - Vu Gia catchment is a highly flood prone region. Floods frequently occur in this area and destroy critical infrastructure. This study compares Multilayer Perceptron (MLP) networks and Long Short-Term Memory (LSTM) networks in forecasting floods at Thu Bon-Vu Gia catchment. Discharges at the downstream point are predicted by utilizing periodic rainfall and flow data at upstream locations. Both models do not use other hydrologic, geological and meteorological data, which have low quality at the study site. Both models are reliable to forecast the flood in the catchment when the values of RMSE and NSE of the models are about 320 m^3/s and 0.5 respectively.

Keywords: Multilayer Perceptron (MLP) · Long Short-Term Memory (LSTM) · Thu Bon-Vu Gia catchment

1 Introduction

Floods create large social, economic, and environmental disruption, adversely affecting both individuals and communities. For example, in 2007, the flood in Quang Nam province, Vietnam caused approximately US$ 53 million worth of property and crop damage [1]. To help people better respond to floods appropriately, hydrological models, such as forecasting flood ones, are considered one of the workable solutions [2].

There are three types of hydrological models, comprising conceptual models, physical models and empirical models in which each model has its own advantages and

N.-S. Vo et al. (Eds.): INISCOM 2021, LNICST 379, pp. 393–402, 2021.
https://doi.org/10.1007/978-3-030-77424-0_32

disadvantages. First, conceptual models are suitable to predict floods in different phys-iographic regions, even ungauged catchments [3]. Second, physical models offer deep insight into real hydrological systems [3] and require large volumes of accurate data, such as meteorological and hydrological data. Third, without analyzing hydrological processes, empirical models are able to simulate relationships between inputs and out-puts by utilizing mathematical equations. Therefore, the empirical models are suitable for this catchment because they do not require many kinds of data, such as geological and meteorological data, which have low quality at the study site.

In empirical models, various architectures and algorithms are adopted in forecasting floods. As mentioned by Thirumalaiah and Deo [4], all training algorithms should be tested in a specific condition to ensure their validity. Meanwhile, currently, there is a lack of applications of neural networks to Thu Bon-Vu Gia catchment. Therefore, this paper aims to compare the prediction ability of the LSTM model and the MLP model which are empirical models at the area.

2 Study Area and Data

The Thu Bon-Vu Gia river system is one of the largest river systems in Vietnam. The catchment area is over 10,000 km^2, partly meeting water requirements of Quang Nam province and Da Nang city. However, frequent floods and droughts in the Thu Bon-Vu Gia river system make water supplies come under increased stress. Furthermore, natural disasters cause 6.3% damage to Quang Nam province's GDP annually, even 20% in years with severe floods [5].

The paper aims to establish a model to generate discharge from rainfall at Nong Son gauging station in the catchment. Due to insufficiency of rainfall and discharge data for less than 24 h in this catchment, we use daily data provided by the Mid-Central Region

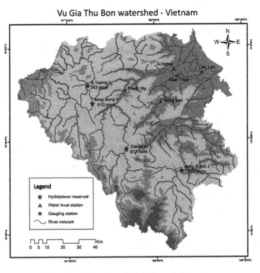

Fig. 1. Thu Bon-Vu Gia catchment.

Centre for Hydrometeorological Forecasting, which are normalized before being used. The input data include rainfall data in Tra My, Nong Son, Tien Phuoc and Hiep Duc station, and discharge data in Nong Son station from 1991 to 2010 (Fig. 1).

3 Methodology

3.1 Introduction to MLP

MLP has been popular in recent years. It has a wide range of applications, such as handwritten character recognition [6]. It includes an input layer, an output layer, and one or more hidden layers. This technique does not include any direct data-flow loop.

The nodes in the layers are fully or partially connected to each other. The relationships between nodes are presented by the weights. In the input layer, the nodes receive input data. In the hidden layers, input data of a node is multiplied by the weight and then added with a bias value. It is then transferred via an activation function. The outcome is sent to the output layer (Fig. 2).

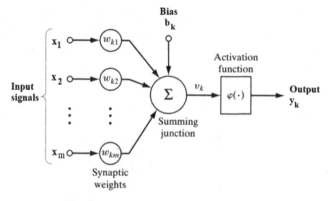

Fig. 2. An MLP with one hidden layer [7]

The operation of a node k at the hidden layers is calculated as:

$$I_k = \sum w_{ki} x_i + b_k \tag{1}$$

$$y_k = \varphi(I_k) \tag{2}$$

in which y_k is the output of the node k; φ is an activation function; x_i is an input i of the node k; w_{ki} is the weight; b_k is the weight.

There are some kinds of the activation function, such as Log-sigmoid transfer function, Hyperbolic tangent transfer function, and Purelin transfer function Training.

To modify the weight values, the backpropagation through time (BPTT) algorithm is recommended. There are four main steps in BPTT. First, the initial weight values are generated randomly. Second, the weight values are used to produce the output values.

Third, the error values between the observed outputs and modeled outputs are calculated as

$$E = \frac{1}{2}(Y_{obs} - Y_{mod})^2 \tag{3}$$

where E is the global error function; Y_{obs} is the observed output; Y_{mod} is the modeled output. Finally, the error values are used to adjust weights to minimize the error. The gradient of the error term is calculated as the formula (4). The model parameters are modified using the gradient descent rule as the formula (5).

$$\frac{\partial E}{\partial W} = \sum_{t=1}^{T} \frac{\partial E_t}{\partial W} \tag{4}$$

$$W \leftarrow W - \alpha \frac{\partial E}{\partial W} \tag{5}$$

3.2   Introduction to Long Short-Term Memory

Recurrent Neural Networks (RNN) has developed since the 1980s. It's applications range from generating text [8], language modeling [9] to forecasting time series [10]. The RNN model builds a directed cycle based on connections among nodes. It helps the RNN model remember prior important information in the data.

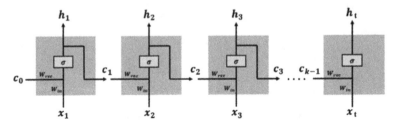

Fig. 3. Unfolding of recurrent neural networks [11]

A basic RNN model shown in Fig. 3 includes one input layer, one hidden layer and one output layer. At time step t, the model input includes an input x_t and a network state c_{t-1} storing previous information. Afterwards they are transferred to the hidden layer. Weight matrices, W_{rec} and W_{in}, go with c_{t-1} and x_t respectively. The activation function is the sigmoid function in the hidden layer. The output h_t is used to calculate the prediction error E. Next, a backpropagation through time (BPTT) training algorithm is also used to update the weight matrices.

BPTT has two common problems, which are the vanishing gradient and the exploding gradient. While the vanishing gradient makes the gradient quickly move to zero, the exploding gradient causes the parameters become too large.

LSTM, a kind of RNN, is recommended to help the model avoid the vanishing gradient problem. LSTM is applied in many topics, from prediction to face detection.

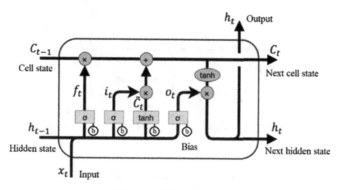

Fig. 4. LSTM cell [11]

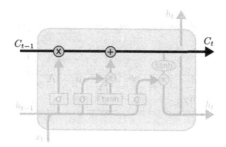

Fig. 5. Cell state in LSTM [11].

LSTM can remember prior important things and forget unnecessary information [12]. A basic LSTM model has three gates: an input gate, an output gate and a forget gate. The gates have different weights and biases (Figs. 4 and 5).

In the forget gate, f_t, input, h_{t-1} and x_t, are passed or forgot. Output of this gate being from 0 to 1 is computed as

$$f_t = \sigma(W_t.[h_{t-1}, x_t] + b_i) \tag{6}$$

where σ is the sigmoid function; w_t is the weight value; h_{t-1} is output of the module at the last time $(t-1)$; x_t is input at time t, and b_i is the bias value. When f_t is 1, the module completely stores the whole information. In contrast, when f_t is 0, the module completely forgets the received information (Fig. 6).

The input gate controls what information is transferred to the cell state. The output is determined by using the following equations:

$$i_t.\tilde{C}_t = \sigma(W_i.[h_{t-1}, x_t] + b_i) \cdot tanh(W_c.[h_{t-1}, x_t] + b_c \tag{7}$$

$$C_t = f_t \cdot C_{t-1} + i_t \cdot C_t \tag{8}$$

where C_t and C_{t-1} are the cell states at time t and t−1 respectively (Fig. 7).

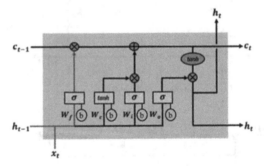

Fig. 6. The *LSTM forget gate* [11].

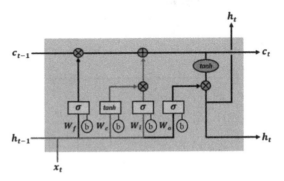

Fig. 7. The LSTM input gate [11].

The output gate controls the data flow in the cell state transferred to the next step. The output value, h_t, is computed as

$$h_t = O_i \tanh(C_t) \tag{9}$$

$$O_t = \sigma(W_0[h_{t-1}, x_t] + b_0] \tag{10}$$

where b_o is the bias value; and W_o is the weight value at the output gate (Fig. 8).

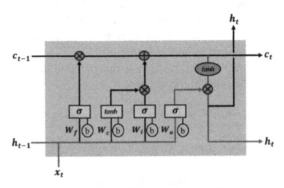

Fig. 8. The LSTM output gate [11].

4 Model Development

The research builds both the MLP model and the LSTM model. They generate the daily discharge data from the daily rainfall data in the catchment between 1991 and 2010. The rainfall data at Tra My, Tien Phuoc, Hiep Duc and Nong Son station, and the discharge data at Nong Son station are divided into three parts, namely training, validation and testing set. The training process uses the training data set (from 1991 to 2008) to generate a relationship between rainfall and discharge. The validation process aims to evaluate how well the current model performs while tuning the parameters of the models. The validation process uses the data from 2008 to 2009. It also helps control the learning rate, avoid overfitting, and select a model among different trained models. Finally, the last year (2010), which is the testing set, is used for performance evaluation.

This paper adopts Python being an open source programming language with libraries, namely Numpy, Pandas, Matpolib, Math and Keras.

4.1 Model Training and Evaluation

There are some aspects that this paper carefully considers while training the models. First, it is the hyperparameters selection including learning rate, timesteps, the number of input neurons, hidden layers, batch size, and epochs. Second, during the training process, overfitting is considered as a serious problem. Dropout regularization is a brilliant solution to prevent the model from overfitting [13]. Finally, both models are Adam which is the optimization algorithm. Adam is a recommended way to update the weights iteratively when it has different successful applications, such as computer vision [14] and natural language processing [15]. The algorithm is computationally efficient, also requires little memory. The trial and error method is adopted to choose the suitable hyperparameters, based on the model evaluation criteria. The training process is repeated and stopped when the evaluation criteria reach an acceptable value.

The Nash–Sutcliffe model efficiency coefficient (NSE) and Root Mean Square Error (RMSE) are used as the model evaluation criteria. NSE is used to indicate the efficiency of the model. The value of NSE ranges from $-\infty$ to 1. NSE value getting closer to 1 indicates a perfect model with an estimation error variance equal to zero. The RMSE measures the differences between the modeled values and the observed values. The RMSD value is always non-negative. If the value of RMSE is 0, it is a perfect fit to the data.

$$NSE = 1 - \frac{\sum_{i=1}^{n}(\hat{y}_t - y_t)}{\sum_{i=1}^{n}(\hat{y}_t - \bar{y}_t)} \tag{11}$$

$$RMSE = \sqrt{\frac{1}{n}\sum_{i=1}^{n}(\hat{y}_t - y_t)} \tag{12}$$

Where $\hat{y}_t$ is observed discharges, y_t is modeled discharges, and $\bar{y}_t$ is mean of observed discharges at time t.

4.2 Validation Results

In the validation, the project uses the values of RMSE and NSE to find the optimal LSTM and MLP models from the proposed models with the different hyperparameters (Table 1).

Table 1. The selected LSTM models and MPL model

Items	The LSTM model	The MPL model
Timesteps	6 days	5 days
The number of hidden layers	1	1
Training parameter	- Learning rate: 0.001 - The number of epochs: 138 - batch_size: 73 - Dropout rate: 0.1 - Early stopping: yes	- Learning rate: 0.001 - The number of epochs: 93 - batch_size: 73 - Dropout rate: 0.1 - Early stopping: yes
The number of neurons at input, hidden, and output layer	5, 4, and 1	5, 7, and 1

4.3 Test Results

The above selected models use the unseen testing dataset, the year 2010, to evaluate their forecasting ability. The data in 2010 is selected for testing because a historic flood occurred in November 2010. The comparison between two models is shown in Table 2 and Fig. 9. The values of RMSE are not high, about $320 \ m^3/s$ compared to the maximum peak discharge of $6,520 \ m^3/s$. The values of NSE are closer to 1. Moreover, there are small differences in the model evaluation criteria between both models.

Table 2. The results of the models in the testing phase.

Model	RMSE (m^3/s)	NSE	Modeled peak (m^3/s)	Observed peak (m^3/s)	Error (%)
LSTM	321.607	0.524	6,262	6,520	4
MLP	315.172	0.592	6,064	6,520	7

Figure 9 illustrates the relationship between the modeled discharges and the observed data from January 1991 to December 2010. There are similar trends among the observed data and modeled data. Both the LSTM and MLP model have the ability to produce the same pattern with the observation in the catchment. They also capture the flood peak. The modeled peak flow rate is closer to the observed data, $6,262.3 \ m^3/s$ and $6,520 \ m^3/s$ respectively on 16th November 2010.

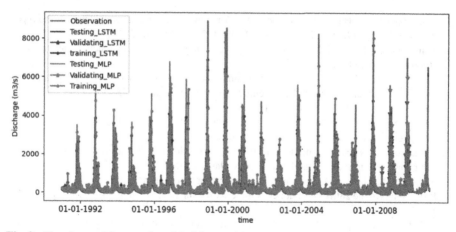

Fig. 9. The observed flows and modeled flows at Nong Son station in the training, validating and testing phase from January 1991 to December 2010.

However, the LSTM and MLP models often underestimate the historical flood peaks. The reason can be from operation of reservoirs, which makes discharge unexpectedly bigger in the points on flood events. Therefore, the next research should consider the reservoir operation in this catchment.

5   Conclusion

This study develops and compares the ability of the LSTM and MLP models to forecast discharge in Thu Bon-Vu Gia catchment. It proves that both LSTM and MLP have the same ability to forecast floods in the catchment.

They require only rainfall and discharge data, but they can produce accurate results. These models are good solutions because they do not require many kinds of data, which have low quality in the catchment. Moreover, although there are differences between the modeled data and the observed data, both models are useful for giving early warning in the catchment.

Operation of reservoirs effecting the results should be considered in future studies.

Acknowledgment. This research is funded by University of Technology and Education - The University of Danang under the project number T2020-06-155.

References

1. Navrud, S., Tran, T., Tinh, B.: Estimating the welfare loss to households from natural disasters in developing countries: a contingent valuation study of flooding in Vietnam. Glob. Health Action **5**, 17609 (2012)
2. Yoshimura, K., et al.: Development of flood forecasting system over Japan and application to 2018 Japan floods event. In: Geophysical Research Abstracts, vol. 21 (2019)

3. Jajarmizadeh, M., Harun, S., Salarpour, M.: A review on theoretical consideration and types of models in hydrology. J. Environ. Sci. Technol. **5**(5), 249–261 (2012)

4. Thirumalaiah, K., Deo, M.: River stage forecasting using artificial neural networks. J. Hydrolog. Eng. **3**(1), 26–32 (1998)

5. Chau, V., Cassells, S., Holland, J.: Economic impact upon agricultural production from extreme flood events in Quang Nam, central Vietnam. Nat. Hazards **75**(2), 1747–1765 (2014). https://doi.org/10.1007/s11069-014-1395-x

6. Pal, A., Singh, D.: Handwritten English character recognition using neural network. Int. J. Comput. Sci. Commun. **1**(2), 141–144 (2010)

7. Choi, M.: [ANN] Making model for binary classification (2018). https://www.kaggle.com/mirichoi0218/ann-making-model-for-binary-classification

8. Sutskever, I., Martens, J., Hinton, G.E.: Generating text with recurrent neural networks. In: Proceedings of the 28th International Conference on Machine Learning (ICML-11), pp. 1017–1024 (2011)

9. Mikolov, T., Zweig, G.: Context dependent recurrent neural network language model. In: 2012 IEEE Spoken Language Technology Workshop (SLT), pp. 234–239. IEEE (2012)

10. Rout, A.K., Dash, P., Dash, R., Bisoi, R.: Forecasting financial time series using a low complexity recurrent neural network and evolutionary learning approach. J. King Saud Univ.-Comput. Inf. Sci. **29**(4), 536–552 (2017)

11. Arbel, N.: How LSTM networks solve the problem of vanishing gradients (2018). https://medium.com/datadriveninvestor/how-do-lstm-networks-solve-the-problem-of-vanishing-gradients-a6784971a577

12. Yuan, Q., Wei, S.: Aligning network traffic for serial consistency and anomalies with a customized LSTM model. In: 2018 IEEE International Conference on Progress in Informatics and Computing (PIC), pp. 322–326. IEEE (2018)

13. Srivastava, N., Hinton, G., Krizhevsky, A., Sutskever, I., Salakhutdinov, R.: Dropout: a simple way to prevent neural networks from overfitting. J. Mach. Learn. Res. **15**(1), 1929–1958 (2014)

14. Liu, Z., Cao, Y., Wang, Y., Wang, W.: Computer vision-based concrete crack detection using U-net fully convolutional networks. Autom. Constr. **104**, 129–139 (2019)

15. Radford, A., Narasimhan, K., Salimans, T., Sutskever, I.: Improving language understanding by generative pre-training (2018). https://s3-us-west-2.amazonaws.com/openai-assets/researchcovers/languageunsupervised/languageunderstandingpaper.pdf

Fast and Simple Method for Weapon Target Assignment in Air Defense Command and Control System

Nguyen Xuan Truong[1]($\boxtimes$), Phung Kim Phuong[1], and Vu Hoa Tien[2]

[1] Institute of System Integration, Le Quy Don Technical University, Hanoi, Vietnam
truongnx.isi@lqdtu.edu.vn

[2] Faculty of Control Engineering, Le Quy Don Technical University, Hanoi, Vietnam

Abstract. The assignment problem is a fundamental optimization problem which can be applied in many real-life automation tasks including weapon target assignment (WTA) as a basic functional module of automated command and control centers. The WTA problem is a class of optimization problems in the field of optimization and operation research. It consists of finding an optimal assignment of a set of weapons of various types to a set of targets in order to maximize the total expected damage to the opponent. In this paper, we propose an optimal air target distribution method in a mixed air defense cluster scenario. Our mathematical formulation is built with both weapons units and targets which are diverse in types in the practical complex anti-aircraft combat conditions. Then, we proposed a method based on Kuhn-Munkres assignment algorithm which has low computational cost and complexity, allowing quick estimation of the optimal distribution plan based on the criterion "efficiency: maximum hostile target destruction, minimum cost of weapon consumed and surface target damage". The experimental results have clarified that the proposed method has a great efficiency in real-time and optimal requirements.

Keywords: Assignment problem · Weapon targets assignment · Command and control · Air defense system

1 Introduction

Experience in wars and conflicts since the World War II shows that most of the victories were achieved by one side owning the superiority in the air. Therefore, air defence systems are the most sophisticated and specialized defense systems in any modern army. The air defense systems is a combination of technical measures including weapon systems, associated sensor systems, command and control arrangements. The air defense automated command and control systems ensure the complete implementation of the following tasks in real-time:

- collecting, processing and fusing sensor information on air and ground situations;

N.-S. Vo et al. (Eds.): INISCOM 2021, LNICST 379, pp. 403–415, 2021.
https://doi.org/10.1007/978-3-030-77424-0_33

- forming the most accurate model of the real situation in the combat area from sensors data, GIS and reports;
- automatically analyzing aerial situations and provide operational decision-proposals on the basis of available options.

One of the key parts of the operational decision is the allocation of defense weapons to threatening enemy targets, this process will be called weapon target assignment (WTA) further in this paper. In an air defense situation, operators have to evaluate the most cost-effective WTA in real-time. Due to human factors, operators tend to perform worse as the number of targets increase [1]. This is the reason there is a need for semi-automated and automated decision support systems, that can evaluate the air situation and find the optimal assignment decision to control weapon terminals.

The weapon target assignment problem is a class of computational optimization problems present in the fields of optimization and operations research. It consists of finding an optimal assignment of a set of weapons of various types to a set of targets in order to maximize the total expected damage done to the opponent. The WTA problem can be formulated as a nonlinear integer programming problem and is known to be NP-complete. There are constraints on weapons available of various types and on the minimum number of weapons by type to be assigned to various targets. The constraints are linear, and the objective function is nonlinear. The objective function is formulated in terms of probability of damage of various targets weighted by their military value [2].

In this paper, we propose an optimal air target distribution method for the weapons unit of a mixed air defense cluster. The key difference of assignment problem in our formulation is both weapons units and targets are diverse in types in real life complex anti-aircraft combat conditions. The proposed method is built on the basis of Kuhn-Munkres assignment algorithm, features with low computational cost and complexity, allowing quick estimation of the optimal distribution plan based on the criterion "efficiency: maximum hostile target destruction, minimum cost of weapon consumed and surface target damage". Thanks to the simplicity of Kuhn-Munkres assignment algorithm [3], the computational cost and complexity are reduced, allowing quick estimation of the optimal distribution. In the next part of this paper, we will evaluate the algorithm on typical WTA scenarios and compare the computational cost of the algorithm in different problem sizes.

2   Conventional Approaches for Solving WTA Problems

There are several popular methods to solve the WTA problem, such as:

- Dynamic programming methods include linear programming, stochastic programming, and mixed-integer programming [4]. Linear programming is an optimization technique of a linear objective function, subject to linear equality and linear inequality constraints. It is a mathematical method that is used to determine the best possible outcome or solution from a given set of parameters or a list of requirements, which are represented in the form of linear relationships. Stochastic programming offers a solution by eliminating uncertainty and characterizing it using probability distributions. A mixed-integer programming problem is a mathematical optimization in which some of the variables are restricted to be integers. There are many methods of solving programming problems, but in general, these problems are very complex in computational cost, especially with large size.

- Meta-heuristic optimization algorithms for static WTA [5], including the algorithms Ant Colony Optimization (ACO), Genetic Algorithm (GA), Enhanced Maximal Marginal Return (EMMR) and Particle Swarm Optimization (PSO). In [6], the authors proposed to use a hybrid algorithm including the improved algorithm Artificial Fish Swarm Algorithm (AFSA) and Harmony Search (HS) to solve the problem of WA for anti-air weapons. The comparison of heuristic WTA algorithms may seem trivial, but there are a number of aggravating circumstances. Firstly, there is a lack of unclassified real-world data sets on which to evaluate the algorithms. For this reason, it seems to be standard procedure to evaluate the algorithms on randomly generated synthetic data sets. Secondly, most heuristic algorithms have a large degree of inbuilt randomness. It is therefore important to base the evaluation of such algorithms on a statistically sufficient number of runs, rather than a single one. Thirdly, algorithms for static WTA only have a very limited time available for searching for good or optimal solutions, due to the real-time requirements, thus an algorithm can generate very good solutions after a long search time can return quite bad solutions when the available search time is shorter.

- In addition to these complicated methods, a study in [7] has proposed the target distribution algorithm for fast-response weapon systems in multi-target and multi-weapon scenarios. The target distribution is built based on the target's azimuth range, distance and threat level value. However, for the purpose of simplicity, the author has assumed that all fire powered targeted vehicles are of the same type. This is not feasible when being applied to a mixed air defense formation with many types of weapons and heterogeneous features.

Our method differs from the above listed approaches in the manner that we propose an optimal and fast assignment solution for the WTA problem of a mixed air defense cluster with strict-deadline real time requirements, which means the algorithm has determined computational time for each problem size. The method is to be applied in mixed-weapons systems with each weapon having different cost and effectiveness, and each target having different threat levels and kill probabilities.

3   Mathematical Formulation of WTA Problem

The target distribution problem is illustrated in Fig. 1, [2, 8], where: $\mathbf{T} = \{T_1, T_2, \ldots, T_N\}$ - set of hostile air targets; $\mathbf{O} = \{O_1, O_2, \ldots, O_K\}$ - collection of objects to be protected; $\mathbf{W} = \{W_1, W_2, \ldots, W_M\}$ - collection of anti-aircraft weapon systems. Each dashed arrow represents a possible assignment between a target and a weapon unit. The number of possible assignments is $N \times M$.

In mixed air defense cluster, each weapon unit is characterized by the boundaries of the affected area in height H_i max, H_i min and range D_{near} and D_{far}. Determining the range of impact of the weapon unit, the possibility of firing at the target by speed v_i and by the course parameter S_i, the probability of hitting the target P_i, firing time t_i. Each

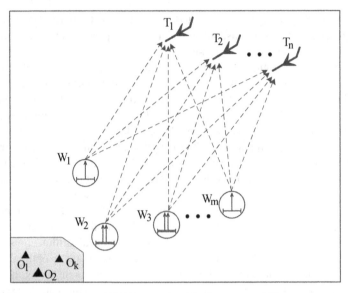

Fig. 1. Illustration of WTA scenario with N targets and M weapon units.

air target is characterized by flight altitude H_j, speed v_j, course parameter S_j and flight time t_j of reaching the $j - th$ target of the impact boundary of the $i - th$ weapon unit.

The firing process of the target by a weapon unit is possible under the following restrictions [9]:

$$\begin{cases} H_{i\ min} \leq H_j \leq H_{i\ max} \\ v_j \leq v_i \\ S_j \leq S_i \\ t_j \geq t_{i\ min} + t_{i\ (j-1)} \end{cases} \tag{1}$$

where, $t_{i\ min}$ - minimum firing cycle of weapon unit W_i; $t_{i\ (j-1)}$ - time of occupation of the weapon unit W_i by firing the previously assigned target T_{j-1}.

Killing probability is a joint probability of independent events, in this case including possibility of firing and possibility of hitting. If one of listed restrictions is not satisfied, the firing process is impossible and the kill probability of an assignment is equal to zero. Otherwise, the joint probability of a target kill event is formulated as follows [10]:

$$P_{unit\ ij} = 1 - (1 - P_{1i})^n \tag{2}$$

where: P_{1i} - kill probability of a single missile in weapon unit W_i.

In regard to given condition, impact level of fire command can be measured from kill probability $P_{unit\ ij}$ and target threat level V_j as follows:

$$F_{impact} = \sum_{j=1}^{N} \sum_{i=1}^{M} (P_{unit\ ij} \times V_j)\, m_{ij} \tag{3}$$

In this case effectiveness of a fire command can be formulated as subtraction of impact to cost of the assignment. According to typical tactic requirements, F_{impact} is usually considered as a constant value, as the weapons unit can fire multiple times to an object to achieve the required P_{unit}. The required number of missiles to be fired per target can be calculated as follows:

$$n = \frac{(1 - \log P_{unit\, ij})}{(1 - \log P_{1\, i})} \tag{4}$$

In this condition, the cost of a WTA assignment can be estimated according to the following expression:

$$F_{cost} = \sum_{j=1}^{N} \sum_{i=1}^{M} \overline{C}_{ij} m_{ij} \tag{5}$$

The global function to optimization is called loss function, which can be calculated from cost value and impact value as follows:

$$F_{lost} = F_{cost} - F_{impact} = \sum_{j=1}^{N} \sum_{i=1}^{M} \overline{C}_{ij} m_{ij} - \sum_{j=1}^{N} \sum_{i=1}^{M} (P_{unit\, ij} \times V_j) m_{ij}$$

$$= \sum_{j=1}^{N} \sum_{i=1}^{M} (C_{1i} \times n - P_{unit\, ij} \times V_j) m_{ij}$$

$$= \sum_{j=1}^{N} \sum_{i=1}^{M} \left[C_{1i} \times \frac{(1 - \log P_{unit\, ij})}{(1 - \log P_{1i})} - P_{unit\, ij} \times V_j \right] m_{ij} \tag{6}$$

where:

$P_{unit\, ij}$ - tactical minimum required kill probability (>0.75);

V_j - individual target value estimated for each target T_j.

C_{1i} - cost of one missile in weapon unit W_i.

m_{ij} - specific assignment parameters for the T_j target and W_i weapon, $m_{ij} = 1$ if weapon W_i is assigned to target T_j, $m_{ij} = 0$ otherwise [11].

The optimization problem is now formulated as finding assignment values m_{ij} to minimize value of F_{lost}. The main purpose of the assignment problem is to minimize the cost of WTA decision, represented mathematically as F_{lost}. Decision variables of F_{lost} function are the values of the matrix of control parameters m_{ij} regarding to the following constraints:

$$\sum_{i=1}^{M} m_{ij} = 1 \quad (j = \overline{1; N}) \tag{7}$$

$$\text{and} \quad \sum_{j=1}^{N} m_{ij} = 1 \quad (i = \overline{1; M}) \tag{8}$$

The constraint in (7) indicates that only one weapon can be assigned to a target at the current moment of time. Similarly, the constraint in (8) allows only one target to be assigned with a weapon in the current moment of time.

4 Proposed Air Target Distribution Method

In this section, we propose a method to solve the air target distribution problem based on the criteria: maximizes effective protection of objects on the ground; minimizes the cost of using weapon units to destroy air targets; minimizes computation time for consistent application in real-time command and control systems. Due to the air defense combat situation constantly changing, resolving all control tasks in repeated after a specified time, called the control task resolution cycle. The proposed target distribution method is to be performed in each control cycle according to the following steps (illustrated in Fig. 2).

1) Based on sensor information about the targets, such as flight direction, speed, altitude, distance, type… and status of protected objects, it is possible to calculate the threat values $V_{jk} \in [0, 1]$ of each target in relation to each protected object (T_j, O_k). Using these threat values, formation of the threat values matrix for target-protected pairs [8]

$$\mathbf{V} = \begin{bmatrix} V_{11} & V_{12} & \dots & V_{1K} \\ V_{21} & V_{22} & \dots & V_{2K} \\ \dots & \dots & \dots & \dots \\ V_{N1} & V_{N2} & \dots & V_{NK} \end{bmatrix}$$

An individual target value V_j is estimated for each target T_j. To compute the target value is to simply go through all threat values for a specific target T_j and pick the largest one

$$V_j = \max(V_{jk} w_k), \quad k = 1, \dots, K \tag{9}$$

where $\omega_k \in [0, 1]$ is a weight representing the important of the protected object O_k, K is the total number of the protected objects.

2) Generation of the air target impact matrix $\mathbf{A}$ on based on the target value V_j and target kill probability $P_{unit\ ij}$

$$A_{ij} = P_{unit\ ij} \times V_j. \tag{10}$$

3) Generation of the lost matrix $\overline{\mathbf{C}}$ based on the weapon cost and impact value A_{ij}

$$\overline{C}_{ij} = C_{1i} \times n - A_{ij}. \tag{11}$$

4) Applying Kuhn-Munkres optimization algorithm to find m_{ij} in (6) in 6 substeps as follows (Fig. 3):

    In the input of Kuhn-Munkres algorithm, we are given a non-negative $m \times n$ matrix $\overline{\mathbf{C}}$, where the element $\overline{C}_{ij}$ in the $i - th$ row and $j - th$ column represents the cost of assigning the $j - th$ target to the $i - th$ weapon unit. We have to find an assignment of the target to the weapon unit, such that each target is assigned to one weapon unit and each worker is assigned one target, such that the total cost of assignment is minimum.

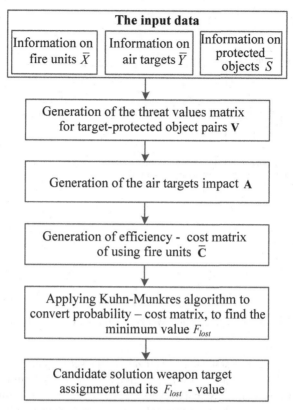

Fig. 2. Flowchart of proposed method to solve the WTA problem.

Step 1: Then we perform row operations on the matrix. To do this, the lowest of all $\overline{C}$ is taken and is subtracted from each element in that row. This will lead to at least one zero in that row (We get multiple zeros when there are two equal elements which also happen to be the lowest in that row). This procedure is repeated for all rows. We now have a matrix with at least one zero per each row. Go to Step 2.

Step 2: Find a zero (Z) in the resulting matrix. If there is no starred zero in its row or column, star Z. Repeat for each element in the matrix. Go to Step 3.

Step 3: Cover each column containing a starred zero. If K columns are covered, the starred zeros describe a complete set of unique assignments. In this case, Go to END, otherwise, Go to Step 4.

Step 4: Find a non-covered zero and prime it. If there is no starred zero in the row containing this primed zero, Go to Step 5. Otherwise, cover this row and uncover the column containing the starred zero. Continue in this manner until there are no uncovered zeros left. Save the smallest uncovered value and Go to Step 6.

Step 5: Construct a series of alternating primed and starred zeros as follows. Let Z0 represent the uncovered primed zero found in Step 4. Let Z1 denote the starred zero in the column of Z0 (if any). Let Z2 denote the primed zero in the row of Z1 (there will always be one). Continue until the series terminates at a primed zero that has no starred

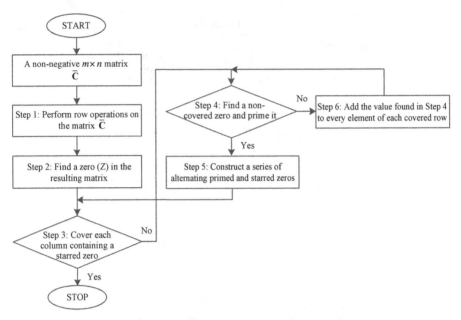

Fig. 3. Flow chart Kuhn-Munkres optimization algorithm.

zero in its column. Remove star each starred zero of the series, star each primed zero of the series, erase all primes and uncover every line in the matrix. Return to Step 3.
Step 6: Add the value found in Step 4 to every element of each covered row, and subtract it from every element of each uncovered column. Return to Step 4 without altering any stars, primes, or covered lines.

5 Experimental Results

For testing and evaluation, the target distribution algorithm was implemented in a computer CPU Intel(R) Core i3-4150, 3.50 GHz, RAM 4 GB, Windows 10 OS and Python 3.8 development environment. In the tests we evaluate the accuracy and effectiveness of the proposed method for different air defense scenarios. The input parameters of the problem such as the target's threat value, the kill probability and the cost of use of a missile for each weapon unit are randomly generated with independent distribution in the segment [0; 1]. As follows:

We create a matrix of threat value of an aerial target regarding to ground-protected objects ($0.5 \leq V_{jk} \leq 0.9$) and a weight vector representing the important of the protected object ($0 \leq \omega_k \leq 1$). To calculate the required number of missiles of weapon unit W_i to destroy target T_j with the probability ($P_{unit\,ij} \geq 0.75$), we create a matrix of 1 missile kill probability ($0.5 \leq P_{1i} \leq 1.0$), and the required number n of fire units is calculated according to the formula (4). From the required number of fire units we calculate the average cost of using weapon W_i to destroy target T_j.

Experiment 1: In the first test, we simulate an air defense scenario and apply the proposed method to solve the scenario target distribution problem to analyze and evaluate the accuracy of the proposed method. In this scenario, we create 6 aerial target, 6 surface weapon to protect ground objects. The size of the target distribution problem is 6 × 6. From the randomly generated input parameters with independent distribution in the range of values as shown above, we calculate the lost matrix of using weapon W_i to target T_j as follows:

$$\overline{C} = \begin{bmatrix} 0.18115 & 0.180771 & 0.476646 & 0.324114 & 0.0691015 & 0.123247 \\ 0.321566 & 0.399824 & 0.232902 & 0.673997 & 0.451779 & 0.505241 \\ 0.480866 & 1.023720 & 0.714871 & 1.268250 & 0.861215 & 0.921880 \\ 0.233978 & 0.597722 & 0.314498 & 0.467106 & 0.198332 & 0.260932 \\ 0.234936 & 0.677352 & 0.320142 & 0.435908 & 0.292508 & 0.429728 \\ 0.298668 & 0.484624 & 0.757474 & 0.761298 & 0.504243 & 0.254476 \end{bmatrix}$$

Applying Kuhn-Munkres algorithm to convert lost matrix, to find the minimum value, the matrix after transformation is as follows:

$$\overline{C} = \begin{bmatrix} 0.112049 & 0 & 0.407545 & 0.054040 & 0 & 0.054145 \\ 0.088665 & 0.055253 & 0 & 0.240124 & 0.218878 & 0.272340 \\ 0 & 0.431184 & 0.234005 & 0.586410 & 0.380349 & 0.441014 \\ 0.035645 & 0.287720 & 0.116166 & 0.067802 & 0 & 0.062599 \\ 0 & 0.330746 & 0.085206 & 0 & 0.057572 & 0.194792 \\ 0.044191 & 0.118478 & 0.502998 & 0.305850 & 0.249766 & 0 \end{bmatrix}$$

From the above matrix, we find the WTA solution as follows:

```
----------------------------------------------------
Candidate WTA solution and its F_lost-value
(1, 2) -> 0.18077090531346085
(2, 3) -> 0.232901549508034
(3, 1) -> 0.4808662061728568
(4, 5) -> 0.1983324667735118
(5, 4) -> 0.43590779964434334
(6, 6) -> 0.25447647156617825
----------------------------------------------------
Total  lowest lost: 1.7832553989783853
```

The solution can be interpreted as: First weapon is assigned to 2nd target with cost value 0.180771, second weapon is assigned to 3rd target with cost value 0.232902, third weapon is assigned to 1st target and so on.

Experiment 2: Evaluate the calculation time complexity of the proposed method. We created various air defense scenarios with increasing complexity to calculate execution time.

As shown in Fig. 4, the time complexity of proposed method obeyed the $O(n^3)$ complexity. For WTA scenarios, with the required time for generating assignment problems about 2–3 s, the algorithm can generate solution for up to 90 targets and 90 weapon units shown in Fig. 5.

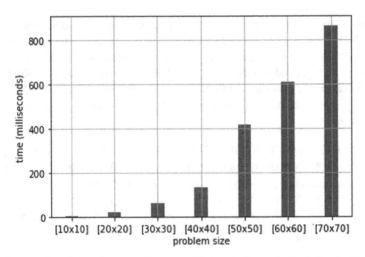

Fig. 4. Computational time for generating a candidate solution and calculating its F_{lost} value.

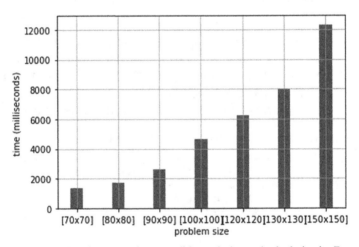

Fig. 5. Computational time for generating a candidate solution and calculating its F_{lost} value with large problem size.

Experiment 3: Experiment with different quantity combination of weapons and targets.

In [11], the real-time condition is assumed the solutions which are obtained in about one second. Hence, to satisfy this condition, the size of a WTA problem which is solved in the static form using exhaustive search algorithm should be smaller than 7×7 (weapons $\times$ targets) (Table 1).

Table 1. Computational time (in milliseconds) for 25 different scenarios.

Weapons	Targets				
	6	12	18	24	32
6	4	5	7	10	11
12	5	10	14	16	21
18	7	15	18	26	37
24	8	17	28	37	53
32	10	21	44	61	98

The comparison of calculation time with the same assignment problem size on the algorithm categories [4–6] (Search algorithms, MMR algorithms, evolutionary algorithms and suggested algorithm) is demonstrated in Fig. 6. Although the implementation of the MMR algorithms is simpler, they produce better performance than search algorithm and evolutionary algorithm. Among the listed method, the proposed method (using Kuhn-Munkres algorithm) is significantly faster.

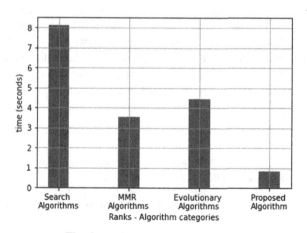

Fig. 6. Ranks – algorithm categories.

Applying our real-time requirement (less than 4 s calculation time in a single core of usual x86 PC) and optimal requirement (guaranteed convergence to global optimum solution), we can sum up the general comparison of WTA algorithms in the aspects of being real-time and optimal in Table 2.

Table 2. A general comparison of weapon assignment algorithms.

Weapon assignment algorithms	Real-time	Optimal
Maximum marginal return algorithm	Yes	No
Genetic algorithm	Yes	No
Ant colony optimization algorithm	Yes	No
Exhaustive search algorithm	No	Yes
Proposed algorithm	Yes	Yes

6 Conclusion

In this paper, we have analyzed the WTA problem in simulated real-combat situation. This is a typical problem for optimizing and planning methods. Finding solutions to this problem in real-time is a high practical research for the military, since these kinds of allocation problems are present in many real-world air defense situations. A mathematical formulation of the real-world problem was proposed to convert WTA problem to a matrix assignment problem. We also proposed an application of a simple and effective assignment algorithm which can guarantee minimization of calculation time for real-time requirement of combat scenarios. In the experiments, the method can generate WTA solution proposal to operator for most air situation (with assignment problem size up to 90×90) in less than seconds. In our future work, the mathematical model and proposed method can be further improved to be more realistic regarding the importance of protected objects and status of weapon units using probability models.

References

1. Roux, J.N., Van Vuuren, J.H.: Threat evaluation and weapon assignment decision support: a review of the state of the art. ORiON **23**(2), 151–187 (2007)
2. Hasan, M.B., Barua, Y.: Weapon target assignment. Licensee IntechOpen, 6 October 2020
3. Kuhn, H.W.: The Hungarian method for the assigment problem. Naval Res. Logist. Q. **2**, 83–97 (1955)
4. Ahuja, R., Kumar, A., Jha, K., Orlin, J.: Exact and heuristic algorithms for the weapon - target assignment problem. Oper. Res. **55**(6), 1136–1146 (2007)
5. Johansson, F., Falkman, G.: A suite of metaheuristic algorithms for static weapon - target allocation. In: International Conference on Genetic and Evolutionary Methods. CSREA Press (2010)
6. Chang, Y., Li, Z., Kou, Y., Sun, Q., Yang, H., Zhao, Z.: A New approach to weapon-target assignment in cooperative air combat. Math. Probl. Eng. **2017**, 17 (2017). Article ID 2936279
7. Yoon, M.: A Weapon assignment algorithm for rapid reaction in multi-target and multi-weapon environments. J. Korea Contents Assoc. **18**(8), 118–126 (2018)
8. Johansson, F.: Evaluating the performance of TEWA systems. Örebro University (2010)
9. Бурмистрова, С.К.: Справочник Офицера Воздушно-Космической Обороны, Тверь: Военная Академия Воздушно-Космической Обороны, 564 p (2006)

10. Занкин, Р.Н., Пересыпкин, Д.А.: Методика выбора типа и количества боевых средств частей (подразделений) зенитных ракетных войск смешанного состава для выполнения задачи непосредственного прикрытия аэродрома. Оперативное Искусство и Тактика **12**, 28–35 (2019)
11. Johansson, F., Falkman, G.: Real-time allocation of defensive resources to rockets, artillery, and mortars. In: 13th Conference on Information Fusion (FUSION) (2010)

A Vision Based System Design for Over-Sized Vessel Detecting and Warning Using Convolutional Neural Network

Xuan-Kien Dang[✉], Viet-Chinh Nguyen, Trieu-Phong Nguyen,
Thi-Duyen-Anh Pham, and Cong-Phuong Vo

Ho Chi Minh City University of Transport, Ho Chi Minh City, Vietnam
dangxuankien@hcmutrans.edu.vn

Abstract. In this work, we aim to investigate the problem of automatically detecting, and warning of an oversize vessel traveling through the Water lock of the flood-holding system. First, the image processing technique based on camera vision using Convolutional Neural Network (CNN), which has the potential to detect the oversize included the length and width of the vessel, is used to help the sailors to prevent this vessel crashed into the Water lock. Second, a model named Oversized Vessel Detector (OVD) was built to detect the vessel in the streaming video and to calculate the size relatively accurately of the vessels based on the proposed math function. Then, the system automatically compares the estimated sizes of the detected vessel and allowable sizes of the flood-protecting system (FPs) to determine the oversize condition, and the result will be displayed on the monitor and warning with alarm devices when decided that the vessel is oversized. Finally, to show the effectiveness and implementation performance of the proposed approach, an experiment is carried out based on Raspberry Pi 4 hardware for coding all the mentioned algorithms.

Keywords: Water lock · Flood-protecting system · Oversized vessel detection · Convolutional neural network

1 Introduction

Climate change is a serious challenge to humanity, profoundly affects, and altogether changes the global social life, especially in marine countries including Viet Nam. Therefore, each country demands implementation climate to proposed change adaptation solutions. Ho Chi Minh City is at risk of flooding, even under normal climatic conditions. Related to responding to climate change, the proposed plan is to deploy a dikes system around the city and tidal sluices while ensuring water traffic. This system, named the flood-protection, used modern technologies [1–5] that involve two possible approaches: to ensure safety for nation waterway traffic system (including vessels and construction) and to adapt to climate change already.

Artificial Intelligence (AI) alongside the Internet of Things (IoT) and Big Data are the core elements of digital technology in the Industrial Revolution 4.0. in the world.

© ICST Institute for Computer Sciences, Social Informatics and Telecommunications Engineering 2021
Published by Springer Nature Switzerland AG 2021. All Rights Reserved
N.-S. Vo et al. (Eds.): INISCOM 2021, LNICST 379, pp. 416–430, 2021.
https://doi.org/10.1007/978-3-030-77424-0_34

Focus on the maritime industry, AI is studied and applied in many fields, most of which are automatic control [6, 7], transportation and Maritime safety assurance [8], video streaming [9, 10], and camera vision-based neural network [11, 12]. In general, AI has many positive and effective points, especially increasing safety in operating and managing marine transportation systems.

In this paper, we focus on the given possible approach, some studies [3–5] provided evidence of damages that happened when the monitoring systems are installed without insufficient alarm functions. The over-height vehicles (OHVs), usually a truck, crane, a double-decker bus, or boats try to travel through bridges or tunnels which have a height lower than the size of OHVs caused collisions for the general transport system, as same as the national water system. These collisions lead to traffic delays, damage to bridge structures, bridge foundations, and fatal harm to drivers. In the worst case, derailment, the immediate collapse of the bridge structures, and fatalities of road users can occur [5, 13]. Moreover, Shanafelt & Horn showed that OHVs were the leading cause of the damage (81%) for the prestressed concrete bridge over 5 years, and about 95% of the damage to the steel bridge in America is due to OHVs [9]. Therefore, the development of new technologies in traffic monitoring and warning systems is necessary at the moment.

Considering the designed models on the traffic monitoring, detecting, and warning system, many authors have studied and applied image processing algorithms to observe and coordinate traffic [1–4]. The authors presented a new method for preventing oversize vehicle collisions by using a camera, and the idea is an improvement to the existing laser projection method [1]. The camera mounted on the side of the road or bridge is used to replace the transmitter, receiver, and distance sensor. The camera is installed at the maximum allowable height of the bridge on all lanes in each traffic direction.

Related to the methods and technologies, the advent of modern improvements in AI and deep learning [1–3] has a significant in camera vision based on computer technology in recent years. Object detection is a computer technology linked to computer vision and image processing that deals with combination object classification and object positioning. Most recent research concentrated on designing the complicated network for object detection based on a neural network to intensify accuracies, such as single-shot detector (SSD) [4] and faster R-CNN [5]. Therefore, the performance of object detection models using deep learning methods has been improved a lot. However, limited by the amount of training data and high computational costs, these frameworks are difficult to be implemented practically.

Related to the hardware of the traffic monitoring system, the authors [14] used some instruments, a laser range sensor, a radar speedometer, and a digital camera, to build a vehicle's exterior contour identification and detection system. According to measured data from the vehicles on the highway, six characteristics, such as vehicle length, height, width, height variance, the ratio of peak length, and body length, are extracted [15]. Then, vehicles are classified into sub cars, mini-buses, trucks, buses, large rails, and large buses automatically using the BP neural network. Test results showed that the system is more effective at classifying existing outcomes, especially being able to differentiate between trucks and buses of similar shape more effectively. Deal with design a height limit warning system based on the road coordination of the vehicle, the proposed method in [16] applied directional coordination in the direction using the SSD algorithm mounted on the camera, vehicle network, GPS, and altimeter algorithm to assist the driver in assessing the height limit and informing the driver in advance. Therefore, a safe way to safely pass the high limit section for vehicles that ignore warnings and do not slow down or change lanes within a safe distance.

Based on the discussion aforementioned, the motivation of this paper is to design the automatic detection and warning of an oversize vessel traveling through the flood-protecting system, for the reasons as follows: 1) Due to climate change, the rising water level seriously affects people's life in Ho Chi Minh City. A new flood protection system is currently in the improvement, the development of the detecting and warning an oversize vessel system is necessary, 2) Selected the image processing technique based on camera vision using Convolutional Neural Network (CNN) has the potential to detect the oversize included the length and width of the vessel, 3) The experiment is carried out based on Raspberry Pi 4 hardware for coding all the mentioned CNN algorithms. The experiment results not only perform the effectiveness but also implement the performance of the proposed approach.

The rest of this paper is organized as follows. In Sect. 2, we introduce the motivation of the paper with the overview of current situation of flood-protection system of Ho Chi Minh City and some remarks. To design the OVD model based on camera vision using Convolutional Neural Network is presented in Sect. 3. Section 4 is dedicated to showing the experiment results, analysis, and evaluation of the proposed model. Finally, we conclude the paper in Sect. 5.

2 Motivation

2.1 Overview of Current Situation of Flood-Protection System of Ho Chi Minh City

Ho Chi Minh City has a dense river system, a system of rivers connecting and circulating to the East Sea of Vietnam. Moreover, the Saigon River water level is highly dependent on two factors: the seasonal rain discharge and the tidal influence. Then, the rivers discharge into the East Sea of Viet Nam, and the lower river limits are subject to tidal influence. Due to climate change, the rising water level seriously affects people's life in Ho Chi Minh City. A new flood protection system is currently in development and under construction, the actual pictures of the flood protection system under construction in HCMC are shown in Fig. 1. The flood-protection system is shown in Fig. 2 comprised six major floodgates including Ben Nghe, Tan Thuan, Phu Xuan, Muong Chuoi, Cay Kho, and Phu Dinh. The barrier widths of floodgates are in the range of 40 m to 160 m. The pumping stations were installed at Ben Nghe, Tan Thuan, and Phu Dinh floodgates, the respective capacities of 12 m^3/s, 24 m^3/s, and 18 m^3/s.

In the context of the gradual completion of the flood protection system, there will be a lot of ships and boats passing through the water locks of these structures caused collision. Therefore, the development of the detecting and warning an oversize vessel system not only assists to protect the system's structure but also helps vessels pass through safely.

Fig. 1. The actual pictures of the flood protection system under construction in HCMC

Fig. 2. The flood-protection system comprises six major floodgates in Ho Chi Minh City

2.2 Some Statistics Related to Bridges and Marine Construction Collisions Caused by Vehicles

In general, Network Rail reported 12,829 incidents in the transport system between 1995 and 2003 in the UK [17]. In their most recent statistics, Network Rail summarized approximately 1,708 bridge collisions in 2014, an increase of 9.9% over the previous year. Especially, bridges and marine construction collisions pose significant risks to the safety and operation of the transport infrastructure. In the United States, it is estimated that more than 7,000 bridges suffer a total of more than 5,000 collisions per year, resulting in more than $ 100 million in damage to public and private property [18]. According to the Federal Highway Administration (FHWA), collisions by vehicles or boats were the third cause of marine construction and bridges failures [19]. The marine construction structure crash issue is widespread globally with OH bridge collisions reported in Canada, Ireland, UK, Western Australia, Japan and 14 European Union Member States, all of which consider the collisions are a significant safety risk [20].

First of all, marine construction collapse is regularly a complex process that results from a combined effect of many different factors. Therefore, it is hard to identify the leading factor that has directly resulted in the destruction. Furthermore, to perform the field tests to study the collision of the vehicle to the marine construction is difficult due to safety concerns and cost issues (Zhang et al. 2013 [21]; Piran Aghl et al. 2014 [22]). In recent years, the progress of finite-element methods and computer technologies have provided useful devices for researchers to study marine construction collapse on a numerical basis. While experimental studies were conducted to understand the collapse status of structures of marine construction included bridges. Although much improvement is used for understanding the action and breakdown of marine construction, many challenging issues remain.

3 Oversized Vessels Detector Model Based on Camera Vision Using Convolutional Neural Network

In recent years, the Convolutional Neural Network (CNN) based methods have been used for ship detection [23], and land target detection [24], and CNN displayed a better achievement than the traditional methods. In [25], the authors divided the images into tiny patches, and then they used a pre-trained CNN model to classify those patches, after which the distribution patches are mapped again onto the original images. However, this method does not take the edges of targets into account to get a low target location precision. Moreover, the structure of Faster-RCNN improved the detection performance for small boats [26, 27].

In this paper, we aim to detect and analyze over-sized vessels automatically from the streaming videos. A comprehensive system is needed to identify the over-sized vessels, estimate the dimensions. The result is displayed and warned on the monitor and alarm devices. Therefore, we deal with using a CNN for detecting and analyzing over-sized vessels, and the overall framework of the proposed model shows in Fig. 3.

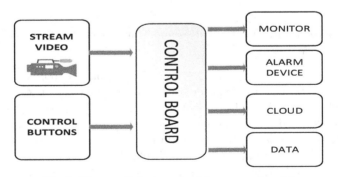

Fig. 3. The overall framework of the proposed model

To detect and estimate the size of a moving object. We selected SSD_Mobilenet_V2 to detect the vessels, and a motion interactive field method used to estimate the vessels' sizes. A framework for Oversized Vessel Detector (OVD) was created and showed in Fig. 4. The control board, selecting the Raspberry Pi 4, is the main computer used to code all algorithms, and the camera is directly connected to the control board and takes image data in the water lock. The signals are processed by using the improved convolutional neural network [4] for the vessel's image processing and detection. The OVD is designed based on the following sequence of steps:

Step 1: To detect the vessels from the streaming video using the improved cnn algorithm.
Step 2: To estimate the sizes of the detected vessel.
Step 3: To display an alert with alarm devices or monitor when the system decided that the vessel is oversized.
Step 4: To process and save the data to the local storages (SD card) and cloud storage.

3.1 Detecting the Vessels from the Streaming Video Using the Improved CNN Algorithm

We aim to develop the OVD model for real-time applications with extremely effectual configuration (GPU/CPU) for embedded systems (Raspberry Pi, Nano PC). Therefore, we select to build a model like SSDLite-MobileNet hybrid helped to achieve high accuracy while low computation time lies in the hybrid structure from SSD and MobileNet structure. Moreover, SSD (Structure of Single Shot Multi-Box Detector showed in Fig. 4) is an object detector that performs two main actions: Extract feature maps of features (from the video streaming) and apply convolution filters to detect vessels.

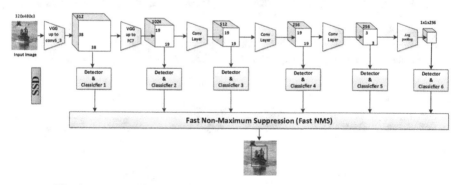

Fig. 4. Structure of single shot multi box detector used to detect the vessels

In this work, we use the loss function presented by Dang et al. [11]:

$$L(x, c, l, g) = \frac{1}{N} \left(L_{conf}(x, c) + \alpha L_{loc}(x, l, g) \right) \qquad (1)$$

$$L_{loc}(x, l, g) = \sum_{i \in Pos}^{N} \sum_{m \in \{cx, cy, w, h\}} x_{ij}^k \, smooth_{L1}(l_i^m - \hat{g}_j^m) \qquad (2)$$

where $\hat{g}_j^{cx} = (g_j^{cx} - d_i^{cx})/d_i^w$, $\hat{g}_j^{cy} = (g_j^{cy} - d_i^{cy})/d_i^h$, $\hat{g}_j^w = log(\frac{g_j^w}{d_i^w})$ and $\hat{g}_j^h = log(\frac{g_j^w}{d_i^w})$; L_{loc} is the localization loss caused by the parameter error between the predicted box and the ground-truth box.

$$L_{conf}(x, c) = -\sum_{i \in Pos}^{N} x_{ij}^p log(\hat{c}_i^p) - \sum_{i \in Neg} log(\hat{c}_i^0) \tag{3}$$

where: L_{conf} is the confidence loss, and α is set to 1 by cross validation. $\hat{c}_i^p = \frac{exp(c_i^p)}{\sum_p exp(c_i^p)}$; $x_{ij}^p = \{1, 0\}$ is an indicator for matching i-th default box to the j-th ground truth box of category P. The default boxes of each feature map computed as Eq. (4) [11]:

$$s_k = s_{min} + \frac{s_{max} - s_{min}}{m - 1}(k - 1), k \in [1, m] \tag{4}$$

The parameters are configured in detail: s_{min} is 0.2; s_{max} is 0.9; s_k is *0.1, 0.2, 0.375, 0.55, 0.725. 0.9* means *32, 64, 120, 176, 232, 290* pixels and some of them have an input resolution of *320 × 480* pixels.

Process of Building the Database of Images: We have taken photos of vessel types sailing on rivers in Ho Chi Minh City in Fig. 5, and some surrounding areas. In this work, we choose small vessels that match the allowed sizes of vessels to be sailed through the flood-protection system.

Fig. 5. Some images collected in Saigon river

We collected 450 pictures to train the recognition model, and the remaining 50 images were used to test in the designed model to hold it is within the allowed limit of memory of selected hardware. To conduct identity modeling training, the author chooses the TensorFlow framework as a template for the data. Known as a framework for building identity models, the TensorFlow APIs provides a full range of intuitive data computation, processing, and evaluation tools.

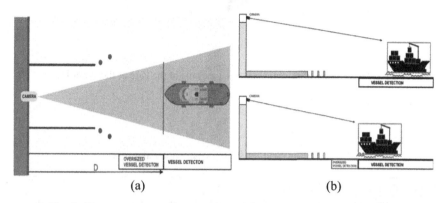

(a)   (b)

Fig. 6. The camera recording area (a) and distance start to get an image (b)

Regarding the problem of the Camera recording area and starting distance to get the image from the video streaming, the camera usually mounted in the center of the water locks, as shown in Fig. 6. The distance to start working is dependent on the position and length of each flood-protecting gate. After identified the vessel, the TensorFlow APIs will intercept the images from the videos and record their locations in each frame. Finally, the identification process finished and moved on to the next step, estimating the sizes.

3.2   Estimating the Sizes of the Detected Vessel

The estimation of vessel sizes (including height and width) is used as the method of converting the object recognition frame height and actual dimensions. Suppose the camera recording area captures from video streaming an area a(m) wide and b(m) length, equivalent to an x * y (pixel) frame. The description of the camera's image frame at the gate of the water lock present in Fig. 7.

The object identification frame coordinates are located at the corners shown in the figure. Hence, we have the width and height of the vessel that can be calculated as follows:

$$Width\,(m) = (X_{max} - X_{min})\frac{a}{x} \tag{5}$$

$$Height\,(m) = (Y_{max} - Y_{min})\frac{b}{y} \tag{6}$$

Where: a is recordable camera frame width (meter), b is recorded camera frame height (meter), and x is frame width and y is frame height (pixel), respectively.

Therefore, we propose the Vessel sizes estimating algorithm in Table 1 as below:

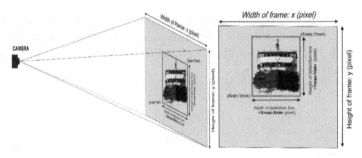

Fig. 7. Description of the camera's image frame at the gate of the water lock

Table 1. Proposed Vessel sizes estimating algorithm.

Vessel sizes estimating algorithm
Input: Bounding box (X_{max}, X_{min}, Y_{max}, Y_{min}), allowable limits of the construction (W_C;H_c)
Output: Vessel Sizes (**Width, Height**)

1.	Creating computed starting position (when the vessel starts entering the virtual line area with preset position) *if (ymax in range(200, 220)[*]):* *self.__width__.setText(str(**width**) + " M")* *self.__heigh__.setText(str(**heigh**) + " M")*
2.	Filtering noise detection frames if ___final_score___ ≥ ___min_score_thresh___ then proceed to measure the size.
3.	Computing the sizes (pixel) of bounded box *width_pixel = ($X_{max} - X_{min}$)* *heigh_pixel = ($Y_{max} - Y_{min}$)*
4.	Creating the bounded box sizes (pixel)
5.	Estimating the sizes of vessel (meter) following equations (5) and (6) **width** *= width_pixel *a /x* **heigh** *= heigh_pixel *b/y*

6.	Comparing set thresholds to deliver notifications
	 *if (**width** > W_C or **heigh** > H_C):*
	   self.Dangerous()
	 else:
	     *if(**width** != 0 and **heigh**!= 0):*
	       self.Safe()

7.	Extracting parameters and writing to history file
	 log = 'Log.txt'
	 with open(log, 'a') as logfile:
	     *logfile.write('Score:' + 'FPS: ' + '**width of vessel**: ' + str(width) + ';*
	     heigh of vessel: ' + str(heigh) + '; Stage: ' + s + '\n')*

8.	End

where: WC is allowable width and HC is allowable height of the construction (meter), [*] noted for the starting position depend on each water lock designed.

4 Experimental Result and Discussion

4.1 Testing the Designed OVD in HCMC University of Transport LAB

a.   The designed hardware of OVD   b.   The tested model of OVD in HCMC
                                               University of Transport LAB

Fig. 8. The overall of designed hardware and tested in HCMC University of Transport LAB

We build the embedding OVD system on the experimental model, which's structure and specification present in Fig. 8, a. This real-time system realizes the program directly into the Raspberry Pi 4 Model B. This model is the latest product in the popular Raspberry Pi range of computers. It offers ground-breaking increases in processor speed, multimedia performance, memory, and connectivity compared to the prior-generation Raspberry Pi 4 Model B+ while retaining backward compatibility and similar power consumption. For the end-user, Raspberry Pi 4 Model B provides desktop performance comparable to entry-level x86 PC systems.

- Broadcom BCM2711, Quad core Cortex-A72 (ARM v8) 64-bit SoC @ 1.5 GHz; 8GB LPDDR4-3200 SDRAM, 2.4 GHz and 5.0 GHz IEEE 802.11ac wireless, Bluetooth 5.0, BLE Gigabit Ethernet; 2 USB 3.0 ports; 2 USB 2.0 ports;
- Raspberry Pi standard 40 pin GPIO header (fully backward compatible with previous boards).

The OVD model are tested in HCMC University of Transport LAB (Fig. 8, b). Under ideal working conditions in the Lab, the OVD system showed the ability to identify the model vessel very accurately.

4.2 Testing the Designed OVD in Cay Kho Floodgates in Ho Chi Minh City

The OVD model are tested in Cay Kho floodgates in Ho Chi Minh City (Fig. 9, a), The vessel is in "oversize" condition in Fig. 9, b. Experimental results and evaluation are discussed in the next section.

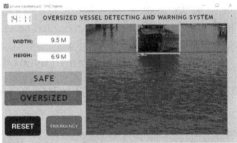

| a. Mounted the Camera on the designed position | b. Images captured and tested sized of the vessels |

Fig. 9. Testing the designed OVD in Cay Kho floodgates in Ho Chi Minh City

4.3 Summary Experimental Results

Images captured through the Logitech C270 camera are then processed using the CNN based on object detection algorithms. The output is the processed image, extracted the frame around the detected object, and the confidence in percent. For vessels within the permissible sized limits, the system display is "Safe" (Fig. 10, (a)). On the contrary, "Oversize" is displayed (Fig. 10, (b)) in case of the system decided that the vessel height and width exceed the permissible traffic allowance of the water lock, a warning will be issued by a light and sound signal in the control room at the water lock. The monitor displayed parameters related to width and height and saved them in the history file. Hence, to confirm and turn off the alarm signals, the supervisor needs to press the "RESET" button on the monitor screen or physical button in the control room. Moreover, the warning actions will be decided by the monitoring specialist through the radio system.

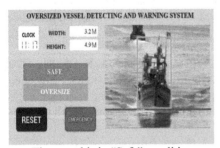
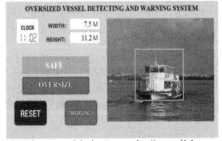

| a. The vessel is in "Safe" condition | b. The vessel is in "oversize" condition |

Fig. 10. Displayed the "safe" and warned "oversize" states of the vessel

Highly configurable models running on TITAN X GPUs produced processing speeds between 17 and 37 frames per second. However, when experimenting on COCO data sets and mean average precision (mAP) calculations on all object classes, the results only reached 21–28%. The experiment used the selected hybrid SSDLite-MobileNet algorithm, and the mAP of the system was firstly tested on the flood-lock model with laboratory working conditions to calibrate the vessel sizes. The high performance attained in the range of 86%–99% accuracy. Then, the experiment was directly tested in Caykho flood-lock in Ho Chi Minh City in normal working conditions, and the performance showed in Table 2, and the mAP achieved from 76% to 97% accuracy.

Table 2. Compare the testing performance of models in experimental

Model name	Test on GPU TITAN X		Real time on water lock area test on Raspberry Pi 4		Laboratory test on Raspberry Pi 4	
	Speed (ms)	COCO (mAP)	Speed (FPS)	(mAP)	Speed (FPS)	(mAP)
ssdlite_mobilenet_v2_coco	27	22	2.39	85	2.23	81
faster_rcnn_inception_v2_coco	58	28	0.12	96	0.12	90

This impressive result is achieved when installing the camera in the bridge in a convenient position while the hardware is a mobile device with only an ARM CPU and no integrated GPU. The highest processing speed is only approximately 3 FPS. The discussion of the experimental results focuses more detail in Table 1. The result showed that 2 models tested on our hardware (Raspberry Pi 4) using our method better than GPU TITAN X hardware (difference hardware) about speed (ms) and mAP. So that, the FPS speed of the test methods is indicated in Fig. 10, and mAP showed in Fig. 11. These results illustrated the good response rate for a monitoring system.

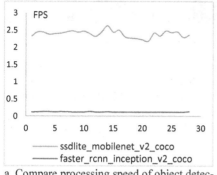

a. Compare processing speed of object detectors on system hardware

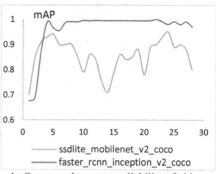

b. Compare the output reliability of object detectors on system hardware.

Fig. 11. Compared the FPS speed and mAP

4.4 Discussion

As for the detection task, the output reliability reached the highest with the Faster RCNN detector. However, it is not possible to meet on a monitoring system. Object detectors based on the hybrid SSD_MobileNet structure (in brown color) produce highly reliable results and meet processing speed requirements. Meanwhile, the results of SSD_MobileNetV1 (yellow) and SSD_MobileNetV2 (green) sets are almost equivalent, but the load time of the model is slow due to large capacity and actual output. There are still certainly deviations. Thus, the improved SSDLite_MobileNetV2 solution gave good results relating to quality, processing speed, fast model load time (stable running on Raspberry Pi 4), and has higher accuracy than the other solutions.

Regarding the FPS, the result presented in Fig. 10 is our experiment compared with the TensorFlow tool used Faster_RCNN_inception_V2_CoCo by the Google team. Extremely powerful hardware performs high FPS, but when considered on the whole COCO data set (about 40,000 images and 90 object layers), the (mAP) for a group of subjects) only attained 58%.

Related to the estimating process, the proposed OVD using a neural network with limited hardware tested in a water lock in the open space environment giving an intermediate accuracy average of about 80–90%. Moreover, the system needs more testing to evaluate the feasibility in real applications when we add extra size errors in the calculating and estimating process.

Fig. 12. Image processing and Vessels' sizes estimation

The results in Fig. 12 are shown with an identification processing level of about two frames per second while with the mobile device hardware only ARM CPU and no integrated GPU. This picture indicated an immeasurable response speed for a surveillance and vessel recognition system that does not require high speed as in the subject's goals.

5   Conclusion

In this paper, we studied and applied the CNN algorithm to design the Oversized Vessel Detector for the Flood-protecting system. The hardware used Raspberry Pi 4, an embedded single board computer with CPU smartphone level, limited RAM without CUDA GPU, for coding all the mentioned CNN algorithms. The experiment results not only perform the effectiveness but also implement the performance of the proposed approach.

The rising water level seriously affects people's life in Ho Chi Minh City due to climate change. Thus, the new Flood-protecting system is currently improving built to help the city clean, beautiful, and safer in the future.

Acknowledgements. This study was supported by the Applied Basic Research Program of Ministry of Transport of Vietnam DT203036 (2020).

References

1. Krizhevsky, A., Sutskever, I., Hinton, G.E.: Imagenet classification with deep convolutional neural networks. Commun. ACM **60**(6), 1097–1105 (2012)
2. Liu, W., et al.: SSD: single shot multibox detector. In: Leibe, B., Matas, J., Sebe, N., Welling, M. (eds.) ECCV 2016. LNCS, vol. 9905, pp. 21–37. Springer, Cham (2016). https://doi.org/10.1007/978-3-319-46448-0_2
3. Rustam, Z., et al.: Pulmonary rontgen classification to detect pneumonia disease using convolutional neural networks. TELKOMNIKA Telecommun. Comput. Electron. Control **18**(3), 1522–1528 (2020)
4. Ning, C., Zhou, H., Song, Y., Tang, J.: Inception single shot multibox detector for object detection. In: 2017 IEEE International Conference on Multimedia & Expo Workshops (ICMEW), Hong Kong, pp. 549–554 (2017)
5. Ren, S., He, K., Girshick, R., Sun, J.: Faster R-CNN: towards real-time object detection with region proposal networks. IEEE Trans. Pattern Anal. Mach. Intell. **39**(6), 1137–1149 (2017)
6. Do, V.-D., Dang, X.-K.: Fuzzy adaptive interactive algorithm design for marine dynamic positioning system under unexpected impacts of Vietnam Sea. Indian J. Geo Marine Sci. (NISCAIR) **49**(11), 1764–1771 (2020)
7. Dang, X.-K., Dong, V.H.: Time-delay estimator design based on neural network for ship control. J. Transp. Sci. Technol. **25**, 20–25 (2017)
8. Le, V.-T., Dang, X.-K., Nguyen, V.-T., Nguyen, N.-L.: Designing a safety assessment model of waterway transportation in Ganh Rai Bay - Vietnam based on fuzzy logic. In: 19th Annual General Assembly – AGA 2018, pp. 220–231. International Association of Maritime Universities (IAMU), October 2018
9. Vo, N.-S., Phan, T.-M., Bui, M.-P., Dang, X.-K., Viet, N.T., Yin, C.: Social-aware spectrum sharing and caching helper selection strategy optimized multicast video streaming in dense D2D 5G networks. IEEE Syst. J. 1–12 (2020). https://doi.org/10.1109/JSYST.2020.2995204
10. Dang, X.-K., Nguyen, V.-C., Phan, T.M.: Applying hybrid convolutional neural networks for image processing to bridge navigational watch & alarm system. J. Transp. Sci. Technol. **32**, 47–53 (2019)
11. Dang, X.-K., Truong, H.-N., Nguyen, V.-C., Pham, T.-D.-A.: Applying convolutional neural networks for limited-memory application. TELKOMNIKA (Telecommun. Comput. Electron. Control) **19**(1), 244–251 (2021)
12. Phan, T.-M., Dang, X.-K.: Current challenges in communication and 5G networks for autonomous marine systems. In: The 18th Asia Maritime & Fisheries Universities Forum (AMFUF2019), pp. 138–148, November 2019
13. Nguyen, B., Brilakis, I., Vela, P.A.: Vision-based over-height vehicle detection. In: Conference: Transportation Research Board 95th Annual Meeting, At Washington, DC, vol. 16-3550 (2016)
14. Xu, L., Lu, X., Smith, S., He, S.T.: Scaled model test for collision between over-height truck and bridge superstructure. Int. J. Impact Eng. **49**, 31–42 (2012)

15. El-Tawil, S., Severino, E., Fonseca, P.: Vehicle collision with bridge piers. J. Bridg. Eng. **10**(3), 345–353 (2005)

16. Fu, C., Burhouse, J., Chang, G.L.: Vehicle collisions with highway bridges. Transp. Res. Rec.: J. Transp. Res. Board **1865**, 80–88 (2004)

17. Network Rail: Prevention of strikes on bridges over highways: a protocol for highway managers and bridge owners, p. 40 (2007)

18. Low clearances GPS data get the most effective low clearance alert system for the US. http://www.lowclearances.com. Accessed May 2017

19. Mineta, N.Y.: 2004 status of the nation's highways, bridges, and transit: conditions and performance. In: Chapter 16, Report to Congress, USDOT, FHWA, FTA, Washington, DC, (2006)

20. Byrne, A.: Special topics report-railway bridges in Ireland and bridge strike trends. In: Railway Safety Commission, Dublin, Ireland (2009)

21. Zhang, J., Peng, H., Cai, C.: Destructive testing of a decommissioned reinforced concrete bridge. J. Bridge Eng. 564–569 (2013). https://doi.org/10.1061/(ASCE)BE.1943-5592.0000408

22. Piran Aghl, P., Naito, C., Riggs, H.: Full-scale experimental study of impact demands resulting from high mass, low velocity debris. J. Struct. Eng. 04014006 (2014). https://doi.org/10.1061/(ASCE)ST.1943-541X.0000948

23. Jiao, J., et al.: Connected end-to-end neural network for multiscale and multiscene SAR ship detection. IEEE Access **6**, 20881–20892 (2018)

24. Cui, Z., Dang, S., Cao, Z., Wang, S., Liu, N.: SAR: target recognition in large scene images via region-based convolutional neural networks. Remote Sens. **10**, 776 (2018)

25. Cozzolino, D., Martino, G.D., Poggi, G., Verdoliva, L.: A fully convolutional neural network for low-complexity single-stage ship detection in Sentinel-1 SAR images. In: Proceedings of the Geoscience and Remote Sensing Symposium, Fort Worth, TX, USA, 23–28 July 2017, pp. 886–889 (2017)

26. Kang, M., Ji, K., Leng, X., Lin, Z.: Contextual region-based convolutional neural network with multilayer fusion for SAR ship detection. Remote Sens. **9**, 860 (2017)

27. Kang, M., Leng, X., Lin, Z., Ji, K.: A modified faster R-CNN based on CFAR algorithm for SAR ship detection. In: Proceedings of the International Workshop on Remote Sensing with Intelligent Processing, Shanghai, China, 18–21 May 2017, pp. 1–4 (2017)

Security and Privacy

How to Develop ECC-Based Low Cost RFID Tags Robust Against Side-Channel Attacks

Manh-Hiep Dao[1,2(✉)], Vincent Beroulle[1], Yann Kieffer[1], and Xuan-Tu Tran[2,3]

[1] Univ. Grenoble Alpes, Grenoble INP, LCIS, 26000 Valence, France
`manh-hiep.dao@lcis.grenoble-inp.fr`
[2] SISLAB, VNU University of Engineering and Technology, Hanoi, Vietnam
`tutx@vnu.edu.vn`
[3] VNU Information Technology Institute, Vietnam National University, Hanoi, Vietnam

Abstract. Radio Frequency Identification (RFID) tags using asymmetric cryptography are more and more proposed to solve the well-known issue of symmetric-based tags, key distribution. In the asymmetric cryptography family, the Elliptic Curve Cryptography (ECC) primitive is often used due to its advantages in security and implementation costs. However, these ECC-based tags must still be hardened against hardware fault attacks (e.g., Side-Channel Attacks and Fault attacks). Balancing between the implementation costs and the security level is challenging since when the security level is improved, the implementation cost also increases much. Finding optimal implementations against hardware attacks is a system-level problem that must be taken authentication protocol security attributes and cryptography primitive costs into account. This paper proposes a methodology to develop low-cost ECC-based tags, ensuring robustness against Side-Channel Attacks. For that, a comparison of various authentication protocols and different ECC algorithms is first given, then an experimental setup is described to allow validating the implementations and measuring the robustness of the tag.

Keywords: ECC · RFID · Side-channel attack · Implementation · Authentication protocol

1 Introduction

Radio Frequency IDentification (RFID) was initially invented in the 1970s to use wireless communication technology is identifying the low cost and low power tags. Theoretically, there are two well-known types of RFID tags: active and passive tags. While the active RFID tags require an internal battery, the passive RFID tags act based on the harvested electromagnetic energy provided by the reader. These passive tags are much constrained in implementation cost, consisting of the number of gates and power consumption.

© ICST Institute for Computer Sciences, Social Informatics and Telecommunications Engineering 2021
Published by Springer Nature Switzerland AG 2021. All Rights Reserved
N.-S. Vo et al. (Eds.): INISCOM 2021, LNICST 379, pp. 433–447, 2021.
https://doi.org/10.1007/978-3-030-77424-0_35

As well as data transmission devices, the RFID systems face many severe threats and security problems. Wireless attacks allow the attackers to illegally access the system to steal or modify the internal tag information by using only wireless communication. There are two classes for wireless attacks: passive attacks (eavesdropping, location tracking) and active attacks (replay attack, relay attack, cloning, etc.). Passive attacks are the most basic methods. They analyze the data transmitted through the channel without modifying the integrity characteristic of the data. By contrast with the former, active attacks consist of modifying, reusing, or generating fake authentication messages to illegally access the system. Consequently, they are often more powerful than passive attacks.

Hardware attacks target the hardware vulnerabilities of the devices. A well-known hardware attack is Side-Channel Attack (SCA). SCA analyzes the Integrated Circuit (IC) radiated information, such as temperature, timing, noise, electromagnetic, and power consumption, when the circuits are processing the data. There are two popular Side-Channel Analysis methods, which provide the most interesting results: Power Analysis (PA) and ElectroMagnetic Analysis (EMA). The difference between PA and EMA is the object to be collected and processed the traces before deriving the bit strings of the key. The PA usually measures the power consumption by measuring the supply current thanks to an added resistor on the supply line of the IC. In the context of RFID tag where no external supply line is easily accessible, EMA is the most adapted method. EMA uses an ElectroMagnetic (EM) probe to collect the leakage EM. After collection, with the different analysis, we will have Simple SCA (SPA- Simple Power Analysis or SEMA- Simple ElectroMagnetic Analysis), Differential SCA (DPA- Differential Power Analysis or DEMA- Differential ElectroMagnetic Analysis), and Correlation SCA (CPA- Correlation Power Analysis or CEMA- Correlation ElectroMagnetic Analysis) [3]. While the SPA exploits the relationship between the executed operations and the collected traces, DPA exploits the relationship between the processed data and the collected traces. CPA uses the correlation calculation to derive the secret key information.

To mitigate wireless attacks, the tags normally use cryptography primitives and authentication protocols to protect the data before transmitting the data through an insecure channel. In RFID systems, there are at least two parties: reader and tag, with one IDentification number (ID) for each tag. With the identification protocol, the readers only verify the ID provided by the tag is either valid or not, whereas in the authentication protocol, the readers and the tags have to prove themselves that they are legal. There are several authentication protocols, but depending on the complexity of the algorithm used to compute the response on the tag side, authentication protocols used for RFID are classified into four categories: heavyweight, simple-weight, lightweight, and ultra-lightweight. Although providing the strongest robustness against the attacks, heavyweight protocols are not suitable for passive tag as complex algorithms used in these protocols are beyond the capacity of these devices. Furthermore, the lightweight and ultra-lightweight are much vulnerable to the attacks mentioned below due to applying the most straightforward computations for computing the communicated tokens. Therefore, in this paper, we consider the simple-weight protocols which use the simple operations or algorithms to create the interrogation tokens.

There are two categories of cryptography primitives: symmetric and asymmetric. Compared to asymmetric cryptography, the symmetric one is much simpler in terms of the complexity of the algorithm, implementation cost, and system performance. However, the most concerning problem of using symmetric primitive such as AES is the vulnerability of the key distribution [7]. Indeed, in the symmetric cryptography, both the sender and receiver must share the same secret key between the data encryption and decryption through a "secure" channel. All channels used in wireless communication are insecure and vulnerable to the attackers; consequently, the adversary could use various attacks mentioned upper to derive the secret key. With asymmetric cryptography, each party owns a pair of keys (public key and private key). While the public key will be known by everyone, the private key is only used on the tag itself, and there is no key distribution vulnerability issue.

Most RFID tag designs deal with security optimizations at the protocol level [12–15] or the cryptography primitive level [4,17,18,21,22]. It leads to an imbalance between the implementation costs and the security level as the countermeasures are not the most efficient. Indeed, a design exploration at the system level focusing on both the protocols and cryptography primitives could be more efficient. Because each protocol or primitive provides different security characteristics and requires different implementation costs, designers must carefully choose them depending on numerous criteria (such as hardware costs, security characteristics) to find the optimal design. This problematic motivate us to propose in this paper a methodology to perform the design exploration for low-cost ECC-based tags ensuring robustness against SCA and wireless attacks. Our methodology consists of comparing the various authentication protocols and different ECC algorithms in terms of security characteristics and costs. An experimental setup is also described for validating tag implementations and measuring tag security level against SCA.

This paper is organized as follows. Section 2 presents the security characteristics to compare the ECC-based authentication protocols used for low-cost ECC RFID tags. Section 3 compares and analyses the vulnerabilities of the low-cost ECC primitives. In Sect. 4, we describe an experimental setup to validate and evaluate the security level of implementation costs. Finally, in the last section, we summarize the paper and illustrate our perspective work.

2 Comparison and Vulnerability Analysis of Authentication Protocols for Low Cost ECC RFID Tags

A general authentication protocol based on ECC consists of two parties: RFID tag and reader. By exchanging the authentication messages created by the ECC

Scalar Multiplication (SM) operation, the tag and the reader can authenticate each other. SM operation provides the discrete logarithm problem, which disables the adversary to perform an inverse computation. Thus, the use of SM allows mitigating various security threats. Here, we mainly focus on the most popular ECC-based challenge-and-response systems that are applied for low-cost ECC-based RFID, such as Schnorr's protocol [12], Chou et al. [13], Zhang et al. [14], or Farash et al. [15]. This section demonstrates the possibility of the vulnerable analysis against both the wireless attack and SCA for these ECC-based authentication protocols, especially, Schnorr's scheme [12].

2.1 Security Characteristics and Threats

There are various characteristics defined to measure the robustness of the protocol against the threatens, such as mutual authentication, confidentiality, anonymity, availability, scalability, forward security, location privacy, and data integrity.

- Mutual authentication: Also called Two-way authentication. This property requires the authentication of both tag and reader.
- Confidentiality: Secret key is kept secret from all but authorized parties.
- Anonymity: Provide protection against discovery and misuse of identity.
- Availability: Assure that the electronic system is reliably available.
- Scalability: the ability of the system to maintain a large number of tags without undue strain and a scalable RFID protocol should avoid any requirement for proportional work to the number of tags [9].
- Forward security: ensures that all the previous secret key cannot be recovered if the long-term key or current session key is compromised, although the data transmitted by RFID is easily captured and may be highly vulnerable to side-channel attacks the stored keys.
- Location privacy: A more subtle attack aims at obtaining information on users and their movements. When using conventional authentication protocols, a tag can be easily identified during verification, which enables readers to trace tags. Therefore, a primary goal of an RFID system is to ensure location privacy by preventing the disclosure of information on users and their movements to all entities that are not trusted by the users.
- Data integrity: In the channel, transmitted data is not modified.

In addition, threats to the authentication protocols being considered are replay attack, Denial-of-Service (DoS), relay attack, cloning attack, and skimming attack.

- Replay attack: An adversary can simply store and replay a previous communication between a tag and reader to impersonate that tag.
- Denial-of-Service (DoS): When there are several illegal tags being deployed in the system, adversaries could abuse or disrupt the computational resource of the system [10].

- Relay Attack: Also named Man-in-the-middle attack. An attacker places an illegal device between the reader and the tag such that it can intercept the information and then modifies it or forwarded directly to the other end. Different from the replay attack, in the sense that the attacker does not store previous messages, nor does he replay them. Instead, the attacker intercepts the communication between the tag and the reader and then tries to relay the interrogation token between them. If the relay attack is performed quickly enough to pass the information to the legitimate tag and respond to the legitimate reader, the adversary can impersonate the legitimate tag or legitimate reader.
- Skimming Attack: In this attack, the adversary observes the information exchanged between a legitimate tag and a legitimate reader. Via the extracted data, the attacker attempts to make a cloned tag that imitates the original RFID tag.
- Cloning Attack: This attack is performed after skimming the tag's information (skimming attack). If the Identification Number of the tag is copied, an impersonal tag is created and acts as the ordinary tag without being detected.

As mentioned above, SCA is also an extremely dangerous threat that allows the adversary to attack authentication protocol. Regarding SPA, the adversary only collects one or a few power traces to derive the secret key; meanwhile, the DPA and CPA need numerous power traces to perform statistical analysis. Of course, these power traces must be collected during the period corresponding to the SM computations involving a fixed secret key. To analyse the protocol security level against SCA the following analysis must be performed. First, the attack requires to trig the start and the end of the SM computations to locate the meaningful information in the traces. Second, all the collected traces must be related to the same secret key. Besides, the attacker must know at least the encrypted data (respectively decrypted data) or the result of the encryption (respective decryption) corresponding to each trace and relative to each SM computation.

2.2 Vulnerability Analyse

Among all the mentioned protocols, Schnorr's protocol, illustrated in Fig. 1, is the least complicated and only provides the identification properties. Before analyzing the Schnorr's scheme, we have to know about the general notations used in the schemes. This authentication protocol is performed in a finite field $GF(q)$ with q is a large prime number. An additive group G with order q consisting of points on an elliptic curve E defined by a generator point P. The ith tag has a pair of keys (x_i, X_i) with x_i and X_i are the private and the public key of the tag. The server owns private key y and its public key Y. Assuming that the ith tag knows the public key of the server, and oppositely, the server also stores the public key of the tag.

Firstly, the tag chooses a random number r and generates an interrogation token $C_0 = rP$ before transmitting C_0 to the server. On the server side, after

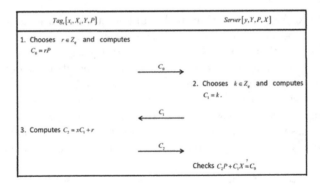

Fig. 1. Schnorr's identification protocol.

receiving the first token, it will send a random number k to the tag. And then, tag hides its private key x_i in the second message C_2 by a calculation $C_2 = xC_1 + r$. In this protocol, the server could check whether this ID being correct or not by comparing the formula $C_2P + C_1X = C_0$, whereas C_i is the communicated token i^{th} in the last step. If the left side of the formula equals to the right side, the identification is legal, and if the formula is not equal, the communication will be refused.

About the vulnerability robustness, due to using the random number r in each communication session to generate the token C_1, C_2, the adversary cannot impersonate tag even they store the token used in the previous sessions. Therefore, Schnorr's scheme is robust against the replay attack. Additionally, this protocol also resists skimming attacks and cloning attacks since they use the SM operation to compute the token C_2, which contains the private key of the tag x_i. However, the adversary can recovery the public key of the tag by computing $C_1^{-1}(C_0 + C_2P)$. As public key X_i is the personal identification, the adversary could extract this value and track the location of the tag.

2.3   Comparison

A performance, security characteristics, and functionality comparison is performed between Schnorr's scheme and other protocols. Table 1 shows the performance comparisons of these schemes. The parameters used for the comparison are the number of Hash function and Scalar Multiplication operations. It is visible that the computation cost of Schnorr's scheme is less than the others; meanwhile the Chou's [13], Zhang's [14], and Farash's [15] protocols require two Hash functions and two Scalar Multiplication operations on the Tag side; meanwhile there are only two Hash functions and one Scalar Multiplication in the server.

Table 2 compares the security features and the robustness against the possible attacks. All protocols have all security characteristics consisting of confidentiality, tag anonymity, availability, forward security, location privacy, and

Table 1. Performance comparison for Authentication Protocols

Scheme	Schnorr [12]		Chou [13]		Zhang [14]		Farash [15]	
	Tag	Server	Tag	Server	Tag	Server	Tag	Server
Hash function	0	0	2	2	2	2	2	2
Scalar Multiplication	1	2	2	1	2	1	2	1

scalability, except Schnorr's identification protocol that does not support the mutual authentication feature. About the robustness against the attacks, all of them are robust against the replay attack by using the random number to generate the tokens. However, only Farash's protocol can be secure against the server spoofing attack. Tag's impersonation and relay attack are not the vulnerable Farash's scheme [15].

Table 2. Comparison table for authentication protocols

Scheme	Schnorr [12]	Chou [13]	Zhang [14]	Farash [15]
Confidentiality	✓	✓	✓	✓
Mutual authentication	-	✓	✓	✓
Tag anonymity	✓	✓	✓	✓
Availability	✓	✓	✓	✓
Forward security	✓	✓	✓	✓
Location privacy	✓	✓	✓	✓
Scalability	✓	✓	✓	✓
Tag's impersonation	-	-	✓	✓
Server spoofing attack	-	-	-	✓
Replay attack	✓	✓	✓	✓
Cloning attack	-	✓	✓	✓
Man-in-the-middle	-	-	✓	✓

After analysing both Table 1 and Table 2, we can realize that the Schnorr authentication is the most lightweight protocol used to implement low cost RFID tags, while it is vulnerable against SCA due to using a constant private key. There is a countermeasure proposed by Naija et al. [16] that protects the system against SCA by changing the private key every session, but this protocol requires more resources. In addition, we can improve the cryptography primitives (ECC algorithm) to avoid leakage data.

3   Comparison and Vulnerability Analysis of Elliptic Curve Cryptography for Low Cost ECC RFID Tags

Elliptic Curve Cryptography (ECC) is one of the most promising algorithms in the asymmetric cryptography family for low cost RFID tag because it features the best trade-off between the security and implementation costs. As discussed in different previous publications, ECC provides the same security level as RSA with considerably shorter operands (approximately 160-bit of the key for ECC versus 1024-bit of the key for RSA). Theoretically, ECC is based on the generalized discrete logarithm problem, which prevents the adversary from performing an inverse computation to find the secret key. In this section, we will discuss the definition of the ECC and countermeasures that help ECC be robust against SCA.

3.1   Definition

Most of the time, in the context of cryptography, an elliptic curve is presented so-called Weierstrass form:

$$E : y^2 + a_1 xy + a_3 y = x^3 + a_2 x^2 + a_6 \tag{1}$$

Normally, when implementing in hardware, the binary form of the Weierstrass Curve, which is presented in Eq. (2) shows the advantages in terms of the number of gates, power consumption compared to the prime form. For the binary field $GF(2^m)$, a Weierstrass Elliptic Curve is defined as a set of points (x, y) satisfying the below formula:

$$E : y^2 + xy = x^3 + ax^2 + b \mod (F(x)) \tag{2}$$

In the Eq. (2), a and b are parameters of the curves with $b \neq 0$; $F(x)$ is the characteristic irreducible polynomial of the binary finite field $GF(2^m)$.

The ECC mainly relies on scalar multiplication kP, where k is an integer, and P is a generator point on the elliptic curve. This computation requires multiple computations of additions, when $P \neq Q$, and doubling, when $P = Q$. Thus, this operation is known as the costliest operation in ECC-based systems. Furthermore, due to using incomplete addition law, this operation becomes the target of SCA. In general, when performing a scalar multiplication, we implement the Double-and-Add algorithm as described in Algorithm 1:

As we can see in Algorithm 1, depending on the value of the bit of key k_i, the processor performs either doubling and addition or only doubling, which leads to consuming different energy patterns. Therefore, the adversaries could analyse the leakage information from the processor and perform (SCA). Furthermore, by inserting an injected fault into the crypto-system in order to move the base point of an elliptic curve to a weaker curve, the problem of solving the discrete logarithm of ECC becomes manageable and thus will lead to the recovery of the secret key.

Algorithm 1. Double-and-Add Algorithm

Input: a point P, an $n-$bit integer $k = \sum_{i=o}^{n-1} k_i 2^i$
Output: kP
    Initialisation :
1: Set register $Q = 0$
    LOOP Process:
2: **for** $i = n - 1$ to 0 **do**
3:    $Q = 2Q$
4:    **if** $k_i == 1$ **then**
5:      $Q = Q + P$
6:    **end if**
7: **end for**
8: **return** Q

In order to resist these attacks, there are several proposed countermeasures in the cryptography primitive level against Side-Channel Attacks. All of these countermeasures will be illustrated and compared in the Sect. 3.2.

3.2 Countermeasures Against SCA

Montgomery Ladder Algorithm: The Montgomery Ladder was presented in 1987 by Peter Montgomery [11] in order to speed up the scalar multiplication in the context of elliptic curves is shown in Algorithm 2.

Algorithm 2. Montgomery Ladder Algorithm

Input: a point P, a bit string $m = (m_{t-1}, ..., m_0)_2$ with $m_{t-1} = 1$
Output: $R = mP$
    Initialisation :
1: Set register $R_0 = 0; R_1 = 2P$
    LOOP Process:
2: **for** $i = t - 1$ to 0 **do**
3:    **if** $k_i == 1$ **then**
4:      $R_0 = R_0 + R_1; R_1 = 2R_1$
5:      $R_1 = R_0 + R_1; R_0 = 2R_0$
6:    **end if**
7: **end for**
8: **return** $R = R_0$

Different from Algorithm 1, in each iteration, the processor executes the same operations, one point addition, and one point doubling. In the case of the nonsupersingular curve, the following properties would be satisfied [4].

– If $P \neq \infty$, A and B are two different points, and $x_A = x_B$, then $A = -B$ and $A + B = \infty$.

- If $A \neq \infty$ and $B \neq \infty$ are two different points of the curve and if $A \neq -B$ then the x-coordinate of addition $A + B$ is:

$$x_{A+B} = x_P + x_B(x_A + x_B)^{-1} + (x_B(x_A + x_B)^{-1})^2 \tag{3}$$

- If A is a point of the curve, then x-coordinate of doubling $A + A$ is:

$$x_{A+A} = \begin{cases} x_A^2 + b/x_A^2 & \text{if } x_A \neq 0 \\ \infty, & \text{otherwise} \end{cases} \tag{4}$$

Consequently, using Montgomery Ladder Algorithm, the Scalar Multiplication can be executed with only x-coordinates of the A and B points. And then, we may recover the y-coordinate of A by the Eq. (5).

$$y_A = x_P^{-1}(x_A + x_P)[(x_A + x_P)(x_B + x_P) + x_P^2 + y_P] + y_P \tag{5}$$

This property not only reduces the requirement of the system in terms of the number of necessary registers, but it also improves the performance of Algorithm 2. The disadvantage of this algorithm is using many inversion operations, which costs many area and power consumption.

To reduce the number of the required inversion, it is possible to use projective coordinates inside Algorithm 2. To perform a Montgomery Ladder Algorithm in the projective coordinates, all Eqs. (3) to (5) have to represent the point A and B under the new coordinates $(X_A, Y_A, Z_A))$ and (X_B, Y_B, Z_B) instead of using affine coordinates (x_A, y_A) and (x_B, y_B). An equivalent relation is defined between the affine coordinate and the projective coordinates, $(x_A, y_A) \sim (X_A, Y_A, Z_A)$ if $x_A = \lambda^c X_A, x_B = \lambda^d Y_B,$ and $z_A = \lambda Z_B = 1$, with c and d are non-zero positive integers. With different pairs of c and d, we can define different projective coordinate systems. For example, with $c = 2, d = 3$, the affine points, which is used to execute the Montgomery ladder will move new projective coordinates, Jacobian Coordinate. The Weierstrass Curve defined in Algorithm 2 will be denoted as:

$$Y^2 = X^3 + aXZ^4 + bZ^6 \tag{6}$$

In this coordinate system, the point doubling is obtained by using these formulas:

$$\begin{cases} X_3 = (3X^2 + aZ_1^4)^2 - 8X_1Y_1^2 \\ Y_3 = (3X^2 + aZ_1^4)(4X_1Y_1 - X_3) - 8Y_1^4 \\ Z_3 = 2Y1Z_1 \end{cases} \tag{7}$$

By storing the intermediate values X_3, Y_3, Z_3, the Montgomery ladder could be executed with six field squarings, four field multiplications, and no inversion. After computing in the Jacobian coordinate, we take the intermediate result and reconvert them back to the affine coordinate by setting a register $R = Z_3^-1$, and thus $x_3 = X_3R^2$ and $y_3 = Y_3R^3$.

There are various implementations that concern reducing the implementation costs in terms of area, power consumption and improve the resistance against SCA, especially SPA, and FA by using the Montogomery Ladder in projective coordinates [4,17,18]. Furthermore, randomizing projective coordinates provide the robustness against the DPA and the CPA due to hiding the base point P [19].

Binary Edward Curves. Edward Curves defined over the field k firstly introduced by Bernstein et al. [20] in 2007 that they provide a complete addition formula for all points belonging to the elliptic curve. When $char(k) \neq 2$, Edward Curves are defined as below:

$$E_B : d_1(x + y) + d_2(x^2 + y^2) = xy + xy(x + y) + x^2 y^2 \tag{8}$$

where $d_1, d_2 \in \mathbb{F}_{2^m}$ with $d_1 \neq 0$ and $d_2 \neq d_1^2 + d_1$. These curves satisfied the Eq. (8) are symmetric over both x-axis and y-axis. It means that, with each point $P_1(x_1, y_1)$ there is always the negative point $P_1'(y_1, x_1)$ belonging to the same curve. Besides, it is clear for us to see that the neutral element of the addition law is the point $P(0,0)$.

In 2008, Bernstein et al. [23] firstly defined Edward Curves over fields k with $char(k) = 2$ and claimed that these Binary Edward Curves (BEC) provide "complete binary Edward curves". A complete Binary Edward Curve is a curve in which there is no exception case in the addition law. Therefore, in order to perform the scalar multiplication, there is only one operation instead of using the Double-and-Add Algorithm. Consequently, when the attacker perform the Simple SCA attack, such as Simple Power Analysis (SPA), they cannot derive any difference in the power traces and then our algorithm is secured.

3.3   Comparison

It is difficult to compare architectures using different elliptic curves and different implementations in terms of implementation cost and robustness against the SCA. Because with different elliptic curves, they provide different security levels in terms of the number of necessary traces to break the key, and they also entail different implementation costs. When we use the same elliptic curve, with different architecture and implementation techniques, the trade-off between implementation cost and the robustness of the design will be worthy of consideration. In order to practically evaluate the trade-off between the implementation cost and the robustness at the system level, we demonstrate an experiment performing CPA on FPGA in Sect. 4 (Table 3).

4   Experimental Setup for Validation and Evaluation of the Security of Low Cost RFID Tag Implementations

There are numerous experimental setups used for validating and evaluating the robustness characteristics of IC against SCA. But they focus only on the cryptography primitives. Thus, they do not allow to archive a good trade-off between the

Table 3. Comparison table for elliptic curve implementations

Design	Field	Curve	Tech	Freq (MHz)
Salarifard [17]	$GF(2^{163})$	Weierstrass	65 nm	6.81
Imran [18]	$GF(2^{163})$	Weierstrass	Virtex-4	64
Sutter [4]	$GF(2^{163})$	Weierstrass	Virtex-e	87.7
Wu [21]	$GF(2^{163})$	BEC	-	1
Rashidi [22]	$GF(2^{163}$	BEC	Virtex-4	-

Design	Area	Runtime (ms)	Energy (uJ)
Salarifard [17]	20.4 kGates	0.146	130
Imran [18]	6.8kSlices + 10kLUTs	0.053	-
Sutter [4]	16 kSlices + 4.7kLUTs	0.019	-
Wu [21]	14.2 kGates	39.8	5.58 nJ/bit
Rashidi [22]	23 kSlices	0.012	-

implementation cost and the security level of RFID tag based on authentication protocols and cryptography primitives. In this section, we introduce an experimental setup to validate and evaluate at system level RFID tag implementations against SCA (in this particular case we choose the CPA). The design implementation of the tag digital parts is done in a FPGA. No wireless communication is implemented. Indeed, the communication components (e.g., antenna, impedance for backscattering) are not validated and as these components are not involved in known security weaknesses. The reader digital part will also be implemented in an FPGA (using FPGA prototyping platform). This will allow us to functionally validate the entire authentication protocol. This validation can be done looking at the exchanged messages between the tag and the reader. Using FPGA allows performing quick area and power estimations thanks to already available design tools. It also allows quickly adding countermeasures. Finally FPGA also allows a good estimation of the security level againts SCA. Indeed, it is well admitted that the results obtained using FPGA are close to the results that would be obtained using a functionally equivalent IC.

In order to perform the CPA, we need an storage oscilloscope, a computer, and a SAKURA-G as depicted in Fig. 2-a. The oscilloscope plays a role of the adversary when they measure the power consumed by the processor and collect the power traces which are the material for the next analysing step. Meanwhile, the computer and the SAKURA-G play as the Reader and the Tag which authenticate each other, the computer also is a tool analysing the collected power traces to find the secret key.

After connecting all the necessary equipment, we use the MATLAB to compute the correlation efficient between the recorded traces and the hypothetical power consumption as depicted in Fig. 2-b. Firstly, MATLAB performs several authentication session by sending several data vectors contained in the

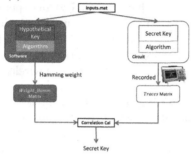

(a) Connection in the CPA Attack

(b) CPA Attack Scenario

Fig. 2. Vulnerable analysing against CPA with SAKURA-G testbench.

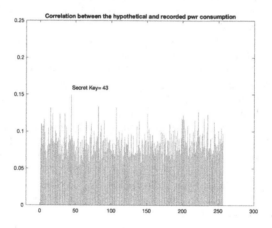

Fig. 3. Result of CPA attack.

"inputs.mat" to the testboard and osicilloscope is used to collect the power and preprocess them before sending to the MATLAB to analyse. Intermediately, by using the Hamming weight model, MATLAB generates a matrix of hypothetical power consumption. Consequently, the adversary uses the Pearson Correlation Coefficient to find the secret key. The result of our experiment is shown in the Fig. 3.

5 Conclusion

In this paper, we have proposed an efficient methodology to develop a security solution against SCA at the system level for ECC-based low-cost RFID tags. This methodology first consists of studying the security level of various authentication protocols against wireless attacks and SCA. For that, we provide a complete list of criteria concerning both wireless attacks and SCA vulnerabilities. Second, adapted cryptography primitives must be designed. Finally, to fairly compare these designs, we have introduced an experimental setup based on an FPGA prototyping platform that can be used for validating and evaluating the robustness characteristic against the SCA of these designs. The perspective of the work is to propose a first authentication protocol and a fair cost ECC primitive that can be secure both against various wireless attacks and SCA.

Aknowledgement. This work is supported by the French National Research Agency in the framework of the "Investissements d'avenir" program (ANR-15-IDEX-02).

References

1. Kocher, P., Ja, J. (n.d.). Differential Power Analysis. 10
2. Brier, E., Clavier, C., Olivier, F.: Correlation power analysis with a leakage model. In: Joye, M., Quisquater, J.-J. (eds.) Cryptographic Hardware and Embedded Systems–CHES 2004, pp. 16–29. Springer, Heidelberg (2004). https://doi.org/10.1007/978-3-540-28632-5-2
3. De Mulder, E., Örs, S.B., Preneel, B., Verbauwhede, I.: Differential power and electromagnetic attacks on a FPGA implementation of elliptic curve cryptosystems. Comput. Electr. Eng. **33**(5), 367–382 (2007). https://doi.org/10.1016/j.compeleceng.2007.05.009
4. Sutter, G.D., Deschamps, J.-P., Imana, J.L.: Efficient elliptic curve point multiplication using digit-serial binary field operations. IEEE Trans. Industr. Electron. **60**(1), 217–225 (2013). https://doi.org/10.1109/TIE.2012.2186104
5. Sklavos, N., Chaves, R., Natale, G.D., Regazzoni, F. (eds.) Hardware Security and Trust: Design and Deployment of Integrated Circuits in a Threatened Environment. Springer, Heidelberg (2017). https://doi.org/10.1007/978-3-319-44318-8
6. Benot, O.: Fault attack. In: van Tilborg, H.C.A., Jajodia, S. (eds.) Encyclopedia of Cryptography and Security, pp. 452–453. Springer, Heidelberg (2011). https://doi.org/10.1007/978-1-4419-5906-5_505
7. Paar, C., Pelzl, J.: Understanding Cryptography: A Textbook for Students and Practitioners. Springer, Heidelberg (2010). https://doi.org/10.1007/978-3-642-04101-3
8. Mangard, S., Oswald, E., Popp, T.: Power Analysis Attacks: Revealing the Secrets of Smart Cards, 1st edn. Springer, Heidelberg (2010). https://doi.org/10.1007/978-0-387-38162-6
9. Song, B., Mitchell, C.J.: Scalable RFID security protocols supporting tag ownership transfer **34**(4), 556–566 (2011). https://doi.org/10.1016/j.comcom.2010.02.027
10. Fu, Y., Zhang, C., Wang, J.: A research on Denial of Service attack in passive RFID system. In: 2010 International Conference on Anti-Counterfeiting, Security and Identification, Chengdu, pp. 24–28 (2010). https://doi.org/10.1109/ICASID.2010.5551848

11. Montgomery, L.: Speeding the pollard and elliptic curve methods of factorization. Math. Comput. **48**(177), 243–264 (1987)
12. Luo, P., Wang, X., Feng, J., Xu, Y.: Low-power hardware implementation of ECC processor suitable for low-cost RFID tags. In: 2008 9th International Conference on Solid-State and Integrated-Circuit Technology, October 2008, pp. 1681–1684 (2008). https://doi.org/10.1109/ICSICT.2008.4734876
13. Chou, J.-S.: An efficient mutual authentication RFID scheme based on elliptic curve cryptography. J. Supercomput. **70**(1), 75–94 (2013). https://doi.org/10.1007/s11227-013-1073-x
14. Zhang, Z., Qi, Q.: An efficient RFID authentication protocol to enhance patient medication safety using elliptic curve cryptography. J. Med. Syst. **38**(5), 1–7 (2014). https://doi.org/10.1007/s10916-014-0047-8
15. Farash, M.S., Nawaz, O., Mahmood, K., Chaudhry, S.A., Khan, M.K.: A provably secure RFID authentication protocol based on elliptic curve for healthcare environments. J. Med. Syst. **40**(7), 1–7 (2016). https://doi.org/10.1007/s10916-016-0521-6
16. Naija, Y., Beroulle, V., Machhout, M.: Security enhancements of a mutual authentication protocol used in a HF full-fledged RFID tag. J. Electron. Test. **34**(3), 291–304 (2018). https://doi.org/10.1007/s10836-018-5725-x
17. Salarifard, R., Bayat-Sarmadi, S., Mosanaei-Boorani, H.: A low-latency and low-complexity point-multiplication in ECC. IEEE Trans. Circuits Syst. I Regul. Pap. **65**(9), 2869–2877 (2018). https://doi.org/10.1109/TCSI.2018.2801118
18. Imran, M., Rashid, M., Shafi, I.: Lopez Dahab based elliptic crypto processor (ECP) over GF(2163) for low-area applications on FPGA. In: 2018 International Conference on Engineering and Emerging Technologies (ICEET), February 2018, pp. 1–6 (2018). https://doi.org/10.1109/ICEET1.2018.8338645
19. Coron, J.-S.: Resistance against differential power analysis for elliptic curve cryptosystems. In: Koç, Ç.K., Paar, C. (eds.) CHES 1999. LNCS, vol. 1717, pp. 292–302. Springer, Heidelberg (1999). https://doi.org/10.1007/3-540-48059-5_25
20. Bernstein, D.J., Lange, T.: Faster addition and doubling on elliptic curves. In: Advances in Cryptology - ASIACRYPT, pp. 29–50. Springer, Heidelberg (2007). https://doi.org/10.1007/978-3-540-76900-2-3
21. Wu, C., Yang, F., Tan, X., Wang, C., Chen, F., Wang, J.: An ECC crypto engine based on binary edwards elliptic curve for low-cost RFID tag chip. In: 2015 IEEE 11th International Conference on ASIC (ASICON), November 2015, pp. 1–4 (2015). https://doi.org/10.1109/ASICON.2015.7517207
22. Rashidi, B., Sayedi, S.M., Farashahi, R.R.: Full-custom hardware implementation of point multiplication on binary Edwards curves for application-specific integrated circuit elliptic curve cryptosystem applications. IET Circuits Devices Syst. **11**(6), 568–578 (2017). https://doi.org/10.1049/iet-cds.2017.0110
23. Bernstein, D.J., Lange, T., Rezaeian Farashahi, R.: Binary edwards curves. In: Oswald, E., Rohatgi, P. (eds.) CHES 2008. LNCS, vol. 5154, pp. 244–265. Springer, Heidelberg (2008). https://doi.org/10.1007/978-3-540-85053-3_16

Pseudo Zero-Watermarking Algorithm Using Combination of Non-blind Watermarking and Visual Secret Sharing Scheme

Le Danh Tai[1,2], Cao Thi Luyen[1,2], and Ta Minh Thanh[1,2(✉)]

[1] Le Quy Don Technical University, 236 Hoang Quoc Viet, Hanoi, Vietnam
thanhtm@lqdtu.edu.vn
[2] University of Transport and Communications, Hanoi, Vietnam
http://fit.mta.edu.vn/

Abstract. This paper proposes a solution for digital image copyright protection technique using the combination of watermarking and visual encryption technique. In our solution, the copyright information (copyright logo) is distributed into n shares using $k - out - of - n$ distributed algorithm, also called (k, n) visual secret sharing method. One of the shares is randomly selected to embed into the original image to prove the user's copyright. The remaining $n - 1$ shares is used to register with Copyright Department. When claiming the copyright belongs to the user, the verifier only needs to extract the watermark information from the watermarked image, then decodes with any registered $k - 1$ shares from $n - 1$ shares for restoring copyright information. Experimental results of the proposed method compared with the method using only digital watermark show that our method has more practical effectiveness in the application of digital product copyright protection.

Keywords: Digital watermarking · Visual secret sharing - VSS · Copyright protection · Discrete Wavelet Transform (DWT) · Discrete Cosine Transform (DCT) · Copyright authority

1 Introduction

1.1 Overview

The number of digital contents delivered over the Internet has been increased in recent years. According to the development of network technologies, the unauthorized copies and manipulation of digital contents have become a serious problem. It also raised the problems of infringing on copyright and affecting the interests of the digital content creators. In order to solve such problems, a lot of watermarking methods have been proposed for protecting the author's copyright. The watermarking algorithms can be applied on the spatial domain and the frequency

N.-S. Vo et al. (Eds.): INISCOM 2021, LNICST 379, pp. 448–464, 2021.
https://doi.org/10.1007/978-3-030-77424-0_36

domain. In general, the watermarking methods used frequency domain are more robust than that of methods used spatial domain.

In the previous watermarking methods, some frequency domains are suitable for robust watermarking methods such as Discrete Wavelet Transform (DWT), Discrete Cosine Transform (DCT), and Discrete Fourier Transform (DFT). The frequency domain based robust watermarking methods have been shown in recently e.g. DCT-based [1–4], DWT-based [5–8], and DFT-based [9,10]. These methods had proved that the frequency domain is efficient for digital right management system. In general, when we embed directly the watermark information into the digital image, its quality may be degraded. Also, the watermark information cannot be extracted when the embedded images are modified under some attacks such as image processing and geometrical processing.

In order to achieve the balance of better quality of the watermarked images and the robustness of watermark extraction, some improved frequency domains are proposed such as q-DCT [11], q-DWT [12], and q-SVD [13]. According to the values of q parameter, those proposed methods could provide a new frequency domain for such purpose. However, the optimization of the values for q parameter is quite complicated, then it depends on many experiments and those of analysis.

With an another approach, the zero-watermarking methods, in which the watermark information is not embedded into the digital contents, are frequently proposed for digital contents [14]. The zero-watermarking methods are mainly employed the robust feature of the content in order to encode with the watermark information, the generate the master share (MS) and the owner share (OS). The MS is used to register to Copyright Office. When the dispute occurs, the feature of the contents is extracted again, then decodes with the owner share to generate the watermark. According to the visual of watermark information, the copyright authority can judge the ownership of the digital contents. However, the drawback of zero-watermarking is to depend on a lot of features extracted from the digital contents. That may be affected when the digital contents are degraded under strong attacks.

The concept of joint visual cryptography and watermarking method [18] is proposed to take a balance of the robustness and the visual quality. In this system, the watermark can only be achieved if all of the shared images are collected. In the other hand, the watermarking method usually embed the watermark information into the digital image its self while preserving the quality of the watermarked image. Based on those merits, the joint visual cryptography and watermarking method proposes a new approach for digital copyright protection.

1.2   Our Contributions

We summarise our contributions in this paper as follows.

We propose a new embedding method utilizing both frequency domain based embedding approach and VSS in order to reduce the amount of watermarking information that is embedded into the digital contents itself. Since our proposed method employs the color watermark image as copyright information, the embedded amount of watermark information should be considered to improve the quality of watermarked contents while remaining the meaning of copyright protection solutions. In our proposed method, the color watermark information is encoded by AES (Advanced Encryption Standard) encryption [27], then created n shares to generate OS and MS by using (k, n) visual secret sharing method. One of the shares, *e.g.* OS, is randomly selected to embed into the original image to prove the user's copyright. Other shares are used as MS to register for Copyright Office. According to our method, the number of watermark bits embedded into the copyrighted contents is litter compared to that of conventional watermarking methods.

In our understanding, in order to achieve the robustness of watermarking method, we need to propose the methods that let not the hackers can break or destroy the watermark information from the watermarked contents. Therefore, our proposed method does not depend on the feature of digital contents, which may be the clues for hackers try to destroy the contents either the watermark information. Since our method uses random one of share as the watermark information for embedding into the DWT frequency domain, it certainly reduces the dependent of the feature of digital contents like zero-watermarking methods. However, our extracted watermarking information can be decoded with MS (remain of $k - 1$ shares) to confirm the registered copyright information.

We also employ AES encryption to encode the color watermark information. After that, we apply (k, n)-VSS method on the encoded color watermark information to separate n shares using in our system. Only the person who has AES key and secret key (k, n) can decode the watermark information and verify the copyright of digital contents. That makes our proposed method more secure comparing with previous zero-watermarking methods.

1.3   Roadmap

This paper is organized as follows. Section 2 gives surveys of related works. Section 3 introduces our proposed pseudo zero-watermarking technique based on non-blind Watermarking and VSS for color images and color watermark image. Section 4 presents the results of the experiments and Sect. 5 concludes our paper.

2   Related Works

There are many image watermarking algorithms using VSS for copyright protection. However, they are tended to follow the same patterns and processed steps to ensure the security of cover image. According to the our survey, we describe the general algorithm of these methods. Then, we also explain the different entities of the integrated system and each role of them.

In general, most of zero-watermarking techniques are proposed based on VSS (*e.g.* visual cryptography - VC) for spatial domain. We call it VZWS. The concept of VSS using in the zero-watermarking is described in paper [19,20]. VC is employed as an extended VSS algorithm for protecting the digital images. Such problem of VC is shown as the special case of a $2 - out - of - 2$ visual secret sharing problem. The secret image is divided into two shares that consist of random dots of the secret images by using the corresponding location of each pixel from secret image. In order to decode the secret image, the secret image can be easily detected when these shares are stacked together.

Firstly, Hwang [28] had built up an zero-watermarking method based on the concept of VC. In his method, the secret information (watermark information) is not embedded directly into the original image. Hwang's method makes it harder to detect/recover from the watermarked image. The watermark information can be obtained by stacking all shares together, without making comparison with the original image. However, since Hwang's method extracts the LSBs (Least Significant Bit) for XOR-ing with the watermark pattern, then its algorithm may not secure and be robust against various strong attacks.

In order to enhance the security of the method [28], Surekha et al. [32] proposed a similar MSB (Most Significant Bit) based algorithm in which a XOR operation is involved for encryption with watermark logo. It achieved better security than that of Hwang, but it could not improve the robustness. Also, Surekha et al. employed the feature of MSBs for encoding, therefore, it increases the probability of false positive. Also, since the increasing of false positive, it leads to ambiguity in authority verification when the depute happens. Hence, such algorithms cannot be applied for copyright protection.

In another approach, Bolla et al. [30] proposed a method by using the statistical properties of sampling distribution of means (SDM) to improve the required security that is mentioned above. This method used the SDM features from original image to create the master share (MS). After that, MS is employed together with the watermark pattern for generating the information of ownership share (OS) using VC(2,2) with a block of 4 subpixels. The results of this method that can resist several processing attacks and geometric attacks.

Since VZWS methods almost employ the spatial feature involving with the watermark pattern, the security issues are not ensured enough. There are some papers focused on proposal of frequency based feature to attain the security and to improve the robustness of their method. We call it VZWF.

In the paper of Wang et al. [31], they proposed a watermarking method that extracts the feature of SVD (Singular Value Decomposition) domain to encode with watermark information in order to improve the security and robustness. In their method, the random 31×31 blocks are selected. After that, the SVD is applied to each block, then the singular value (SVs) is selected to generate the MS. The security of their method is improved by using decomposition into random several blocks, and using a variant of the VC (2,2) with a block of 4 sub-pixels. Based on such approach, the OS is generated. In order to confirm the authority rights, the MS is constructed with the same process, and then superimposed on the OS to extract the watermark. Wang's method focused on using the feature of frequency domain based on the secret key for randomizing the blocks patterns.

To solve the false positive problem (FPP), Surekha et al. [32] proposed a watermarking method using the feature of DWT (Discrete Wavelet Transform) domain. It presented a new VC(2,2) scheme called Pair-Wise Visual Cryptography (PWVC) which measures the security criteria for ensuring the reliability of the method. Also, they used PWVC to avoid the distortion of the watermark information by creating shares with same size as the original watermark. In their method, the LL sub-band of DWT domain is randomly selected by using secret key to reconstruct the feature matrix which contains the averages of selected blocks. According to the feature matrix, the MS is generated by using PWVC algorithm. In order to confirm the authority rights, the same process is repeated to generate the MS, the latter is superimposed on the OS to extract the watermark.

In order to improve more securely, Thanh *et al.* [14] proposed a new image zero-watermarking algorithm based on the encryption of visual map feature (VMF) or permuted visual map feature (PVMF) extractes form original image with copyright information. They employed the robust feature extracted from the cover image by taking the combination of QR decomposition and 1D-DCT. Then, they encrypted the VMF and PVMF feature with the watermark information to generate MS and OS. Therefore, they could improve the security of method by randomizing visual feature of original images. They had demonstrated that their method is robust against common processing and geometric attacks, also it is with low consuming time.

3   Our Pseudo Zero-Watermarking Technique Based on Non-blind Watermarking and VSS

According to above analytic, we found that the mentioned issues can be solved by improving VSS and watermarking technique. This section explains the detail our proposed method.

3.1   Random Bit Sequence Based (k, n)-VSS Scheme

The (k, n)-VSS scheme provides a method where a secret image is separated into n shares. In this scheme, any k or more shares can generate the secret image by stacking them. However, fewer than k shares get nothing about the secret image.

In general, in secret sharing scheme, there exist n users $U = \{U_1, U_2, ..., U_n\}$ and a provider P. A (k, n)-VSS scheme consists of two phases as follows:

(1) *Sharing phase*: the provider P divides the secret image W into n shares $S_1, S_2, ..., S_n$ and sends each share S_i to a user U_i.

(2) *Reconstruction phase*: a group of at least k users collect and submit their shares to reconstruct the secret image.

Based on the *Sharing phase* and *Reconstruction phase*, the information secret sharing method among many users is established. In order to control the security of secret image W for applying on copyright protection solution, we improve the (k, n)-VSS scheme by using random bit sequence. The detail steps are described as follows:

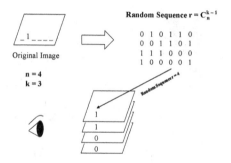

Fig. 1. An illustration of our sharing algorithm.

1. *Sharing algorithm*
   (a) To define the number of shares, the secret key ns is computed by following formula.

$$ns = C_n^{k-1} \qquad (1)$$

   Based on the value of ns, the random bit sequence $\{Sq_1, Sq_2, \cdots, Sq_{ns}\}$ is generated.
   (b) Suppose that the secret image W is divided into n shares $S_1, S_2, ..., S_n$. Such n shares are generated by using our simple algorithm,
      i. All pixels of S_t is set "0" by default values where $(1 \leq t \leq n)$.
      ii. If the value of ith bit of each pixel from the image W is "1", the random value r is generated so that it is between 1 and ns. The corresponding i^{th} bit of S_t is calculated by $S_t(i) = S_j(i)|Sq_r(j)$, where | is OR bit operation, and $1 \leq j \leq n, 1 \leq r \leq ns$. The concept of sharing algorithm is shown in Fig. 1.
2. *Reconstruction phase*
   (a) In order to reconstruct the secret image W, s shares $(k \leq s \leq n)$ are collected. The value of s is randomly created for each reconstruction.
   (b) The secret image W' can be reconstructed by taking the OR operation of all corresponding bit position of each share.

$$W'(j) = S_1(j)|S_2(j)|...|S_s(j), \qquad (2)$$

where $1 \leq j \leq w \times h$, and $w \times h$ is the size of W.

3.2   Our Pseudo Zero-Watermarking Method

The concept of our pseudo zero-watermarking method is shown in Fig. 2. Our method is composed of watermarking technique and $(k - n)$-VSS technique. The detail steps of our method is described as follows:

1. The color watermark image W is firstly encrypted by using AES algorithm [27] in order to enhance the security of our method. Then, the encrypted watermark image is divided into n shares called $S_1, S2, ..., S_n$ by using (k, n)-VSS method explained in Sect. 3.1.

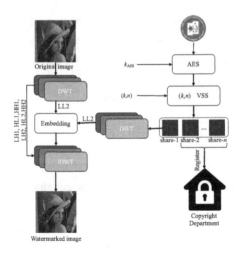

Fig. 2. Our embedding algorithm.

2. A random share is chosen to embed into the original image. For simply, we choose S_1 as the watermark information for watermarking method. The remains (*e.g.* $S_2, S_3, ..., S_n$) are registered as ownership share (OS) for the office of copyright authority (CA) in order to check the copyright of content.
3. Perform the first-level DWT (applied on RGB component) of the input image I and the share image S_1. Then, the LL_1 sub-band of I and S_1 is performed the second-level DWT. The LL_2 sub-band of I and S_1 is achieved to embed the watermark information.
4. The LL_2 sub-band of S_1 is $S_1^w(i,j)$ is embedded into the LL_2 sub-band of I as follows:
$$LL'_2(i,j) = LL_2(i,j) + \alpha S_1^w(i,j), \tag{3}$$
where α is the strength embedding factor.
5. After embedding the watermark information, the embedded sub-band LL'_2 is composed with another sub-bands to perform the inverse DWT (iDWT) and generate the watermarked image I'.

3.3 Copyright Confirmation

Note that, in our method, the master share (MS) is the watermark extracted from the embedded image I'. In order to extract the watermark S'_1, the original image I and the watermarked image I' are required. Therefore, our method is non-blind algorithm. However, since our method is used to register with CA for copyright confirmation, so that it is useful in real applications.

If the property dispute concerning the image I' happens. The CA department needs to judge the rightful owner of the such image. The CA asks the owner to provide the secret key such as α, the key k_{AES} of AES encryption, the key (k,n) of (k,n)-VSS, and the secret key ns.

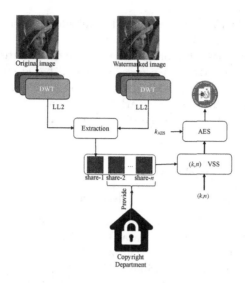

Fig. 3. Our extraction algorithm.

The MS is extracted from the watermarked image by workflow shown in Fig. 3. The explanation is shown as follows:

1. Perform the second-level DWT (applied on RGB component) of the input image I and the watermarked image I'. Then, the LL_2 sub-band of I and I' are retrieved to extract the watermark information $S_1'^w(i,j)$, called MS, by using the following formula.

$$S_1'^w(i,j) = (LL_2'(i,j) - LL_2(i,j))/\alpha \qquad (4)$$

2. The extracted $S_1'^w$ is composed with the remains (e.g. $S_2, S_3, ..., S_n$), called OS. A group of ns shares are used to decoded in (k,n)-VSS scheme, then obtain the AES encrypted image.
3. Finally, the AES encrypted image is decrypted using AES with the secret key k_{AES} to extract the copyright image W'.

According to the extracted image W', CA can judge the rightful owner of the suspected image.

3.4 The DWT-only Method

To justify the utility of combining DWT-based watermark technique with (k,n)-VSS, we propose here a reduced version of our method based only on the DWT domain. That means after encoding the watermark image by using AES encryption with secret key k_{AES}, the encrypted watermark image is performed the second-level DWT on RGB components. Note that, the (k,n)-VSS scheme is not applied on the DWT-only method. The embedding process is treated with same methodology of Eq. (3).

In the extraction phase, the original image I and the watermarked image I' also are required. The extraction process is treated based on the Eq. (4). The extracted watermark image is again decrypted by using AES encryption with secret key k_{AES} to obtain the watermark information.

According to the extracted image W', CA also can judge the rightful owner of the suspected image.

4   Experimental Results

4.1   Test Images and Evaluation Measures

To perform the efficiency of the proposed method, we conduct five color images of the well known Standard Image Data-BAse (SIDBA) database[1]. The size of our test images are $W \times H = 256 \times 256$ pixels.

To evaluate the quality of experimental images, we use $PSNR$ (Peak Signal to Noise Ratio) criterion [14]. The value of $PSNR$ of $W \times H$ pixels image of $I(i,j)$ and $I'(i,j)$ is calculated as follows:

$$PSNR = 20 \log_{10} \frac{MAX(I)}{\sqrt{MSE}}, \tag{5}$$

where $MAX(I) = 255$ and MSE (Mean Square Error) is calculated as follows:

$$MSE = \sqrt{\frac{1}{W \times H} \sum_{i=0}^{W-1} \sum_{j=0}^{H-1} (I(i,j) - I'(i,j))^2} \tag{6}$$

To verify the robustness of watermark information, we employ the normalized correlation (NC) value between the original watermark W and the extracted watermark W' [14]. The NC value is calculated as follows:

$$NC = \frac{\sum_{i=0}^{L} \sum_{j=0}^{L} W(i,j).W'(i,j)}{\sum_{i=0}^{L} \sum_{j=0}^{L}, W(i,j)^2}, \tag{7}$$

where $L \times L$ is the size of W.

In the experiments, the $PSNR$ value for each attacked image and the NC value for each watermark extracted from the attacked images is calculated. In general, if the $PSNR$ value is larger than 35 dB, the quality of the attacked image is considered to be close to the original image. When the NC value is close to "1", it denotes that the proposed method is robust against the attacks.

To define the suitable value of watermark strength factor, we used the same method of paper [35]. In the rest of our experiments, we set $\alpha = 0.2$ as the default watermark strength factor value.

---

[1] http://decsai.ugr.es/cvg/index2.php.

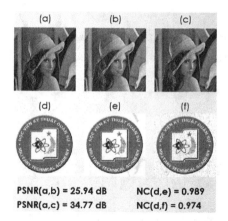

Fig. 4. (a) Lena - original image, (b) DWT-only method based watermarked image, (c) Our method based watermark image, (d) Original watermark logo, (e) DWT-only method based the extracted watermark, (f) Our method based the extracted watermark

Table 1. The values of PSNR and NC for experimental images

Image name	PSNR	NC
Lena	34.7672	0.974729
Pepper	34.7935	0.975822
Couple	34.8068	0.975416
Mandrill	34.8077	0.976204
Parrots	34.9288	0.973707

4.2   Quality of Evaluation

Firstly, we evaluate the quality of the watermarked image after applying our method for embedding the color watermark image shown in the Fig. 2. Our proposed method embeds only S_1 share into the original image instead of embedding all shares in DWT-only method, therefore, the quality of the watermarked image can be improved.

The comparison results are shown in Fig. 4. Since our proposed method only embeds litter amount of watermark comparing with DWT-only method, the quality of watermarked image is better than that of DWT-only method. That shows in the values of our method (34.77 dB) and DWT-only method (25.94 dB). Also, the watermark that is extracted from such DWT-only method and our method show that it is almost the same. NC values are 0.989 and 0.974, respectively.

The values of $PSNR$ and NC are shown in Table 1. Such results show that our proposed method is suitable for the real applications of copyright protection.

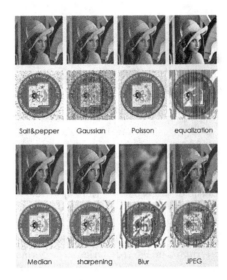

Fig. 5. The extracted watermark image based on corresponding attacks.

Table 2. The NC values computed from attacked Lena image.

Type of attacks	NC
Salt and pepper	0.92044
Gaussian	0.82326
Poisson	0.91805
Equalization	0.70237
Median	0.9567
Sharpening	0.95019
Blur	0.8814
JPEG	0.78889

4.3   Robustness of Comparison

In the following, we evaluate our proposed method against some attacks such as noise addition, low pass filtering, image enhancement, etc. Table 2 shows the NC values of the extracted watermarks under several image processing attacks on Lena image. Figure 5 also shows the extracted watermark image based on corresponding attacks. We can observe that the proposed method is fairly robust against image processing attacks.

In order to prove the efficiency of our method, we compare our experimental results with that of DWT-only method. Table 3 demonstrates that the proposed method is robust against Salt and pepper noise, Gaussian noise, Poisson noise, histogram equalization, Median filtering, Laplacian sharpening, Blur filtering and JPEG compression attacks. Based on these experimental results,

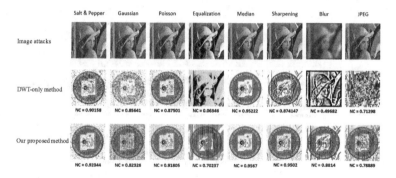

Fig. 6. The comparison of extracted watermarks between the DWT-method and Our method on Lena image.

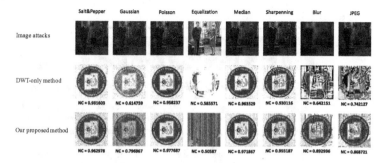

Fig. 7. The comparison of extracted watermarks between the DWT-method and Our method on Couple image.

our proposed method outperforms the reduced DWT-only method for almost testing attacks. This can conclude that the combination of the two technique (DWT-based watermarking and VSS) is more practically helpful than the use of one domain only (DWT) especially if the watermarked images are intended to undergo these types of attacks.

Figure 6, Fig. 7, Fig. 8, Fig. 9, and Fig. 10 describe that the extracted watermarks from our proposed method are more superior than that of DWT-method. The visualization of watermark logos are clear for confirmation the copyright of digital images. The reason is that, in the DWT-method, all bits of color watermark image are embedded into the original images, therefore the quality of the watermarked images is degraded. Also, when the watermarked images are edited undergo some attacks, that makes the extracted watermark images are not so clear.

For robustness confirmation, our values of NC parameters are better than the DWT-method. Therefore, all these experiments show that the proposed method is robust against common image-processing attacks.

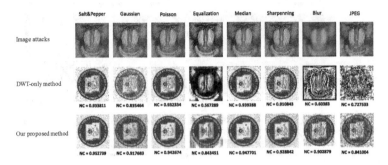

Fig. 8. The comparison of extracted watermarks between the DWT-method and Our method on Mandrill image.

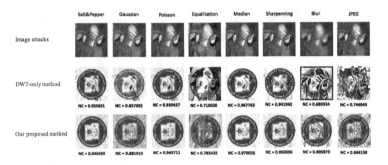

Fig. 9. The comparison of extracted watermarks between the DWT-method and Our method on Parrots image.

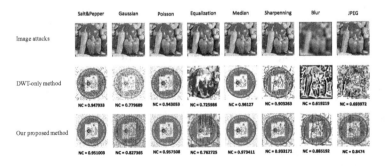

Fig. 10. The comparison of extracted watermarks between the DWT-method and Our method on Pepper image.

Table 3. Comparison of other images.

Attack types	Lena		Pepper		Couple		Mandrill		Parrots	
	DWT-only	Ours	DWT-only	Ours	DWT-only	Ours	DWT-only	Ours	DWT-only	Ours
Salt and pepper	0.90158	**0.92044**	0.94793	**0.95103**	0.9316	**0.99298**	0.93381	**0.95273**	0.93565	**0.94549**
Gaussian noise	0.85641	**0.82326**	0.77968	**0.82737**	0.61476	**0.79696**	0.83546	**0.98768**	0.83709	**0.88191**
Poisson noise	0.87501	**0.91805**	0.94305	**0.95751**	0.95824	**0.97769**	0.93233	**0.94267**	0.93043	**0.94571**
Histogram equalization	0.06346	**0.70237**	0.72598	**0.7627**	0.58557	**0.50587**	0.56728	**0.84345**	0.71602	**0.78542**
Median filter	0.95222	**0.9567**	0.96127	**0.9734**	0.96353	**0.97186**	0.93928	**0.9477**	0.96776	**0.97002**
Sharpening	0.87414	**0.95019**	0.90326	**0.93317**	0.93011	**0.95518**	0.91084	**0.92884**	0.94194	**0.95003**
Blur	0.49682	**0.8814**	0.61922	**0.88519**	0.64215	**0.89293**	0.60383	**0.90287**	0.68032	**0.90587**
JPEG	0.71298	**0.78889**	0.69397	**0.84741**	0.74213	**0.86872**	0.72753	**0.841**	0.74494	**0.84613**

5   Conclusion

In this paper, a robust and simple watermarking scheme based on the combination of DWT domain and VSS is presented. In our solution, the copyright information (copyright logo) is distributed into n shares using $k - out - of - n$ distributed algorithm, also called (k, n) visual secret sharing method. Then, random one share is chosen to embedded into the original images and reduce the degradation of watermarked images.

The experimental results demonstrate that our proposed method provides better robustness against multiple image attacks such as Salt and pepper noise, Gaussian noise, Poisson noise, histogram equalization, Median filtering, Laplacian sharpening, Blur filtering and JPEG compression attacks. Besides, the quality of the watermarked image is satisfactory in terms of imperceptibility for real applications.

In the future works, we plan to extend the watermarking involving visual secret sharing approach to video watermarking domain. It is clear that the embedding and the extracting processes are of low complexity and do not require any specific features of the input image, the extension to video watermarking will be suitable for applying on.

Acknowledgements. This research is funded by Vietnam National Foundation for Science and Technology Development (NAFOSTED) under grant number 102.01-2019.12.

References

1. Hsu, C.T., Wu, J.L.: Hidden digital watermarks in images. IEEE Trans. Image Process. **8**(1), 58–68 (1999)
2. Das, C., Panigrahi, S., Sharma, V.K., Mahapatra, K.K.: A novel blind robust image watermarking in DCT domain using inter-block coefficient correlation. AEU Int. J. Electron. Commun. **68**(3), 244–253 (2014)
3. Zear, A., Singh, A.K., Kumar, P.: A proposed secure multiple watermarking technique based on DWT, DCT and SVD for application in medicine. Multimedia Tools Appl. 1–20 (2016)
4. Singh, A.K., Kumar, B., Singh, S.K., Ghrera, S.P., Mohan, A.: Multiple watermarking technique for securing online social network contents using back propagation neural network. Future Gen. Comput. Syst. (2016)
5. Barni, M., Bartolini, F., Piva, A.: Improved wavelet-based watermarking through pixel-wise masking. IEEE Trans. Image Process. **10**(5), 783–791 (2001)
6. Singh, A.K., Kumar, B., Dave, M., Mohan, A.: Robust and imperceptible dual watermarking for telemedicine applications. Wireless Pers. Commun. **80**(4), 1415–1433 (2015)
7. Singh, A.K., Dave, M., Mohan, A.: Robust and secure multiple watermarking in wavelet domain. J. Med. Imaging Health Inform. **5**(2), 406–414 (2015)
8. Singh, A.K., Dave, M., Mohan, A.: Hybrid technique for robust and imperceptible multiple watermarking using medical images. Multimedia Tools Appl. **75**(14), 8381–8401 (2015). https://doi.org/10.1007/s11042-015-2754-7

9. Urvoy, M., Goudia, D., Autrusseau, F.: Perceptual DFT watermarking with improved detection and robustness to geometrical distortions. IEEE Trans. Inf. Forensics Secur. **9**(7), 1108–1119 (2014)
10. Cedillo-Hernandez, M., Garcia-Ugalde, F., Nakano-Miyatake, M., Perez-Meana, H.: Robust digital image watermarking using interest points and DFT domain. In: 35th IEEE International Conference on Telecommunications and Signal Processing (TSP), pp. 715–719 (2014)
11. Thanh, T.M., Tanaka, K.: The novel and robust watermarking method based on q-logarithm frequency domain. Multimedia Tools Appl. **75**, 11097–11125 (2016)
12. Thanh, T.M., Tanaka, K.: A proposal of novel q-DWT for blind and robust image watermarking. In: Proceeding of IEEE 25th International Symposium on Personal, Indoor and Mobile Radio Communications - (PIMRC), Washington D.C., pp. 2066–2070 (2014)
13. Thanh, T.M., Hiep, P.T., Tam, T.M.: A new spatial q-log domain for image watermarking. IJIIP: Int. J. Intell. Inf. Process. **5**(1), 12–20 (2014). ISSN 2093–1964
14. Thanh, T.M., Tanaka, K.: An image zero-watermarking algorithm based on the encryption of visual map feature with watermark information. Multimedia Tools Appl. **76**(11), 13455–13471 (2016). https://doi.org/10.1007/s11042-016-3750-2
15. Rani, A., Bhullar, A.K., Dangwal, D., Kumar, S.: A zero-watermarking scheme using discrete wavelet transform. Procedia Comput. Sci. **70**, 603–609 (2015). ISSN 1877–0509. https://doi.org/10.1016/j.procs.2015.10.046
16. Liu, X., Zhao, R., Li, F., Liao, S., Ding, Y., Zou, B.: Novel robust zero-watermarking scheme for digital rights management of 3D videos. Sig. Process.: Image Commun. **54**, 140–151 (2017). ISSN 0923–5965. https://doi.org/10.1016/j.image.2017.03.002
17. Abdelhedi, K., Chaabane, F., Ben Amar, C.: A SVM-based zero-watermarking technique for 3D videos traitor tracing. In: Blanc-Talon, J., Delmas, P., Philips, W., Popescu, D., Scheunders, P. (eds.) ACIVS. LNCS, vol 12002. Springer, Heidelberg (2020). https://doi.org/10.1007/978-3-030-40605-9_32
18. Fu, M.S., Au, O.C.: Joint visual cryptography and watermarking. In: 2004 IEEE International Conference on Multimedia and Expo (ICME) (IEEE Cat. No.04TH8763), vol. 2, pp. 975–978 (2004)
19. Naor, M., Shamir, A.: Visual cryptography. In: De Santis, A. (ed.) EUROCRYPT 1994. LNCS, vol. 950, pp. 1–12. Springer, Heidelberg (1995). https://doi.org/10.1007/BFb0053419
20. Shamir, A.: How to share a secret? Commun. ACM **22**(11), 612–613 (1979)
21. Blakley, G.: Safeguarding cryptographic keys. In: Proceedings of AFIPS National Computer Conference (1979)
22. Asmuth, C., Bloom, J.: A modular approach to key safeguarding. IEEE Trans. Inf. Theory **29**(2), 208–210 (1983)
23. Kandar, S., Dhara, B.C.: k-n secret sharing visual cryptography scheme on color image using random sequence. Int. J. Comput. Appl. **25**(11), 0975–8887 (2011)
24. Kumar, S., Sharma, R.K.: Threshold visual secret sharing based on Boolean operations. Secur. Commun. Netw. (2013). https://doi.org/10.1002/sec.769
25. Elbasi, E., Eskicioglu, A.M.: Naïve Bayes classifier based watermark detection in wavelet transform. In: Gunsel, B., Jain, A.K., Tekalp, A.M., Sankur, B. (eds.) MRCS 2006. LNCS, vol. 4105, pp. 232–240. Springer, Heidelberg (2006). https://doi.org/10.1007/11848035_32
26. Huang, S., Zang, W.: Blind watermarking scheme based on neural network. In: The 7th World Congress on Intelligent Control and Automation, Chongqing, pp. 5985–5989 (2008)

27. Joan, D., Vincent, R.: AES Proposal: Rijndael, National Institute of Standards and Technology (2003). https://nvlpubs.nist.gov/nistpubs/FIPS/NIST.FIPS.197. pdf

28. Hwang, R.J.: A digital image copyright protection scheme based on visual cryptography. Tamkang J. Sci. Eng. **3**(2), 97–106 (2000)

29. Surekha, B., Swamy, G.N., Rao, K.S.: A multiple watermarking technique for images based on visual cryptography. Int. J. Comput. Appl. **1**(1), 78–82 (2010)

30. Bolla, V.R., Gopal, V., Amancha, S.: A two phase copyright protection scheme for digital images using visual cryptography and sampling methods. In: International Conference on Electrical, Electronics, and Optimization Techniques (ICEEOT), pp. 2041–2046 (2016)

31. Wang, M.S., Chen, W.C.: Digital image copyright protection scheme based on visual cryptography and SVD. Opt. Eng. **46**(6) (2007)

32. Surekha, B., Swamy, G.N.: Sensitive digital image watermarking for copyright protection. Int. J. Netw. Secur. **15**(1), 95–103 (2013)

33. Fu, M.S., Au, O.C.: Joint visual cryptography and watermarking. In: IEEE International Conference on Multimedia and Expo (ICME), pp. 27–30 (2004)

34. Tharayil, J.J., Kumar, E.S.K., SusanAlex, N.: Visual cryptography using hybrid halftoning. Procedia Eng. **38**, 2117–2123 (2012)

35. Benoraira, A., Benmahammed, K., Boucenna, N.: Blind image watermarking technique based on differential embedding in DWT and DCT domains. EURASIP J. Adv. Sig. Process. **2015**(1), 1–11 (2015). https://doi.org/10.1186/s13634-015-0239-5

Post-layout Security Evaluation Methodology Against Probing Attacks

Sofiane Takarabt[1,2]([✉]), Sylvain Guilley[1,2], Youssef Souissi[1], Laurent Sauvage[2], and Yves Mathieu[2]

[1] Secure-IC S.A.S., 35 510 Cesson-Sévigné, France
sofiane.takarabt@secure-ic.com
[2] Télécom Paris, Institut Polytechnique de Paris, 91 120 Palaiseau, France

Abstract. Probing attack is considered to be one of the most powerful attack used to break the security and extract confidential information from an embedded system. This attack requires different bespoke equipment's and expertise. However, for the moment, there is no methodology to evaluate theoretically the security level of a design or circuit against this threat. It can be only realized by a real evaluation of a certified evaluation laboratory. For the design house, this evaluation can be expensive in term of time and money. In this paper, we introduce an innovative methodology that can be applied to evaluate the probing attack on any design at simulation level. Our method helps to extract the sensitive signals of a design, emulate different Focused Ions Beam technologies used for probing attacks, and evaluate the accessibility level of each signal. It can be used to evaluate precisely any probing attack on the target design at simulation level, hence reducing the cost and time to market of the design. This methodology can be applied for both ASIC and FPGA technology. A use-case on an AES-128 shows the efficiency of our methodology. It also helps to evaluate the efficiency of the active shield used as a countermeasure against probing attack.

Keywords: Probing attack · FIB · AES · Active shield · Exposed area.

1 Introduction

Nowadays, embedded systems are omnipresent in our daily life and contain more sensitive and confidential information. Because of this trend, many physical attacks are developed in order to break and extract sensitive information from these systems. The best known attacks are Side-Channel Attack (SCA), fault injection and probing attacks [3,10]. The latter is the most powerful one. Using a Focused Ion Beam (FIB) [1] station allowing to access the internal signals of the device at the micro-metric or even nano-metric scale, this attack removes the measurement noise and properly retrieves the target information, such as

© ICST Institute for Computer Sciences, Social Informatics and Telecommunications Engineering 2021
Published by Springer Nature Switzerland AG 2021. All Rights Reserved
N.-S. Vo et al. (Eds.): INISCOM 2021, LNICST 379, pp. 465–482, 2021.
https://doi.org/10.1007/978-3-030-77424-0_37

secret keys or encrypted data. The attacker may target buses to read the memory content, or combinatorial signals to read an intermediate sensitive values. There are two major countermeasures used to protect against this type of attack (or attacker model). The first is based on masking scheme, where the attacker needs to combine d wires to retrieve the secret [8] (known as d-probing model). The principle is to share the secret into several parts, so the attacker must probe more signals to be able to reconstruct the secret, which makes the attack more difficult. The second is based on active shield [4]. It is integrated into the chip itself on metal layers. The goal is to detect any physical intrusion by activating an alarm, when a shield wire is cut. However, this approach is a race between the precision of the FIB (or performance) and the characteristics of the used shield. The most important parameters for the latter are; the wire width and the spacing. The denser it is, the more efficient is the shield to detect intrusions.

The FIB performance depends on several parameters. From an attacker perspective, it is the resolution of the spot that is decisive. It depends on the technology of the FIB, the voltage and current limits. With the size and the shape of the spot, we can model the holes as a cone [1], and hence the ratio of the FIB. It is the ratio between the diameter and the depth of the hole. Several experiments have shown that for holes with a diameter higher than 100 nm, a ratio of 10 can be achieved. For diameters lesser than 100 nm, the ratio decreases to 1, and even at lower values [5]. This decrease is due to the fact that when the diameter is small, it becomes difficult for the extracted particles from the surface to come out, and it would be more difficult to increase the depth without increasing the diameter [5]. To enhance the ratio, Helium ion (He^+) beam can be used instead of Gallium ion beam (Ga^+) [18].

Despite the advanced technology used in the new generation of devices, probing attacks remain a serious threat, using a high resolution and a high aspect ratio FIB. To ensure an acceptable security level, a rigorous evaluation of the device is fundamental. For the moment there is no effective methods for evaluating probing attack. To be very effective, we must place ourselves within the framework of the best attacker having a very broad knowledge of the target device.

For this reason we propose an advanced methodology for evaluating a circuit at pre-silicon level, based on its post-layout description and by combining SCA primitives and geometric notions to deal with the circuit layout. This is validated on a real use-case involving an Advanced Encryption Standard (AES) IP protected with an active shield. In the following we presents in detail our approach, and contributions.

1.1 Contribution

In this paper, we give an end-to-end methodology to evaluate a circuit against front-side FIB probing attacks. Based on a full pre-silicon model of the circuit, we give an automated evaluation of sensitive signal identification, location and complexity access given a FIB configuration. Our main contributions are:

- Automatic identification of sensitive signals
- Improved method for exposed area detection [17]
- An adapted metric for evaluating the security in term of exposed area

The sensitive signal identification is based on Normalized Inter-Class Variance (NICV) SCA metric [2], that we apply to each signal individually, using the critical parameters of the implementation. Only a few knowledge of the target IP is required, which allows testing third-party IPs, since the layout file description (Library Exchange Format (LEF) and Design Exchange Format (DEF) files) are provided. For exposed area search, our approach is fully bottom-up and supports angled holes (which is not supported in [17]). It delimits the attack zones according to the presence of wires at each metal layer, thus it makes possible to track all the possible attack paths, and to determine the contribution of the shield on a given implementation. Besides, no interaction is needed with the routing tool and it is fully autonomous. This allows a quick evaluation of custom countermeasures without re-running the whole routing process. We demonstrate our approach on a real implementation of an AES protected with one shield, and we evaluate the different ways that may improve the security of the device.

1.2 Outline

The paper is organized as follows. In Sect. 2, we start by giving some related and previous work about probing model and probing attack. In Sect. 3, we describe the different step of our methodology about sensitive signal identification, location and evaluation against probing attacks. In Sect. 4, we give some results on protected implementation using a shield, and we discuss how the security can be improved by inserting new (virtual) shield.

2 Related Work

2.1 Probing Model

In probing model, the attacker is allowed to probe d signals [8]. It is said to be secure at order d if no information about the secret can be learned up to d probes. If we consider a powerful attacker who can record a given signal of the circuit, the number of needed measurements to recover the key depends on the function that computes this value [6].

For example, if we probe the value of the *AddRoundKey* output, we can recover only one bit of the secret key. The attacker needs to probe each bit to recover the whole key (which is very complex and time consuming). The best way to minimize the number of measurements is to probe a non-linear function [6]. In the case of AES or Data Encryption Standard (DES), we probe the Substitution Box (S-Box) output (or the input if we target the last round) [15].

2.2   FIB for Probing Attack

To achieve a real probing attack, a FIB workstation is required. The attacker need to follow three main steps:

- Reverse engineering: The goal is to reconstruct the target circuit or gain knowledge about the structure of the design. Thus, identify the vulnerable signals or area for probing attacks [11]. It is based on a chemical process to properly decapsulate the chip, and a microscope imaging to reconstruct each layer. This process is performed on a sacrificial chip.
- Probing pad creating: When the design is reversed, the attacker creates connections with the sensitive signals on the target chip, located thanks to the previous step.
- Extract secret: The attacker record the value of the sensitive signals and compare with an hypothetical value involving the secret data [21].

The complexity of the probing attack depends on many parameters. Mainly, the step of reverse engineering is the most complex one. The attacker should identify each block and the vulnerable signals of the implementation [19]. This process is highly dependent on the performance of the workstation. The performance of a FIB is determined by the following parameters:

- Ion Beam: It depends on the voltage V, the current I and the aperture of the Ion column. The voltage varies generally from hundreds to few thousands volts (1 kV to 30 kV), and the current varies from few pico to few nano amperes (1 pA to 50 nA).
- Electron Beam: used for imaging.

Those two parameters determine the resolution and the performance of the FIB station [18,22]. For example at 30 kV and 1 pA, the resolution of the ion beam, or the spot size may reach 7 nm. The distribution of the ions follow a Gaussian Probability Density Function (PDF) [9]. It is the main factor involved in the milling process to access sensitive signals [12]. In [1], the authors gives mathematical model for the ion beam profile and different equations to estimate the diameter, the depth and the dwell time. It is also important to mention that the smaller the diameter, the lower the sputtering yield. This can be explained by the fact that among the sputtered particles, some are redeposited on the substrate, which leads to a lower hole ratio [23].

The ling step can be enhanced to achieve higher aspect ratio as presented in [13], by activating the Electron Beam (EB) to reduce the Coulomb interaction, and fix to a very low current for ions. In [7], the authors show a different technique to achieve high aspect ratio and sub-micro diameter holes. By fixing the dwell time to 0.1 ms and the current at 48 pA they achieved an absolute depth of 1.8 μm with a relative diameter less than 300 nm, which gives a ratio of six ($R_{FIB} = \frac{depth}{diameter} = 6$).

In [17,20], the authors described a methodology allowing to analyze a hardware implementation protected by an active shield against probing attack. They showed on a protected implementation with an active shield, the optimal ratio necessary to bypass the shield, or conversely, deduce the ratio for which the shield remains effective.

3   Methodology of FIB for Probing

As described in the previous section, FIB probing is an advanced, complex and extremely expensive attack. Therefore, there are just few entities that can realize a FIB testing on their circuits. For this reason, we propose a new methodology to simulate the FIB attack at an early stage of the design life cycle. With this methodology, the designer can simulate and correct all vulnerabilities that can be exploited by the attacker using a FIB. The new methodology is composed of the following steps that we detail in the sequel:

1. Sensitive signals identification
2. Sensitive signals location
3. Exposed signals

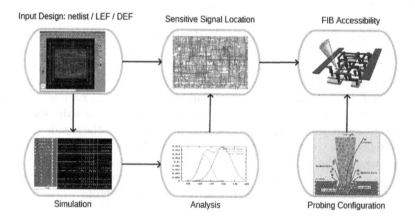

Fig. 1. Global workflow for probing evaluation threats

The global workflow of our approach is presented in Fig. 1. In term of FIB attack, we can address three main types; by-passe attack, re-routing attack and disable shield attack.

When an implementation is protected by a shield, the easiest way for an attacker is to avoid cutting its wires, which is the first attack (by-passe attack). The last two attacks require more effort on the attacker side. They require more investigation for the reverse engineering step, and the routing of certain wires. This increase the attack time and its complexity. In the following, we address only the by-passe attack, which do not require editing the circuit.

3.1   Sensitive Signals Identification

The FIB allows probing and monitoring the internal signals of the circuit during its operation. With the retrieved data, the attacker can recover the sensitive information hidden inside the circuit. The question is which signal the attacker needs to probe. In a complex circuit, with thousands of internal signals, he can not probe them all. For this purpose, the first step of our methodology consists in creating a method to select a group of sensitive signals that could be interesting for a FIB attack. The workflow of our method is the following:

- Tag the critical parameters
- Create the testbench
- Launch the logic simulation
- Create the simulated traces
- Analysis

The first step of our method consist in tagging the critical parameters. In this step, the designer needs to define all critical parameters that he want to protect against the FIB attack. For example, they could be the value of the secret key, plaintext or masks of cryptographic IPs.

Once the critical parameters are selected, they will be used as the input for the second step: Creating the appropriated testbench. In this testbench, we will create a test process which varies these values. It will be used to evaluate the propagation of these values into the design.

The third steps consists in launching the simulation of the new testbench using a digital simulator. During the simulation, all internal signals states are stored and used for the evaluation. In the fourth step, we use the simulation results to generate the activities traces of each signal. Once the simulated traces of each signal are generated, we can launch the last step; analysis. For this purpose, we use the NICV as a metric for the evaluation. This metric allows detecting the dependency of each simulated signal with the sensitive parameters which are defined above by the designer. The NICV is given by:

$$NICV(X, Y) = \frac{\mathbb{V}[Y|X]}{\mathbb{V}[Y]} \qquad (1)$$

This metric is applied for each internal signal and each sensitive parameter. At the end, we will obtain the NICV coefficient of each signal for each time sample. Then, we can apply a threshold to select the signals where the NICV is greater than this selected threshold. It means that these signals are correlated with the sensitive values that the designer wants to protect. Hence, by probing these signals, an attacker can retrieve these sensitive values. At the end, a list of sensitive signals for each sensitive value is obtained.

3.2   Sensitive Signal Location

Once the sensitive signals are identified, we need to know if these signals are accessible. First, we need to identify the physical location of these signals in the layout. It is done using a layout parser. This parser is able to analyze all kind of layout (ASIC or FPGA design) and extract the location of each physical segment of the signals. It will allow identifying how many segment a specific signal (or net) has, on which metal they are located and their corresponding coordinates. The procedure of this parser is the following:

1. Take the layout file as input
2. Find the information related to the technology (number of metal layers, wires width, Vias etc.)
3. Parse the name of all wires used by the devices (including the power wires Vdd and Gnd)
4. For each wire, retrieve the following information:
   - The different segments
   - The metal layer related to each segment
   - Different Vias of the layer
   - The metal layers related to each Via

At the end of the parsing step, we get the whole information of each wire. All these information will be stored in a database. Then, a customized program is used to select the desired signal and show all these information. Note that, this parser can be applied for both ASIC and FPGA layouts. It gives the information of both sensitive and non-sensitive wires (signals). The information of non-sensitive wires is also important. It will help us to determine the real sensitive areas for probing attack. More details about the sensitive areas will be presented in the next section.

3.3   FIB Probing Model

A FIB is composed of different components that allow scanning and milling specimens. An electronic microscopy is used to scan the surface of the sample, and an ion beam for milling and lamellae preparation. In the case of milling, a flow of ions are emitted with specific current I ($5\,nA; 30\,nA$)), accelerated at a specific voltage U ($5\,kV; 30\,kV$), and focused into a point of the sample. The ions hit the surface of the target and weakens the focused zone and tear atoms from the sample. The depth and the diameter of the left hole depends on the Dwell time (fixed time at single point), the beam current and the voltage. Another factor which depends on the sputtered yield is the incidence angle to the surface. Experiments shows that the maximum yield is reached when the angle is between 65° and 85°. The spot size of the beam is obviously the most important parameters which defines the FIB resolution. The best knows resolution is about 5 nm [18].

The purpose of probing attack is to be able to access to some sensitive signals of the circuits. To access these signals, we need to identify an appropriate area, that optimizes the milling step. This can be defined as the dimension of the cone that we must make to achieve that, and decide if a such cone is feasible with a given FIB.

3.4   FIB Access Methodology

In the circuit layout, we have different layers that contains the targeted signal. For a given signal at position $X = (x, y, z)$ (or a list of positions of wires), we try to access this signal without damaging the circuit (or with minimal damage). We describe our method applied to a wire, which can be seen as a list of positions at different layers. The principle idea of this method is a bottom-up process, which is based on two principle steps:

- Projection: The wire will be projected recursively to the layers above.
- Delimitation: This step consists in eliminating the region that is crossed with other wires, or select the one that has the less number of wires (minimal damage).

We start from the wire position, and give the surface from where it can be accessed. Note that in this method, we assume that all wires have either $0°$ or $90°$ with respect to the X axis.

Algorithm 1: Projection and delimitation process

Input: Design: (LEF, DEF files) , Signal target: S
Output: Accessibility paths

1 $Segments \leftarrow shape(S)$
2 **for** $segment \in Segments$ **do**   // For each segment in Segments
3 $\quad current\_layer \leftarrow get\_layer\_index(segment)$
4 $\quad layer\_above \leftarrow current\_layer + 1$
5 $\quad height \leftarrow Design.get\_distance\_between\_layers(current\_layer, layer\_above)$
6 $\quad rectangle \leftarrow first\_projection(segment, height)$ // Projection
7 $\quad wires\_at\_layer\_above \leftarrow Design.get\_wires\_at\_layer(layer\_above)$
8 $\quad sub\_rectangles = rectangles.split(wires\_at\_layer\_above)$
   $\quad$ // Delimitation
9 $\quad new\_sub\_rectangles = empty\_list()$
10 $\quad$ **for** $r \in sub\_rectangles$ **do**
11 $\quad\quad current\_layer \leftarrow layer\_above$
12 $\quad\quad layer\_above \leftarrow current\_layer + 1$
13 $\quad\quad height \leftarrow$
   $\quad\quad Design.get\_distance\_between\_layers(current\_layer, layer\_above)$
14 $\quad\quad r.update\_projection\_angles(segment)$
15 $\quad\quad r.project\_up(height)$ // Projection
16 $\quad\quad wires\_at\_layer\_above \leftarrow Design.get\_wires\_at\_layer(layer\_above)$
   $\quad\quad new\_sub\_rectangles.add(r.split(wires\_at\_layer\_above))$
17 $\quad sub\_rectangles = new\_sub\_rectangles$
18 $\quad$ **while** $layer\_above < top\_layer$ **do**
19 $\quad\quad$ *goto* step 9

20 **return** $sub\_rectangles$

In Algorithm 1, we give the projection and delimitation steps that give us the list of all surfaces allowing to access any sensitive wire.

Projection. A wire can be seen as a list of positions in a given layer. Here, we describe the whole process for one segment of the wire (for the whole wire, we apply the same method for each segment). The normal projection of the wire gives its image at the top layer, and by varying the projection angle θ from $[0, \theta_{max}]$ along x and y axes from the normal angle, we get a rectangle image which represents the surface from where the targeted wire can be reached from the layer above. If the segment is determined by two positions (x_0, y_0) and (x_0, y_1) (here we suppose that is vertical), then the boundaries of the rectangle can be computed as follows:

$$r = z \times \tan(\theta_{max})$$
$$R = \{(x_0 - r, y_0 - r), (x_0 - r, y_0 + r), (x_0 + r, y_1 + r), (x_0 + r, y_1 + r)\}$$

where z is the distance between metal layers. It depends on the level of the metal layer and the used technology.

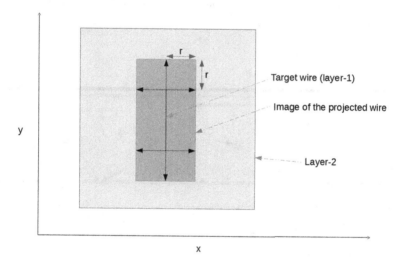

Fig. 2. First projection of a sensitive wire to the top layer.

The whole area allows accessing the target wire by different angled holes. Figure 2 shows the projection phase of a wire located at layer $M1$. The image of the projection gives a rectangle at layer $M2$. We consider that, from any point from this rectangle, the sensitive signal can be accessed by the FIB.

The rectangle may be crossed with some signals located at layer $M2$. Thus, it should be divided into smaller sub-rectangles. This is the second step of our method, and will be detailed in the next section.

Delimitation. The purpose of the delimitation step is to check if the projected rectangle is crossed by some wires in the layer above. For each wire, we need to split and delimit the area to form other sub-rectangles, thus we obtain a new list of independent areas. Once the delimitation is done as illustrated in Fig. 2, and the list of rectangles are determined, we can project them again to the layer above, and so on, to reach the surface of the layout. In this step, we can eliminate the region where the diameter of the hole exceeds the size of the area (we cannot mill through this area without completely cutting a wire).

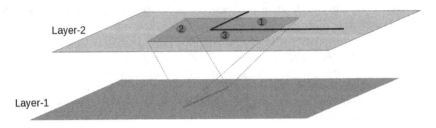

Fig. 3. The projected area is crossed by one wire. It will be divided into small rectangles.

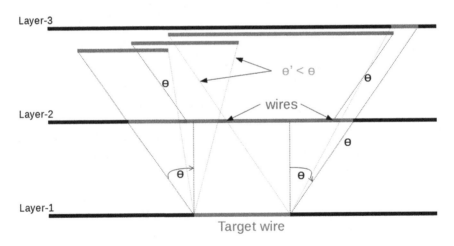

Fig. 4. Cross-section of projected sensitive wire to the top layers: the projection angle θ is adapted following each situation. (Color figure online)

The projection angle has to be determined by the limits of the targeted wire, and the maximum realisable angle. We illustrate in Fig. 4 the process of the projection of each area. Each rectangle becomes independent, and the accessibility of the signal should be determined by the projection path. In fact, many rectangles can be projected to some surface to make a bigger area, but this should not be considered as a contiguous one. The angles of projection for each sub-rectangle should take into a account its location. The angles of projection also depend on their location. For each rectangle, this angle is determined by either its maximal value ($\theta_{max} = \theta^*$), or the extremities of the targeted wire and the rectangle location, as illustrated in Fig. 4 in green. Therefore, each area has its own projection angle computed after its creation.

FIB Model. Once the phase of projection and delimitation are done, one needs to see how much is difficult to access the sensitive wire. This basically depends on two parameters; the surface of the access path and the performance of the FIB. Obviously, the larger the surface is, the easier the access is. So as a priority, we will sort all the available access paths according to their surfaces. It allows us to find the optimal set-up to access the sensitive wire. Once this phase is completed, we can estimate the setting of the FIB as well as the complexity of milling (or milling time).

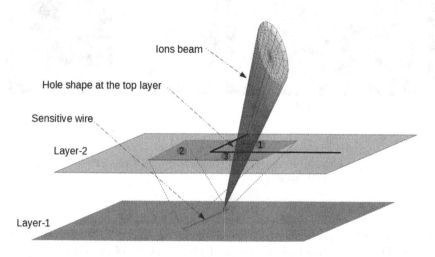

Fig. 5. Illustration of the FIB model for milling.

Depending on the best found surface, we can determine the shape and the volume of the optimal cone that allows to access the sensitive wire, and thus fix the voltage and the current of the ions beam. With those information we can estimate the time needed to make the hole.

4 Study-Case on AES

To demonstrate the reliability of our methodology on a concrete case. We apply our method to evaluate an ASIC circuit, implementing an AES protected with an active shield.

4.1   Target IP

The circuit is composed of different IPs including AES, a Physical Unclonable Function (PUF), Digital sensors and also an active shield used to protect the circuit against probing attacks.

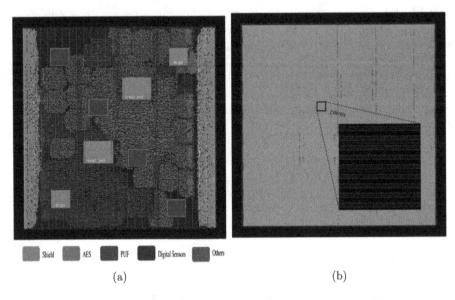

Shield   AES   PUF   Digital Sensors   Others

(a)   (b)

Fig. 6. Circuit used for the evaluation: (a) Logic part of different IPs, (b) Shield mesh located at top-most metal layer [4].

An overview of this design is presented in Fig. 6. As explained in [14], it is composed of 8 IPs, particularly, an active shield, an AES, a PUF and two digital sensors. The active shield (described in [4]) is composed of three parts:

– ALICE (transmitter), which embeds a SIMON block cipher to generate 128 random bits.
– BOB (receiver), which also embeds a SIMON block cipher.
– Shield mesh (Fig. 6(b), which is composed of n lines on the last metal layer. It is used as a communication channel between ALICE and BOB, and achieves the anti-tamper protection of the integrated circuit located below it, with a 128 bits comparator.

This design uses the CMOS 65 nm technology from STMicroelectronics. The core size is 560 μm × 560 μm. The shield mesh is composed of 640 parallel lines with 0.4 μm width and 0.4 μm spacing.

4.2   Sensitive Signal Location

To identify the sensitive signals, we run a leakage detection analysis with the NICV as described in Sect. 3.1, using the intermediate value computed by the

S-Box. There are 9448 signals (wires) at all in the AES block (without counting logic gates). After the analysis, we have only 256 sensitive signals, which correspond to the output of the S-Box, and the input of *MixColumns*, as detailed in Table 1. The result of parsing is shown in Fig. 7, where the signals around the circuit are plotted with the right positions from the DEF file.

Table 1. Result of parsing and sensitive signal identification.

Block	#Signals	#Sensitive signals
AES	9448	256
S-Box	6511	128
MixColumns	268	128

It is therefore those signals that are vulnerable against a probing attack. We note that the *ShiftRow* block is not present in the design, as it is just a wiring of the S-Box output into the input of *MixColumns*.

4.3 FIB-probing Evaluation

We have selected the output of the S-Box. This signal is routed over layers $M3$, $M4$ and $M5$. To compare the FIB attack with an implementation without shield, we consider only the metals at levels lower than 6. For the performance of the FIB, we have fixed the ratio to 5 ($R_{FIB} = 5$). The criticality of a probing attack can be measured by the number of exposed areas, their surfaces and the angle to the target wire. The larger the angle is (compared to the normal angle), the greater the relative hole depth becomes. Thus, more time will be needed to complete the hole.

To heuristically estimate the difficulty of the FIB attack, we have defined a metric taking the different parameters into account, namely the surface of each exposed area and its relative depth. The bigger the area is, the easier the attack is. Moreover, the bigger the angle (or the depth) is, the more the attack is difficult. Hence, this heuristic I can be calculated as follows:

$$
\begin{aligned}
I_i &= \frac{R_i}{D_i} \\
I &= max_{I_i}\{I_i\}
\end{aligned}
\tag{2}
$$

where R_i are the exposed rectangles surfaces, and D_i is the relative depth from R_i to the sensitive signal. This latter is computed from the center of the rectangle. The larger I is, the easier the probing attack is.

Table 2. Results for different angles. For each angle we show the number of exposed areas and the value of I (μm) (Eq. (2)).

Implementation	θ_{max}		
	$\frac{\pi}{3}$	$\frac{\pi}{4}$	$\frac{\pi}{6}$
w/t shield	143 (23.784)	39 (21.632)	16 (13.543)
w shield (M7)	525 (2.101)	142 (1.643)	61 (1.635)

We reported in Table 2, the number of exposed area for different realisable angles. These angles can be chosen by the evaluator relatively to the capacity of the FIB station. The targeted segment of the sensitive signal is the one at level $M3$. We can see that the number of exposed areas is higher at $M7$, because each exposed area at $M6$ will further be divided at $M7$ according to the shield wires, but the surfaces are smaller. The indicator I is significantly lower when considering $M7$ (as expected). This shows that the attack becomes difficult at $M7$, but still feasible with the chosen ratio in this case ($R_{FIB} = 5$). The exposed areas that do not verify the FIB ratio are ignored. Furthermore, for bigger angles the indicator is bigger, because more susceptible (larger) areas can be found, with a relative low depth.

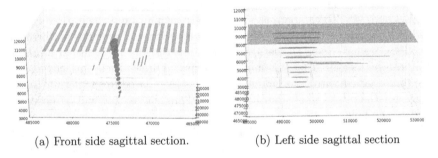

(a) Front side sagittal section.   (b) Left side sagittal section

Fig. 7. Best area to mill. The sensitive signal is presented at layer $M3$. The path of the hole is presented as small (gray) ellipses.

For a signal taking the output of the S-Box, we illustrate in Fig. 7 the best exposed area for the attacker to mill. Interestingly, at this position, there is no much signals at layer $M6$. This allows us to get larger exposed areas when running Algorithm 1. As we can see, the hole could have an ellipsis shape $(0.800\,\mu m \times 12.8\,\mu m)$. As there is no wire at layer $M6$, the hole can be extended further (if needed) along the shield wire direction and thus, allow making a deeper hole. As we can see in this evaluation, the shield did not provide significant protection. We note an improvement in the difficulty of the attack in the case where no shield is added, but the attack remains feasible and it is only the depth of the hole which increases, without making its realization impossible with the chosen ratio.

4.4   Security Improvements

To see possible improvements, we can imagine adding a second layer of shield ($M8$). We considers two ways for that:

1. A second parallel shield, but with an *offset* relatively to $M7$.
2. A second *orthogonal* shield with respect to $M7$.

We then calculate the score I to find the best area in both cases. We find that in case (1), there is a very negligible (or even no) improvement. We always get rectangles with a very large length, around 15.8 μm and a width of 0.800 μm. The latter is limited by the characteristics of the shield (wire width and spacing). The second solution offers more protections. Surfaces with a very large width at $M7$ level are forced to be divided when projected to $M8$. All holes that can be milled from $M8$ must be restricted to a diameter less than 800 μm at $M7$. By limiting the diameter, the depth that could be reached is restricted.

Table 3. Evaluation with a second shield $M8$. For each angle we show the value of $I(\mu m)$ (Eq. (2)).

M8	θ_{max}		
	$\frac{\pi}{3}$	$\frac{\pi}{4}$	$\frac{\pi}{6}$
Parallel with offset (1)	2.174	1.452	1.421
Orthogonal (2)	0.214	0.196	0.198

As expected, we can deduce from the value reported in Table 3, that a second shield with an orthogonal orientation relatively to $M7$ is more efficient. Besides, with the same chosen ratio ($R_{FIB} = 5$), the signal shown in Fig. 7 cannot be accessed. As the highest diameter that we can achieve at layer $M7$ is less than 0.8 μm, the ratio of the FIB should be higher than 9 to be able to access that signal.

In Fig. 8, we show the improvement of the security level estimated by Eq. (2) when there is no shield, after the insertion of two parallel shields and then, after the insertion of two orthogonal shields. The results show that the security level increases more significantly with two orthogonal shields.

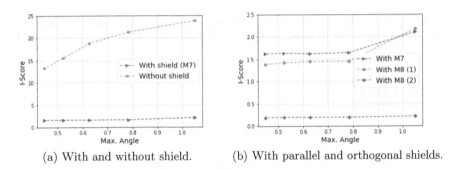

(a) With and without shield.   (b) With parallel and orthogonal shields.

Fig. 8. I score with different shield configurations.

With this procedure, we can determine the available ways to secure a given implementation against probing attacks. For example, manual re-routing of excessively exposed signals to lower levels makes these attacks more difficult as demonstrated in the last test, but still, we can also move other signals (not necessarily sensitive ones) in empty areas above the sensitive signals, which force the size of the exposed areas to be reduced.

5   Conclusion

In this paper we have presented an end-to-end methodology, allowing to evaluate a hardware implementation against a probing attack. The selection of sensitive signals is performed automatically, with minimal configuration (random or fixed input). We have shown an example of an attack on an implementation protected by an active shield, considering the parameters of a typical FIB. This later can be adapted to model a more powerful attacker, being able to make smaller holes at higher depth as shown in the state-of-the-art with different techniques. By analyzing the possible angles of attack identified exhaustively, the designer can choose to modify the routing in the most optimal way according to the performance of a given FIB, such as re-routing over lower metal layers, moving some signals to empty areas, or inserting a second layer of shield. Besides, our framework is autonomous, and no interaction is required with the routing tool, thus he designer can test some countermeasures and re-routing without launching the full routing process, and estimate the security gain more in advance.

Acknowledgments. This work has been funded in part by the bilateral French-German "APRIORI" project (MESRI-BMBF call). The tool presented in this paper is implemented in Secure-IC VIRTUALYZR product [16]. VIRTUALYZR is an electronic design automation (EDA) software tool dedicated to pre-silicon security evaluation.

References

1. Ali, M.Y., Hung, W., Yongqi, F.: A review of focused ion beam sputtering. Int. J. Precis. Eng. Manuf. **11**(1), 157–170 (2010)
2. Bhasin, S., Danger, J.-L., Guilley, S., Najm, Z.: NICV: normalized inter-class variance for detection of side-channel leakage. In: 2014 International Symposium on Electromagnetic Compatibility, Tokyo (EMC 2014/Tokyo), pp. 310–313. IEEE (2014)
3. Brier, E., Clavier, C., Olivier, F.: Correlation power analysis with a leakage model. In: Joye, M., Quisquater, J.-J. (eds.) CHES 2004. LNCS, vol. 3156, pp. 16–29. Springer, Heidelberg (2004). https://doi.org/10.1007/978-3-540-28632-5_2
4. Cioranesco, J.-M., et al.: Cryptographically secure shields. In: 2014 IEEE International Symposium on Hardware-Oriented Security and Trust (HOST), pp. 25–31. IEEE (2014)
5. Fu, Y., Ngoi, K.A.B.: Investigation of aspect ratio of hole drilling from micro to nanoscale via focused ion beam fine milling (2005)
6. Handschuh, H., Paillier, P., Stern, J.: Probing attacks on tamper-resistant devices. In: Koç, Ç.K., Paar, C. (eds.) CHES 1999. LNCS, vol. 1717, pp. 303–315. Springer, Heidelberg (1999). https://doi.org/10.1007/3-540-48059-5_26
7. Hopman, W.C.L., et al.: Focused ion beam scan routine, dwell time and dose optimizations for submicrometre period planar photonic crystal components and stamps in silicon. Nanotechnology **18**(19), 195305 (2007)
8. Ishai, Y., Sahai, A., Wagner, D.: Private circuits: securing hardware against probing attacks. In: Boneh, D. (ed.) CRYPTO 2003. LNCS, vol. 2729, pp. 463–481. Springer, Heidelberg (2003). https://doi.org/10.1007/978-3-540-45146-4_27
9. Jamaludin, F.S., Sabri, M.F.M., Said, S.M.: Controlling parameters of focused ion beam (FIB) on high aspect ratio micro holes milling. Microsyst. Technol. **19**(12), 1873–1888 (2013)
10. Kocher, P., Jaffe, J., Jun, B.: Differential power analysis. In: Wiener, M. (ed.) CRYPTO 1999. LNCS, vol. 1666, pp. 388–397. Springer, Heidelberg (1999). https://doi.org/10.1007/3-540-48405-1_25
11. Kömmerling, O., Kuhn, M.G.: Design principles for tamper-resistant smartcard processors. Smartcard **99**, 9–20 (1999)
12. Li, H.-W., Kang, D.-J., Blamire, M.G., Huck, W.T.S.: Focused ion beam fabrication of silicon print masters. Nanotechnology **14**(2), 220 (2003)
13. Luo, H., Wang, H.L., Cui, Y.M., Wang, R.M.: Focused ion beam built-up on scanning electron microscopy with increased milling precision. Sci. China Phys. Mech. Astron. **55**(4), 625–630 (2012)
14. Ngo, X.T., et al.: Cryptographically secure shield for security IPs protection. IEEE Trans. Comput. **66**(2), 354–360 (2017)
15. Schmidt, J.-M., Kim, C.H.: A probing attack on AES. In: Chung, K.-I., Sohn, K., Yung, M. (eds.) WISA 2008. LNCS, vol. 5379, pp. 256–265. Springer, Heidelberg (2009). https://doi.org/10.1007/978-3-642-00306-6_19
16. Secure-IC. Virtualyzr tool (VTZ). https://www.secure-ic.com/solutions/virtualyzr/ and https://cadforassurance.org/tools/design-for-trust/virtualyzr/. Accessed 4 Mar 2021
17. Shi, Q., Asadizanjani, N., Forte, D., Tehranipoor, M.M.: A layout-driven framework to assess vulnerability of ICs to microprobing attacks. In: 2016 IEEE International Symposium on Hardware Oriented Security and Trust (HOST), pp. 155–160. IEEE (2016)

18. Sidorkin, V., van Veldhoven, E., van der Drift, E., Alkemade, P., Salemink, H., Maas, D.: Sub-10-nm nanolithography with a scanning helium beam. J. Vacuum Sci. Technol. B: Microelectro. Nanometer Struct. Process. Meas. Phenomena **27**(4), L18–L20 (2009)
19. Skorobogatov, S.: Physical attacks on tamper resistance: progress and lessons. In: Proceedings of of 2nd ARO Special Workshop on Hardware Assurance, Washington, DC (2011)
20. Wang, H., Shi, Q., Forte, D., Tehranipoor, M.M.: Probing assessment framework and evaluation of antiprobing solutions. IEEE Trans. Very Large Scale Integr. (VLSI) Syst. **27**(6), 1239–1252 (2019)
21. Wei, L., Zhang, J., Yuan, F., Liu, Y., Fan, J., Xu, Q.: Vulnerability analysis for crypto devices against probing attack. In: The 20th Asia and South Pacific Design Automation Conference, pp. 827–832. IEEE (2015)
22. Wu, H., et al.: Focused helium ion beam deposited low resistivity cobalt metal lines with 10 nm resolution: implications for advanced circuit editing. J. Mater. Sci.: Mater. Electron. **25**(2), 587–595 (2014)
23. Zhou, J., Yang, G.: Focused ion-beam based nanohole modeling, simulation, fabrication, and application. J. Manuf. Sci. Eng. **132**(1) (2010)

Combined VMD-GSO Based Points of Interest Selection Method for Profiled Side Channel Attacks

Ngoc Quy Tran[1], Hong Quang Nguyen[1], and Van-Phuc Hoang[2(✉)]

[1] Faculty of Electronics and Telecommunications, Academy of Cryptography Techniques, Hanoi, Vietnam
[2] Institute of System Integration, Le Quy Don Technical University, Hanoi, Vietnam
phuchv@lqdtu.edu.vn

Abstract. Nowadays, one of the most powerful side channel attacks (SCA) is profiled attack. Machine learning algorithms, for example support vector machine, are currently used for improving the effectiveness of the attack. One issue when using SVM-based profiled attack is extracting points of interest, or features from power traces. So far, studies in SCA domain have selected the points of interest (POIs) from the raw power trace for the classifiers. Our work proposes a novel method for finding POIs that based on the combining variational mode decomposition (VMD) and Gram-Schmidt orthogonalization (GSO). That is, VMD is used to decompose the power traces into sub-signals (modes) of different frequencies and POIs selection process based on GSO is conducted on these sub-signals. As a result, the selected POIs are used for SVM classifier to conduct profiled attack. This attack method outperforms other profiled attacks in the same attack scenario. Experiments were performed on a trace data set collected from the Atmega8515 smart card run on the side channel evaluation board Sakura-G/W and the data set of DPA contest v4 to verify the effectiveness of our method in reducing number of power traces for the attacks, especially with noisy power traces.

Keywords: Profiled attack · Side channel attack · Support machine learning · Variational mode decomposition

1 Introduction

Side channel attack (SCA) is one of the most powerful cryptoanalysis technique for revealing secret key or sensitive information stored on cryptographic devices. The conducting of SCA is based on the analyzing of unintended side channel leakages observed from the devices during cryptographic algorithms run on. There are so many forms of the observed leakages, but the time of operation, the power consumption of the devices, or electromagnetic radiation are the most common uses. SCAs based on the power consumption are known as the power analysis attacks first proposed by Kocher et al. in the late 1990s [1]. These attacks rely on the physical nature that the instantaneous power

N.-S. Vo et al. (Eds.): INISCOM 2021, LNICST 379, pp. 483–503, 2021.
https://doi.org/10.1007/978-3-030-77424-0_38

consumption of a cryptographic device depends on the data being processed and the operation being executed. This dependency can be used to expose the data that contains the secret key of a cryptographic device. Depending on the knowledge of attacker about the device under attack as well as the statistical method of analysis and extraction of information from the power consumption traces, SCAs are classified into two main classes: non-profiled attacks and profiled attacks. DPA [1], CPA [2], Mutual Information Analysis (MIA) [3] attacks belong to the first class. These are considered as effective attack methods when the attacker has only an attack device and information of its implementation. The profiled attacks are used when the attacker has the same device as the attack device with full control over. By this device, the attacker is able to accurately characterize the power consumption of the device so that the attack efficiency is much higher than non-profiled attacks in the term of the needed number of power consumption measurements for revealing the secret key successfully.

So far, there is a lot of attention on profiled attack in SCA research community. The first one is called template attack, as proposed in [4] by Chari et al., which relies on an assumption that power consumption characteristic follows multivariate Gaussian distribution. However, in general, this assumption might be not met, so that machine learning (ML) techniques are introduced for profiled attacks. Consequently, several works have applied machine learning techniques to profiled SCA attacks [5, 6]. These works all indicate that ML based profiled attacks are more efficient and SVM is commonly used as ML algorithm. ML based profiled attacks relax the need for probability distributions of side channel leakage traces but still require specific extraction techniques to identify points of interest (POIs) on the traces or feature selection in ML domain. In SCA, POIs are time sample points from the power traces that correspond to the calculation of the sensitive variables being targeted and their values change according to those variables [7]. The POIs selection, as input features to machine learning algorithms is critical for two main reasons as follows: (1) the power traces are usually acquired by a measurement equipment with high sampling rates and so consist of a large amount of time samples. However, often only a relatively small range of these time samples is informative or statistically dependent on a sensitive target variable; (2) power traces are considered as highly multi-dimensional data that results in the curse of dimensionality issues with ML algorithms. That is, computational and runtime complexity for them to solve a task increase. Therefore, POIs selection is critical to the effectiveness of the profiled attacks. The more precisely the POIs are selected, the better the ability to characterize the power consumption of a profiled device, resulting in increasing attack efficiency and vice versa. Our work focuses on a method for finding POIs for SVM-based profiled attacks.

Some studies in the side channel community focus on methods of finding POIs for profiled attacks, which can be classified into four classes: filter methods, dimensionality reduction method, wrapper and hybrid methods, and ML based methods. In filter methods, POIs selection process operates on the base of computation of some sample-wise statistics, whose aim is to quantify a sort of signal strength. The signal-strength estimates are derived from classical SCA distinguishers computed under the right key hypothesis, such as the Difference of Means [4] or Correlation Power Analysis (CPA) [8]. Other deployed estimates are the Sum of Squared Differences [9], the Signal-to-Noise Ratio [10, 11], and the Sum of Squared t-differences, corresponding to the t-test [9]. Once the chosen signal-strength estimate is computed, all time samples for which the signal strength is higher than a certain threshold are selected as POIs. Of these, the POIs selection method based on CPA estimates is the most common use.

Principal component analysis (PCA), as dimensionality reduction method, is another technique for POIs selection. The time samples on traces have the maximize the variability in the projection space of PCA are remained as POIs. So far, the effectiveness of PCA-based profiled attack is not clear and selecting the number of retained components as well as the threshold of determination in PCA process is also not an easy task [12].

Profiled attacks, as presented in [13], use the wrapper method for finding of POIs. In the wrapper method, subsets of time samples on the power traces are evaluated by the prediction performance of a classifier and the subset has the best performance is selected as POIs. To reduce the number of subsets of the wrapper, hybrid method is used. That is, candidate features are first selected by a filter then furthered refined by an accuracy wrapper. As claimed in [13], wrapper and hybrid methods gave slightly better results. The issue with this approach is that computational complexity and search space increase exponentially as the length of trace increases. Because of the capability of ML algorithms in determining the most informative features from raw data inputs, ML algorithms can be used to finding POIs of power trace. In the first work in this approach [14], SVM has been trained and the sample points of trace which correspond to highly absolute value of weights are selected as POIs. This method is also called normal-based feature selection and strongly recommended by authors in [14].

As our knowledge, there are only few works on finding POIs with noisy traces. Furthermore, there have been no more studies on feature engineering in the machine learning domain as applied to profiled attacks. For noisy traces, the authors in [7] claim that the goodness of POIs selections depends significantly on the noise level: as noise level increases the goodness of POIs selection decreases, while at the same noise level, CPA estimation based POIs selection method is the best. This drawback of the POIs selection method is confirmed by the authors in [13] regarding the wrapper and hybrid method. Inspired by the success of VMD [15] in feature engineering in machine domain, in this work, we propose the method of combining VMD and GSO to find the POIs of power traces. That is, VMD is used to decompose a trace into sub-signals, or modes and POIs are selected from these modes by using GSO as the filer feature selection method. Then, the selected POIs are used for SVM-based profiled attack. We denote SVM_{VMD} for our proposed attack. To demonstrate the efficiency of our proposed attack method, we compare our method with two other SVM-based profiled attacks using the SVM classifier. The first attack uses CPA as the POIs selection method as in [5], so called SVM_{CPA} and is currently considered to be the best method, and the second one uses a normal-based feature selection method as in [14], so called SVM_{NB}. We also investigate the effectiveness of our method with noisy power traces, which often happens in the real attack scenarios.

Our contributions are follows. Firstly, we investigate the ability of combining VMD and GSO for finding POIs of the power traces. Secondly, we propose an SVM-based profiled attack method that uses our POIs selection method. This is a different approach for conducting profiled attack and it is efficient for noisy power traces. The remainder of the paper is structured as follows. In Sect. 2, we describe the background to this research:

the profiled attacks, variational mode decomposition and Gram-Schmidt Orthogonalization and SVM. In Sect. 3, we present our proposed SVM-based profiled attack. The experiments and their results are presented in Sect. 4. Finally, the conclusions of our research are presented in Sect. 5.

2 Background

2.1 Profiled Attack

For profiled attack, the attacker must have a device with full control over that is similar the attack device. This device is called profiling device and used for leakage information characterization by the attacker. In this work, an attack device that runs a block cipher is used for our attack scenario and leakage is in the form of power consumption. The implementation of profiled attack consists of two phases: profiling phase on profiled device and attack phase on attack device.

In the profiling phase, a dataset of N_p profiling traces is acquired from the profiled device. The dataset is seen as the realization of the random variable $S_p \triangleq \left\{(x_1, z_1), \ldots, \left(x_{N_p}, z_{N_p}\right)\right\} \sim Pr[X|Z]^{N_p}$, where x_i are the traces obtained from the device processing the respective intermediate values $z_i = \varphi(P, K)$. Based on S_p, a model is built to characterize the side channel leakage of the cryptographic device for each hypothetical value z_i. This can be modeled as $F(X|Z) : X \rightarrow P(Z)$.

In the attack phase, a dataset of N_a attack traces are acquired from the target device. The dataset is seen as a realization of $S_a \triangleq \left(k, \left\{(x_1, p_1), \ldots, \left(x_{N_a}, p_{N_a}\right)\right\}\right)$ such that $k \in K$, and for all $i \in [1, N_a], p_i Pr[P] \wedge x_i Pr[X \vee Z = \varphi(p_i, k)]$. Subsequently, a prediction vector is computed for each attack trace, based on a previously built model: $y_i = F(x_i), \forall i \in [1, N_a]$. A score, for example the probability, is assigned to each trace for each intermediate value hypothesis z_j, $with j \in$. The j-value of y_i describes the probability of z_j according to the model when the attack trace is x_i. These scores are combined over all the attack traces to output a *likelihood* for each key hypothesis and the candidate with the highest likelihood is predicted to be the correct key. The maximum likelihood score can be used for prediction. For every key hypothesis $k \in K$, this likelihood score is defined by Eq. (1) with the key assigned the highest score predicted as being the most likely.

$$d_{S_a}[k] \triangleq \prod_{i=1}^{N_a} y_i[z_i] \ where \ z_i = \varphi(p_i, k) \tag{1}$$

2.2 Variational Mode Decomposition (VMD)

VMD is a method used to decompose a real valued signal into narrowband sub-signals, also known as intrinsic mode functions (IMFs) or simply VMD modes [15] by Eq. (2). In that $x(t)$ is the orginal signal and $u_k(t) = A_k(t)cos(\phi_k(t))$, called the kth mode, is the amplitude-modulation and frequency-modulation signal where $A_k(t)$ is the slowly varying, positive envelope and $\phi_k(t)$ is the phase. Each mode has a central frequency f_k that its instantaneous frequency $\phi'(k)$ varies around.

$$x(t) = \sum_{k=1}^{K} u_k(t) \tag{2}$$

The finding simultaneously a set of modes and their central frequencies by VMD is done by solving the optimization problem given by expression (3). This is the constrained minimization process of sum of all mode's bandwidth. The bandwidth of each mode is estimated by 3 steps: compute the analytic signal of each mode by using Hilbert transform so its spectrum is positive; multiply the analytic signal with a complex exponential for shifting its frequency spectrum to baseband; compute the squared 2-norm of the gradient of the baseband signal.

$$\min_{u_k, f_k} \left\{ \sum_k \left\| \frac{d}{dt} \left[\left(\delta(t) + \frac{j}{\pi t} \right) * u_k(t) \right] e^{-j2\pi f_k t} \right\|_2^2 \right\} \tag{3}$$

$$\text{s.t.} \sum_k u_k(t) = x(t)$$

The solution for (3) provides the optimal point of an unconstrainted augmented Lagrangian given by (4) where α is the penalty factor and $\lambda(t)$ is Lagrangian multiplier. This optimization could be solved by using the alternate direction method of multipliers algorithm [16]. All modes of $x(t)$ are computed in frequency domain by (5) and (6) at each iteration of algorithm until the condition (7) is met.

$$L\{u_k(t), f_k, \lambda(t)\} = \alpha \sum_{k=1}^{K} \left\| \frac{d}{dt} \left[\left(\delta(t) + \frac{j}{\pi t} \right) * u_k(t) \right] e^{-j2\pi f_k t} \right\|_2^2$$
$$+ \left\| x(t) - \sum_{i=1}^{K} u_k(t) \right\|_2^2 + \left\langle \lambda(t), x(t) - \sum_{k=1}^{K} u_k(t) \right\rangle \tag{4}$$

$$U_k^{n+1}(f) = \frac{X(f) - \sum_{i<k} U_k^{n+1}(f) - \sum_{i>k} U_k^n(f) + \frac{\lambda^n}{2}(f)}{1 + 2\alpha \left\{ 2\pi \left(f - f_k^n \right) \right\}^2} \tag{5}$$

$$f_k^{n+1} = \frac{\int_0^\infty \left| U_k^{n+1}(f) \right|^2 f df}{\int_0^\infty \left| U_k^{n+1}(f) \right|^2 df} \approx \frac{\sum f \left| U_k^{n+1}(f) \right|^2}{\sum \left| U_k^{n+1}(f) \right|^2} \tag{6}$$

$$\sum_k \frac{\left\| u_k^{n+1}(t) - u_k^n(t) \right\|_2^2}{\left\| u_k^n(t) \right\|_2^2} < \epsilon \tag{7}$$

After the convergence of this optimization, the inverse Fourier transform is applied to (5) to obtain the waveform of each mode. Because of the combination of Wiener filtering, Hilbert transform and ADMM in VMD, VMD modes are highly accurate in describing the different components of the original signal and robust to noise.

2.3 SVM Method

SVM algorithms [17] is used to construct classifiers. The basic form of SVM is the binary classifier which can classify two class by the largest-margin separating hyperplane between them. Let $D_M = \{(x_i, y_i) \vee x_i \in R^N, y_i \in \{-1, +1\}, i = 1, 2, .., M\}$ represent a training set, where x_i is a training vector, and y_i is the label of x_i. The training vector x is mapped into feature space by the nonlinear function $\phi(.)$. Consequently, the maximum margin of a binary-class SVM classifier is a constrained optimization problem as follows:

$$\min_{\omega,b,\xi} \left(\tfrac{1}{2}\|\omega\|^2 + C \sum_{i=1}^{M} \xi_i \right), s.t. y_i\left(\omega^T \phi(x_i) + b\right) \geq 1 - \xi_i, \xi_i \geq 0, \tag{8}$$
$$i = 1, 2, \ldots, M$$

where $\omega \in R^N$, $b \in R$, and $C > 0$ is the penalty parameter which evaluates the trade-off between training error and margin size, and ξ_i is the training error of x_i. After the Lagrange multiplier is introduced, the optimization problem in (8) is simplified as follows:

$$\min_{\alpha} \tfrac{1}{2} \sum_{i=1}^{M} \sum_{j=1}^{M} \alpha_i \alpha_j y_i y_j K\left(x_i, x_j\right) - \sum_{i=1}^{M} \alpha_i, s.t. \sum_{i=1}^{M} \alpha_i y_i = 0, 0 \leq \alpha_i \leq C, \tag{9}$$
$$i = 1, 2, \ldots, M$$

where α_i are Lagrange multipliers and the kernel function is $K\left(x_i, x_j\right) = \phi(x_i)\phi(x_j)$.

The kernel function maintains the reasonable computational complexity of SVM in feature space. The common kernel functions are linear kernel and RBF kernel.

$$K_{Linear}\left(x_i, x_j\right) = x_i^T x_j$$
$$K_{RBF} = \left(x_i, x_j\right) = exp \tag{10}$$

where γ is the hyperparameter in (10) and the notation $\|.\|$ represents the L^2 norm between two vectors.

For consideration of training time and accuracy, the one-against-one strategy can be used to train an SVM classifier for each pair of possible classes. In order to use the maximum likelihood estimation to recover the secret key, an attacker is more interested in the probability of an instance x_i belonging to the class c. Accordingly, we give the posterior conditional probability $P_{SVM}(x_i \vee c)$ of each instance [18].

2.4 GSO-Based Feature Selection

As mentioned above, the finding of POIs on the power trace is also known as the feature selection in ML domain. In this paper, Gram-Schmidt orthogonalization based feature selection method is used to select the POIs of the traces. This method is in the form of filter method, independent of the advance classifiers and is effective in ranking he features contained in the traces based on criteria computed directly from the traces. Indeed, this method allows the features to be determined without weighting all of features in the traces. It ranks features based on the correlation between features and the output target of a prediction model or the pre-assigned label of features. Let $x_k = [x_{k1}, x_{k2}, \ldots, x_{kN}]^T$ be the kth feature vector of N instances, $y = \begin{bmatrix} y_1, y_2, .., y_N \end{bmatrix}^T$ be the output target and Q is the number of features. This results in (N, Q) matrix feature data set. To define the relation between each feature and output target, the correlation is calculated by (11) [19].

$$cos(\alpha_k) = \frac{\langle x_k.y \rangle}{\|x_k.y\|} \tag{11}$$

In formula (1), x_k is a column vector containing N values of the kth feature in all Q features, α_k is the angle of vectors x_k and y. If they are perpendicular to each other, the cosine of α_k equals 0 meaning there is no correlation between them, whereas when the angle between them becomes smaller, this correlation increases and the maximum value is 1 when they are completely correlated.

The GSO-based feature selection process uses the formula (11) to quantify the degree to which features are related to the output target. The first selected feature is the most correlated input features with the output target by the cosine calculation. The next features are selected according to the iteration process as follows until all input features are ranked, or until a stopping condition is met [19]: (1) the rest input features and output target are projected on the subspace orthogonal to the selected feature; (2) the cosine calculations are done on this subspace for all projected features and target output to find out the most correlated feature. This feature is added to selected feature list.

3 Proposed Method

In this part, we present our proposed SVM-based profiled attack that uses the combination of VMD and GSO for POIs selection of power traces.

3.1 SVM-Based Profiled Attack

The proposed SVM-based profiled attack, as shown in Fig. 1, is carried out in two phases: a profiling phase and an attack phase. In the profiling phase, power traces are collected from the profiled device while it is executing a cryptographic algorithm to form a trace data set. This trace data set is labeled according to the Hamming weight of targeted value of the algorithm that needs to be profiled $Z_1, \ldots, Z_m$. Usually these targeted values are taken at the output of the S-box. Because, they are 8-bit values that result in 9 Hamming weight classes from 0 to 8 denoted as $c_0, c_1, \ldots, c_8$. This labeled set of traces is fed to the feature extraction and selection block for mapping traces into feature space and the best features are selected. These selected features are considered as POIs of the power trace in feature space that should describe the statistical dependency of the Hamming weight of the targeted value Z_i with the power consumption. In the final step of the profiled phase, POIs of all traces are used to train SVM to model the power consumption characteristic of the profiled device. For training SVM classifier, its parameters are selected as follows: the kernel function is RBF, the penalty factor and width of kernel of RBF are optimized by Grey wolf optimization algorithm as presented in [20].

During the attack phase, unlabeled traces collected from the attack device are fed into the feature extraction and selection block to select POIs and they are next classified by the trained SVM model to determine the probabilities of the traces for classes $c_i \in \{0, 1, \ldots 8\}$. Finally, we compute the log likelihood for each hypothesis value of the key byte that is used by attack device as follows:

$$logL_k \equiv log \prod_{i=1}^{N_a} P_{SVM}(x_i|c_i) = \sum_{i=1}^{N_a} log\, P_{SVM}(x_i|c_i) \qquad (12)$$

where k is a hypothesis key byte value, $c_i = Hammingweight(Sbox(p_i, k))$, p_i is the plaintext associated with trace x_i, and the number of attack traces is N_a. The key k_c that maximizes the log likelihood in (13) is predicted to be the correct key.

$$k^c = \underset{k \in K}{argmax}\, logL_k \qquad (13)$$

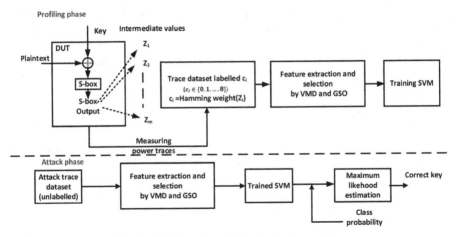

Fig. 1. SVM-based profiled attacks framework.

3.2 Feature Extraction and Selection

Features or POIs selection is critical to the effectiveness of the profiled attacks. The more precisely the features are selected, the better the ability to characterize the power consumption of a profiled device, resulting in increasing attack efficiency and vice versa. This section presents a new method for finding features of power traces for SVM-based profiled attack. First, power trace characteristics are discovered as follows:

The power trace collected during the operation of a cryptographic device describes its power consumption. It consists of many components in which dynamic power dissipation is the most important [10]. This component depends on the processed data of the circuit and is useful information leakage for power analysis attack. The dynamic power dissipation mainly caused by the switching activity of logic gates in a circuit which is controlled by the operating clock frequency so the dynamic power consumption is driven by the clock frequency of circuit. Therefore, in spectrum of power trace, it is expected that the clock frequency component has significant magnitude compared to the other components. The information leakage is nearly in the form of a both amplitude and frequency modulation signal and the central frequency of its spectrum is the clock frequency. Generally, in a device, the different parts of its circuit are controlled by different operating frequencies through the clock division system, so the dynamic power dissipation is the combination of some amplitude - frequency modulation signals with different center frequencies. So, if it is possible to separate the dynamic power dissipation to the amplitude - frequency modulation signals with different center frequencies, one of these signals contains significant information leakage related to target circuit part while the other does not.

As a result, the feature extraction process from power traces should ensure: (1) the remaining features contain the most important information of the trace which is the dynamic power dissipation caused by the targeted circuit; (2) it could remove the other components of power traces; (3) it could reduce noise in the power traces. Fortunately, these requirements can be fulfilled by using VMD method because VMD decomposes a trace into different components and it is robust to the efects of sampling and noise.

In our proposed method, VMD is used for extracting features from power traces. VMD decomposes the signal into sub-signals, called VMD mode in this paper, which are amplitude-modulated frequency modulated signals so each mode contains a specific frequency spectrum with different center frequency. So, the VMD mode which center frequency relates to clock frequency could be use as feature of the power trace. Indeed, VMD can discover signal changes more accurately so that features of power traces can be recognized more accurately. Moreover, VMD is robust to noise thanks to the use of Wiener filter technique. Thus, VMD should be useful for using noisy traces.

Unfortunately, VMD mode still contains redundant features which not related to target variable that has been profiled. Therefore, they must be eliminated for increasing the generalization capability of the classifier and reducing the volume of training data. The elimination of redundant features is known as the feature selection. In previous related works, all features that is higher than a certain threshold are selected. In this paper, we recommend using GSO to selection feature of selected VMD mode.

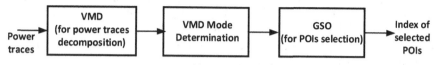

Fig. 2. Feature selection procedure of power trace.

To sum up, there are three phases in the proposed features extraction and selection method as illustrated in Fig. 2. Firstly, VMD is used to decompose original traces to VMD modes. In the VMD process, it is necessary to set parameters. VMD needs to preset the value of number of decomposed modes (K). If K is too small, all the decomposition modes cannot be captured. In contrast, if K is too large, the interfering signal will be over decomposed such that the center frequencies of modes will be mixed. The penalty factor (α) affects the bandwidth of the decomposed signal. To decompose the traces by the VMD, the number of IMFs (K) and the quadratic penalty factor (a) should be determined beforehand. In this work, the parameters, K and a, were determined according to the following steps: (1) Decompose a power trace into modes for different $K = [1, 20]$ and $a = [5, 2000]$; (2) Add up the modes for each of the K and a values to obtain the reconstructed power trace and estimate the values of Pearson correlation coefficient for the reconstructed and original power trace; (3) Select the sets of K and a values for maximum of Pearson correlation coefficient. Others input parameters of VMD including update rate (τ) and convergence condition (ϵ) are selected by standardization values in range of $(0 : 1e - 6)$ [15].

In VMD mode determination phase, the frequency range that containing the clock operating frequency of our attack device is selected. This VMD mode can be used as features of the power trace and contains the most useful information for the SCA. Therefore, CPA attack on the selected VMD mode should give the best results among all VMD modes. Hence, the method for determination of VMD mode is as follows: perform CPA attacks on all the VMD modes and based on the results of these CPA attacks, the VMD mode that has the largest correlation coefficient is selected.

In GSO feature selection phase, it is necessary to set the number of selected features (N). Our principle of finding the value of N is to find a trade-off between the accuracy and the computation cost or execution time. So, the value of N that SVM has the highest accuracy together with the lowest execution time is selected.

4 Experimental Results

In this section, we show the experimental results of implementing profiled attacks with the proposed new SVM$_{VMD}$ approach, which is based on SVM and the combining of VMD and GSO for feature extraction and selection. We compared the effectiveness of the proposed method with the two profiled attacks based on SVM with points of interest selection by CPA in [5] called SVM$_{CPA}$, and the normal-based feature selection method in [14] called SVM$_{NB}$. The following parameters are used to evaluate the effectiveness of an attack:

- The ability to reveal the correct key: To confirm that our profiled attacks can reveal the correct key used by AES-128, we figure out the probability of each key being the actual key used. The key with highest probability is the most likely one.
- Guessing Entropy [21]: This score is also known as average rank of correct key is widely used to rate the effectiveness of side channel attack according to number of attack traces. By conducting the attack several times independently, guessing entropy is calculated as follows: (1) the rank of correct key in all guessing keys are computed. This is the index of the correct one in the list of all ranked keys; (2) calculate the average indexes of the correct key. In this paper, this guessing entropy is estimated over 10 independent attacks.

4.1 Dataset

Dataset 1: The set consists of 60000 traces collected while AES-128 processed inter-mediate values at S-box output. AES-128 was implemented on a Smartcard Atmega8515 runing on Sakura G/W. A sample of one of the collected power traces has 2500 time-samples which is titled '**Original trace**' in Fig. 3.

Dataset 2: This data set consists of 100000 traces downloaded from public DPA contest v4 website at: http://www.dpacontest.org/v4. There is 4000 time-samples in a trace of a first-order masked AES implementation which the output of S-box is $Sbox(P_i + k) \oplus M$, where M is a mask [22]. When the mask values are known, this data set are considered as an unmasked case.

4.2 Results

4.2.1 Feature Selection Phase

In this section, we investigated the effect of the feature selection on the classification accuracy of the proposed method. First, VMD is used to decompose original traces to VMD modes. For VMD, two main parameters: the number of VMD modes (K) and penalty factor (α) are initialized with $K = 5$, $\alpha = 1000$ according to procedure as described in Sect. 3.2. The VMD modes of both Dataset 1 and Dataset 2 are depicted in Fig. 3 and Fig. 4, respectively. As expected, VMD modes contain different components of the original signal at different central frequencies. For selection of VMD mode as feature of the power trace, we conduct CPA attacks on all the VMD modes and the results are shown in Table 1. VMD mode 1 and VMD mode 2 are selected as the extraction feature of power trace in Dataset 1 and VMD mode 2 because the CPA attack gives the highest correlation value.

Table 1. Results of correlation power attack on VMD modes.

Mode	Dataset 1		Dataset 2	
	Max correlation	Key found	Max correlation	Key found
VMD mode 1	0.64	63 (correct)	0.52	108 (correct)
VMD mode 2	0.62	63 (correct)	0.87	108 (correct)
VMD mode 3	0.54	63 (correct)	0.80	108 (correct)
VMD mode 4	0.37	255 (wrong)	0.37	188 (wrong)
VMD mode 5	0.35	246 (wrong)	0.34	135 (wrong)

Table 2 represents the classification accuracy of SVM on Dataset 1 when extracted features are VMD mode 1 and the selected features are chosen by GSO. Table 3 represents the classification accuracy of SVM on Dataset 2 when extracted features are VMD mode 2 and the selected features are chosen by GSO. The selected features are put into an SVM classifier for the training phase. As the feature dimension increases, so does the accuracy of the classification, but with too many features the accuracy decreases because the features do not generalize the power consumption characteristic well when used by the classifier. Therefore, the subset of features with the highest accuracy and lowest feature dimensions are selected and shown in bold font.

Table 2. Acquired results considering extraction of features by VMD and selection by GSO on Dataset 1.

Dim	Selected features	Classification accuracy (%)
2	1036 509	18.2
4	1036 509 2261 2262	30.12
6	1036 509 2261 2262 2263 2260	50.31
8	1036 509 2261 2262 2263 2260 2264 2265	81.56
10	1036 509 2261 2262 2263 2260 2264 2265 2259 861	81.78
12	1036 509 2261 2262 2263 2260 2264 2265 2259 861 2267 1038	89.22
14	**1036 509 2261 2262 2263 2260 2264 2265 2259 861 2267 1038 411 577**	**95.03**
16	1036 509 2261 2262 2263 2260 2264 2265 2259 861 2267 1038 411 577 886 1687	95.02
18	1036 509 2261 2262 2263 2260 2264 2265 2259 861 2267 1038 411 577 886 1687 1211 1670	94.27
20	1036 509 2261 2262 2263 2260 2264 2265 2259 861 2267 1038 411 577 886 1687 1211 1670 1576 216	92.84

Table 3. Acquired results considering extraction of features by VMD and selection by GSO on Dataset 2.

Dim	Selected features	Classification accuracy (%)
2	1804 3201	22.6
4	1804 3201 1664 2389	31.89
6	1804 3201 1664 2389 689 3231	60.38
8	1804 3201 1664 2389 689 3231 1524 1556	80.24
10	1804 3201 1664 2389 689 3231 1524 1556 3093 3192	86.66
12	1804 3201 1664 2389 689 3231 1524 1556 3093 3192 2766 2282	90.35
14	1804 3201 1664 2389 689 3231 1524 1556 3093 3192 2766 2282 1244 852	95.68
16	**1804 3201 1664 2389 689 3231 1524 1556 3093 3192 2766 2282 1244 852 2392 1797**	**96.62**
18	1804 3201 1664 2389 689 3231 1524 1556 3093 3192 2766 2282 1244 852 2392 1797 2251 3113	94.58
20	1804 3201 1664 2389 689 3231 1524 1556 3093 3192 2766 2282 1244 852 2392 1797 2251 3113 3108 1095	90.28

4.2.2   Key Recovery Phase

In order to verify our proposed SVM_{VMD} profiled attack has the ability to reveal secret key of attack device, In the attack phase, SVM_{VMD} is used to reveal the secret key when classifying 9 Hamming weight classes of S-box output. Instead of predicting the class HW of each trace, we gave the posterior conditional probability $P_{SVM}(X_i \vee c)$. The estimated probability of the hypothetical keys is determined by the maximum likelihood estimation. The correct key is defined as the key with the highest probability. For Dataset 1, which was collected in this experiment, the first byte of the AES-128 key is 63, and that is assigned the largest probability value, as depicted in Fig. 5. With Dataset 2, the recovery key is 108 which is identical to the key used to install AES in the DPA contest v4 (Fig. 6). These results prove that our attack method could correctly recover the key used by AES-128.

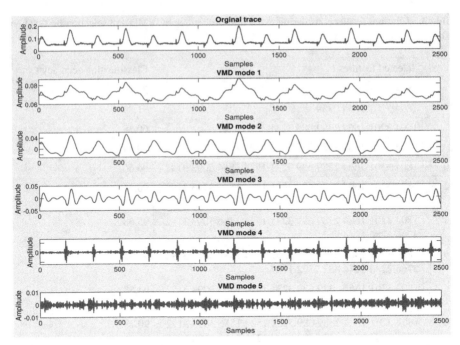

Fig. 3. VMD mode of the power trace on Dataset 1.

Figures 7 and 8 report the GE corresponding to different numbers of traces used for attacks with Dataset 1 when SVM_{VMD}, SVM_{CPA} and SVM_{NB} are used to predict the Hamming weight classes. As expected, the GEs of all attacks decrease as the number of traces increases. Moreover, the larger the size of the training set, the lower the GE. The reason for this is that the performance of SVM is determined by its parameters, and the size of the training set is critical to find the best parameters for the SVM. With Dataset 2, we performed the same experiments as for Dataset 1, and the GE calculated in the attack phases are presented in Fig. 9 and Fig. 10. The overall performance of all attacks are the same as those for Dataset 1. Again, SVM_{VMD} achieves the best GE values.

As shown in Table 4, for each dataset we give the number of traces required by the profiled attacks based on SVM for guessing entropy to reach 0. SVM_{VMD} requires the minimum number of traces to recover the key, 10.2 and 5.3 traces on average, corresponding to 100 and 200 profiling traces, respectively. These empirical results indicate that the SVM-based profiled attack with the VMD feature extraction technique is more effective than the attacks with the CPA and normal-based feature extraction techniques. This can be explained by the VMD extraction technique allowing more effective selection of trace characteristics than the CPA and normal-based POI selection methods.

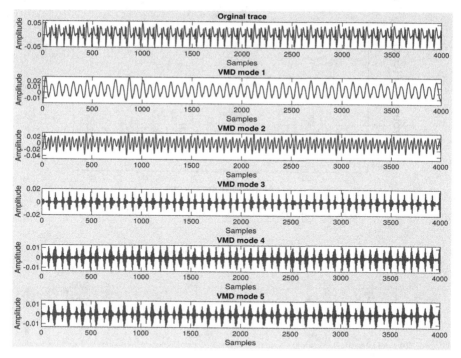

Fig. 4. VMD mode of the power trace on Dataset 2.

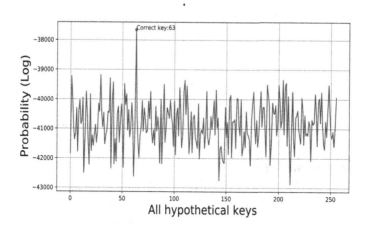

Fig. 5. Probability of all hypothetical keys on Dataset 1.

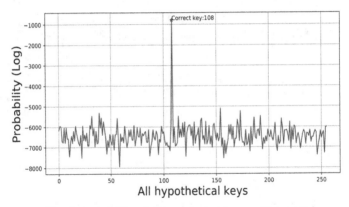

Fig. 6. Probability of all hypothetical keys on Dataset 2.

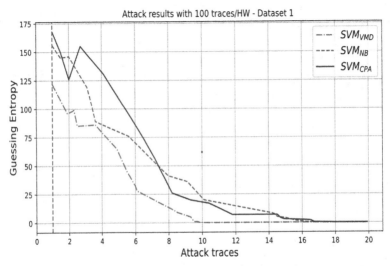

Fig. 7. Attack performance with 100 traces/HW class on Dataset 1.

4.2.3   Results with Noisy Traces

The power traces are usually polluted with noise in practice. To examine the effectiveness of our proposed SVM$_{VMD}$ profiled attack in noisy condition, additive Gaussian noise is added to the power traces. In our experiments, two noise level of standard deviation $\sigma_1 = 5$ and $\sigma_2 = 10$ are added to both Dataset 1 and Dataset 2. In addition, different feature extraction techniques were used for the SVM-based profiled attacks to investigate their effects on the efficiency of the attacks in the presence of noise. Overall, the guessing entropy of all the attacks increase with the level of noise, but the attack based on SVM with combining of VMD and GSO is the least sensitive to noise. The results of our attacks with 200 profiling traces per Hamming weight class, presented in Figs. 11, 12, 13 and 14 and Table 5, show that out of SVM$_{CPA}$, SVM$_{NB}$ and SVM$_{VMD}$, the proposed method, SVM$_{VMD}$, has the best performance at both noise levels while SVM$_{CPA}$ and

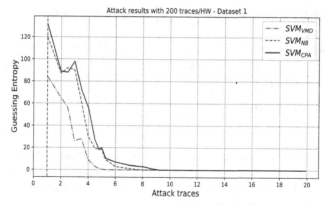

Fig. 8. Attack performance with 200 traces/HW class on Dataset 1.

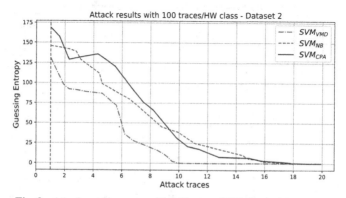

Fig. 9. Attack performance with 100 traces/HW class on Dataset 2.

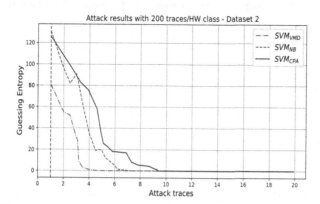

Fig. 10. Attack performance with 200 traces/HW class on Dataset 2.

SVM_{NB} are comparable to each other. After adding noise to the power trace, the number of traces required for GE to reach 0 increased by only 25% approximately with the

Table 4. Number of traces used by the attacks to attain GE = 0.

No. of profiling traces	Dataset 1			Dataset 2		
	SVM_{VMD}	SVM_{CPA}	SVM_{NB}	SVM_{VMD}	SVM_{CPA}	SVM_{NB}
100	10.2	18.1	17.6	10.3	19.2	18.3
200	5.3	9.2	8.7	4.7	9.4	7.3

proposed attack, while it increased by over 100% for the other methods. This proves that the VMD signal is insensitive to noise so the SVM_{VMD} attack should work well under noisy conditions. This property is very useful in real attack scenarios where collected measurement traces invariably contain noise.

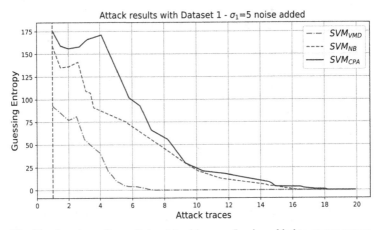

Fig. 11. Attack results on Dataset 1 with $\sigma_1 = 5$ noise added to power traces.

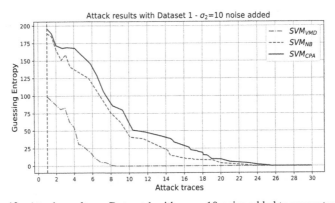

Fig. 12. Attack results on Dataset 1 with $\sigma_1 = 10$ noise added to power traces.

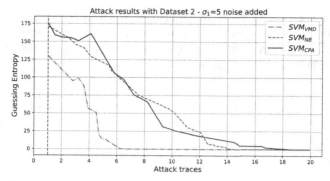

Fig. 13. Attack results on Dataset 2 with $\sigma_1 = 5$ noise added to power traces.

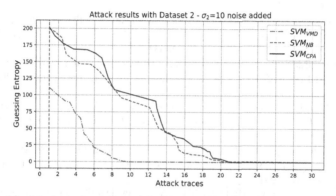

Fig. 14. Attack results on Dataset 2 with $\sigma_1 = 10$ noise added to power traces.

Table 5. Number of noisy traces used by the attacks to attain GE = 0.

Noise level	Dataset 1			Dataset 2		
	SVM$_{VMD}$	SVM$_{CPA}$	SVM$_{NB}$	SVM$_{VMD}$	SVM$_{CPA}$	SVM$_{NB}$
$\sigma_1 = 5$	7.4	19.0	17.0	6.7	18.8	14.6
$\sigma_2 = 10$	8.6	25.7	23.6	9.8	21.6	20.2

5 Conclusion

In this work, the combining of variational mode decomposition and Gram-Schmidt was proposed as a feature extraction and selection method for the power traces. The VMD mode that has central frequency related to clock operation frequency of the attack device can be used as features of power traces and GSO can be used as a feature selection method. Experimental results show that an acceptable classification accuracy can be achieved when SVM classifier uses these selected features as its input. Compared to other SVM-based profiled attacks, the SVM$_{VMD}$ required the minimum number of traces for successful key recovery. Furthermore, SVM$_{VMD}$ is less sensitive to noise so can be used well with noisy power traces. In our opinion, this work suggests a new approach for feature extraction from power traces using variational mode decomposition, and this method should also be tested in combination with other feature selection method and learning algorithms for the profiled attacks.

Acknowledgment. This research is funded by Vietnam National Foundation for Science and Technology Development (NAFOSTED) under grant number 102.02–2020.14.

References

1. Kocher, P., Jaffe, J., Jun, B.: Differential power analysis. In: Wiener, M. (ed.) CRYPTO 1999. LNCS, vol. 1666, pp. 388–397. Springer, Heidelberg (1999). https://doi.org/10.1007/3-540-48405-1_25
2. Brier, E., Clavier, C., Olivier, F.: Correlation power analysis with a leakage model. In: Joye, M., Quisquater, J.-J. (eds.) CHES 2004. LNCS, vol. 3156, pp. 16–29. Springer, Heidelberg (2004). https://doi.org/10.1007/978-3-540-28632-5_2
3. Gierlichs, B., Batina, L., Tuyls, P., Preneel, B.: Mutual information analysis. In: Oswald, E., Rohatgi, P. (eds.) CHES 2008. LNCS, vol. 5154, pp. 426–442. Springer, Heidelberg (2008). https://doi.org/10.1007/978-3-540-85053-3_27
4. Chari, S., Rao, J.R., Rohatgi, P.: Template attacks. In: Kaliski, B.S., Koç, K., Paar, C. (eds.) CHES 2002. LNCS, vol. 2523, pp. 13–28. Springer, Heidelberg (2003). https://doi.org/10.1007/3-540-36400-5_3
5. Heuser, A., Zohner, M.: Intelligent machine homicide. In: Schindler, W., Huss, S.A. (eds.) COSADE 2012. LNCS, vol. 7275, pp. 249–264. Springer, Heidelberg (2012). https://doi.org/10.1007/978-3-642-29912-4_18
6. Lerman, L., Bontempi, G., Markowitch, O.: A machine learning approach against a masked AES. J. Cryptogr. Eng. **5**(2), 123–139 (2014)
7. Zheng, Y., Zhou, Y., Yu, Z., Hu, C., Zhang, H.: How to compare selections of points of interest for side-channel distinguishers in practice? In: Hui, L., Qing, S., Shi, E., Yiu, S. (eds.) ICICS 2014. LNCS, vol. 8958, pp. 200–214. Springer, Cham (2015). https://doi.org/10.1007/978-3-319-21966-0_15
8. Rechberger, C., Oswald, E.: Practical template attacks. In: Lim, C.H., Yung, M. (eds.) WISA 2004. LNCS, vol. 3325, pp. 440–456. Springer, Heidelberg (2005). https://doi.org/10.1007/978-3-540-31815-6_35
9. Gierlichs, B., Lemke-Rust, K., Paar, C.: Templates vs. stochastic methods. In: Goubin, L., Matsui, M. (eds.) CHES 2006. LNCS, vol. 4249, pp. 15–29. Springer, Heidelberg (2006). https://doi.org/10.1007/11894063_2
10. Mangard, S., Oswald, E., Popp, T.: Power Analysis Attacks: Revealing the Secrets of Smart Cards. Springer, Heidelberg (2007)
11. Lomné, V., Prouff, E., Roche, T.: Behind the scene of side channel attacks. In: Sako, K., Sarkar, P. (eds.) ASIACRYPT 2013. LNCS, vol. 8269, pp. 506–525. Springer, Heidelberg (2013). https://doi.org/10.1007/978-3-642-42033-7_26
12. Hettwer, B., Gehrer, S., Güneysu, T.: Applications of machine learning techniques in side-channel attacks: a survey. J. Cryptogr. Eng. **10**(2), 135–162 (2019)
13. Picek, S., Heuser, A., Jovic, A., Legay, A.: On the relevance of feature selection for profiled side-channel attacks. Cryptology ePrint Archive (2017)
14. Bartkewitz, T., Lemke-Rust, K.: Efficient template attacks based on probabilistic multi-class support vector machines. In: Mangard, S. (ed.) CARDIS 2012. LNCS, vol. 7771, pp. 263–276. Springer, Heidelberg (2013). https://doi.org/10.1007/978-3-642-37288-9_18

15. Dragomiretskiy, K., Zosso, D.: Variational mode decomposition. IEEE Trans. Signal **62**, 513–544 (2014)
16. Stephen, B., Parikh, N., Chu, E., Peleato, B., Eckstein, J.: Distributed optimization and statistical learning via the alternating direction method of multipliers. Found. Trends® Mach. Learn. **3**(1), 1–122 (2011)
17. Cortes, C., Vapnik, V.: Support-vector networks. J. Mach. Learn. **20**(3), 273–297 (1995)
18. Platt, J.C.: Probabilistic Outputs for Support Vector Machines and Comparisons to Regularized Likelihood Methods, pp. 61–74. Advances in Large Margin Classifiers MIT Press, Cambridge (1999)
19. Stoppiglia, H., Dreyfus, G., Dubois, R., Oussar, Y.: Ranking a random feature for variable and feature selection. J. Mach. Learn. **3**, 1399–1414 (2003)
20. Eswaramoorthy, S., Sivakumaran, N., Sekaran, S.: Grey wolf optimization based parameter selection for support vector machines. Int. J. Comput. Math. Electr. Electron. Eng. **35**(5), 1513–1523 (2016)
21. Standaert, F.-X., Malkin, T.G., Yung, M.: A unified framework for the analysis of side-channel key recovery attacks. In: Joux, A. (ed.) EUROCRYPT 2009. LNCS, vol. 5479, pp. 443–461. Springer, Heidelberg (2009). https://doi.org/10.1007/978-3-642-01001-9_26
22. Nassar, M., Souissi, Y., Guilley, S., Danger, J.: RSM: a small and fast countermeasure for AES, secure against 1st and 2nd-order zero-offset SCAs. In: Design, Automation & Test in Europe Conference & Exhibition (DATE), Dresden (2012)

A Study on IDS Based CMAC Neuron Network to Improve the Attack Detection Rate

Trong-Minh Hoang[1]([✉]) and Trang-Linh Le Thi[2]

[1] Posts and Telecoms Institute of Technology, Ha Noi, Vietnam
hoangtrongminh@ptit.edu.vn
[2] Electric Power University, Ha Noi, Vietnam

Abstract. The massive growth of the Internet of Things has brought a lot of attractive benefits because it is going to have a positive impact on life and work through many applications. Besides its advantages, the adoption of massive applications also points the door for attackers to gain cyberattacks on the system. Hence, needed solutions to detect attacks from the edge of the network must be considered to reduce the pressure on the computing elements in core networks. Therefore, approximate approaches to low computational complexity in an Intrusion Detection System (IDS) are being studied to favor limited-resource devices. In this study, a novel IDS based intelligent computation is proposed, the Cerebellar Model Articulation Controller (CMAC) neuron network is chosen to tailor various hardware edge devices. Moreover, to approach edge processing, a feature selection reduction scheme is proposed to reduce the time complexity of the training phase while keeping reasonable accuracy. The experimental results are compared to other previous studies in the same input conditions to high-light the proposed advantages.

Keywords: Security · IDS · Neuron network · Machine learning · Dataset

1 Introduction

Today, Internet of things (IoT) applications are being developed in mass to meet the needs of automation for the economic, medical, or agricultural industries. Communication network architectures force the processing hierarchy to move closer to the end-users for faster processing and reduce the pressure on the core network infrastructure. Therefore, intelligent computing solutions and information processing at the edge of the network are considered key technologies for new generation networks such as 5G and 6G [1].

Security for the IoT network is becoming more and more important as the number of devices increases rapidly with a variety of devices. Attacks can come from any device and lead to serious damage to network infrastructure. Moreover, attacks based on smart IoT devices can cause rich vulnerable issues. Hence, IDS based on intelligent methodologies is needed for such scenarios.

These solutions are intended to deal with the intelligence of attacks in open environments. Historical data streams are identified and regionally sorted to confirm current

© ICST Institute for Computer Sciences, Social Informatics and Telecommunications Engineering 2021
Published by Springer Nature Switzerland AG 2021. All Rights Reserved
N.-S. Vo et al. (Eds.): INISCOM 2021, LNICST 379, pp. 504–511, 2021.
https://doi.org/10.1007/978-3-030-77424-0_39

unusual events. In it, neural networks are trained and classified for threshold values. However, the time and algorithmic complexity of AI solutions is always a big challenge [2]. Therefore, finding a solution suitable for edge network computing characteristics is a research direction recently. Along with this approach, this study provides an intelligent edge processing solution to deal with attacks with a feature reduction method while still ensuring the accuracy of the model. The results proving the validity of the proposal presented in the paper have been compared with the previous research results. The proposed model gives high accuracy and less feature number than the recent proposals on the UNSW-NB15 dataset. The paper structure is organized as follows: The next section presents related work; Sect. 3 briefs the primary and base principles; The detailed proposal is illustrated in Sect. 4; in the last section, our conclusions and future works are presented.

2 Related Work

In recent years, the need to compute and manage huge IoT devices has become imperative to adapt to massive application growth. Therefore, cloud computing systems have been decentralized towards the edge of the network. Along with that, security systems also transfer some functions to different cloud layers to ensure the safety and efficiency of the whole system [3]. To early prevent attacks from IoT devices and reduce compute load to the processing center, IDS intrusion detection systems are migrated to the network edge to detect and predict device or traffic anomalies [4, 5].

IDS systems were developed to identify attacks and to avoid attacks if possible. Using the effectiveness of machine learning and artificial intelligence strategies, IDS becomes smarter and gets more accurate in dealing with its decision that comes decision tree techniques, fuzzy logic techniques, support vector machines, or neural networks are applied [6, 7].

In deployment scenarios at the edge of the network, IDS systems face new challenges including fast response times and the high dimension of data sizes. That is also the biggest obstacle of traditional ML algorithms and needs to be carefully considered nowadays. Therefore, the approach to finding new algorithms is very urgent in the goal of IoT network protection. With certain advantages of CMAC which are fast calculation and easy deployment on hardware [8], the proposed IDS based on CMAC is a deal to tailor with edge computing scenarios. Moreover, to reduce the computational complexity when the input data is a high dimension, feature selection techniques are selected as a preprocessing step for the intelligent algorithms of the IDS system. This solution eliminates redundancy and improves system IDS performance [9]. Different from the previous approaches, a solution proposed in this study to reduce the number of traits for decision trees according to the Gini index is proposed. Experimental results on the UWNB data set show that the proposed solution gives more accurate results with some properties less than the previous solutions.

3 Premier

a. **The feature selection approach**

The purpose of feature selection is to find a subset of attributes from the original set sufficient to represent the data. Among wrapper, filter, and embedded approaches we use the filter approach to get efficient data based on the statistics expressed by the Gini index [10]. Gini index is used to determine which feature/attribute gives us the maximum information about a class. For the dataset X which contains n class, the *Gini* index is determined by the formula [10],

$$i(X) = 1 - \sum_{i=1}^{n} p_i^2, \tag{1}$$

where p_i - the probability of an object being classified to a particular class.

After splitting of dataset X with A selection features into two subsets X_1 and X_2 with some records respectively N_1 and N_2. The *Gini* index is determined by the formula,

$$i_A(X) = \frac{N_1}{N} i(X_1) + \frac{N_2}{N} i(X_2), \tag{2}$$

where $i(X_1) = 1 - \sum_{i=1}^{n} p_i^2(X_1)$, $p_i(X_1)$ *is* the probability of an object being classified to a particular class in the dataset X_1, $i(X_2) = 1 - \sum_{i=1}^{n} p_i^2(X_2)$, $p_i(X_2)$ is the probability of an object being classified to a particular class in the dataset X_2.

The feature is considered the best if $\Delta i(A) = i(X) - i_A(X)$ has reached the maximum value.

In this study, the feature is selected by using the random forest algorithm over the Gini impurity index, which attributes with the highest Gini impurity will be the most important value.

b. **The CMAC proprieties**

The structure of CMAC was originally composed of two inter-layers (a, p) mappings illustrated in Fig. 1. The mathematical formulation to express the relationship between input vectors and output vector of CMAC model and multilayer perceptron (MLP) model is the same. However, CMAC has several interesting different features as below.

- The input vectors are only accepted integer values;
- Only output for multiple inputs;
- The parameter p is the key parameter that determines network performance through memory capacity and convergence time.

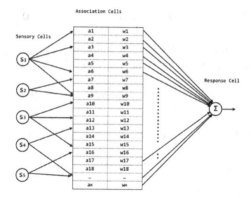

Fig. 1. The CMAC structure

4 The Proposed Model and Experimental Validations

a. The proposed model

To build and validate our proposal, the UNSW-NB dataset 15 is used in this study [11]. The main characteristics of the dataset include 44 attributes for each attack type, 2,540,044 records stored in four CSV files. The percentages of the number of attack types are shown in the second column of Table 1.

Table 1. Components of attack types in the UNSW-NB15 dataset

Attack types	Num of records
Normal	1959775
Reconnaissance	13357
Backdoor	1983
DoS	5665
Exploits	27599
Analysis	2184
Fuzzers	21795
Worms	171
Shellcode	1511
Generic	25378

The input vectors of the CMAC neural network only accept integer values so they must first be quantized. For quantization, it is necessary to determine the maximum and minimum values of each attribute. These values are described in Table 2.

The maximum value in order to quantize for each feature applied to CMAC neural network is: 17, 257, 257, 1025, 9, 65. The set of values of 6 input vector features is:

$$X = \{x^{(1)} = \overline{1, 17}; x^{(2)} = \overline{1, 257}; x^{(3)} = \overline{1, 257}; x^{(4)} = \overline{1, 1025}; x^{(5)} = \overline{1, 9}; x^{(6)} =$$
$$\overline{1, 65}\}.$$

The values of the 6 input vector features are quantized according to formula (1).

The learning process of the CMAC neural network depends on the value of the general parameter p, only receiving the p = 2, 4, 6, 8, 16, 32. Furthermore, the accuracy depends on the threshold ϑ. The number of training steps is 10 000 000.

Table 2. The minimum and maximum value of each feature

№	Feature	Minimum value	Maximum value
1	Service	21	33
2	Sttl	0	255
3	Dttl	0	252
4	Smeansz	24	1504
5	Ct_state_ttl	0	6
6	Ct_srv_dst	1	62

The training process will be done when the input vector is quantized, the number of DoS attack records is 4412, the non-DoS attack is 126485 (accounting for 80% of the number of DoS attack records and the DoS attack of UNSW-NB dataset 15).

When the training process is done, the testing process will be carried out. The data of the testing process are also quantized like the training process. The number of DoS attacks and non-DoS attack records that will be tested is 1103 and 31616 respectively (accounting for 20% of the DoS attack records and non-DoS attack records of the UNSW-NB 15 dataset). Each record will be labeled:

- 1 - when the record is a DoS attack,
- 0 - when the record is a non-DoS attack.

The process of testing the CMAC neural network is performed with different threshold values from 0.1 to 0.9 with a jump of 0.01. When comparing the obtained results, the number of identified attacks reached the highest result when the threshold value is 0.57, the percentages of the identities for a DoS attack and a non-DoS attack are 86.13% and 85.13% respectively.

b. **The validation**

The two networks used for comparison are MLP and Support Vector Machines (SVM). SVM is another kind of machine learning technique. Based on the principles of linear classification, SVM creates a hyper-plane to maximize the distance between two layers.

The training process of the MLP network and SVM were implemented in a MAT-LAB environment, by using the application package Neural Network Toolbox. The learning process of the CMAC neural network is done in Visual Studio 2013 and/or the programming language is C++.

During the training process, the SVM network uses 2 functions: Gaussian Radial Basis Function (RBF) and polynomial to select the best results. The experimental results are listed in Table 3.

Table 3. Test results

Type of neural network	Parameters				
	Methodology	The number of layers and neurons in each layer	Threshold value	Identification rate of DoS attack, %	Identification rate of non-DoS attack, %
NN CMAC	NN CMAC		0.566	86.49	85.1
MLP	Trainlm	30–20–10–1	0.72	85.31	84.71
SVM	Rbf	-	-	56.3	89.45

c. **The proposed feature selection to apply CMAC neural network**

The selection of features by using the random forest algorithm to determine the Gini impurity index [10], in which the feature with the highest Gini impurity will be the most important. By applying the above method, the results obtained 9 features with the highest Gini impurity index are Proto, Service, Sttl, Dttl, Synack, Smeansz, Ct_srv_src, Ct_state_ttl, Ct_srv_dst.

The records from the UNSW-NB 15 data set with the 9 selected above features were added to the MLP network to compare the results with the MLP network by using 42 features. If the result by using 9 features is higher or equal to the result by using 42 attributes, it will reduce 1 feature. The reduction process of a feature will be finished when the obtained result by applying the number of feature drops is lower than the result by using 42 features.

The training process MLP network was performed on 4.412 DoS attack records and 12.6485 non-DoS attack records (accounting for 80% of the number of records of the UNSW-NB15 data set). The input MLP will use 42 features of all types of attacks and the used algorithms are trainlm, traingdx, trainscg, trainbfg. During the learning and testing process we used 3 layers (15–10-1, 30–20-1, 50–30-1, 100–50-1, 100–100-1, 150–100-1, 200- 100–1, 200–150-1) and 4 layers (30–20-10–1). The threshold for classification will run from 0.1 to 0.9 with a jump of 0.01. The testing process was performed on 1.103 DoS attack records and 31.616 non-DoS attack records (accounting for 20% of records from the UNSW-NB 15 dataset). After testing all the cases, the highest classification accuracy for DoS and non-DoS attacks are 85.31% and 85.71% respectively. The proposed feature selection algorithm is illustrated below.

The proposed feature selection algorithm

Begin

1. $i := [1,...9]$, (i: the number of features in the attribute set F)

2. $j := [1,...c_9^i]$, (j: numerical order in i)

3. $F = \{F_{ij}\}$, (F: the attribute set)

4. For $i = 9 \rightarrow 1$ do

5. Set threshold [0.1 − 0.9] and step parameter [0.01]

6. Compare $B_{ij} \diamondsuit A_{42}$ (B_{ij} : experimental value, A_{42} : original MLP value)

7. If $B_{ij} < A_{42}$, go to the end

8. If $B_{ij} \geq A_{42}$, go to next step

9. Select a feature set with the highest accuracy

10. $i := i - 1$, return to step 4.

End

The above results show that, when using the input vector with 6 features, the result is no worse than when using 42 features. Therefore, 6 features: Service, Sttl, Dttl, Smeansz, Ct_state_ttl, Ct_srv_dst were selected to include in the CMAC neural network used to identify DoS attack on UNSW NB 15 dataset.

5 Conclusion

The aim of improving IDS system performance for edge computations is an interesting problem in currently researched problem because of its topicality. The research results show that IDS based CMAC is an effective tool to detect attacks. To overcome the limitation of the CMAC as the input of the network is limited by the number of features, we proposed a novel method based on the combination of the MLP network and the Random forest for reducing input features that also degraded its complexity. Experimental results show that when reducing the number of features from 42 to 6 for DoS attack on dataset UNSW NB 15, the NN CMAC gave higher results than MLP and SVM networks. In the next research, we will present the NN CMAC test on other real attack dataset and will propose a multi-expert system in which the component is neural networks.

References

1. Letaief, K.B., Chen, W., Shi, Y., Zhang, J., Zhang, Y.-J.A.: The roadmap to 6G AI-empowered wireless networks. IEEE Commun. Mag. **57**, 84–90 (2019)
2. Fang, H., Qi, A., Wang, X.: Fast authentication and progressive authorization in large-scale IoT: how to leverage AI for security enhancement. IEEE Netw. **34**(3), 24–29 (2020)
3. Cao, K., Liu, Y., Meng, G., Sun, Q.: An overview on edge computing research. IEEE Access **8**, 85714–85728 (2020)

4. Mudgerikar, A., Sharma, P., Bertino, E.: Edge-based intrusion detection for IoT devices. ACM Trans. Manage. Inf. Syst. **11**(4), 21 (2020). Article 18 https://doi.org/10.1145/3382159
5. Almogren, A.S.: Intrusion detection in edge-of-things computing. J. Parallel Distrib. Comput. (2019). https://doi.org/10.1016/j.jpdc.2019.12.008
6. Nguyen, V.-T., Nguyen, T.-X., Hoang, T.-M., Vu, N.-L.: A new anomaly traffic detection based on fuzzy logic approach in wireless sensor networks. In: Proceedings of the Tenth International Symposium on Information and Communication Technology (SoICT 2019), pp. 205–209. Association for Computing Machinery, New York (2019). https://doi.org/10.1145/3368926.3369714
7. Zhang, H., Wu, C.Q., Gao, S., Wang, Z., Xu, Y., Liu, Y.: An effective deep learning-based scheme for network intrusion detection. In: 24th International Conference on Pattern Recognition (ICPR), pp. 682–687. IEEE (2018)
8. Xing, F.: A Historical Review of Forty Years of Research on CMAC. In ArXiv, abs/1702.02277 (2017)
9. Moustafa, N., Slay, J.: A hybrid feature selection for network intrusion detection systems: Central points. In arXiv preprint. arXiv:1707.05505 (2017)
10. Breiman, L.: Random forests. Mach. Learn. **45**(1), 5–32 (2001)
11. https://www.unsw.adfa.edu.au/unsw-canberra-cyber/cybersecurity/ADFA-NB15-Datasets/. Accessed 18 Oct 2020.

Author Index

Printed in the United States
by Baker & Taylor Publisher Services